The Life & Legend of

E. H. Harriman

The Life & Legend of

by Maury Klein

The
University of
North Carolina
Press
Chapel Hill &
London

E. H. Harriman

© 2000

The University of North Carolina Press

All rights reserved

Set in Minion and Miehle types

by Keystone Typesetting, Inc.

Manufactured in the United States of America

The paper in this book meets the guidelines for
permanence and durability of the Committee on
Production Guidelines for Book Longevity of the
Council on Library Resources.

Library of Congress Cataloging-in-Publication Data

Klein, Maury, 1939–

The life and legend of E. H. Harriman / Maury Klein.

    p.   cm.

Includes bibliographical references and index.

ISBN 0-8078-2517-4 (cloth: alk. paper)

1. Harriman, Edward Henry, 1848–1909. 2. Capitalists
and financiers—United States—Biography. 3. Railroads—
United States—History. I. Title.

HE2754.H2K54   2000

385′.092—dc21

[B]   99-28864

            CIP

04   03   02   01   00   5   4   3   2   1

For Kathy, again . . .

My one and Olneyville

Contents

Illustrations

Acknowledgments

The research and writing of this book owe much to people in many capacities who contributed freely of their time and energy. Although it would be impossible to name them all, the following individuals stand out for their efforts and cooperation. Donald D. Snoddy of the Union Pacific Museum was a rock on whom any researcher could lean for support. In this project, as in previous ones, he provided a full measure of help and good cheer. Ken Longe of the Union Pacific's public relations staff also responded to every request with alacrity. I am especially grateful to Jim Ady of Salt Lake City, who brought to my attention certain invaluable records of the Los Angeles & Salt Lake Railroad that he had personally saved from destruction.

William J. Rich III helped me gain access to the materials stored at Arden Farms, which turned out to be a mine of useful information. At Arden Farms, George Paffenbarger generously gave me complete access to the Kennan and other materials, office support, and useful advice. Frank Allston of IC Industries granted me access to the early minute books and records of the Illinois Central Railroad still in possession of IC Industries.

Librarians in several locations provided their expertise as well as access to key collections of papers. Foremost among them were Florence Lathrop of Baker Library at the Harvard Business School, W. Thomas White of the James J. Hill Reference Library in St. Paul, John Aubrey of the Newberry Library in Chicago, Mary Ann Jensen and Andy Thomson of the Firestone Library at Princeton University, Andrea Paul of the Nebraska State Museum and Archives, Bernard J. Crystal of the Butler Library at Columbia University, Richard Crawford of the National Archives, and Margaret N. Haines of the Oregon Historical Society.

The staff of my "home" library at the University of Rhode Island fielded my every request with their usual efficiency and helpfulness. In particular I wish to thank Marie Beaumont, Vicki Burnett, John Etchingham, Mimi Keefe, Sylvia C. Krausse, Kevin Logan, John Osterhout, and Marie Rudd. Several friends and colleagues were generous with their advice and support on various subjects. Their ranks include William D. Burt, Don L. Hofsommer, Priscilla Long, Albro Martin, Lloyd J. Mercer, and Glenn Porter. Frank A. Vanderlip Jr. helped me understand his banker father. I benefited, too, from interviews with Elbridge T. Gerry, W. Averell Harriman, and Robert A. Lovett in my earlier Union Pacific project.

My editor, Lewis Bateman, has been uniformly helpful, as have Pamela Upton and other members of the staff at the University of North Carolina Press. Trudie Calvert's fine copyediting rescued me from numerous bloopers.

Finally, I wish to pay tribute to my wife, Kathy Klein, who endured with patience and understanding the perpetually vacant expression of the writer lost in thought.

Introduction

At this end of the twentieth century the name of E. H. Harriman may be less familiar than that of his son W. Averell Harriman, who followed an already impressive career in business with long and distinguished service in diplomacy and politics. To any American living in the first years of this century, however, the name and face of E. H. Harriman were as familiar as those of his fellow titans J. P. Morgan, John D. Rockefeller, and Andrew Carnegie. Like them, he had become to the public the very essence of what he did. Morgan stood for banking, Rockefeller for oil, Carnegie for iron and steel, and Harriman for railroads. But where the first three men had achieved their lofty reputations through a lifetime of steady achievement in their fields, Harriman burst onto the railroad scene like a comet at the age of fifty and worked his magic on the industry in a single decade.

Harriman differed from the others in personality as well. Morgan was aloof and aristocratic, Rockefeller secretive and reclusive, and Carnegie voluble and hungry for the limelight. Harriman was intense and combative—the forerunner of an age when speed and efficiency would replace grace and charm. On duty he was a human computer, his mind racing so quickly over data to conclusions that others could hardly follow him. Coming late to railroads, the oldest and most hidebound of major industries, he looked at its hoary traditions with fresh eyes and with startling speed literally reinvented the business. In one decade his innovations shoved an industry made moribund and dispirited by the depression of 1893–97 into the twentieth century. The railroads under his control became models for others to emulate. He modernized not only their physical plant but their organizations, business practices, financing, and safety records.

He began in 1898 with the Union Pacific Railroad, the once-proud transcontinental line then emerging in pieces from nearly five years of bankruptcy. In only a few years Harriman rebuilt the line, reorganized its management, reacquired its lost subsidiaries, and turned it into one of the most profitable properties in the nation. In 1901 he acquired the Southern Pacific, then the largest transportation system in the world, and worked the same formula on it. To the newly integrated Union Pacific–Southern Pacific system he brought a bold management structure that shocked traditional railroad men because it seemed to violate all the known principles of how such things were done. The Harriman touch was extended to other roads and with it the formula that became the mantra for railroad success in the twentieth century: long hauls of high volume at low rates. Harriman did not invent the formula, but he applied it more rigorously and with greater speed and efficiency than anyone else.

Harriman's vision did not stop at the water's edge or the national boundary. He built lines into Mexico and looked to extend them deep into Central America. Late in life he envisioned a combined rail-water transportation system that would circle the globe. To that end he visited Japan and negotiated for rights to construct lines in China, Manchuria, and elsewhere that would complete such a system. Nothing stirred him more than a challenge. In 1899 he transformed a vacation cruise to Alaska into a major scientific expedition that left a lasting legacy of knowledge about the region. When the earthquake of 1906 devastated San Francisco, Harriman rushed to the scene to direct Southern Pacific operations personally. When the Colorado River overflowed its banks and threatened to immerse the entire Imperial Valley of California, he ordered the Southern Pacific's long and expensive campaign to force the river back into its bed.

In everything he took up, Harriman tended to be ruthless and single-minded. His abrasive style and personality made enemies almost as rapidly as did the novelty of his approaches. Impatient of those slower and duller than himself, he charged ahead to his goals without bothering to explain or mollify. Having thrust himself into the public arena, he found himself engulfed in one controversy after another. A well-publicized split with his onetime friend Theodore Roosevelt blackened his reputation for a time and generated some of the myths about Harriman that endured for many years. Before his death in 1909 he had reclaimed public recognition for his many accomplishments, but he remained a controversial and misunderstood figure.

It seems odd that no full biography of so seminal a figure in American business history has appeared since George Kennan produced his two-volume work in 1922. The story of that work is found in the prologue and is a natural place to begin the quest for the real E. H. Harriman. Kennan had access to most of the men who were closest to Harriman, but his work was both sponsored and supervised by the Harriman family and advisers. Moreover, Kennan had a distaste for the intimate and the familiar and was careful to avoid dealing with any aspect of Harriman's personal life beneath the surface. The result was a work that perpetuated as many myths about Harriman as it tried earnestly to correct. But Kennan did have access to materials that no one has seen before or since, and which most people believed had been destroyed in a 1912 fire. The lack of good primary source material has long been a deterrent to any study of Harriman, as it was with Jay Gould.

Those readers familiar with my biography of Gould will notice that I have recycled the title for use here. As this device suggests, the lives of both men have become so intertwined with myth as to require major reclamation, and there are a surprising number of similarities between them. Both were small, unimpressive-looking men who made their way to the jungle of Wall Street at a tender age. Both men launched the pivotal phase of their careers by rescuing the Union Pacific Railroad from the depths of depression and breathing new life into it. Both had quick, agile minds that baffled those around them with their audacity and unorthodoxy.

Gould and Harriman alike were ruthless engines of efficiency in business and utterly devoted to their families off duty. Their similar blends of boldness and brilliance gave them an air of mystery that led others to dislike and distrust them even while admiring their ability. Both men were misunderstood in the most literal sense and so made enemies easily. At the dawn of the age of media they learned too late in life the importance of cultivating good relations with the press. And both men worked themselves to death, refusing late in life to ease up and enjoy their accumulated fortunes. Neither man put his funds into safe investments but stayed instead at the riskier work of development because that was to them the essential work of life. They died relatively young and in harness, leaving behind them legacies piled high with achievement and controversy.

There are important differences between them as well. Where Gould was frail and self-deprecating, Harriman was athletic and combative. Gould's quiet, retiring style made him adept at compromise and the art of suggestion; Harriman was brash and overbearing. If Gould's voice and manner had the insinuating lilt of the oboe, Harriman's was the clarion call of the trumpet. As a young man Gould burst into public prominence with a string of episodes on Wall Street that were as wild and breathtaking as their perpetrator was tame and unassuming. So great was the notoriety earned by these maneuvers that he spent the rest of his life trying to live down his former reputation and convince observers that he was in fact a constructive businessman. By contrast, Harriman's early years on Wall Street earned him a reputation as a shrewd but cautious, careful, and utterly reliable broker. Where Gould was an outcast, Harriman was an establishment man at home with the social elite. His relative obscurity until the age of fifty made his entrance onto the broader stage of business affairs all the more spectacular and mysterious because he seemed to come from nowhere.

Gould spread himself across several key industries, most notably railroads and the telegraph. Although Harriman made investments elsewhere, he confined his attention mainly to railroads. Born a dozen years apart, the two men knew each other slightly and came in the end to represent the first two eras of railroad history. Gould was a developer, eager to lay track into virgin regions to open up unsettled areas. He was also a master strategist, adept at the art of piecing together large roads from smaller ones and transforming larger roads into systems through a mixture of acquisition and construction. In all this work

Gould also had to play the role of agile diplomat, threading his way through a world of shifting alliances and balances of power among emerging systems.

Harriman arrived on the scene after the depression of the 1890s had shaken the industry to its core. While he too found it necessary to weave his way through a reorganizing battleground of alliances and powers, he lacked Gould's patience and gift for negotiation. He was more the field marshal, ready to fight for what he wanted and confident always of victory. His most enduring contribution was in quite another area. Where Gould put down lines and helped fill the railroad map, Harriman transformed them into well-built, efficient operations. He modernized and reorganized old systems into new, often larger, and always more profitable ones. Put another way, he carried the work begun by Gould and others to another level, one that ensured the survival of railroads in an era that would produce new forms of competition in transportation.

As was true with Gould, the story of Harriman's life and career contains more questions than answers. Although Harriman's reputation never reached the depths of desecration and odium reserved for Gould in his day, it hit surprisingly low levels for a time and never fully recovered. Like Gould, he became a figure admired for his achievements and deplored for his methods. In writing Gould's biography I noted in the prologue that one objective was to "square the legend with the facts as we now know them, to determine what he actually did or did not do, what powers he did or did not possess, what the effects of his actions were, and why he did what he did." That statement holds equally true for this study of Harriman. The goal here, as before, has been to integrate Harriman's career into the broader context of his life and the era in which he lived. Only then does it become possible to separate fact from legend or grasp some sense of the complexity of history itself in an age when popular culture has increasingly twisted the past into a pastiche of cartoons and soap operas.

The Life & Legend of

E. H. Harriman

Prologue: Mr. Kennan Writes a Biography

The trend of my rather eventful but comparatively unimportant life was determined,
mainly, by the fact that my father was born with a latent taste and a decided aptitude
for applied science, and was then trained and educated as a school-teacher and a
lawyer.

—George Kennan, *Autobiography*

If in the bleak winter of 1913–14 George Kennan had paused to draw a balance sheet of his life, he would have found cause for the anxiety that gnawed at him. To all appearances he had enjoyed great success in his mixed career as explorer and journalist. At sixty-nine he was an elder statesman in the literary, diplomatic, and scientific circles that had been his home for three decades. Presidents and editors alike had long considered him the foremost American authority on Russia and sought his views on every turn of that country's erratic political wheel.[1]

"George Kennan," said an admiring friend, "was a peculiarly lovable man and a remarkably attractive one." Tall and gaunt with thick brows and a formidable mustache beneath his bald head, Kennan still stood ramrod straight as an old man. His dark, fierce eyes were alert and restless like those of an eagle scouting prey, and his intellect covered no less ground in its quest for nourishment. Since the 1860s he had roamed the globe searching out mysteries and recording them with remarkable clarity and objectivity.[2]

From middle-class beginnings in Norwalk, Ohio, where he caught his father's passion for the telegraph (his mother was related to Samuel F. B. Morse), Kennan had first ventured out into the world at seventeen as a substitute operator in a Cleveland office of Western Union. Two years later he applied for a position with the Western Union Extension, which was about to string wire across Alaska and Siberia. Thus began his lifelong love affair with Russia. He arrived at Petropavlosk in August 1865 and remained in Russia nearly three years, roaming across as much of the country as he could while doing his work.[3]

In January 1860, nine months after his return, Kennan produced his article and gave his first lecture. By the spring of 1870 he had delivered more than sixty lectures and found a publisher for his first book, *Tent Life in Siberia*. He made enough money to go back to Russia that summer. After visiting St. Petersburg and Moscow he toured the Caucasus, roaming the hills until his money ran out, then hitching a ride to the coast on a flour train. He followed a stream of pilgrims to Mecca, gradually working his way back until he landed in London with empty pockets.[4]

Everywhere his keen eye captured detail for future lectures. Reserved and dignified at home, Kennan seemed another person on his travels, his lean, angular frame stalking through native grounds with the self-effacing dedication of a monk seeking truth in whatever form it took. He poked and pried everywhere, talked to anyone who might tell him something, and recorded what he saw and heard with an extraordinary precision that enabled him to describe it vividly years later. Kennan had found his life's classroom. Years later, asked where he had earned his degree, he replied, "Russia."[5]

When at last he came home, his career as writer and lecturer seemed well launched. But the need for security still tugged at him, and his family depended on him for support. In the summer of 1871 Kennan bought some stock in the Union Bank of Medina, New York, and became its cashier. Emeline Rathbone Weld, whom Kennan met in Medina that same summer, also spurred his desire to get ahead. For five years Kennan toiled at the bank. He became a model citizen, the leader of his Sunday school class, yet all the while he continued to lecture and write in hopes of earning enough to quit banking forever. The response to a western lecture tour in January 1876 so encouraged him that in May he left the bank and moved to New York with little more than his books and fifty dollars in his pocket.

Kennan broke with his past but could not escape it entirely. For six months he scraped by on $5.50 a week while struggling to find work with a newspaper, wire service, or scientific organization. When all these efforts failed, he meekly signed on as a clerk for a life insurance company. Meanwhile, he wrote and translated Russian furiously, waiting for the chance that finally came in November 1878 when the Associated Press (AP) sent him to Washington to cover the Supreme Court. Within a few months he had become AP's night manager in Washington.

By September 1879 Kennan felt secure enough to marry Emeline (or Lena, as she was called) Weld. Their long life together turned out to be more alone than they had hoped; their only child died at birth. Whatever vacuum this lack of children created the Kennans soon filled with work, causes, travel, simple pleasures, and the eccentricities any couple develops over time when their lives are so self-centered. Lena was a strong-willed, possessive woman who once drove away Kennan's namesake, young George F. Kennan, at their only meeting because she was afraid her husband would give the boy some of his treasures.[6]

Diplomat Willard D. Straight, after enduring a dinner party with the Kennans in 1904, decorated his diary with a caricature of Lena brandishing a hammer in each hand. "A dozen hammers would better describe her knocking power," he wrote, "and mean—small hurt rending." Nor was Straight much impressed with Kennan himself. "He . . . knows the methodist local lecture bureau's idea of the Real Hero," Straight sneered, "and the financial public's ideas on how he should act. He does."[7]

After his marriage Kennan's career took off, spurred by a knack for jumping on big stories and an ability to turn out thoughtful, incisive prose in a hurry. He gained attention through a series of articles on the ill-fated *Jeannette* polar expedition and handled the wires at the White House when President James A. Garfield was shot. But his eye never strayed far from Russia. In 1884 he returned for another long stay; the following year he contracted with *Century* magazine to undertake an expedition to Siberia.

By 1890 Kennan was widely recognized as an authority on Russian affairs. He churned out articles for major magazines like *Century* and worked the lecture circuit so intensely that in 1889 he felt bold enough to quit the Associated Press and live on his own free-lance efforts. He kept a rugged schedule, giving one hundred to two hundred lectures a season, often decking himself out in native Siberian garb, and sometimes collapsing from its rigors. In 1888 he and Lena found their perfect haven in Baddeck, a tiny settlement in the remote reaches of Cape Breton Island. For the rest of their lives the rhythm of their seasons revolved around summer and fall in Baddeck and winter in Medina.

In 1898, when the United States stumbled into war with Spain, Kennan hurried to Cuba as a war correspondent for *Outlook*. He was in Santiago during the surrender and stayed until the last Spanish troops sailed home. Six months later he returned to Cuba to explore the aftermath of war, then rushed home to launch a new lecture tour. He fell ill from fever during the tour but struggled on, complaining only to his diary.

The Cuban adventure clinched Kennan's reputation as a specialist in foreign affairs. *Outlook* asked him to write on the situation in China and then the Philippines, giving him claim to being present at the dawn of American empire. He became *Outlook*'s staff correspondent in Washington even while negotiating with S. S. McClure to underwrite another trip to Russia. Kennan was eager to go back to gather material for a biography of Lev Tolstoy, whom he had met and deeply admired.[8]

Unfortunately, the trip and the project fizzled because of the worsening political climate in Russia. Kennan had made himself unpopular with the czarist regime by championing the cause of political prisoners held captive in Siberia. Twenty days after his arrival in St. Petersburg, just as he was on the verge of completing arrangements with Tolstoy, the police ordered him to leave. Kennan never returned to Russia.

Foreign policy, long the sleepy hollow of affairs in Washington, sprang to life during these turbulent years. The rivalries for empire among European powers grew more explosive and were aggravated by the sudden emergence of the United States as an imperial force with its victory over Spain and acquisition of the Philippines as a footstool for its revived interest in the Far East. Germany blossomed as a formidable rival of England. Japan had scrapped its feudal traditions in favor of industrialization, and Russia struggled to modernize enough to stave off revolution.

These developments thrust Kennan into a limelight he relished. A vigorous new president had come to office who was keenly interested in foreign affairs. Theodore Roosevelt had a habit of enlisting anyone who could be of service to him and was quick to draw Kennan into his orbit. There were luncheons and receptions at the White House as well as private sessions in which Kennan briefed the president on Russia, Cuba, Japan, or whatever interested Roosevelt at the moment.

When the Russo-Japanese War erupted in 1904, *Outlook* dispatched Kennan to cover it. Unable to get into Russia, he went instead to Japan for a stay that lasted two years. Although his contact with Russians was limited to the inmates of two prisoner of war camps he visited, Kennan managed to travel extensively in China and Korea as well as Japan, bolstering his credentials as a Far Eastern expert. In Japan he interviewed and socialized with leading political and business figures. By the war's end he knew everybody who mattered.

After Kennan's return in 1906, S. S. McClure tapped him for the staff of his muckraking magazine. He was sent to California to cover two major stories: a sensational graft investigation in the Bay area and growing tension over Japanese students in California schools. For two years Kennan kept a frantic pace as McClure shoved him about the country like a piece on a chessboard, then abruptly dispatched him to England. Kennan returned home in July 1908 and simply collapsed.

The nervous breakdown forced him to stop. For six months Kennan rested in Baddeck with Lena, trying to heal his frayed nerves and exhausted body. Although his spirit remained undiminished at sixty-three, the pace was wearing him down. He left *McClure's* and returned to the more congenial pace at *Outlook*, but he did not give up the lecture circuit or slow his writing output because he could not afford the luxury of repose. He had not laid up much money, and old age was fast approaching.

And Kennan was brilliant at what he did. People flocked to his lectures because few rivaled his ability to paint a scene with words. Everywhere he traveled—the Siberian tundra, the Cuban swamps, the jungle trails of Central America, the angry volcanic mouth of Mt. Pelee (where he had covered an eruption), the mountain slopes of Mt. Altai—he took meticulous notes that

Explorer turned biographer: George Kennan in 1903, before the rigors of exploring and lecturing wore him down. (Library of Congress)

enabled him to describe an adventure in vivid detail. One man who heard Kennan's talk on the Caucasus complimented him many years later on the splendid pictures he had shown to illustrate the lecture. There had been no pictures.[9]

Lawrence Abbott of *Outlook* told Kennan in 1911 that he had been an uplifting influence on his life. Kennan was flattered, but praise did not pay the bills. Every winter he girded up for another season of lectures while continuing to grind out articles for the twenty-five or fifty dollars they fetched. While his reputation ensured him work, his lack of security meant little rest. "It hurts me to let work go not as good as I can make it," he sighed in May 1912, but he had little choice. During that year Kennan penned 37,200 words for *Outlook* alone; in 1913 he churned out 20,000 words in two months.[10]

He could not keep up this pace indefinitely, but a solution to the problem eluded his weary eyes. In fact, it slipped in unnoticed through the back door, disguised as a request from Will Dall, an old friend, to stand in for him at a dinner given in honor of Mary Harriman.[11]

At sixty-one Mary W. Harriman was one of the richest and most powerful women in the world. As the widow of railroad baron E. H. Harriman, whose estate had been worth anywhere from $70 million to $100 million, she was well provided for financially. But Harriman had given her something else that set her apart from any other widow of a financial titan. In one of the shortest wills on record, he had made Mary the sole beneficiary and executrix for his entire fortune. Suddenly, in September 1909, she had found herself atop a vast business empire.[12]

The Harrimans had always been more a clan than a family—close, proud, fiercely loyal to one another. Henry (as he was called at home) had shared his business secrets with Mary and had full confidence in her ability to manage the huge fortune he had left behind. His decision was deliberate; he had not died suddenly but in slow, painful agony from cancer. No one expected Mary to enter the business world, and she did not. The fortune became a passive one, but she took an active role in its management with help from family agent C. C. Tegethoff and Henry's lawyer and most trusted adviser, Judge Robert S. Lovett.

At first, she did nothing. Crushed by grief, she languished in seclusion at Arden, the huge estate in the Ramapo Mountains of New York that Henry had not lived to complete. Then, in January 1910, she confided to friends that she was ready to take up life again. She came back to New York City, reopened the family brownstone at 1 East 69th Street, and took up the one business that had pursued her even in mourning. During the months after Henry's death thousands of "begging" letters had poured into Arden. Some were genuine; others fraudulent, but one thing became clear to Mary: her lifelong interest in philanthropy was about to become a profession.[13]

She was well suited to it. Her father had been a prominent businessman and banker in Ogdensburg, New York, where Mary had spent most of her childhood. He had long been active in civic and welfare activities, served for years as a vestryman of St. John's Church, and took part in state and local politics as a Democrat. After a stay at finishing school in New York City, it was only natural

Devoted couple: Mary and E. H. Harriman pose for photographers just before leaving for Europe in 1909. (Union Pacific Museum Collection)

that Mary come home to immerse herself in charitable work. So successful did she become that the minister at St. John's who presided over her wedding complained that the ceremony cost him "the services of a young lady who had become a leader in every good work, especially in helpful ministries, to the ignorant, the distressed and the poor."[14]

Good works, then, was a business Mary knew well. She needed all the help she could get; within six months of Henry's death the requests for money pouring in on her totaled $247 million. Like Henry, she had a passion for efficiency and a horror of waste. Like him, too, she left a personal stamp on everything she did. Mary moved quickly to systematize her charitable work, but she gave not a dime to any cause that did not interest her personally. She showed no detachment, no professional distance from the causes she supported. Not until 1925 did Mary bother to establish a charitable trust, and even then the fund remained in the tight control of her two sons and her lawyer.[15]

During the first year after Henry's death Mary put money into causes dear to him and herself: the Boys' Club, the tuberculosis sanitarium of old friend Dr. E. L. Trudeau, the work of John Muir, another good friend, to save Yosemite Valley, the efforts of C. Hart Merriam, who had edited the volumes on the Alaskan expedition Harriman had sponsored, to collect data on the animals of North America. Although the family never admitted that Henry died of cancer, Mary gave the chief surgeon of the Southern Pacific Railroad $60,000 for bacteriological and pathological research. Closer to home, she completed a project begun by Henry to donate nearly half of Arden's acreage along with a $1 million endowment to the state of New York as an extension of the Palisades Interstate Park.[16]

One cause above all others obsessed Mary Harriman, indeed fueled all the good works she sustained: the memory of her husband. In many respects her life became a monument to his memory, to preserving what she deemed a true image of it. Like good clansmen, too, the Harrimans were slow to forgive those who had wronged them. The last years of Henry's life had been wracked with controversy. In the generic attack on big business during the Progressive era his name had been dragged through the mud on several transactions that became the target of reformers.

Nothing had damaged Harriman's reputation more than his break with Theodore Roosevelt, who denounced his old friend as an undesirable citizen, a malefactor of great wealth, and a liar. There followed an Interstate Commerce Commission (ICC) investigation of Harriman's roads and a host of attacks by what Otto H. Kahn later called the "Harriman Extermination League." Press, pulpit, and polticos alike scourged him as an engine of greed who held the law in disdain. Gradually the fickle gyroscope of public opinion tilted back from this hysteria to admiration for Harriman and his achievements, but the fight cost him the last of his fragile health.[17]

Kahn had called the last year of Harriman's life a "triumphal procession," but that did not satisfy Mary. She never forgave Roosevelt for what she considered a dishonest and treacherous act. Her thirst for vengeance still burned in 1910. When the Republicans got walloped in the off-year elections in New York despite some arduous campaigning by Roosevelt, she crowed to her diary, "Everyone jubilant over Roosevelt's defeat, a vindication of all Henry suffered." But Mary wanted some more positive and permanent memorial, a biography of Henry that would set the record straight by putting down the "true" story of his vast accomplishments. History would be Henry's judge, but someone had to call court into session.[18]

Shortly after returning to New York in 1910, Mary found the man she thought right for the job. George W. Batson had been a reporter for the *Wall Street Journal* before joining the banking firm of Eugene Meyer & Company. He was regarded as a railroad expert and had got to know Harriman in that context. Still a young man eager to make his mark, Batson admired Harriman greatly and was willing to tackle the assignment. In May 1910 he published an adulatory magazine article on Harriman. The piece appeared anonymously, with the author described as one who was closer to Harriman in the last years than anyone outside the family.[19]

Mary personally opened every door for Batson to family friends, Wall Street men, acquaintances, and key people in the companies Henry had dominated. Nearly everyone agreed to be interviewed, and even some of Harriman's old foes such as James J. Hill filled Batson's ear with tales of bygone clashes. In November 1910 Batson commenced writing the biography even as he continued to interview people and collect material. By the following March he had carried the story down to the Northern Securities panic of 1901, where he stopped cold. "It is unwise, if not impossible," advised Mary, "to go any further until I have an opportunity to see such of Mr. Harriman's private correspondence and papers as throw light on his business career."[20]

For some reason, these papers were slow in coming. Although Batson diligently interviewed the people who had been close to Harriman, he could not get close to Harriman's own papers. Why Mary held them back is not clear, but Batson kept writing anyway. By September 1911 he had completed sixteen chapters, all of which were sent to Mary and Judge Lovett for careful scrutiny. In December rumors leaked out that the manuscript was complete and would be published in time for the forthcoming election.[21]

The rumors were wrong. The manuscript was far from complete, more a collection of fragments than chapters. Batson was anxious to finish it, but the effort was wearing him down. "While it is a pleasure," he told Mary wearily, "it is also a responsibility & a strain on top of many others." Then disaster struck. On January 9, 1912, a fire swept through the Equitable Life building at 120 Broadway, which also housed the Union Pacific Railroad offices. The company was in the midst of moving to new offices, but the blaze hit before most of its records had been transferred. Most of the company papers for the Harriman era, along with many of Harriman's own papers, went up in flames.[22]

In later years both Harriman sons, Averell and Roland, perpetuated the story that all their father's papers had gone up in the Equitable Building fire. By then they may well have believed it, but at the time they knew better. Judge Lovett, a man renowned for his rectitude, said the same thing, as did others familiar with the event. Yet on the day of the fire Lovett assured reporters that Harriman's papers had not been lost because they had already been moved to the Fifth Avenue office of the Harriman estate. Why this story changed over time remains a mystery.[23]

Batson never got a chance to find out. In March 1912 he fell ill and underwent an operation for mastoiditis. Two months later he was dead, leaving the biography unfinished and its future in doubt. Ironically, the project fell into limbo just as Theodore Roosevelt was mounting a desperate bid to regain the presidency. Mary Harriman never lacked determination, but she did not know where to turn. Who now would tell Henry's story as she wanted it told?[24]

The dinner party for Mary Harriman in March 1912 was given by C. Hart Merriam, who had invited some fellow members of the 1899 Alaskan expedition to join them at dinner or afterward. Will Dall was one of them but could not attend. Since George Kennan happened to be in Washington and was at home among scientists, Dall asked him to escort Mrs. Dall to the dinner. There Kennan met Mary Harriman for the first time and with her the doorway to a destiny he had never even remotely contemplated.[25]

Kennan attached no significance to the evening because nothing happened for nearly two years. Then in January 1914 he received a letter from Merriam saying that Mary Harriman wished to discuss something important with Kennan the next time he was in New York. On February 4 Kennan went to 1 East 69th for lunch; the only other guest was one of Mary's nieces. Mary described the Batson manuscript and asked Kennan to read it and give her an opinion on it. The next day Kennan went to Mary's office at 475 Fifth Avenue, where he met Tegethoff and began reading the manuscript.[26]

Why Mary chose Kennan is unclear. He was unknown to her and knew nothing of railroads or finance. Although he had met Harriman when they both happened to be in Japan, he was not familiar with his career. Possibly Merriam recommended him to her; certainly she liked what she saw. They were of similar age (Kennan was six years older) and tastes—conservative, reserved people who shunned display. Kennan had an excellent reputation as a writer; he could be counted on to be fair, painstaking, and discreet. Harriman's life was full of prickly, controversial episodes. To Mary's displeasure, Batson had been prone to lapse into what she deemed sensationalism in describing them. Kennan would surely avoid that temptation.[27]

Whatever her reasons, Mary came quickly to a decision. On March 1 Kennan mailed off his report, which had little good to say about the manuscript. Privately he called it "badly arranged and faulty in style and good taste." Back came a special delivery letter asking him to rewrite the biography on his own terms. Startled by the offer, Kennan agonized for days over his reply. Here at last was an opportunity for the financial security that seemed always to elude him, but what should he seek? Finally, on March 26, Kennan sent off a long letter saying he would undertake the work for $6,000 a year with a three-year limit. Two days later Mary replied that a "family council" had unanimously approved the terms.[28]

She agreed that Kennan need not give up his other duties at once but could work half-time on the biography until October. That summer, when war erupted in Europe and rang down the curtain on an era of Western history, the shift in Kennan's life became apparent even though it had scarcely begun. Normally so monumental an event abroad would have absorbed his attention and swamped him with work. Instead, he remained aloof from the crisis, gathering material for the Harriman biography while penning occasional articles for *Outlook*, which still had him under contract.[29]

In October Kennan returned to New York City, leased a friend's apartment on Fifth Avenue, and dug into the biography. Mary invited him to spend a weekend at Arden, giving him a first look at the estate. On the train he ran into young Roland Harriman, who had been thrown from his horse while fox hunting and was encased in a plaster cast from chin to waist. He was traveling home with his doctor. It was dark when the train arrived at Arden Station. As they got off, the doctor pointed to a cluster of lights alongside the stars and said, "There's Arden House."[30]

"Do you mean those lights on the very top of the mountain?" asked an astonished Kennan.

"Yes," replied the doctor. "It isn't far in the air line, but it is 1300 feet above us, and five miles away by road."

To Kennan's surprise, Roland drove the car, grasping the wheel crablike around his plaster shell. They passed what Kennan thought was a large country house, only to be told it was the stable, and zigzagged up the mountain along a road that reminded Kennan of a favorite bridle path in the Caucasus. The mountainside was a shroud of unbroken forest, but on the valley side constellations of village and farmhouse lights twinkled in the distance. At the top stood Arden, which Harriman had insisted be built by American workmen (mostly his own) with American materials. The house was a huge, irregularly shaped mansion of cut stone bounded by a high wall covered in Japanese ivy on one side and with a view across the treetops on the other.

A wide corridor of colored marbles led into a giant room with a marble floor softened by rugs and bearskins. Kennan peered at a fireplace as tall as himself flanked by sofas, easy chairs, and two or three tables with stacks of magazines and newspapers. All the rooms at Arden were cavernous and bordered a central court with a fountain, shrubbery, and some statuary. Vases and tubs of flowers lined the corridors and spilled over into every room. A grand stairway of unpolished white marble led Kennan to his bedroom, where, after a brief chat with Mary, he found his suitcase unpacked, his things put away, and his evening clothes laid out on the bed.

The dinner was delicious, the servants to Kennan's fussy eye well trained and unobtrusive. Afterward they went into the organ room, which to Kennan's amazement was about the size of the Episcopal Church in Medina. Another huge fireplace dominated one end, and a giant loft concealing the organ stood at the other beneath a high, vaulted ceiling. Kennan thought the room could seat at least two hundred people. An immense bas relief of an Indian hunting buffalo, done by Mary's son-in-law Charles Cary Rumsey, loomed above the fireplace.

Kennan was grateful to find no other visitors. Besides Mary, her daughter Carol, and Roland, there was only the doctor and a Miss Pritchett, who had been Carol's chaperone in Europe. After coffee and liqueurs were served, the women knitted while the men smoked. They sat and talked until just before eleven, when everyone went to bed. Kennan used the opportunity to chat with Mary about the war, politics, *Outlook*, and Theodore Roosevelt, taking care to remain circumspect on every topic.

The whole weekend was pleasant in every respect and served to draw Kennan more deeply into the Harriman orbit. After services at Arden Church on Sunday morning, Mary took Kennan to the graves of Henry and his namesake son, who had died at age four. They lay beneath plain rough slabs of granite smothered in fresh white chrysanthemums. There was something elegant in the simplicity of the site. The family plot occupied the far corner of the churchyard, the only spot in the enclosure where the bluestone reached the surface. It was only fitting that Harriman's grave had been blasted from solid rock; in death as in life, he had let no obstacle deter him from his chosen course.[31]

Once back in New York, Kennan found Mary generous with small favors despite her busy schedule. She took the Kennans to the symphony, lent them her box at the opera, had them to tea. Tegethoff escorted him to the Harriman National Bank on Fifth Avenue to open an account. Kennan plunged happily into the work, prowling the New York Public Library for days at a time. Reluctantly he declined all lecture invitations, but he could not entirely let go of his other life. That fall he agreed to furnish several stories to *Century* and occasional two-thousand-word articles to *Outlook*.[32]

At least one friend warned Kennan that his task would be difficult. Harriman was hard to capture, said Joseph Stanley-Brown at dinner one evening, because there was so much good and so much bad in him. Moreover, the cancer that killed Harriman affected his temper toward the end and made him bitter. Stanley-Brown's views could not be taken lightly; he had spent three years in Harriman's employ before going into banking. Nor did time soften his views; six years later, at a dinner party, he growled that Harriman "had not the soul of a peanut." He had treated Tegethoff like a dog, alienated Jacob Schiff, James Stillman, and his other close friends except Otto Kahn, was niggardly with money, selfish, secretive, and disagreeable in the extreme.[33]

At every turn Kennan found mysteries, contradictions, fragments of stories spewed angrily by partisans on both sides of the Harriman legend. It intrigued him that Harriman aroused such passions. Those close to Mary were fiercely loyal to Henry's reputation and expected Kennan to vindicate it fully. Could he be co-opted without being compromised? If this question troubled Kennan, he gave no sign of it. In fact, he decided to enter the debate over Harriman at its most sensitive point. Stanley-Brown had warned that the Chicago & Alton deal in particular would be hard to explain. Batson had not even touched the episode. Finding this to be the lightning rod of controversy, Kennan started his work with it.

Mastering the Alton's intricacies helped plant Kennan squarely in Harriman's financial and railroad affairs. In August 1915 he completed a twelve-thousand-word piece, which was then read by Mary, Judge Lovett, Otto Kahn of Kuhn, Loeb, Paul Cravath, the Wall Street lawyer who had been Harriman's counsel in the fight, and Samuel M. Felton, the railroad man Harriman had put in charge of the Alton. Everyone was impressed. Lovett marveled that "one not brought up in the railroad world could have written it," Kahn that "one not brought up in the financial world" could have produced it. Kahn offered some incisive suggestions, Felton a packet of new data and ten pages of comments.[34]

Originally Kennan intended the work as a chapter in the biography. A quirk of fate, however, led him into the eye of a storm that would redefine the entire project. That same summer Professor William Z. Ripley, a Harvard economist and noted railroad authority, published a book titled *Railroads: Finance and Organization* in which he depicted the Alton transaction as a showcase for all the abuses and depredations of unscrupulous railroad operators. Along the way Ripley called Harriman a "conspirator" who "crippled" the Alton with his "piratical" and "fraudulent" tactics.[35]

This was too much for Kennan, who had explored the same episode in far more detail. "I'm sick of seeing the Alton transaction referred to every little while as a classical illustration of wrecking, looting, piracy & fraud," he told Tegethoff. If Mary would give him a free hand, he wanted nothing better than to go after Ripley. Mary was quick to agree, and Kennan set about turning the chapter into an article rebutting Ripley's charges.[36]

The logical place for the piece was *Outlook*, but Kennan ran into trouble there. His article took a swipe at Theodore Roosevelt, who had been associated with the magazine since leaving the White House. Caught between two longtime friends, Lawrence Abbott squirmed in misery before rejecting the article because it was too long. Instead he asked Kennan for a shorter piece praising Harriman's "great constructive railroad genius" rather than one steeped in criticism. "If such an idea interests you," he added pointedly, "I would strongly advise against referring to the controversy with Mr. Roosevelt. It would be awkward for us to take that up."[37]

Kennan got the message: whatever Abbott's regard for him, he would do nothing that offended Roosevelt. Mary brushed the setback aside, saying, "We shall have to try, try again." They went next to the *North American Review*, and Mary decided to have the piece published privately as a small book as well. Thus began a pattern in which certain episodes of the biography also saw life as independent volumes. The Alton fracas alone produced two such books.[38]

The *Review* accepted a shortened version. By chance, both the article and the full account in book form appeared in January 1916. Mary had five thousand copies of the book printed and distributed them broadside to newspapers, libraries, banking and brokerage firms, railroad officials, and friends. Letters of praise flowed in from admirers of Harriman who believed he had long gotten a bum rap. Some politicians too conceded that Harriman's role had been misunderstood. Secretary of the Interior Franklin K. Lane, who had been on the ICC commission Kennan criticized, told Kennan that "Harriman was doing what the commercial conscience of the time approved of."[39]

If Kennan thought he had laid the Alton controversy to rest, he was soon undeceived. The pompous Ripley was furious over the article and took refuge behind a wall of academic arrogance. "I have received the interesting and presumably rather expensive defense of Harriman which you have permitted to appear over your name," he wrote Kennan haughtily. "The substance of it interests me not at all. You have too evidently marred a well-deserved literary reputation for money." After three more paragraphs of labored contempt, Ripley added, "Why not write Harriman's life by emphasizing the good work and passing over his crimes lightly. You can't whitewash them. Forget them."[40]

Although the letter outraged Kennan, he dismissed it for what it was: ill-mannered and ill-advised. But Ripley had only begun. Samuel Felton was astonished to receive an ingratiating letter from Ripley seeking information on the Alton episode. Roberts Walker, a Wall Street lawyer who had investigated the

Alton on behalf of the interests who wrested the road from Harriman, got a similar inquiry. Both passed copies along to Kennan. A month later Walker saw Kennan and warned him that the professor was still "pretty well wrought up by your article and has also been prodded to reply to it by the Interstate Commerce Commission and by a very eminent gentleman at Oyster Bay."[41]

The flinty Kennan was not about to back down. "The C. & A. case ought to have been threshed out long ago," he insisted, "and if Mr. Ripley makes a rejoinder, we can thresh it out now." The passions aroused by the stirring of bones that were fifteen years old had caught him up, and, as Walker observed, the stakes were going up. Kennan's book had shaken the credibility not only of a distinguished Harvard professor but also of the Interstate Commerce Commission and the president, whom some thought had put the ICC up to the investigation in the first place.[42]

Mary's dander was up as well, and she made a formidable adversary. After seeing Ripley's letter, she sought the views of several leading academics: President Arthur T. Hadley of Yale, himself a transportation expert, the historian Charles A. Beard of Columbia, and the economist E. R. A. Seligman of Columbia. Beard praised Kennan's book except for what he called its "little spirit of bitterness." The tactful Seligman suggested that the best way to approach Harriman's life was to praise his achievements and "omit references to his questionable actions."[43]

None of them knew what to make of Ripley's intemperate letter, but Kennan understood perfectly. The Ropes Professor of Economics had been caught with his scholarly pants down. In what he intended as a magisterial work on railroads he had seized on the Alton legend as a bad example without looking at it closely. No amount of prestige could conceal the fact that he simply had not done his homework. To make matters worse, his sloppy work had been challenged by a man Ripley deemed a mere amateur, a journalist. His professional feelings bruised and his reputation threatened, Ripley lashed out with more venom than good sense.

While preparing a rejoinder that in his view would demolish Kennan, Ripley wrote Seligman a letter obviously intended for Mary Harriman's eyes. He praised Harriman's "great constructive ability" but warned against raking up old scandals. Kennan, he suggested, should either tackle the biography "in a more dignified way, or else it should be done by an expert in work of this kind." Kennan hardly needed lessons in dignity, and Mary scoffed at Ripley's advice. "Either he is stupid," she said in exasperation, "or conceited beyond belief." Otto Kahn examined the letters and deplored Ripley's "exhibition of temper, unfairness, and ill breeding."[44]

Ripley's vaunted rejoinder in the *North American Review* proved a high horse that pulled up embarrassingly lame. The professor gave a very unprofessional performance, resorting to ad hominum attacks, appeals to authority ("it takes years to master these affairs," he sneered privately to Kennan), digressions, vague generalizations, innuendos, irrelevancies, and mishandled evidence. He pounced on one of Kennan's sources as a "third-rate hack" without acknowledging the very full list of other creditable references. Never did he engage Kennan's main points or refute his arguments.[45]

Mary Harriman may have been partisan, but her reaction to Ripley's article was right on target. "It is patchy and incoherent," she observed. "I can not make anything out of it." It was also nasty, mean-spirited, and blustering—a perfect target for Kennan to skewer, which he did in a reply as precise and specific as Ripley was vague and dismissive. Ironically, it was Kennan who proved more the scholar and Ripley the journalist in this dispute. On his first page Ripley included this breathless passage:

> [Harriman] was a dominant factor in the inner circles of the greatest banking institutions. The vast resources of the New York Life Insurance companies were at his disposition. Ramifications of his political power, Federal and State, extended to every quarter of the land. State and even national conventions took his orders. Members of Congress did his bidding. Laws were enacted at his will. Only two men ever dared to block his path. The late J. P. Morgan stood between him and the possession of the Northern Pacific Railroad in 1901; and Theodore Roosevelt thwarted his purpose to become an absolute dictator of the transportation affairs of the United States.

By contrast, Kennan had done his homework well and consulted the men who had been there. He may have been a hired gun, as Ripley kept belaboring, but his aim was precise and he used live ammunition.[46]

To bolster his position, Ripley solicited help from Roosevelt, who in 1916 was eyeing yet another run at the presidency. Roosevelt furnished a letter that Ripley reprinted in his article. Referring to the piece written by "a Mr. George Kennan" as if he had not known the author for years, Roosevelt dismissed its arguments and blasted the suggestion that he would prompt an investigation because of a personal disagreement as "monstrous in its iniquity, and equally monstrous in its absurdity." Undaunted, Kennan responded by hoisting Roosevelt on his own petard of past performance in a short but effective piece titled "The Psychology of Mr. Roosevelt."[47]

By any measure both Ripley and Roosevelt got the worst of the exchange, and both soon retreated in silence. Kennan wanted to publish a volume with both his articles along with Ripley's. The professor first gave his permission, then changed his mind a few days later. He did, however, send a copy of his piece to Judge Lovett and asked "whether I have fairly represented the situation so far as any outsider can do so." The judge assured him that he had not. "I find it impossible," Lovett said bluntly, "to account for the utter recklessness of many of your assertions upon any theory consistent with fairness."[48]

Ripley's version of the Alton affair was discredited, yet even the loyal Lovett had some misgivings. "I would never write an estimate of Harriman for Mrs. Harriman," he admitted to Clarence Barron in June 1915, "for as a woman she would not appreciate the facts I set down. Harriman was not a man without his faults. My idea is that you praise Harriman if you set forth his faults and his great qualities." But he conceded that the Alton was Harriman's Achilles' heel: "We tried many times to explain the Alton matter but we never could reach any satisfactory explanation. . . . I do not think there could be any explanation made. Harriman declared it was the one blot on his record."[49]

If Kennan shared this broader view of Harriman, he kept it to himself. The Alton fight made him more than ever a partisan—a meticulous and careful one, but a partisan nevertheless. Increasingly he came to view his task as shaping the major episodes of Harriman's career in the most favorable light within the bounds of the known facts. This was precisely what Mary and all the old family friends wanted, and the Alton fight showed them conclusively that Kennan was their man. It also reaped him two important rewards, one expected and the other wholly unexpected.

From the outset Kennan realized that he had to overcome the handicap of venturing into fields in which he had no credentials. "Now that the little book is out," he told Mary in January 1916, "it will be easier to get everybody to talk freely. Before it seemed to be tacitly assumed that I, as a mere literary man & an expert on Russia, couldn't be expected to understand railroad affairs." The Alton imbroglio firmly established his credibility in both railroad and financial affairs. He had routed one of the foremost authorities in the field, made him look foolish. Whatever else happened, he would be taken seriously.[50]

The second benefit went beyond the fringe. Kennan saw that he had won Mary's complete trust, but he could not know what this meant. As late as November 1915 he complained, "In studying Mr Harriman's life nothing has surprised me more than the almost complete lack of letters & documents. Nobody seems to have preserved anything." Now and then something turned up. Melville E. Stone of the Associated Press, who had known Harriman well, talked to Kennan about the Alton affair. Later Stone recalled that Harriman had once given him a statement he had dictated but never used. Stone rummaged through piles of old junk at his house and produced what purported to be Harriman's only defense of the Alton affair. But was it? It bore no identification, and no one else, not even Harriman's closest friends, knew of its existence.[51]

Kennan made good use of the statement in his Alton piece, but such finds were disappointingly rare until March 1. On that date Mary surprised him with a bundle of short memoirs on Henry that she had personally solicited from his close friends. Many of them were little more than syrupy panegyrics, but some contained revealing and useful anecdotes. "There are many interesting documents at my office," Mary hinted on the card attached to the bundle. A few days later she asked Kennan to meet her at Tegethoff's office. When he got there, Tegethoff had already arranged nineteen large manila envelopes on the desk, all with headings related to Harriman's major activities. Before Kennan could examine them, Mary arrived and led him to the basement of Farmers Loan & Trust Company. There she fetched out a large tin box filled with more envelopes.[52]

Kennan's eyes widened in surprise. Here spread before him were many of the papers supposedly burned in the Equitable fire: letters, telegrams, testimony, printed matter, clippings—even an Alton letterbook and a second copy of Harriman's Alton statement. Scarcely able to contain his excitement, he plunged eagerly into the mass of material despite a turn in the weather that forced him to trudge home in a blizzard. Not even the cold he caught dampened the enthusiasm he expressed that night in his diary: "Nothing since I began this work has astonished me more than this sudden disclosing of this mass of material. When I asked Mrs. Harriman, more than a year ago, if she did not have letters of Mr Harriman and documentary material generally I understood her to reply in the negative. I have never even suspected before that there was such a quantity of stuff in existence. Whether she didn't fully trust me at first & has been trying me out or not I don't know." There had been a test, and Kennan had passed with flying colors. Three days later Mary called at the Kennans' apartment for the first time, a gesture that was symbolic in more than social terms.[53]

A turning point in the project had been reached. Mary now trusted Kennan completely and was confident he was the man to redeem Henry's memory. There was a subtle irony in her delivering over the mass of papers on Harriman: she was giving Kennan the means to write a fuller biography under conditions, however implicit, that they be used to write the right kind of biography. In one stroke she had freed Kennan and bound him to her more than ever. She did not expect him to be dishonest, but she did expect him to be discreet and, above all, loyal. Time would prove her judgment to be thoroughly sound.

The original three-year time limit was forgotten as the project grew larger. When Kennan found that he had underestimated the cost of living in New York and was struggling to make ends meet, Mary picked up the rent on the Fifth Avenue apartment so he could work undisturbed. She did the Kennans countless favors, most of them unasked, and commissioned two more separate volumes, one on Harriman's saving of the Imperial Valley from flooding and the other on his ambitious plans for a Far Eastern transportation system circling the globe.[54]

Personally she began to treat Kennan as if he were an old family friend. In January 1917 she received him for the first time in an upstairs room of her town house that Kennan found far more pleasant than the cold downstairs parlors. It was, he told Lena, "the kind of room that we should have if we owned the house." Mary looked worn from a siege of the grippe, yet she impressed Kennan with her grasp of a wide range of topics, as if she felt freer to discuss her views. Averell and Roland were there, too, and joined in a discussion of the Imperial Valley book. "The whole Harriman family seems to be far more satisfied with all the work I have done thus far," he said after the visit, "and I felt tonight more than at any previous time, an atmosphere of cordial approval."[55]

They had reason to be pleased. Kennan had produced the two little volumes on the Imperial Valley and Far Eastern episodes during the summer and fall of 1916 while studying and indexing the mass of new material in Tegethoff's office. Kennan's way of organizing a project was to create an elaborate index, using business envelopes instead of cards to record and cross-reference each item, and tucking relevant clippings or notes inside the envelope. Eventually the file swelled to more than eight thousand envelopes, neatly stacked, arranged, and coded in Kennan's monklike script and private shorthand.[56]

The Far Eastern volume took Kennan for the first time into an area on which Batson had written. A close look at Batson's work convinced Kennan anew that it was riddled with errors and could not be used without checking every fact. He pursued the biography in the same piecemeal way that he had come into it, taking up the major episodes in no particular order other than to gratify Mary's wishes or his own curiosity. As the work progressed, Averell Harriman took a closer interest, digging up new material, critiquing chapters, providing Kennan access to people he needed to see. So did Jacob Schiff, the venerable head of Kuhn, Loeb, who was impressed by Kennan's ability and offered himself as both source and critic.[57]

Everything Kennan wrote went first to Mary and then to Averell, Judge Lovett, or other family friends who knew something about the subject. In this way every chapter got direct feedback from participants whose memories were sometimes more convenient than accurate. Although Kennan was a stickler for verifying the facts, he could hardly dispute the word of a trusted family friend who had been there unless he had contradictory information. Not surprisingly, Kennan found his way to very few sources unfriendly to Harriman's career beyond those that already existed in print. Those who talked frankly about Harriman did not expect to see their reservations put into print. Besides, anything that Kennan wrote had to run the gauntlet of Mary's approval.

Nothing betrayed Kennan's dilemma more than his handling of Harriman's personal life. During the last year of his life Harriman had sat for a bust by Auguste Rodin. Kennan spent some time one January day studying the piece, yet what could he do with any insights he gleaned? Mary was an intensely private person who shuddered at the idea of making public any detail, however trivial, of her life, and she felt the same way about Henry's life. Such was her horror of the personal that she did not even want Kennan to say explicitly that Harriman had died of cancer. There could be mention of pain and suffering because it affected his work, but the cause must go unmentioned.[58]

This attitude would have created an insuperable barrier for most biographers but not for Kennan because he felt exactly the same way. "I am in perfect sympathy with all you say about giving to the public one's intimate life," he assured Mary. "I have a horror of such revelations myself, and I have been begging my wife for years to let me destroy hundreds of my letters to her, for fear that we might both be killed suddenly in an automobile accident, and that our letters to each other might fall into the hands of our executors."[59]

The result was a biography with a subject but not a character. In taking up Harriman's business career Kennan was partisan but thorough, building his case with careful research and painstaking care. In treating the man, however, he stayed at arm's length, sculpting a monument instead of a figure, casting him in stone instead of flesh until he began to assume mythic proportions. The final product was not a man cloaked in mystery and contradiction but a noble shrine undisturbed by blemishes.

Through the dark years of war and peace Kennan toiled at his task, watching events only from the corner of his eye. In 1917 the revolution in Russia tugged incessantly at his attention, but not even a siege by reporters could pull him from the biography. Here was yet another savage irony. Years later Soviet president Mikhail Kalinin told young George F. Kennan that he had grown up reading his namesake's books on Siberia, which had become the bible for radical students. At the time of the revolution, however, America's best-known Russia watcher missed that country's most historic moment because he was preoccupied with recounting the career of America's premier capitalist.[60]

The reason was not hard to find. Wartime inflation had made the Kennans more dependent on Mary's largesse than they cared to admit. They clung gratefully to the comfortable apartment on Fifth Avenue for which she paid the rent. "I don't know how we could have got along without it," Kennan admitted to her. In May 1919 he asked for one more year of free rent to finish the project. Mary granted it readily, assuring him that she was in no hurry.[61]

The one year stretched into two as illness dogged Kennan and the handling of controversial episodes slowed his pace. He also had a problem with audience that most authors never face. Mary had originally conceived the biography as a memorial for her children and had not yet decided whether the public should have it. "It is possible," Kennan told Schiff in May 1920, "that the biography may not be published in your lifetime or mine." The break with Roosevelt offered a classic example of the dilemma. "It may not be expedient to publish all of it now," he told Mary, "because it will hit Mr Roosevelt very hard."[62]

The same held true for Harriman's much publicized break with his longtime friend Stuyvesant Fish, which had aroused almost as much bitterness and censure as the clash with Roosevelt. Friends advised leaving an ugly pot unstirred, but Kennan disagreed. He balked at detailing what he called "the ambitious & lavish extravagance of both Mr & Mrs Fish (in style of living, personal expenditures, &c) which led him into his speculations," but he insisted on clearing Harriman of the charge that he had betrayed an old friend.[63]

In August 1920 Kennan finally surrendered his New York apartment and moved back to Medina with all his material. His pace of writing had picked up during the past year despite severe attacks of diarrhea that left him weak and dispirited. Time had begun to work against him in several respects. Schiff died in September 1920, having lived long enough to critique Kennan's account of the Northern Pacific fight but not the dissolution of Northern Securities. At seventy-five Kennan himself no longer possessed his old energy, yet he drove the work forward despite repeated bouts of illness.[64]

By October he had produced about 165,000 words treating all the major episodes in Harriman's life. "There are several chapters already written," he told Mary, "such as Boyhood and Early Life at Arden, that I would like to go over with you when you have time. They need revision and editing in the light of your personal knowledge and taste." There were also some minor episodes to cover and a summary of Harriman's character and business methods that Kennan was eager to do if Mary approved. Not until July 1921 did Kennan declare the manuscript finished.[65]

By then Mary had made her decision. A dozen years had passed since Henry's death. Many of the participants, including Roosevelt, had gone to their graves, and Mary herself had just turned seventy. But some of Henry's antagonists still lived; Judge Lovett was reluctant to let the chapter on Stuyvesant Fish go unless Fish himself had a chance to comment on it. After some hesitation Mary brushed these objections aside and in April 1921 told Kennan to look for a suitable publisher. Her monument to Henry would be a public one, thanks in large measure to the skill and dedication of its sculptor.[66]

Once decided, Mary pushed to get the book in print as soon as possible. She applauded when Kennan negotiated a contract with Houghton Mifflin, a house that prided itself on publishing American biographies and autobiographies, and willingly assumed the cost of composition and plates (about $3,000) to help Kennan obtain a higher royalty. Through the months of preparation she rained letters on Kennan, prodding, agonizing over every detail with him, impatient to get the final product into reviewers' hands. Kennan showed no resentment but remained as deferential as ever. "It will always be a source of pride to me," he told Mary, "that I have had an opportunity to associate my name, even as a recorder, with the name of the greatest and most useful business man who has lived in my time."[67]

On February 28, 1922, Kennan read the last proof and signed off on the work that had occupied eight years of his life. "It is not perfect," he told Mary, "but it represents the best work I can do." In reply Mary poured out her gratitude "for satisfying my hopes & desires. You have been so faithful & loyal to Mr. Harriman & to my wishes that I shall never forget or appreciate enough your devotion." When the handsome, two-volume work actually appeared in April, Mary pronounced herself "pleased & satisfied beyond expectation." Although the work was done, she cheerfully kept Kennan on the payroll until October, when their contract year ended.[68]

Kennan needed all the help he could get. The book earned critical success despite the inevitable charge that he was biased in Harriman's favor, but it sold only about twenty-seven hundred copies the first year. The arrangement with Mary had earned Kennan a total of $49,200, from which he had saved $20,000. Investments brought him about $2,800 a year, which was his only income outside of writing. Although Kennan was careful with money, he had never fared well financially. His father had been as inept in providing for his family as Harriman's had, forcing Kennan to shoulder that burden well into manhood. Much of the money he had made lecturing had gone to helping political exiles and their families escape from Siberia and later to aiding destitute fugitives.[69]

Worst of all, no one seemed to want his work anymore. The *Outlook* never forgave his attack on Roosevelt and snubbed him despite his long association with the magazine. Hopefully he put together a collection of his best essays with some new material only to have two publishers reject it. The requests for commentary on world events, once so frequent, stopped coming, and at seventy-seven Kennan could no longer stand the rigors of the lecture circuit. Things had changed greatly since the war, and Kennan was not in tune with the new ways. He was an old man outflanked by time, who found it ever harder to endure the harsh winters of Medina.[70]

Once again Mary came to his relief. In November 1923 she sent him a thousand dollars disguised as a "bonus" to enable the Kennans to spend the winter in Florida. Gratefully they fled to the isolation of Sanibel, a small island in the Gulf, where, Kennan reported with satisfaction, he found "a unique colony of cosmopolitan people, all of whom . . . hate crowds, noise, jazz music, fashion & display." The winter passed pleasantly for him, and he did not have the worry of coping with another one. He died that May after returning to Medina. Mary Harriman lived on to 1932 and Lena Kennan to 1940, by which time a new generation of Harrimans and Kennans had begun to make their mark on world affairs.[71]

Ever mindful of his place in history, Kennan had not neglected his duties as an archivist. The documents and papers given him by Mary, the Batson interviews and chapter fragments, and Kennan's own materials, including the index on envelopes that he called "an encyclopedia of information with regard to railroad history, economics and finance," were dutifully bundled up and re-turned to Arden, where Mary promised to preserve them. "I found a snug place in one of my bookcases at Arden House for your indexes," she assured Kennan, "& put them away with care myself." She asked Kennan to destroy the Batson manuscript, but he could not bring himself to do it and Mary never got around to it.[72]

The memorial to Henry was finally complete, the book published and the sources from which it had sprung safely deposited in the family's hands. Even-tually Kennan's index and all the material he had collected got moved into an enormous wicker trunk and was pushed out of the house into another building. There it lay undisturbed, its existence unknown outside the family and forgotten within, until now.

Part I. Duchy

1848–1898

1 Sources of Pride and Strength

The circumstances and conditions that have a determining influence upon a man's
life and character often antedate, by many years, his own conscious existence. . . .
When he first becomes conscious of himself and his environment, he is already caught
in a web of external relations, conditions and circumstances from which he seldom
afterward escapes.

—George Kennan, *Autobiography*

For a time early in the nineteenth century the Harriman family seemed destined to an inglorious end in a watery grave. Three of William Harriman's sons met with death at sea in very different ways. The eldest, William, died in a naval clash between English and French ships. Alphonso drowned in the waters off the Battery after the family moved to New York, and Edward simply vanished. His father had made him master of cargo on one of the vessels he fitted out for the West Indies, but the ship never reached port and was never heard from again. Three other sons had died in childhood, leaving only one to carry on the family name. Orlando did not need his mother's fervent pleas to spurn adventure at sea in favor of joining his father in business. Upon that frail reed rose the Harriman dynasty.[1]

From the first it was shrouded in mystery. No one knows what induced William to leave his comfortable life as a stationer in London. He was said to be in sympathy with the colonial cause, yet he did not sail for America until April 1795, long after the issues of war and peace had been decided. He was not a poor man; some of his neighbors in New Haven, where he first resided, liked to refer to him as "the rich Englishman." Nor was it a move to be lightly considered. William brought with him the baggage of a full life: a wife, six children, and his wife's sister, Rosamond Holmes. Whatever pushed or pulled him across the sea had to be of more than ordinary force.

Once settled in New Haven, William tried his luck at the West Indies trade until the treacherous currents of commerce swallowed most of the money he had brought from England. After a few years he took his family to New York City, where he gradually shifted from shipping to a general commission business. There William prospered in a modest way, and young Orlando did well enough to open his own office on Pearl Street in 1811. By the time of William's death around 1820, Orlando had built well on the foundation provided by his father.[2]

Like his father, Orlando possessed a cold, practical nature that suited a merchant, but he did not neglect the social graces entirely. He met his wife at a dancing school they had both attended since childhood. Anna Ingland was the pampered only daughter of a good family, accomplished in needlework and music as well as dance, and surprisingly practical despite having been indulged all her life. Orlando married her in 1810 when he was only nineteen and just starting out in business. Some thought him rash, but the Harrimans showed a knack for marrying wisely and well that endured for generations.[3]

Their marriage produced twelve children, eleven of whom survived to adulthood. The matter of names counted for much to families of ambition, who always had an eye cocked toward posterity. This posed a delicate problem for Orlando. He had been named by his aunt Rosamond after a favorite character in Shakespeare's *As You Like It*. The fit could not have been less appropriate; there was nothing of the romantic in Orlando, who came to loathe his name. With great reluctance he passed it along to his eldest son but thereafter used his influence to fill later generations with Williams and Edwards and other conventional names befitting good businessmen.[4]

Destiny seemed intent on mocking his intentions. The only child he lost in infancy was named William. Orlando then passed the name to his next son, who died unmarried at the age of thirty. His remaining sons were given the prosaic names of Edward, James, Charles, and Frederick. Only the youngest, Oliver, received a name that smacked of the unusual, and he amassed a larger fortune in business than any of the others. It would have amazed Orlando to know that the Harrimans who left the greatest mark on history descended from his namesake son, the least successful of them all, and that neither Edward nor his sons, William and Edward, ever used those names.

His growing family kept obliging Orlando to find larger quarters. After a siege of yellow fever quarantined the family, Orlando moved them to a stately old house on Broome Street. Sheltered by rows of maple and elm trees, the house sat in the middle of a large, sloping lawn that became the gathering place for the children and their friends. At the nearby Dutch Reformed Church the Harrimans entered a new social circle that included Herveys, Van Alens, Livingstons, and Lows, who remained their friends for generations.[5]

The children grew up in this comfortable, idyllic setting until a devastating fire ravaged New York's business district in 1837 and dealt Orlando a blow from which he was slow to recover. As the boys came of age, they joined their father in business except for young Orlando, who showed a flair for scholarship. He was sent off to Columbia, where he did well enough to graduate with honors. Lacking any talent for business, Orlando chose the ministry. In the spring of 1841 he was ordained a deacon in the Episcopal Church, the first Harriman to eschew commerce for the professions.[6]

It proved an unhappy precedent. Young Orlando was as ill suited for the ministry as he was for business. Like so many of the Harrimans, he possessed a cold, austere personality that seldom warmed or moved his parishioners. The name "Orlando" mocked him as it had his father; he had not a shred of that character's charm or spirit, for which intellectual diligence was a poor substitute. At nineteen he had penned an essay on happiness in which, like St. Paul, he ruled out wealth and glory in favor of goodness and contentment, "the practice of every virtue and the abstaining from every vice." These words served as a perfect epitaph for a life that practiced virtue dutifully without ever veering close to wealth or glory.[7]

The one gift Orlando did reveal was the family knack for marrying well. Cornelia Neilson was the daughter of a well-known physician and elder of the Dutch Reformed Church. One of her ancestors had served on George Washington's staff, and the family tree was intertwined with Stuyvesants, Fishes, Bleeckers, and Livingstons. Cornelia was a strong, proud woman with a fierce sense of family. Why she accepted Orlando is a mystery unless at twenty-six she had no other offers and prospects looked bleak.[8]

Their life together got off to a rocky start. The marriage was planned for the spring of 1840, but Orlando's health forced a postponement. By the time it finally took place two years later, Orlando had been ordained and was seeking a position. All his life the one thing that constantly eluded him was a place suitable to his needs. In 1843 he finally found a post as assistant rector at a church in Tarrytown. It took him another year to get a parish of his own, St. George's at Hempstead, Long Island.[9]

The marriage produced six children, all of whom survived. It says much about Cornelia's influence that the first son, John Neilson (1843), received her father's name while the second son, born a year later, got his father's unwanted name. Anna (1846) was named after Orlando's mother. Not until the fourth child arrived in 1848 did Orlando resort to the family store of prosaic names; he was called Edward Henry and in later years never cared much for either name. He was followed by Cornelia (1850) and William (1854).

As in most small country parishes, the pay at St. George's was meager and often in arrears. As his family grew, Orlando found himself in a losing struggle to make ends meet. In 1849 he quarreled with his vestry over back salary still owed him. Shortly afterward a post as assistant rector opened up on Staten Island, but Orlando could not support his family with the pay. With prospects in the East so grim, he began looking for a place in the West. In 1850 he received an offer from a small parish in the California mountains, where the gold rush had created a frenzy of migration. Unable to find anything better, Orlando decided to try it.[10]

Cornelia Harriman must have blanched at the news. Her strong sense of family and social pride were firmly rooted in the East. That was where she and her children counted for something, where she hoped to see them prosper. In the West they would be one more batch of nobodies, and poor ones at that. If one had to be poor, better to be among family and friends who knew your social worth. Orlando understood these things, and he realized the perils offered by the trip itself. There were only three ways to reach California: the long overland trek, the still longer sea journey around Cape Horn, and the shorter sea journey with its dangerous overland hike through the jungle at the Isthmus of Panama. All of them required stamina and a healthy dose of good luck; for a family with small children the odds got much longer. Orlando could see only one way to manage it. Leaving his family in Hempstead, he sailed alone for Panama in May 1850.

The rugged trip across the isthmus left Orlando weak and exhausted. He fell ill with fever and lay helpless for a month in Panama before he was strong enough to board a steamer for San Francisco. Once arrived in California, he was stunned to learn that the parish, having heard nothing from him for so long a time, had hired another minister. The next year sorely tested his faith in God as he wandered about the state, preaching in mining camps and raw frontier towns, founding a small church in Stockton, and braving a cholera epidemic to start another one in Sacramento.[11]

During those months everything was a struggle and nothing seemed permanent. Slowly, painfully, Orlando came to the harsh truth that there was nothing for him in California. Broken in health and spirit, he climbed aboard a steamer in March 1851 and endured the long journey back to New York. If, as his youthful essay stated, happiness consisted in large measure of contentment, Orlando was not a happy man. After a year's absence he came home to tell his anxious family that the whole adventure had been a dismal failure.

The search for a place resumed. Orlando brought his family from Hempstead to a small house on Hamilton Square in Jersey City, where he found work for meager pay as a semiattached curate in one of the city's churches. While Orlando floundered, his brothers had commenced their careers in business. William and Edward joined their father in the family firm of William Harriman & Company, which had an office at 128 Front Street. Young Oliver started out as a commission merchant on his way to earning a fortune in dry goods.[12]

The family did what it could to help Orlando. In his earnest, fumbling way he grew desperate enough to try his hand at business in partnership with his brothers. During the early 1850s he juggled his duties as curate with work in the family firm, struggling to learn matters utterly foreign to him. When William's untimely death dissolved the firm in 1856, Edward continued it with Orlando as his partner. But Edward also had his own drug import company to run, and Orlando proved as inept in business as he had in managing his own affairs. The arrangement lasted only about a year before a chastened Orlando gave up the experiment and went back to the dreary hunt for a parish of his own.[13]

The search brought him two churches. So wretched was the pay at these small parishes that Orlando was obliged to take both, preaching at Clairemont in the morning and walking to West Hoboken every Sunday afternoon. After he had served for seven years, the West Hoboken church owed him nearly two years' back salary. Unable to collect more than verbal praise from his congregation, he left the post in October 1866.[14]

The pattern of Orlando's life had become painfully clear. While his brothers climbed steadily to prosperous careers, he failed at everything he tried except marriage. The needs of his own family threw Orlando onto the charity of both the Harrimans and the Neilsons. His ineptness doomed him to the role of poor relation in proud and distinguished families that could not have entirely concealed the disdain they felt over his bumbling. When he finally achieved some semblance of financial security well into middle age, it came in the form of a final humiliation: a modest inheritance left his wife by one of her relatives.

It was only fitting that Orlando find himself dependent on his wife's family at the end. Through these years of tribulation it was Cornelia Harriman who kept the family together through sheer strength of character. Herself a creature of tradition, she impressed this sense of pride and place on all her children. Hardship, poverty, even humiliation could be borne so long as they remembered who they were and where they belonged. The worse their prospects, the taller they stood in defiance of them.

While all the children absorbed this lesson, one learned it especially well. The rigors of a childhood in which the family was constantly dependent on the largesse of others left a deep imprint on Edward Henry Harriman. Two lessons in particular were drilled into his character: the importance of family sticking together and sustaining one another and the determination never to be dependent on others. He would never suffer the petty slights and humiliations endured by his father because he could not make his own way in life. Orlando was a good but impractical man in a world that belonged to the practical. His son would not make that mistake. Indeed, the third and perhaps most important lesson he absorbed was learning the importance of finding ways to get things done.

Edward Henry Harriman never talked about these matters later in life when the public lusted greedily for details of his youth. The dogged efforts to cast his upbringing in the Horatio Alger mold got no help from him, but he revealed something of his feelings in a less obvious way. He named a daughter after his mother, but no son bore his father's name. To his thinking, the world had more Orlandos than it needed; certainly he wanted no more reminders of their presence.

The child born February 25, 1848, to Cornelia Harriman would never be an imposing physical specimen. All his life Henry was the runt of the litter, a large-eared, weak-eyed bantam who made up in scrappiness what he lacked in size. Where others intimidated through size or strength, Henry did so through sheer force of will fueled by volcanic bursts of energy. An acquaintance from school days remembered him as "the worst little devil in his class, and always at the top of it."[15]

He was not much of a student except when he put his mind to it, and he seemed to excel at anything he put his mind to. At the public school in Jersey City he took more to sports than to books. When Henry was twelve, his parents scraped together the funds to send him to Trinity School in New York. Every day he rose at dawn, trudged to the ferry, crossed the river, and hiked another mile to school. Legend has it that the trip took him through the turf of some street toughs who let no newcomer pass unchallenged, but Henry learned to hold his own against them. Whether true or not, the image fits: Henry grew up streetwise in every sense of the term.[16]

Even this story stands out as an exception. The most striking thing about Henry's childhood is the absence not only of information but of legend as well. Several writers trying to strike the trail of Harriman's past in the 1900s could pry nothing out of his old friends and acquaintances about the early days. There seemed to be a conspiracy of silence led by Harriman himself for reasons that had nothing to do with modesty. A decade later Kennan encountered the same vacuum and managed to wring only dollops of information from family and friends. In the end he was forced to rely on the material gathered by Batson, who had not done much better.[17]

There is little doubt that Henry's childhood scarred him in ways he did not wish to confront later in life. He was the son of two aristocratic parents forced to endure a life below their station. One journalist seeking to unravel the Harriman mystery thought he understood what this meant: "Both [parents] had that terrible bane of the poor—pride of family. They lived in a haughty exclusiveness, teaching their children to follow social lines closely. As they grew older, and as they grew more comfortable, this feeling intensified; their circle narrowed, they knew few people, and cared to know no more. Within the circle the warmest feelings reigned, but to the world outside the Harrimans were cold, reserved, haughty."[18]

The Harrimans responded to this unpalatable mix of pride and poverty by drawing closer together, but the effect on Henry took quite another form. Despite the protection given by his mother, he could hardly escape the stigma of being a poor relation or miss the example of a father who, for all his erudition, had gone nowhere in life. Henry showed himself to be far more combative than his parents or any of his brothers. Something in the chrysalis of his childhood transformed these humiliations into a determination to succeed, to erase the blot on the family name with crushing finality.

The obvious solution was to make enough money to ensure the financial security he had always lacked. For any Harriman the logical arena was business, where family and friends could be useful. School offered little to satisfy a restless and ambitious boy like Henry. After enduring Trinity for two years, he informed his father that he intended to quit and go to work. Orlando was appalled but could not budge the boy. To every objection Henry merely fidgeted impatiently and said, "I am going to work."[19]

But Henry did not simply enter the business world. Not for him the slow, steady climb up the rungs in a mercantile house, even though his uncles had done well at it. Instead he went straight to the fastest lane around: Wall Street. In 1862, at the age of fourteen, he started with a small firm, then got a place as office boy in the firm of DeWitt C. Hays, a broker who held membership number three on the New York Stock Exchange and later served as its treasurer for thirty years. After a brief stint as a messenger carrying securities in a bag to other firms, he became a "pad shover." These were boys who scurried from office to office with stock prices and buy-or-sell orders scribbled on pads of paper.[20]

In an age without tickers or electricity, the brokerage business was a gigantic paper chase. Being a pad shover offered any bright, alert boy the chance to observe every aspect of the business from the purely technical nature of how transactions were made to the psychology of behavior under stress as revealed by the men who gave and received orders. Henry found himself in a classroom offering lessons he was eager to learn, and he proved an apt pupil. In addition to possessing a keen eye for detail and a phenomenal memory, he proved himself trustworthy and reliable in a place where these qualities counted for everything.

He had come to Wall Street at a momentous time. During the past decade the nerve center of American finance had undergone a revolutionary change. Thanks to the newfangled telegraph and the emergence of intercity express service, every major eastern city gained access to New York markets. Business news and stock prices became regular features in major urban newspapers. The California gold rush and an orgy of railroad construction had sparked a boom in mining and rail securities that sent the financial district into a speculative frenzy until the panic of 1857 flattened it.[21]

From the rubble of that disaster emerged a new breed of traders less genteel and more aggressive than the older generation they displaced. The newcomers flocked to New York from distant states, where they had piled up fortunes in mining or railroads or commerce, eager to try their hand in the biggest casino of all and willing to play for stakes that made older hands blanch. They knew little and cared less about the traditions of the street. For them the only two rules of the game were success and survival.

Under any circumstances this new breed of trader would have changed the tone of Wall Street, but their arrival coincided with the most extraordinary event of the age. The Civil War plunged the country into a era of abnormality that proved an ideal training ground for a new generation of businessmen and speculators alike. Wall Street gamblers feasted on the uncertainties of war as every market twitched in tune to news from the battlefield. "The war," said one denizen of the street, "which made us a great people, made us also a nation in whom speculative ideas are predominant."[22]

Get-rich-quick mania swept Wall Street in epidemic form. All day long crowds of brokers swarmed through the stock, mining, and gold exchanges, flooding out onto the curb in their incessant quest for riches. At dusk, wrung dry and exhausted, they still did not quit but stalked the reading room and corridors of the Fifth Avenue Hotel until the exasperated proprietor evicted them. Since the stock exchange limited its membership and confined its trading to two sessions a day despite the enormous leap in volume, most of the action took place on the curb or in some place set up for continuous trading. Nothing short of the limits of human endurance slowed the ritual.[23]

As a result, Henry got his initiation to the street amid a school of sharks caught up in a feeding frenzy. By age twenty-one he had seen the market convulsed by war, Lincoln's assassination, Reconstruction, the feverish speculation over the relative values of gold and greenbacks, the Morse panic, the Harlem, Hudson, and Prairie du Chien corners, the Erie war, and Black Friday. From these episodes Henry gleaned enough material for an advanced course in finance and speculation. As tutors he had the machinations of such luminaries as Cornelius Vanderbilt, Daniel Drew, Jay Gould, Jim Fisk, the Jerome brothers, Anthony Morse, and Henry Keep.

His own employer was a broker of the old school who survived through conservatism rather than daring. The dignified Hays, whose smooth, morose features were wreathed in straggly side-whiskers, thought enough of Henry's ability to make him managing clerk at a salary of $2,000 a year. This promotion merely spurred a growing desire to strike out on his own. He was hardly the type to be content in someone else's employ, and he had seen enough to believe that his future lay in Wall Street. Henry liked to be where the challenges were great, where victory went to the fleet of mind and staunch of heart. He had nerve, knew how to hustle, was indefatigable, and had accumulated a useful store of knowledge and acquaintances during his days as a pad shover.[24]

For role models he looked past his father to his uncles. Oliver was doing well in dry goods, Charles in imports and sugar refining, and Edward as a merchant and drug importer. During the war Uncle Edward had been a broker and gone partners with Larry Jerome, whose nimble mind and flashing wit made him a favorite on the street. When that partnership dissolved after the war, Edward had formed a new firm with his brother John and possibly James as well. But none of the Harrimans who tried Wall Street had yet left a mark. Here was Henry's chance to blaze a trail.[25]

On August 13, 1870, at the age of twenty-two, Henry became member 281 of the New York Stock Exchange. Memberships that year sold at prices ranging from $4,000 to $4,500, plus a $500 initiation fee. Henry did not have this much money in addition to capital for his new venture, so he borrowed most of it from his uncle Oliver. It proved to be the wisest investment Oliver ever made.[26]

There was something altogether fitting in the manner of Henry's debut as a broker. He joined the club on money rented from his family, and to succeed he would need more than a little help from his friends. Whatever capital he had came from those same sources. An old friend recalled Henry pulling a hundred-dollar bill out of his pocket just after he had opened his new office and shrugging, "Well, I can't lose much, anyhow; that's all I've got."[27]

But he knew what to do. Henry launched his career not as a lone wolf eager to prowl the treacherous haunts of the street with a keen nose but as one of the boys hoping to make their way in life by helping each another whenever possible. Short of cash but long on social connections, Henry learned early to maximize the assets at hand.

2 Sources of Advancement

Membership of the New York Stock Exchange is the equivalent of a liberal education. It costs quite as much in hard cash and brain wear, and is worth neither more nor less when acquired.

—James K. Medbery, Men and Mysteries of Wall Street

The firm of E. H. Harriman began life in a cramped office on the third floor of a building at the corner of Broad Street and Exchange Place. Henry did not long stay at the top of two flights of stairs, thanks to Richard Schell, a prominent operator who had close ties to Commodore Vanderbilt. The portly Schell came to like young Harriman as a broker but hated to wheeze his way up the stairs. He offered to give Henry enough business to cover his rent if he would move to the ground floor. Henry did so willingly and became an instant marketing genius. How many brokers got more business from important clients by having a poor location?[1]

For that matter, how many newcomers even survived on Wall Street? Henry set up shop only three years before a major depression blighted the economy for most of the decade. Between 1870 and 1879 a total of 401 firms failed on the New York Stock Exchange. Harriman's was not one of them, largely because he tacked a cautious course even before heavy weather engulfed his fragile enterprise. The boldness for which he was later renowned did not show itself during these years. On Wall Street it was the plungers and the peacocks who got the headlines but the slow, steady plodders who survived the whims and vagaries of a fickle market. Henry stayed resolutely within the latter's ranks.[2]

Harriman's firm thrived during rocky times for two reasons. He had a knack for attracting good clients, men of wealth and influence who valued a trustworthy broker. These included the Schell brothers, banker August Belmont, and Charles J. Osborn, one of the brightest and most fearless speculators on the street. Big rollers like the Schells and Osborn employed whole armies of brokers when conducting an operation and soon learned who was reliable. So did Jay Gould and Commodore Vanderbilt, both of whom were reputed to have thrown some orders Harriman's way.[3]

But Henry was shrewd enough not to rely on so unstable a foundation as the big operators. He also developed a more solid clientele from the connections possessed by his family for decades. The Livingstons, Fishes, Neilsons, Cuttings, Van Burens, and Clarks were people he socialized with as well as cultivated for business. For a time in the early 1870s he took his friend James Livingston as a partner, and the firm's name expanded to E. H. Harriman & Company.[4]

Contacts helped win customers, but a second factor kept both the big rollers and social acquaintances as steady clients. Henry was the right broker for uncertain times: alert, energetic, loyal, and utterly reliable. He never abused privileged information for his own gain and was content to earn commissions rather than speculate on the side. No one on Wall Street was immune to the occasional plunge. As street savant James Medbery observed, "Probably there cannot be found a single house in Wall Street, no matter how wealthy or bound up in traditions, which could show books clean of stock speculations made in the firm interest."[5]

Nothing is harder to trace than the activities of a small dealer on Wall Street. Later accounts talk of Harriman's speculative exploits during these formative years, but none of them offers hard evidence. Certainly the opportunities were there. During Henry's first years on his own he saw the market react violently to the last stages of the Erie war, Gould's corner in Chicago & Northwestern, the great Chicago and Boston fires, the failure of Jay Cooke that triggered the depression, S. V. "Deacon" White's anthracite corner, and the telegraph war, among other events.[6]

Henry may have taken an occasional flyer, but his real talent lay in making commissions off the speculations of others. Years later he was accused of being one of the stingiest traders on the exchange floor. Probably the charge was deserved, for Harriman loved nothing more than to drive a hard bargain and was unrelenting on the attack. He was an active but not reckless trader, looking always to take a profit as soon as it appeared and ready to cut a loss before it grew large, shaving close in both directions.[7]

Ever the realist, Harriman realized that he was a small player who could not afford to take chances until he had built up his original stake. Family considerations also inclined him toward conservatism. Henry was not alone in starting a new business during the summer of 1870. His brother Orlando went partners in a cotton brokerage firm; a year later he continued it alone as Harriman & Company. The other brothers had already dissolved their brokerage, and the eldest, John, was at loose ends over his future.[8]

None of the brothers took hold of their careers as quickly as Henry. Orlando worked hard at the cotton business but had little experience and less capital. In September 1872 Henry joined him as a partner for three months, then gave way to Louis Livingston. Before the new partnership could make much headway, however, the panic of September 1873 sent the economy spiraling into depression. Livingston held on until February 1874, then left the firm. Henry was obliged to rejoin Orlando in the cotton firm and also take his brother John into E. H. Harriman & Company as a broker.[9]

Despite Henry's help, his brothers found it hard going. John stayed with Henry only until November 1874, then switched over to Orlando's cotton brokerage. For nearly two years Henry helped nurse his brother's firm through hard times. But Orlando could not keep it going. By December 1876 he was flirting with failure, and Henry left the partnership. Orlando hung on for another year or so, then folded up and moved to Savannah in search of better prospects. The youngest brother, William, had already come into Henry's firm after an apprenticeship with D. C. Hays and another house. In 1875 Henry made him a partner.[10]

The inability of his brothers to secure their futures could not help but influence the way Henry handled his own business. All his life he was driven by a fierce drive to succeed, but during these years he was fueled more by its darker twin: he dared not fail. In the fumbling efforts of his two older brothers he could not miss an eerie echo of his father's pathetic inability to take hold. Moreover, it behooved any newcomer to play a cautious game, especially during a depression. Wall Street was a place where failure came swiftly and without warning to the reckless or unwary.

In 1876 a credit reporter for R. G. Dun noticed E. H. Harriman & Company for the first time and called it a "good conservative & reliable House." Henry did not have a large capital, but he was active and stood well with the banks. He maintained this reputation through the lean years of the depression, working hard but taking few chances, squeezing a profit from close trading wherever he could, waiting patiently for the larger opportunities he hoped would turn up one day.[11]

The man who would later be called the "human business machine" was anything but that as a young broker. He had not yet developed the Jekyll-Hyde personality that characterized his later career: warm and personable off duty, cold, aloof, and relentless when at work. Henry seemed no different from hundreds of other young men just starting their careers. He was full of fun and pranks, and laughter came easily to him.[12]

Small of stature and wiry, his prominent forehead framed by large ears and his dark myopic eyes enlarged by thick wire spectacles, Henry looked the part of a Dickens clerk. But photographs caught him only at rest, which he seldom was. His movements were brisk and lithe; he had the coordination and the stamina of an athlete, which he had been since childhood. Far from being an office mole, he reveled in sports and the outdoors, both of which whetted his competitive edge.

These activities happened to be the tastes of the social set in which Henry ran, but there was nothing contrived about his love of them. His combative nature found a natural outlet in sports. As a young broker, perhaps inspired by his boyhood scrapes with street toughs, he took up boxing and got the brother of light-weight champion Billy Edwards to give him lessons. He became a crack shot with a rifle and won awards for his marksmanship, played billiards well, liked gymnastics, and developed a passion for horses, especially trotters. One of the first luxuries he permitted himself was the purchase of a trotter at a country fair.[13]

In all his activities Henry was the complete social animal. A snappy dresser and lively companion, he joined the fashionable Traveler's Club and was a regular at the Saturday night dinners that brought together a crowd of the young social elite. He belonged to the Union and Racquet Clubs and to Company K of New York's Seventh Regiment, a militia unit known as the "society company" because its ranks were filled with bluebloods like his friend Augie Belmont the younger. Henry's prowess at shooting developed in large measure from this playing at soldier with his friends.

Above all, Henry loved the outdoors, hunting and fishing or simply roaming the woods in search of adventure. Nature was for Harriman a tonic like no other, a perfect counterpoint to the pressures of his work in the city. His friends shared this passion and went camping together much as they went to parties and dinners. No one knows exactly where Henry acquired his love of the outdoors. He had always been a city boy, and it may well have been his friends who introduced him to the pleasures of the Adirondacks. Whoever showed him the way, he remained an ardent convert all his life.

By far the favorite haunt of Henry and his crowd was Paul Smith's camp, a tiny outpost tucked away in the northernmost reaches of the Adirondack wilderness. To get there required a train trip to Saratoga and then Whitehall, a boat journey to Plattsburg, a short hop on a branch rail line to the mines at Ausable Forks, and then a forty-two-mile trek by coach through the forest over a rough corduroy road. No one went to Paul Smith's who did not really want to be there, and anyone who did expected to rough it. There was no running water and no amenities beyond the wilderness itself and the strong presence of Paul Smith and his family.[14]

Smith was an original: a physically imposing specimen with a jovial personality, somewhat indolent of temperament but vigorous when engaged in his perpetual love affair with the outdoor life. A laugh came easy to his face, and he loved nothing more than to taunt his guests for their pretensions and book learning. There was, he liked to say, no fool like an educated fool. Smith showed himself to be anything but a fool; in later years he grew rich on land speculations and by buying up water power on the Saranac River. The image of the shrewd investor, however, seemed worlds away from the brawny figure standing in the small lodge dining room, chains still slung over his shoulder from letting out the hounds after the morning hunt, joking easily with the guests while he carved a roast or venison.[15]

Paul Smith's camp may well have been Henry's introduction to the great outdoors, and he probably learned of it through his close friends Jim and Lou Livingston. They were wild and reckless enough to appeal to Harriman. Like Henry, they were always up for fun or a new challenge and felt as at home in the forest as in a Fifth Avenue drawing room. Through them Henry met E. L. Trudeau, a young doctor who had known the Livingstons since boyhood. With Harriman's help, he would later found a famous sanitarium on Saranac Lake.[16]

When Trudeau fell ill with tuberculosis in 1873, Lou Livingston took him to Paul Smith's in May. No one in those days looked on the rough wilds and rugged climate of the Adirondacks as anything but a death warrant for consumptives. Trudeau went only because he imagined himself dying and wanted to be near the scenes he loved best. To his surprise, Trudeau began to recover. Lou Livingston stayed with him until the end of July, then returned to New York. When he left, Henry volunteered to look after Trudeau. "Head me," he telegraphed the camp, "here I come."[17]

A short time earlier Paul Smith had bought a gilt ball and hung it proudly atop the flagpole in front of his lodge. Trudeau warned him that Harriman would use the ball for target practice the moment he saw it, but Smith paid no attention. The doctor knew his man. When the stage pulled up to the lodge, Harriman jumped out, caught sight of the new ornament, reached back for his rifle, and blasted a hole through it. Then he bounded up the porch stairs to shake the hands of a grinning Trudeau and a stunned Smith.

This was the Harriman that Trudeau knew: carefree, full of fun, eager to plunge headlong into the next adventure. They spent long, joyous days together fishing and floating in their boat on the lake or tramping the woods in search of game, pitching camp whenever it suited them to stop for the night. Henry loved to hunt loons from a boat because it was nearly impossible to hit one in the few seconds it surfaced. The greater the challenge, the more he relished it, even in his pleasures. Not a serious thought stirred their brains during those languid August days. For both men it was a idyllic time they would never again fully recapture.

At the month's end Henry had to return to work, just in time to catch the panic triggered by the failure of Jay Cooke, and Jimmy Livingston came up to keep Trudeau company. His health improved so much that the doctor moved his family to Saranac Lake village permanently in November 1876. Harriman and his friends kept returning as if drawn by a magnet. "A more light-hearted and better companion and friend," Trudeau acknowledged gratefully, "I could not have had."[18]

The lighthearted Henry overlooked no chance for a prank and loved nothing more than deflating windbags. One summer Paul Smith had among his guests a pompous Englishman who bored everyone with tales of his exploits hunting big game all over the globe. Harriman quietly sent to New York for a giant bear's paw, which he used to make tracks along the soft, muddy rim of the lake and nearby streams. The mighty English hunter soon found them and, cheered on by Henry and the others, occupied himself for weeks in tracking the most elusive game ever to challenge him.[19]

Nor did Harriman spare Paul Smith's own guides. When some of them boasted too much of their prowess at boxing, he brought up to the camp lightweight champ Billy Edwards disguised as one of his Wall Street friends. The burly guides guffawed when Henry suggested they all put on the gloves but were finally goaded into it. Their astonishment was exceeded only by their pain as the slight, smooth-faced stranger punched them silly. Henry then assuaged their battered pride by telling them who they were up against.[20]

This incident betrayed more of Harriman than even his close friends knew. Apart from his mischievous streak, Henry loved nothing better than pitting bigger, stronger foes against a seeming underdog who overcomes them with superior skill and guile. It was in fact the central paradigm of his life: the small but gritty underdog tackling bigger and bigger challenges against odds that grew steadily longer. Harriman was all of one piece; the same instincts drove him at play as at work.

He showed the same qualities in his charities. Henry was a man whose interests never extended far beyond himself. During his early years as a broker he got involved in a project that revealed more about his boyhood than anything else. Through the Union Club he had become friends with George C. Clark of Clark, Dodge & Co., one of the most respected houses on the street. Clark's mother had long taken an interest in the Wilson Mission School, which offered industrial training to girls in the tenement district around Tompkins Square. One day in 1875 Henry went with her to the school. While there, he heard the school matron complain about the way gangs of neighborhood boys harassed the girls and the school.[21]

A year or so earlier Henry had gone with another friend, Samuel Blagden, to visit another charity, the Newsboys' Lodging Club. Shortly afterward Harriman toured the lower East Side with Blagden, and as they were leaving he said, "Sam, why can't we do something for the boys there similar to what you have been doing with the newsboys?" Perhaps that incident ticked in his mind during the visit to the industrial school, or perhaps Henry responded to the matron's belief that if the young girls could be civilized, so could the boys. Whatever his source of inspiration, Harriman jumped on the notion of helping both the school and the boys.[22]

Henry went to a policeman in the precinct and asked him to recruit some of the boys for a meeting at the mission. Most of the boys knew about the matron's complaints, however, and were wary of a trap. Only three of them let curiosity overcome their fear and ventured into the mission. Henry plied them with sandwiches and coffee while laying out his idea: what would the boys think of having a place where they could come to amuse themselves? Not for classes but for fun? The notion appealed to them almost as much as the free food, and the boys promised to tell their friends about it.[23]

After more conferences with the boys, Henry rented the basement of the industrial school and had it fixed up as a clubhouse where the boys could come in the evenings to talk, sing, play games, or be entertained by some modest show. The Tompkins Square Boys' Club was the first of its kind in the world. There were no dues or requirements, and boys of any age, race, or religion were welcome. Some social reformers frowned on the notion of a program devoid of spiritual uplift, moral instruction, and educational classes, but Harriman knew better what was needed to get boys into the place, where they could then be reached in other ways.[24]

Henry interested some of his Union Club friends in the venture, and together they footed the bills and took turns keeping order in the evenings. There were no managers or employees, and the club closed from May to October. During the late 1870s fewer than fifty boys came on a regular basis, but after 1880 the membership climbed steadily until Henry was obliged to rent another floor of the building to sort out the younger boys from the older ones.[25]

This venture was remarkable not only for its originality but for its intensely personal nature. Harriman started the club, financed much of it, and devoted many of his evenings to running it. On at least one occasion he also served as bouncer. There was always an undercurrent of fear that neighborhood toughs would get out of hand when thrown together in tight quarters. This rarely happened, but one night a local bully made himself obnoxious during an exhibition of tricks given by one of Henry's Union Club friends. Harriman set precisely the example he wanted by personally throwing the boy out. He knew the others would be impressed by someone who backed up his words with action.[26]

Years later George Kennan puzzled over why an ambitious young broker would devote so much time to such an activity. Many society people interested themselves in social work out of noblesse oblige, but Henry's involvement went far beyond writing a check or performing brief, dutiful ministrations to the unwashed. The answer lay beyond Kennan's narrow bounds of propriety. Something in the experience with the East Side boys touched Henry deeply and directly. He knew their nature from his own rowdy boyhood, especially from those lonely treks through their turf to Trinity School. He knew what their lives lacked because he had once felt a similar lack.[27]

Whatever else the Boys' Club did for Harriman, it marked a crucial step in coming to terms with the pain of his own boyhood about which he remained so tight-lipped in later life. The club enabled him for the first time to confront in a positive, constructive way the loneliness and misery he had felt as a boy struggling to make himself the success his mother always hoped he would be. He identified with the boys just as he identified in some way with every cause or charity he took up. Nor was his concern for boys confined to the club. A decade later, when he was associated with the Illinois Central Railroad, he donated $6,000 to create a fund for the benefit of boys working in the company shops.[28]

Nothing moved Harriman unless it connected directly to him in some way. This quality often made him seem indifferent or insensitive to the suffering of others. His mind and his feelings were like the fierce, straight glare of a locomotive lamp, illuminating everything in its path with striking clarity while ignoring all that lay outside its beam. The outer world of darkness seldom aroused his interest.

As more boys flocked to the club, Henry recruited more of his society friends to help out. Young men from good families, who were just coming out of college, donated their evenings and athletic ability as group leaders. Harriman also began hiring a staff, and he incorporated the club in 1887. As its activities expanded, books and periodicals were collected for a small library, and a program of steamer excursions gradually evolved into a permanent summer camp.[29]

By 1898 the Boys' Club had outgrown its facilities in the mission building. Harriman was just then injecting himself into the affairs of the Union Pacific Railroad, a move that would catapult him to the top of the railroad world. Still, the club got his close attention. After a lengthy search, he finally found the right man to serve as superintendent. Francis H. Tabor was an Englishman with impeccable credentials who had done social work in London as well as New York. Henry promised him not only ample support but a new building if Tabor would take charge of the club.[30]

Tabor took the position, and Harriman delivered on his promise. In 1901 he erected a new five-story building at a cost of $185,000. The money came out of his own pocket and the work came during the busiest year of his rocketing career, but he laid the cornerstone early in the year and watched the work through to completion in December. The new facility housed a gymnasium, carpenter shop, showers, library, auditorium, reading room, natural history room, and plenty of extra space for classes and activities. Harriman gave Tabor carte blanche in furnishing the club.

After the new building opened, Harriman visited the club less often, but he followed its progress closely. He never refused a request from Tabor for funds or help. During the panic of 1907, when subscriptions dropped, he carried the club out of his own pocket. In 1904 he paid to send the club's top wrestlers to the world's fair at St. Louis, where they won two championships. Every year he attended the opera staged by the Junior Singing Club and made it a point to congratulate the boys not on their performance but on the hard work they had put into the production.[31]

Whole generations of East Side boys had good reason to thank E. H. Harriman. They had even better reason to thank the ghosts of his childhood, some of which lay entombed in the cornerstone of the new Boys' Club building.

George Clark exerted a profound influence on Harriman's life without the slightest intention of doing so. It was his mother who took Henry to the East Side, where his inspiration for the Boys' Club took root, and it was in Clark's home that Henry first met the woman who became his life's companion.

Mary Williamson Averell was a cousin of George Clark's wife and a frequent visitor to their house. She lived in Ogdensburg, a small town on the St. Lawrence River in northernmost New York, where her family had been prominent for generations. Her father, William J. Averell, and his brother James built on their father's profitable liquor, commission, and forwarding business. They were already rich when the elder Averell died in 1862, and wartime business made them even richer.[32]

By the war's end the brothers had enough money to live as gentlemen of leisure, but idleness was not the Averell way. After a brief fling as a broker on Wall Street, William went into banking at home with his brother and another partner. In 1873 the brothers closed up the family firm to concentrate on banking; by the decade's end their Ogdensburg Bank was prosperous, well managed, and the only bank in town. Like the Harrimans, the Averells were shrewd, cautious, secretive, and careful to look out for their own. But William was more than Ogdensburg's leading banker and one of its wealthiest citizens. He was also a vestryman in the Episcopal Church, an alderman in city government, and served a year as mayor. The Averells were a conservative, genteel family who believed in the gospel of public service and who happened to be Democrats instead of Republicans.[33]

These influences were deeply ingrained in Mary Averell. One of only two children, she grew up a bright, dutiful daughter whose life revolved around family, friends, church, and civic activities. After her education at home she was sent to finishing school in New York with the usual expectation that one day she would become a fine wife and mother for some young man of equal or greater social standing than the Averells. Like many genteel young ladies, she did not rush to her destiny. She was in her late twenties when she met Harriman.

At thirty Henry did not quite fit Averell's wish list, but he came close. He had the right social connections, and his firm was deemed reliable and trustworthy. Although he had not achieved any distinction, he stood well on the street. At five foot four he was hardly an imposing physical specimen except for the prominent forehead exposed by a hairline that had already begun to recede and a formidable mustache. His face had a sensitive cast on those rare occasions it was at rest, but usually it bristled with intensity.[34]

Even as a young woman Mary had a matronly air. Her face was pleasant but heavy-featured, with brown hair pulled back. Like Henry, her intelligence and strength of character were more striking than her looks. Three years younger than Henry, she was interested in many of the same things he was and had the energy to stay with him. Early in their courtship Henry took her down to see the Boys' Club, of which he was more than a little proud. It was not the ordinary evening out for a young couple, but it suited them more than mere socializing.[35]

They were well matched in every respect. Apart from shared values, tastes, and interests, they complemented each other well. Mary's proper upbringing included a healthy dose of subservience that enabled her to live with a man who insisted on dominating everything he did, yet she was also strong enough to earn his respect as well as his love. Never did Mary become the doormat that Henry made of so many other people in his life. He remained devoted to her all his life and carried on the one family tradition that even his hapless father had managed to achieve: he married wisely and well.

The wedding took place in Ogdensburg on September 10, 1879. Afterward William Averell provided an unwitting glimpse into his new son-in-law's destiny. He arranged a special train for their departure and surprised Henry by having the workmen paint "E. H. Harriman" on the engine. Averell could do this because he was president of the small Ogdensburg & Lake Champlain line. Already he had given Henry the more substantial gift of a seat on the Ogdensburg's board. It was Henry's first formal connection with a railroad.[36]

The wedding set in motion what seemed no more than the natural evolution in a young man's life. Except for brief periods, Henry had continued to live in New Jersey with his parents and his brother Willie. Brother John and both his sisters had long since married, and young Orlando had gone to Georgia. After his honeymoon trip Henry found a place at 25 East 44th Street in New York. Sometime around his father's death in 1881, however, Henry moved uptown to 14 East 55th Street, a few short blocks from the residence of the man who became first his friend and then his nemesis, Theodore Roosevelt. Soon afterward his mother found a place nearby at 36 West 55th. Willie came to live with her, and the family circle resumed its familiar closeness.[37]

The closeness extended to business, where Willie had acquitted himself well under his brother. About the same time Henry moved to 55th Street, he also took a larger office at a more prestigious address, 2 Wall Street. The fun-loving, impish social animal bade farewell to his bachelor lifestyle and stepped into greater responsibilities at home and at the firm. Nothing impressed this change on Henry more than the arrival of three children: Mary (1881), Henry Neilson (1883), and Cornelia (1884).

In the years after 1880 nothing shaped Henry's world more than his family. He doted on his wife and children, did everything with them, and insisted they do everything together. A family physician later declared that he never seen a more perfect family. No day, he added, was "too short or too full of affairs, that [Harriman] did not find time for the children . . . and when conferences with men of affairs lasted at his house through the afternoon, and the children's hour came, the men and affairs gave way to his children."[38]

Gradually there developed between Henry and Mary a bond that was as much intellectual as emotional. "His attitude toward her was more than devotion," recalled Judge Robert S. Lovett, who later became Harriman's closest adviser. "It was profound admiration, respect and unfailing attention and courtesy." Henry was not merely acting out some Victorian ideal. He had found the center of his personal life, the source of strength that would always sustain him. After 1880 family became more than ever the closed universe it had been when he was a boy, only this time he and not Orlando sat at the head of the table.[39]

In the spring of 1880 Henry enlarged his firm by bringing in his first outside partner since James Livingston. Although William McClure brought little capital to the business, he was an ornament to the house's conservative reputation. Formerly of Winslow, Lanier, he had served two years as vice-chairman of the New York Stock Exchange before joining Harriman. He was considered a safe, prudent broker, exactly the sort Henry needed to manage the house's affairs while he hustled business for it and pursued other interests of his own.[40]

After 1879 the economic gloom lifted and brightened rapidly into sunny expansion until curbed by the shooting of President James A. Garfield in July 1881. "The news from Washington," said a distraught financial editor, "was an element de novo, something never thought of or calculated upon in the stock market." During the next three years the market ran ragged, pushing doggedly upward only to be cut down again and again until a brief but severe panic in May 1884 injected a decisive note of restraint.[41]

Through these vagaries Harriman steered his usual careful course, unshaken by the sirens' call of speculation that swept many other houses into ruin. He was the most steadfast of brokers in the most erratic of times, insisting that his firm do strictly a commission business. He never disclosed the amount of his capital—one estimate placed it at between $100,000 and $150,000 in 1881—but his solid reputation for conservatism earned him a sound line of credit at the banks. By 1883 a credit reporter was referring to E. H. Harriman & Co. as "an old & well established house."[42]

Respectable and reliable. These were the words most often applied to Harriman and his firm. By the mid-1880s he had become the very model of a sound, respectable broker. He made a good living, enjoyed a happy home life, and traveled in the most proper of social circles. Not yet forty, he had achieved all his mother could have asked of him. Above all, he had gained the solid footing in life that had eluded his father and, to some extent, his older brothers as well. He had done nothing great, but greatness was not expected of him.

In every respect Henry had become exactly what a staid, solid family hoped he would be. By any measure his life had been a success, and yet he was not satisfied. The fierce energy that had driven him this far had not found rest, and the dark hunger that fueled it had not been sated. Some vague, inchoate ambition burned relentlessly in him, tormented him because he could find no way to give it voice or release.

It was as if his life had been a climb up the face of some huge, uncharted mountain. He had struggled past the first formidable obstacles and established a base camp where he need no longer fear falling back. Getting to that point was an impressive accomplishment, but he could not remain there indefinitely. What others viewed as the peak of their ambitions was for Henry but a way station where he could pause long enough to consider what perils lay ahead and what route should be taken to overcome them.

McClure stayed with the firm five years before leaving in May 1885. By then Willie had gained enough experience to take charge of the office, a stature he celebrated in September by acquiring his own seat on the exchange. Henry found himself faced with an intriguing dilemma. He had been in business fifteen years and done well at it. The future promised more of the same, but he was growing restless, bored by the repetition in what he did. He wanted fresh challenges, fresh opportunities to test his ambition.[43]

While Willie minded the store, Henry began exploring other interests, joining with some of his friends in investments that might pan out to something more than profits. As usual he moved slowly, cautiously, searching for the right path to lead him to a destination he had not yet defined. One avenue in particular looked promising: railroads.

3 Sources of Growth

The friends of [Harriman's] youth describe him as frank, open, fond of gaiety

and fun. The twenty-odd years of the Stock Exchange had effectually removed the

frankness and the openness. In their place he had a studied reserve, a careful holding

of himself in leash, a fixed resolve that no man should be able to guess the real

thoughts and motives that lay within his mind.

—C. M. Keys, "Harriman: The Man in the Making"

Railroads were the obvious arena for a man of ambition in the 1880s. As the largest and most dynamic industry in the nation, they were the catalyst for an industrial revolution that was transforming American life with bewildering speed. More track would be laid during the 1880s than in any other decade. Expansion wars of unparalleled ferocity raged well into the depression of the 1890s, giving rise to the systems that would dominate the railroad scene for much of the next century. A man entering the field during these years could find himself overwhelmed and confused by the sheer rush of events, as if he had wandered unexpectedly into the swirl of a vast and desperate battle.

For a man of uncommon intelligence and clarity of vision, however, the panorama unfolding before his watchful eyes offered a classroom of exceptional value. Anyone who learned the correct lessons there would be well prepared for the conditions that followed. Like Wall Street, where the industry's roots ran deep, the railroad arena was no place for the timid or unwary. The challenges were great, the risks even greater. In one sense at least they were inescapable for Harriman. As a broker he had little choice but to learn the intricacies of rail securities because they were the lifeblood of the New York Stock Exchange.

The exchange accepted its first rail stock in 1830 and then watched the list mushroom. By 1885 it contained 125 railroad issues compared to only 26 nonrail stocks. Railroad bonds also dominated that market, where they competed only with state and federal securities. The orgy of mergers that would create a new breed of industrial securities was still a decade away, the utilities even further in the future. With the list so top-heavy in one area, no broker could afford to be less than expert in rail issues.[1]

But railroad securities were not the same thing as railroads. Dealing in the one did not provide an education or even insight into the other unless one sought it out. In Henry's case the opportunity first arose when William Averell put him on the board of the Ogdensburg & Lake Champlain, a 118-mile road running between Ogdensburg and Rouse's Point on Lake Champlain, just below the Canadian border. The position was not merely a gesture; Averell needed Henry's financial expertise and saw a way to give him some business as well.

Henry was not the only new director in June 1879. He was joined by Stuyvesant Fish, who came from an old and socially prominent family connected to the Harrimans through the Neilsons. His father, Hamilton Fish, had served New York as governor and senator before becoming secretary of state under Ulysses S. Grant. His mother was a descendant of William Livingston, the first governor of New Jersey. When Henry first met Fish is unknown. The families had known each other for years, and Henry may well have met Fish socially through the Neilsons or Livingstons. Certainly he knew him from Wall Street, where Fish worked for Morton, Bliss & Company. No association was to have a more profound influence on Harriman's life.[2]

The contrast between them could not have been more striking. Three years younger than Harriman, Fish had grown up with every advantage. As a boy he was educated in the best private schools and lived two years in Europe with his family. He followed his father to Columbia, but his mind turned to business rather than politics or the professions. After graduating in 1871, Fish worked briefly for the Illinois Central Railroad, then entered a position awaiting him at Morton, Bliss. Tall and blond, a genial giant whose blue eyes and heavy features spread easily into a smile, Fish had a pleasant manner born of social assurance. At work, however, he could be a martinet.[3]

By 1877 Fish had decided that his future lay in railroads rather than banking. He left Morton, Bliss that March to join the board of the Illinois Central, where he remained for nearly thirty years until ousted by his old friend Harriman. The company had just made the pivotal decision to buy the bankrupt connecting lines between the Ohio River and New Orleans and reorganize them into the Chicago, St. Louis & New Orleans Railroad. Since Fish handled financial matters for the New Orleans road, he needed friendly firms to sell securities, arrange loans, and take care of other needs. Harriman was a logical man to use, given the long family association, their circle of mutual friends, and Henry's reputation for conservatism.[4]

By the late 1870s Fish was throwing some business Henry's way and had already cast his lot with the railroad industry while Harriman still pondered his future. During the next few years Fish provided the model if not the inspiration for Henry's own change of career. The fact that Fish turned up on the Ogdensburg board with Henry in June 1879 indicates clearly that they were looking to expand their mutual interests. Fish had no connection to the road other than through Henry, who had been put there by his father-in-law. Here was the classic tiny acorn that was destined to yield a mighty oak. From this first modest venture together Fish and Harriman learned that they made a good team in certain respects.

The Ogdensburg had a peculiar history that previewed the pattern of so many later western roads. Chartered in 1845 as the Northern Railroad of New York, it was promoted as the last link in a chain of roads running from Boston north to Montreal and west to Lake Ontario. Five years later the road opened to a chorus of enthusiasts predicting a vast flow of traffic away from New York City to Boston via the northern route. But the vast flow never materialized. Twice before the Civil War the road failed and was reorganized. In 1876 the hapless line slid back into bankruptcy again, and William Averell became its receiver.[5]

Averell had been on the board since 1873 and knew just how dismal the road's prospects were. Net earnings had tumbled 42 percent between 1870 and 1876. The road needed new rails and equipment, and its capital structure was saddled with bonds and preferred stock that paid 8 percent. Averell managed to take the line out of receivership in April 1877 and became its president a year later, but the road continued to flounder. He needed a fresh infusion of capital to revitalize the road just as he was about to acquire a new son-in-law who worked in the money market. Harriman was put on the board to help raise money and restructure the company; he brought with him Fish as a friend who commanded wide resources.[6]

By the end of 1880 Harriman and Fish had put together a plan to refund the existing bonds at a lower rate of interest. This was Harriman's first stab at the kind of restructuring that later became his trademark, and it had little effect. Money was spent to improve the Ogdensburg, but it faced a future with too few options. In 1881 Harriman and Fish left the board, having made their imprint on the road's finances but not its future. Five years later the road was leased to the Central Vermont, which had acquired control of its stock.[7]

What had Harriman learned from this first venture into railroads? Probably not much, other than getting his feet wet. That same summer of 1881 he and Fish turned their attention to a more promising opportunity. The Sodus Bay & Southern was a small road running from Sodus Bay, a harbor on Lake Ontario midway between Oswego and Rochester, to the town of Stanley thirty-four miles to the south. It too was a derelict of grand schemes gone unfulfilled. The road opened in January 1873 just in time to catch the depression and went into receivership a year later.[8]

The receiver was Sylvanus J. Macy, a shrewd New Yorker with impeccable business credentials. His grandfather Josiah Macy had built a flourishing oil business in New York, and his father, William, also served as president of Seamen's Bank. The Macys were Quakers with a reputation for shrewdness and integrity. In the spring of 1872 the Macys sold their company to Standard Oil; a few months later William Macy died, leaving Sylvanus and his brothers a large estate. The firm of Macy & Sons continued to prosper. By 1874 Sylvanus had become a senior partner and was thought the richest of them.[9]

Something attracted Sylvanus to the town of Sodus Point and its railroad. He bought a large block of the road's bonds and went to Sodus Point, where he astonished the locals by buying real estate and putting up buildings out of his own pocket. In September 1875 he helped reorganize the railroad as the Ontario Southern; fifteen months later he left Macy & Sons to concentrate on Sodus Point. He became a presence in the little town, a leading citizen and driving force in its economy. But he could not make the railroad go. The line still failed to earn even its expenses, let alone pay interest or dividends.[10]

In December 1879, Macy and the other major bondholders surrendered the road to a fresh group of optimists who projected an extension toward the bituminous mines in Potter County, Pennsylvania. But the scheme flopped. Despite the return of good times, the wretched line ran only one train a day each way and barely earned expenses. The discouraged Macy moved to Rochester in 1881, but that October he formed a syndicate to buy back the original thirty-four-mile road. This time his partners included Harriman and Fish.[11]

Here was another of those countless small lines destined for the graveyard of lost dreams, where a plot had already been reserved for it until a quirk of fate brought it to Harriman's attention. Apparently Mary's brother William Averell, who lived in Rochester, had invested in the Sodus Bay; possibly some other relatives had too. Uneasy over the prospect of losing their money, they asked Harriman to look into the road's affairs.[12]

This was the story Harriman told years later, and it fits the circumstances well. All his life Henry was obliged to bail out family or friends who had made unwise investments. But he also had a way of arranging his past to suit him when confiding it to others, and he may have done just that with the rest of the story. Legend has elevated this episode into the moment of epiphany for Harriman's future career, and his own words reinforced that status. "It was a lesson for me that I followed in after life," he said later, "that the only way to make a good property valuable is to put it in the best possible condition to do business."[13]

Kennan swallowed this version whole, but the known facts, though sketchy and contradictory, do more to deny than confirm. For one thing, the road was not a good property but a proven dog. Harriman in his prime could not turn a sow's ear into a silk purse, and he was still an acolyte in 1881. For another, there is no solid evidence that he was the decisive factor in bailing the road out. He may have devised what proved to be the winning strategy—or it might have been Fish—but Macy remained the main man in the property.

In October 1881 Henry became vice-president of the road with Macy as president. For the first time Harriman was an officer of a railroad, but Macy remained head of the syndicate. He also joined with Macy, Fish, and R. Fulton Cutting in erecting a grain elevator at Sodus Point in hopes of reaping a profit from the lake traffic to come. In this venture, too, Macy remained the largest owner. During 1882 the syndicate reorganized the road as the Sodus Bay & Southern, cut the stock and bonds nearly in half, and refunded the bonds at a lower interest rate. Still the road failed to earn even its expenses. At this point, according to legend, Harriman came up with a brainstorm. He bought out his discouraged partners, then plowed money into improvements and sold the road to the Pennsylvania for a handsome profit.[14]

Particles of truth are sprinkled through this legend. Someone saw what eluded the other syndicate partners: the road's chief (and perhaps only) asset was its potential as a pawn on the chessboard of rail strategy. The Pennsylvania Railroad lacked an outlet on Lake Ontario while its most bitter rival, the New York Central, touched the lake at several points. The Pennsylvania did not want to be shut out of lake traffic, and the New York Central did not want the Pennsylvania to gain access to the lake. If Henry could play on the mutual fears of these rivals, he might unload the road on one of them at a hefty price. Packaged properly, the tiny Sodus Bay could become the object of a bidding war between the two richest railroads on the continent.

According to the legend, Henry made his move in October 1883 by offering either to sell his own shares or buy those of the other syndicate members at a price he named. There were only twelve stockholders; several jumped at the chance to get out, and Harriman found himself in possession of his first railroad even if it was shared with his friends. He organized a board that included his brother Willie, Fish, Macy, and Mary's brother William. "I soon recognized that if I wanted to dispose of this property," he said years later, "I would have to put it in good shape so that the rival lines at each end of my road would want to purchase it."[15]

From this sprang another myth of the Sodus Bay as the experience that taught Harriman the lesson of spending for improvements as the key to making money on railroads. But the evidence tells a different tale. Harriman held the road only nine months before selling it, hardly enough time to overhaul even a small line. During that time there is no record of funds spent for improvements or indication of work done. The only sharp increase in expenditures came after the Pennsylvania took control. Nor did Harriman replace Macy, who remained president until the road was sold.[16]

Harriman and his friends did manage to drum up more business. In 1883 the Sodus Bay hauled nearly twice the tonnage it had carried two years earlier and half again as many passengers. The new business produced the largest gross earnings the road had seen since the depression and its first modest surplus because none of it went for improvements. In 1884 the road was still laid with its original fifty-six-pound rail. It also had the same rolling stock as when it opened for business in 1873 except for one more locomotive, a new baggage car, and forty-eight fewer freight cars. If Harriman bought any new equipment (and there is no evidence that he did), he did not expand the fleet. The locomotives in 1884 were of the same weight as those running in 1880.[17]

Harriman did bring in a new superintendent to improve operations and drive the business, but he invested little money in the road. Maintenance outlays under Harriman were only 24 percent of earnings compared with 39 percent in 1881 and 38 percent in 1879. The road did spend more on repairs to engines and cars during those months than for any year since the depression. This suggests that, far from upgrading the road and rolling stock, Harriman was trying to hold the old equipment together long enough to unload the property.[18]

The Sodus Bay under Harriman looked very much like the same old derelict, except that in 1884 it actually earned $8,726 more than its expenses, by far its best performance. Henry managed this profit not with a program of improvements but with the tried-and-true tactic of skimping on upkeep. The object was to create the appearance of improved performance as an inducement for buyers. In short, the Sodus Bay experience looks less like Harriman's moment of revelation than like a financial campaign managed with impressive skill for maximum profit. It also reveals his willingness to recast his image in a likeness he preferred.[19]

Once business picked up, Harriman dangled the Sodus Bay before the two rival giants, telling Frank Thomson of the Pennsylvania that his system needed an outlet on the lake and officials of the New York Central that they could not afford to let the Pennsylvania acquire the road. This simple tactic was effective in an industry where roads nearly always justified expansion in defensive terms and officers lived in mortal terror that rival lines would steal a march on them. The Central paid willingly for an option on the Sodus Bay until its agents could investigate the road. Frank Thomson then offered to buy the road outright only to learn that he was blocked by the Central's option.[20]

The option expired at noon on July 1. The Central waited until that morning before sending an official to Harriman's office to get the option renewed. Henry already had a good offer in hand from the Pennsylvania, however, and stayed away from his office all morning. When the option expired, he telegraphed Thomson that the road was his. After cleaning up some legal problems over right-of-way, Henry took his pay in Pennsylvania Railroad bonds and walked away with a tidy profit for himself and his friends. Later he bought control of the grain elevator at Sodus as well, and the hard times of 1894 found him scrounging for wheat to fill it.[21]

The most important result of these early forays into railroads was not the education of E. H. Harriman; rather, it was the success of his collaboration with Fish, which tightened a business association that thrust Harriman into the arena he was destined to conquer. In a sense Fish not only arranged for Henry's education in railroads but also provided him with a scholarship to a much larger campus where his learning experience truly commenced.

No western railroad owned a better reputation than the Illinois Central. It was the bluest of blue chips in a region where the ledgers of many roads bled a steady stream of red. Completed in 1856, it was the first land-grant railroad and at 705 miles the longest railroad in the world. It was also an anomaly, the only major north-south line in a nation where overland transportation flowed east-west. On a map the Illinois Central resembled a "Y" with one arm anchored in Chicago and the other stretching to Dunleith in the northwest corner of Illinois. The arms joined just above Centralia, and the stem ran southward to Cairo on the Ohio River.

After the Civil War the Illinois Central expanded in two directions. It joined the railroad frenzy in Iowa by leasing some small roads extending from Dunleith to Sioux City on the Missouri River. This line gave the Illinois Central a modest share of the east-west traffic between the rivers. It also won a lengthy battle to acquire the roads reaching from the Ohio River to New Orleans. Once perfected, this addition would give the Illinois Central a through line from the lakes to the Gulf of Mexico.[22]

By 1880 the system embraced 1,320 miles and carried a diversified traffic that made it an impressive cash cow paying regular dividends through the depression of the 1870s. Analysts heaped praise on what one called "the conservative spirit so dominant in the company's affairs." The management was honest, capable, and dedicated to keeping the debt low; in 1880 the company had outstanding only $29 million in stock and a paltry $12 million in bonds. The operation was efficient and maintenance standards high. Since 1877 the company had invested heavily in improvements, upgrading the new lines in Iowa and south of the Ohio River to the same standard as the parent road. Earnings remained remarkably stable through the lean 1870s, thanks to general manager James C. Clarke's careful husbanding of resources.[23]

The management regarded its conservative reputation as a badge of honor. But as the competitive environment exploded into an orgy of expansion, pressure mounted on every major road to rethink its strategy. This debate split the Illinois Central board in predictable fashion. One faction clung doggedly to the ways of the past, believing as so many businessmen do that the old formula for success would continue to work regardless of changing conditions. Another group argued that the company could not afford to stand still or more aggressive systems would swallow it.

As the depression wound down, the traditionalists still dominated the management. The revolution that was about to transform American railroads into giant systems was a speck on the horizon, visible only to the most acute eyes. Its approach infiltrated the boardrooms of every major road, triggering debates over policy that often led to turmoil and turnover of managements, yet few rail executives understood what was happening. It was as if they were victims of a spreading epidemic and helpless to diagnose its nature or find a cure.

Stuyvesant Fish returned to the Illinois Central in 1877, just as this debate over the company's future was taking shape. A new president, William K. Ackerman, was chosen that October, and James C. Clarke was promoted to Ackerman's old post of first vice-president. The two men complemented each other well. Ackerman was a meticulous, scholarly man who had spent his entire career in the business office, while Clarke was a lifelong railroader with a gruff, profane manner that endeared him to the men he commanded. Although cautious and careful by nature, both men were convinced the Illinois Central had to expand if it were to remain prosperous.[24]

It was from Ackerman and Clarke that Fish gleaned much of his education in railroads and probably his point of view as well. Gradually he emerged as the leading advocate of progressive policy on the board, a strong voice growing stronger as his confidence increased. In effect, he blazed the trail Harriman later followed, joining the board as a young financier and transforming himself into a railroad manager.

As the depression lifted, two basic issues confronted the Illinois Central board: expansion and internal reorganization. Although the decision to extend to New Orleans had been made in 1872, the long struggle to gain control of the southern lines had not reconciled some of the conservatives to taking them over. The moves south and into Iowa made them uneasy because of the costs and extended obligations involved. While conceding the need to keep the system in top shape, they balked at anything that might jeopardize the road's proud dividend record. So too did they resist the notion that the company's management structure needed revamping. Every action met with resistance, every vote was divided, and the officers felt the strain.[25]

Through these conflicts Fish grew in both knowledge and stature, steadily extending his influence until he emerged as the leader of those directors favoring more aggressive policies. But he did not have a majority with him, and the board split badly on most crucial votes. Much depended on how heavy a financial burden the new lines proved to be. This problem opened a door for Fish. If he could find creative ways of handling these obligations, he might disarm the fears of the conservatives. The logical man to help him do this was his friend Harriman.

In June 1881 the Illinois Central was looking to sell some bonds issued by its New Orleans line. Probably at the urging of Fish, E. H. Harriman & Co. bid on the $2.5 million lot and got them along with an option for another $1.5 million. This first transaction with the Illinois Central proved fateful for Harriman in two respects. It launched his brokerage on a course away from general commission business and toward a deeper involvement in railroad finance, and it set in motion the chain of events that lured Harriman away from banking into railroading.[26]

This first venture turned out to be anything but routine. Just before Harriman received the bonds, a crazed office-seeker shot President James A. Garfield. The markets plunged sharply and then twitched uneasily until Garfield's death on September 19. After a difficult struggle, Harriman managed to unload the bonds in a depressed market. Although legend insists that Harriman profited handsomely from this transaction, no one knows how much he actually made. What he did make was a reputation for reliability, which proved far more lucrative in the long run. With Fish's blessing, he got involved in the road's financial affairs, hoping to become its American agent.[27]

Fish had more than friendship in mind. With the clash over policy heating up, he was looking for allies to help him gain control of the board. Among the twelve directors he had only two consistent allies, his old friend W. Bayard Cutting and John Elliott. Ackerman and Clarke sided with Fish on most policy matters but had to hew a careful course because of their positions as officers. To complicate matters, the board held staggered elections in which only three directors stood for election each year.[28]

Disagreement still raged over what to do with the New Orleans line. Clarke, who had managed it since 1877, argued repeatedly that it should be upgraded and integrated into the Illinois Central system. By 1881 he had accomplished the first goal, but it took another year to gain approval for a perpetual lease of the New Orleans road. Fish and Clarke then pressed hard for vigorous expansion south of Cairo to stake out territory before competitors grabbed it. The company was also constructing branches in the north and grappling with the Iowa lines as well. The scale of this expansion alarmed some directors, who fretted over how the board could pay for it, let alone manage things coherently.[29]

Fish concluded that an enlarged system required a new management structure, preferably one with himself in charge. While agonizing over expansion policy, the board also created a committee to tackle the problem of reorganization. With the president and vice-president located in Chicago and the financial office in New York, there had long been friction over who held what responsibilities in the latter office. In November 1882 the committee unveiled a plan with two key changes: Clarke would become first vice-president and chairman of the executive committee, while Fish would assume the new position of second vice-president. Fish got his new post, but Clarke wanted no part of the intrigues in New York. He agreed to stay only after the board let him remain in Chicago with title of first vice-president and general manager.[30]

By 1883, then, the Illinois Central found itself at a crisis in its history. While analysts praised its prudent management, turmoil rocked its boardroom. During this year Fish reached a fateful decision: the solution was to replace the old guard on the board with his own social and business friends, who would support the policies he advocated. Every new vacancy on the board became for Fish an opportunity to elect an ally. The death of one director enabled him to bring aboard Sidney Webster; his next recruit was Harriman.[31]

Henry was happy to comply. His short association with the Illinois Central had been profitable and looked to be more so. Whether he saw anything more in it at this early stage remains doubtful. By 1883 he and Fish had wrapped up their Ogdensburg road project and were deep into the Sodus Bay venture. He was a natural ally for Fish's larger ambitions on the Illinois Central, and the more prominent Fish grew in the company, the more likely it was that Henry's firm would become its financial agent. Dutch interests owned a large amount of Illinois Central stock and entrusted most of it to Boissevain Brothers, which in turn used American agents. Harriman persuaded them to use his firm.[32]

As the election approached, Fish rounded up proxies for a ticket that included Harriman in place of one of the old directors. Henry had no trouble getting his seat, but the election of officers took an unexpected turn. Ackerman shocked the board by declining to serve and suggesting that Clarke take his place. Thrown into confusion, the board postponed the election a month, then reluctantly took his advice, leaving Fish as the lone vice-president.[33]

Suddenly the takeover envisioned by Fish seemed on the verge of reality. As president, Clarke was strictly an operations man who took his cue on policy matters from Fish. With Harriman on the board, Fish had a valuable ally and conduit to the money market. All he needed was one or two more loyal directors to complete his coup. In December 1883 he had Harriman move creation of a committee to look anew at the organization in New York. The motion had two objectives: to place the New York office firmly under the vice-president's control and to raise the salaries of officers there.[34]

The first point made good sense with Clarke residing in Chicago. Harriman and Sidney Webster made up a majority of the committee; the third member was Frederick Sturges, a longtime director who opposed their views and submitted his own minority report. At the decisive board meeting Harriman and Webster carried their recommendations by narrow margins. Fish was given command of the New York office force and a hike in salary along with the secretary and treasurer.[35]

This clash marked the opening of a power struggle that raged for three years as Fish and Harriman fought to oust the old-timers who opposed their policies.

Sturges was the first to go. Indignant over his defeat and upset at the direction the company was heading, he resigned despite pleas that he stay. The tug of disagreement in boardrooms was gentlemanly but no less grim or serious for its civility. "I am sorry that there is any difference among the Directors," sighed Clarke to Fish. "I should greatly regret to see any difference arise that might lead to any estrangement or that want of harmony and co-operation which is so essentially necessary in the successful operation of a great Railroad."[36]

Fish also regretted the want of harmony and moved to restore it by replacing dissonant voices with others more in tune with his own. Another old-timer, treasurer L. V. F. Randolph, also stepped down as a director, and Ackerman's seat was still empty, giving Fish three vacancies on the board. He brought in banker Walther Luttgen of August Belmont & Co. (a friend of Harriman's) and two society friends, Robert Goelet and S. Van Rensselaer Cruger. Although Cutting was an ally of Fish's, he could not reconcile himself to the Sturges incident and resigned as director a month after the election. Fish replaced him with William Waldorf Astor.[37]

Analysts were quick to sense what was happening. One called attention to a lack of the "conservative spirit so long dominant in the company's affairs" and linked it to "rumors connected with some of the late changes in management." Sam Sloan, a crusty old railroad man who was a neighbor of both Fish and W. H. Osborn, the grand old man of Illinois Central, minced no words in his assessment. "I don't like that Harriman," he growled. "He and 'Stuyv' Fish are going to get Osborne [sic] in trouble with the Illinois Central, if he don't look out."[38]

How much of the change was Fish and how much was Harriman is not clear, but there is no doubt that Fish led and Harriman followed. Having solidified his hold on the board, Fish got another raise in salary on a motion put forth by his friend Henry. When Randolph retired as treasurer, Fish took over his office as well with another hike in pay to $12,000. Harriman got his reward in the form of more bonds to sell.[39]

Fish needed the money despite his own personal wealth because he was being dragged into a very expensive lifestyle. His wife Marian (or Mamie) liked to refer to Fish as "The Good Man" in the old Knickerbocker style, but there was nothing old-fashioned about her. A bright, strong-willed woman as chatty as Fish was silent, she had plunged with gusto into the rapidly escalating arms race of New York and Newport society. The Fishes had a fine house on East 78th Street in New York, a Stanford White creation with one of the largest ballrooms in a private residence, and a Newport estate called Crossways, where Mamie entertained lavishly.[40]

The place Fish liked best, however, was Glenclyffe Farms, his country place at Garrison. He had always been proud of his lineage through an old Puritan family stretching back to the *Mayflower*. The simple, austere character of his

Mentor and friend turned foe: Stuyvesant Fish, who helped launch Harriman's railroad career and later fought an ugly battle against him. (Culver Pictures)

ancestors appealed deeply to him, as did their strong, silent ways. The "Rose-bud" of his soul was no mystery to anyone. At Glenclyffe he liked to haul his guests up the stairs to a plain, old-fashioned bedroom without running water that he and his brother had shared as boys. "None of the maids will sleep in it," he murmured with a shake of his massive head, "it is not good enough for them; yet I spent some of the happiest hours of my life here."[41]

But he had married Mamie Anthon, whom he adored and who thrived on a very different lifestyle. Fish cared little for society but tolerated its amusements to please his wife. More than once he shuffled wearily home from a business trip to find the house crowded with people who had taken over the place and sometimes even his shaving gear. "It seems I am giving a party," he would shrug diffidently. "Well, I hope you are all enjoying yourselves."

Mamie appreciated her husband's devotion but could not resist teasing him. "Where would he be without me?" she asked in mock innocence. "I put him on the throne." It was an expensive throne, however, and the cost of extravagance soared at a pace that challenged even Fish's ample resources. There was no doubt what he needed from the Illinois Central or the investment advice given him by Harriman. The unanswered question was rather, What did Harriman himself want?

4 Sources of Education

But his knowledge—that was what built the rungs of his golden ladder. . . . With his craving for knowledge, his amazing memory, his genius for detail and a downright blindness for non-essentials, he was not long in acquiring a reputation for solid ability and solid knowledge. An intimate friend says that Harriman literally burned the midnight oil mastering details.

—Edwin Lefevre, "Harriman"

No photograph ever captured the true Wall Street of the nineteenth century because it could not record the sheer energy of a spectacle in constant motion. Wall Street was a still life only under the mantle of darkness or in those few fleeting moments of morning gloom when Trinity Church loomed like a nagging conscience above its empty streets.

Through these narrow, crooked streets Harriman wound his way most days, still the financier looking to expand his horizons, released at last from the prod of failure and driven now by mounting ambition to climb beyond his firm into broader realms of business. Fish had opened a door through which he had scurried eagerly without yet knowing what it would bring beyond mutual profit.

Harriman's connection with his firm and with Wall Street has long been misunderstood. Those who view it as a prelude to later greatness forget that in a real sense he never left the street. He remained a financier all his life. What he left was the active management of his firm and a career as a trader. Even then he simply moved to dealing in more specific operations with rail securities, at which he became a master. At the height of his power he delegated more of this work but did not abandon it entirely; instead he piled other activities on top of financial ones.

Legend has it that Harriman crossed the Rubicon of his career by retiring from his brokerage in 1885. In fact, he did no such thing. What happened that year was rather that William McClure left the firm and Willie Harriman replaced him as the partner in charge of the office. In June 1887 Henry took in Stuyvesant Fish's eldest brother, Nicholas, as a partner and changed his own status to special partner. Nick Fish had been in the diplomatic service before trying his hand at banking. His presence tightened the bond between the Fishes and the Harrimans; it also gave Henry another partner to mind the house's business.[1]

The new arrangement was supposed to last five years but was dissolved on February 1, 1888. Not until then did Henry wind up his firm and transfer all its outstanding contracts to the other family house, Harriman & Co., where Willie went to work. There is no evidence of trouble between Nick Fish and the Harriman brothers; the partnership was terminated because Henry's own position with the Illinois Central had taken a radical turn. After 1888, Harriman & Co. held the same close relationship to the Illinois Central that Henry's own firm had, and he kept an active interest in it.[2]

Later Henry would be quoted as saying he had wasted fifteen years of his life on Wall Street. Of course that was not true. Apart from making himself a wealthy man and developing skills that he used brilliantly all his life, Harriman also laid the foundation for many ventures to come. The point was that he had outgrown his trade and wanted greater challenges than the buying and selling of securities. But he never left Wall Street; no one who dealt in railroad finance got very far from the street. Rather, he became more specialized in what he did there.[3]

This change in Harriman's life came gradually. The man who later seemed so indifferent to what others thought of him still took pains during these years to ingratiate himself with the right people. The man who later gained notoriety for being tactless and impatient was careful and patient during these years because he could not afford to be otherwise. Perhaps financial insecurity continued to gnaw at him, or perhaps he was feeling his way to some unknown destination. Whatever the case, he tested the waters slowly enough that the transition in his interests went unnoticed even by those few people who bothered to notice what he did.

By 1886 Fish was only one step away from completing his takeover of the Illinois Central board. Two lone directors remained as last vestiges of the old guard; in March he informed Clarke that they would be dumped at the forthcoming election. Clarke was distressed but powerless to save them. In their place Fish brought aboard Oliver Harriman and Levi P. Morton of the banking house Morton, Bliss & Co., whose London office represented many English holders of Illinois Central.[4]

A new era in the Illinois Central's history had dawned, and Clarke was not comfortable with it. Although his own position was secure, things were going too fast for him and not always in directions he liked. In May 1887 he left the company despite pleas from the board for him to stay; a few months later he turned up as president of the Mobile & Ohio Railroad. Ultimately his place on the board went to another of Fish's blueblood friends, John W. Auchincloss. Fish assumed the presidency and in September had Harriman elected vice-president. A year earlier Henry had been put on the executive committee, giving him a taste of policymaking; now he found himself for the first time an officer of a major railroad. With his and Fish's rise to the top positions, the revolution was complete.[5]

The struggle involved far more than a palace overthrow by ambitious young Turks. Fish wanted to implement policies that he and Harriman believed would turn a strong system into a great one. These were dangerous times for railroads. By mid-decade the expansion wars were raging all around them, and rates were dropping despite frantic efforts by the warring parties to sustain them. By the 1890s overbuilding would be cursed as a disease for which bankruptcy was the only known cure. Timing and selectivity were crucial in a game where most of the players tended to be impatient and indiscriminate.

Fish and Harriman proceeded in a vigorous but systematic manner. They launched a three-pronged program to restructure the company's financial obligations, enlarge and streamline the system, and institute improvements to make the road as efficient as possible. To underwrite expansion, Harriman resorted to refunding old bonds at lower rates. Although the Illinois Central had done this for years, he added a new wrinkle by tying expansion needs and refunding into one tidy package. The idea was to issue new bonds at the lowest possible rates and use the proceeds not only to retire older issues but also to pay for new lines.

This approach could work only for a conservative road with solid credit and strong earnings like the Illinois Central. Earlier the company had aroused envy when it sold 5 percent bonds. In November 1885 it floated 4 percent bonds for the first time, and these did so well that three months later Fish got approval to try some at 3.5 percent. As financial agent, Harriman and his firm handled most of these transactions. "I think this is a good time to buy some money," he liked to say, and he was hard-nosed in getting what he wanted. In one negotiation he waited nine months to save a charge of one-eighth of 1 percent a year.[6]

But Harriman also knew when not to wait. He had his own approach to timing. "We never will have a better opportunity for sale of this class of bonds," he advised Fish during one protracted negotiation. "I mean that during easy call money is the time to sell & not wait for fear of a turn to higher rates and also the [market] becomes overstocked with bonds at such times."[7]

For most railroads equity financing had long since become wistful thinking, yet so secure was the Illinois Central's credit that during 1886–87 it sold $11 million worth of stock, mostly to its own stockholders, to raise cash for extensions and improvements. Harriman handled these transactions for the company. He also borrowed money and put the road's surplus funds into short-term loans, in effect relieving Fish of his chief responsibilities as treasurer. It is doubtful that Fish could have held both offices without Harriman at his elbow.[8]

Harriman also took charge of a delicate function that thrust him into the heart of expansion policy: negotiating the purchase of securities in other lines the Illinois Central wished to acquire. He liked this work because it was instructive as well as profitable and allowed him to use his formidable skills as a bargainer. The deals ranged from long and tortuous affairs with obstinate sellers to intrigues fanned by rival bidders to routine paper shuffling. Through these operations Harriman gradually evolved from an agent of financial policy to a shaper of it.[9]

During Harriman's first four years on the board the company added 428 miles of new track and brought it up to standard. South of the Ohio River the Illinois Central expanded its main stem by acquiring a route into Memphis and extending a branch line into the cotton-rich Yazoo delta. North of the river the company added several small branches and built one major road, the Chicago, Madison & Northern.[10]

The cost of this expansion policy was what had driven Clarke to seek his future elsewhere. There was reason for concern. At the time, the policy did not look as cautious and well-considered as it would in retrospect. Nor had Harriman and Fish yet demonstrated their ability to oversee it. In an age of falling rates, the cost of this expansion program might have scuttled the credit and certainly the dividends of a road that lacked the intelligent financing Harriman devised. He looked to save money as well as spend it, and one of his efforts drew him into a fateful encounter with a man who would cross his path many times in the future, J. P. Morgan.[11]

Twenty years earlier the Illinois Central had secured its Iowa connection by leasing the Dubuque & Sioux City Railroad on terms that paid its owners 36 percent of gross earnings. This arrangement soured as Iowa filled up with competing railroads, rates declined steadily, and the Dubuque's losses mounted. The road might get more business by extending its two subsidiary lines, but under the lease the Illinois Central would have to pay for such work and then give 36 percent of all future earnings to lessors who had risked nothing.[12]

The lease was due to expire in October 1887 but would be renewed in perpetuity unless the Illinois Central terminated it by April 1, 1887. Fish and Harriman agreed that the best solution was to cancel the lease and buy outright control of the road. Although there was danger in this strategy, they saw that the Dubuque road needed the Illinois Central as badly as the Illinois Central needed it. Without a reliable connector it would be reduced to an impoverished local road.[13]

The Dubuque board included two formidable bankers, J. P. Morgan and Morris K. Jesup. In April 1886 Jesup formed a committee that by December had gained control of well over a majority of the road's stock and deposited it with Drexel, Morgan & Co. as trustee. The plan was to hold the stock until it could be sold for at least par or produced a new lease paying at least 4 percent a year.[14]

While Jesup's committee gathered its forces, Harriman tried to scrounge

Dubuque shares in the open market. His efforts yielded only about 15,000 shares compared to 32,680 controlled by the committee. He scattered shares among a hundred Illinois Central employees to give him vocal support at the Dubuque's annual meeting on February 14, 1887, then went to Dubuque in person to oversee the fight, as did Charles Coster of Morgan's firm. Both sides had hired local attorneys as front men to wage the battle.[15]

Harriman's cause looked hopeless until he stumbled onto a way to snatch victory through a technicality. Three times he wired Fish for permission to try it and got no reply. Well might Fish hesitate; Morgan and Jesup were dangerous men to antagonize. The stakes were high for the Illinois Central, however, and at last he turned Harriman loose.[16]

It happened that the laws of Iowa contained no provision for voting stock by proxy. For years company elections had ignored this fact, but two weeks before the Dubuque meeting Harriman had a friendly stockholder bring suit against the road and the committee to void their shares on that ground. When Harriman's lawyers raised this point at the annual meeting, the proceedings broke down into the gleeful wrangling over technicalities indulged in by lawyers who love nothing more than to be paid for the pleasure of splitting hairs as finely as possible. When the fog of rhetoric cleared, the only stock allowed to vote produced a board friendly to the Illinois Central. During the noon recess, the enraged Morgan forces held a rump meeting and elected their own board.[17]

The clash moved to the courts, where it lingered for months. Meanwhile, the Illinois Central board gave formal notice of terminating the lease, and Harriman offered to buy the Jesup committee's stock at 80 with a strong hint that the offer would not be renewed. The committee hesitated, then accepted on April 7. The bankers had little choice; with the lease about to expire, they were aware that the road had little value as an independent line. Fish and Harriman had won a stunning victory for the Illinois Central.[18]

But the long-term costs were huge for Harriman. This first clash with Morgan cast a pall over their relationship that was lifted only on Harriman's deathbed. For Morgan the issue was not the Dubuque property but his personal code of honor. He never forgave Fish for what he considered an affront to his sense of propriety, and his resentment flashed past Fish to Harriman, whom he considered a nobody. Years later Morgan's son-in-law recounted how the banker drew from this episode "a prejudice against Harriman that kept him in later years from cooperating with him when it might have been better had he done so." What had offended him was Harriman's resort to the "Jay Gould method" of taking refuge in "the devices of lawyers and technicalities." In Morgan's book, men of honor did not stoop to trickery, from which he concluded that Harriman had no sense of honor.[19]

But there had to be something more, for Morgan had actually got along well with Gould and worked closely with him in several enterprises. The clash involved not only values but personalities. Morgan's stolid, Tory instincts had to be handled carefully. Gould's quiet, unassuming manner and gift for tact kept him on the right side of Morgan even during disagreements. By contrast, Harriman's combative nature and abrasive style guaranteed friction with a man like Morgan.

The purchase of the Dubuque road left only one loose end in Iowa. A branch line called the Cedar Falls & Minnesota was leased to the Dubuque road under terms that cost the Illinois Central $90,000 a year. The branch had been losing large sums since the lease was signed in 1866. Fish and Harriman suspected fraud in its origins and wanted out, but how to break a lease that had gone unchallenged for twenty years? Sidney Webster offered a thoughtful analysis that encouraged them to test the lease in court.[20]

Once again Harriman acted as point man, handling the effort in Iowa while trying to buy as much Cedar Falls stock as possible. Resorting to yet another legal technicality, he pushed the suit so aggressively that an offended Cedar Falls bondholder issued a circular blasting his method of operation. In his attack, the bondholder coined a term that would delight a later generation of critics. "Cedar Falls bond holders and others," began the circular, "may learn from the following account how the Illinois Central Harrimanizes branch lines."[21]

The Cedar Falls resisted Harrimanizing longer than most. For eight years the case wound its glacial path toward the Supreme Court until Fish cut a deal with the branch's security holders. Long before this affair reached its end, Fish merged the Iowa lines and began improving them. By the time Harriman became vice-president in September 1887, the new regime had impressed even the editor who had expressed reservations about it three years earlier. "It cannot be said that the company has abandoned its old-time conservatism," he admitted, "but it has developed a somewhat more aggressive disposition."[22]

Improvements got the same close attention. In January 1886 Fish got the board to adopt a policy of investing in work projected over a fifteen- to twenty-year period. The crown jewel of this program was a bridge over the Ohio River at Cairo, creating an unbroken line from Chicago to New Orleans. When the new bridge opened on October 29, 1889, Fish and Harriman went to Cairo for the festivities. The local hotels bulged with rail officials, engineers, reporters, railroad employees, and spectators who had come to see this latest marvel in engineering. Along with the usual speeches and ribbon-cutting, Fish and Harriman treated the crowd to another quaint custom for inaugurating a new bridge. Nine seventy-five-ton Mogul locomotives coupled in tandem lined the track approaching the bridge, their stacks belching smoke in anticipation of the demonstration to come. The object was to prove that the 518-foot span was sturdy enough to withstand the most severe test—in this case a combined engine weight of nearly seven hundred tons.[23]

There was a circus element to this test. Protocol required dignitaries to show their faith in a new bridge by literally staking their lives on it. At nine that morning, therefore, Fish and Harriman climbed into the cab of the lead engine behind the crew as lesser officials swarmed aboard the other locomotives. While the crowd held its breath, the chain of huffing beasts groaned slowly onto the main span until it stretched from pier to pier, then stopped dead in a massive exhale of steam. The bridge stood firm, the crowd cheered loudly, and the engines wheezed their way back onto terra firma to discharge their high-priced cargo.

From this ceremony another, more subtle symbolism could be glimpsed. As their presence in the lead cab suggested, Fish and Harriman were in firm command of the Illinois Central and willing to take large risks on its behalf. There was no doubt about the relationship between them. Fish continued to lead and Harriman to follow except in financial matters, where his advice was usually heeded. Both men recognized not only who was president but who had brought Harriman to the Illinois Central in the first place. Once Harriman became an active officer, Fish expected this dutiful relationship to continue. Like so many others, however, he reckoned without Harriman's phenomenal capacity for growth.

During these years the partitioning of Harriman's life that would later become so conspicuous began to emerge. Most businessmen in the industrial era developed a form of split personality. Doctor Jekyll was the dutiful, considerate husband and father, the genial master of the household, who could be the soul of kindness and hospitality to his friends. At work, however, he became Mr. Hyde, the cold, lynx-eyed businessman who prided himself on his single-minded dedication and ability to shut feelings or sentiment out of decisions.

The difference revealed itself in the names people used to address him. At home he was still Henry to his wife and family, but at work he was called "Ed" or "Ned." Later the public and most of his associates would know him only by his initials, the name pared down as his style grew more brusque in dealing with people. To Mary, however, Henry was ever the devoted husband, eager to share with her all that he did. He grew close to her family as well and often went to Ogdensburg during the summer with his own growing brood. Sometimes they went to Paul Smith's, where it must have pleased and amused the host to watch his old friend introduce his children to the mysteries of the wilds.[24]

By 1887 young Mary was nearly seven, little Henry—or Harry, as he was called—four, and Cornelia three. Harriman delighted in their company and their antics. He loved nothing better than romping with them. There was still something of the child in him: a boyish enthusiasm for everything he did, a restless energy that sometimes exploded into mischief, an elemental nature that relished this most elemental stage of life. In certain ways that were revealed as he grew older, he had not really grown up at all.

Harriman's love of nature led him to a major decision in 1886. He had done well enough to afford a summer place of his own, and that year a rare opportunity presented itself. A large property in the Ramapo Highlands, about forty-five miles north of Jersey City, was coming up for auction. It belonged to the Parrott family and had a history steeped in the early iron industry of the Ramapo Valley.

As early as 1811 the Greenwood furnace began producing iron, using charcoal taken from the surrounding forests as fuel. In 1837 William and Gouverneur Kemble took over the ironworks and a few years later started the West Point foundry as well. Eventually the Greenwood Iron Works embraced nearly eight thousand acres of magnificent wilderness, with extensive forests to provide charcoal and mountains to mine for iron ore. The Kembles did well at the iron trade but preferred society to the rigors of business. As their interests expanded, they leased the West Point foundry and then the Greenwood Iron Works to another pair of brothers, Robert and Peter Parrott.[25]

The short but severe panic of 1857 hit the Parrott brothers hard. They failed unexpectedly but managed to pay off all their debts by the decade's end. Then came the Civil War. Overnight the foundry and Greenwood found themselves swamped with more orders than they could handle. Robert designed a new kind of cannon known as the Parrott gun and turned them out at the foundry along with ammunition. Government contracts lifted the brothers from embarrassment to large fortunes and even more sterling reputations.[26]

After the war the expanding iron industry caught up with the small Parrott operation, and the onset of depression in 1873 dealt it a crippling blow. Then, on Christmas Eve in 1877, Robert died suddenly, depriving Peter of the brother on whom he had leaned heavily for advice. Peter borrowed heavily to keep the business going. He formed the Parrott Iron Company and transferred all of Greenwood's assets to it along with most of his real estate except for a small parcel around his house. Still the business swallowed more money than he could raise. Fighting doggedly against his fate, Peter watched his firm slide toward failure. In August 1885 the Greenwood Iron Works closed as a prelude to bankruptcy.[27]

The receiver appointed for the property was none other than Stuyvesant Fish. By September 1886 it was ready to be sold under foreclosure. The court stipulated that the land could be sold in parcels or as a whole provided the latter fetched a price exceeding the sum bid for the parcels. How Harriman learned about the sale is unclear, but he jumped at the chance. Here was a tract of 7,863 acres, most of it dense forest, set in a site of breathtaking beauty. It would be like having a miniature Paul Smith's much closer to the city, complete with majestic hills offering spectacular views of the highlands and the Ramapo River.[28]

On September 17 Harriman arrived at the Goshen courthouse to find that the only other interested bidders were timber speculators eager to strip the Ramapo hills. They were no match for Harriman's determination; he bid $52,500 for the entire property and found himself the owner of a country estate. The Parrotts kept only their homestead, which stood on a large clearing alongside a small lake between two sets of small hills near the western boundary of the estate. There was also a small cottage once occupied by a married daughter, where the Harrimans began to stay on weekends. As he grew more fond of the area, Harriman began to enlarge and improve the cottage. He gave the estate the name Arden, which Kennan traced back to the family name of Mrs. Parrott.[29]

But there was a deeper, more personal connection. Arden was the forest where Shakespeare had set *As You Like It*, the play from which Harriman's father had drawn his ill-fitting name. Harriman was not a well-read man, but it is hard to believe he did not know the play or draw his inspiration from it. He was in fact quoted late in life as saying, "Arden to me is the Arden of 'As You Like It' . . . a retreat from the world worries [*sic*]. Here I seek to free myself from all business cares, and so far I have been successful. My guests here are made to understand that they are most welcome if they abstain from talking shop."[30]

Arden forest was a place at once fanciful and down to earth, free of dragons, goblins, giants, and other creatures of myth but not of romance. Nature itself was for Harriman a romantic, even mystical realm where he stepped out of time and character to regenerate his energy. There he became literally a child of nature, bubbling with enthusiasm and eager for the challenge of pitting his elemental character against the elements. Only one prominent figure outdid Harriman in his fanatical embrace of wilderness as a source of personal catharsis: Theodore Roosevelt.

Arden served Harriman in many ways. To outward eyes it was his country place, an ornament befitting any successful man of means. But it was also his preserve against the world, a timeless and private playground where he could be himself with family and friends, an immutable fortress against the darker, blighting side of civilization's advance that he not only guarded jealously but expanded steadily over the years until the estate embraced thirty square miles of forest. Gradually Arden also became something else that revealed another side of Harriman: a working dairy farm organized socially like a medieval manor with Henry as the benign lord overseeing his flock with paternal eyes.

This return to nature was not the usual way of either the upper crust or successful businessmen. To see the difference in striking relief, one had only to look just south of Arden, where tobacco heir Pierre Lorillard created for his wealthy friends a suburban playground called Tuxedo Park, a compound so elegant and exclusive that it gave the modern formal dinner jacket its name.[31]

Breaking ground in September 1885, a year before Harriman bought Arden,

Lorillard constructed a miniature village of twenty-two enormous English-turreted "cottages" served by thirty miles of road, a water and sewage system, grocery store, pharmacy, and its own private telephone exchange and police station. To supply the needs of its demanding residents, Tuxedo Park included four lawn tennis courts, a swimming pool, a bowling alley, an icehouse, a club-house, a boathouse, immense stables, a trout pond, and a hatchery. An eight-foot fence helped preserve its exclusive character, and the formidable entrance gates were always guarded. The gatehouse, declared its architect modestly, re-sembled "a frontispiece to an English novel."[32]

Lorillard completed his fantasy island in the spring of 1886, and Tuxedo Park soon became the most formal and exclusive address on the continent. Most of the elite families who bought "cottages" occupied them only during the spring and fall, when they enjoyed a constant round of teas, dances, concerts, dinners, and the annual ball for debutantes. Two of the inmates were men who sat on the board of the Illinois Central: William Waldorf Astor and Robert Goelet.

Nothing of the pretension of Tuxedo Park seeped into Arden. Although Harriman moved in the best social circles and liked to rub elbows with the elite at their own playgrounds in the city or Newport or Bar Harbor, he brought little of it home with him. The cottage at Arden began life as the real item. Harriman transformed it into a big, sprawling manor that was far more comfortable than elegant and looked as if people actually lived in it. A long wraparound veranda flowed into an enclosed sunroom and overlooked Echo Lake.[33]

Other than enlarging the cottage, Harriman found little time to do much more with Arden in the first few years after he acquired it. The frenzy of activity surrounding the revolution in the Illinois Central kept him on the road much of the time. When he became vice-president in October 1887, his career reached a turning point in more ways than one. He already served as president of such subsidiary lines as the Mississippi & Tennessee Railroad, but these were nominal offices that could be filled from New York. His new position, however, required him to move to Chicago.[34]

5 Sources of Revelation

His consuming thirst for knowledge at first hand, his ceaseless study of the science
of railroading, both the "practical" and the financial sides of it, his training in stock-
gambling and stock-market methods and procedure, all made him a valuable man,
a daring man, but one whom the most conservative financier would not call a
dangerous speculator—he knew too much and thought too logically, too
dispassionately.

—Edwin Lefevre, "Harriman"

Harriman in Chicago was a fish out of water, a stranger in a strange land where he could not monitor Wall Street directly. Although the family traveled extensively, this was the first time they had lived for any time outside New York. Chicago struck their eastern eyes as a crude cowtown despite the progress it had made as a city. To make matters worse, tragedy struck only a few months after their arrival in Chicago. Little Harry, not yet five years old, contracted diphtheria and died in February 1888.[1]

The sudden, wrenching loss of his only son devastated Harriman just as he was struggling to make the transition not only from Fifth Avenue to Michigan Avenue but also from broker to railroad official. Given his devotion to family and his passion for children, it was fortunate that the press of work left little time to grieve. That the loss lingered with him was obvious; on the first anniversary of Harry's death he made a gift of $6,000 for "aiding and encouraging the boys" who worked in the Illinois Central shops.[2]

"My father always said that [Harry's death] was the thing that made him feel he should make railroading his career," recalled Averell Harriman decades later. "He felt his son had died because he was working on the railroad, and he wanted to justify the sacrifice of his son by dedicating himself to railroading."[3]

It is a poignant tale but only partially true. Averell was born three years after his brother's death and so never knew him. More likely, the loss of Harry reinforced a process already begun, the real catalyst for which was wrenching Harriman away from Wall Street. Why else would he have come to Chicago if not to immerse himself in the details of railroading? Harry's death spurred Harriman to accomplish what he had already decided to do.[4]

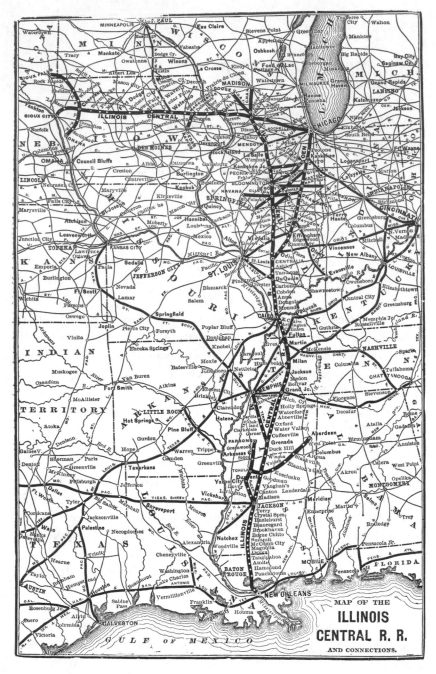

Heartland: A map of the Illinois Central system. Unlike most major roads, it ran north-south instead of east-west. (Baker Library, Harvard Business School)

A curious paradox soon emerged. By being in Chicago, Harriman had less voice in the making of policy in New York. At the same time, his separation from Fish gave him a certain independence. He was on the scene, observing firsthand conditions he formerly knew only by hearsay, learning the complexities and subtleties behind the reports sent to New York. This new perspective had a predictable effect on Harriman: the more he learned, the more he grew and the more confident he became that his judgment on matters was superior to that of his friends in New York.

The problem was that Harriman did not yet know what he could do in Chicago. Great progress had been made toward expanding and integrating the system, but it still lacked an efficient organization. Fish's revolution had rendered the old structure obsolete. Past presidents had always resided in Chicago, which left no doubt about the chain of command in the West. Now the president was in New York and the vice-president in Chicago. The latter's duties had never been defined; neither had those of the general manager, who ran the railroad. New relationships had to be worked out between the president and vice-president in one direction and the vice-president and general manager in the other.[5]

The board also wanted to overhaul procedures throughout the system. Like most railroads, the Illinois Central still conducted its business according to practices honed by custom. Although railroads were by far the largest and most complex business organizations in the world, few of them functioned on the basis of written rules. The keeper of custom was not the board or president but the chief operating officer, who oversaw every aspect of the road in the field. On the Illinois Central that man was Edward T. Jeffery.[6]

Harriman occupied a vacuum between Fish and Jeffery, and he was not a man to suffer a vacuum for very long. In April 1888 the board created a committee to consider three major issues, including "a new distribution of executive duties at Chicago, and along the railway." It also asked Harriman, Fish, Jeffery, and general solicitor B. F. Ayer to report in writing on what duties the vice-president should have. At first, Harriman was distracted by Harry's death and the illness of a daughter. That same month he took the family with him on a business trip south to escape one of the worst winters on record. They went first to Memphis and then to New Orleans, where Henry lingered, tending to company matters while his family basked in the warmth.[7]

Then Fish summoned him to New York for an important board meeting. Mary urged him to go, but Harriman hesitated. "I do not think it would be prudent to leave my family here alone at this time," he protested. "Besides the nurse seems just now to have lost her head & I dont know what to expect from her." He wanted the family safely back in Chicago, yet he also feared taking his daughter back to a cold climate. The tone of this exchange shows Harriman to be unusually anxious and high-strung. Nothing agitated him more than a threat to his family's well-being, and Harry's death inflamed this sensitivity. Reluctantly he went to New York.[8]

When he finally returned to Chicago, his uneasiness did not vanish so much as transfer itself into a feverish outburst of energy directed at reforming procedures in both the New York and Chicago offices. "It seems almost impossible to wire the New York office and receive an answer the same day," he complained to Fish at one point. He also revamped the way statements were prepared by the auditor and cleaned up other routines that had grown inefficient or aimless.[9]

When it came time to submit the statement on the duties and powers of the vice-president, however, Harriman suddenly turned coy. While he had no intention of limiting his scope by defining his powers too specifically, he could not bring himself to cry, "All power to the vice-president." Instead, he mouthed some vague mush and hoped New York would let him fill the vacuum in his own way. But Fish refused the bait and pressed for a more definite statement. This time Harriman seized on the major flaw. Under existing procedures, the general manager and department heads reported directly to the president, who had always been in Chicago. With Fish in New York, however, all business went directly there and then had to come back to the vice-president. This left Harriman out of the decision-making loop, and Fish compounded the problem by constantly yanking him back to New York to deal with financial matters instead of assigning him duties in Chicago and leaving him there.[10]

The obvious solution was to make the vice-president the chief officer in the West and channel all business through him to New York, but this presented Fish with a nice dilemma. There was in his nature an imperious streak that made him reluctant to delegate authority. To retain power in his own hands, he would have to move to Chicago—an idea repugnant to him. If he wished to stay in New York, he had no choice but to delegate authority to Harriman in Chicago and quit summoning him to New York.

Neither option appealed to Fish, and the matter was complicated by Jeffery's demands. The general manager agreed that with the president in New York, the vice-president in Chicago should be the chief officer in the West. But Jeffery too was anxious to preserve his own autonomy and submitted a description of his duties that matched Harriman's in vagueness. The subtext of his message was plain, however: he would serve as the vice-president's subordinate provided the vice-president did not interfere with his work. Jeffery's ploy to protect his power base disturbed general solicitor B. F. Ayer. "I do not see," he despaired, "how any distribution of administrative functions can be made between the Vice President and General Manager, without causing dissatisfaction and perhaps considerable inconvenience and trouble."[11]

In New York the astute Sidney Webster, sifting through the correspondence on the subject, was bothered by the inability of Harriman, Jeffery, and Ayer to specify the vice-president's duties. "Perhaps the three officers named . . . cannot define those matters," he concluded. "If they cannot, how can the Committee?" After grappling with the issue for a year, the committee admitted defeat in May 1889 by declaring that either the president or vice-president should reside in Chicago and "exercise actual supervision."[12]

This decision by default did nothing to clarify the chain of command, leaving a vacuum that controversy would soon fill. In April, however, the board had revised its own structure by replacing the executive committee with three new committees: finance, law, and rates, revenues, and expenditures (RRE). The press of business had grown too great for a single committee to handle, especially with the indefatigable Harriman absent from New York. Under the new arrangement, duties were shared among nine directors instead of only three or four.[13]

A sense of urgency underlay these efforts to find a structure that would enable the Illinois Central to run smoothly. During 1888 earnings continued to crumble beneath the pressures of rate wars and competitive overbuilding that were ushering American railroads into a new and dangerous era. No issue since the Civil War proved more politically explosive than railroad rates, partly because its complexities defied ordinary logic. There were two distinct kinds of rail rates. Local rates covered traffic moving along a company's line that was not subject to competition from other roads. Through rates applied to traffic that started or ended beyond the company's line and had to compete with other roads for all or part of the journey. Local rates were vulnerable to the charge of monopoly, through rates to cuts by rival lines seeking to attract more business.*

During its early stages the American rail system consisted mainly of independent connecting lines that lived off their local business and cooperated in moving through traffic along their combined routes. Gradually, however, strong roads absorbed their connections and integrated them into larger systems. As these systems expanded, they reached more towns in common and competed at more places for through traffic. The orgy of railroad construction after the Civil War intensified these struggles, multiplying competitive points and triggering rate wars that reached new heights of bitterness during the depression of the 1870s, when roads fought desperately for their share of a dwindling traffic.[14]

Rate wars among railroads were unlike any other form of industrial conflict. Every road had a published rate schedule divided into classifications based on the different value of diverse cargoes. (For obvious reasons, the rate was much higher on a pound of silk than a pound of lumber.) But traffic officers did not hesitate to offer special rates or rebates to large shippers or others whose busi-

*A large amount of traffic paid a mixed rate—that is, a combination of the local rate for the distance moved on the road's line and the through rate for the distance beyond it.

ness might go elsewhere. These lower rates were secret and fluctuating, which made them inviting targets for political attack.

Rebates infected the rail industry like a pernicious disease, undermining its health and defying all attempts at a cure. Since every line needed a steady flow of business to stay solvent, it made sense to fill empty cars with something, even at reduced rates, rather than have them run empty. If one line had a longer, more roundabout route between two points than another, it could compensate by offering lower rates. The return of prosperity after 1879 brought more traffic but also the greatest expansion of the rail system in history. As new lines appeared and old ones extended their tracks into new territory, the rate wars increased in scale and ferocity.

In their desperate attempt to impose stability, railroad leaders everywhere formed pools among competing roads to maintain rates by sharing business. But pools were fragile alliances with no standing in law and were violated regularly despite strenuous efforts to maintain them. Then in 1887 the Interstate Commerce Act changed the game entirely by outlawing pools, thereby depriving carriers of their only vehicle for curbing rate wars. State railroad commissions also lowered rates, and competitive wars kept them low.

In 1888 the first symptoms of a financial epidemic that would later ravage railroads burst forth, aggravated by slumping business in the West, where a cycle of summer drought and winter blizzards shattered the cattle boom and ruined crops. As traffic and earnings declined, dividends were cut or omitted altogether. The value of rail securities plummeted, making capital harder to secure. Public hostility toward the carriers rose as steadily as rates fell. Frenzied efforts to curb the wars led to long, tortuous rounds of negotiation producing agreements that crumbled at the touch. The Illinois Central did better than most roads but in 1888 still suffered a drop of 10 percent in gross and 17 percent in net earnings. Fish could no longer protect the company's dividend record, which had earlier been cut from 8 to 7 percent and faced a steeper drop that winter. Pressure mounted on Fish to the point that he lamented, "I am liable to be out of my present position at any time."[15]

The rate question had begun to haunt Fish and Harriman. Repeated attempts to maintain them in Illinois and Iowa had failed miserably. During the summer of 1888 Jeffery ordered company agents to give no rebates without his direct approval. Fish did not learn about this edict until January 1889, when he asked Jeffery for an explanation of how special contracts were handled. He let Jeffery continue approving any deviation from set rates but instructed him to forward details of every case to New York. In pondering the difficulties facing him, Fish concluded that he had no choice but to assume direct authority over all rate decisions.[16]

The board shared this belief. In April 1889 it added a new clause to bylaw XI stating that no rate could be reduced without the approval of the president. The message sent to Jeffery could not have been plainer. The granting of special rates and rebates had always been the province of traffic agents and officers, with only occasional interference from their superiors. Now the amended bylaw XI forbade giving any such rate without advance approval from top management.[17]

Unfortunately, the board's right hand took this swipe at virtue without consulting its left hand. Jeffery saw the flaw in the plan at once: the system could work only if an officer with the necessary power resided in Chicago. Harriman was there, but the board had yet to resolve who had what duties in which place. Within months this vacuum in the structure of management plunged Harriman into the first major crisis of his career as a rail officer.

The year following little Harry's death was an ordeal for Harriman in many respects. Apart from the painful adjustment to a household without a small boy to enliven it, there was the constant struggle to rationalize the managerial and financial structure of the Illinois Central at a time of turbulence in the industry. Although he could not know it, Harriman was witness to the dawn of a momentous new era in railroading: the rise of giant systems spanning half the continent. Like the evolution of feudal Europe into nation-states, the transition was a jarring, inchoate experience as individual roads accustomed to fighting one another in their own backyards suddenly found themselves clashing at remote points all over the continent in wars that grew ever larger and more destructive in scale.

Harriman's distracted eye caught only passing glimpses of this furor. Through the winter and spring of 1888 he ran a constant circuit between Chicago, New Orleans, and New York, trying to define his position while helping Fish nurse along some complicated bond negotiations. Their relationship continued to smack of master and protégé. For all his affability, Fish was a hard taskmaster who shifted abruptly from addressing Harriman as "My dear Ed" to reprimanding him for some error. "I sincerely trust the circular which you handed me late this afternoon will not be published," he noted coldly on one occasion. "With a view to stating the facts with some degree of exactness, permit me to suggest substituting the enclosed." Harriman bore these rebukes with clenched teeth because he had no choice. With the bond negotiations stalled, he fled gratefully to Arden in May and to Ogdensburg in July, never more than a telegraph key away from summons by Fish.[18]

After the bond sale was made in September, Harriman still had to scramble for money, peddling bonds and seeking loans on good terms. Through the dreary winter of 1888–89 he kept at the hunt until the strain wore down even his relish for dickering. His patience finally snapped in one test of wills with a Jewish banker. "I am not much astonished at Goldsmith's action as it is about what his class might be expected to do," he growled. "I have had to struggle for the past three years against these shylocks & they dont feel at all friendly because of so many former defeats."[19]

This outburst of anti-Semitism was typical of Wall Street but less so of Harriman. It was a prejudice that usually came out under duress, as it did here, but Harriman later grew close to several Jewish bankers, notably Jacob H. Schiff of Kuhn, Loeb. His real frustration was less with the Goldsmiths of the world than with Fish, who persisted in keeping him busy at his old financial duties without defining his position in Chicago. As long as Fish needed his financial expertise and was reluctant to grant him autonomy in other areas, Harriman could see no way out of his dilemma.

Hard times revived old doubts about the direction Fish and Harriman had taken the company. Stockholders who had been uneasy over expansion policy seized on the dividend cut as evidence of poor management. Some newspapers picked up the dispute and gave Harriman an early taste of notoriety. The *New York Sun* compared the Fish-Harriman bookkeeping practices to those of a scoundrel currently in vogue, Henry S. Ives, and demanded to know the size and source of Harriman's fortune: "He was not accounted a wealthy man when he went into the Illinois Central management, but his fortune is now generally estimated at several million dollars. According to the reports current in Wall street, he and Fish stand to increase their respective piles materially or to diminish them, according to the course of the market. . . . Some of the foreign houses assert that there is not an arbitrage house in the street that has not sold Illinois Central stock for their account or upon orders from Harriman & Co."[20]

Stockholder grumbling over the reduced dividend and growing financial obligations of the company erupted into controversy at the annual meeting in March 1889. Fish went to Chicago for the sessions and told Harriman to remain in New York. When a dissident stockholder named F. B. Cooley charged that Harriman had stayed home to avoid being questioned by his critics, the accusation got into all the morning papers in New York. Harriman was hopping mad when he read it and fired off a telegram to Fish. "Please state without fail at today's meeting," he asked, "that I intended to be present but remained here at your request."[21]

Fish did so, and after the meeting he assured Harriman that "Cooley is a mere trader and not a straightforward man of business." But something else began to tick in Fish's mind. "Jealousy and personal dislike of Mr Harriman," he confided to the Dutch bankers, "is at the bottom of a great deal of this abuse, which is most unmerited." Harriman seemed to have a knack for being a lightning rod of controversy even when serving in a capacity that normally attracted little attention. He was incapable of sitting still and wanted to poke into everything. That spring, for example, he decided the New York offices needed reorganizing and presented Fish with a plan for the work.[22]

Fish was tired of it all and anxious to get away for a long rest. He planned to sail for Europe on July 10, to be gone until October. This would leave Harriman in charge as acting president with no immediate restraint on his bent for constant action. The thought must have given Fish more than one shiver. Diligently he went about trying to put the house in order so that Harriman would have little to do.

The rate conundrum resisted every effort at finding a solution or even a truce. What it did create was a clash between Fish and Jeffery that caught Harriman in the middle. During the spring of 1889 rates deteriorated as one road after another withdrew from yet another agreement that was to end the wars among them. From Chicago Jeffery watched grimly as major lines launched a new round of cuts. To agents of other roads he protested that many rates being offered were so low that they amounted to self-inflicted wounds. But the struggles erupting on all sides shattered attempts to hold rates steady, and the unresolved power vacuum in the Illinois Central hampered efforts to match cuts given by competitors who did not have to lose time asking New York for approval.[23]

Fish offered Jeffery little comfort. As rates softened, he twice reminded the general manager of the amended bylaw XI requiring the president's approval for any special rate. Early in May, while Fish was visiting Chicago, Jeffery collared him for long talks in which Fish promised that he would urge the board to restore bylaw XI to its original form. But nothing was done. A month later, he went west again and found Jeffery even more adamant. It was impossible to function without authority to make rates on his own, he insisted; the delay of obtaining approval from New York was intolerable to shippers, who took their business elsewhere.[24]

Fish replied that he had to abide by the bylaws. A few days later, Jeffery sent Fish his resignation. "The Company's business cannot be satisfactorily managed under the eleventh By-Law, as it now reads," he protested, "unless the President resides here and assumes direct charge." The decision did not come easily to Jeffery, who had started work for the Illinois Central at the age of thirteen. But he had been unhappy since Clarke's departure and had tried to quit a year earlier only to have Fish talk him into staying. Now he offered to remain until the year's end, "exercising the same powers and performing the same functions as heretofore."[25]

Fish received this letter only a few days before he was to sail for Europe and found himself in a quandary. The board had a proposal to revise bylaw XI as Jeffery wished, but it had not come from Fish and was referred to the RRE committee, which would not act on it for weeks. Fish did not have weeks; he had a boat to catch. He asked Jeffery to stay through December and quoted Jeffery's own terms back to him. Unfortunately, this vague phrase meant something different to each man. In his haste Fish may have overlooked the potential for misunderstanding, or he may simply have left it for Harriman to thrash out with Jeffery. After scribbling off some instructions for Harriman on a variety of topics, Fish climbed gratefully aboard the *City of Paris* on July 10.[26]

"I am now in harness," the new acting president chortled to an officer, but he lingered in New York only a week before taking his family off to Bar Harbor for a vacation. Five days after Fish left, another tragic blow struck Harriman: his mother died suddenly. Neither Harriman nor his biographers even mention the loss of this strong woman to whom he was so close, but there is no doubt it had a profound effect on him. The mainstay of his youth, the woman who had instilled in him the values he held so strongly, was gone. It is revealing that he did not inform Fish of her passing until September 2, when he was caught up in his first crisis.[27]

While mourning his loss, the matter most on his mind was a charge from the board to revamp the organization. In May a committee headed by Fish and Harriman had been created to prepare a new scheme of departments for the company. Fish did not expect anything to be done until his return, but Harriman was eager to get started. It was, he told general solicitor James Fentress the day after Fish departed, "one of the most important matters we have had before us for some time." He did not yet have a specific plan in mind, but he was insistent on one point. "We should first adopt a plan & then make our officers fit into it as best we can," he argued, "& not make a plan to fit our officers."[28]

This observation offers a glimpse at the germ of an idea Harriman would later implement on a colossal scale. It was the product of a mind that searched relentlessly for the most efficient way to put something together without concern for how personal dynamics affected its operation. It recognized frankly that any change in organization would weaken the autocratic hold of the general manager. The object was to find a plan that suited the board, not Jeffery.

Meanwhile, in Chicago Jeffery reverted to his old practice of deciding special rates on his own. Harriman discovered this when he asked Jeffery for some examples of special rates. Although Harriman noticed that Jeffery was not obeying bylaw XI, he did nothing more than ask for details, probably because he saw the futility of challenging Jeffery from afar. Nevertheless, Jeffery sensed that something was brewing. A proud, stubborn man, he let pride lead him into a rash act. Late in July he told several friends that he had resigned before Fish's departure. Within days the story leaked to the newspapers, leaving Harriman with an awkward public relations problem.[29]

The last thing Harriman wanted was a crisis suggesting that he could not mind the store in Fish's absence. Uneasily he reported the incident to Fish almost as an afterthought, adding, "I don't anticipate much inconvenience from that cause." Fish's reaction was anything but casual. Amid the sunny, serene surroundings of Interlaken he exploded at "this piece of egotism, not to speak of it as a breach of discipline and of confidence. . . . It is astounding that so intelligent a man should be guilty of such a stupid impertinence." Before Harriman even received this outburst, however, the affair boiled into the crisis he had so dreaded.[30]

Once Jeffery went public, Harriman handled him gingerly and even took pains to compliment his work in a difficult negotiation with another road. But he also saw in Jeffery's stand a streak of arrogance that needed curbing. On a sultry day late in August Harriman boarded a train for Chicago to face Jeffery in a confrontation that could no longer be avoided. Early on the morning of September 2, Jeffery stopped by Harriman's office to discuss the purchase of some locomotives. After that topic was exhausted, Harriman said abruptly that while he was in Chicago he expected Jeffery to refer all special rates to him in accordance with bylaw XI.[31]

Jeffery stiffened in his chair. He glared at Harriman for half a minute, then jumped up and said, "If that's your decision, I quit, and will turn the road over to you at twelve o'clock to-day." A startled Harriman urged him not to act hastily. "Well," Jeffery countered, "I quit at five o'clock, and turn the road over to you." He told Harriman of the arrangement with Fish, which in his view had given him authority to handle rates in the old way. Without that power, Jeffery emphasized, he would not remain in office for even one day. Harriman shrugged and said he could see no alternative to enforcing bylaw XI. "All right then, I quit," Jeffery repeated, and stormed out of the office. "He was very much excited," Harriman reported to Fish, neglecting to add that he was no sea of tranquillity himself. This was his first crisis as a railroad officer, and on the surface it put him in a bad light. He was a mere caretaker, a novice at the game, who had just driven from the company one of the most respected operating men in the country. Jeffery lost no time giving news of his abrupt departure to the papers along with copies of the relevant correspondence, which sounded as if he had been pushed out. Predictably, most editors showered him with praise and sympathy.[32]

Harriman maintained strict silence in public and ordered other officials to do likewise, but privately he was quick to justify his action. He offered the board a muted defense, saying, "I regret very much that it fell to my lot to perform this trying duty, as it was very much against my inclination." To Fish, however, he admitted being surprised that Jeffery "took the position he did as I had always understood that he did not object to the Bylaw if the Prest or Acting Prest was in Chicago." Then he added a revealing disavowal: "You must know that I would not, if I were able, undertake to manage the affairs of this Company, but I will hold everything in good shape until your return or the Board makes some change; so you need not feel at all uneasy."[33]

These words suggest how insecure Harriman felt in his position and how dependent that place was on Fish. Obviously he feared Fish would think he was overreaching his power, a suspicion that later events would confirm. They also show how well Harriman understood that Fish regarded his presidency with a fierce possessiveness and brooked no rivals. For the moment, however, he need not worry. Fish issued a strong defense of Harriman's action. This was hardly surprising; he was, after all, actually defending himself from Jeffery's charge that he had gone back on his word. "You did right to let him go," Fish cabled from Paris. He denied vehemently that he had ever promised to amend or suspend bylaw XI. "Pride and incapacity to submit to control," he concluded, "were the real sources of [Jeffery's] trouble."[34]

A few weeks after Jeffery's departure, Harriman quietly authorized traffic manager T. J. Hudson to use his discretion in arranging coal rates, but he personally approved other reductions under bylaw XI. The real issue had never been bylaw XI but rather the lines of power. By letting Jeffery go, Harriman signaled that the Illinois Central was no longer a fief for the general manager to rule in the old absolute way. If the message was not yet plain, he aimed to deliver it anew with his plan for shuffling the organization.[35]

This first crisis affected Harriman more deeply than he knew. While Jeffery's departure alarmed him, it also liberated him in an unexpected way. On any matter dealing with the railroad he could not help deferring to Jeffery's formidable knowledge and long familiarity with the road. Jeffery had become an institution on the Illinois Central who, like most practical railroad men, embraced the folklore of experience as the canon for how things should be done. With Jeffery gone, Harriman was free to act without the weight of tradition peering over his shoulder. C. A. Beck, the acting general manager, was also an old railroad man but lacked Jeffery's prestige. New to his post and hoping to keep it, Beck was eager to please.[36]

John G. Mann, the superintendent of southern lines, waited only a few days before tossing back at Harriman one of his own suggestions. The system was too centralized, Mann observed, because every action had to await approval from the general manager in Chicago. Why not give the superintendents on the northern, southern, and Iowa lines the authority to act on most matters while still holding them accountable to the general manager in Chicago?[37]

In effect, Mann was proposing an organization based on divisions rather than departments. As one railroad man described the difference, the departmental approach "spread the working organization . . . over the entire system; the other makes a number of different working organizations, or units." The Pennsylvania Railroad had pioneered the divisional system, and debate was then raging among railroad men over which one was superior. Harriman liked the divisional idea, which, as Mann pointed out, had another virtue. If a new general manager was needed on short notice, the divisions groomed superintendents for the place.[38]

Harriman's enthusiasm for fresh ideas quickly became contagious. Traffic manager T. J. Hudson checked in with a blueprint for revamping his organization, as did the freight agents, passenger agent, and other superintendents. In New York the Organization Board, chaired by Harriman in Fish's absence, spent a full day discussing and revising a new plan it had drawn up to reform the operating system and close the power vacuum between New York and Chicago. From its labors emerged a new "Code of Rules for Conducting the Business of the Illinois Central Railroad Company."[39]

A sense of revelation and exhilaration flooded through Harriman during these last weeks before Fish's return. As he worked feverishly on the new plan, it dawned on him that the much respected Illinois Central was still in many ways a stodgy, conservative company. The new board had accomplished much, but much more remained to be done. The social register that constituted its membership were all good fellows but hardly the sort to be inspired by a vision and the desire to fulfill it. Harriman was inspired, not only by the tasks before him but also by a growing confidence in his own ability, and he rushed after his vision with a ferocious burst of energy.

Along with devising the new code and supporting Mann's plan for a divisional organization, Harriman launched intensive investigations of the traffic, operating, and machinery departments. Everywhere he saw the need for more and better facilities. "I could write a book full on what might have been done & lost opportunities," he enthused to Fish, who was then in London, "but will keep it until you return & lay it all before you & see if we cannot make better provision for the future."[40]

This explosion of activity must have puzzled Fish. Why was the man who had disavowed any desire to run the company suddenly pushing for action on every front? Having lost touch with affairs, Fish found it hard to get back into the flow when he returned on October 24. His sense of displacement was not helped by Harriman's irrepressible enthusiasm. While Fish struggled to get back in harness, Harriman raced ahead at full speed, dragging his friend along with him.[41]

"The whole machine has now got a fresh start," Harriman exulted, "and we should not allow it to stand still or again to get in such a rut as it has been for some years past." Breathlessly he poured out a torrent of suggestions for more changes, oblivious to the implication that the entire system had been moribund until he had taken hold of it. Fish buried whatever resentment he felt; instead, he supported the proposed reforms and gradually made them his own by differing with Harriman on details or timing. For his part Harriman found it difficult to settle back into his role as second fiddle, a position in which he was never again comfortable.[42]

In December 1889 the board approved the new code after lengthy debate. The Jeffery affair left one major legacy: under the new setup, the president's office moved back to Chicago. Fish cringed at the prospect and at the thought of leaving Harriman to handle matters in New York, but he saw little choice. Before Fish could move, however, Harriman fell ill with the grippe and was confined to his house for a month. This was nothing new; he was forever honking or rasping with a cold or the flu. While he languished this time, events took a surprising turn.[43]

During the summer the RRE committee had been asked to study the company's long-term needs and resources. That same December Fish and Harriman joined in asking the board to increase outlays for improvements over the next three years. The board in turn asked them how much would be needed, and the RRE committee wanted the same figures before submitting its report. All this work had to be done while Harriman lay ill, which forced Fish to remain in New York and throw something together on his own.[44]

A year earlier Fish had asked Jeffery for an improvements wish list only to have him come up empty. In Jeffery's opinion, the road needed no new ballast or heavier rails, no sidings, double tracks, grade reductions or new alignments, no major buildings or terminal facilities. Fish was appalled at this lack of vision on future needs. Now, with Harriman hors de combat, he had to formulate a list with little help from the sources he needed most.[45]

Despite this handicap, Fish devised an impressive statement. The company had in his view reached a turning point in improvements policy. Since 1883 it had financed more than $3 million in betterments from current income, but the gap between needs and available income kept widening. It was clear to Fish that the scale of improvements had outgrown this method of financing. The time had come for the board to choose between leaving the road in its present state or making improvements "to put the railway in a condition to compete success-fully . . . [for] all the traffic possible."[46]

Fish estimated the price tag for the second alternative at $7.8 million. This sum could not be paid from earnings; most of it would have to be financed from the sale of stock or bonds. The company, argued Fish, had reached a crossroads and must decide whether to meet the challenge of new competitive conditions by modernizing its physical plant on a grand scale. Following this course meant increasing its financial obligations, but Fish thought the investment vital to protect the road's future business.

The RRE committee agreed. After three days of meetings it endorsed a policy of "improving the physical condition of the property . . . with a view of making the Illinois Central one of the most thoroughly equipped and constructed railroads in the country." The committee wanted the work extended over a period of more than three years and asked Fish for more detailed information on what was needed.[47]

Harriman received both the Fish and RRE committee reports while still sick in bed, but he summoned the strength to pen a response. He ducked Fish's statement by pleading, "I have been too ill to go over the President's report as carefully as I would like," but he did not hesitate to dispute the committee's conclusion. "I . . . think it would be unwise at this time to pass *any* resolution adopting a policy for large expenditures of money," he said flatly. "Our organization is not prepared for it, we haven't sufficient information. It might lead to extravagance. Our whole force should be directed towards *making* and *saving* money." Lest anyone miss his point, Harriman added, "If I were present to-day I would vote against any resolution for the adoption of a *policy* as recommended by the Committee."[48]

Only five directors attended the meeting that Friday, but the others got copies of the letter. All were baffled by this abrupt change of front by one who had always supported the improvements policy. But Harriman had not changed position; his point was that the timing was wrong to declare such a policy. Rates were falling, the competitive wars were heating up again, and the bond market was glutted with offerings. The Illinois Central's new organization was just coming on line and not yet ready to handle so ambitious a program.

This episode evolved into a cornerstone of the Harriman legend, especially after Kennan credited Harriman with uncanny foresight in anticipating the depression that struck three years later. Rather than revealing Harriman as a prophet, the incident has an ironic twist that eluded Kennan entirely. Fish was proposing in 1890 the very policy for which Harriman would become famous eight years later while rebuilding the Union Pacific, yet on this occasion Harriman vigorously opposed it.[49]

It is a fallacy to assume, as Kennan and many later writers do, that because the Illinois Central pursued policies later used by Harriman, he was instrumental in developing them. In many cases he learned them from his experience with the Illinois Central, sometimes from opposing them only to find that he was wrong. Like most bright people, he was capable of profiting from his mistakes as well as his triumphs. He did not invent the notion that the proper policy for the newly emerging era of railroads was to put a road in the best physical condition to haul the largest possible traffic at the lowest possible cost. What he did was gauge with remarkable accuracy the point in time when that policy would pay handsome returns.

Harriman finally returned to work on February 11, still weak but eager to get back in harness. Eight days later the board debated the improvements question at length, then tabled the RRE committee report until Fish and Harriman could submit the report requested of them earlier. Instead of conferring on the matter, however, Fish sent Harriman to attend the meeting of a subsidiary company in New Orleans, where trouble from some minority stockholders was expected.[50]

When their signals got crossed on this business, Fish fell into a snit and delivered one of his scoldings. Harriman retorted that he didn't like the way Fish was handling him. "It will be a very long time before a definite report can be made on all the matters you have requested me to handle at New Orleans," he grumbled. And why should he handle it personally? "I think I can give material aid in bettering the Company's position by working through others, even better than if I attempted to do the actual work myself."[51]

It especially annoyed Harriman that Fish had sent him to New Orleans instead of conferring on the improvements report. Uneasy that Fish might be ignoring him, Harriman reminded him, "We have at last gotten our finances in almost perfect shape, & I hope now we will go very slow about expending any excessive amount of money." But when they finally got together to work on the report, Fish ignored this advice and urged improvements totaling nearly $2.5 million for 1890 alone. Harriman fought to curtail the list and signed the report only after itemizing one specific dissent over how much to spend on ballast.[52]

A confused board studied the report, then authorized Fish to determine the outlay for ballast. After some wrangling, however, it dumped the RRE committee's policy recommendation and approved only $612,500 of the requests plus the ballast. This setback proved the last straw in Fish's running battle with Harriman. The president was furious that both his policy statement and many of his specific requests had been rejected. He was even more irate with Harriman for opposing what Fish expected him to support. On any critical policy issue the top officers were supposed to march in unison.[53]

Fish was still struggling to regain the reins of leadership that had in subtle ways slipped from his hands since the trip to Europe. Things had gone much smoother when Harriman took care of financial matters and Fish ran the railroad. Once Harriman had become vice-president, however, he had made steady inroads into Fish's turf and showed no sign of slowing down. Harriman had changed in ways Fish did not understand. He was no longer as deferential and did not give ground as easily when their views disagreed. It never occurred to Fish to see in this behavior symptoms of growth. On the contrary, he concluded that illness and overwork were driving Harriman toward a nervous breakdown.[54]

Aware that rumors of discord within the Illinois Central were already circulating, Fish saw what must be done to rectify the mistake he had made. Harriman was simply not capable of working under the direction of others; he must be put back in his old sphere, where his strengths would shine and friction between the two friends would be minimized. The price of such a change, Fish realized gloomily, would be that his own move to Chicago could be delayed no longer.

The showdown took place a few days after the board meeting on improvements policy. It could not have come as a surprise to Harriman, but that did not make the confrontation any less tense or uncomfortable. Exactly what passed between them is not known, but Harriman accepted the outcome quietly even though it must have bitterly disappointed him. Afterward Fish breathed a sigh of relief and hurried to confide the news to his most powerful backer, William Boissevain of the Dutch banking house.

Since his return from Europe, he wrote Boissevain, "very decided differences of opinion" between Harriman and himself had reached a point where "an open rupture was imminent & it was deemed best to avoid this by his applying for temporary relief from duty on the score of his health, which has been precarious for several weeks past. It is now understood that he is, at a suitable time, to withdraw from the Vice Presidency." Everything had been done "very quietly and in a dignified and decorous manner and so to admit of his dropping out with credit, all of which can now be done with good feeling & respect on both sides." Their differences, Fish emphasized, were not personal but concerned "the general policy and administration of the Company." No one knew about the problem except the directors, and only a few of them realized how serious the breach had grown. Fish was pleased at how well a delicate situation had been resolved and (though he did not tell this to Boissevain) even more pleased at how favorable the resolution had come out for himself.[55]

Harriman's feelings were another matter. His first attempt at railroad management had ended in a humiliating retreat. The clash did not rupture his friendship with Fish even though it left the latter solidly in control of the Illinois Central. It does demolish the myth that Harriman's foresight saved the Illinois Central from possible ruin during the depression, for the simple reason that his views went unheeded. Fish pushed hard for the improvements program and got most of what he wanted. Between 1890 and 1892 the Illinois Central spent $7.3 million on improvements, and it kept spending right through the depression. During the next five years the company sank another $11.4 million into capital outlays.[56]

The Illinois Central sailed through the depression unscathed not because Harriman was a prophet but because he had returned to the role that best suited him: the deft handler of finance in difficult times. On that front Fish sorely needed his help, and their mutual desire to keep the company strong did much to heal old wounds and restore the partnership to good working order.

6 Sources of Opportunity

The seven-year period from 1889 to 1896 may be passed over briefly. Mr. Harriman played no prominent part in it. . . . In fact, by 1894 even his part in the Illinois Central had been largely forgotten, except by the closest students of events. He was doing what he had so well trained himself to do—lying back and waiting for his time. . . .

Through the long night that came upon the business world in the early nineties he rested, making himself strong for the day that was to follow.

—C. M. Keys, "Harriman: The Man in the Making"

The black hole of Harriman's career lies in the years between the crisis of 1890 and 1898, when he emerged as a factor in the newly reorganized Union Pacific Railroad. It is, like his boyhood, a time about which he never spoke in later years, as if he had willed it out of existence. His biographers and critics touch these years only in passing because they can find little in them to unlock the most vexing riddle of all: how did the financial wizard and failed vice-president of the Illinois Central Railroad emerge from obscurity to become the most dominant and spectacular figure in the transportation industry?

Part of the answer lies in a classic formula for success: Harriman was the right man in the right place at the right time. Such accidental forces exert a larger influence on destiny than self-made men or biographers care to admit. Harriman in 1897 was no butterfly sprung from the chrysalis of the Harriman of 1890. During these years he continued to grow and to spread his wings into new ventures, gleaning what he could from every activity, keeping an eye cocked for new opportunities and preparing himself to take advantage of them.

The hurt from his confrontation with Fish he buried deep within himself as he did all pain until it became invisible to others and possibly to himself as well. The most revealing key to Harriman's personality is his refusal to admit weakness or frailty. Whereas most people liked to advertise their suffering, Harriman boasted of his ability to ignore it. Nor was there during these years any long night of the soul in which he wrestled with the dark torments of his life and emerged triumphant over old demons. Harriman was not a reflective man. He was too busy living his life to spend much time philosophizing on it, and he still clung fervently to most of the values imbued in him as a child.

Above all, Harriman was a man in motion, searching for things to do. He gathered new challenges as others collected silver or stamps. No amount of work seemed to sate this urgent need. All his life the polar extremes of caution and boldness waged constant war within him. Until he was fifty, caution won most of the big battles and orchestrated the course of his career. This was not surprising, given the circumstances of his upbringing. Caution had been bred into him and took the form of an overpowering need to give his own family the financial security his parents had never had.

Once Harriman secured his financial and social position, however, the drive that had spurred him toward those goals began to prod him in new directions. The beauty of his involvement with the Illinois Central was that it fulfilled both needs at once. It brought his firm a bonanza of new business and himself an entry into the most dynamic industry in the country. In 1889 the war within him tipped steadily toward the side of boldness until he seemed on the verge of shedding his banker's skin for that of rail executive.

The confrontation with Fish terminated this movement with brutal suddenness and revealed for the first time a side of Harriman's nature that grew increasingly prominent. At bottom the episode involved a clash between Harriman's breeding and his instincts. Of necessity, breeding had prevailed and continued to rule him, though with mounting difficulty, through the depression years. But his instincts pushed ever harder against its restraints, especially one that had reared its head in the fight with Fish: a love of power. It had been crushed just as his eyes had been opened to its possibilities. He saw that he could not possess it as long as he remained subordinate to Fish, and on the Illinois Central he would always be subordinate to Fish.

For a time, then, the practical, conservative side of Harriman's nature reasserted its dominance. Although frustrated by the manner in which his quest for new horizons had been cut short, he recognized that the time was wrong to fight against his fate. The downturn in the economy required all his skills as a financier to keep the Illinois Central stable and his own fortune intact.

Hard times also offer opportunities of their own. Harriman poked at some new ventures but not in a way that might shove his destiny in new directions. He was content to wait until the depression eased and to extend his knowledge of railroad affairs through his work for the Illinois Central. The taste of power, fleeting as it had been, still lingered in Harriman's mouth, however, and he found ways to keep its irresistible flavor alive.

Although Harriman's work as vice-president ended in March 1890, he did not formally resign until June and the board did not accept until October, when it could put him back on the finance committee as chairman. A few papers used the occasion to revive the rumor that Harriman, in the *New York Tribune*'s words, "had been practically suspended from office before he resigned." Harriman resisted the urge to reply; he had plenty to do as the financial scene grew steadily gloomier.[1]

The shifting pattern of the railroad industry had become painfully clear. Rates continued to decline and costs to rise. Lower rates required a higher volume of traffic to keep earnings stable, which in turn meant more wear and tear on the physical plant and larger outlays to keep it up. Fish and Harriman agreed that Jeffery had not put the road in shape to meet these changing needs. Fish was anxious to upgrade the system as rapidly as possible because he had glimpsed a crucial aspect of the future that still escaped many of his peers. "Competition among Western Railways," he warned in 1890, "which has heretofore been almost entirely on the line of a reduction of rates, is coming to be . . . one of adequacy and frequency of service, and . . . in such a struggle success lies in furnishing the best service."[2]

Fish won the battle for his improvements program, but how to pay for it in a capital market saturated with offerings by other railroads starved for cash? He tried issuing $10 million in new stock, but shareholders took only $1.8 million and Harriman's firm was obliged to peddle the remainder in an unreceptive market. Within a few months the improvements outlays sent Harriman scurrying in search of short-term loans. He managed to sell some bonds and refund some old obligations at lower rates, but a cut in the dividend could no longer be avoided. The rate dropped to 6 percent in 1890 and then to 5 percent in 1891, raising howls of protest from stockholders.[3]

All of Harriman's efforts to get cheap money and keep the company's credit sound depended on the road's earnings; if they slumped badly, his work would be undone. To his dismay, the financial outlook grew even more bleak during 1892. Early in October, when Harriman got the preliminary earnings figures for July, his reaction belied the later image of him as imperturbable under fire. That evening he and Mary went to the theater with the Fishes. Henry barely noticed the show; his brain burned with the disaster of the July figures. He kept trying to discuss them with Fish but could never find a time. Frustrated and distraught, he dashed off a note late that night begging Fish to meet him in Tuxedo the next afternoon. "I am more than worried about I. C. earnings," he admitted, and his anxiety poured out in a torrent: "It would be fatal to have them published until some change is effected. We ought to do something at once all of us doing what we can. I'm ready to do my share in any way you can make me of service. . . . I made statement of earnings for June & July 1892. Compared with the previous year it is startling & I am badly scared but believe it can & will be made all right."[4]

The final figures turned out to be more respectable and were published. During the next year earnings revived, thanks in part to a surge in passenger business from the World's Fair in Chicago. While the income of other roads shriveled, the Illinois Central sailed through the depression of 1893–97 with solid earnings and its dividend record intact if reduced. For this achievement Harriman deserves much of the credit. "It was a well known circumstance among bankers," said Otto Kahn of Kuhn, Loeb & Co., who later fell under Harriman's spell, "that the Illinois Central's finances were managed with remarkable skill and foresight."[5]

But it did not come easily. Harriman worried his way through the gloomy fall of 1892, handling every monthly earnings report like a time bomb waiting to explode in his face. Through the depression years he managed to peddle bonds in the Illinois Central's prime market, London, and even refunded some at lower rates. Between sales he made ends meet with time and sterling loans arranged at low rates. When markets were tight in July 1896, a group of leading bankers tried borrowing money in Europe against a pledge of collateral, which amounted to buying gold. Harriman smiled indulgently at their effort. "As you know," he told Fish, "we have been quietly doing this very thing for some time back."[6]

While Illinois Central finances remained sound, other roads were going bankrupt and falling into the hands of what Harriman called "Banker Syndicates," some of which were reaping enormous profits out of reorganizations. Harriman had strong feelings on the issue. "I've been a 'Crank' on this subject as you know for years," he wrote Fish, "& it looks now as tho the whole country was so aroused by the abuses arising from this state of things that there must soon be a change."[7]

Two years later Harriman involved himself in a syndicate to reorganize the Alton that would expose him to the same scathing criticism, but there is no doubt his views were sincere. "Financing of RRs has been looked upon as the least important department," he noted, "when in reality it's all important. And the good properties have been brought into the 'Bankers' . . . hands by poor financing." This was more than a passing observation on railway management; it was also an expression of the pride he felt in the job he had done for the Illinois Central and a reminder for Fish to give credit where it was due.[8]

Harriman's performance is all the more remarkable in that the road not only pushed the improvements program through the depression years but also expanded aggressively at a time when weaker roads around it were failing and could be bought at cheap prices. Harriman had definite ideas on the best policy in such cases. "It pays better to invest in roads already built rather than build new ones," he argued to a dubious Fish, because someone else would buy the older line and do something with it. "Better buy our neighbors' than build new," Harriman repeated. "Better do that than have to support two properties with one business."[9]

This notion was hardly original, but few railroad men accepted it. Most preferred building their own line because it was cheaper, could be put where it was wanted, and incurred no onerous past obligations. For large projects Harriman's strategy had less value, but for branches in many regions it made good sense. Any rival line, however ramshackle, remained a smoking gun so long as it ran trains and could be scooped up by some stronger company and transformed into a competitor.

The expansion work occupied Harriman in months of tough negotiations. The Illinois Central had leased its Memphis branch, the Mississippi & Tennessee, for example, but wanted to merge it into the New Orleans road through a permanent lease. As president of the subsidiary road, Harriman spent four months dickering with minority holders before getting the new lease in place. More months went into negotiating the purchase of the financially troubled Louisville, New Orleans & Texas, an 807-mile system lying between Memphis and New Orleans, which was finally acquired in June 1892.[10]

These efforts paled before Harriman's struggle over another road, the Chesapeake, Ohio & Southwestern. Since its main line ran between Louisville and Memphis, the Illinois Central and the Louisville & Nashville (L&N) agreed to purchase the road jointly. The transaction was a complex one in which the L&N was to get the road and the Illinois Central would have only trackage rights between Memphis and Fulton, Kentucky, but nothing went smoothly. Fish got into a bitter dispute with August Belmont, chairman of the L&N board, over the terms of their agreement that was resolved only when the court barred the L&N from acquiring control of the Southwestern.[11]

The legal battle dragged on until 1896, when the Supreme Court upheld the decision against the L&N. In July the Illinois Central took control of the entire 456-mile Southwestern system, which then had to be foreclosed and reorganized because it was in receivership. Much of this work fell to Harriman, who tended it closely. Not until October 1897 did he have the Southwestern ready to lease to the parent road. He also spent considerable time arranging for the foreclosure and reorganization of two small branch lines of the Southwestern. The legal and financial snarls of minor projects were often as intricate of those on larger roads, but Harriman became masterful at the work.[12]

By 1896 Fish and Harriman had greatly enlarged the presence of the Illinois Central in its territory. The system embraced 4,390 miles of track, nearly four times what it had been in 1877. The transformation envisioned by Fish when he enlisted the help of Harriman and others had come to fruition. The Illinois Central was not only larger but stronger as well. Expansion did not weaken or undermine its health as it did so many other systems. The company did not merely grow; it devised new methods of organization and management to support the enlarged system.[13]

Above all, it financed growth in an orderly and creative manner. For this Harriman was chiefly responsible, and he was just as busy at the work in 1896 as he had been in past years. When the Illinois Central celebrated its golden anniversary in 1901, Fish declared, "The measure of success which has been achieved by the company in the last twenty years, with regard to finances is due to no man more than to the chairman of our finance committee, Mr. Harriman." By that time Harriman had moved beyond the Illinois Central to become a dominant force in the railroad world. The apprentice had become the master.[14]

The depression of 1893–97 affected Harriman's career in two contradictory ways. On one hand, the pinch forced him to keep a close eye on the family banking firm even though he was not fully responsible for it. His ties to Wall Street had shifted but not radically; if anything, they had been enhanced by his growing reputation as an astute railroad financier. On the other hand, hard times created opportunities for him to roam beyond his usual sphere of activity. During these years Harriman joined his friends in a variety of ventures, some in far-flung places and others in his own backyard. In these peripheral excursions he sought not only profit but new directions for his career to take.

One venture found him. In July 1893 the hapless Erie Railroad joined the procession of roads swept into bankruptcy by the depression. The task of reorganizing its complicated affairs fell to J. P. Morgan, whose New York office shared the burden with its London counterpart because so many Erie securities were held in England. One problem in particular divided the two offices. The Erie had a second consolidated mortgage with terms so peculiar that they had triggered many of the road's problems. Since many of these bonds were held abroad, the London office wished to protect their status in the new plan. But Morgan was convinced that a sound reorganization demanded large sacrifices from these holders, and this view shaped the final plan.[15]

When the plan went public in January 1894, the provisions for the second mortgage bonds became the flash point of protest. The outcry came not only from England but also from an array of American houses, including Kuhn, Loeb, August Belmont, and Harriman & Co. The dispute was over terms, not objectives. All sides agreed that the Erie's capital structure had to be simplified and scaled down. The dissidents argued that Morgan had not gone far enough in this direction and that his plan imposed an unfair burden on one class of holders. Although his own holdings in the Erie were small, Harriman took up the fight with his usual relish. The Erie was his friendly neighborhood railroad; Arden had its own depot at which Erie trains stopped on request.

Morgan brushed the objections aside and kept his original plan intact. His stance divided the protesters. The more cautious among them, such as Kuhn, Loeb, decided not to fight the plan; others formed a protective committee to oppose it. Harriman agreed to head the committee. When the Erie plan gained enough support to go into effect, he promptly filed suit to block it. There is a famous story about Harriman going to Morgan's office and laying out his objections to the plan. When Morgan's partners asked whom he represented, Harriman snapped, "Myself!"[16]

The tale is apocryphal but not out of character. The court denied Harriman's request for an injunction, and the Morgan plan went into effect. Within months, however, the Erie's earnings proved so dismal that Morgan's firm was forced to scrap the original plan and impose a new one along the lines demanded by the Harriman committee. The revised version, put into effect in November 1895, gave Harriman the satisfaction of having lost the battle but won the war. It would not be the last time he and Morgan tangled over the Erie.[17]

Unfortunately, the clash also added another layer of friction between Harriman and Morgan. The outcome, noted Kennan, vindicated Harriman's foresight and gave "a number of leading bankers a higher opinion of his judgment and courage." To Morgan and his partners, however, the episode merely demonstrated anew that, as his son-in-law observed, "Harriman always wanted to get terms which were a little better than other people's."[18]

Who was right? Which one was the real Harriman: the public-spirited banker of courage or the sharpster trying to beat better terms out of Morgan for his own holdings through the usual tactic of harassment? The man of vision or the terrier nipping at Jupiter's heels? The only answer even close to correct was all of the above.

During these years Harriman did not confine his business ventures to railroads. His outside investments fell into three broad categories: those related to the Illinois Central Railroad; unrelated opportunities that caught his attention, and projects in which his relatives had an interest.

It made good sense for men like Fish and Harriman to invest in businesses along the railroad's line. Apart from any profits they might glean, the object was to develop new sources of traffic. After absorbing one branch road, for example, the Illinois Central subsidized an experiment to grow sugar beets in its territory. Fish and Harriman took stock in a New Orleans company called Grammercy Sugar, which hoped to use the raw sugar planted in the Delta region. They also invested in a textile firm that used cotton from the Illinois Central region. Neither enterprise made them rich.[19]

In the course of business Harriman often got invited to put money into projects only marginally related to the railroad. Since the Illinois Central received a large traffic from the Gulf, many of these solicitations came from Latin America. They ranged from a bank in Honduras to some banana plantations that prompted Fish to ask Harriman wryly, "Do you want to buy a 'pig in a poke'?" Sometimes Fish bit, but Harriman usually kept his money at home.[20]

Occasionally Harriman took up a project for family or personal reasons. When one of his brothers got in over his head with a streetcar line in St. Joseph,

Missouri, Henry bought control of the company and sorted out its affairs. He went to St. Joseph, looked over the property, and ordered improvements made. Once this was done, Harriman sold the company. Later he claimed that he had never made a cent while he owned it.[21]

Another bailout involved Mary's brother William, who had gone partners with his cousin in the Furnaceville Iron Company, located in that small town between Rochester and Sodus Point. Despite backing from his father and uncle, the venture failed. Harriman ended up as president of the company by 1889, but it did little business after the depression struck. In 1895, however, the state legislature authorized an expenditure of $9 million to enlarge the Erie Canal. Harriman decided to submit bids for all the work between Rochester and Lockport and came away with five contracts covering thirty-four miles of canal. By December 1897 his manager had assembled the machines, tools, and men needed for the project. Then, five months later, the state abruptly ordered work to cease. The original appropriation had been too small, there had been cost overruns, and an investigation hinted at scandal among some contractors.[22]

Litigation over the unfinished work dragged on for years. Through this long ordeal Harriman stood firm even though the Furnaceville Iron Company meant little to him. By 1898 he was preoccupied with other matters, yet he pressed the suits until the state paid Furnaceville more than $100,000 for its claims. In part, his stubbornness stemmed from loyalty; as with most of his activities, he had sold Fish (and probably other friends) some stock in the iron company.[23]

The largest and most satisfying project Harriman undertook during these years was literally in his own backyard. He expanded the original three-room cottage at Arden into a large, rambling, comfortable house, then set about transforming the estate itself into what amounted to his private duchy. Arden became a striking example of Harriman's ability to mix business with pleasure.

The cottage had to be enlarged because the Harrimans were spending more time there, and the family was growing. Three new children helped ease the still painful loss of little Harry. A third daughter, Carol, arrived in December 1889, followed in November 1891 by the son Harriman had craved so desperately since Harry's death. He received the name William Averell. Four years later, on Christmas Eve, Mary delighted Henry with a special present in the form of another son. He was named Edward Roland Noel Harriman, honoring his father, grandfather (Roland was the closest thing to Orlando that Henry could abide), and the season.[24]

The growth of his family and the enlargement of the house at Arden revealed Harriman's growing determination to sink deep roots in Orange County. Three of its proudest traditions were dairying, mining, and horse breeding; after 1890 Harriman plunged eagerly into all three activities. Arden may have been a retreat, but like all of Harriman's activities, it quickly became an active rather than a passive pleasure. Milk and dairy products had been the staple of Orange County farmers throughout the nineteenth century. A new frontier opened in 1842, when the Erie Railroad carried the first consignment of milk to reach New York City by train. Five years later the first regular milk train from Orange County made its maiden run.[25]

Harriman could not resist getting into the business because it used Arden's resources so nicely. He created a new company called Arden Farms, which leased everything it used from Arden. The estate grew hay and fodder for feed, and the surrounding villages served as market along with Tuxedo Park. Harriman also tried to distribute his milk to the poorer districts of New York around the Boys' Club. He had the milk packed in sanitized cartons and offered it for a penny a quart less than other milk to get it to children. But his tactics backfired: the tenement people thought something must be wrong with the cheaper milk and refused to buy it.[26]

Horse breeding suited both Harriman and Arden even better than dairying. The lay of the land in Orange County was ideal for breeding. The quality of grasses was superb, especially for the light harness horse or trotter in which Orange County had long excelled. At Arden Harriman's passion for sports moved easily into horse breeding and racing. His approach showed the same single-minded purpose he brought to business. Surveying the venerable stables that dotted Orange County, he concluded that what he needed most was a prize champion and stud. Without hesitation Harriman plunked down $41,000 for a horse named Stamboul, which more than repaid him as a winner on the turf, in the show ring, and as a stud. Despite the horse's value, Harriman was not prissy about using him. One winter he wired Arden's stablemaster from New York, "Send Stamboul." When the horse arrived, Harriman hitched him to a sleigh to race on Harlem River Drive.[27]

Once in the fall of 1895 he was eager to see an important race at Goshen but missed the Erie train that stopped there. The only other train was the Chicago express, which made local stops only to pick up passengers. Harriman asked an Erie official to have the express drop him at Goshen as a courtesy; the official refused curtly. Undaunted, Harriman wired a friend in Goshen to buy a ticket for Chicago and got on the train himself in New York. When the train stopped to pick up his friend, Harriman jumped off and got to the race in time. Here again he exhibited the trait that had so offended Morgan. Harriman did whatever he had to do to get what he wanted, and he did not care what anybody else thought of it. If bruised feelings or smoldering resentments were left in his wake, he took little notice. As he was reputed to have told Morgan, he represented himself. Everybody else could do the same, and may the best man win.[28]

In mining, Harriman's activity extended beyond the little Furnaceville company. Arden had, after all, begun life as a mining and iron-making enterprise.

Harriman made no effort to revive the Parrott ironworks, but he did acquire a mine at Sterling, just west of Arden, along with twenty thousand acres of forest that remained in the family until the 1950s. The lure of mining may have had a more profound influence on his career than anyone has realized. His first interest in the West concerned mines rather than railroads, notably some copper properties in Idaho and a gold mine in South Dakota.[29]

Arden contained a small village filled with people who had once worked the mines or were employed on the property. To these people Harriman became the patriarch as the estate and dairy replaced the mine. Gradually Squire Harriman emerged as the father figure that Orlando had never quite been, overseeing everything and taking care of everyone. He provided the jobs and backed the local store. To outside eyes he craved money and power, but at Arden he aspired to be the rock on which the residents could anchor their lives.[30]

Harriman enlarged and improved not only his house but the estate itself. He gobbled up adjacent land until the original holding nearly quadrupled and was twice the size of Manhattan Island. "He collects mountains," groused one unimpressed neighbor, "as other men collect china." To provide power for the village, Harriman installed a small water-driven power plant. When the demand for electricity outstripped its capacity, he built a larger, coal-driven plant in the nearby village of Turners to serve both communities and the Sterling mine.[31]

A large estate required good roads. Harriman developed a passion for building and improving them, first at Arden and then for the county. He was elected road supervisor for Orange County and quickly overspent his budget. On his own Harriman built a new road along the west bank of the Ramapo River. To learn firsthand how things were done, he willingly paid his tuition. When bids were requested for a few miles of macadamized road near Arden, Harriman offered to do the work for $25,000 a mile even though the going rate was around $100,000 a mile.[32]

Like any proper manor, Arden had its own Episcopal church. St. John's had been built in 1863 with backing from the Parrotts and others. The Harrimans were adamant that the church serve as the center of village life even though the local men showed little interest in religion. Determined to change their habits, Harriman brought in a new minister to preside over his growing flock. The amiable J. H. McGuinness served his new master well and got vigorous support for his good works.[33]

Shortly after McGuinness's arrival in September 1895, Harriman scolded the men from the estate for their religious sloth. "The lack of interest on your part," he wrote, "is discouraging to those who provide the means whereby you can have the important privilege of attending church services." The men got the message quickly. When attendance improved the next Sunday, Harriman invited the men to create a church organization for the winter months and offered to pay for three-fourths of the entire expense himself.[34]

The Harrimans were usually in residence all summer and most weekends, and Henry wanted the men to commit themselves to sustaining the church in his absence. He made no bones about what he expected from them: "The religious work cannot be carried on permanently, without active and continued help by the men. Women and children must not be left to do it all. Boys attend Sunday School and Church and are no doubt benefitted thereby. But by the example of the men they only expect to do so while boys. Under the influence of your indifference they get to believe that, when they grow up it is unmanly to attend church and show any interest in religion. You should change this. Make it a pleasure as well as benefit and do the thing in a whole-souled way."[35]

The squire practiced what he preached. He and his family were in church every Sunday, filling their reserved pew up front, chanting the responses and singing the hymns in lusty voices. Once Harriman had to miss church because his daughter Cornelia suffered an attack of appendicitis the night before and required an immediate operation. In the midst of his anxious vigil Harriman dashed off a note to McGuinness explaining their absence from church and asking that a prayer be said "for the sick child & us all."[36]

After church Harriman usually took the parson home with him to have lunch and discuss the parish's mission work, in which the whole family took a keen interest. Already he and Mary were training the older girls in good works, giving them cases of their own and saying, "That's yours to attend to. Investigate the case, find out if it's deserving, give what you think is right." Henry believed in philanthropy but not in extravagance, which he could no more abide at home than at the office. Sometimes he impressed on the children the harsh lessons of his own childhood. "Money comes hard," he liked to tell them. "It should go wisely."[37]

There was not a single false note in Harriman's attitude toward religion. Both he and Mary had been reared in families steeped in the traditions of worship and service. As a minister's son, Henry could hardly have escaped it, but he never rebelled against it. He prodded (some would say coerced) the men of Arden into religious worship out of a stern sense of duty as well as a desire to impose order on his manor. Some resented Harriman's way of doing things, but no one doubted the sincerity of his convictions.

Unlike his business persona, the squire was not an aloof figure at Arden. Social services were delivered with a personal touch, and Harriman took immense pleasure in the village characters—a blacksmith from Chester, a black preacher, and the old-timers living out their last years as pensioners on the estate. Harriman kept them on the payroll doing something just to preserve their self-respect. One day he stopped to give a lift home to one named Stevens, who was pushing ninety years old.

"Do you drink?" he asked Stevens as they rode along.

"Yes sir, but not to interfere with my work," said Stevens without hesitation.

"Well," said Harriman, smiling, "if ever you're sick and need a little bracer, let me know."

"I'm sick now, sir," answered Stevens at once.[38]

Harriman loved to tell this story along with one about a sixteen-year-old boy named Lukey, whose spunk he admired. Once he had noticed Lukey smoking and asked him sharply, "Do you think it's good for you?"

Lukey looked him in the eye, which pleased Harriman, and asked coolly, "Why do you sell tobacco in your store?"[39]

On another occasion Harriman was trying to hurry an old German to a cab. When the old man dawdled, Harriman snatched up his bag impatiently and carried it on ahead. "It's some satisfaction," grinned the pensioner later, "to have had a millionaire carry your bag for you."[40]

These vignettes do not suggest that Harriman spent his days mingling with the masses, but neither did he keep himself remote from them. "If more wealthy men were democratic," he liked to say, "the public wouldn't be so down on them." The difference was that Harriman liked to impress people with what he did rather than with who or what he was. He never worried that someone might take advantage of him or make him look foolish. No one doubted who was lord of the manor, but few lords enjoyed the company of their flock with such relish.[41]

He demanded much of his workers and could be hard on them when they did not perform. Like others of his class, Harriman had trouble keeping good servants. Once in 1888 the butler went to town and came back to Arden "drunk & 'sassy,' " in Harriman's words. "I bounced him & he had to walk to Southfield," he told Fish, who was planning to visit Arden with his wife later that week. While Henry assured Fish that everything would be ready for them, Mary hurried to the city in search of fresh recruits.[42]

The squire took care of his flock in many ways, including medical needs. When a scrubwoman fell ill, Harriman asked McGuinness to summon a nearby doctor whose practice was limited to more fashionable people. The doctor put off coming for a mere menial despite five calls from McGuinness. When Harriman heard this, he dialed the doctor himself and said in steely tones, "Go to Mrs. M— and go at once!" It was two o'clock on an icy winter morning, but the doctor hurried to Arden without delay.[43]

Christmas at Arden always delighted the Harrimans, who saw to it that every person on the estate received a present selected by some member of the family. Mary usually did the honors with Henry at her side. One year it was discovered that a small boy with a drunken father had been overlooked by mistake. A chagrined Harriman barged through the house, found a good sled, and tramped four miles through the woods in the stinging cold to deliver it personally. It was not nobility or a flair for the grand gesture that impelled him so much as his fierce determination to do things right and to brook no obstacle in the doing of them.[44]

At Arden Harriman counseled and lectured his flock, played baseball and hockey with them, rode and hiked about with them, and adjudicated their disputes. Whatever game he played, the competition was savage and waged according to one inviolable Harriman commandment: the rules must be obeyed at all times. He provided uniforms for the village baseball team and in 1900 built a social hall above the school for basketball, parties, and plays, which he invariably attended as he did those of the Boys' Club. When the Driving Association planned to fence its track at Goshen, Harriman objected. "What if some do steal in and see the races for nothing?" he argued. "They couldn't pay their way in—so we don't lose, and, anyway, they need the fun."[45]

Unlike many busy people, he knew how to play and how to release himself entirely to the pleasure of simple things. In middle age no less than in youth, nothing gave him more pleasure than nature. On that score, Arden was for him truly paradise. He loved not only to ride or drive his horses but even more to walk and thought nothing of tramping miles through the forest. Little Echo Lake in front of the house was too shallow and muddy for swimming, but three miles into the woods lay Forest Lake, a spring-fed beauty with waters ninety feet deep. Harriman built a crude stable to house the horses and Adirondack-type tents with wood floors.[46]

There Harriman would ride with some of the family or friends, leave the horses, row to one of the small islands in the lake, and set up camp to fish or swim or loaf beneath the trees as he had at Paul Smith's. He had a passion for trees and, believing that each one had its own personality, would not let one be chopped down without a forester's advice. At the edge of Echo Lake stood a special tree where he sat motionless for hours, staring at the distant forest while his mind churned with plans and prospects.[47]

At Arden Harriman came into his own during the depression years. He reveled with his family and friends in the clean, elemental life of the outdoors, and he grew comfortably into the role of squire. He learned to rule a duchy before he ever ruled a business kingdom, and the experience both revealed and deepened his passion to manage. Years later, having decided to build a great new house at Arden, he told a friend, "You are a minister's son, and I'm a minister's son. Minister's sons never have homes. I'm going to have a home here."[48]

He had long since made Arden a home and a sanctuary from the cares and hostility of the outside world. The squire loved his manor and his flock and believed they loved him. "Go to Arden," he told a reporter defiantly years later, after he had become a national target. "Don't tell me when you go; go by yourself and ask questions of the people there. There isn't a man or woman in Arden that wouldn't go to hell and back for me, if I asked them." Harriman might be at war with the world, but at home he was always at peace.[49]

Part II. Kingdom

1898-1900

7 Going West

The name of Mr. Harriman first appeared in an official notice in January, 1898. . . .
No one but Mr. Schiff knew exactly what sort of man Mr. Harriman was. He had
worked quietly with the syndicate, yet his was the master mind that had conceived
and guided its gigantic project. . . . At this juncture Mr. Harriman stepped from the
ranks. One day he was simply one of the directors of the Union Pacific; the next he
was chairman of the executive committee.

—C. M. Keys, "A 'Corner' in Pacific Railroads"

Most of what has been written about Harriman bears a tone of inevitability, as if he was destined to have a spectacular career. This same tone carries over to his use of the Union Pacific as the vehicle for his leap to greatness, but there was nothing inevitable in either case. Nobody seems to have asked the obvious question of what first attracted Harriman's attention to the Union Pacific. Nor has anybody raised an even more basic question: what drew Harriman's attention to the West?

Given Harriman's later career, it is easy to forget that he had no experience with the West before 1896. He had always been an easterner to the core, finding his wilderness pleasure not in the West as Theodore Roosevelt did but in the forests of upstate New York. There is no record that he had even ventured beyond the Missouri River except in 1890, when he escorted his sister to Fort Worth. The move to the Union Pacific was a jump not only into a new company but a new arena. While Americans have always headed west to seek fame and fortune, something more personal drove Harriman. His father, the hapless Orlando, had gone west in search of a fresh start and come home an abject failure. Here were footsteps less to be followed than covered over, scars that still needed healing. Harriman had a score to settle with the West that no one else even suspected.

Although the evidence is sketchy, mines seem to be what first drew his attention to the West. In 1895 he looked into some copper mines in Idaho; four years later he turned up as owner of the Golden Reward mine in Deadwood, South Dakota. Exactly when his involvement began is not known, but in April 1896 Harriman took his family on what was apparently their first trip west. Their destination was Deadwood, hardly a place one would visit without some compelling reason.[1]

These forays served to whet Harriman's curiosity about the West and its possibilities. There was also a connection to the Union Pacific that has gone unnoticed. After the Illinois Central secured control of its Iowa lines, it was eager to reenter the transcontinental business it had abandoned years earlier. The logical partner for this arrangement was the Union Pacific. Unfortunately, the Illinois Central reached Sioux City while the Union Pacific terminated at Omaha, just across the river from Council Bluffs, where the four Iowa or Granger roads met.[2]*

In November 1888 E. T. Jeffery explored the idea of a connection between the systems, but the Union Pacific was too wracked by inner turmoil and financial woes to build the branch. Five years later the Union Pacific toppled into a receivership that threatened to dismember the entire system. One of its five receivers, John W. Doane of Chicago, also sat on the Illinois Central board. "It seems a little strange to me," he wrote Fish in January 1894 while in Omaha on an inspection trip, "that the Illinois Central should run so close to the largest city in this section of the country without getting a slice of the large business that centers here, and . . . it might be to the interest of the Illinois Central to compete for its portion of this business."[3]

Fish did not respond because he was preoccupied with other problems. As the Union Pacific reorganization dragged on, however, Fish found himself drawn into the fray, spurred by a renewed interest in the proposed connecting branch. Harriman too got involved in its intrigues, little suspecting that he had come to the Rubicon of his career.

To eyes less keen than Harriman's, the Union Pacific offered nothing but trouble. The reorganization of any railroad is a complicated affair, but none rivaled the Union Pacific in complexity or acrimony. It was a unique road in American history, part of the first transcontinental line, and had been created under a federal charter. Of all the roads swept into receivership during the depression, it was the only one in which Congress had a direct voice in its destiny. A quarter-century of bitter controversy had made it a political football. To make matters worse, its lines ran through the plains states, where sentiment ran deep against railroads.[4]

The government held what amounted to a second mortgage on the Union Pacific. As a creditor with more than the usual clout, it could cancel the debt, extend it, refund it at a lower rate of interest, or demand cash payment and get out altogether. While the last alternative was the most desirable, it meant raising

*The four Iowa lines were the Chicago, Burlington & Quincy, the Chicago & Northwestern, the Chicago, Milwaukee & St. Paul, and the Chicago, Rock Island & Pacific.

$52 million in a depressed market. Instead a campaign was mounted to pry a refunding bill from Congress even though several earlier efforts had failed.

Given the obstacles strewn before them, few bankers were willing to touch the Union Pacific. J. P. Morgan, already involved in several other reorganizations, shunned it as a lost cause. The first reorganization committee fumbled more than a year away trying to get a refunding bill from Congress before disbanding in March 1895. Meanwhile, a procession of foreclosure suits lopped off one branch line after another into the hands of separate receivers. A system that had totaled 7,691 miles in October 1893 shriveled to only 4,537 miles by the winter of 1895. The stock dipped below 8, the lowest it had fallen since the dark days of 1873.[5]

For months the reorganization drifted aimlessly while interested parties tried to cobble together a new approach. The foreclosures that pulled the Union Pacific system apart at least simplified the problem: a new plan did not have to cope with all the branch-line holders but could deal only with the main line and Kansas division. Nor did it have to wait for a refunding bill from Congress; instead it could proceed toward a foreclosure sale and set aside enough securities to buy out the government's interest.[6]

One thorny question remained: who would undertake the reorganization? Morgan remained cold to the project, and few other banking houses had the resources or prestige to tackle so large a project. The lone exception was Kuhn, Loeb & Company, which had grown impressively during the past decade under its senior partner, Jacob H. Schiff. The small but lithe Schiff dwelled in Morgan's portly shadow in every sense and preferred it that way. A quiet man of formal manner and elaborate courtesy, Schiff looked every inch the aristocrat. He stood ramrod straight and masked his handsome features with a neatly trimmed white goatee that complemented his thinning white hair. His large blue eyes surveyed the world with a knowing and sardonic shrewdness. An impassive demeanor helped conceal the fact that he was hard of hearing.[7]

One contemporary described Schiff as "a patient, skillful man, a suave diplomat with a complex Oriental nature." He was also a deeply religious man, what his daughter called "a whole-hearted Jew," who said his prayers every morning, partly in Hebrew and partly in German, and afterward took from his wallet a frayed envelope with fading photographs of his parents to kiss reverently. After meals he always said a grace of his own composition, and he practiced the ancient custom of blessing his children on Friday nights.[8]

Schiff's roots lay in Frankfort-on-Main, where the family had resided for more than two centuries before Jacob's birth in 1847. His merchant father gave the boy an education in more than commerce; Jacob Schiff was a man of culture in the old-fashioned sense. He first came to America in 1865 but went back to Germany when his father died. Late in 1874 he returned to New York at the

Cautious visionary: Jacob Schiff of Kuhn, Loeb, the banker who became one of Harriman's closest friends and financial supporters. (Baker Library, Harvard Business School)

invitation of Abraham Kuhn to join the firm of Kuhn, Loeb. He sealed this connection in May 1875 by marrying the daughter of Solomon Loeb.[9]

Although his English was excellent, Schiff filtered it through a heavy German accent and what his daughter described as "a certain thickness of speech." First names were not in his vocabulary. Dapper in appearance, he always adorned his buttonhole with a fresh flower. Like many of his class, Schiff was a creature of habit, punctual to a fault and fastidious in his tastes. He carried in his vest pocket a small silver notebook with two ivory tablets in which he recorded everything he had to do. As each task was completed, Schiff crossed it off, and at bedtime he carefully checked to see whether everything had been done before wiping the tablets clean for the next day's work.[10]

Schiff loved the solitary pleasures of reading and of nature. A firm believer in exercise, he regularly walked the first three miles to work from his home at 74th Street and Fifth Avenue before surrendering to his driver or climbing aboard the El. His other outlet for exercise was the bicycle, which he rode with more zeal than style. While he shared Harriman's love for children as well as nature, he did not engage them in play with the same abandon.[11]

For all his elegance, Schiff was a prisoner of small economies. Instead of notepads he relied on whatever scraps of paper he could find. As a director of Western Union he had a telegraph frank, which prompted him to use telegrams instead of the telephone even when time was of the essence. At home he kept a pad near the telephone and insisted that everyone list their calls. But there was nothing oppressive about these quirks; Schiff leavened them with a sense of humor that lightened his formality.

Kuhn, Loeb was a close family firm that prided itself on having as few part-ners as possible. When Solomon Loeb retired in 1885, Schiff became its un-disputed head at the tender age of thirty-eight. Although a decade younger than Morgan, he had by 1895 amassed impressive credentials in railroad finance. His list of clients included the Chicago & Northwestern, the Louisville & Nashville, and the Missouri Pacific, now dominated by the late Jay Gould's son George. In recent years Schiff had also done a little business with the Illinois Central, which introduced him to Fish and Harriman.[12]

It was George Gould who sent his chief counsel, Winslow S. Pierce, to sound Schiff on reorganizing the Union Pacific, in which Gould had large holdings. The cautious Schiff balked at touching the project until Morgan assured him that he wanted nothing to do with it. So pessimistic was Morgan over the Union Pacific's prospects that he refused even to join the underwriting syndicate. De-spite Morgan's gloomy sentiments, Schiff decided to take the chance. The risks were great, but so was the promise of profit if Kuhn, Loeb could pull off the reorganization. Homilies were a disease among bankers to which Schiff was not immune. To make the reorganization a success, he chirped, the firm would "have to paint the whole thing over fresh."[13]

Schiff put together a new committee, which in October 1895 unveiled a streamlined reorganization plan. It proposed a capital structure for the Union Pacific consisting of $100 million in 4 percent bonds, $75 million in preferred stock, and $61 million in common stock. Of these new issues $35.8 million in bonds, $20.8 million in preferred, and a small amount of common were set aside for settlement of the government debt. By late January 1896 the committee had received enough old securities to declare the plan operative. A new refunding bill was introduced in March amid predictions that passage had a better chance than ever before.[14]

This optimism did not reckon with the vagaries of an election year. The campaign of 1896 turned out to be a watershed in American politics. In the hotly contested fight between William McKinley and William Jennings Bryan the issue of government ownership of railroads took a back seat to that of free silver, but in the plains states, where Populism was strong, it aroused fierce passions. McKinley's victory ended months of uncertainty, and when Grover Cleveland's final message to Congress emphasized the need to settle the Pacific railroad issue, the committee redoubled its efforts to get a refunding bill and avoid the need for a foreclosure sale.

Just when prospects looked bright, however, mysterious obstacles began to crop up. There were problems with the press, with minority holders, and in Washington—none of them large but all of them harboring ripples of antagonism that were hard to pinpoint but which succeeded in slowing the momentum toward a settlement with the government. Was someone strewing obstacles in the committee's path? Schiff heard from a friend that Morgan was doing it out of jealousy over the plan's progress, but Morgan emphatically denied any interest in the reorganization. A relieved Schiff then confided that some "powerful but subtle influence" was blocking progress on the plan. Did Morgan know who was behind it? Morgan shook his head. He was not the problem and did not know who was, but he agreed to see what he could find out. Some weeks later he sent for Schiff and told him that the source of opposition had been discovered. "It's that little fellow Harriman," he said scornfully, "and you want to watch him carefully."[15]

Schiff was no stranger to Harriman. They had become acquainted in 1884, after Harriman joined the Illinois Central board. A decade later they got to know each other better when Kuhn, Loeb entered into lengthy negotiations to handle some bonds for the Illinois Central. During the winter of 1896–97, when Schiff was encountering obstacles to the reorganization, they met several times to discuss the proposed Illinois Central connection to the Union Pacific. In this affair Harriman was acting on behalf of the Illinois Central. By December 1896

Fish had revived interest in the connector and for that reason injected himself into the reorganization scuffle. This raises several questions. Did the idea of tying the connector to the reorganization come from Fish or from Harriman? What inspired Harriman to make the leap from the connector to the Union Pacific itself? Was he playing a double role in these intrigues or did his interest in Union Pacific simply evolve out of them?[16]

To complicate matters, Harriman was ill much of that winter with his usual siege of colds and flu. Being laid up didn't stop him from doing business. Fish had already discovered the habit for which Harriman soon became notorious. "You seem to do more work by telephone than by personal interview," he acknowledged to Harriman in January. And while illness kept Harriman from getting around as much as usual, it also gave him more time to scan the papers and financial journals, which had some very interesting things to say about the Union Pacific that winter.[17]

One of the hoariest myths about the Union Pacific is that in 1896 it was a junk pile of a railroad with a bleak future. This tale contained just enough truth to deceive contemporary and later observers alike, and it gained impetus from Harriman's own meteoric rise after 1898. Shrewder minds on Wall Street knew better, however, and took a different slant on the road's prospects. No one was more bullish than the *Wall Street Journal*, which hammered steadily at one theme: Union Pacific was the most undervalued stock on the street because the road had been kept in good shape by its receivers and would do an immense business once the depression lifted and the reorganization was completed.[18]

Harriman always had his ear to the street, and amid the usual mixed signals he could not have missed this insistent argument that the Union Pacific was stronger than most people suspected and a great speculative buy. Signs of better times were already budding before the election, and to conservatives like Harriman the presence of William McKinley in the White House ensured that prosperity would soon flower. Once this happened, the long moribund West had the potential to deliver a massive flow of goods to the railroads.

Fish and Harriman understood this potential clearly. Why else would their interest in the connector have revived at just this time if not to prepare for a cornucopia of traffic to come? When the lame-duck Congress convened in December 1896, Fish sent an agent to Washington to lobby for a plan he favored as an alternative to the refunding bill desired by the reorganization committee. In effect, he wanted the government to give all the Iowa roads—including the Illinois Central—equal access to the Union Pacific as a connector.[19]

The plan gained the support of several congressmen and was surely the "obstacle" in Washington mentioned by Schiff. During the talks over the connector, Fish took care to brief Harriman on developments in Washington while withholding the same information from Schiff and from Marvin Hughitt of the

Northwestern, which had long been the Union Pacific's closest ally among the Iowa roads. Meanwhile, Harriman drew from Schiff a pledge that the Illinois Central would have access to the Union Pacific equal to that of the Northwestern. When Schiff suggested that the Illinois Central put its engineers to work surveying the new connector, Fish did so at once.[20]

"I have marked this letter confidential," said Harriman at the end of one report to Fish, "as I have agreed that no one, except yourself, should know of my talks with Mr. Schiff." But how much ground did these talks cover, and how much of that ground did Harriman actually relay to Fish? Sometime during these same weeks Schiff, following up the lead given him by Morgan, asked Harriman whether he was the unknown force opposing the reorganization committee's efforts.

"I am the man," Harriman retorted at once.

"Why are you doing it?" Schiff asked.

The answer came in a flash. "I want to reorganize the Union Pacific myself."

Schiff permitted himself a small smile. "But how are you going to do it? We have all the bonds in, and what means have you to reorganize this company?"

"The Illinois Central Railroad ought to have that property," snapped Harriman. "In the Illinois Central we have the best credit in the world. I am going to issue $100,000,000 of 3% bonds at close to par and with the proceeds reorganize the Union Pacific. At the best you can not get money at less than 4½%. I am stronger than you are."

Schiff blinked in astonishment. It was, he said later, a "brutal conversation," from which his genteel style recoiled. "Well, you will have a good time doing it, Mr. Harriman," he replied blandly, "but in the meantime, what is your price?"

"There is no price to it. I am interested in the Union Pacific Railway and I am determined to take charge of the reorganization."

Not blackmail? This was a new wrinkle to Schiff. "Are there no terms on which we can work together?" he persisted.

"If you will make me chairman of the executive committee of the reorganized company," Harriman said at once, "I will join forces with you."

Schiff shook his head. "That is out of the question. Mr. Pierce is to be chairman of the new company. I think he deserves it."

"Very well, Mr. Schiff, go ahead and see what you can do. Good day."[21]

It seems probable that this exchange occurred during their discussions over the connector. Did Harriman assert in this context that the Illinois Central should control the reorganization? Nothing in the surviving letters between Fish and Harriman mentions any such idea. If Schiff's version of events is accurate, it raises the intriguing possibility that Harriman launched this bold proposal on his own.[22]

Fish did not get his bill, but he helped prevent Schiff from getting one. On

January 11, 1897, the House decisively rejected the refunding bill after months of debate, forcing President Grover Cleveland to insist on a cash sale. Schiff had no choice but to cut a deal with the government on a foreclosure plan by which the committee guaranteed a bid of $45.8 million for the government lien. A foreclosure sale would rid the Union Pacific of federal influence; however, it also required Schiff to form a second syndicate to raise the cash needed for the bid. Nor could he count on the incoming administration to honor the deal.[23]

To help carry the financial load, Schiff recruited a powerful ally, James Stillman of the National City Bank. Despite Stillman's presence, however, the new syndicate met with little enthusiasm at home or abroad. A fellow banker watched Schiff struggle and was convinced he would "have to carry a big chunk himself, and use all his friends." Late in February the chunk got bigger when the new attorney general, Joseph McKenna, dismissed the proposed bid as too low, obliging the committee to raise the ante to $50 million.[24]

Schiff had also been rattled by his meetings with Harriman. The little man's boundless confidence and brash, staccato style unsettled him, the more so because Harriman seemed to be holding a weak hand. Then, shortly after the deal with the government was announced, rumors swirled that another bidder would offer $10 million more than the committee for the Union Pacific. Speculation ran rampant over the identity of the mystery challenger, but no one mentioned the name that tossed uneasily in Schiff's mind.[25]

In May a new obstacle appeared in the form of a Sioux City company representing more than twenty creditors who threatened to intervene in the foreclosure. Schiff probably did not know that Fish and Harriman were in league with the company's managers, but he was in no mood to leave any flank exposed. Without knowing exactly what role Harriman had played in the difficulties plaguing the reorganization, Schiff called on him and explained why Winslow Pierce should be made chairman of the executive committee. As Gould's counsel, Pierce represented large interests, some of them cool if not hostile to Harriman. Moreover, Pierce had brought the reorganization to Kuhn, Loeb in the first place.[26]

But there was another possibility. "If you will join with me," Schiff said carefully, "I will put you on the executive committee as soon as the company is reorganized. Very likely, if you prove to be the best man on the committee, you will get the chairmanship."

This was the moment Harriman had been waiting for, the one to which all his calculations had aimed to bring Schiff. "All right," he replied at once, "I'm with you."[27]

By June 1897 Harriman had taken a $2.2 million share in the underwriting syndicate; during the next year he added another $1.1 million. This was the only role he played in the reorganization other than as obstacle, but it proved a fateful encounter for both Harriman and the Union Pacific. He had come into the business on behalf of the Illinois Central connector, but his eyes had been opened to vast new horizons of possibility beyond the Missouri River.[28]

That same June he traveled west to see for himself what was happening. For the first time he saw at close range what some analysts were already chanting: the depression was lifting and with it the blight on rail earnings. Signs of prosperity were everywhere—in the crops, livestock, merchandise orders, shipments, and the mood of a region where hard times had eroded confidence along with bank accounts. Smiles were returning to lined, leathery faces that for many years had seen nothing to smile about. Glints of hope radiated from eyes long glazed by defeat and from voices that had long been silent or talked in hushed, faltering tones.

The West was springing to life again, and the Union Pacific ran a long, straight route through its prosperous underbelly. Here was an extraordinary opportunity to take charge of a unique property that nobody wanted. To most observers the road was little more than a dinosaur with a colorful past. As the first transcontinental, it had paid the inevitable price of a pioneer by costing far more to build than newer, more efficient lines. How could an old railroad with a bloated capital structure compete with modern lines?

Harriman saw the germ of an answer, one drawn of necessity from the road he knew best. For all its problems, the Union Pacific still owned the best transcontinental route. The reorganization would pare its capital structure down to manageable size, and the foreclosure sale would get the government out of its affairs. The task then would be to create a modern, efficient line capable of wringing the utmost advantage from its strategic location—in short, to transform the Union Pacific into an Illinois Central.

These thoughts occupied Harriman as the reorganization struggle drew toward a close. The pundits who had long praised the Union Pacific's possibilities chirped even louder that summer as speculators boosted the stock from a low of 4½ in April to just below 25 in September. "The country this year is a perfect garden," confirmed a Union Pacific officer who had toured the line. Harriman bought the stock heavily at cheap prices and made no secret of it.[29]

The foreclosure sale took place November 1 in Omaha, and the new Union Pacific Railroad was born, free of the federal government for the first time. The new company had a Utah charter granting far more liberal provisions than the old federal charter, but it did not yet have a new management. Schiff was anxious to get one in place. The long ordeal of reorganization had taken its toll on him. Years later he confessed that on the night of the foreclosure sale, he had paced the floor of his dreary hotel room in Omaha fretting over whether he had bitten off more than he could chew. The leadership vacuum in both New York and Omaha did nothing to assuage his fears.[30]

Schiff kept his promise to Harriman by putting him on the executive committee, which convened early in December with Winslow Pierce at its head. Later that month the committee chose Horace G. Burt of the Chicago & Northwestern as president. On January 31, 1898, the new Union Pacific opened its New York office in the Equitable Life Building at 120 Broadway. Everything was in place, yet one key question remained unanswered: who wielded power in New York?[31]

The new board was a mosaic of interests. Gould held a seat along with Pierce, who served as both chief counsel and chairman of the board. Marvin Hughitt was president of the Northwestern and Roswell Miller of the Milwaukee road. Henry B. Hyde, the head of Equitable Life, was an old Gould ally. Oliver Ames represented his family's large interest, while Schiff, Otto Kahn, Louis Fitzgerald, James Stillman, and T. Jefferson Coolidge were all bankers who had participated in the reorganization. George Q. Cannon filled the place reserved for Utah interests, and John Doane had been a government director.[32]

Then there was Harriman, the mystery man. Why was he on the board? What role was he expected to play? No one paid any attention to his presence, in part because so little was known about him. His association with the Illinois Central was highly regarded, but he had no past connection with the Union Pacific or the West. He was a wild card whose impact on the game would exceed anyone's wildest dreams.

The other directors did not tender Harriman a warm welcome to their circle. Some regarded him as an interloper who did not measure up to them in wealth, position, or achievement. To their eyes he was, in Otto Kahn's words, a sort of "free lance, neither a railroad man nor a banker nor a merchant." James Stillman, the quiet but ambitious head of National City Bank, had been warned by a friend to "look out for Ed Harriman. He is not so smart as some people think, and he is not a safe man to have business with." Ever cautious, Stillman heeded this advice, using his detached style to keep his distance from Harriman while remaining ever watchful.[33]

This reception was predictable. Harriman was, after all, a brash, combative newcomer who had elbowed his way onto the board. Why should the other directors trust a man who had forced his company on them? They knew he was a good banker but had no idea what else he was capable of. Nor did they know his reasons for wanting to be in the Union Pacific management. It was only natural for them to regard him with suspicion until he had proven otherwise. If their hostility bothered Harriman, he handled it in his usual way—as a challenge—and set about earning the board's respect with a demonstration of his ability and demonic energy.

Schiff had predicted that Harriman would get the chairmanship if he showed himself the strongest man on the executive committee, but there was also a power vacuum working in his favor. Those who understand and crave power are usually quick to sense its absence, and Harriman was no exception. The very nature of boards and committees create such vacuums because their labors are divided and their members distracted by other interests. On the Illinois Central Fish had filled this vacuum. No strong figure had yet emerged in the Union Pacific, and no one on the executive committee seemed a likely candidate.

The other members included Pierce, Stillman, Hughitt, and Otto Kahn of Kuhn, Loeb. All of them were better known in business circles than Harriman, but his relative obscurity proved an advantage. The others had their hands full elsewhere. Pierce's primary concern was to look out for the Gould interests; on the Union Pacific it was all he could do to serve as chairman of the board and chief counsel, let alone manage the executive committee. Stillman and Kahn were bankers who had no time or inclination to run a railroad, while the venerable Hughitt had his own railroad to manage.

None of them wanted the job Harriman coveted, and all were eager to find someone who could do it well. Harriman understood that the right man could lift a heavy burden from their shoulders. He still performed his duties for the Illinois Central, but his commitments were minor compared to those of the other committee members. If he could impress them with his knowledge of railroads as well as of finance, the position of chairman would be his almost by default. To that end he bent his energies during the winter of 1898.

It did not take Harriman long to become indispensable to Pierce, who was distracted by the mountain of legal work attached to the start of the reorganized company. While Schiff badgered Pierce to get the paperwork done, Harriman volunteered to handle such chores as the delicate diplomacy over Union Pacific connections in the Northwest. The new company had not reacquired its Oregon line, and some doubted that it could. This uncertainty left relations tense among competing roads in a volatile region. Although new to the western game, Harriman mastered its essentials in short order and plunged into the negotiations in mid-January 1898.[34]

Through the winter Harriman repeated this pattern, impressing Schiff, Pierce, Stillman, and the other directors with his ability to take hold of something new and become expert at it in a remarkably short time. To their relief, the interloper proved not only talented but willing and able to do the difficult tasks none of them had time to do. On May 23, 1898, Harriman was rewarded by being named chairman of the executive committee with Pierce as chairman of the board.[35]

The news attracted little attention outside the company. Harriman was still unknown in railroad circles, and Wall Street could divine no meaning from the elevation of the Illinois Central's financial wizard to a top management position on the Union Pacific. Did it mean closer relations between these two powerful roads? The connector between them did get built, finally opening in December 1899. By then Harriman had crossed fully to the other side. He had used the connector as a bridge to his destiny in railroading.[36]

James J. Hill, the railroad titan of the Northwest, had scanned the original list of Union Pacific directors and drawn a blank at one name. "Now, who the hell is Harriman?" he had asked a friend. He would soon find out, as would many other rail managers who did not yet know that a cyclone had landed in their midst.[37]

With scarcely concealed glee Harriman settled into a drab office on the Pine Street corner of the Equitable Building. His window peered down on the yard of Trinity Church, near where he had attended school as a boy. In reminiscent moods his gaze swept down the crooked length of Wall Street and across the river to distant Jersey City, where so much of his youth had been spent. How far he had come from the failures of his good-natured but inept father! And how much there was for him to do in his new position!

On his first day in the new office he summoned the Union Pacific's secretary, Alexander Millar, and announced that he had come to take charge of the company's affairs. A short time later Millar told him hesitantly of an inquiry from the president of a rival system asking discreetly who Harriman was; they did not seem to know him. "Oh well," Harriman laughed in reply, "they'll know me better by and by."[38]

What, then, sent Harriman west to find his destiny? The answer was a mixture of ambition and opportunity. At fifty the fires of many men have banked into the pleasures and rewards of comfortable middle age. In Harriman, however, the flame of ambition burned with an unsated fury. More than ever he yearned to accomplish great things, and at fifty the time for doing them was fast running out. The time was right for the economy as well as for him, and the Union Pacific offered a rare opportunity to prove his mettle in a great arena. The road cried for leadership, and Harriman longed to lead.

And the place was right. The West was in many ways still wilderness, a vast canvas awaiting the touch of a master hand. Harriman adored wilderness in both the literal and figurative senses. The deep woods were one form of it; an undeveloped economy or an enterprise in disarray was another. Both offered him similar mixtures of pleasure and challenge. They were frontiers to conquer, and Harriman sought frontiers as a moth seeks flame or Icarus the sun. The rest of his life would be devoted to exploring new frontiers, each one larger and more formidable than the last, each one expanding his horizons until they embraced the bounds of empire.

8 Going for Broke

The Union Pacific of that day was a melancholy imitation of a railroad. Of the whole system he found only about 400 miles of road that was graded at all, the rest being merely a collection of ties and rails laid down on a dirt foundation. The station buildings were tumble-down shacks. The cars, as he whizzed past them, looked old and battered, and eloquent of economy in the purchase of paint. West of Cheyenne, on the main line of traffic from the Missouri to Ogden, his train climbed hills by the hundred, hills that would compel every heavy freight train to call upon two engines for its haulage. The engines were old and light. Everything was dirty, decrepit, low-class.
—C. M. Keys, "Harriman: The Man in the Making"

Nothing has done more to shape the Harriman legend than the myth that he found the Union Pacific a dilapidated wreck. What better way to demonstrate Harriman's genius than to portray him as the Merlin whose magic touch transformed a decrepit antique into the very model of a modern railroad? Everyone from journalists to Schiff to Kennan perpetuated this story over the years. Averell Harriman, who was only six years old when his father took charge of the Union Pacific, insisted late in life that "its rusting rails were sinking into mud; its ties were rotted and broken, its rolling stock falling apart."[1]

Observers at the time took a different view. Since a bankrupt road did not have to pay interest on its bonds, it could devote most of its earnings to upkeep. The Union Pacific receivers did just that and thereby earned praise from all sides. For two years the *Wall Street Journal* hammered at the themes that the Union Pacific was well maintained and the stock undervalued. In October 1897, just two months before Harriman joined the board, the *Journal* issued its most emphatic statement on the road's condition: "Under the receivership the whole property has been put in the most extraordinary fine condition. . . . It is no secret that instead of buying a worn-out property, the new company will get a system in as fine condition as anything in the West. New rails, new bridges, new rolling stock, passenger and freight, in fact everything that goes to make up a first-class railroad line."[2]

Those who knew the Union Pacific from the inside, such as secretary Alex

Millar and operating official W. H. Bancroft, scorned the "two streaks of rust" myth and insisted that the road compared favorably with other western lines. Western railroads did not match eastern lines in their physical condition because they were usually longer and carried much less business. Bancroft made clear what he meant by a typical western road: light rails, little or no ballast, heavy grades over mountain ranges, and light equipment.[3]

The myth erred in two respects: it described the Union Pacific as a rundown road and measured it by the standard of eastern roads. What Harriman found was not a derelict but a typical nineteenth-century western road, old-fashioned in both its equipment and operating procedures.

The task facing Harriman, then, was more subtle than the myth has portrayed. By prevailing standards, the Union Pacific was in decent shape to do what it had done in the past. Most directors and observers, their thinking dulled into caution by hard times, saw this minimum as all that was needed. The long depression had blinded them to the potential for a bonanza from the recovering western economy. But Harriman's trip west had stirred his mind to a daring conclusion: traffic was there in huge quantities and could be handled only by transforming a tolerable nineteenth-century road into an efficient twentieth-century one.

Harriman was not alone in this vision of what the future held, but he was the only man willing to bet the store on it. He was going for broke on an idea that was not as obvious as it seemed later, and he had somehow to persuade the rest of the board to follow him.

Less than a month after becoming chairman of the executive committee, Harriman set out to inspect the entire Union Pacific system. He borrowed Fish's private car from the Illinois Central and put it at the head of a special train consisting of some Union Pacific private cars and a baggage car with the locomotive at the rear. This arrangement provided a nice breeze and allowed Harriman to inspect the roadbed, buildings, equipment, and countryside. For most of the trip the train ran only in daylight because Harriman wished to see everything.

On any excursion Harriman had an inimitable way of mixing business with pleasure. He took along the five Union Pacific officers who had the most to tell him: president Horace Burt, chief engineer J. B. Berry, general manager Edward Dickinson, freight traffic manager J. A. Munroe, and general passenger agent E. L. Lomax. But he also included his two oldest daughters, Mary and Cornelia, and old friend Dr. E. L. Trudeau. The frail, sickly Trudeau had already founded his famous sanitarium at Saranac Lake for which Harriman had served as a trustee since 1891. Since their early days together at Paul Smith's, Harriman seldom missed a chance to invite the doctor on an outing.[4]

Everyone gathered at the Union Depot in Kansas City, where the train had been readied. Harriman and the girls were in high spirits, the rail officers quiet and deferential. They could not help but feel apprehensive over being locked in close quarters for more than three weeks with the man who held their destiny in his hands. At the same time, they were curious about him and eager to take his measure. Harriman was still a mystery to the men in the West, who knew him vaguely as a financier connected with the Illinois Central. What, if anything, did he know about railroads?

At two o'clock on the afternoon of June 17, 1898, the train chugged slowly out of Kansas City, "backing up" as railroad men said when the engine pushed from the rear, and rolled onto the Kansas division of the Union Pacific. The pace was leisurely, allowing Harriman to scrutinize everything in sight. The first night was spent at Wamego and the second at Ellis, where the visitors were treated to an outdoor band concert. By late afternoon on the third day, as the train ran toward Denver, the endless prairie dissolved into vistas of distant green forests and mountain peaks.

The train rolled past Denver through a lush valley wedged against a mountain wall until it reached Colorado Springs that night. There Harriman paused for two days to take the girls sight-seeing. He liked to visit every local attraction as if he had all the time in the world and nothing else to do with it. They went to Manitou, gaped in awe at the Garden of the Gods, then made the drive up Pike's Peak. The next day they ran through Clear Creek Canyon, where the roaring water had carved the rocky cliffs into dozens of grotesque shapes that lined the track. In the sixty-mile crevice with sides rising five hundred to fifteen hundred feet, the sky loomed like a narrow strip of cobalt above the jagged rock.

On June 22 the train returned to Denver and hurried to Cheyenne, where it picked up the Union Pacific main line. On the rolling prairie the girls saw herds of antelope and caught distant glimpses of coyotes. They paused for the night at Laramie, huddled between the Laramie and Medicine Bow ranges, then pushed on to Rock River in the middle of stock-raising country, the coal-mining town of Hanna, the continental divide at Creston, and the formidable Red Desert, once a favorite Indian hunting ground but now prowled mostly by sheep. Beyond the twisted sandstone cliffs called Point of Rocks lay Rock Springs, another Union Pacific coal town where the infamous massacre of Chinese miners occurred in 1885. That night they stopped at Green River, opposite some imposing bluffs that had eroded into all forms of weird figures.

Green River was the gateway to the Uinta Mountains and Utah, which had finally been admitted to the Union two years earlier. At Echo City Harriman learned that a small branch line had been ravaged by fire the day before. He hunted up the mayor and walked the town with him until satisfied that his help was not needed. On they went to Ogden, where the Union Pacific connected with the Central Pacific, and down to Salt Lake City, where Harriman and the girls roamed eagerly around the tabernacle and other attractions of Temple Square. The night was spent at Saltair, a new resort with a huge concert and dancing pavilion on the shore of the lake. Next morning they enjoyed a dip in the clear salt water.

They were the perfect tourists, willing to go anywhere to see anything, yet the rail officials found it hard to relax because they were being introduced to the Harriman style. His energy and insatiable curiosity overwhelmed them. As J. B. Berry noted tactfully, "He was keenly alive to all the surroundings." Harriman seized on details others missed and fired questions nonstop until even veteran rail officials had to rack their brains on matters that had never occurred to them. Nor could they duck the line of fire, for Harriman had a way of pressing until he got an answer that satisfied him.[5]

At every stop the local superintendent and other officers climbed aboard and got the same intense grilling. Harriman's sharp eye and tough, persistent questions jolted them. He could not be fooled because he seemed to know so much already, and smart officers saw quickly that it was dangerous to trifle with him. While riddling others with questions, Harriman said little in return, leaving them to stew in uncertainty. No one could follow his thinking or divine its direction.

North of Ogden lay the Oregon Short Line and the Oregon Railway & Navigation road over which the Union Pacific reached Portland. The company had lost control of both lines, and Harriman was already deep into negotiations to reacquire them. This remote corner of the West had long tantalized entrepreneurs with its vast potential for wealth, and Harriman wanted to see it for himself. His train headed over the Short Line, then turned north at Pocatello to visit the huge mining complexes at Butte and Anaconda.

At Butte Harriman met Marcus Daly, the mining baron of whom one Montana paper grumbled, "If Christ came to Anaconda he would be compelled to eat, sleep, drink and pray with Mr. Marcus Daly." Harriman was happy to share those activities with the genial Daly and quickly fell to arguing over who owned the best trotter. Before parting they agreed to settle the debate with a race for $10,000. When the race was held, Daly won and collected the bet. Harriman later insisted on a rematch, however, and this time his horse won.[6]

While Harriman poked around the mines, the girls ventured down the Anaconda chute and took snapshots of Indians. Later they all rode bicycles around the camp and then horses through the countryside. Harriman also got in some trout fishing on the ride back to Boise, where everyone plunged eagerly into the giant indoor natatorium for a swim. From Boise the train moved on to Umatilla, where it picked up the breathtaking Columbia River line into Portland. The stately peaks of Mount Rainier, St. Helens, and Adams on one side and Mount

Hood on the other fired their imaginations, as did the Multnomah Falls and the fish-wheels along the river.

All this was frontier for Harriman. The vast spectacle of the country unfolding before him filled his mind with bold, immense ideas. Every new experience seemed to open his eyes to how much more could be done and to ignite within him the desire to do it. Even before he had conquered a kingdom there burned within him grand visions of empire. There was so much more to the West than he had ever dreamed, and once impressed with its majesty he never forgot the lesson.

The line terminated at Portland, but Harriman wanted to see more. After pausing only a few hours to explore Portland, the train rattled southward on Southern Pacific track toward Ashland, where the travelers spent the night of June 30. The next day they visited Mount Shasta, which offered views the girls found "exquisitely beautiful, and can not be excelled on the American continent." They gasped in delight at the Rogue River Valley, Strawberry Valley, and the Sacramento River curling about the mountain's base.[7]

After reluctantly leaving Shasta, the Harrimans spent the night at Delta, California. Shortly after their departure the next morning, the train was derailed, injuring the fireman and causing a delay of ten hours. While the crew waited for a wrecking train to rerail the cars, an unruffled Harriman hunted up a pole and went off fishing for a couple of hours. Next day they chugged into Monterey, where more magnificent scenery awaited them. Groves of oak, pine, and cedar trees draped the distant mountains and flanked the bay along the peninsula, where they enjoyed a long drive. That night Horace Burt hosted a dinner at the palatial Hotel Del Monte.

On Monday, July 4, the Harrimans arrived in San Francisco and were enchanted by it. Reluctantly they pushed on to Burlingame, where the next day they were guests at a luncheon hosted by Julius Kruttschnitt of the Southern Pacific. This was Harriman's introduction to the man who later became indispensable to him. The stolid, burly Kruttschnitt, a walking encyclopedia of knowledge on railroads and the West, obliged Harriman with a steady stream of information. After lunch the Harrimans returned to play tourist for two more days in San Francisco before starting the long trip home.

On this homeward journey Harriman traveled the entire original transcontinental route for the first time. For three days his tireless eyes scanned the track and the country. He marveled at the ascent through the rugged Sierras and long, desolate stretches across the Humboldt desert to Ogden, where they switched from the Central Pacific to the Union Pacific. Through Weber's Canyon, past the glowering Uinta Mountains and the sullen Red Desert, the Wyoming prairie and the Black Hills, the scenery mattered less to Harriman than the terrain. While the girls recorded its beauty, he calculated the cost of transforming it into a road comparable to the Illinois Central. He crossed the heart-stopping Dale Creek bridge and felt the engine struggle up Sherman's Hill, the highest point on the road and the biggest obstacle to efficient operation.

Once into the flatlands of Nebraska, he studied the curvature and weight of the track, the bridges, depots, and outbuildings, looked over the repair shops at Grand Island, and took note of the lush crops filling the broad Platte River valley. On the afternoon of July 9 the train rolled into Omaha, having covered 6,236 miles in twenty-three days. They proved to be the most important miles Harriman ever traveled. His mind had gone much farther, leaping to possibilities he had scarcely imagined before the trip.

Harriman had headed west relishing the challenge of bringing a moribund railroad to life but knowing little of what the work entailed. He had examined the road, estimated what was needed to modernize it, and taken the measure of the men who ran it. Aware that they barely knew who he was, let alone what he could do, he had blown in like a whirlwind and stamped on them the indelible imprint of his authority before rushing out as abruptly as he had come. He had also surveyed the country, talked to shippers as well as bankers and business-men, gauged the mood of the farmers on what their crops and livestock promised. In little over three weeks he had learned the West and come home a convert to its potential. The West became a shrine at which Harriman never ceased to worship. The reconstruction of the Union Pacific remained his major goal, but it also became the first step in a much larger vision of empire. The design had not yet unfolded to him, but the inspiration was there.

On the last evening of the trip, while everyone was enjoying dinner in his private car, Harriman announced, "I have today wired New York for 5000 shares of Union Pacific preferred at 66, and any one of you are welcome to take as few or as many shares as you like." This was a revelation to the railroad officers, to see a financier actually put his own money into an enterprise before it had even shown what it could do. Those impressed enough to take Harriman up on the offer were not disappointed at the results.[8]

Harriman did more than invest his own money in the company. He also telegraphed New York for authority to spend $25 million at once for new equipment and improvements. The signs of prosperity he saw everywhere along the route convinced him that the road was about to receive more business than it could possibly handle. Labor and materials could still be had at depression prices; the time to act was now, before a revived economy drove them upward. So determined was Harriman to steal a march that he let some contracts for work on his own responsibility even though he knew the board would balk at a request of such magnitude.[9]

Harriman's telegram fell like a bombshell on the board. The railroad was barely six months out of receivership and struggling to earn a dividend on its preferred stock. To entertain such a huge expenditure seemed the height of madness; it was, cried one director, an extravagance that would hurl the Union Pacific back into bankruptcy. The request was tabled until Harriman could argue his case in person. On July 14 he took on the executive committee in a long and heated session. The other members hammered away at Harriman with their misgivings but could not shake his confidence; in the end, with much shaking of heads and uttering of dire prophecies, they approved the request.[10]

Harriman had no illusions as to what some of the board members thought of him or, as Otto Kahn put it, "the fatal consequences to his career in case his forecast should turn out to have been mistaken or even premature." He had also been buying Union Pacific common stock for months at prices ranging up to 25 even though no one believed it would pay a dividend for years to come. "You see," sneered one financier to Kahn, "the man is essentially a speculator. . . . He will come to grief yet." When Kahn mentioned this to Harriman, the little man retorted, "Union Pacific common is intrinsically worth as much as St. Paul. With good management it will get there."

St. Paul was then selling around par. Kahn merely nodded and walked away. It sounded to him, he later admitted, like "the wildest kind of wild talk."[11]

Schiff had walked the floor of his hotel in anguish the night he had purchased the Union Pacific, but Harriman seemed unfazed by the enormous gamble he was taking. There was a toughness and certainty of purpose about him that unnerved even hardened financiers, but no one doubted that in this case the once conservative banker was putting his own future on the line as well as that of the Union Pacific.

In going for broke Harriman had one advantage that was in many eyes a liability. The railroad industry was the nation's first big business, and by 1890 it had already grown hidebound in many respects. Railroad men dwelled in a world of eternal verities shaped by one immutable belief: experience was the best if not only teacher. To them Harriman lacked the hands-on experience necessary to run a large railroad. He had no "practical" background in how things were done.

It never occurred to most railroad men that this lack of experience was an asset in a rapidly changing world where yesterday's habits became today's obstacle. Harriman's lack of experience in the nuts and bolts of operations meant that he had little to unlearn before he could begin to learn. With a mind free of the shibboleths that blinded so many rail officers, he could look at things as they were instead of how someone told him they were supposed to be.

And he was a fast learner. The speed with which his mind assimilated, sorted, and collated data seemed inhuman to those around him, as did his ability to pick something up much later at exactly the point where he had left it. Asked to explain how he managed it, Harriman thought for a while and then said, "I think that the mind is like these—what d'ye call 'em on this desk?—these pigeon holes. A man comes to me. I listen and decide on what to do; and then—it goes into a pigeon-hole."

"And it's always there?" asked the interviewer. "No trouble in finding it again at any time?"

"It's always there." Harriman pondered the matter, as if curious to know the answer himself. "It's always there," he repeated at last. "Whenever I need it again I find it there."

"And you don't know how you do it?"

"I don't know how I do it."[12]

The Harriman brain became a source of fascination among those close to him. What awed them was his ability to be so quick and incisive and still reach sound conclusions. Judge Robert S. Lovett, who later became one of Harriman's closest friends and associates, marveled at this gift: "His mental processes were unlike any that I have ever seen. He never arrived at conclusions by reason, or argument, or any deliberative process that I could observe. His judgments seemed to be formed intuitively. The proposition was presented to him and he saw it. It was much like turning a flashlight on a subject. If interested, he saw it, and did not care and probably did not know how it was revealed. And his vision and measure of it was almost unfailingly clear and correct."[13]

James Stillman, who overcame his early doubts to become one of Harriman's closest friends and admirers, agreed that the little man's brain was "a thing to marvel at. And yet it was that kind of brain which, if you could take it apart as you would a clock, and put it on a shelf to look at, would be distinguished by the incredible simplicity of its mechanism, and its ability to make the most complex problems solvable and common unto itself."[14]

This ability to flash from insight to conclusion with lightning speed led to his being dubbed the "Human Business Machine." But Harriman was much more than a calculator. He prided himself on his imagination and liked to say that lack of it was a serious defect in any man. Unlike most men, he never let experience glaze his vision. For Harriman the conventional wisdom was a point of departure, not a refuge.[15]

Few outsiders understood how Harriman's mind worked. As a result, he has long been portrayed as a man who mastered the intricacies of railroading by immersing himself in detail. Nothing could be farther from the truth. Details were for him merely springboards to understanding how things should be done, and his gift for finding larger truths in the smallest incident was uncanny. From these insights flowed a grasp of the principles on which a railroad should be run.

During his first trip over the Union Pacific, Harriman happened to notice at one stop that it took a long time for the engines to take on water. His eye wandered up to the narrow pipe feeding the boiler. Why, he asked, were the discharge pipes only four to six inches in diameter? Because, came the railroader's stock answer, they had always been that way, for reasons nobody knew. Harriman ordered new pipes with twelve-inch diameters installed, and crews were astonished to find that water stops took much less time.[16]

In upgrading the Union Pacific, what mattered most to Harriman was how well he trusted the officer in charge. He realized that it was crucial to have the right men in key positions if he was to accomplish great changes. In business as in war the general was always at the mercy of his staff. Harriman was slow to place his trust in a man, but once given he relied heavily on the man's judgment. "Unless he could trust a man implicitly," said Julius Kruttschnitt, "he would soon replace him with a man he could trust."[17]

One of those key men arrived in June 1898, just before Harriman departed on his inspection trip. Judge William D. Cornish had served the Union Pacific as master in chancery for the long receivership ordeal before being tapped as the new first vice-president. A shrewd, patient negotiator, the tactful Cornish proved to be the perfect balance wheel for Harriman's curt, abrasive manner. His sound judgment and skillful handling of subordinates enabled Harriman to concentrate on larger matters.[18]

Harriman's business style demolishes the myth of him as a prisoner of detail. He told subordinates what he wanted, sought their advice, scrutinized their reports, decided what to do, and left the execution to them. Far from demanding piles of data, he insisted that even complex reports be pared down to a page or two. "While Mr. Harriman thoroughly understood the details of railroad work," noted Kruttschnitt, "his policy was to select men who were competent to supervise and control the details, and then to give himself no further trouble about them."[19]

If the officers did their job well, Harriman let them do it their own way. "He always said to the railroad people," emphasized J. B. Berry, "that he looked to them for results and that he did not expect to instruct them in it." Samuel M. Felton worked for ten years in important positions for Harriman yet saw him only once every month or two. "He analyzed men," declared another officer, "much as he analyzed facts." Sometimes he picked the wrong man, but incompetents did not last long under his system. Harriman was slow to praise and quick to criticize. He expected high-quality work and insisted that officers work together. Cost overruns never bothered him if he got the results he wanted.[20]

Nobody found it easy working for Harriman. "I say work for," stressed Felton, "because no one worked with him. He was always the sole director, and sometimes imperious and arbitrary." The most energetic officer scrambled to keep up with him; one auditor grumbled that Harriman would wear out any man in ten years. This edge of desperation was made worse by Harriman's

Man at work: E. H. Harriman at his desk, the omnipresent telephone at his elbow.
(Union Pacific Museum Collection)

unfathomable way of leapfrogging from one topic to another without any obvious connection. He seemed to carry the office in his head—in those invisible pigeonholes that even he couldn't explain.[21]

His mind flashed across a subject so quickly that no one could follow it. Once Harriman rattled off to Felton a string of figures nonstop for ten minutes, then tossed out another number as the conclusion to be drawn from the others. "Isn't that so?" he demanded. "Wait a moment, Mr. Harriman," pleaded the dazed

Felton. "If I could understand all that as quickly as you do, then I should be sitting where you are." Harriman laughed at that and repeated the figures more slowly.[22]

As Fish discovered early, Harriman wore out the telephone in his zeal to save time and transact business when he could not be present—a handy tool for one who fell ill often. When the telephone was not available, he used the telegraph, firing off messages in the same staccato style. Instead of scanning telegrams himself, he had the secretary read them to him and usually had an answer framed before the reading was finished. He grew to dislike writing letters as much as reading them and gradually reduced his output to a minimum as the telephone allowed him to do business faster.[23]

One reason Harriman avoided letters was the toll it took on both the stenographer scrambling to keep up with him and his own concentration. In his haste to spew out a message, he often produced wildly convoluted sentences like this one to Horace Burt, which outlines his relationship to the Union Pacific president:

> Your telegram of the 4th regarding answer to Mr. Stubbs letter of the 3rd to me received here this morning, and I have answered Mr. Stubbs as per copy enclosed. The substance of his letter was communicated to me over the telephone on Saturday, at which time I directed Mr. Millar to wire you requesting that you advise me by wire what attitude I should take and answer make to Mr. Stubbs, but his message seems to have been put so that it indicated that I intended to take the matter up here, which I certainly do not unless it should be necessary in order to help settle the matter and save you so long a journey as coming here for this purpose and I desire you to understand that that is the attitude which I want you to consider me in towards this company and yourself,—that is, where I can take up a matter which would tend to help the Company & its officers I will be glad always to do it.

The sentence reads like a road map of Harriman's mind at work: everything hangs together perfectly if you can follow its breathless twists and turns. But few of his officers could. Railroad men were methodical by nature and incapable of following the leaps Harriman's mind took.[24]

Although this gap in intellect made subordinates uneasy in Harriman's presence, it led them to believe in his genius. But something more attracted them even as he worked them to exhaustion: a magnetism born of his towering confidence in his plans. "He would not only convert you but would keep you converted," insisted Felton. "The better you knew him, the more confidence you had in him. He had unbounded confidence in himself, and probably this confidence was so overwhelming that few could resist it."[25]

Otto Kahn got a taste of this confidence early. Harriman came to Kuhn, Loeb one hot summer day in 1897 to persuade the bankers to take an interest in a certain deal. When Kahn showed no interest, a pale, haggard Harriman argued in vain to change his mind. Finally, he got up and stumbled to the door, then turned around and rasped, "I am dead tired this afternoon, and no good any more. I have been on this job uninterruptedly all day, taking no time even for luncheon. I'll tackle you again to-morrow, when I am fresh. I'm bound to convince you, and to get you to come along." To Kahn's surprise, Harriman appeared the next day and pleaded his case until Kahn yielded as much to his persistence as his arguments. "His power of will was nothing short of phenomenal," marveled Kahn. "I have seen him perform veritable miracles in the way of making people do as he wanted." This was Kahn's first lesson about Harriman; the second was that the deal turned out to be very profitable.[26]

9 Going Modern

He found in the Union Pacific a completely broken-down property. . . . There was absolutely but one thing he could do . . . and to do it required the courage that all of us that are not Harrimans lack. That was, not to wait for things to happen . . . but to do something that none of our railway speculators had ever done before him; namely, to borrow huge sums of money and build up his property physically; to cut down granite grades, fill mountain valleys, provide the heaviest rails, the best engines—in a word, to buy for his new line, even at enormous cost, high efficiency.
—Frank Spearman, "Building Up a Great Railway System"

Harriman understood earlier than most men the basic formula for success in the new era: to make money, a road had to haul greater loads at lower rates as cheaply as possible. This prime directive was simple but costly, especially in the vast, lightly populated West, where roads had been built as cheaply as possible to handle a modest traffic at high rates. To capitalize on the economic revival, they had to be made into modern lines like those in the East, where traffic density had always been much heavier. Since western roads were much longer, the cost of reconstruction would be greater.

There was a domino effect that made modernizing hard to tackle piecemeal. Bigger payloads required longer trains with larger cars and heavier engines, which in turn needed a straighter line, lower grades, heavier rails, better ballast, sturdier bridges, updated signals, more sidings, and newer facilities. The Illinois Central had taught Harriman that these improvements formed a seamless web where any gain in one area would always be limited by a lack of progress in the others. To undertake the whole package at once meant a huge investment from which most rail managers shrank.

But Harriman was not intimidated. During the winter of 1898, while still only a director, he had asked chief engineer J. B. Berry for data on what costs and savings would flow from reducing grades, straightening curves, and shortening the line. Berry scratched his head in dismay. Since few railroads had bothered to examine these matters, he would have to generate the figures from scratch. This task occupied him through most of 1898. To display the data's meaning clearly, Berry created a special map showing the present line and proposed changes with tables itemizing the cost of changes and probable savings from them on each section. He also factored in savings from the use of heavier power and larger cars. When he tried to include interest costs, however, Harriman snapped, "Leave that off. I prefer to figure out what the interest account will be myself."[1]

Harriman liked the concise way the map presented what he wanted to know. The total price for its wish list came to $8.7 million, which staggered Berry. To his astonishment, Harriman seemed unfazed by the amount. In January 1899 Harriman summoned several officers to New York and, map in hand, led them into an executive committee meeting. The discussion lasted only fifteen minutes before the request was referred to the chairman with authority to act.

This phrase soon became the standard litany of executive committee meetings, and the chairman was not one to dawdle. Harriman gave the Omaha officers their marching orders before they had left the room. For railroad men accustomed to seeing expenditures doled out like relief rations, the performance was a revelation. Berry came away from New York convinced that no project was too big for Harriman if he could be shown that it would save money. Nor did the board balk at his requests, for by then he had mesmerized the hand-wringers with the belief that he could make money by spending it.[2]

How well Harriman had consolidated his power became clear on December 1, 1898, when the directors abolished the position of chairman of the board, leaving Harriman de facto head of the board as well as the executive committee. Schiff, Pierce, Stillman, and Hughitt remained on the executive committee, and a seat was added for George Gould as well. A year earlier Harriman had come onto the board as an unknown quantity; now he had been given command of a major railroad by a group of financial heavyweights who had come to trust his judgment in a remarkably short time. They had yielded power willingly to Harriman because he got things done, but none of them dreamed how much he was to do.[3]

During the weeks after his inspection trip Harriman worked feverishly on a dozen projects at once. By September 1898 he was exhausted but reluctant to quit. He took his family off to Paul Smith's, intending to leave them there, then decided to stay a week himself. "I find I'm a little used up more than I realized while working under pressure," he explained to Burt. A week later Harriman was back pushing Burt to get everything done yesterday.[4]

Of the $8.7 million approved by the board, $2.7 million was marked for new equipment. Harriman knew that much of the Union Pacific rolling stock consisted of old twenty-ton wooden boxcars. To imprint his guiding principle on the officers, he collared one and asked, "How much does a boxcar weigh?"

"About 40,000 pounds," came the reply.

"And what load does it carry?"

"Also about 40,000 pounds."

Harriman snorted. "Then you use 40,000 pounds of dead weight to carry 40,000 pounds of paying weight. Wouldn't it be well to make the car weigh less in proportion to the paying freight that it carried?"[5]

The official conceded that it would, and Harriman made this the policy for modernizing the fleet. So too with the older, lightweight locomotives, which weighed about fifty tons but could not muster even ten tons of tractive power. Larger cars made of steel instead of wood and bigger, more powerful engines could double the capacity of a train with only a small increase in operating costs. A trickle of orders for new equipment in 1898 turned into a cascade over the next decade.[6]

Harriman's aim was not merely to increase the fleet but to modernize it. The key to his approach was less what he bought than what he discarded. In his haste to leave the past behind, he junked old engines and cars faster than he replaced them; for as many years as not, the Union Pacific showed a net decrease in equipment. Officials got this message early when Harriman scrapped 1,094 cars in his first eighteen months. The audacity of this policy astonished observers. "It is now clear," wrote one reporter in August 1899, "that the Union Pacific rolling stock is to be replaced as fast as possible by the Harriman management."[7]

To handle larger payloads, the Union Pacific needed a straighter, wider road-bed with heavier rails and more ballast. Little of the main line had decent ballast despite the treasure trove of disintegrated gravel at Sherman Mountain. The problem had always been a lack of heavy equipment to dig the gravel and work trains to haul it. Harriman moved at once to rectify this problem. His first equipment order in 1898 included two sixty-ton steam shovels and three hundred Rodger ballast cars, which Harriman knew from his Illinois Central days. A year later he doubled the fleet of Rodger cars as entire trains of ballast began moving east and west from Sherman.[8]

For five years Harriman concentrated on upgrading the roadbed. By 1903 the Union Pacific had widened 1,032 miles of road and ballasted 2,246 miles with Sherman gravel or good local material. As always, he let officials take nothing for granted. On one inspection trip his eye was drawn to the shoulder of the ballast—the distance from the rails to the point where the ballast began to slope off. Harriman asked an officer what this distance was.[9]

"Eighteen inches," replied the officer.

"Why eighteen inches?"

"That is our standard."

There it was again, the conventional wisdom of tradition that allowed railroad men to do their work by rote. "That is no answer," snapped Harriman. "Why is it our standard?"

The big dipper: A steam shovel near Buford, Wyoming, loads a string of cars with Sherman gravel to be used for ballast. (Union Pacific Museum Collection)

The official shook his head in dismay. "I presume they want a good quantity of ballast outside the rails so that a part of it could be used if necessary in filling in between the rails when it got shaken down."

"But isn't it likely that the outside ballast would slide off down the slope," persisted Harriman, "so that a good deal of it wouldn't be there when you wanted it?"

"It might," conceded the official.

"Suppose that the ballast shoulder was only eight inches; wouldn't that do just as well?"

"It might."

"Then get a pencil and a piece of paper," growled Harriman, "sit down, and figure up the quantity and the cost of an eight-inch shoulder of ballast, as compared with an eighteen-inch, on 9,000 miles of track."

For officers facing this inquisition whenever Harriman swung down the line, every question was a bullet too swift and true to dodge, boring relentlessly into its hapless target. "Going on an inspection trip with him was an ordeal," sighed Felton. "I have been on many of them, and was always glad to get out more or

Cold work: A track crew, working ahead of the track-laying machine, lays rails on the frigid Wyoming plains in 1900. (Union Pacific Museum Collection)

less alive. He noticed everything; he asked you about everything, and he compared what he saw and what he heard with what he had seen and heard on all previous trips over the same line."[10]

Ballast was but one component of a good roadbed. Larger equipment required heavier rails to bear the load, and a good railroad kept its track stable by replacing worn ties on a regular basis. The usual practice was to lay heavier new rails on the main line, then use the old rails taken up to replace still older ones on branch lines or sidings. Through this domino effect the entire line got upgraded over time if the company kept steadily at the work.

According to myth, Harriman inherited a road still laid mostly with the lightweight fifty-six-pound rail that had once been the standard on western roads. In fact, the Union Pacific of 1899 had only 5 miles of this rail on its entire 1,929-mile main line. About 40 percent of this track had sixty- or sixty-seven-pound rail, and 59 percent had seventy-pound or more rail. What Harriman did was nudge these standards even higher and apply them to other roads he absorbed into the system that were in much worse shape than the Union Pacific main line.[11]

In this area the real Harriman revolution took place less on the Union Pacific than on the Oregon lines he recaptured for the company. By 1902 the system's main-line mileage had expanded to 3,895, of which about 25 percent still had less than seventy-pound rail. Seven years later, 63 percent of the system's 4,045 miles had eighty-pound or heavier rail; the rest had seventy- or seventy-five-pound. Large sums also went to renewing ties every year until the entire system conformed to the high standard demanded by Harriman.[12]

Creating a fast, smooth-riding track was a huge project, but it didn't go far enough for Harriman. The line itself was flawed in several places. During the spring of 1899 Harriman came home from another inspection trip and announced that the road needed still larger expenditures to make it first-rate. He was ready to transform Berry's enticing map of line changes into reality despite the enormous costs and engineering difficulties. In this work Harriman relied heavily on Burt and Berry, driving them in his usual relentless way first to decide which projects to take up and then to push the work along. "He never measured what the capacity of a man might be," observed Berry wearily, "but just simply piled on work, expecting it to be taken care of."[13]

Berry withstood the pressure because the work was enough to make any engineer sing with joy. Few of his breed ever got the chance or the resources to redesign a major railroad. The work would be fiendishly difficult because on a single-track road like the Union Pacific construction trains and crews would have to operate around the normal flow of traffic and compete with it for equipment. The project would be a feat of logistics no less than of imagination.[14]

The greatest challenge lay in the Black Hills west of Cheyenne. Sherman Hill, the highest point on the line, stood 8,247 feet above sea level and required a fleet of helper engines to assist trains up the slope. The nearby bridge at Dale Creek, 130 feet high and 650 feet long, floated like a gossamer apparition. Both were bottlenecks on a division that had the most traffic and worst weather on the system. At altitudes averaging above 6,000 feet winter descended in September and lingered until May, punctuated by storms of unbelievable ferocity.[15]

The way to deal with Sherman Hill and Dale Creek, Berry concluded after looking at the profiles, was to eliminate them altogether. By relocating thirty miles of track and boring an 1,800-foot tunnel through solid granite, he could cross the hill at a point 236 feet lower than the original line. In the spring of 1900 the silence of the Black Hills was shattered by the arrival of a work force at Sherman that ultimately totaled 131,332 men. Eight giant steam shovels swung into place followed by fifteen locomotives each hauling a string of dump cars. A two-mile spur was built to handle supplies from the main line. Electric lights strung along the site enabled crews to dig around the clock.[16]

On paper, the tasks were elemental: bore through Sherman Hill and fill up Dale Creek. From May until December one shift of workmen after another gouged at the tunnel headings with powerful pneumatic drills, averaging less

The big dig: Work goes forward on the tunnel at Sherman Hill, the highest point on the Union Pacific line. The opening is visible at the center of this J. E. Stimson photograph. (Union Pacific Museum Collection)

than five feet a day and blasting where possible. The rock had to be hauled out by teams, the dirt chewed up by horse-drawn plows. At Dale Creek endless trains of Rodger cars rumbled across trestles, dumping their loads of fill into a crevice that swallowed 475,000 cubic yards of gravel. Once completed, the new embankment stood 120 feet high and 900 feet long.

When the new line opened in June 1901, it was a third of a mile longer but had a standard grade of 43 feet compared with 68 to 98 feet per mile on the old line. Much curvature had also been eliminated, and W. L. Park skirted objections by other officers to convince Harriman that the original line should be upgraded into a second track over the summit. Once presented with the argument, it took Harriman about a minute to decide that Park was correct.[17]

Whole armies of engineers and crews swarmed across Wyoming and Utah, tackling one project after another, dodging trains and sometimes tripping over each other. One engineer named T. J. Wyche, sent to make a report, hunted up a foreman he knew and asked, "Jerry, when do you expect to finish this part of the work?"

"Bejabbers, Tommy, I don't know," sighed Jerry, mopping his brow. "If y'ill take away these al-jay-bray min, I'll do it in tin days."[18]

Wyche took the hint and pulled off the younger engineers who were getting in the way. Some of the engineers thought even less of the crews. "One of the greatest annoyances to which the contractor is subjected in this section," sniffed one, "is the worthless, thriftless class of men he has to depend upon for labor."[19]

The "spider web" bridge: A train crosses the notorious "spider web" bridge across Dale Creek, erected in 1876 as the second of three spans, all of which gave passengers a heart-stopping thrill. (Union Pacific Museum Collection)

Everyone felt the lash as the work became another of those tests of manhood that railroad men relished. "Of course, men fell by the wayside," snorted Park. "The pace was terrific; those without brain and brawn got out of the way. The elimination was, however, the survival of the fittest; there was no favoritism; those who made good were remembered, those who did not were forgotten."[20]

The survivors sweated and shivered their way across the bleak, rugged terrain, altering the line in a dozen places between Laramie and Ogden, Utah. Three cutoffs between Howell and Dana in Wyoming swallowed a staggering 5.4 million cubic yards of fill. So much curvature was eliminated that in one four-mile stretch the new line crossed the old one seven times. Three miles west of Green River the new line carved its way through some heavy shale ledges embedded with petrified fish. The weary crews hacking out this longest cut on the line promptly dubbed it "Fish cut."[21]

On one bad section between Leroy, Wyoming, and the Bear River, Berry hit upon a way to reduce twenty-one miles to ten, cut the grade by a third, and eliminate 1,371 degrees of curvature by boring a tunnel 5,900 feet long. When work began on the Aspen tunnel in the spring of 1899, however, it soon turned

The big fill: Train no. 5 pauses while two unidentified men have some fun on the new Dale Creek fill. The line was shifted and the bridge torn down and replaced with this fill 900 feet long and 120 feet high. (Union Pacific Museum Collection)

into a nightmare. The early borings revealed limestone on the east portal and shale on the west, with seams of coal, oil, and water in between. Openings drilled one day shifted or closed up entirely by the next. The reason soon became clear: carboniferous shale, once exposed to air, tended to swell with devastating force in unpredictable directions.[22]

Doggedly the crews attacked the tunnel again and again only to be frustrated. Gas explosions hurled men, mules, and beams out of the tunnel like toys. When the gas abated, flooding overwhelmed the pumps and drove the men out. The shifting surfaces required constant reinforcement to stay in place. It took two and a half years before the Aspen tunnel, with rails embedded in thick concrete, finally opened. Harriman exulted in this triumph because results mattered more to him than cost or even casualties.

Between 1899 and 1902 large appropriations sailed through the executive committee with a speed that made their approval little more than a formality. Harriman trampled over every obstacle, beat down every objection, listened eagerly to every proposal to modernize the road. By 1903 the only major blemish

Something old, something new: A train glides along the new line through the shale backdrop of the Fish cut. The old line can be seen just below it. (Union Pacific Museum Collection)

still on the main line was the infamous "oxbow" just west of Omaha. This legacy of unwise meddling in the original survey had become a bottleneck for the traffic flowing through the road's eastern terminus. Berry had no trouble selling the project to Harriman; he had long since figured out how the boss's mind worked. A modern double-track line could shorten the line from twenty-one to twelve miles, cut the grade eighteen feet, and eliminate 260 degrees of curvature. Current business did not justify so large an expenditure, Berry conceded, but a traffic increase of 25 percent would make the investment pay.[23]

That was all Harriman needed to hear. His thinking always raced past current conditions to future needs. The project got swift approval but inched along because of the heavy work required. To cross the Big Papillion and Little Papillion Creeks, for example, the engineers had to construct one embankment 65 feet high and 5,600 feet long and another 89 feet high and 3,100 feet long. By one estimate, the crews had to excavate a total of 2.9 million cubic yards of earth and fill 4 million cubic yards of embankment. When the new Lane cutoff finally opened in May 1908, it was the last link in Harriman's modernized line.[24]

The transformation was astonishing. By 1909 the Union Pacific had rebuilt 253 miles of its main line and Kansas division alone. The new railroad was 54

How it was done: Cars in a long string take turns dumping their loads onto a large fill for the Lane cutoff. (Union Pacific Museum Collection)

miles shorter, had 4,470 feet less grade, and lost enough curvature for nearly twenty-six complete circles. The roadbed had been widened to a standard of 20 feet and ballasted. Most of it had been laid with eighty- or ninety-pound rail on new ties of uniform size with heavier tie plates. Veteran railroaders shook their heads in wonderment. No less distinguished a passenger than President William McKinley paid Harriman the highest tribute. Traveling over the Union Pacific in 1901 with his invalid wife, McKinley pronounced its smooth ride the equal of the Pennsylvania.[25]

Sometimes the change caught Harriman himself by surprise. In May 1906 he

The big picture: A broader view of the ninety-five-foot-high fill being constructed for the Lane cutoff. (Union Pacific Museum Collection)

made what proved to be a record dash across the continent, running from San Francisco to New York in seventy-one hours and twenty-seven minutes, an average speed of 45.6 miles an hour including all stops. Early one morning east of Cheyenne he sent for the superintendent, who arrived at the stateroom to find Harriman shaving. "Why are we running so slowly?" growled Harriman between strokes.

"Slowly?" stammered the superintendent. "Why, we are running sixty-five miles an hour."

Harriman paused, then raised his window shade and looked outside for a few moments. "Are we on time?" he asked.

"Yes sir, to the minute."

There was another pause. "This track rides a little smoother than I expected it would," Harriman said finally, returning to the mirror.[26]

Heavier equipment and a wider roadbed required larger and stronger bridges. Under Harriman the Union Pacific replaced nearly nineteen miles of old wooden bridges with either embankments or new steel or concrete spans. Double-tracking also posed a problem for bridges, and its day had come. "For a long time it has been evident," noted Burt in November 1899, "that the West has outgrown single-track trunk lines and was ready for such roadbeds as are the rule in the East." Other transcontinental roads had ducked this task because of the cost, but Harriman merely piled it on top of all the other work without flinching at the price tag. By the spring of 1910 half the main line had a second track in operation. It also got longer side tracks and more of them.[27]

Every aspect of the railroad's operation took on a fresh look as Harriman goaded his officers to replace not only old equipment but old ways of doing things as well. At water stops the road used huge tubs holding about twenty-five thousand gallons set in an enclosed shed with a stove underneath to keep the water from freezing. Windmills pushed the water to the locomotive; when the wind failed, section hands or the train crew had to man the pumps. Harriman retired the tubs in favor of steel vats with a capacity of sixty thousand gallons using small steam or gasoline engines to pump the water. Pipelines were built into regions lacking good water, and water softeners were installed to keep impurities out of engines.[28]

Coal chutes got similar treatment. The old ones were little more than platforms where coal was either shoveled into engines by hand or carried aboard in boxes by the brakeman. The new breed used chutes with a double track that received coal in huge bins and ran it via conveyor to the top of another chute, where crushers reduced it to engine size. There were also sand bins allowing locomotives to take on sand at the same time and sometimes a water crane as well.[29]

Nothing dramatized the transformation more than the emphasis given to installing a system of automatic block signals on the line. Automatic signals were still a rarity on American railroads when Harriman became a convert to them. "Without electric block signals it is impossible to move our trains closer together than forty-five minutes," he explained. "With the electric block signals we can move trains ten minutes apart. That will give us more use of our tracks, permit the handling of a greater volume of freight and passengers without additional expense for main line, and also increase the safety of both passengers and freight."[30]

As the major line changes wound down, Harriman stepped up the installation of block signals. Within four years the new signals covered the entire main line and most of the Kansas division. Here too Harriman blazed a trail. By 1909 his lines already had five thousand miles of automatic block signals; twelve years later, the amount on all American railroads totaled only thirty-nine thousand miles.[31]

Nothing on the Union Pacific escaped the chairman's eye. The Omaha shops were enlarged and given electric lights, central heating, and new machinery to improve efficiency. Along the line the company erected 58 new stockyards, a dozen icehouses, 45 section houses, 36 depots, 7 roundhouses, and 274 other

Repair central: An uncharacteristically quiet and tidy view of the refurbished Omaha machine shop in 1903. (Union Pacific Museum Collection)

buildings. Old section houses, most of them little more than weathered shacks, were knocked down in favor of two-story buildings with stone foundations and plaster walls. Laborers got comfortable bunkhouses, agents and dispatchers cottages with such amenities as indoor plumbing. Some older depots were little more than shacks on the weather-beaten doors of which could still be found horses, wild animals, and other graffiti carved by passing Indians. In their place Harriman installed modern buildings with steam heat and pleasant waiting rooms.[32]

The telegraph line had not gone far beyond the original system of two wires on small, odd-sized poles and powered by gravity batteries with repeating offices (which received messages and repeated them) every two hundred miles. Harriman had larger poles put up and strung with heavier copper wire, thirty thousand miles worth, run by dynamos instead of batteries, with circuits every five hundred to a thousand miles. While the railroad needed the telegraph, Harriman wanted something faster and got the company busy installing telephone lines on the system.[33]

Appearance also mattered to Harriman. He prodded officers to install parks at terminals along the line. Not even the alkali desert of Wyoming could thwart his zeal. On one inspection trip he paused at the coal-mining town of Rock Springs and eyed the barren landscape in disgust. "Why don't you put in a little park here?" he asked the superintendent. "Some green grass and a little shrubbery would freshen things up wonderfully."

A local resident standing next to him shook his head. "Mr. Harriman, there is not a sprig of grass in Rock Springs," he said mournfully. "The percentage of alkali in the soil is an absolute bar to its growth."

"Nothing is impossible," snapped Harriman, his eyes behind their thick lenses gleaming at the challenge.

Before long a procession of cars filled with good quality soil began rolling into Rock Springs. Their load was spread around the depot until there was enough to sustain grass, shrubs, and even small trees. The same treatment was applied to Green River, Rawlins, and other spots until the depots became little oases of greenery in the desert. Harriman liked these parks because they also served as a vivid example to employees of doing things the right way and taking pride in the results.[34]

Nothing pleased Harriman more than to see the road match the state of perfection imprinted in his own mind. While running down the line on an inspection tour, he came to a section of track that had been put in top-notch shape. He stared at it beaming with pride, then crowed to superintendent W. L. Park, "a man who would not gladly pay to ride over a railroad line like this ought to be forced to pay to ride in a vehicle with an oxteam furnishing the motive power."[35]

In that moment of pride could be found a reflection of Harriman's creative vision. The one perfect section of track became the model for a whole railroad, for entire systems of railroads. It embodied Harriman's demonic urge to transform chaos into order by applying imagination, common sense, and unflagging energy. He would remake the Union Pacific as he had Arden, as he would any human endeavor that caught his attention. The only thing Harriman was content to leave alone was nature, perhaps because he saw in its beauty and majesty a symmetry all its own.

The new line at Sherman Hill suffered one casualty in the form of a large stone monument erected by the company in 1882 to honor Oakes and Oliver Ames, the shovel manufacturers who had played leading roles in building the original Union Pacific. The monument had been placed at the highest point on the line, where it now stood in isolation, an abandoned relic of another era, no longer even visible to passing trains. Harriman neither needed nor wanted any such display; the new Union Pacific itself was the only monument he required.

Harriman's own monument was far more impressive. In one decade he lavished $160 million on the Union Pacific: $40 million for new equipment, $18 million for line changes, $8 million for second track, $32 million for other betterments, and $62 million for the construction and acquisition of other lines. In return he got the most efficient railroad for its size in the West and probably the entire nation. On its smoother, straighter roadbed a new breed of equipment ran in longer trains with larger loads on faster schedules at a time when traffic poured onto it in unprecedented volume.[36]

Harriman was right in his belief that a flood of business was coming, and his modernization enabled the Union Pacific to cope with it better than most roads. Between 1899 and 1909 the mileage operated rose 36 percent and the amount of tonnage carried more than tripled. Yet the company handled this crush of traffic despite increasing its fleet of engines only 11 percent and cars of all types 20 percent, thanks to larger payloads. An average train in 1909 hauled 552 tons of freight, nearly double the 280 tons it had carried in 1898. While the number of loaded cars per train rose 26 percent, the amount of freight hauled jumped 97 percent. The new freight cars averaged 20.4 tons of payload per car in 1909 compared to 11.9 tons in 1898.[37]

The blend of new equipment and an efficient roadway reduced the operating ratio (ratio of operating expenses to gross earnings) from 63.6 percent in 1898 to 47.2 percent in 1909 even though costs rose steadily and rates were held in check. In the old days railroad managers kept the operating ratio low by spending as little as possible on maintenance and letting the road run down. Harriman did it by modernizing the property so that trains could run at the lowest possible cost. This enabled the Union Pacific to reap large profits even at low rates.

Nothing proved the value of Harriman's foresight more than the fact that even the new Union Pacific had to scramble to meet the demands on it. The traffic crashing down on railroads dwarfed the wildest predictions of managers and swamped facilities everywhere. In the East the mighty Pennsylvania and New York Central systems staggered beneath the load. "Traffic is so heavy now on all roads," noted one analyst in 1905, "that no old car can be spared so long as it hangs together, and the demand for new equipment is so heavy that no road can begin to get what it wants from the equipment companies. The Harriman companies are in better condition in this respect than any others."[38]

In vain did Harriman's officers struggle to keep ahead of the demand. In 1900 they were told to prepare estimates of all items their departments would need during the next five years. "We grew so fast," sighed Berry, "that this statement was not worth the paper it was written on at the end of twelve months." A crisis gripped the entire American rail system in mid-decade that led to clogged schedules and soaring accident rates. The Union Pacific did not escape this gridlock, but it fared better than most, as can be seen by looking at an obscure factor called meeting points.[39]

In 1897 fifteen freight and four passenger trains ran daily on the Union Pacific main line. By 1909 the number had increased to twenty freight and seven passenger trains. This meant that train density (number of trains per mile of road) had increased 82 percent while traffic density (gross ton miles per mile of road) had leaped 186 percent. A key to efficient operation on a crowded single-track line lay in the number of meeting points or places where two trains meet and one must lose time giving way. Nothing slowed schedules more than too many meeting points.[40]

Between 1897 and 1909 the number of meeting points on the Union Pacific rose 235 percent. Enormous as this increase seems, its effect was mitigated by the company's new ability to run fewer trains carrying heavier loads, thereby cutting the number of meeting points. If the improvements wrought by Harriman are factored out and the Union Pacific operated in 1909 as it had in 1896, train density would have increased 180 percent and meeting points a staggering 689 percent.

Harriman's faith in the revival of the West paid off long before the congestion crisis hit. By May 1898 earnings on the Union Pacific looked so solid that talk of a dividend on the preferred stock surfaced only three days after Harriman became chairman of the executive committee. Before he returned from his fateful inspection trip in July, Wall Street was convinced that a dividend would be forthcoming. Harriman's own views are unclear and may reflect the fact that he did not yet have enough power to get his way. The Dutch holders were pushing hard for a dividend and skeptical about all the work being done on the road. At one point Harriman had to summon Berry to his office to explain to a Dutch banker the necessity for plowing so much money back into the property. The executive committee and the board were both divided on the subject.[41]

In September, after returning from his brief vacation at Paul Smith's, Harriman proposed to the executive committee a 1½ percent dividend on the preferred. Stillman protested that it was sheer folly for a reorganized company with an unproven track record even to think of paying a dividend. Such a course, he added ominously, would soon land the Union Pacific back in the hands of the receivers. But Stillman was too good a team player to split the committee. Rather than oppose the dividend outright, he simply abstained.[42]

Within a few months Stillman had occasion to smile at the recollection of this debate. As traffic swamped the railroad and earnings continued to soar, the surging tide of McKinley prosperity carried Union Pacific stock prices steadily higher. From a low of 45⅞ in March 1898 the preferred topped 74 by the year's end, while the common moved from 16⅛ to 44⅝. Those who had bought early reaped large rewards; those who bought early and continued to hold would see these first returns dwarfed.[43]

The brash newcomer had impressed the bankers and other directors in the manner they most appreciated. The thoughtful Stillman soon discarded the advice to be wary about Harriman and formed his own impression. Gradually his suspicion thawed into trust and then admiration. Schiff too found his opinion of Harriman growing steadily. Here was a man who might do great things not only for the Union Pacific but also for its new banking ally, Kuhn, Loeb.

10 Going Back Together

Almost immediately after the purchase of the Kansas lines, steps were taken to
induce the owners of the Oregon Short Line and the Oregon Railroad & Navigation
Company to exchange their stock for the stocks of the Union Pacific. In the fall of 1898,
to help this exchange along, the first dividend was declared on the Union Pacific
preferred stock. For the first time the credit of the Union Pacific was called upon to
acquire a railroad.

—C. M. Keys, *"Harriman: The Man in the Making"*

Harriman's rage for order extended into every corner of his life, including his family. No one was a more devoted or attentive father even at the busiest times. Every evening after supper, before Harriman plunged into work, he played with the boys in the study of the brownstone at One East 55th Street in New York, where the family lived for a time. One of their games required scattering pieces of paper around the room. Afterward Roland had to pick them all up and put them in a special drawer of his father's desk.[1]

The children knew their father's demand for order only too well. He loved to bring them presents but never let them cut the string to open them. It had to be untied and wound up, the paper removed and folded, and then both put away before the gift could be enjoyed. "In everything he did," said Averell, "he took command, no matter what was going on. Even if we went for a walk, he'd tell us where he wanted to go. He knew what he wanted to do."[2]

This overpowering sense of direction filled the vacuum of those who lacked it, including friends who fell into his orbit. During the summer of 1907 Harriman took the family up to their Pelican Bay lodge nestled on Klamath Lake in southern Oregon. He invited a friend, the celebrated naturalist John Muir, to spend the summer with them. Muir hesitated, saying that he had a book to write.

"Well, you come up to the Lodge and I will show you how to write a book," countered Harriman. "The trouble with you is that you are too slow in your beginnings. You plan and brood too much. Begin, begin, begin! Put forth what you have to say in the first words that come to mind, just as you talk, until all that's to go into the book is got down. Then correct, transpose, add, strike out and change as much as you like. Hammer away at it until it suits you. Come on and get something begun." Muir went to the lodge, where Harriman put his private secretary at the naturalist's disposal with orders to take down everything he said. Before the summer's end, Muir found that he had the beginnings of more than one book.[3]

The lodge itself was a monument to that peculiar twilight zone in Harriman's mind where wilderness and order merged. Getting there required a trek more daunting than that to Paul Smith's. The family rode the train to end of track, then drove fifty miles by coach to the rough little town of Klamath Falls. Next morning they took a launch twenty-five miles up Klamath Lake to the lodge, where the only other visitor was a steamboat that periodically dropped mail and provisions.[4]

There Harriman found his wilderness paradise. The lodge stood near some magnificent crystal springs at the head of Pelican Bay, with Klamath Lake on one side and lush meadows on the other, their serene colors rolling into distant hills and mountains crowded with trees. Flocks of waterfowl and leaping trout skimmed the mirror surface of the lake, while deer and bear prowled the nearby forest. The weather was cool even in summer, the air fresh and invigorating for any kind of outing. Harriman reveled in long tramps through the woods or boat rides across the lake, stalking game or nagging fish beneath the pristine waters.[5]

He could not have been more removed from the grind of the business world, yet he was not distant at all. Harriman could not leave paradise entirely untouched by civilization; despite the lodge's remote location, he had a telegraph wire strung to it so that he could keep abreast of affairs. He could turn off the telegraph whenever he pleased, but it was always there—a reminder of that other world where nature had not imposed so perfect an order.

The Union Pacific lacked system in every sense of the word. Five years of receivership marred by financial and legal wrangling had dismembered the original system like a body at autopsy, leaving only the trunk intact and other parts scattered about the West with no assurance that they would ever be put back together again. The dissection had been messy and prolonged, but for Harriman it served one useful purpose: he could assess each lost limb on its merits and retrieve only those he really wanted.

The reborn Union Pacific owned 323 miles of small branch lines that the reorganization committee had acquired. By the end of 1899 Harriman had recaptured another 1,182 miles of branch line for the company. Other roads were left to their fate because they had seldom earned their way, especially the Union Pacific, Denver & Gulf, an amalgam of twelve roads that had been merged in

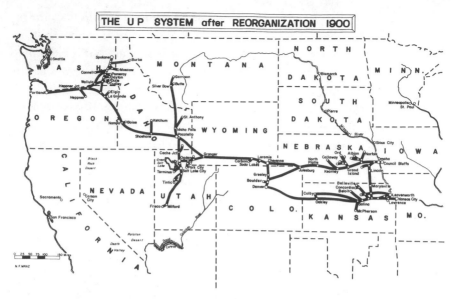

THE U P SYSTEM after REORGANIZATION 1900

Together again: The Union Pacific system reconstructed by Harriman as of 1900.
(Union Pacific Museum Collection)

1890 and never lived up to expectations. Harriman let it go except for one 152-mile branch he spent a year negotiating to get back. He let another road, the St. Joseph & Grand Island, drift until its performance improved, then scooped it up in 1902.[6]

The difficulties in reassembling this part of the system paled before the struggle to regain the most valuable limb of all: the Oregon lines. For thirty years the image of the Northwest as a cornucopia of traffic had enticed railroad men into spending huge sums to build roads on the promise of what was to come. The quixotic Henry Villard, a journalist turned entrepreneur whose vision inspired German investors to sink millions into his companies, was the first to open the region by patching together a motley assortment of rail and steamer lines known as the Oregon Railway & Navigation Company from Portland to Huntington at the Oregon-Idaho border. His bold gamble had spurred the Union Pacific to build the Oregon Short Line, a branch from its main line to Huntington.[7]

Reckless and careless of details in the way of dreamers, Villard paid too much for everything in a frontier region where traffic would not flow freely for years. When the long dormant Northern Pacific Railroad sprang to life and began laying rails toward Tacoma, Villard created a holding company to control both the Northern Pacific and Navigation only to see his empire collapse in 1884. After losing most of his fortune in a vain effort to stem the disaster, he fled to

Europe, leaving behind a jumble of corporate debris that haunted the Union Pacific and the region for decades.[8]

Through the 1880s the Northwest raged with convoluted intrigues and fierce railroad wars as the Union Pacific and Northern Pacific struggled for supremacy. After a lengthy battle, the Union Pacific managed to gain control of the Navigation Company and its line into Portland, but the cost nearly sank the company. In 1893 both roads toppled into receivership, leaving the field open to a formidable new competitor, James J. Hill.[9]

The best known and most respected railroad man in the nation, Hill staked his claim to the Northwest by driving his Great Northern line through the rugged Cascades to Puget Sound. Unlike Villard, he was worthy of the challenge. A short, stocky man with a large head dominated by a grizzled beard, Hill had made his reputation by building top-quality roads and managing them efficiently. His earthy, no-nonsense manner appealed to the public, and he had grown adept at using his popularity to promote himself and his railroads.[10]

Extending his Great Northern to the Pacific Coast had been a bold and brilliant gamble. Hill spared no effort to find the best route west so that he would always have the edge in operating costs. In this aim, and in his zeal for good management, he had no peer among railroad men until Harriman came onto the stage. During the hard times of the 1890s Hill quietly fortified his position in the Northwest for the clashes he knew must come when the depression lifted. He was content to watch the Oregon Short Line and Navigation Company drift out of the Union Pacific system and resisted overtures to involve him in reorganizing the Union Pacific.[11]

But Hill did inject himself into the Northern Pacific reorganization and in the process drew closer to the banker who ultimately did the work. J. P. Morgan welcomed the help and assured Hill that the reorganized Northern Pacific would be his to run once the legal barriers were removed. Control of the Northern Pacific and his own Great Northern would allow Hill to forge in the Northwest the rational harmony of interests he and Morgan craved. And should any dispute arise, Hill had a decisive hole card to play: he owned the best built, most efficient railroad and could win any rate war.

This duet to harmony, however, soon struck some sour notes. The key to the Northern Pacific reorganization was a pet Morgan device known as a voting trust, which gave him undisputed control of the new company for five years. Hill chafed at the voting trust, especially when Morgan proceeded to run the company as an independent system despite his earlier pledge. Then Morgan named as president of the Northern Pacific Charles S. Mellen, a man nobody liked except Jupiter himself. As prosperity returned and the Northern Pacific thrived, Mellen took seriously his charge of pursuing an independent course in the Northwest. Friction soon arose over several issues. While Hill scowled in frustration, a wild card in the form of E. H. Harriman unexpectedly reshuffled the balance of power.[12]

From the start of his tenure at the Union Pacific Harriman eyed the Northwest with keen interest. On his first inspection trip in 1898, while the train rattled over the Oregon Short Line from Butte to Salt Lake City, he sat up late one evening listening to W. H. Bancroft wax eloquent on the prospects of the road. Then a superintendent, Bancroft soon became one of Harriman's most able and trusted lieutenants.

"How much will the Short Line earn this year?" asked Harriman.

"Six million dollars," replied Bancroft.

"Aren't you putting it too high in your enthusiasm?" Harriman challenged.

"No sir," Bancroft insisted. "Not only will it earn six million this year, but in ten years it will earn twelve million."

Harriman demanded to know the grounds for this assertion. He was not familiar with the country, but the more Bancroft talked, the more its possibilities fired his mind. His observations reinforced Harriman's conviction that the Union Pacific must reclaim its line to Portland and find a way to end two decades of warfare that had resolved nothing. Here was a challenge worthy of Harriman's zest for battle, a wilderness crying for the order he could give it. As always, he thought less of the obstacles than of the opportunities and plunged into the arena without regard for who or what might oppose him.

Harriman got involved in recapturing the Short Line even before he became chairman. Once reorganized early in 1897, the Short Line had pursued an independent course by canceling its old traffic contract with the Union Pacific. Harriman joined the reorganization committee in quietly buying up a majority of Short Line stock during the winter of 1898. By September Harriman could proclaim Union Pacific ownership of the Short Line "closed beyond all doubt."[13]

The Navigation Company was a nightmare of complexities thanks to Villard's tangled legacy. Although the Short Line owned two-thirds of Navigation's common stock, control of the company rested with the $11 million of preferred stock. These shares had been locked up in a voting trust for the joint interest of the Union Pacific, Short Line, Great Northern, and Northern Pacific. The trustees had the power to dominate Navigation's board for ten years or until the company paid 20 percent in dividends on the preferred. Under this arrangement Navigation remained an independent line ruled jointly by three competing systems.[14]

The object was to make Navigation a kind of Switzerland, serving all its connectors impartially and remaining neutral in times of war. Unfortunately, this Switzerland was ruled by suspicious rivals with conflicting agendas for their futures. For two decades rail diplomacy in the West had groped for ways to reduce competition by sharing facilities. Too often the result was not peace but the construction of duplicate lines on routes where the business could barely support one. It was this dreary pattern that the combatants in the Northwest hoped to avoid, but the three men on whom peace depended, while very different from one another, were all tough, ambitious leaders accustomed to having things their own way.

By the summer of 1898, then, forces were gathering to disrupt an uneasy balance of power. The prize at stake was the burgeoning flow of traffic from the triangle formed by Spokane, Portland, and Seattle along with western Idaho. Although both northern roads had breached the mighty Cascades, the best route into Portland remained Navigation's low-lying line along the south bank of the Columbia River. At Umatilla on its eastern end the line formed a "Y," with the southern fork meeting the Short Line at Huntington and the northern fork connecting with the Northern Pacific. The territory between the forks had been hotly contested by Navigation and the Northern Pacific for years.[15]

Peace among the rival systems depended on their ability to obtain equal access to Navigation's line on reasonable terms and settle disputes over who had the right to build what branches where. If either northern road grew unhappy over existing arrangements, it could build another line to Portland along the north bank of the Columbia. There was also friction over connections between Portland and Puget Sound. The only existing route, owned by the Northern Pacific, was an inefficient one. In 1890 Hill had signed an agreement with the Union Pacific to build a joint line. The project was abandoned when the Union Pacific ran into financial trouble, but it could be revived at any time.[16]

Hill was especially anxious to keep Navigation neutral because it enabled him to reach Portland without the expense of building there. But Hill also liked neutrality with an edge, and in this case he hoped the edge was A. L. Mohler, the capable president of Navigation. Mohler had spent fifteen years on Hill's roads and was widely regarded as Hill's man.[17]

The first round of confrontations came during the summer of 1898, when Harriman was still preoccupied with modernizing the Union Pacific. The slithery Mellen was the only major player who did not control the road he managed. While ultimately responsible to Morgan, he dealt mainly with Charles H. Coster, Morgan's able but overworked partner, who had done most of the spadework in the Northern Pacific reorganization. Aware that Coster was too busy to peer constantly over his shoulder, Mellen pursued an aggressive policy of putting down new branches wherever he could get away with it. This tactic brought him into conflict first with Hill and then with Harriman.[18]

Both leaders were furious over Mellen's tendency to throw down branch lines like gauntlets in disputed territory. Harriman complained that Mellen seemed "to want to get a line through the heart of the Navigation System without giving any proper consideration therefor." When Hill offered to mediate one dispute with Mellen in July 1898, Harriman agreed to join him in Chicago. This may have been their first extended meeting, and both were anxious to get a feel for the other's ability. Harriman left no record of his impression, but he was quick to stake out his own agenda. A few days after the parley, he told Horace Burt that the most important matter facing them was "obtaining absolute control" of Navigation.[19]

As a first step, Harriman agreed to a conference to settle outstanding issues. The disputes traced back to an 1897 contract in which bankers representing the Northern Pacific and Great Northern roads agreed to keep Navigation neutral and open to all connecting lines. They also authorized selling some of the Navigation stock acquired by the northern lines to the Union Pacific if they thought it would expedite the peace process. Harriman was eager to get hold of this stock, but no agreement could be reached with so many controversies hanging fire.

On the morning of October 3 ten distinguished gentlemen assembled at the Northern Pacific office on Broad Street for what amounted to a summit conference on two sticky issues: the territorial or branch matter and the relationship of the two northern roads to Navigation. Joining Harriman, Hill, and Mellen were Coster, Schiff, banker W. L. Bull, chairman of Navigation's board, Northern Pacific vice-president Daniel S. Lamont, railroad managers Samuel Spencer and E. B. Thomas, and corporation lawyer Francis Lynde Stetson.[20]

The internal dynamics of this group had some subtle shadings. Lamont, the former secretary of war, was an old confidant of Hill's. Schiff too was a longtime friend of Hill's, but the Union Pacific reorganization had moved him closer to Harriman. Stetson had been the legal architect of Standard Oil; he and Spencer lent their expertise to Morgan's firm. Thomas headed the Erie Railroad, another reorganization that had brought Morgan into conflict with Harriman. The brilliant but frail Coster was more the voice of Northern Pacific than Mellen, to the latter's chagrin.[21]

Coster led off by explicating the 1897 contract and the disputes that threatened to nullify it. For the Northern Pacific, these involved territorial issues. Hill chimed in with a plea for peace and a warning that it could not be obtained without a guarantee of Navigation's neutrality. "Any contract that does not cover the matter desired to be covered," he lectured, "is not worth signing." But when pressed for specific suggestions, Hill had nothing more to offer than his standard demand that all parties should have "equal relations and equal terms with the Huntington gateway."

Schiff then turned to Coster and said he understood what the Union Pacific and the Great Northern wanted when they bought their shares of Navigation stock, but what was the Northern Pacific after? "It was to establish good connections with the Navigation," replied Coster, "but above all that it was to co-operate in a scheme which was supposed to insure . . . permanent harmony in that territory."

Schiff nodded, then asked, "Now, what do you propose to do to get this harmony?"

The primary issue, Coster stressed, was territory. The Northern Pacific had several lines south of the Snake River, a region Navigation claimed as its own; Navigation had put branches north of the river, which the Northern Pacific regarded as its domain. The logical solution was a division of territory: since the river was a natural boundary, why not have each company agree to keep out of the other's territory?

Harriman listened intently to this exchange, his eyes darting back and forth behind the thick spectacles and his teeth biting absently at the straggly mustache drooping over his lip. "Mr. Coster," he asked abruptly, "when you say that Snake River seems to be a fair boundary division of territory, do you mean it with respect to traffic going east or west?"

"I consider all that territory in that triangle to be Northern Pacific territory," answered Coster.

"Whether it be for business going east or west?" pressed Harriman.

"Both; east and west."

Why? asked Harriman. Navigation was, after all, "the shorter and more natural line." Shifting topics, Harriman admitted being a newcomer to the situation, but to his eyes the February 1897 contract called for joint ownership of Navigation by the Short Line, Great Northern, and Northern Pacific.

"No, I want to dispute that emphatically," said Coster. "That agreement was in my mind based upon the assumption that the Navigation Company was for all time to be an independent company."

But if the bankers intended selling Navigation stock to the Union Pacific and Short Line, countered Harriman, they must have assumed ownership would rest there.

"It was contemplated that the Union Pacific should acquire the Short Line stock," Schiff reminded Coster.

The possibility was recognized, Coster conceded, but he would not yield the point Harriman wanted: that eventually the Short Line and the Union Pacific would control Navigation outright. "The object of the purchase," insisted Coster, "was to delay the consummation of that possibility."

They sparred over the issue for a while longer, the others listening with puzzled expressions, trying to fathom where Harriman was going. Finally he coaxed out of Coster an admission that the bankers thought control of Navigation for five years would enable them to work out some harmonious arrangement before the Union Pacific reacquired the company.

Harriman nodded in satisfaction. "I am not enough of a railroad man to propose a plan," he demurred, "but it seems to me that the Oregon Railroad & Navigation Company should be placed in a position where all three companies should have equal rights." The others looked at him expectantly. "But I do not want to divide territory. That did not seem to be in contemplation when any of these agreements were made."

Coster looked dumbfounded. There would be some kind of agreement, Harriman assured him, but the Union Pacific would not agree to any division of territory.

"Then I do feel very apprehensive," said the crestfallen Coster. Doggedly he resumed his argument for a territorial agreement, but an impasse had been reached. Harriman agreed that harmony was important but added, "I think it inadvisable for political reasons, to agree upon absolute territorial lines." Spencer asked if he had any alternative plan to present; Harriman admitted he did not. The discussion rambled on without changing anyone's views. After agreeing on a carefully worded memorandum that resolved nothing, the grim-faced participants left Broad Street having learned little more than that a tough bargainer had joined their circle.

Without an agreement to restrain him, Mellen went back to his old trick of dangling peace overtures while sending survey teams into the field. Bolstered by support from both Harriman and Hill, Navigation retaliated in November 1898 by chartering a new road to build eight branches in western Idaho and eastern Washington. A month later the company added plans for ten more branches and started work on some of them. As the fight heated up, Harriman rebuffed all efforts by Hill and Coster to get a settlement of the territorial issue.[22]

Late in May 1899 Harriman left on the trip that became the celebrated Alaskan scientific expedition. Although he did not return until August, his shadow loomed over the struggle. In July Navigation's board guaranteed payment of the required dividend on its preferred stock, thereby returning control of the company to the common stock. Since the Short Line owned two-thirds of this stock, no one doubted that the Union Pacific intended to reclaim control. Did this mean that the territorial dispute would burst into open war? Mohler brushed aside inquiries with a cryptic observation that Navigation's construction activities would soon speak for themselves.[23]

Ten months earlier Harriman had not even met Mohler; now he was drawing him and Navigation into his orbit. This shift in allegiance led Hill to complain that Navigation was "no longer neutral as between the Short Line and ourselves." Beneath his alarm lay an ominous feeling that events were fast slipping from his hands. Only a year earlier he had asked who Harriman was; now he was getting an answer he did not like. The question began to haunt him: did Harriman possess the ability to shift the balance of power in the Northwest?[24]

Workhorse: A. L. Mohler, the former Hill lieutenant who became Harriman's tough, hard-driving executive in the Northwest and later president of the Union Pacific. (Union Pacific Museum Collection)

On July 30 the ship bringing Harriman back from Alaska docked at Seattle. He stayed with the scientists until they reached Portland, then joined Burt, Berry, Mohler, and Mellen for a trip across the Navigation line. During this whirlwind journey he came to terms with Mellen on a six-month truce halting the branch construction war between the Northern Pacific and Navigation. The

Northern Pacific then agreed to sell its Navigation preferred stock to "friends" of the Union Pacific, thereby ensuring control by the latter.[25]

Within a few months Navigation returned to the Union Pacific system with Harriman as chairman of its board. "Hereafter," stressed the *Wall Street Journal*, "the Union Pacific Railroad Company is to be considered as owning the entire line from the Missouri River to the Pacific." Long before the formalities wound up, Harriman set about whipping Navigation into shape. "My desire," he informed Mohler, "is that there shall not be the least shadow of suspicion as to our living up in every way to the spirit, as well as the letter, of the agreement between Mr. Mellen and myself." The reason was clear: Harriman wanted Mohler to concentrate on modernizing Navigation's line.[26]

Mohler was about to be introduced to the Harriman formula. As always, it was a breathtaking revelation. Harriman asked for a report on "what expenditures should be made to put our existing railroads in proper condition for economical operation, as well as the collecting of business to best advantage. This should include perhaps some relocation, reduction of grades and curvatures, improvement of terminals, shops, water tanks, motive power, and—particularly favor turning special attention to the improvements already begun on the Columbia River Line. . . . The money thus expended will produce better results than if expended in new and additional lines, and will materially strengthen our position." This request staggered Mohler as it had Berry. Mohler was told not to be deterred by the scale or cost of the work. If, for example, he agreed that work on the Columbia River line should go forward at once, he was to push it "irrespective of whether the expenditures are to be made from income or from some other source." Put simply, Mohler was to do the work and Harriman would find the money.[27]

What is most remarkable about these instructions is their context. Harriman wrote this letter only a week after his return from Alaska. He had been out of touch with events for two months, had discussed matters with no one in New York, and had no authority from the executive committee for such bold and decisive action except that attached to his position as chairman. Yet in those first few days home he defused a conflict with Mellen that had raged for well over a year and driven Hill to despair, toured the Navigation line, talked to the officers on the scene, and issued orders that would cost millions of dollars to implement.

Hill continued to press him for joint ownership of Navigation. In a long letter he reminded Harriman that "with Five million dollars I could build a much better line from our road into Portland and with say Two million more reach the most productive sections of the Navigation Company." This veiled threat so irritated Harriman that he did not even bother to reply. It was left to Schiff to smooth ruffled feathers on both sides.[28]

The whole affair left Schiff apprehensive. As the conflict deepened, he felt himself being pushed into the role of buffer between two men he admired. Hill was an old and cherished friend, but Harriman was fast becoming the mother lode of Kuhn, Loeb. Schiff shuddered at the thought that events might one day force him to choose between them, but his shrewd, clear-sighted mind recognized the possibility as a real one. If a collision of ambitions occurred, Schiff realized in dismay, he would be caught between them.

Once Navigation returned to the fold, Harriman faced the task of integrating the three lines. The key lay in applying economies of scale with a vengeance. He wanted every practice rationalized, simplified, and standardized. Aware that new techniques and technologies were transforming many areas of railroading, Harriman prodded his officers to stay on top of developments. Any innovation, applied to the whole system, could save the company enormous sums.[29]

The task was formidable because togetherness was not a tradition in railroading. The merging of several roads into a system did not necessarily unify them even when management tried to impose harmony. Most were broken down into units presided over by superintendents, who tended to view each other as rivals and operate as autonomously as they dared. Individual identities died hard, and personal ambitions fueled competition as each unit guarded its prerogatives jealously.

Harriman had to cut through these hoary practices if he was to unify operations, cut expenses, and simplify relations between units. He could not afford to have the Union Pacific, Short Line, and Navigation behaving like separate companies or their officers throwing obstacles in the way of one another from force of habit. The trick was to stress the advantages of cooperation and coordination at every level. As a start, he insisted that the officers of all three lines agree on common standards for bridges, buildings, depots, rails, ties, roadway signs, ballast, air brakes, car trucks, locomotives, rolling stock, and a host of other items.

Journalists were fond of dubbing top rail entrepreneurs the "Napoleons" of their field. In this work Harriman deserved the title more literally than most. Every American railroad operated under its own set of rules, which varied widely among companies. Just as Napoleon codified the laws of France, Harriman ordered his general managers to standardize their rules so that everyone operated under the same code. Under Harriman, declared Julius Kruttschnitt, "a uniform policy was followed in all branches of the railroad service on all of the constituent companies. Methods found to be the best on any one of the systems could be applied to all."[30]

The advantages of standardization were great. Equipment could be easily exchanged to relieve temporary shortages. Purchasing and maintenance costs could be slashed, the number of parts stocked reduced, and heavily used items bought in huge quantities for the entire system. Harriman made the mass buying of key items a major priority. In September 1899 he told Burt to discuss tie needs with Mohler and Bancroft. "One party should control the matter for all three companies," he ordered, "and make purchases for benefit of whole system."[31]

Harriman applied the same procedure to everything from rails to rolling stock to bridge material. He shopped carefully for the best price, using the size of his order as leverage even in such supplies as stationery and telegraph blanks. Samples of stationery collected from the different systems were found to range in cost from $1.90 to $11.50 per thousand sheets. A stationer was hired to help design common letterheads for everyone at the $1.90 cost. The same approach was used for telegraph blanks. By adopting a standard size for all the roads and simplifying headings, the company lowered typesetting and printing costs as well as getting more telegram blanks from each standard sheet. It also got better prices by ordering as many as twenty million blanks at one time. The savings from these reforms alone paid for the cost of the stationer twenty-five times over.[32]

No one doubted that the drive for economy and order came directly from the top. Harriman was a hard bargainer who loved to dicker over prices, whether at home or at the office, and who would not pay the smallest bill without knowing it was correct. On one occasion a clerk brought him a bill for some candy along with a check for him to sign. "Who got this candy?" he asked the clerk abruptly.

"The girls," answered the surprised clerk.

"Then get them to initial it, and never bring me a bill that has not been signed by the persons who got the goods."[33]

Difficult or unusual problems always aroused Harriman's competitive fires. One in particular piqued his interest: the gangs who preyed on the Wyoming division of the Union Pacific. There was nothing fancy about their raids. They robbed passing trains and then fled into the rugged North Park country or Brown's Park or the Hole-in-the-Wall country, where posses had no chance of picking up a cold trail. Some, like Butch Cassidy and the Sundance Kid, became the stuff of legend, but to Harriman they were simply a nuisance he determined to put out of business.[34]

If a posse could not reach the scene in time to pick up the bandits' trail, he reasoned, then the logical solution was to put the posse right on the train. He knew a little something about horses, and he could afford to hire the best guides and trackers as special agents. His idea was to put horses capable of traveling a hundred miles a day on trains with the best men he could find as a mobile posse. This strike force could pick up a trail within hours and pursue it relentlessly for days.

So brilliantly did the mobile posse do its work that train robberies ceased on the Union Pacific even though they continued to plague other western roads.

The mobile posse became almost as famous for its exploits as the gangs it tracked. To a later generation, the man enshrined in film as "Mr. E. H. Harriman of the Union Pacific Railroad" was a cold-blooded businessman driving the romance and flavor of the Old West to extinction. In his own time, however, he was simply a cold-blooded businessman imposing his own brand of order on an industry desperately in need of fresh thinking.

11 Going Elsewhere

Practically all of the possible abuses or frauds described in the preceding pages under the caption of stock-watering are found combined in a single instance in recent years—the reorganization of the Chicago & Alton road by the late E. H. Harriman and his associates during the eight years following 1898. The case is an illuminating one; for it shows how an unscrupulous management may, at one and the same time, enormously enrich insiders at the expense of the investing public, and prejudice the interests of shippers, both by crippling the road physically and by creating the need of high rates for service in order to support the fraudulent capitalization.

—*William Z. Ripley,* Railroads: Finance and Organization

When Harriman joined the Union Pacific in 1897, he was an obscure banker whose only railroad connection was the Illinois Central. Three years later he stood on the threshold of a business empire that would catapult him into being the dominant figure in the transportation industry. While his achievement with the Union Pacific would have satisfied the ambitions of most men, it was for him merely a prelude to the foundation of an empire.

Like an alert scout, Harriman had struck a promising trail through the dark and tangled forest of the modern industrial system. He already understood the symbiotic relationship between the financial and rail industries and the ways in which each enriched the other. The more he learned about the essentials of modern railroading, the more he began to probe the riddle of its larger nexus of relationships. He had the ability to examine its character with the cold eye of a clinician, unfettered by conventional wisdom and without regard for political or social obstacles. Nor did financial considerations detain him; they were simply another technical problem to be solved.

At no time did the Union Pacific occupy Harriman's full attention. He remained in charge of the Illinois Central's finance committee and took the job seriously. Although this work took a backseat to the Union Pacific, it continued to influence his strategic thinking. Less than a year after taking charge of the Union Pacific, Harriman got involved in the reorganization of three major railroads: the Baltimore & Ohio, the Kansas City, Pittsburg & Gulf, and the

Chicago & Alton. In each case he applied the formula of modernization that was already beginning to revamp the Union Pacific.

Harriman could not have moved to the national arena without vast financial resources behind him. To reorganize and overhaul rail systems required huge sums of capital, which put Harriman even closer in league with the two giants of finance who became his lifelong associates: Jacob Schiff and James Stillman. The significance of these three ventures went far beyond their effect on the railroads. Like the Union Pacific, they enhanced Harriman's reputation and bound the bankers to him for greater things to come.

By 1900 a formidable alliance had been forged among the three men in which each played a distinctive role. Harriman managed the property, used his formula to modernize it, and arranged its new capital structure. Schiff's firm underwrote the security offerings and handled most of the financing, while Stillman, through his National City Bank and close connections with men like William Rockefeller, mobilized capital for the venture by bringing powerful backers to it. Apart from bringing immense profits to the three allies, this division of labor also redefined the transportation map of America and ultimately provoked a political hailstorm.

The reporters covering the financial beat came early to agreement over the enigmatic James Stillman. He was, in the words of one of them, "the coldest proposition in America." The banking brethren were notorious for being remote and aloof, but none except George F. Baker rivaled the glacial facade of Stillman. Laughter came to his lips with the frequency of leap years. He was an iceberg whose smooth, pleasant features revealed absolutely nothing of the dark complexities swimming beneath their surface.[1]

A short, dark man with small, well-shaped hands and feet, Stillman dressed immaculately and wore a full mustache. His large ears and prominent nose made less impact on those around him than the piercing brown eyes and the sardonic curl of his mouth. He was, said banker Henry Morgenthau, "a perfect example of the well-built man of the world, sartorially correct, soft spoken, with a tendency toward cynical humour, and with a tongue capable of devastating sarcasms." His tastes were urbane and cultivated. He loved the sea and the hills, admired beautiful things but lacked Morgan's passion for buying them, and enjoyed the rituals of an ordered life.[2]

Two years younger than Harriman, Stillman was born in Texas but came to New York as a child. The shy young man showed a remarkable gift for ingratiating himself with older men who came to value his ability. James Woodward, his partner's brother, headed the Hanover National Bank and made young Stillman a director. A seat on the board of the Chicago, Milwaukee & St. Paul Railroad introduced him to the road's major stockholder, William Rockefeller, who be-

Silent partner: The brilliant, velvety James Stillman, who masterminded the rise of National City Bank and became one of Harriman's closest friends and allies. (Baker Library, Harvard Business School)

came one of his closest friends. The alliance between them was later sealed when both of Stillman's daughters married sons of William Rockefeller.[3]

At forty-one Stillman found himself head of a small, sound bank of excellent reputation. Building it up became for him a form of religion. His dream was to do for banks what Harriman was trying to do with railroads: push them into a new era by transforming what they did and how they did it. This meant moving City Bank into investment banking, the fastest growing and most profitable area of finance. The top investment houses like Morgan and Kuhn, Loeb already dominated the origination of security issues and used their extensive overseas connections to peddle them. Some large banks, allies of these firms, took large chunks of their offerings to sell to their own networks of correspondent banks.[4]

Stillman and his bank came late to both ends of the investment business— originating and marketing—but that did not deter him. Apart from being a brilliant financier, he had a gift for forging alliances with men of means. He liked the company of bright, farsighted men who could teach him things, and he filled the board of City Bank with the heads of giant enterprises. By doing this, he tapped the best business minds in America for the absurdly low fee of $400 a year.[5]

Like Harriman, Stillman rose from obscurity to titan in less than a decade, creating by 1907 the prototype of a modern big business bank. In 1895, however, he was still a banker of solid but modest reputation seeking the doorway to his destiny. His first major entry into investment turned out to be the most significant transaction of his career. It was the reorganization of the Union Pacific Railroad.[6]

The alliance with Schiff was a perfect fit for Stillman. Kuhn, Loeb, unlike Morgan, had no large commercial banking business and could not support large issues; instead, it relied on a network of other houses at home and abroad. City Bank offered the resources, Kuhn, Loeb the ability to originate, and both could place securities. Together they could underwrite huge issues not possible by either of them alone. The success of the Union Pacific reorganization demonstrated this ability and cemented their relationship.[7]

The reorganization also brought an unexpected bonus to both bankers. There were two basic sources for large security offerings: rail reorganizations and the wave of mergers that had begun to sweep all sectors of industry. To place these recapitalized ventures on a sound financial footing, the bankers needed someone capable of giving them efficient management. The Union Pacific experience introduced them to the ideal man for the rail industry. Harriman was for them the final piece in an intricate puzzle that promised enormous profits and exciting times for all of them.

Harriman did not have to seek out other projects. His growing reputation as a railroad wizard among his newfound friends brought them to him. Two distinct sets of associates looked to him for help. One revolved around Schiff and his circle; the other consisted of prominent Chicago businessmen and bankers Harriman had come to know through the Illinois Central, including meatpacker Philip D. Armour, Marshall Field, and financier Norman B. Ream. Both groups wanted Harriman in the Baltimore & Ohio Railroad.

The B&O was one of the four trunk lines that dominated traffic between Chicago and the eastern seaboard.* During the depression it too had undergone a reorganization managed in part by Kuhn, Loeb. It was probably Schiff who invited Harriman to join the B&O board. In his deft and graceful way he was looking to solve two problems at once. The B&O needed a management that would modernize the road, and, since Hill was already on the board, Schiff hoped that working with Harriman on the B&O might improve their relationship. He soon discovered that any boardroom was too small to hold both Harriman and Hill.[8]

Hill sent the B&O one of his best operating men, Frederick D. Underwood, to become its general manager. His first task was to examine the road thoroughly to see what improvements were needed. Hill cautioned him to remember that "while money can be well expended to reduce grades and increase the load on a road with a heavy traffic like that of the Baltimore and Ohio, there is of course a limit to which this should be carried." Here was a difference that grew painfully obvious over the years: whereas Harriman never thought in terms of limits, Hill was more flexible, more attuned to political and personal influences on policy.[9]

In seeking funds from the board, Underwood found himself depending more on Harriman than on his mentor, Hill. When an expenditure for improvements was on the agenda, he would take the matter to Harriman. "Have you been over these figures personally," Harriman would ask while giving the papers his usual quick study, "or are they the figures of some clerk?" Underwood assured him that he had gone over them with the chief engineer. Satisfied, Harriman would say when the matter came up in the meeting, "Gentlemen, I have been through these figures and I know that they are right." Before the others could debate the question, he added, "I have an engagement and cannot stay but I move that the budget be approved."[10]

This routine helped Underwood wheedle some $32 million for improvements out of the B&O board, but it did not bring Harriman and Hill together as Schiff had hoped. Hill approved the policy but grew increasingly annoyed with the tactics. By 1900 he suspected Harriman of trying to dominate in his usual manner. Fortunately, there was a solution to the conflict. To survive, the B&O had to resolve its longtime struggles with the other trunk lines. The Pennsylva-

*The four eastern trunk lines were the Pennsylvania, New York Central, Erie, and Baltimore & Ohio railroads.

nia was eager to buy into the B&O and forge what became known as a "community of interest." Harriman did not oppose this move, and by 1901 the B&O was safely tucked away under the Pennsylvania's influence.[11]

Later Harriman declared that he had "put in eighteen months of hard work" at the B&O, and he was not yet done with it. To make room for Pennsylvania representatives on the B&O board, Hill and some other directors resigned their seats. But Harriman stayed on and kept his seat for the rest of his life.[12]

The other two projects that engaged Harriman's attention were closer to home. One of them, the Kansas City, Pittsburg & Gulf, was a classic example of a good plan badly executed. A quixotic promoter named Arthur E. Stilwell had put together a 762-mile railroad from Kansas City to an outlet on the Gulf of his own creation, modestly named Port Arthur. Stilwell was not the usual entrepreneur; late in life he attributed his major decisions to the appearance of "spirits" or "brownies" in his dreams. His hunch in this case was a good one: to build a line that would haul grain to deep water cheaper than it could go to eastern ports.[13]

Through sheer drive and personal magnetism, Stilwell pushed his projects to completion despite enormous obstacles. Having scrounged money to finish the road in the throes of a depression when no one else was laying track, he seemed poised to reap the harvest of improved business conditions in 1897. In the end, however, his "brownies" betrayed him. Like most visionaries, Stilwell was neither a good manager nor a capable financier. He built an old-fashioned road the old-fashioned way. The line meandered more in search of promising town sites than the best route for cheap transportation. It lacked equipment to handle the crush of business, and the flimsy roadbed turned to goo in torrential rains.[14]

Stilwell tried valiantly to hold out against the Wall Street interests he later termed the "Cannibals of Finance." By the year's end, however, he saw no choice but to seek a reorganization. Unfortunately, refinancing the road proved as muddled as constructing it. Stilwell's creditors included some Dutch investors and John W. Gates, the flamboyant head of Illinois Steel Company who had fed rails and money to the cash-starved Gulf road in exchange for its securities. In January 1899 a reorganization committee was formed in New York. Weeks passed without it producing the expected plan; then in March the committee added three new members, including Harriman. Later it brought in Stillman as well.[15]

Although Harriman later claimed that he was reluctant to get involved, he surely saw the possibilities that had beguiled Stilwell. As one of his officers stressed, "No one had a clearer idea of the strategic value of railroad properties than did Mr. Harriman." The Gulf line occupied a territory between the two systems in which he was most interested. It was a sort of miniature Illinois

Central, running north-south from a major rail center to deep water. Its northern terminus, Kansas City, had already emerged as a primary grain market. Huge shipments of grain could be funneled from the Union Pacific's Kansas division to the Gulf at lower cost than to eastern ports.[16]

Once Harriman got involved, he took a radically different view of the road than Stilwell. Feeling his control of the road slipping away, Stilwell had a friend sneak into court to ask for a receivership under his own men. This shady tactic drew harsh criticism and was overturned by a federal judge, who named impartial receivers. Thwarted in his plan, Stilwell quit the committee and formed a new one with friendly Philadelphia interests. "The whole trouble," he muttered, "is that we dared to build a railroad out west without having first consulted Wall Street."[17]

Stilwell failed to grasp that he was an old-style promoter trying to play the game in a new setting that Harriman understood but he did not. Two issues were at stake in the reorganization: how much to reduce fixed charges and how much to spend on improvements. The conventional wisdom espoused by the Philadelphia committee looked to scale charges down moderately and limit spending on betterments until earnings improved enough to pay for them. Harriman's approach, which the New York committee adopted, emphasized spending money now to earn more later. He favored a steeper reduction in fixed charges and much larger outlays for improvements to put the road in shape.[18]

To find out how much this would cost, Harriman sent Samuel Felton to inspect the Gulf line. Felton's report described a western railroad that could have been built thirty years earlier. He figured $1.8 million was needed at once to bring it up to standard, along with a massive infusion of new equipment. His report reinforced what the receivers had said a few weeks earlier when they warned the court that the road was in terrible shape and required $3.7 million for improvements and equipment. The court authorized them to spend only $800,000, and when the Philadelphia committee issued its plan late in August, it pronounced this sum along with net earnings "ample to place the whole system in good working order and with adequate equipment."[19]

This approach suited investors who wanted to sacrifice as little as possible in the scaling down of securities and spend as little as possible out of pocket to improve the road's earning power. Its short-term view contrasted sharply with the New York plan, but the latter was delayed by Harriman's trip to Alaska that summer of 1899. In his absence, the situation changed drastically. The desperate Stilwell again turned for funds to Gates, who shrewdly bought more shares in the Gulf road, then demanded a place on the Philadelphia committee and soon gained control of it. Stilwell was unceremoniously shoved aside and reduced to a pawn between forces much stronger and smarter than himself.[20]

Harriman was livid at finding the Philadelphia committee in control of the reorganization with Gates at its head. In his eyes Stilwell had broken faith by selling out to Gates. Even worse, the cautious Dutch investors had lined up behind the Philadelphia plan, which by late September won support from a majority of the outstanding securities. Otto Kahn of Kuhn, Loeb, who had played a small role in the affair, assumed Harriman had lost the fight and offered his condolences.[21]

"Hold on. Not so fast!" barked Harriman. "I am not through with this thing yet, by any means. I can't be played fast and loose with like this. I did not care particularly to go into it, as you know; but . . . having done so, I am in it to stay."

Kahn cocked an eye in surprise. "But it's done," he replied; "the newcomers are in rightful control, it's no use making a fuss, and it seems to me that the best, and indeed the only thing for you to do is to look pleasant and get out."

When Harriman repeated his determination to stay, Kahn asked what he was going to do. Harriman shook his head. "I don't know yet," he admitted. "I'll just stand pat and not budge and watch."

So Kahn told the story two years after Harriman's death, embellishing its details and mislaying some of the facts. As he confessed to Kennan much later, the episode lingered in his memory only as an example of "the irresistible force of Mr. Harriman's personality and the workings of his mental processes." What impressed him most was Harriman's refusal to submit even though his opponents had complete control of the reorganization and could do what they pleased. His presence at a time when he ought to have retreated caused them to hesitate, to wonder if they had overlooked something.[22]

Gates was an erratic figure who trampled on the sensibilities of more staid financiers, but he was a tough bargainer. An inveterate gambler, he was only months away from a trip to England, where his spectacular antics at the race tracks would earn him the sobriquet "Bet a Million." He had come up the hard way, climbing from a village hardware store in Illinois to selling barbed wire in Texas. Twenty years of hard work and brassy maneuvers had put him atop an empire in wire and into the presidency of the Illinois Steel Company. In 1898 he took his operations to a new level by organizing the American Steel & Wire Company, a combine capitalized at a well-watered $90 million.[23]

For all his success at business, Gates was at heart a plunger who liked to use the securities of his companies as ammunition for market raids. "Gates was all nerve—and no nerves," observed Bernard Baruch. "Beneath his roughness lay a cool, bold, penetrating intelligence." He had two things in common with Harriman: a love of horses and the enmity of J. P. Morgan, whose recent creation of a giant combine called Federal Steel had embraced Illinois Steel but pointedly left Gates off the new board. His penchant for short-term hits made him unpredictable and therefore dangerous.[24]

The Gulf line struggle, however, was Gates's first venture into railroads, and he was smart enough to realize that Harriman had forgotten more about railroads than he would ever know. Preoccupied with clashes in his own bailiwick of wire and steel, he offered Harriman enough concessions to bring the two committees together on a compromise plan. A new company called the Kansas City Southern was created with an executive committee consisting of Harriman, Kahn, Gates, and two Gates cronies. Stilwell was dumped altogether because, he claimed, "I had refused to surrender the road to Harriman."[25]

Gates agreed to sell half his interest to Harriman provided he could name two-thirds of a committee formed to control the road. This shadowy arrangement allowed Harriman to dominate even though he lacked actual control. The Union Pacific pattern repeated itself: Gates, finding Harriman's arguments and force of will hard to oppose, made him chairman of the executive committee in June 1900. Two weeks later Harriman brought in a new president of his own choosing. No one on Wall Street knew what to make of it.[26]

One major reason for the compromise, and for Harriman's presence in the first place, escaped notice. Stilwell had enraged the other roads in his region by cutting rates to get business, and the receivers had followed suit. The connecting roads retaliated with a boycott against freight from the Gulf line. To Harriman and other rail managers seeking some form of stability that would prevent a recurrence of the old rate wars, Stilwell was a menace. Within days after Gates and Harriman came to terms, the dispute was patched up and the Kansas City Southern did no more rate cutting.[27]

Harriman took charge of the Southern, and Gates sailed off to Europe. When he returned from testing the race tracks, his attention was diverted by a complex web of intrigues that led to the formation of the giant United States Steel Company. With stakes of such magnitude boiling in his brain, Gates had little time for the Southern, yet he was reluctant to let go. With control of the road locked up for five years in a voting trust he dominated, Gates realized he must either manage the road himself or let Harriman do it. The problem was that their goals were irreconcilable: Gates wanted to manipulate the road for quick market profits, while Harriman insisted on making it a first-class line.[28]

Once again Harriman waited patiently for Gates to make the next move. In October he accepted an offer from Gates for his holdings. Two weeks later, he was summoned to another conference in which Gates, still haunted by uncertainty, did most of the talking, as if trying to thrash out the whole business for himself. By the time Gates finished, the deal was reversed. Harriman kept his shares, and Gates agreed to turn control of the voting trust and the board over to him.[29]

Puzzled observers in both New York and Chicago assumed wrongly that Harriman had bought Gates out. "The Harriman interests and mine are working in harmony," said Gates blandly, "and we have turned over the active management to railroad men." Three Gates cronies were replaced by Harriman, Kahn, and George Gould, head of the Missouri Pacific. Along with Stillman and a Gould ally, the newcomers made up five of the seven trustees for the Kansas City Southern. By acting together, they could ensure harmony among a half dozen or so of the leading rail lines in the region.[30]

During 1901 the Southern's earnings grew steadily amid constant rumors that Harriman was about to sweep it into some combination with the Alton and other roads. That January, only fifteen miles north of Port Arthur, the first gusher of the fabulous Spindletop oil field blew in, assuring Texas of a boom in oil and the Southern of a bonanza in traffic.[31]

Harriman's involvement with the Southern had deep roots in what he was doing with the Alton. It was a road he knew from his Illinois Central days and one that for twenty years had pursued a different course than the major Chicago lines. While the others evolved into systems reaching the Missouri River and beyond, the Alton remained an overgrown local road between Chicago and St. Louis with a cutoff branch to Kansas City. Although other local roads had been swallowed up by their neighbors, the Alton survived because its tracks ran through a territory that fed it a steady traffic of coal, iron, wheat, corn, oats, flour, cattle, and hogs.

Since 1864 the Alton had been managed by the same man, a Connecticut Yankee named Timothy B. Blackstone, who kept the road on a steady, prosperous course through the wild swings of the postwar economy. The railroad was Blackstone's baby in more ways than one; his only two children had died in infancy. He took care of both its financial and operating needs, serving a quarter-century without pay, nursing the road through rate wars and two depressions without missing a dividend. Since 1881 the Alton had paid a steady 8 percent on both its preferred and common stock. Analysts hailed the road as a model of sound, conservative management.[32]

The Alton was more popular with stockholders and analysts than with other railroads. Blackstone survived by pursuing a maverick course: he refused to integrate the Alton with a rail network that was growing increasingly unified. The Alton was notorious as a disturber of stability. It cut rates, juggled schedules, ignored rate associations, and ran light, fast trains that pleased customers while driving connecting roads to despair. During the 1890s it blithely paid 8 percent dividends while larger systems sank into bankruptcy.

Although no one denied Blackstone's impressive achievement, by 1898 some stockholders wondered if his day had not passed. The old president, nearing seventy and ill, clung fiercely to the same policies, but his tenacity could not conceal a decline in performance that traced back well before the depression of the 1890s. Both tonnage carried and freight earnings had been slipping since

1883; net earnings peaked that same year and had slumped 35 percent by 1898. Even more revealing, earnings per ton-mile slid inexorably downward from 1.24 cents in 1881 to 0.78 cents in 1898.[33]

While rates were declining for every road, larger systems could compensate by carrying heavier volumes of traffic on longer hauls more efficiently than before. The Alton, however, was unprepared to embrace this credo of the new age of railroading. An expert accountant summarized its condition in unsparing language: "It had not added one mile of road in seventeen years. It had little or no reserve capacity to conduct a larger business. Its cost of operation, per unit of traffic, was very high in comparison with similar roads. Its grades were uneconomical. Its shops and equipment were uneconomical and old."[34]

The Alton was another example of how policy that succeeds under one set of conditions becomes a bar to success when conditions change. By standing still through two of the most tumultuous decades in railroad history, it had become an anachronism. Its dividend had been maintained by skimping on maintenance and improvements, leaving the road ill-equipped to compete in a faster game. The Alton was neither a bad nor badly managed road; it was merely an obsolete one. But as long as it paid 8 percent every year, analysts and investors praised it as a conservative, well-managed property.[35]

During 1898 Alton common sold for nearly $167 a share. That winter, however, an analyst pinpointed its stagnation and warned that changes must be forthcoming. By the fall a fluid situation had evolved. The Gulf line and other roads showed interest in buying the Alton, and a new company threatened to build yet another line from St. Louis to Chicago. With Blackstone too ill to give more than token attention to his duties, some Alton stockholders craved new leadership. One of them, John J. Mitchell, president of a powerful Chicago bank, took his case to Harriman. Mitchell believed that the stock was undervalued, that earnings could be increased by modernizing the road, and that large profits could be made by whoever handled the refunding and improvements programs.[36]

The main obstacle was Blackstone, who owned about a third of the Alton's stock and opposed selling on anything less than a cash basis with all stockholders getting the same price. A cash deal would require nearly $40 million up front for the purchase. From a coldly financial point of view, the issue was clear to Harriman: could the Alton be bought for a price below the intrinsic value of the stock and earning capacity of the railroad? If it could, did he want to devote time to the deal? He was hardly looking for things to fill idle hours.[37]

Although Harriman was always eager to make money, the crux of any deal for him was what else it had to offer. In this case Harriman saw two other compelling factors: he could stamp his brand of progress on another archaic railroad and civilize a historic disturber of rates in a strategic region where he had large interests. With prosperity returning, this last reason may have been decisive. The bloody rate wars of a decade earlier were still vivid in every rail manager's mind, and nobody wanted a repeat of that costly debacle. Here was an opportunity to bring warring parties together in a deal that could eliminate several threats at once.

Every account of the Alton episode describes it as the most controversial episode of Harriman's career. Most also label it his biggest mistake, a view shared by Harriman himself. The broader significance of the Alton experience, however, has gone unnoticed: it introduced Harriman to the possibilities of what became known as "community of interest." From this first venture flowed the insights and connections on which Harriman erected an unprecedented transportation empire.

Harriman's first step was to send Samuel Felton, who was then receiver for a midwestern road, to examine the Alton and make the first of what proved to be a string of reports on different lines. Felton hardly knew Harriman, had met him once a decade earlier and done a favor for him. "I was surprised," he confessed, "for I thought surely he had forgotten all about me. He had not forgotten; I learned later that he never forgot anything."[38]

Felton went off to inspect the Alton in his usual thorough way, but Harriman couldn't wait for him to finish. By December 1898 rumors were already circulating that a deal was near; the *Wall Street Journal* even listed the exact prices Mitchell had proposed. Felton was barely half done when a telegram arrived from Harriman: "Wire report on one telegraph blank." The engineer swallowed hard. Never mind that he had not finished his work; how could he possibly cram his report about a major rail line onto one sheet?[39]

For hours Felton wrestled fitfully with a stack of blanks, ripping up one after another until in desperation he let one go to New York. Then he hurried to complete his inspection, wrote up a lengthy report, and took it to Harriman with some trepidation. "Yes, I am very glad to have this," breezed Harriman. "I bought the road on your wire."[40]

This was almost certainly not true, but it was vintage Harriman, a side of his personality that those close to him seldom mentioned. He loved staging brief, telling scenes to impress those around him with his boldness and decisiveness. Of course, he was bold and decisive, yet he could not resist framing a suitable vignette to emphasize the point. Harriman had already decided to tackle the Alton; Felton's telegram merely reinforced his belief that it could be done. The timing of events is crucial here. That same December the Union Pacific board abolished the position of chairman, leaving Harriman as its de facto head. This change was a clear sign that his view of railroad policy had won over both Schiff and Stillman. George Gould had also been added to the executive committee, strengthening the ties between the Union Pacific and Gould's Missouri Pacific system.

Felton's report, boiled down to its essence, depicted a road that was in decent shape but required $5 million at once for improvements and equipment to modernize it. In Felton's opinion, this outlay could improve net earnings by as much as $1 million. Aware that a large supply of cash would be needed for the deal, Harriman took Mitchell's proposal to Schiff, Stillman, and Gould. There is little doubt that he persuaded them to join him in raising the money to buy the road, improve it, and refund its securities. The total amount needed came to about $54 million.[41]

A few months later Harriman outlined his reasoning in a confidential letter to Fish. "The scheme under which the purchase of the Chi & Alton was undertaken," he explained in one his convoluted sentences, "was mainly for purpose of eliminating it as a factor, more or less, from the situation as a competitor in the South & Southwestern territory, and also through the personel [sic] of its management, to cement the various roads together & prevent to a great extent the buying of business [rebates] & stop largely the running trains at unnecessarily high speed and too many of them."[42]

To accomplish this, Harriman wanted the leaders of the Union Pacific, Illinois Central, Wabash, Missouri Pacific, and Katy roads on the Alton board. Harriman dominated two of these companies, Gould another two, and John D. Rockefeller the Katy. In a novel twist Harriman also wanted the other directors selected from the operating departments of the five roads. This bold departure from convention, he argued, would "tend to bring them into closer relations & enable them to adopt methods for saving much in expenses." It was, he scribbled breathlessly, "all a very big & very important matter & can be turned to good account to bettering the whole situation. It's a great big opportunity for us doing." First, however, he and his friends had to get control of the Alton. Mitchell sent a circular to all stockholders offering to buy their shares at $175 for common and $200 for preferred. The ailing Blackstone could do little more than promise that if the offer was refused, he would declare a stock dividend to represent the earnings invested in improvements over the years. This point was to loom large in the later controversy; in effect, Blackstone was proposing an action similar to one that would bring severe criticism to the Harriman syndicate. At the time it drew scant notice, however, for the stockholders ignored the plea. Early in March 1899 Blackstone conceded defeat and joined the ranks of those depositing their stock.[43]

About 98 percent of the Alton shares came in under the offer. Harriman assumed the presidency and announced a major improvements program to put the Alton on "the same standard as the other big roads of the West." In paying for the purchase and betterments, Harriman and his associates assumed the transaction personally. This meant they had to carry at their own risk for an indefinite time obligations totaling $63 million.* Later the Alton syndicate was expanded to a hundred individuals and firms, but most of the load fell on Harriman, Stillman, Schiff, and Gould. It was the series of transactions they devised for easing this burden that later aroused a storm of criticism—though at the time little complaint was made about them.[44]

As a first step the syndicate refunded old obligations by issuing $40 million in new 3 percent bonds. About $32 million of these were taken by the stockholders; the rest were left in the treasury. Since the syndicate owned 98 percent of the stock, this amounted to selling the bonds to themselves at a price of 65, which realized about $20.8 million for the company. Kuhn, Loeb, acting for the syndicate, then sold these bonds to another firm, which later sold them to some insurance companies at a price of 96. It is not known what price Kuhn, Loeb paid for the bonds or got for them.[45]

Finding a market for these bonds took some doing. Their value would be enhanced dramatically if the state of New York added them to its list of approved investments for savings banks. A bill to that effect went through the wringer at Albany and emerged in February 1900, when it was signed by Governor Theodore Roosevelt. The irony of that act would not become clear for several years. According to Melville E. Stone of the Associated Press, Harriman's role in procuring this bill was what first drew him into the orbit of New York State politics and Benjamin B. Odell, who succeeded Roosevelt as governor and became a close friend of Harriman's.[46]

The new issue of bonds was approved at a special board meeting of the Alton shortly after Harriman's return from Alaska. Felton assumed the presidency and launched the improvements program. By the year's end he had whittled down the organization and spruced up its physical plant. "This road," marveled one observer, "is undergoing a metamorphosis under its new management." That fall the board also declared dividends on both the preferred and common stock.[47]

To eliminate the threat of a new Chicago–St. Louis line, the syndicate bought the small St. Louis, Peoria & Northern and sold part of it to the Illinois Central. Since the Alton's charter did not permit it to absorb the new road, a holding company called the Chicago & Alton Railway was created and made into a vehicle for more creative financing. It acquired the Peoria line outright and leased the Alton Railroad for a long term. To pay for them, it issued $19.5 million in preferred stock, a like amount of common, and $22 million of collateral trust

---

*This sum included $38.8 million for the stock, $20.8 million for the 3 percent bonds mentioned below, $3 million for the purchase of the St. Louis, Peoria & Northern line, and $500,000 for commissions and other expenses.

bonds. For this $61 million in securities the holding company gained control of both roads.[48]

At the same time (May 1900), the syndicate carried out a version of the transaction promised by Blackstone if the Alton remained in his hands. Shortly after taking charge, it had credited to the Alton's surplus account the sum of $12.4 million representing the amount invested over the years in improvements and paid for out of earnings. Instead of the stock dividend Blackstone proposed, however, the syndicate declared a 30 percent cash dividend on both classes of stock, paying it with proceeds from the earlier bond sale. Most of this $6.7 million went to the syndicate.[49]

These transactions recapitalized the Alton at a much higher level. Harriman figured the interest on its bonds and a 4 percent dividend on both classes of stock at $3.5 million. During the lean depression years the Alton's net earnings had averaged $2.7 million annually. Felton estimated that $5 million worth of improvements and more efficient management would boost the net at least $1 million a year on existing traffic. The new Peoria line and $5 million more in betterments, Harriman thought, would add another $1 million, making $4.7 million in all. This would be more than ample to support the enlarged capital structure.[50]

If all went well.

At the time, these transactions aroused much interest but little criticism. Seven years later, however, they became the target of an ICC investigation that condemned nearly every aspect of Harriman's management. In 1915 the righteous Professor Ripley used this ICC report as the basis for his own attack, adding little more than a generous garnish of moral indignation. Both the commission and later critics such as Ripley were guilty of the same fallacy: they wrenched the issues out of their historical context.[51]

The primary charges leveled at Harriman and the syndicate were that they impaired the Alton's credit by giving it a bloated capital structure; they aggravated this problem by paying themselves the 30 percent dividend and taking the new bonds at prices well below their market value; they deceived those who bought Alton securities by concealing the true nature of these transactions; and they skimmed exorbitant profits while the overcapitalized Alton ultimately sank.

Although the charges contain elements of truth, they were not probed deeply because the ICC and later critics were less interested in what actually happened than in using Harriman as a whipping post for their own agendas. The ICC wished to show the perils of allowing men like Harriman to wield such power over the rail system, while Ripley and others used the Alton to illustrate unsavory financial practices a later era had disowned. Kennan, who defended Harriman vigorously, was of course no more impartial on the subject than the critics and borrowed most of his argument from Harriman's own statement.[52]

No one has bothered to look at some basic questions that got buried in the mud-slinging. What did Harriman try to do? Why did he do it? In what ways did his handling of the Alton differ from his treatment of other roads?

The letter to Fish cited earlier reveals clearly what Harriman had in mind with both the Alton and the Gulf line. Already the vision of imposing order on the region between the Mississippi and Missouri Rivers had seized him; soon it would be extended to the Pacific coast. With prosperity returning, it was imperative that the earnings bonanza not be dissipated by rate wars. As Schiff explained to George Gould, "If all interests involved combine to clear up the railroad situation in the Middle West, great results can . . . be accomplished, which will be of lasting benefit . . . to all the different railroads which divide this territory."[53]

Again the timing is crucial. Convinced that he had the correct formula for whipping any road into shape to make money, Harriman had applied it first to the Union Pacific. By late 1898, when he went into the Alton, the results of that experiment were promising but by no means certain. Having sunk huge sums into the Union Pacific, the syndicate members then shouldered the Alton (and later the Gulf line) before the outcome of their venture was clear. The high degree of risk made them anxious to hedge their investment, especially since the money was going to be tied up for a while.

This sense of caution applied more to the bankers than to Harriman. Even at this embryonic stage of their partnership can be seen its later pattern of Harriman rushing headlong into new projects while the bankers struggled to assimilate the last one. But how free a hand did he have at this early stage? How much of the Alton's financial scheme was devised by Harriman and how much by the bankers? Melville Stone, who grew close to Harriman in later years, said that one day, while the two of them were chatting under the pagoda at Arden House, Harriman told him that Schiff had arranged the recapitalization of the Alton while Harriman was away in Alaska. After his return Harriman found much in the scheme that he did not like, but he acquiesced and never tried to duck his share of responsibility for the results.[54]

While this might explain why Schiff defended the deal so vigorously, it does not clarify Harriman's role. He was not yet a prominent financier; indeed, many writers argue that it was the Alton transaction and not the Union Pacific that first thrust Harriman into the limelight on Wall Street. How, then, did the Alton deal differ from the Union Pacific and the group's later investments?[55]

At first glance, Harriman seemed to follow his familiar formula with the Alton. He recapitalized the road at a much larger figure just as he did the Union Pacific and later enterprises, sank huge sums into modernizing the road and its equipment, streamlined its management, got it to hustle harder for business, and tried to arrange favorable interchanges of traffic with connecting lines.

But there were differences, some of them subtle at first but looming larger over time. Harriman's formula enlarged the capital structure to raise the funds for upgrading a road so that increased business could carry its greater financial burden with ease. This approach worked best for the larger transcontinental systems with long hauls and untapped resources to exploit. The Alton was an intermediate road through well-developed country, which meant that the bulk of any new business had to come from connecting roads rather than its own territory. This proved far more difficult to do than Harriman anticipated.

The Alton's earnings did in fact increase as Harriman projected, jumping 32 percent by 1904. Net earnings rose only 17 percent during those years but averaged $3.5 million between 1900 and 1904. Although earnings continued to rise for the next few years, expenses soared even faster. Harriman's plan for the Alton was scuttled by twin economic forces that also hurt his other roads less severely: steadily rising costs and flat or declining rates. Harriman insisted that these factors were decisive; his critics discounted their influence. On this point Harriman was more right.[56]

The whole point to taming maverick roads was to stabilize rates in two ways: keep them level or rising slowly and develop new sources of traffic paying higher rates than bulk products like coal and lumber that required huge volumes at low rates to break even. To run economically, the Alton needed not only more traffic but better traffic and more tonnage in every car. A key to accomplishing this, argued Felton, was "removing the present disabilities of the property in securing traffic from connections."[57]

Felton understood these factors and analyzed them in his reports on both the Alton and the Gulf lines. His conclusion for the latter fit the former equally well. "Unless the average rate per ton per mile can be raised materially without seriously curtailing the traffic movement," he wrote, "future results probably will justify but a small fixed charge." Unfortunately, neither road did well in comparison with rival roads in their territory.[58]

Two forces that could not have been anticipated combined to frustrate this objective. For more than thirty years after the Civil War prices fell in the longest period of deflation in American history. After 1897, however, the trend reversed as the cost of labor and materials climbed steadily. Railroads, like other businesses, found themselves needing higher rates just to keep pace with inflation, but political pressures at both the state and federal levels kept rates down, thereby squeezing strong and weak carriers alike. On the Alton the earnings per ton-mile declined steadily from ninety-two cents in 1894 to sixty cents in 1907. Harriman estimated that the fall in rates between 1898 and 1907 alone cost the Alton nearly $19 million, or $2 million a year, in income.[59]

As a result, net income chased gross earnings in an upward spiral, but the gap between them widened steadily. The Alton could not stand this squeeze as well as larger systems; nor did Harriman manage to integrate it with neighboring roads. Since the concept of real or adjusted prices had not yet entered the economists' repertory, critics paid little attention to Harriman's argument on this point. He could hardly be held responsible for the broader trends of the economy or for a political mood that let its hostility to giant enterprises in general blind it to the railroads' situation in particular.[60]

These factors guaranteed a decline in the Alton's performance, yet they are not the whole story. Harriman's critics were right on one point: he weakened the Alton by deviating from his formula in ways that aggravated these external problems. On his other roads he used earnings to pay for improvements and resolutely held off paying dividends in order to divert as much money as possible to the work. The object was always to increase earning power enough to justify the larger capitalization he imposed on the road. In nearly every case this was exactly what happened.[61]

But not with the Alton. Here the syndicate resorted to old-style financial tactics for taking back some of their investment early. In addition to the special 30 percent dividend, it started paying regular dividends at once. The reason for this deviation lay in the fact that the Alton had to be a cash deal requiring greater risks and more money up front, and it came at a time when the syndicate's leading members were already carrying heavy financial loads.

From several angles, then, the Alton was an exception to the norm of Harriman's policies. Most of his critics attacked the episode for the wrong reasons and committed the fallacy of applying the prevailing standards of their era to an earlier time in which those standards did not apply. On the surface there appeared to be reasonable counterarguments to the charges, their force heightened by the absurdity of some of Ripley's accusations. The charge that the transactions were concealed to deceive investors, for example, simply is not true. They received full coverage in every major financial organ, often in more detail than other transactions, precisely because they were so complex.[62]

Yet the doubts and ambiguities lingered. Harriman's rebuttal never went public because in this one case he could not persuade himself to believe in the deal. Years later he talked about the transaction with Clarence W. Barron of the *Wall Street Journal* and asked him to write up something on it. Barron was willing because personally he believed the refinancing of the Alton had "not a financial or moral error in the whole transaction." But when he produced a draft statement, Harriman told him that someone wiser than both of them had advised him to say nothing on the subject. Barron thought the advice had come from Harriman's lawyers and that they were wrong.[63]

So Barron confided in May 1915, six years after Harriman's death. A week later he dropped by the office of Judge Robert S. Lovett, who had been Harriman's most trusted adviser. What Barron heard during the next hour gave him an entirely different slant on the transaction, one that remained confidential until two years after his death in 1928.

Shaking his head sorrowfully, the judge admitted that the critics had been right on one main point. "The crime of the Alton," he said, "was that instead of the Alton credit being improved the Alton credit was destroyed and the benefit of that credit transferred from the company to the syndicate." The syndicate had put only about $1.3 million of its own money into improvements, and it created the holding company just to get the profits from the bonds it sold itself at a bargain price. In doing this, the syndicate had not increased the Alton's fixed charges, but it had skimmed for itself profits that ought to have gone to the railroad.

"We tried many times to explain the Alton matter," sighed Lovett, "but we never could reach any satisfactory explanation. When we thought we had something I would show Harriman how from the facts it could be picked to pieces. He would lose patience and throw it up. There never was any explanation made and I do not think there could be any explanation made. Harriman declared it was the one blot on his record."[64]

12 Going North

Hardly less important than the actual fruit of the expedition is its value as a sign-post to our multi-millionaires. A little while ago a Western man of vast wealth was heard to complain to a friend that he did not know how to spend his money satisfactorily. ... Mr. Harriman's Alaska Expedition and its magnificent results seem to indicate one true solution to the problem. ...

—Will Dall, "Discoveries in Our Arctic Region"

Between October 1898 and April 1899 Harriman solidified his hold on the Union Pacific, launched his improvements program, went after the Short Line and Navigation companies, plunged into the intricate diplomacy of the Northwest, secured control of the Alton, bought into the Gulf line, and joined the board of the B&O. He had formed an alliance with Schiff and Stillman in which the bankers furnished the capital for buying or merging railroads and put them in Harriman's charge. Despite all these moves, Harriman was still largely unknown to the public. His name seldom appeared in the papers and attracted scant recognition when it did.

A summer earlier, fresh from his first tour of Union Pacific, Harriman sagged with fatigue and took refuge at Paul Smith's. Since then his burdens had grown heavier and his pace even quicker. This time Harriman sought his relief in a two-month sabbatical that may have been the most remarkable vacation ever taken by a man of business. His idea of rest was to organize, underwrite, and direct what became the last major scientific expedition of the nineteenth century.

Of all the mysteries surrounding Harriman's life, none is more elusive than the origins of the Alaskan expedition. Kennan, whose curiosity was always curbed by emotional reticence as well as allegiance, offered Harriman's own simple explanation. In seeking relaxation, Harriman decided to take his family on a chartered cruise to Alaska. His attention had been drawn to the region by the prospect of hunting for the world's largest bear, the Kodiak. When it became clear that the ship he required for comfort and safety could hold many more people, Harriman got the idea of inviting a party of scientists as well.[1]

Perhaps that was all there was to it. As Kennan has demonstrated, Harriman's life can be interpreted at face value without probing into deeper motives. But this approach explains nothing, and there is much to explain. Why would a man of driving ambition who had, at the age of fifty, just burst into the highest circles of wealth and business power interrupt the busiest and most productive year of his life to undertake a diversion wholly unrelated to anything else he was doing? For Harriman to drop out of the business scene for two months at this critical point in his activities is more than curious; it is positively jarring. It was as if Caesar, approaching the Rubicon, stepped back and sailed instead to Egypt for a lengthy junket with a party of friends. There has to be some more compelling reason than doctor's orders to seek rest, some deeper connection to Harriman's inner landscape.[2]

Part of it was certainly the old appeal of wilderness. Having recently sampled the most spectacular scenery the United States had to offer, Harriman was naturally attracted to the stark, forbidding beauty of the North. No one knew how long its serenity would remain intact, for the gold rush of 1895 had already carved the first scars of civilization on its pristine landscape. Alaska was both a mystery and a treasure, a vast, rugged space filled with resources waiting to be cataloged and then exploited.

The business potential of Alaska interested Harriman, if only because of Navigation's boat lines that plied the Northwest waters. Yet it is doubtful that the developer's urge was what drew him north. In 1899 he already had his hands full of projects, and there is not a shred of evidence that he had already begun to think about the round-the-world transportation project that later occupied him. More likely it was the other way around: the journey north helped nurture the germ of such an idea.

What Harriman did need was time to reflect on the intricate web of enterprises into which he had plunged. The railroad industry was at a turning point that offered vast opportunities to those with the nerve to gamble huge commitments on tough strategic decisions that took them into uncharted legal and financial waters. Harriman was eager to commit, but he needed time to ponder and plan. To do that, he had to get away from the firing line, where the press of detail, meetings, and other demands interrupted constantly. He also needed his own particular brand of relaxation. For Harriman even diversion was a test, a challenge pitting him against nature or some competitor. Nature did more than nurture Harriman; it toughened and refreshed him for the plunge back into the business arena.[3]

This would explain why Harriman sailed away to Alaska at this critical juncture, but not why he turned the trip into a full-blown scientific expedition. Alaskan cruises had already become a fad among the upper classes; Harriman and his family might simply have joined the procession of tourists. But Harriman was never an ordinary tourist, and he led processions rather than joining them. Like everything else, he wished to see Alaska in his own way on his own ship. Accordingly, he had an old Navigation Company steamer, the *George W. Elder*, refitted into a comfortable modern cruiser.[4]

Harriman's keen interest in technology did not extend to science; he was always more attuned to the practical than the theoretical. But his mind was active and voracious. There was ample room aboard the *Elder* for scientists, and Alaska offered a bonanza of hidden treasures for exploration. The presence of scientists would turn the ship into a floating classroom, and the children would profit greatly from the experience. Society would benefit from the findings of the expedition, and Harriman himself would gain something he never admitted to wanting: public recognition. He could do something no individual—not even such profligate philanthropists as Andrew Carnegie and John D. Rockefeller—had done and take an active personal role in it.

This was a side of Harriman rarely mentioned, partly because he liked to leave the impression that it did not exist. He wanted not only to do great things but to be known as a doer of great things, and preferably one indifferent to public recognition or his reputation. He was like a man pretending not to notice that other people are watching him or to care what they think of him. Occasionally, however, he let slip a clue that he did know and care about such things. During the train trip across the continent after his return from Alaska, Harriman basked quietly in the publicity given the expedition and submitted willingly to interviews on the subject. Once back in New York, he was quick to ask Omaha for copies of the articles in the local papers.[5]

If the expedition sprang from Harriman's need for a little rest, he anticipated the need well in advance. The Alaska venture was no spontaneous event but a tightly planned outing put together months before the May 31 sailing. It began on March 25, when Harriman and his physician, Dr. Lewis R. Morris, called unannounced at the Washington office of C. Hart Merriam, head of the biological survey of the Department of Agriculture. In his matter-of-fact way Harriman said that he was planning a trip along the Alaska coast in a private steamer and wished to take along a party of scientists. Would Merriam help select them?[6]

Merriam eyed him cautiously. He did not know Harriman, had never even heard of him, and so was inclined to think him a crank. Harriman mentioned casually that he was associated with railroads, and after his departure Merriam sounded a railroad official about him. Harriman was the real item, the officer assured him, a man of means and a rising power in the industry. When Harriman visited Merriam's home later that day, therefore, the scientist took him seriously.

A ship had already been engaged and was being fitted out, Harriman told him. While his plans were still in their infancy, he liked the idea of having two top men from every field along with an assistant for each one. Merriam remarked delicately that he doubted many scientific men could stand the expense of such a trip. Harriman brushed the objection aside; they would all be his guests. Merriam then offered two names at once: paleontologist Will Dall, whose trips to Alaska had made him an authority on the region, and G. K. Gilbert, an eminent geologist and explorer of the West. Fine, replied Harriman, bring them to my hotel room.[7]

The next day in Harriman's room, the scientists were so impressed by his frank, no-nonsense way of doing things that they joined the expedition on the spot. After some more meetings, Harriman brought Merriam and Dall to New York for a lengthy discussion over dinner at the Metropolitan Club. There he entrusted Merriam with the task of choosing the other expedition members. With such associates, Harriman said later, "there was much pleasure and recreation in working out the details of the expedition, and almost imperceptively its scope expanded and its membership grew."[8]

In seeking out the best men in each field, Merriam leaned heavily on those he knew personally from the Academy of Sciences and from the Cosmos Club in Washington, which had been a meeting place for top scientists since its founding in 1878. His roster included twenty-three scientists from a dozen fields, two photographers, three artists, two taxidermists, and a scout. To this list Harriman added two physicians (Morris and his old friend E. L. Trudeau), a chaplain, his own family, William Averell (Mary's brother), his wife and daughter, two secretaries, and three maids. In all the passenger list totaled fifty.[9]

Merriam did not limit himself to the academy. Two of his choices were renowned "naturalists," that breed of amateur belonging to an earlier, simpler America when credentials and formalisms did not yet dominate the professions. John Muir and John Burroughs, the "two Johnnies" of the expedition, were beloved public figures. Muir's writings had awakened many Americans to the importance of wilderness and its preservation, while the gentle prose of Burroughs had charmed even Theodore Roosevelt, whose way with nature was anything but gentle. The suspicious Muir had to be coaxed into accepting the largesse of an unknown businessmen, but he was eager to go after learning the ship would visit parts of Alaska he had never seen. The elderly Burroughs, a devout homebody who had been a boyhood chum of Jay Gould, was even more reluctant but agreed to go as the expedition's historian.[10]

Nothing like it had ever been conceived. No individual or even government had gathered together experts from so many fields on a private ark and taken them to explore wilderness from their own perspectives in a setting where they were free to interact, exchange ideas, and determine their own agenda. Even more remarkable, the benefactor who had made the venture possible was himself going along to share the adventure.

The expedition brought more men closer to Harriman for a longer period of time than any other episode of his life. For two months this phalanx of scientists were cooped up aboard ship with Harriman and his family. Given the events that followed his return as well as Harriman's legendary power of persuasion, it is tantalizing to wonder what course railroad history might have taken if the passengers aboard the *Elder* had been top railroad men and bankers instead of scientists.

The *Elder* was scheduled to sail from Seattle on May 31. While Merriam put together the team of scientists, Harriman took care of the travel arrangements. For those journeying west from New York, he turned the trip itself into an adventure. The Omaha officers scrambled to put together a special train of Pullman cars and arrange its passage over other lines from New York to Omaha. After some juggling they hired two sleepers, a diner, and a combination baggage car/smoker from Pullman, adding to it Union Pacific business car number 100 for Harriman's personal use.[11]

Harriman did not yet own his own railway car. He was having one built, but it would not be ready until the return trip. He planned to call it the Arden, as if it, like the estate, would be a pleasant, fanciful retreat from the pressures of the world. On the special he installed a library of books and maps in the smoking car along with several brands of fine cigars. The car had comfortable wicker chairs and settees for reading or gazing at the scenery or conversing quietly. It was called the Utopia.[12]

The name had an ironic twist. Harriman was embarking on a venture that would test his inner landscape no less than his stamina. A man of quick, decisive action with a nose for the practical, he had for thirty-five years dealt with men as hard and knowing as himself. Now he had caged himself up with a cargo of academics and artists, woolly thinkers and sensitive souls who had never cut a deal or met a payroll. They were men who liked to ruminate and contemplate, who understood every aspect of an egg except how to cook it. Harriman knew the breed, but the knowledge touched painful chords of memory. In some respects, especially their blend of naïveté and impracticality, they were men very much like his father.

The special was scheduled to depart from Grand Central Station on the afternoon of May 23. At the appointed hour the expedition members threaded their way through the bustling crowd to an unmarked gate where the doorman let them through when told who they were. When Harriman arrived, artist Frederick Dellenbaugh was struck by the way he "walked in as unconcernedly as if this sort of princely tour were an everyday matter with him." It never occurred to Dellenbaugh how often Harriman boarded a special train with special guests for a long-distance journey.[13]

As the train chugged out of the station and the scientists settled back in their seats, Harriman came through the car to greet them. Some were too eager to make a good impression and banged their heads on the upper berth as they jumped up from their seats. When botanist Thomas Kearney did so, Harriman laughed and said, "You are the fifth man who has done that." Most of the scientists were impressed at once with Harriman's sharp, penetrating gaze and his peculiar blend of calm and bristling energy. The next day they were introduced to the Harriman style of management.[14]

Calling the group together, Harriman emphasized that he did not want to interfere with anyone's work. He wanted the decisions about route, itinerary, and other matters made by those who knew most about them. To facilitate this task, he proposed creating an executive committee and several special committees. Before the train reached Chicago, this had been done and every member assigned a place. Dr. Morris marveled at how he managed this "without any Member feeling that it was thrust upon him."[15]

While his guests enjoyed the scenery, Harriman sent a steady stream of telegrams to Omaha taking care of last-minute details. Horace Burt arranged a special trolley to take them to the Omaha Exposition, then hitched his car aboard the train for the ride to Cheyenne. Overnight the billowing prairie turned into a raw, rugged landscape that struck Burroughs as "the dumping ground of creation, where all the refuse had been gathered." In Idaho Bancroft rigged up a trip to the spectacular Shoshone Falls even though the hotel there had not yet opened for the season. They jounced merrily across the lava plain in a motley assortment of horses, buckboards, wagons, even a stagecoach, to the canyon, then boarded a ferry for the ride to the towering falls. After their return, Harriman took everyone to Boise for a dip in the natatorium.[16]

At Pendleton, Oregon, Harriman arranged another side trip. The train looped through the Palouse country to Colfax, Washington, where a Northern Pacific special took everyone to Lewiston, Idaho. There Mohler met them with a stern-wheel steamer for a cruise down the Snake River. While the scientists reveled in the beauty of nature, Harriman and Mohler studied a different sort of scenery. This area was part of the battleground between Navigation and Northern Pacific, where Mohler was laying branch lines to counter Mellen's. Harriman wanted a look at the work and was not above mixing business with pleasure even on this jaunt.[17]

The steamer glided through the long canyon of the Snake River to a bridge near its junction with the Columbia River, where the travelers found their train waiting to carry them along the magnificent river route to Portland. The West Coast members of the expedition climbed aboard at Portland for the trip to Seattle. One of the newcomers was John Muir, who met Harriman for the first time. Despite his reluctance to be beholden to anyone, Muir's dark suspicions about businessmen began to thaw. "I soon saw that Mr. Harriman was uncommon," he admitted later. "He was taking a trip for rest, and at the same time managing his exploring guests as if we were a grateful soothing essential part of his rest-cure, though scientific explorers are not easily managed, and in large mixed lots are rather inflammable and explosive."[18]

At Seattle the sense of anticipation grew keener as the departure time drew near. Beneath the damp fog and drizzle Harriman stood on the dock watching a steady stream of supplies and equipment pour onto the *Elder*: baggage, cameras, canoes, painting and surveying equipment, guns, ammunition, lantern slide projectors, traps, a piano, books, cases of cigars and champagne, a graphophone capable of both playing and recording voices, a menagerie of horses, chickens, steers, turkeys, sheep, and a milk cow, giving the whole scene a flavor of Noah's ark. Up the gangplank strode the scientists two by two and behind them the Harriman entourage with the little boys in sailor suits.[19]

"Since Vitus Hehrings [*sic*] set out in 1725," burbled an Omaha paper, ". . . there have been many expeditions to the Land of the Midnight Sun, but none probably have been more novel or important than that now nearing the Alaska coast." This bit of puffery, like some others, was orchestrated from Omaha, where the officer in charge urged his underling to "lay great stress upon the scientific importance of this excursion and what they hope to accomplish."[20]

Once the gangplank lifted, however, and the *Elder* steamed up Puget Sound, Harriman threw himself into the expedition with a zest that no amount of puffery could exaggerate. Whether it was a lifeboat drill or a trek across a glacier, Harriman was always ready for the outing. The scientists did not know what to expect from such a man, but they did not expect what they found. His energy and enthusiasm were unquenchable, his stamina astounding. On the train trip he had displayed his ability as a swimmer and diver as well as a hiker and mountaineer. Aboard ship he relished the daily sports on deck or the board games below, especially his favorite—Crokinole.[21]

Throughout the voyage he remained alert and venturesome, exposing himself to every hardship and taking risks the others thought no one in his position should take. "If anything were worth seeing he wanted to see it," marveled Merriam. "If a difficult or dangerous trip were to be taken, by launch or foot, he was almost certain to be in the lead." He took a childlike glee even in small things. Muir's most vivid image of Harriman was his keeping trot-step with little Roland (then only three) while helping him drag a toy canoe along the deck with a string.[22]

Burroughs watched Harriman race his children along the deck and decided that he was a man to like. "He seems very democratic," Burroughs wrote, "and puts on no airs." In the cramped quarters of a ship, his unaffected manner and willingness to shoulder any responsibility deeply impressed the scientists. They encountered the enigma that puzzled everyone who came to know Harriman: he seemed so ordinary yet separated himself out by his ability to do so much so quickly without fumbling or complaint. He was a man of strong views yet knew how to listen and to digest what he heard so rapidly that it seemed as if he had known it all along. His presence seemed unassuming until he swung into action; then his dynamism made him loom like a giant.[23]

The rest of the family also confounded the scientists' expectations. Those who think of Victorian women as staid, sedentary creatures will have their assumptions jolted by the behavior of the Harrimans during the expedition. Mary and her daughters endured every hardship willingly and thought nothing of tramping two or three miles across a glacier or braving icy winds to visit a mine or Indian village. Their eagerness to learn impressed the scientists as much as their hardiness. A father as formidable as Harriman might overwhelm his children, but he did not allow them to be passive or withdrawn.

On its way north the *Elder* paused at Victoria on Vancouver Island for some sight-seeing, then headed toward Princess Royal Island, where the expedition got its first look at two starkly contrasting scenes: a small Indian village and a salmon cannery manned by Chinese workers. At their next stop, New Metla-kahtla, they observed what chaplain George F. Nelson called a unique experi-ment in "civilizing the savages." A Scottish missionary named William Duncan had brought a group of fierce Indians there to teach them the ways of religion and free enterprise, erecting a cannery as well as a church and making both prosper under his stern supervision. Harriman was impressed by the natives' industry and intelligence. If they could learn to speak English, he remarked, they could be useful in the development of the territory.[24]

From New Metlakahtla the ship threaded its way northward through the tangle of islands and inlets to Wrangell, Farragut Bay, Taku Village, and Douglas Island across from Juneau. As they floated through the icy waters with whales splashing and diving playfully near the ship, the beauty of this natural spectacle was shattered by the deafening roar of machinery and explosions from the Treadwell Mine on Douglas Island. A quick tour of the island showed its once dense forest hacked into forlorn stumps by the expanding mine operations.[25]

As the expedition members climbed gratefully aboard the *Elder* and steamed away, Harriman noticed a stray dog wandering about the deck. Told that the animal had followed a crewman, he decreed, "As long as this dog remains on board, he is our guest." He hunted up the dog's friend and ordered him to feed the animal until he could be returned to Juneau. The dog was assured of hospi-tality, for as entomologist Trevor Kincaid noted, Harriman was a man "of the type that issues orders and expects them to be obeyed."[26]

The expedition pushed on to Skagway, one of the boom towns spawned by the mad rush for gold. Harriman had arranged for the group to ride the newly completed White Pass Railroad, which carried prospectors and supplies twenty-one miles into the rough interior. As the ship docked, a throng of men and boys swarmed onto its deck to welcome the startled visitors. Gratefully they headed for the railroad to ride along one of the most infamous routes in Alaska: the Dead Horse Trail.[27]

The new rail line tamed the horrors of a route drenched in tragedy and defeat only a winter earlier, when it was jammed with eager prospectors unprepared for the hardships facing them. Disease and exposure had thinned their ranks and broken their spirits, and the harsh climate still preserved the carcasses of horses littering the trail. Harriman and his guests stared aghast at what looked like the frozen rubble of a battlefield. At the top of White Pass Ridge the expedition found a forlorn village of shanties and tattered flags marking the boundary between the United States and Canada.[28]

The bleak, jagged landscape stunned them all. "I felt," murmured Burroughs, "as if I were seeing for the first time the real granite ribs of the earth. . . . Here were the primal rocks . . . that held the planet together." The railway officials hosted a lavish picnic in one of the ramshackle buildings. Afterward, as the train eased back down the pass, someone noticed a prominent face was missing. The cars hurried back up the track to find Harriman and William Averell, who had wandered off to explore the area around the ridge.[29]

After leaving Skagway, the *Elder* steamed through the network of islands toward Glacier Bay, where the ship would anchor for five days. Muir knew the region, had discovered a glacier there that bore his name. The small cabin he had built on his earlier trip still stood beneath a wall of ice soaring two hundred feet high. Enormous chunks of ice snapped off the glacier and crashed into the water with a frightening roar. While the scientists set out eagerly to gather specimens, the hunters readied an expedition—lured on by Muir's tale of wolves and bear he had seen at a place called Howling Valley. Harriman led a party of six hunters and six packers across the jagged, treacherous glacier while his wife and four of the girls joined another group in a three-mile hike along the glacier.[30]

Lugging twenty-pound packs, the hunters and packers trudged all day across thick, jagged ridges of ice and collapsed in exhaustion only to be driven from their sleep by cold that penetrated the sleeping bags. Wearily they resumed the hike despite being pelted by freezing rain. After tramping sixteen miles Luther "Yellowstone" Kelly, who had once scouted for General George Custer, knew a bad bargain when he saw it and turned back, but Harriman insisted doggedly on continuing until they reached the valley Muir had described. Roping themselves together as protection from crevices in the deep snow, they slogged onto a divide that looked down on Howling Valley. Seeing no sign of animals, Harriman gave up and they dejectedly retraced their steps.[31]

After covering twenty-four miles on foot, the soaked and exhausted hunters arrived back just in time to witness the birth of a new iceberg. Enormous chunks weighing hundreds of tons slid downward, sending even more colossal bergs, some of them two hundred feet above the water, crashing into the sea with a roar. "The dancing, clashing, clapping, lapping of bergs, big and little," exulted Muir, "welcoming the newborn as it slid ahead . . . were sublime, glorious." Merriam thought otherwise after seeing a tsunami-like wave spawned by the crash roll toward two photographers in a frail canoe and the spectators along the shore.[32]

Three small boats lay less than a mile from the waves. The photographers were closest and seemed doomed as the huge wave curled toward them. But the dancing bergs dissipated some of its power, and the men boldly paddled into its face and rode up to the crest and down again. They handled each wave the same way, saving themselves at the expense of the negatives in their gear. Behind them the spectators fled as the waves crashed thunderously on the gravel shore.

The futile trek put Merriam in bed to rest his swollen, arthritic knees, but Harriman lured him out the next day for some sight-seeing in the launch while the girls remained on the glacier helping Henry Gannett, chief geographer of the U.S. Geological Survey, place his measuring instruments. Muir took a small party to camp on Hugh Miller glacier and in his wanderings discovered that the Grand Pacific glacier had split into three smaller ones. With a flourish he named one of the newborns "Harriman glacier." Some of Harriman's business associates would find the image all too apt: a looming presence of ice nearly a mile wide.[33]

After three days on the glacier the scientists were eager to get back to the *Elder*, but they got delayed on the hike back to shore and missed the rendezvous time. Harriman sent out two of the launches to find them, piloting one himself through the ice until he located the missing party. "Running the launch was one of his favorite diversions," said Merriam, "and . . . we were not long in learning that we were safest when in his hands." The scientists were soon back aboard the *Elder* nursing sunburns along with a glass of wine or whiskey before dinner. At the evening lecture session Muir took the podium to report the new glacier named in their host's honor. A cheer went up, followed by the chant that became the expedition's war cry: "Who are we? Who are we? We are, we are, the H. A. E.!"[34]

A strong bond of camaraderie had developed among the expedition members, tested by the usual petty rifts and annoyances but seldom strained by them. For this Harriman deserved much of the credit. On the voyage no less than in the office he had forged a strong organization through intelligent planning, careful attention to detail, and the sheer imprint of his personality. The only difference, and an important one aboard a crowded ship, was that the cold, detached side of his personality did not emerge when he attended to business—in part because this business, with all its perils, was a source of great pleasure for him.

A night's run down Peril Strait brought the *Elder* to the town of Sitka, where the group disembarked in a driving rain. Then capital of Alaska, Sitka was a regular tourist stop where visitors could buy Indian trinkets in the store of the Alaska Commercial Company. It was also an outpost of civility with a core population of educated elite (the governor was a Yale man). Most of the old buildings built by Russian traders had been replaced with charmless American structures. An old Russian church still survived, however, and the expedition members flocked inside to inspect its lavish decor.[35]

That same evening the governor and other local notables dined aboard the *Elder*, where the conversation soon turned to the local Tlinkit Indians. Fascinated, Harriman asked that their chief and some other tribe members be invited to a reception at the governor's mansion. He brought along the graphophone and persuaded the chief and his friends to talk and sing into the machine. Afterward Harriman startled the Indians by playing back their voices, which so intrigued the governor that he asked to make a speech into the gadget.[36]

The next day, before leaving Sitka, Harriman gave the Indians another chance to hear their voices. The Indians in turn surprised Harriman by marching on him with a brass band playing the same tunes he had recorded. Harriman yelped with glee and captured the renditions to play back for the band. As the *Elder* steamed out, the band stood on the dock in the rain saluting the ship with snappy versions of "Yankee Doodle" and "Three Cheers for the Red, White, and Blue."[37]

During the stay at Sitka a tourist ship arrived, bringing mail for the expedition and flooding the town with visitors prowling the shops and dickering with the native peddlers. Sitka was the northernmost stop for the tourist ships, but the *Elder* had only begun its journey. For the first time the steamer left the sheltered coastal channels and headed into the Pacific for a long day's cruise to Yakutat Bay. Gradually the thick spruce forests and rolling green mountains around Sitka gave way to a bleak landscape of rock and ice. Harriman spotted a glacier that interested him and, joined by a gaggle of the scientists, put down a launch to investigate it.[38]

Towing a smaller boat in case of emergency, Harriman eased the launch toward the face of the glacier. Nothing went right on the approach. One of the boats got caught on rocks and sprang a leak, spraying the men with ice water. In trying to maneuver the boat, Harriman gashed his hand on a nail and spent most of the trip using the other hand to staunch the bleeding. After a futile effort to repair the damage, the group retreated wearily to the *Elder* and confined their viewing of glaciers to the deck chairs for a time.

At midnight the ship reached the entrance of Yakutat Bay, which was lined with glaciers. One of them, the Malaspina, boasted a face fifty miles wide. The ship anchored opposite a tiny village settled by Indians under the care of a

Swedish missionary. Next day the *Elder* dropped off a party on the north shore near Malaspina to scout the moraine for bear and other game. Another group headed by Merriam landed nearby to collect specimens. Harriman took the steamer deeper into the bay to a small inlet called Disenchantment Bay. As the *Elder* tried to skirt thick ice floes, some Indians paddled out to sell the visitors furs and skins.[39]

Delighted at their presence, Harriman invited them aboard and quickly struck up a friendship with one named James, who wore a bright red patch over his left eye and a weathered, broad-rimmed felt hat. Impressed by James's knowledge of the region, Harriman asked him to stay on as adviser to the pilot. He then hauled out the graphophone and entertained the Indians by playing the recordings made earlier at Sitka. Finally, the ice opened enough for the *Elder* to crawl into Disenchantment Bay. At dinner that night Captain Peter A. Doran informed the others that the *Elder* was the first large ship to enter the bay. So deep were its waters that he could not drop anchor until "Indian Jim" suggested a place.[40]

It was worth the trip. Around the bay lay an incongruous blend of tree-covered mountains and islands drenched with wildflowers with a scent so powerful Muir could smell them half a mile away. For five days the group frolicked in the area, hiking and climbing or collecting samples. Cornelia and her cousin Elizabeth Averell helped Dall and Gannett with their measurements and in the bargain learned the rudiments of surveying, struggling across rough ground undeterred by the trail of their long skirts. Harriman went off looking for the elusive Kodiak and came back with only a fine pelt bought from an Indian who drove a harder bargain than some of Harriman's business foes.

By the time the *Elder* left Disenchantment Bay, the ice had closed in again, isolating the two parties still camped on the shore near Malaspina. The *Elder* circled about in a vain search for an opening while the scientists waited anxiously, seeing only the ship's stacks and smoke. Finally, Harriman ordered two small boats lowered and took command of one of them. Threading his way laboriously through the sharp floes and grounded bergs, he rowed a circuitous route to shore against a pounding surf. Half a century later Thomas Kearney still recalled the blisters he got from rowing. The men and gear were loaded aboard, and the boats maneuvered their way back through the dangerous pack ice.[41]

Harriman was beginning to relish his role as rescuer, having only the day before braved a roaring surf to fetch Muir and three others stranded near an Indian village. As the *Elder* headed out of Yakutat Bay for Prince William Sound, a huge albatross floated in the sky above it, dipping and soaring in the wind until it tired of the sport, its flight so effortless that it struck Burroughs as "weird . . . like the spirit of the deep taking visible form and seeking to weave some spell upon us or lure us away to destruction."[42]

At Prince William Sound the ship docked at Orca, a small town dominated by a large salmon cannery. Mounds of salmon heads and fins clogged the waters for miles along the shore, and the air reeked with the stench of rotting fish. A disgusted Muir watched the Chinese toiling long hours for low wages in the cannery, faces stolid and thin, sharp knives flashing in swift, precise strokes against the army of fish marching at them. "Men in the business," he muttered privately, "are themselves canned." There were also miners in the town, many of them gaunt survivors of a scurvy epidemic that had ravaged the trail from Valdez to the Klondike. Stranded without money, the ragged men waited forlornly until a steamer captain agreed to take them to San Francisco.[43]

Harriman invited officers from the Pacific Steam Whaling Company and Alaska Commercial Company aboard for the cruise along Prince William Sound. Under clear blue skies the *Elder* steamed a leisurely course, depositing scientists on shore before anchoring at Golofnin Bay. Harriman went ashore with "Indian Jim" for a day's hike over the mountains in search of bear. Next day he nosed the *Elder* toward the northeast corner of the sound, where a narrow channel near Port Wells was supposed to harbor huge glaciers and hidden animal life. The spectacle was magnificent. "We were in another great ice chest," enthused Burroughs, peering down a lengthy fjord at a procession of glaciers. With a touch of whimsy the scientists dubbed it College Fjord and named the glaciers around them Harvard, Yale, Radcliffe, Smith, Bryn Mawr, Vassar, Wellesley, and Amherst.[44]

The glaciers were the most active they had seen, discharging volley after volley of ice into the channel with deafening thunder, clogging it with pack ice so thick the *Elder* could get no closer than twenty miles to its head. They tried the launch and still got only to within ten miles of the most active glacier. The ship backed away and veered instead into an arm of Port Wells west of College Fjord. To starboard loomed the mighty Barry Glacier. Captain Doran informed Harriman that, according to the U.S. Coastal Survey maps, navigable waters ended there.[45]

Since the Barry Glacier extended across the head of the fjord, there seemed to be no reason to go farther. It was a formidable barrier with a high sea wall two miles long that pushed farther out into the water than any they had seen before. Undaunted, Harriman had Doran ease the ship deeper into the fjord. As they drew closer, a sliver of open water popped into view beyond the glacier. They approached the Barry to examine its caves and pinnacles and saw to their surprise that the open water beyond stretched for miles, with two other glaciers breaking its surface in the distance.

Was this a new and unknown fjord? A wave of excitement swept through the ship as everyone rushed on deck for a glimpse at the teasing waters. Without hesitation Harriman ordered Doran to steer toward the open space, crying, "We shall discover a new Northwest Passage!" The pilot balked. "Here, take your ship," he told Doran. "I am not going to be responsible for her if she is to run into every unsounded uncharted channel and frog marsh." Doran also objected to being responsible for navigating uncharted waters. What was the point, added Captain Omar Humphrey of the whaling company, in charging recklessly into "every little fish pond" where hidden rocks could scuttle the ship? He knew the area, and in his expert opinion there was nothing worth chasing.[46]

This one moment loomed as a microcosm of both Harriman's character and his career. He knew what it was to play safe and had done so most of his life. During the past year, however, he had burst from the cocoon of caution to become the most daring of butterflies, as if something had impressed upon him that great things could not be accomplished without great risks. He had always been willing to risk, but never in so many ways and on such a scale. The boldness that had galvanized him in recent months was not confined to his career but extended to everything he did, and the success that flowed from it infused his every action with a fearless confidence.

In this sense the expedition was not a departure from his business activities but merely an extension of them. The same brash confidence that vaulted him to power could be seen in Alaska, and his success there in turn presaged the still more daring deeds he would perform on his return. For Harriman, business and pleasure sprang from the same wellspring: an insatiable zest for living life to its fullest, staring down its challenges with a glee bordering on insolence.[47]

Doran crept to within half a mile of the glacier face, then stopped. Harriman asked Muir if he had seen all he wished and was ready to turn back. "Judging from the trends of this fjord and glacier there must be a corresponding fjord or glacier back of the headland, to the southward," replied Muir, "and although the ship has probably gone as far as it is safe to go, I wish you would have a boat lowered and let me take a look into the hidden half of the landscape."

"We can perhaps run the boat in there," said Harriman. Since Doran wanted no part of it, Harriman took the wheel himself and headed slowly into the dangerously narrow passage. Everyone stood tense, their ears straining to catch the sound of unseen rocks scraping against the hull. A chilling clang told them that contact had been made. It cost the ship one of its propellers, but Harriman pushed forward. Gradually the passage widened until it revealed a beautiful fjord twelve miles long with a phalanx of stately glaciers stretching as far as the eye could see. Rugged, snow-capped mountains rimmed the fjord like sentinels guarding its isolation.

It proved to be the most spectacular geographical find of the expedition. Later it went onto the map as the Harriman Fjord, and its largest glacier would be known as the Harriman Glacier. Eagerly Muir led a party of scientists ashore to camp and collect for a few days on the edge of a forest of thick mountain hemlock. After they had gone, a sudden snowstorm isolated the ship from the wall of mountains. On board, the group celebrated with a dinner of Welsh rarebit while Captain Doran pondered how to ease his way back through the strait to Orca for repairs.[48]

Cautiously the captain hugged the side of the Barry as he eased through the passage to Port Wells, wincing every time he heard the hull scrape ice. Below deck Harriman relaxed by playing a vigorous game of Crokinole with doctors Morris and Trudeau, seemingly oblivious to the tension around him. Just before the *Elder* cleared the passage, the incoming tide caught the ship and shoved her toward the glacier wall. Doran pushed the rudder hard to port but got a sluggish response. For a few minutes it looked as if the ship would slam against the ice; then it broke free of the tide's grip and crawled toward Orca with a school of dolphins playing in its wake.[49]

While the propeller was being repaired, Harriman took his family on a picnic to a nearby bay. When the ship was ready, they returned to pick up the party camping at the fjord and then steamed toward Cook Inlet in search of bear. Harriman paused to inspect a copper mine on LaTouche Island before moving to Saldovia Point. When a Russian native told him that Kodiak Island offered both a nicer climate and a better chance to bag a bear, Harriman promptly turned the ship toward the island. After dropping a group of scientists at Kulak Bay on the Alaska Peninsula and depositing some of the hunters at Uyak Bay on Kodiak, the *Elder* anchored opposite the village of Kodiak, nestled against rolling green hills that startled the visitors in their contrast to the bleak, rugged fjord.[50]

It was, murmured Burroughs, a "pastoral paradise" in the North. While he basked in the lush greenery, Harriman took his daughter Mary, Elizabeth Averell, and Merriam to set up camp at Eagle Bay, eight miles from the village. Others streamed back and forth from the camp, but Harriman ignored them as he did the mosquitoes, which Merriam called "fearful." He left almost at once in quest of a bear, the supreme trophy that had so far eluded him. The others knew this was the main reason he had come and were loath to see him disappointed. Harriman took along a large party, including a Russian villager who was an expert bear hunter.[51]

This time they found a bear, a small female and her cub. Harriman saw her munching grass like a cow; nevertheless, he wanted her. The hunters drove them into a narrow gorge, where Harriman stood poised with his Winchester. The others, anxious for his safety, stationed themselves around him with enough firepower to rip the bear to shreds. But when the bear charged, Harriman coolly dropped her with one shot while one of the others shot the cub. Merriam thought it was the first Kodiak ever measured and photographed in the flesh.[52]

The next day was the fourth of July, giving the celebration an even more joyous tone. On the *Elder* the crew stuffed rags into a small brass cannon and shot them off in lieu of fireworks. The graphophone blared out "Stars and Stripes Forever" as prelude to the program of speeches, music, and recitations arranged by the Committee on Music and Entertainment. Afterward the group went over to Wood Island to watch two teams of natives play a baseball game. When the competition turned to boats, Harriman joined a four-man canoe team to race a naptha launch and barely lost. The host was in fine spirits, buoyed by his new trophy and holiday festivities that were marred only by an ill-timed denunciation of American policy in the Philippines by Charles Keeler.[53]

Unruffled, Harriman looked next to an excursion across the Bering Strait to Siberia. As the *Elder* turned toward the Aleutian Islands seeking passage into the Bering Sea, strange mirages danced over the chain of islands, creating bizarre effects none of the scientists could explain. The ship anchored at Sand Point to deposit five of the scientists, who went to gather specimens at a remote village, then steamed to Unalaska Island, where a town called Dutch Harbor had arisen to serve a firm dealing in seal fur, the North American Commercial Company. The town was a strange mix of contrasts, brightened by a profusion of flowers through which flowed a steady stream of prospectors defeated in their struggle with the implacable Yukon. It was, marveled Merriam, "a veritable flower garden—like all the rest of this country."[54]

From Unalaska the *Elder* pushed on to the craggy volcanic Bogoslof Islands, where Harriman piloted a launch to shore to observe the breeding grounds of sea lions and murres. The scientists shot some specimens before moving on to the Pribilof Islands, where the North American company harvested seals at a government-controlled rookery. Harriman had secured a permit to visit the rookery on St. Paul Island, and he followed with keen interest the company guides who showed them where the seals bred and the company gathered its quota of kills allowed by the government. Merriam had been there eight years earlier and saw to his dismay that the number of animals had shrunk to less than a quarter of what had been there before. The senseless slaughter had devastated the seal population until the government stepped in with regulations mostly written by Merriam himself. After the tour they retired to a nearby village to discuss the problem with the company officials over whiskey and cigars.[55]

A thick fog had closed in by the time the *Elder* lifted anchor to head for Plover Bay in Siberia. Everyone was at dinner, the ship running full speed, when suddenly a series of rough jolts climaxed in a rasping crash. The ship had struck a reef. Fear of shipwreck swept through the dining saloon; Harriman rose calmly from his seat and went on deck, followed by the alarmed scientists despite the steward's plea that they remain seated. Merriam was convinced the ship's hull had been smashed and asked the engineer for assurance that it would not sink.

As the group milled about anxiously on deck, someone suggested that Harriman be taken off in a boat for his own safety. He gave the person a scornful reply, then muttered to Merriam, "Can you conceive of such a suggestion? What would a man want to live for if his family were drowned?" He stayed with Doran and the pilot, who finally eased the ship off the rocks and found to their relief that the hull had not been damaged. Those who hoped the incident might induce Harriman to turn back were quickly disappointed. He ordered Doran to proceed on a new course despite the treacherous Bering Sea and dense fog. All night long the expedition members were jolted awake by the shrill cry of the ship's whistle bellowing its warning through the thick mist.[56]

After missing St. Matthew Island because of the fog, the ship put in at Plover Bay on the Siberian coast. Scarcely had the anchor dropped when several boatloads of Eskimos paddled toward it, eager to sell their wares. The scientists fetched out their cameras and took pictures before heading ashore in the launch. The small village at Plover was a dismal sight, its inhabitants pocked and scarred by syphilis, the gift of visiting Russian whalers. While his comrades shivered in the icy wind that sliced through their cloth coats, Harriman stood proudly in a warm reindeer coat he had bought at Unalaska.[57]

There was little to see at the grim village. The natives were friendly and allowed themselves to be photographed. Harriman gave them gifts of tobacco and glass beads, and some of the scientists did a little trading. But the novelty of a foreign shore vanished quickly in what Merriam called "the most barren and desolate place of its size" he had ever seen. Gratefully the scientists hurried back to the Elder. That night, as the ship made for the whaling outpost of Port Clarence, some of the group sat up on deck all night to enjoy the midnight sun and listen to Will Dall's endless supply of tales about the Siberian natives.[58]

Finding no less than ten whaling ships at Port Clarence, the Elder dropped anchor several miles away. Still the indefatigable natives paddled out to greet them with furs for sale. Their lively, cheerful disposition reminded Muir of "a merry gypsy crowd." Harriman allowed some of the whalers to come aboard but not the Eskimos. While he bounded off to tour a whaling ship, his family went to Port Clarence in a surf so rough they had to be carried ashore. When Harriman returned to the Elder at half past six that evening, he learned that Merriam and two of the other scientists had gone ashore to visit the Eskimos and were still there. Wearily he took the launch to shore, found his friends, and started back.[59]

The sea was running high from a strong offshore wind, and the Elder lay fourteen miles away. About halfway there, with only the masts and stack of the Elder visible, a crewman told Harriman that the supply of gasoline was so low it might not get the launch home. The wind grew stronger, reaching gale force and driving waves large enough to capsize the boat if it lost power and drifted. Harriman stayed grimly at the wheel, using the wind to push through the waves. His luck held and the launch made it to the Elder, but he could not get too close or the sea would smash the launch against the larger ship. Using poles to keep the launch away, the crewmen tossed down a rope ladder and helped pull everyone aboard.

Exhausted but relieved, Harriman started toward his quarters when someone told him that his family was still ashore along with a few others. Without a murmur he fetched a fresh supply of gasoline and jumped back into the launch. Twice again he made the dangerous run to shore in gale-force winds and pitching waves until he had brought both shore parties safely home. It was past nine o'clock by the time he returned from the second run, but no one had eaten dinner. The others were not about to sit down at table before their host and his passengers were ready to join them.

Harriman's love of horses and prowess with them was well known, but his skill as a sailor was less familiar. The Alaska expedition honed and challenged those skills in precisely the sort of confrontation with nature Harriman loved. He came to be as home on the sea as he was on the surging iron horses he used to roam the vast American interior. The great advantage offered by the sea was that he did not have to follow the straight and narrow but could change course and direction whenever he pleased.

Port Clarence marked the northernmost point reached by the expedition. Beyond it pack ice closed the way to the Arctic Ocean. On July 13 the *Elder* turned south to begin the trip home. During a brief pause at St. Lawrence Island the Harriman daughters joined the scientists in gathering more specimens while Merriam chased eagerly after two polar bears that turned out on closer inspection to be swans. The hunters tried again at St. Matthew Island, then resigned themselves to the fact that the Smithsonian would not have its halls lined with the looming presence of fresh bears.[60]

As the ship plowed southward, the mood of the group swung between relief at going home and nostalgia for the unique adventure they had shared. Already each member had begun to assess the value of the project. Harriman made it clear that he wanted all photographs given to him so that he could prepare souvenir albums for everyone. He also asked that no articles on the expedition be written without his approval so that advance publicity would not undercut the two volumes he planned to publish.[61]

Privately Muir thought the two volumes would amount to "much twaddle about a grand scientific monument of this trip." What it boiled down to, he added scornfully, was that "game-hunting, the chief aim, has been unsuccessful. The rest of the story will be mere reconnaissance." Time would prove him spectacularly wrong. The series of studies subsidized by Harriman continued long after his death and reached a total of thirteen volumes. Merriam was to devote twelve years of his life to this project, transforming it into a scientific team effort that extended far beyond the expedition itself.[62]

Harriman himself was well satisfied with the results. After one of the evening lectures he followed the speaker to the podium. "Let nobody think anything about repaying Mr. Harriman," he said in his crisp way. "Mr. Harriman has been amply repaid by the pleasure he has had out of it." But he was also growing restless. Once the ship turned south and the adventure began to wind down, his mind in his usual fashion raced more and more to the intricate web of business matters awaiting him. Gradually his focus shifted from the wilderness to the hard decisions that lay ahead.[63]

Few stops were scheduled on the return run. One of them was Dutch Harbor, where Harriman invited Joseph Stanley-Brown of the North American Company to return with them to Seattle. Stanley-Brown did and later became Harriman's secretary. The *Elder* also paused at Kodiak Island, where Harriman savored his earlier conquest of the bear and helped Cornelia celebrate her fifteenth birthday. A few days later her mother was honored in the same way with champagne toasts and entertainments prepared by the expedition members.[64]

Harriman joined in heartily, but his mood swings grew more frequent. At the Malaspina Glacier Harriman ran the ship in close and led a hunting party ashore. They returned empty-handed and in a sour mood. "No bears, no bears, O Lord!" chided Muir privately. "No bears shot! What have thy servants done?" Next day, as the ship cruised past the magnificent Fairweather mountain range, Harriman sat with his wife on the opposite deck while the others marveled at the majestic sight. Merriam came to fetch them, shouting, "You are missing the most glorious scenery of the whole trip!"

Harriman glared at him. "I don't care a dam [*sic*]," he snapped, "if I never see any more scenery!"[65]

But the mood did not linger. As the *Elder* sailed through the straits south of Juneau, Harriman recalled a story he had heard from Fred Dellenbaugh about a deserted Indian village and decided to investigate. Drawing the launches up on a smooth white beach north of Cape Fox, the group found an entire village of abandoned cabins fronted by a row of nineteen beautifully carved totem poles. There were no signs of life; no one knew why the inhabitants had fled. Decorations, crockery, even clothing could be found inside the cabins, but the poles were the prize.[66]

While the scientists ransacked the cabins for artifacts, Harriman brought deck hands ashore to dig out several of the totem poles. Everyone sweltered in muggy heat they never expected to find in Alaska. Some of the scientists claimed poles for their institutions; Harriman helped himself to a pair of large carved bears adorning graves. It took an entire day to gather the treasures and float them back to the *Elder*. Afterward Harriman brought everyone back to the village for a group photograph.[67]

That evening the group celebrated with an entertainment that turned into what Dall wryly called a "love feast" as one speaker after another rose to praise Harriman amid cries of the familiar "H. A. E." chant. Harriman acknowledged the cheers with thanks and admitted that he had not dreamed how huge an undertaking the expedition would be when the train first left Grand Central Station. It was, noted Muir, a night of "wild glee and abandon," a fitting capstone for a unique and remarkable expedition.[68]

More than three decades later, a grown Averell Harriman, introduced to Josef Stalin, startled the dictator by saying that the first time he had stepped foot on Russian soil it was without passport. All the Harriman children bore the imprint of this experience in later years, as did most of the others. The scientific results of the expedition proved even more enduring than the lavish supply of anecdotes and tall tales it produced. The bond formed among the participants was renewed in periodic reunions over the years. "What a tie the trip furnished," Burroughs later enthused. "What a peculiar interest we are likely always to have in each other!"[69]

The *Elder* steamed into Seattle on July 31, its hold empty of animals except for the still productive milk cow. After stevedores unloaded its groaning cargo of luggage, specimens, totem poles, and artifacts, the ship pushed on to Portland. The Harrimans and a few others made the trip by rail and greeted the *Elder* at the dock. The expedition members said their farewells and went their separate ways. The easterners climbed aboard Harriman's special train for the return trip, but Harriman took a different train to tour the battlefield of eastern Washington, Idaho, and Montana with Mohler.[70]

Newspapers across the country heaped praise on the expedition. It was this publicity after the ship's return that first thrust Harriman into the public limelight. Before then he was barely known outside of business and financial circles. The *New York Times* introduced him to the public as a man who "has had an influential voice recently in shaping the relations and policies of certain Western railroads." That voice was about to grow much louder and attract considerably more attention. Harriman stepped off the ship and plunged directly into what soon emerged as a major turning point in the nation's railroad history. Harriman would do much to shape its course. To all appearances, he had come back from Alaska rested and fit, ready to take up the wars without missing a beat. In fact, much more had happened.[71]

The Alaska expedition was more than a vacation or even a scientific milestone. It had toughened and hardened Harriman in ways few other experiences could. Time and again he had pitted himself against nature's wrath and come away bloodied but triumphant. The ordeal had whetted his competitive edge, fed his zest for challenge, and broadened his already expansive vision of what could be done. Nothing would ever seem as difficult to him again. Compared to the elemental clashes of will with the frozen North, Wall Street and the business arena were soft adversaries for his renewed spirit.

Part III. Empire

1900–1904

13 Seeking Order

There was probably never a time in the history of railway enterprises when there were more schemes and negotiations with reference to the rearrangement of the railway map than are going on now. . . .

The combinations proposed are of extraordinary importance. Under whatever names and in whatever legal forms they may be brought about, the purpose is to concentrate railway power in few hands for the double purpose of securing stability and perhaps advance in railway rates with resulting profits for those who hold railway securities.
—Wall Street Journal, January 3 and 9, 1901

The America to which Harriman returned from Alaska was a new world hurrying to be born. "The decade from 1896 to 1906," enthused banker Henry Morgenthau, "was the period of the most gigantic expansion of business in all American history. . . . In that decade the slowly fertilized economic resources of the United States suddenly yielded a bewildering crop of industries. . . . All these swift growths demanded money: money for new plants—money for expansion—money for working capital. The cry everywhere was for money—more money—and yet more money."[1]

The bankers were happy to furnish the money at enormous profits to themselves. Even young Morgenthau caught his breath at the largesse of his chosen profession. Once he marveled to Stillman at the generous return on a transaction and was told in a tone of gentle rebuke, "You don't understand what profits we are in the habit of making."[2]

So much had happened so fast that observers despaired of keeping a perspective on events. Half a century of wrenching industrial development was hurtling toward the climax of its first phase. Machines replaced manual labor as the dominant source of productivity. The output of goods and services soared as the factory system superseded the home shop. Machines also moved onto the farm, enabling fewer people to produce more food. Large factories and plants in growing cities lured millions of people from the farm and from overseas with the promise of jobs. By 1900 the nation had 160 cities with a population of twenty-five thousand or more, and nearly 40 percent of Americans lived in towns of twenty-five hundred or more people.[3]

A rural, agrarian society was being transformed into an urban, industrial one linked together by a network of rails and telegraph and telephone wires. Regional and local markets were becoming national, enabling firms to manufacture and distribute their products on a giant scale. This opportunity brought once remote firms into bitter competitive clashes for higher stakes than ever before and engulfed the economy in perpetual warfare. The fallout from these fights left whole industries in a state of instability. Reluctantly the federal government entered the fray in ways that threatened to reverse its historic relationship with the private sector.

The uncertainties spawned by these clashes drove most businessmen to conclude that competition was fine in theory but ruinous in practice. It bred waste, inefficiency, and instability. In warfare it brought too many Pyrrhic victories. To survive, much less prosper, managers had to curb competition in their own industry, however much they extolled its virtues in other fields. The most obvious way was to eliminate competitors. As strong firms absorbed or crushed weaker rivals, growth became in part a by-product of the competitive wars. But it was also the result of superior efficiency and organization. The strongest enterprises tended to be those that best pruned waste from their operation. They made a good product at a low price, streamlined the process, and used this advantage to drive competitors to the wall.[4]

As the competitive wars winnowed out weaker firms, a handful of giants emerged to dominate many industries. These corporate leviathans marked the dawn of a new era in American history. Their presence forced small fry to combine in self-defense if they wished to compete. In many sectors of the economy survival boiled down to a harsh imperative: organize or perish. Managers discovered that the sheer scale of corporate warfare made cutthroat competition intolerable not only to the combatants but to society as well.

Once the economic system grew so closely interlocked, competitive clashes moved from limited to total war, sweeping up civilians in their devastating wakes. The failure of one large firm spread quickly to other sectors, throwing thousands out of work, crippling subsidiaries, suppliers, jobbers, retailers, and service firms, blighting security prices and tightening the money market. The wave of contraction launched by a single major failure could swamp banks and brokerages as it crashed down on the shores of distant businesses, perhaps even trigger a panic or depression. Quickly it became apparent that an enlarged scale of operation multiplied the impact of both success and failure on society as well as the economy.

The rapid growth of the stock market revealed this pattern vividly. For thirty years after the Civil War railroad stocks dominated the market as the major publicly held corporations. Most industrial companies were private, family-owned firms or partnerships until the competitive wars drove them to combine with rivals into large enterprises—usually a new public corporation with securities that were traded on stock exchanges. This was what required the huge supply of capital furnished by the bankers and what planted them squarely at the crossroads of the entire process. The result was an outpouring of new stocks on the New York Stock Exchange and a quantum leap in the number of people involved with them. The once private domain of businessmen and traders became the plaything of ordinary citizens charting their investments or dabbling in the sport of speculation. This wider audience elevated the market into a critical barometer of the economy's well-being, thereby making it a political as well as a financial animal.

Once unrestrained competition menaced the larger society as well as businessmen, stability and harmony became the holiest of grails for managers and politicians alike. Three decades of bitter experience had taught businessmen that the key to stability lay in having the size and strength to impose order on an industry and its market. Two approaches to this problem emerged: collusion and combination. The first sought stability through agreements among the major players, the second through outright control. Since the latter smacked of monopoly, which was politically unacceptable, most industries resorted to a mixture of both approaches.

The railroads pioneered both collusion and combination. By 1900 a handful of powerful figures dominated the bulk of railroad mileage in America, but they had yet to find mechanisms for working together within the bounds of law. It was hard enough to get a room full of strong-willed executives to agree on anything, let alone formalize it in a legal manner. To make matters worse, mergers and the sheer size of corporations were fast becoming hot political issues among a populace worried about the power exerted over their lives by the new giant firms. Between 1895 and 1904 there occurred 319 mergers with a total capitalization exceeding $6 billion. During that decade an average of 301 companies vanished every year—1,028 of them in 1899 alone.[5]

As public unrest over this trend grew, so did the potential costs of a political misstep. In 1900 railroads were still the only industry regulated by the federal government; no one was more vulnerable to pressure from Washington. Their high profile made railroads easy targets for many strains of discontent, and railroad bashing had long been a popular sport among politicians playing to the galleries. Unable to find a clear path to their goal, the dominant men of the industry groped uncertainly toward a mixed bag of solutions, the most promising of which came to be known as the "community of interest."

By 1900 the map of railroad competition had boiled down to four major theaters. The northern theater, stretching from the Atlantic seaboard to the

Mississippi River, was the oldest route and carried the heaviest traffic. It was dominated by the four trunk lines, of which the Pennsylvania and the New York Central were considered the strongest roads in the country. The southern theater occupied the region south of the Ohio and east of the Mississippi Rivers. A handful of systems, notably the Southern, Atlantic Coast Line, Louisville & Nashville, and Seaboard, held sway there.

Between the Mississippi and Missouri Rivers lay the midwestern theater, the dark and bloody ground contested by the four Granger roads and a host of smaller foes along with north-south lines like the Illinois Central and Kansas City Southern. The western theater embraced the vast territory west of the Missouri and broke down into three separate battlefields. The Northwest locked the Union Pacific, Northern Pacific, and Great Northern in combat. South of Oregon three systems vied for supremacy: the Union Pacific–Central Pacific original transcontinental road, the Southern Pacific, and the Atchison, Topeka & Santa Fe. A fourth system, the Missouri Pacific, occupied the region south and west of St. Louis and reached as far west as Pueblo, Colorado, and El Paso, Texas, which meant it straddled two theaters.

The third western battlefield involved the traffic of Colorado and Utah. Only the Union Pacific owned a line through the entire region to the coast, but other systems had laid track along parts of the route. The Burlington, Rock Island, and Missouri Pacific had all built into Colorado and could send business as far west as Ogden on the Rio Grande and the Rio Grande Western, which together formed the only alternate route to the Union Pacific between Denver and Ogden.

Looking at the whole map, the eastern theaters appeared to be the most stable in 1900. The trunk lines had made it policy not to cross the Mississippi River and showed no signs of abandoning that strategy. Nor did the southern systems display any interest in venturing beyond the boundaries so conveniently defined for them by nature. The two western theaters were another matter. All four Granger roads had jumped the Missouri River and posed the threat of building through to the Pacific coast. By contrast, none of the systems west of the Missouri owned a line to Chicago except the Atchison, which was also the only one to challenge the Southern Pacific in California. A sprawling giant revived from bankruptcy by an aggressive management, the Atchison was eager to dominate the entire territory from Chicago to the Pacific coast.

Here was a dangerously fluid and volatile arena. The site of countless earlier clashes, it had grown quiet during the dark depression years as many of the roads toppled into receivership. But the return of prosperity had rekindled old rivalries and infused managers with expansion fever. Large systems looked to extend their hold while smaller roads cowered in the shadow of threats to absorb them. Every system eyed its neighbors nervously, hesitant to precipitate a war but fearful that someone might steal a march.

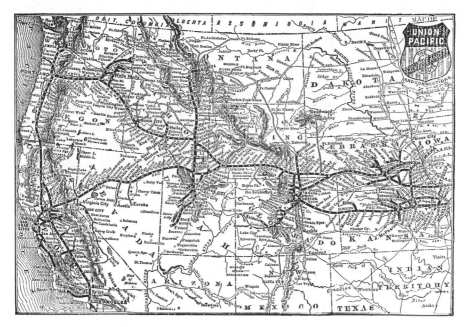

Systems united: This map shows the Union Pacific and part of the Southern Pacific system as put together by Harriman in 1901. (Union Pacific Museum Collection)

The traffic pouring out of the West was a prize worth fighting for: lumber and wheat from the Northwest, fruits and vegetables from California, minerals from the interior mountains. Moreover, the Spanish-American War had planted the United States in the Far East, and large quantities of supplies were heading west to support American troops in the Philippines. The Open Door policy helped American firms wedge their way into the China market. Newly industrialized Japan had emerged as a trading partner of enormous potential.

On this map of railroad strategy Harriman's Union Pacific played the role of Germany: a tough, aggressive power faced with threats on two fronts. To the north lay the Northern Pacific and Great Northern, both anxious to curb the Union Pacific's penetration of northwestern markets. To the south lay a confused situation where war might erupt at any time. The bulk of transcontinental business still moved via the Southern Pacific's Sunset Route despite the Atchison's challenge. Lines belonging to the Granger roads bracketed the Union Pacific on both fronts; one or more of them might decide to extend to the coast or combine with the Rio Grande to form an alternate route to Ogden.[6]

Under these circumstances peace seemed a frail reed. The permutations seemed endless, the threats constant. Harriman was alert to all of them and eager to forestall their effects. The Union Pacific had been whipped into an efficient fighting machine, but Harriman preferred diplomacy to war if it could be managed. Just as the great powers of Europe were groping toward alliances, so the major rail systems desperately sought a balance of power and a mechanism to maintain it before some incident drew them into a devastating war.

Diplomacy among railroads, no less than among nations, was a complex mix of policy and personality. By 1900 only a few of the giants who had built the roads still remained. The best known of them were Hill, who had earned a national reputation as railroad savant, and Collis P. Huntington, the aged but indomitable head of the vast Southern Pacific empire. The Vanderbilts had long controlled the New York Central and the Northwestern, while young George Gould had inherited the sprawling Missouri Pacific system created by his father. The Pennsylvania's management under the autocratic A. J. Cassatt dwelled in its own lofty world.

By far the most significant new element in railroad diplomacy was the enlarged role of the bankers who had reorganized bankrupt systems and then moved onto their boards to exert a conservative influence on policy. The presence of Morgan, Stillman, and Schiff in the management of so many systems helped tone down the acrimony that characterized relations among imperious, stiff-necked rail managers. Since the bankers' interests extended across the entire industrial spectrum, they took a dim view of belligerence and were anxious to preserve peace at nearly any price.

Anyone familiar with railroad affairs knew that major changes loomed on the horizon, but no one dreamed that within two years a series of violent clashes would restructure western rail systems into radically new configurations. Nor did anyone suspect that Harriman would become the catalyst for this change. In 1899 he was still a newcomer to the ranks of the major players. The Union Pacific stood in the eye of this gathering storm. Strong leadership would enable it to exert a decisive influence on events; vacillation might cause it to crumble beneath the pressure from all sides. Here truly was Harriman in the role of a railroad Napoleon, risen from obscurity to a position of power in which the destiny of his world rested in the choices he made between war and peace.

Observers credited the eastern trunk lines with originating the community of interest in January 1900, when the Pennsylvania bought large blocks of stock in the Baltimore & Ohio and some other roads. Actually its roots traced back to the Alton deal and the attempts to carve out peace in the Northwest during 1898 through joint control of Navigation. Harriman had played a prominent role in both events, rejecting shared rule in the Northwest while taking the initiative to achieve it in the Midwest, where there were many more players and relationships were more complex. As one of its authors, he was keenly aware of its value and limitations in bringing harmony to disputed areas.[7]

Community of interest involved the major players not merely buying stock in rival or connecting roads but also sitting on their boards to learn firsthand what was going on. This exchange of hostages provided a forum for mediating conflicts before they erupted into crises. The bankers sat on the boards as well and used their influence to smooth over differences. Critics denounced this cozy arrangement as one more conspiracy to stifle competition and jack up rates. Not so, answered conservatives; the object was simply to avoid the reckless overbuilding and rate wars that had disrupted the industry earlier.

Both were right; the difference lay in the contrasting views they held about competition. Conventional wisdom extolled it as the lifeblood of the American economic system, which meant that no politician could afford to ignore the clamor for it. The rail leaders of Harriman's generation, however, equated competition with low rates, overexpansion, and perpetual strife, all of which they regarded as obscenely wasteful. The bitter wars of the 1880s, followed by the bankruptcies of the next decade, had frightened them into a determination to prevent such a thing from ever recurring. They had been to the slaughterhouse in their youth and did not care to go again. It had been their Munich—the pivotal experience that shaped their views of what future policy must never allow to happen again.[8]

Community of interest offered a beguiling alternative to this nightmare. It put the rail network in the hands of a few strong leaders who could maintain order with help from the bankers. Harmony among the systems assured good service for shippers and solid returns for investors. The beauty of this approach was that it seemed to stay within the bounds of law. Formal consolidations could be attacked under state law or the Sherman Antitrust Act, which so far had not been applied to railroad mergers, but no law forbade men of large interests from working together on an informal basis. "They see," stressed an observer, "that the principle of community of ownership is beyond legal interference and that it affords a sure road to the desired end."[9]

But not entirely sure. Community of interest demanded cooperation among powerful, strong-willed, ambitious men accustomed to having their own way. Could they do better than the previous generation of rail leaders who had squabbled and schemed like petty nobles for every scrap of advantage they could gain? The danger, noted the *Wall Street Journal* shrewdly, was that "human nature will be found very much the same in the controllers of great railway systems as it is in other people. Kings when bound together by the strongest political and family ties have not been able to agree."[10]

Therein lay the fatal flaw of community of interest. Kings might be fewer in number than nobles, but they were no better at reconciling their differences or subordinating their ambitions to the greater good. They too had their weaknesses and distractions, their vanities and vices. And kings no less than nobles were fond of posing as apostles of peace while awaiting the right moment to steal a march. For all their good intentions, they had yet to learn that peace was more than a matter of power; it was a matter of attitude.

The strategic situation confronting Harriman in August 1899 varied widely from one front to another. In the Northwest Harriman had seized the initiative with his whirlwind tour. He had ordered Mohler to begin modernizing the Navigation line and had negotiated the truce with Mellen. Although intended to last only six months, the pact was renewed and all sniping over extension lines stopped.[11]

At Ogden the Union Pacific handed over its traffic to the Central Pacific, which was owned by the Southern Pacific. The grizzled Huntington, sitting atop the largest transportation system in the world, had slowed in recent years. His rail lines had not kept up with the times, and plans for improving the Central Pacific were stalled because of the expense involved. He was also exploring the possibility of a joint line with the Atchison from Los Angeles to Salt Lake City. Harriman chafed impatiently at the Ogden bottleneck that neutralized his own gains in efficiency and denounced the proposed desert line as "unfriendly & antagonistic" to the Union Pacific.[12]

The Midwest also demanded his attention. The Union Pacific exchanged business with all four Granger roads. Its historic policy had been to stay west of the Missouri River and play these roads off against one another. To reverse this strategy by acquiring one of the lines would make enemies of the others and drive them into the arms of competing systems. Moreover, all four roads had built west of the Omaha gateway.* The Northwestern and the Milwaukee occupied territory north of the Union Pacific, the Rock Island south of it; the Burlington straddled both sides. If these roads extended westward to the mountains and the coast, they would parallel the Union Pacific and possess a line into Chicago as well.[13]

The Northwestern was wedded to the Union Pacific in what amounted to a most-favored-nation treaty. Harriman knew that the Vanderbilts who controlled it were stolid, unimaginative men more attuned to society than to grand strategy. The New Englanders who dominated the Burlington had made it the most efficient and aggressive of the Iowa roads, but the management had grown old and reluctant to pursue an expansion policy. Charles E. Perkins, its bulldog of a president, was nearing retirement and recognized that the Burlington was destined to be part of another system rather than an independent.

Reckless expansion and consistent undermaintenance had left the Rock Island weak and ripe for takeover. The Milwaukee had large ambitions but an

---

*A gateway is a point where systems terminate and interchange traffic with other systems. Ogden was also a gateway.

indecisive management. Harriman feared it less than the others because the dominant stockholder in the road was William Rockefeller. This was precisely the kind of fluid situation dreaded by seekers of stability: three of the four Iowa roads had aging managements that made them candidates for takeover by someone whose presence might upset the balance of power west of Chicago.[14]

Harriman had old ties to this theater through his long association with the Illinois Central, and he had injected himself back into it by acquiring the Alton and getting into the Gulf line. By the fall of 1899 these disparate interests were converging on him in a way that thwarted his attempts to impose order. The Illinois Central extension to Omaha was nearing completion, and Fish let it be known that he expected to get business from the Union Pacific. "Nor can we afford to take other than a front seat in the Omaha business," he told Harriman pointedly.[15]

Fish's attitude ruffled the feathers of Northwestern officers, who feared losing traffic to the Illinois Central. The other Iowa roads made their displeasure known as well, and Felton expected the Alton to profit from its connection with the Union Pacific at Kansas City. How could Harriman square the demands of Fish and Felton with each other, let alone with the Iowa roads or the Wabash, which traversed the region east of St. Louis and was controlled by George Gould, who sat on the Union Pacific board?[16]

Out of these tangled threads Harriman had to weave a coherent policy. It was the perfect opportunity for a master diplomat, but Harriman was more a general, the bold tactician searching his map for the unexpected thrust that could turn an entire campaign to his advantage. Once victory was assured, the rest could be left to politicians and diplomats. In this sense, too, Harriman was truly a railroad Napoleon, intent on bringing order out of chaos and confident that the only way to do it was according to his own design. For all his gestures toward community of interest, Harriman was at heart a warrior too impatient to pursue peace over one plodding hurdle after another. When he said he wanted to harmonize roads, critics sneered that his real goal was to "Harrimanize" them. Although new to the uppermost circles of power, he was no more capable of acting as one voice among many there than he was in his own family. As George Gould declared, Harriman "aims to dominate, and if he don't like us he'll throw us out."[17]

Harriman craved power unabashedly. Far from sating this appetite, victory only vaulted it to higher ambitions. This drive to achieve, fueled as it was by an indomitable will, indefatigable energy, and sheer tenacity, became an awesome juggernaut to friends and foes alike. Like Napoleon, Harriman saw himself as wielding power to serve not himself but larger, nobler causes. He was an apostle of progress, an engine of modernity sweeping away outmoded thinking. Resistance of the most desperate kind only reinforced his belief in the righteousness of his cause.

His banker friends slowly (and sometimes painfully) learned this side of Harriman and did what they could to temper or restrain him, but in the end they had to concede that he was a force unto himself. The bankers themselves were hardly free of ambition; the difference was that they were more diplomats than warriors. For all their success, Schiff and Stillman had spent their entire careers in the shadow of J. P. Morgan. In Harriman they found an ally who had not hesitated to butt heads with Morgan regardless of the odds against him. It was a quality they could admire if not emulate, and it spurred them to grander ambitions.

Stillman in particular came to appreciate the full range of Harriman's ability during the months after his return from Alaska. Daniel Lamont discovered this in July 1900 while trying to help resolve the dispute over policy in the Northwest. "He is very close to Mr Stillman these days," Lamont reported to his friend Hill, "and the latter rates him very high as a business man and a great railroad leader on broad and comprehensive lines—says we have had no such man in the East in a long time; that he is very rich, can command any amount of money, is independent of any man or any banking house and is very ambitious."[18]

In the year after his return from Alaska, Harriman did more than enough to earn this praise from Stillman. The long voyage had given him time to mull over the complexities of a two-front war. Before the *Elder* docked at Seattle, he had determined a strategy: he would defuse the crisis in the Northwest long enough for what he hoped would be a decisive strike in the Midwest. After his tour with Mohler, Harriman hurried on to Butte, Salt Lake City, and then Kansas City to attend the Alton meeting. Before going on to Omaha, he wired Burt to invite officers from all the major midwestern roads to join him at lunch in Chicago on August 12. By then he had arranged the truce with Mellen, given Mohler his marching orders, inspected key points on the line, and rearranged the Alton management.[19]

Sitting down to lunch at the Chicago Club, Harriman was an affable host to the officers he had assembled. He listened closely to their discussion of rate differentials and other problems. When they had finished, he agreed they should meet again and scheduled another luncheon for September 7. Then he pulled aside George B. Harris of the Burlington for a private talk that nearly sent Harris into shock. In his usual way Harriman wasted no words. He had come to the conclusion that the Union Pacific and Burlington should combine, and he wanted to know if Charles Perkins would entertain the idea. The fit between the systems was ideal, Harriman insisted. He had no specific terms in mind but wished only to explore the idea with Perkins. He swore Harris to secrecy, saying it would embarrass him if other roads had an inkling that he had even made the suggestion.[20]

Bringing the Burlington into the fold would give Harriman the best line into Chicago and eliminate his most dangerous competitor among the Iowa roads west of the Missouri River. It would also revolutionize the structure of relationships at the Omaha gateway, turning the Northwestern from ally to enemy and triggering a mad scramble for merger partners among the other Iowa roads. In flirting with Pandora's box, Harriman was oblivious to the fact that the two rail systems made a far better fit than the personalities; the flinty Perkins did not get along with Harriman as well as he did with Hill. There was also a question of whether the law would permit a merger between two systems with so much parallel track.

Perkins's response was cautious. "The trouble is that the other fellow is so much more heavily capitalized than we are, that it will be difficult to work out any plan," he told Harris, "but the general idea is all right." If Perkins marveled at the audacity of this plan, he would have blanched at the dimensions of the entire scheme Harriman brought back from Alaska. Already he was toying with the idea of a giant system embracing the Union Pacific, Southern Pacific, and Burlington, which he could make so efficient that no one could compete against it.[21]

While Harriman dreamed, Wall Street buzzed furiously with more than the usual crop of rumors about mergers and alliances. The Milwaukee threatened to build its own line to Duluth, a route where three roads already vied for business. Did every road have to go to every place? There seemed no end to the bickering and posturing, the schemes and threats that usually culminated in more duplicate construction as the railroads pursued their own version of the arms race. Harriman, Hill, and other rail leaders shared a desire to end this dreary, wasteful cycle. The problem was that each of them wanted peace and harmony on his own terms. Could some way be found to bring them together, or would their clashes continue to escalate into the formation of ever larger systems until superpowers ruled the arena?[22]

While all of them groped toward an answer, the year of decision came upon them with unexpected suddenness.

14 Seeking an Advantage

In comparison with [Harriman], the Vanderbilts, the Goulds, the Garretts,

the Huntingtons, represent the parochial period in our railroad history. They

consolidated small railroad principalities into kingdoms; Harriman is federating

their kingdoms into an empire.

—Burton J. Hendrick, *"The Most Powerful Man in America"*

The business giants of the Victorian era were notorious for their slavish devotion to work. It was said of Harriman's good friend H. H. Rogers of Standard Oil that the only vacation he needed was "a shave and a trip up the Sound." One railroad president told a friend wearily, "I have been working for fourteen years without a break. I think I deserve a vacation and I am going to take one, a real long one. I am going right away now." A couple of days later the friend stopped by the office on business and was surprised to find the president hard at work. "I thought you were going away on a long vacation," he asked in surprise. "Oh," nodded the president, "I went away yesterday."[1]

As the Alaska trip revealed, Harriman kept his grueling regimen only by taking frequent and sometimes lengthy breaks. He rarely came downtown on Saturdays and often stayed away on Mondays as well to have a long weekend at Arden or Paul Smith's or with Dr. Trudeau at Saranac. Sometimes he took the family to Newport during the summer or south in winter. Play was important to Harriman even if the rigorous forms he favored seemed more like work to those around him.[2]

The breaks were necessary to recharge the energy he spent with such reckless abandon. On the job he was all business, a curt, unsmiling dynamo who resented a wasted minute or dollar. He once boasted that he got through his morning bath, shave, and breakfast in only twenty-five minutes. Sometimes he couldn't wait even that long. One morning the senior partner of a brokerage firm, summoned to Harriman's house on business, found him in the tub, telephone in hand. "Hurry up!" became one of his favorite phrases, leading Alex Millar to call him privately "Harriman, Hurryman."[3]

On drab winter days he could be seen scurrying briskly down Broadway, hands jammed into coat pockets and collar pulled tight against the cold, his mind absorbed in whatever problem occupied it at the moment. The sight was not an impressive one. His thinning hair contrasted with the thick, drooping mustache that was, smirked Frank Vanderlip, "as unkempt as if it had been worn by a Skye terrier." The dark, expressionless face with its deep-set eyes reminded one observer of a "a Frenchman of the small professional type." But the chin had a pugnacious thrust to it, the jaw muscles worked constantly, and the walk had the bow-legged jauntiness of a jockey.[4]

It was the eyes that provided mystery. Many people described them as piercing, yet no one agreed on what color they were. Averell Harriman said they were brown; others insisted they were black or gray. Perhaps the thick spectacles confused observers, or the enigmatic quality many saw behind them. Or perhaps it was simply because the eyes were so often focused on things no one else could see.[5]

The new century opened to a thunderous chorus of hosannas from Americans supremely confident that it would bring even greater progress than the last one. The affable, politically shrewd William McKinley occupied the White House, an ideal figure to preside over the golden age of prosperity that came to bear his name. From modest roots in the factories perched on New England rivers and frail ribbons of iron reaching from the seaboard into the hinterland had risen a new era in human society: the flowering of material civilization. Few people doubted that the flow of goods from shops and factories would continue to swell or that the texture of daily life would grow ever more comfortable and pleasant for those who could afford its amenities.

Only a few troubling blotches marred this rosy prospect. Companies were coalescing into giant firms that wielded too much power for a society accustomed to small aggregations. Labor too showed a disturbing tendency to consolidate into larger units, the better to fight the corporate giants facing it. Wealth itself seemed to be driving a wedge into society, improving everyone's lot but piling up huge, almost obscene fortunes in the hands of those at the top of the heap. Misery seemed to multiply as fast as money and was more visible than ever before, being packed into teeming, squalid slums in the heart of the very cities that had become the showcases of material progress. These festering sores on the urban body politic were literally alien to most Americans—a swarming jumble of strange tongues, customs, and smells.

Against this backdrop Harriman went his way, determined to make his contribution to progress by imposing order on the largest and most unruly industry in America. He was oblivious to the danger signs already flashing, partly because his concentration was so riveted elsewhere and partly because the danger signs lay in his blind spot. His party and his president were in power, the crop reports were good, and business was booming across the land. The trick was to ride the wave of prosperity as far as it would travel.

In any two-front war the obvious strategy is to neutralize one front long enough to gain victory on the other. Harriman tried the Burlington first. In January he sat down with Perkins, who advised him that if the Burlington was for sale, which it wasn't, the price would be $200 a share. Out of the question, huffed Harriman. In mid-March he tried to tempt Perkins with a dual offer: $150 a share in cash or $200 a share if Perkins would take Union Pacific bonds in payment.[6]

The price, replied Perkins stiffly, was $200 cash.

Always a hard trader, Harriman saw that he had a worthy foe in Perkins. Back he came late in April, this time with Schiff at his side. Perhaps, mused the tactful banker, the time was not yet ripe for a merger. When Perkins agreed, Schiff suggested that he let Harriman and Kuhn, Loeb know when the proper time had arrived. Perkins shook his head. He had not put the Burlington on the block but was simply listening to offers. Any move had to come from interested parties, and he was not bound to anyone.

Despite his love of dickering, Harriman was usually willing to pay whatever a property was worth to get it. In the long run the Burlington was worth $200 a share, yet on this occasion he balked at paying top dollar. It was a rare hesitation on his part and one he was to regret for the rest of his life. After the April meeting with Perkins he formed a pool with Schiff, Stillman, and George Gould to buy Burlington stock in the open market. But too much of the stock belonged to small holders—the legendary widows and orphans—who would not sell unless advised by Perkins to do so. By late July the syndicate had acquired less than 9 percent of the outstanding shares and had little hope of getting more.[7]

During these same months Harriman fared no better with Huntington. The wily old bear had consolidated his hold on the Southern Pacific in league with banker James Speyer and showed no interest in Harriman's repeated overtures to take the Central Pacific off his hands. During July, while the syndicate was chasing Burlington stock, Harriman went camping in the Adirondacks for a few days with Huntington and his close associate Edwin Hawley. Nothing came of the trip, and Harriman returned to New York no nearer a solution on either front than he had been at the beginning of the year. Then, on August 14, Huntington died suddenly, leaving his Southern Pacific stock in the hands of his widow and nephew. Everyone on Wall Street expected them to sell; the burning question was who would buy. The king was dead. Long live . . . who?[8]

Harriman saw at once that fate had reversed his priorities. Twice he trekked up to Perkins's summer place in New Hampshire, but only to suggest that it would be good policy for some Union Pacific and Burlington directors to sit on each other's boards. Perkins dismissed the idea, and Harriman let the Burlington go its way. The road had lost none of its appeal for him, but the Southern Pacific demanded his immediate attention.[9]

Huntington's death signaled a momentous shift in the balance of power. The Burlington, Milwaukee, and Northwestern all coveted a line to the coast; if one of them acquired the Southern Pacific, it need only build to Ogden to parallel the Union Pacific and own a route from Chicago to San Francisco. No one knew how serious these threats were, but Harriman dared not ignore them. At the same time, threats were for him a favorite doorway to opportunity. His reluctance to let the Southern Pacific fall into other hands was a perfect rationale for doing what he longed to do anyway: have the Union Pacific buy it and join the two lines together once and for all.

The unknown quantity in Harriman's calculations was George Gould, whose measure at age thirty-seven had yet to be taken. Since early boyhood he had been groomed as the heir to his father, the most brilliant and innovative financier of his age. After Jay Gould's death in December 1892, George became the manager of his vast business empire. He carried this staggering load with help from his brothers and his father's longtime associates. Through the depression years he had nursed the Gould roads carefully, keeping even the weakest of them out of bankruptcy. By 1900 they had emerged as a strong system, and there were whispers on Wall Street that George was flirting with ambitions worthy of his father.

To all appearances Harriman and Gould embodied community of interest. They had been allied in every syndicate from the Union Pacific to the Alton and sat on the boards of each other's companies. But Gould was quietly picking up stock in the Rio Grande, which was in turn buying control of the Rio Grande Western. If he captured these roads, he would own the only road to Ogden besides the Union Pacific. There was also an ironic twist to this threat: the president of the Rio Grande was none other than Edward T. Jeffery, the man who had quit the Illinois Central after his clash with Harriman.[10]

To complicate matters, Senator William A. Clark, one of the Montana copper kings, announced late in August that he would build the long-heralded road from Los Angeles to Salt Lake City. Harriman's mind churned furiously over the whole range of possibilities. If Gould acquired the Rio Grande and the Southern Pacific, he could dictate terms to Harriman at Ogden and to the Atchison in California. If Harriman snatched the Southern Pacific, he would control every transcontinental line south of Washington State except the Atchison. And how would the formidable Clark inject himself into this puzzle?[11]

Harriman did not wait to find out. In December 1900 he approached James Speyer and Edwin Hawley, who had been asked by Huntington's heirs to dispose of the stock. Although the sale was made to Kuhn, Loeb, which pocketed a fat commission on the transaction, Harriman did the negotiating personally. Schiff

Falling short: George J. Gould, who inherited Jay Gould's business empire and presided over its collapse. (Union Pacific Museum Collection)

did not even put in an appearance until the final meeting at Harriman's house late in January. Two weeks later Kuhn, Loeb sold 750,000 shares of Southern Pacific stock (37½ percent of the total) to the Union Pacific.[12]

To pay for the deal, Harriman had to raise $40 million at a time when he was already spending huge sums on the Union Pacific. Investors took a dim view of the Southern Pacific, which paid no dividends and would require heavy outlays for improvements before it did. Undaunted, Harriman had the Union Pacific issue $100 million in 4 percent bonds that could be converted into stock anytime before May 1906. He used $40 million of this amount for the Southern Pacific purchase and reserved the balance for a transaction that would prove even more astonishing. Kuhn, Loeb underwrote the issue, and, to Wall Street's surprise, subscribers grabbed the entire issue within a month.[13]

Six years later, in the glare of an ICC investigation, Otto Kahn insisted that Harriman bought the Southern Pacific to keep Gould from getting it. Gould disputed this, saying indignantly, "I would have considered that disloyal to my associates." Kahn also claimed that Harriman bought the entire system just to get the Central Pacific. No one really wanted the Southern Pacific, he argued, because it was not profitable and required such large sums for improvements. Kahn made few converts, then or later. Harriman's ambitious soul craved the challenge of remaking the Southern Pacific as he had the Union Pacific and putting the two giant systems in tandem. "We have bought not only a railroad," he exulted, "but an empire."[14]

Schiff was no less jubilant, but as always he cushioned his excitement with tact. "We have finally landed the Southern Pacific bird," he told Hill, "and I am sure this has your approval, as it will much simplify the problem in which you yourself take so deep an interest." Hill did not share this enthusiasm, and neither did his close friend, the banker John S. Kennedy, who worried that so many giant mergers would glut the market with securities. "Some people also say," grumbled Kennedy, "that Harriman is posing as the Napoleon of Railways in New York but they think he has at last bitten off more than he can chew and that he ought to be checked."[15]

The news did not catch George Gould by surprise because Harriman had informed him early that he was negotiating for the Southern Pacific, but it did leave him at a loss over what to do. George had begun to betray crucial differences between himself and his remarkable father. Jay had been a man of breathtakingly bold plans and careful judgments based on exhaustive study. George tended to be careless of detail and mercurial in his decisions, as myopic as his father was far-seeing. He lacked both the judgment and the work ethic of his father; some thought he also lacked the backbone. "His preeminent characteristic is indecision of character," noted one critic. "He by no means lacks ability; he is capable of forming great, even grandiose plans . . . but he lacks the physical force, the 'nerve,' to see his operations through."[16]

One reason for this difference could be found in his personal life. George was extravagant and self-indulgent, fond of sports and parties, a denizen of society, in sharp contrast to his father, whose tastes were abstemious and always took a backseat to business. Society was a distraction few business leaders could afford in excess. A dozen years later one critic wrote this epitaph of George and his brothers: "Like the Vanderbilts, they have attempted to do two incompatible things—live lives of idleness and luxury, and at the same time personally control great enterprises."[17]

In 1900 the exhilarating vision of empire had not yet seized Gould as it had Harriman; the Southern Pacific purchase may well have been the spark that kindled it. He told Harriman in his ingenuous way that if Harriman did not want the system, he would buy it for all their interests. When Harriman did take it, Gould asked for a half interest in the purchase. Sharing the Southern Pacific would, after all, exemplify the community of interest spirit. That was not possible, Harriman replied bluntly. Instead, he invited Gould to become a director of the Southern Pacific.[18]

This dash of cold water awakened Gould to the threat posed by Harriman's control of both Pacific systems. Within a few weeks Gould wrapped up his conquest of the Rio Grande. Shortly after hearing the news, Harriman approached Gould and said, "You bought that, I suppose, for both interests—Union Pacific and your own."[19]

"No," answered Gould.

"Well," persisted Harriman, "I would like to have a half interest in it."

"That cannot be arranged," said Gould, "but I would like you to serve on Rio Grande board."

This rare show of grit must have given Harriman pause. On the surface he and Gould preserved the facade of community of interest by taking seats on each other's boards and by joining in yet another attempt to forge an organization capable of enforcing cooperation among the carriers. A series of meetings in 1900 had led to the formation of an advisory committee of five, including Harriman, Schiff, and Stillman. In January 1901 they issued a joint call with Morgan, Hill, Gould, Fish, and James Speyer for a meeting of delegates from all western roads to create a permanent advisory committee.[20]

Some rail presidents greeted the invitation coldly. Perkins suspected it of being "all done for the aggrandizement of Harriman," and snorted, "The idea of the Presidents of all these big Western railroads running down to New York to talk with the bankers whenever the bankers want to talk, seems absurd." The railroads, it seemed, were bigger than their presidents. Like so many past attempts at cooperation, the advisory board wasted much time and energy with no results. This failure of diplomacy impressed anew on Harriman the belief that the surest road to harmony was to weed out the small fry through consolidations and reduce the number of players to a handful of giant systems. The question was whether the fledgling community of interest could survive the rigors of weeding out.[21]

By the winter of 1901 even the dullest observer realized that unprecedented forces had gripped Wall Street. The urge toward acquisition and merger took on a life of its own, creating another of the feeding frenzies that periodically shook the street. During the bull market of 1872, about two hundred thousand shares had changed hands on the liveliest days, most of them in ten active stocks. The bull market of 1881 saw transactions reach seven hundred thousand shares a day, mostly in twenty active stocks. By 1901 the number of live stocks had jumped to sixty, and on January 7 the market recorded its first two-million-share day.[22]

Everyone had to readjust his sense of scale. Harriman's purchase of the Southern Pacific was hailed as a "colossal" transaction only to be dwarfed that same month by the creation of United States Steel. Capitalized at an astounding $1.4 billion, it was by far the largest corporation in the nation and set new heights for the merger mania. Rumors of gigantic rail combinations, which had flooded the papers for months, seemed confirmed by Harriman's grab of the Southern Pacific and Gould's move into the Rio Grande.[23]

Under these pressures the coolest of rail managers wavered between fear and reason. Whatever sense a merger made on its own terms, there remained the old prod that if you didn't do it someone else would. Nothing terrified railroad men more than the thought of being outflanked, isolated, or left standing in the game of musical chairs that passed for strategy in the industry. If the domino theory applied anywhere, it was there, and Harriman had set the dominoes in motion with the Southern Pacific deal.

Knowing observers predicted an explosion in the Northwest, where Harriman continued to resist any settlement based on territorial division, only to be stunned when it occurred on the opposite front. The reason lay in one basic fact: none of the three roads vying for dominance in the Northwest owned a line to Chicago. In the new age of mega-systems, it made sense to redefine a transcontinental line as one controlling its own route from Chicago to the Pacific coast. With the Iowa roads in so volatile a state, the time to shop was now, before some rival scooped up the best line.[24]

The two best prospects were the Burlington and the Milwaukee. Harriman had already sniffed out the Burlington only to be distracted by Huntington's death. During the hectic winter of 1901 Hill took his turn. Morgan preferred the Milwaukee because it was cheaper, Hill the Burlington because it occupied territory claimed by the Union Pacific "over better lines and with better terminals than any other road." Hill sounded out the Milwaukee in deference to Morgan, but when these discussions waned in December, Morgan sent him after the Burlington. The price of war was about to go up.[25]

Like a gathering storm, the merger mania had been hovering over the West for months, illuminating the sky with one sensational rumor after another. Then suddenly the storm burst as Harriman bought the Southern Pacific, Gould took the Rio Grande, and Hill went after the Burlington with Harriman close behind him. Harriman met Perkins in Chicago on February 10 and offered to buy half the Burlington's stock. The next day Hill arrived with a proposal to merge the Great Northern and Burlington through a stock swap. Perkins welcomed Hill as a suitor but stuck by his terms: $200 a share in cash.[26]

As the price of Burlington soared in the market, all the players agonized over who was buying. Back came Harriman to dine with Perkins on February 22, but instead of a new offer he pointed out that Hill and Morgan were buying Burlington stock heavily and asked that someone from the Burlington board negotiate with him. Two days later Perkins huddled with his top advisers to weigh the merits of combining with Hill or Harriman. They agreed unanimously that "if Hill means also Morgan and the Northern Pacific, as he says it does, that would be the stronger and safer place for us to land."[27]

Unaware of this development, Harriman decided to buy only enough Burlington to wield influence in the community of interest spirit. The best way would be a joint purchase by the Union Pacific and Northern Pacific. But he and Schiff grew uneasy that people close to Hill were buying large amounts of Burlington stock regardless of price. Late in March they paid a call on Hill and asked if he was trying to gain control of the Burlington. Hill replied blandly that he was not buying stock and had no interest in acquiring the road. Satisfied that the word of his old friend was good, Schiff left feeling more reassured than did Harriman.[28]

Here, as in so many clashes among titans, truth proved as elusive as understanding. It is possible that Hill was more virtuous than Harriman; certainly he worked harder at cultivating an air of virtue. He denied Schiff's charge not once but several times and insisted that he had told Harriman clearly what he was doing. But Hill's explanations do not even jibe with one another, and their tone leaves the impression that he was trying to persuade himself as much as others. In this game of high stakes he did not hesitate to deceive his old friend. But neither had Harriman and Schiff told Hill about their earlier efforts to buy the Burlington.[29]

Having snookered Schiff, Hill sneaked off to Boston for a series of meetings with Perkins. Between March 27 and April 9 they hammered out terms for the sale of the Burlington to the Northern Pacific. But reporters spotted them, and on March 30 news of their conferences went public. While Harriman steamed, Schiff learned that Hill was on his way to another session with Perkins. Hurriedly he asked the banker George F. Baker to arrange a meeting, then sent his son Morti to intercept Hill at the ferry landing. Morti persuaded the reluctant Hill to come with him to Baker's house, where the elder Schiff and Harriman were waiting. It was neutral ground. Although Baker was close to Morgan, he did not share the latter's grudge against Harriman and was anxious to avoid an irreparable split between Harriman and Hill.[30]

The atmosphere in Baker's parlor was funereal, charged with the tension that overhangs any scene the participants expect to be unpleasant. Hill looked ill at ease at the prospect of being asked questions he did not want to answer. The bristling Harriman strained at the leash of propriety like a terrier, eager to have at it. Schiff struggled to contain the anger and disappointment tugging at his sturdy mask of tact and gentility. He was the first to break the awkward silence. Why, he asked earnestly, had Hill disclaimed any interest in the Burlington?[31]

Hill apologized for misleading his old friend, explaining that Schiff's connection with the Union Pacific made it necessary. Schiff expressed his mortification in wounded tones, then let the matter drop; the real issue was not hurt feelings but the Burlington. He and Harriman pleaded with Hill not to close any deal with Perkins until some agreement had been reached to protect the Union Pacific's interests. Hill regretted that this was not possible. Harriman urged him to reconsider, adding ominously that any such purchase would be regarded by the Union Pacific as an invasion of territory and a hostile act. Hill deflected the request by mumbling a few platitudes.

Harriman was having none of it. "Then you will have to take the consequences," he barked. Hill made no reply and stalked out to catch the Boston train.

A sense of foreboding made Schiff's skin crawl with fear of the repercussions that would flow from a collision between Harriman and Hill. He rushed to Morgan's office to enlist his help, but Morgan was preparing to depart on his annual hegira to Europe and did not want to talk business. Disappointed, Schiff turned to Morgan's partner Robert Bacon, who had earlier told Harriman that he could do nothing until the Union Pacific made a specific proposal. Schiff offered to take a one-third interest in the Burlington purchase; otherwise, he warned Bacon, the merger would "bring the Northern roads, with their great power, at the throat of all trans-Missouri railroad interests, and . . . be a constant danger to the Union Pacific."[32]

"It's too late," replied Bacon. "Nothing can be done."

Schiff struggled to contain the anger welling up inside him. Not the least of it flowed from his resentment at the arrogance of the Morgan men and their condescension toward those they thought inferior to them. Schiff fought these familiar feelings down, as he usually did, and tried vainly to impress on Bacon that the Union Pacific regarded the situation as intolerable and would not hesitate to protect itself. His warning fell on deaf ears.

Later Hill justified the refusal by saying the offer was illegal, but privately he gave a different explanation. The Burlington directors balked at dealing with the Union Pacific, he noted, and "we did not want them." With these words Hill sang a requiem to the community of interest. Both he and Bacon seemed strangely oblivious to the broader ramifications of what they done. There was surely an element of revenge in sticking it to Harriman for the aggravation he had caused them in the Northwest. Morgan himself shared this attitude and regarded the request for a one-third interest as "butting in." Not even Jupiter was above letting personal bias cloud his judgment; never was this weakness to prove more disastrous.[33]

Harriman had behaved no better. He had treated them much the same way he had George Gould. First, he had tried to get the Burlington without telling them; then, having refused to share Navigation with the others, he demanded that they share the Burlington with him. He had spurned the proposals by Hill and Morgan for peace in the Northwest only to insist that they swallow his version of peace on the plains. In short, he had tried to "Harrimanize" them without success.

How could there be community of interest among men so adamant on having things their own way? No suitable answer to this question was forthcoming, and time was running out. The Burlington purchase set in motion a chain of events that would soon swallow all the players and fix the destiny of the rail industry for nearly a century.

Schiff alone sensed that disaster would result from the refusal to share the Burlington. He could not imagine what it would be, but he knew Harriman would not ignore any gauntlet tossed at his feet. In desperation Schiff made a personal appeal to Hill only to be politely but firmly rebuffed. Hill, Perkins, and Bacon wrapped up the transaction by dividing the Burlington equally between the Great Northern and the Northern Pacific. Morgan sailed to Europe secure in the belief that the Burlington was safely tucked away in the hands of the northern lines. It would not prove to be the most serene vacation he ever took.[34]

15 Seeking Trump

When the railway mileage of the country is in the control of ten men, will those ten men be found willing to yield their personal preferences and interests to the general good enough and often enough to maintain unity of purpose? Or will personal ambitions, jealousies, annoyances over outside matters, or other complications disintegrate community of ownership until instead of harmony, railway wars break out between great systems instead of between local roads?

—Wall Street Journal, *April 5, 1901*

One requirement for those who aspire to greatness is the ability to think the unthinkable, conceive plans so audacious that no one suspects they are even being considered, and then execute them fearlessly. During the frantic spring of 1901, as the Burlington slipped into Hill's hands, Harriman jumped to a response that seemed as logical to him as it did fantastic to others: if he could not buy the Burlington directly, he would get it by buying one of the buyers.

The Great Northern was out of the question; Hill and his friends clutched it too tightly. The Northern Pacific had outstanding $80 million in common and $75 million in preferred stock. Hill and Morgan controlled only about $35 or $40 million of this in the belief that no one was demented enough to go after a $155 million railroad in the open market. The flaw in this reasoning was that it underestimated Harriman, who had both the resources and the nerve for such a campaign. He still had $60 million of the $100 million convertible bonds issued to buy the Southern Pacific. More important, he also had Schiff and Stillman behind him.[1]

Shortly after his fruitless appeal to Bacon early in April, Schiff started buying Northern Pacific stock. Ordinarily large purchases attracted attention, but the market had been seized by one of its periodic feeding frenzies. There were large transactions in Milwaukee stock, fueling rumors that the Union Pacific was buying the road, and in Union Pacific itself, sparking rumors that Hill or the Vanderbilts would soon own it. This activity camouflaged Schiff's buying. By late April he had picked up $25 million of preferred and $27 million of common. Harriman sent him back for more, but Schiff could find little on a fast-rising market.[2]

These large transactions aroused no suspicion. Morgan had boarded the

White Star liner *Teutonic* on April 4, leaving Bacon and newcomer George W. Perkins to mind the shop. Hill left St. Paul on April 15 to take an English friend on a tour of the Great Northern. Later writers concocted the tale that Hill learned of huge transactions in Northern Pacific stock while in Seattle and responded with a mad dash across the continent. Albro Martin has demolished this myth by showing that Hill made record runs to Seattle and back simply because his guests were in a hurry and Hill "had nothing in particular to do in Seattle except turn around and come back." After the trip, Hill lingered in St. Paul a week. On Friday afternoon, April 26, a clerk hurried in to tell Hill that Northern Pacific stock had jumped three points that day on a huge volume of 129,900 shares. One analyst attributed most of the buying to Union Pacific "on the expectation that E. H. Harriman would join the board next week." Only then did Hill go to New York, but still without any sense of urgency; he did not leave St. Paul until Saturday evening.[3]

All existing accounts of these events have been muddled by a curious error: they have Hill arriving in New York on Friday, May 3, and going at once to see Schiff, as if the sole purpose of his trip had been the Northern Pacific crisis. But Hill actually reached New York on Monday, April 29, five days before he saw Schiff. The intriguing question is, What did he do that fateful week after checking in at the Netherlands Hotel?[4]

None of the evidence suggests that he had come because of Northern Pacific. His main mission may have been to see his daughters off; they were going abroad, and he packed them aboard ship on Tuesday. That same day Schiff's son Morti was married, but it is not clear whether Hill attended the wedding breakfast at Sherry's. A reporter spotted the Harrimans and the William Rockefellers, but not Hill. There was to be a meeting of the Baltimore & Ohio board on Friday, but it was canceled. On Thursday he went to New London. Beyond this, the trail grows cold. Throughout that crucial week, Harriman and Schiff managed to keep their buying campaign secret.[5]

Whatever else Hill was doing, he could not help noticing that the stock market had gone berserk. By coincidence the exchange opened for the first time that Monday in cramped temporary quarters at the Produce Exchange, and the brokers were greeted with the busiest day in their history. Prices gyrated wildly as a record 2.38 million shares changed hands. Union Pacific soared eleven points and Northern Pacific ten.[6]

Bewildered pundits groped for an explanation. The spotlight had been on Union Pacific since April 24, when it set a new record for transactions in one stock as 662,800 shares were traded. In ten days the stock had jumped from 98½ to 133, convincing analysts that someone was buying for control. But who? Harriman remained tight-lipped to the reporters dogging his heels. On Tuesday,

Man on a mission: The indomitable James J. Hill, in a typical moment on the move and in a hurry. (James J. Hill Reference Library, St. Paul)

while he enjoyed Morti Schiff's wedding, the market smashed the record set the previous day by trading nearly 3.3 million shares, a million of them in the first hour alone. When the smoke cleared, the *New York Times* declared flatly that Harriman had lost the Union Pacific to the Vanderbilts. There were also heavy transactions in Milwaukee and Northern Pacific.[7]

By Wednesday the strain of handling record volumes in jammed, unfamiliar quarters began to tell. Brokers sagged with weariness and anxiety. As confusion piled up faster than the litter on the exchange floor, more analysts edged toward the conviction that Harriman had lost a dogged fight with the Vanderbilts for the Union Pacific. After wild swings on Wednesday the stock closed up thirteen points. Still Harriman remained mum. William K. Vanderbilt himself was in France, where he was said to be conferring with Morgan, and half a dozen other rumors chased each other around the exchange.[8]

On Thursday the volume exceeded 2.8 million, with the heaviest transactions in Atchison. That morning Harriman informed the Union Pacific executive committee that he had purchased large amounts of Northern Pacific securities for the company. Later that day he and Schiff attended a ceremony unveiling a statue of Henry B. Hyde, founder of the Equitable Life Assurance Company. Afterward Harriman put off the flock of reporters hovering around him with the cryptic remark, "I certainly have not let go of anything that I have had."[9]

On Friday speculators sent the market reeling by grabbing profits. The volume exceeded three million shares as Union Pacific and Northern Pacific tumbled with the rest of the list. Still nobody knew what was happening, but Harriman's comment reinforced a general feeling that he had beaten back the attempt to snatch the Union Pacific from him—if indeed there had been one. It had been one of the strangest weeks in the history of Wall Street, and no one suspected that it was but a prelude to even more sensational events.[10]

Biographers of great generals like to portray their campaigns as bold, decisive actions won by daring deeds and deft maneuvers, when in fact victory often staggers out from the bungled efforts of ignorant armies clashing by night. So it is with business titans as well. Campaigns portrayed in retrospect as brilliantly conceived and crisply executed often turn out to be desperate attempts to salvage something from a series of wrong choices made in confused circumstances.

Harriman had triggered this chain of events by seizing the Navigation line while negotiating peace in the Northwest. Hill retaliated by grabbing the Burlington, then refusing to share it just as Harriman had declined to share Navigation. Now Harriman hoped to get an interest in Burlington through the Northern Pacific, which in his hands would become Hill's most formidable rival. Men who professed their desire for peace had made a series of choices leading to war, ignoring at every turn the basic premises on which community of interest rested. Each time the stakes had gone up until what began as an effort to harmonize differences escalated into a showdown. Everything depended now on the swift execution of battle plans to ensure victory. Instead, there followed a succession of blunders that produced a fatal impasse.

By Friday, May 3, Harriman and Schiff were confident that victory lay within their grasp. What happened that day remains a riddle of contradictions. Sometime that morning Hill sauntered into the building at 27 Pine Street that housed the offices of both Kuhn, Loeb and the Great Northern. Schiff was waiting for him, his face pinched with intensity. They stepped inside Schiff's private office, where, in earnest tones, Schiff said that the Union Pacific had secured about 40 percent of Northern Pacific's stock "to bring about the harmony and community of interest which other means and appeals . . . had failed to produce."[11]

"But you can't get control!" cried an astonished Hill.

"That may be," said Schiff, "but we've got a lot of it."

Hill did not yet know that some of his friends along with Morgan associates, the Northern Pacific treasury, and even a Morgan trust fund had sold shares to profit from the rise without suspecting that someone was buying for control. Hill penned several versions of what happened next at the interview with Schiff, each more elaborate than the last. From them emerges a fascinating conspiracy theory without a shred of hard evidence to sustain it.[12]

The real target, Hill claimed, was not himself but Morgan, and the driving force behind the attack was Stillman, for whom Harriman was merely an instrument. But even Stillman did not have the resources for a broadside attack on Morgan, which could only mean he was seconded by his friend William Rockefeller and the Standard Oil millions under his influence. "They offered me . . . control of Un & So Pac as well as Nor Pac &c," Hill related shortly afterward. "They offered me their Nor. Pac proxy for ten years if myself and friends would cooperate with them and throw Morgan overboard, and they actually had the gall to suppose that I would consider such a proposal." Three years later he embellished the story: "On going into our office in Schiff's building I met him, and he told me they had bought sixty millions of Northern Pacific, which, with what myself and friends owned, would give an absolute control, and we would put the whole thing in together with the Union and Southern Pacific, and that I should make my own terms and take general direction of the combined properties. Harriman came in often and repeatedly said, 'You are the boss. We are all working for you. Give me your orders.'" Why would the "City Bank crowd," as Hill labeled them, do such a thing? "I am sure," he asserted, "the main motive was truly expressed by Stillman and others who said, they would show the world that Morgan was not the only Banker in America &c that all other Banking Houses were nothing more than his clerks, and talked of cutting his wings &c."[13]

Was this a campaign so gigantic that it sought to dethrone the mighty Morgan from his leadership of the financial world? Circumstantial elements at least support the possibility. The bad blood between Harriman and Morgan was well known, and it was Morgan whose resources had made the Burlington deal possible. While both Schiff and Stillman had become prominent in banking circles, they could never escape Morgan's shadow. The motive was there, and possibly the ambition as well. Moreover, a combination of the sort described by Hill could dictate peace throughout the West.

The most glaring flaw in Hill's scenario, aside from lack of evidence, is that it simply does not fit the characters. It is hard to imagine men as notoriously conservative and prudent as Schiff and Stillman launching so reckless an assault on a banker whose goodwill they taken pains to cultivate for so many years. To accept Hill's story is to believe that Schiff and Stillman were willing to gamble their reputations, as well as the future of firms to which they were devoted, on one rash fling of the dice. Harriman was far more daring than either of his partners, but Hill reduces his role to that of puppet. It is as difficult to conceive of Harriman playing this docile part as it is to imagine Schiff being so wildly indiscreet about Morgan or making any such brash proposal.

What, then, to make of Hill's story? Like many righteous men with strong convictions, he had a way of adjusting the facts to fit his needs. His dislike of Harriman grew stronger over time, fueled by the mounting bitterness between them. Moreover, Harriman's soaring reputation challenged Hill's supremacy as a railroad man. He had begun to upstage Hill, and strong egos tend to make estranged bedfellows.

The one certainty about Hill's meeting with Schiff is that it alerted him to a serious danger. If the Burlington deal stood, the Hill-Morgan roads would parallel the Union Pacific on both sides, threaten its local business with branch construction, and maintain the possibility of extending the Burlington to California. If Harriman obtained the Northern Pacific and half of the Burlington, he would control the entire region south of the Great Northern to the Pacific coast. This was a battle neither side could afford to lose.

The weak link in any scheme Harriman undertook, the one variable he could never predict or control, was his own body. It was not frail, as many observers thought, but simply inadequate to the demands made on it. The more power he burned, the harder it was for the physical plant to stay with it. He was forever falling prey to colds or la grippe even in his youth, and after 1900 more serious ailments began to plague him. At this critical moment in the Northern Pacific campaign his health again betrayed him. On Saturday, May 4, Harriman was laid up at home with another of his interminable colds. It is not known when he fell ill; if he had also been at home the day before, he could not have been present at Schiff's meeting with Hill.[14]

Lying in bed that Saturday morning, the telephone at his elbow, he rehashed the battle plan repeatedly for flaws or loopholes that might come back to haunt him. One technicality bothered him. He had acquired a majority of Northern Pacific's total stock and its preferred, but not of common. The company's board had the power to retire the preferred any time after January 1, 1902. Harriman could prevent this by electing his own board at the annual meeting in October, but what if the current board somehow postponed that meeting until after the first of the year and retired the preferred before Harriman could put in his own directors? It was a long shot at best, and counsel had assured him that a majority of the total stock was sufficient to control the road.

But Harriman was not satisfied. He needed only forty thousand shares to control the common as well. Between the honking and wheezing, drumming his fingers impatiently, he decided to close the last loophole. Aware that the market closed at noon on Saturdays, he called Schiff at Kuhn, Loeb only to find that he was at synagogue. He talked to a junior partner named Louis Heinsheimer and told him to buy forty thousand shares of Northern Pacific common. Heinsheimer confirmed the order and Harriman settled back on his pillow, unable to conceive of any other weaknesses Hill might exploit. Later that day reports came to him of heavy transactions in Northern Pacific stock, which convinced him that the new shares had been acquired and Northern Pacific was secure.[15]

That same morning while at synagogue, Schiff was surprised to find Louis Heinsheimer beckoning urgently to him. Informed of Harriman's order for forty thousand shares of common, he told the younger man to ignore the order. It was not necessary, Schiff added; he would take full responsibility for the action. The previous evening Schiff had received an odd visit from Hill, who had droned on in his animated way well past midnight without saying much. The performance baffled Schiff, but he saw nothing in it to worry about and did not bother mentioning it to Harriman.[16]

Standing in the elegant lobby of the Regina Grand Hotel in Aix-les-Bains, his mind devoted more to an inventory of art treasures he coveted than to matters of business, the portly but imposing figure of J. P. Morgan made an easy target for the clerk bearing a cable from New York. Morgan liked the old resort, although he was erratic in taking its prescribed cure. Reporters and photographers did not bother him, and the townspeople knew him. On this visit the mayor had come to greet him officially with a large bouquet in thanks for money he had donated to the town hospital. Later the town would also name a street after him.[17]

The cable handed him, however, drained the pleasure from his visit. It told of Harriman's attempt to gain control of the Northern Pacific and of a plan Hill had devised to thwart him. The scheme required buying more Northern Pacific stock—at least $15 or $20 million worth to be safe—and Robert Bacon could not spend that kind of money without direct authority from Morgan. As Morgan absorbed the message, consternation spread like a cloud across his softly rounded but fierce features dominated by an unfortunately diseased nose. Without hesitation he strode to the desk and dictated a reply authorizing Bacon to buy

Jupiter's glare: The stern visage of J. P. Morgan, whose diseased nose was touched up here, as it was in nearly all photographs of him. (Culver Pictures)

at any price all the Northern Pacific common needed to assure control. But the cable did not reach Bacon until Sunday, May 5, too late to have any effect if Kuhn, Loeb had carried out Harriman's order.[18]

Standing in the lobby of the Waldorf Astoria Hotel on a busy day, the lucky tourist might encounter Mark Twain or Richard Harding Davis, Lillian Russell,

Gentleman Jim Corbett, or Admiral George Dewey, the hero of Manila. If the tourist were sharp-eyed enough, he might also spot Diamond Jim Brady or James R. Keene, Edwin Hawley or Bet-a-Million Gates. Along with being a crossroads of glamour and celebrity, the Waldorf was the favorite haunt of prominent Wall Street men. To be labeled one of the "Waldorf crowd" signified that a Wall Street warrior had arrived.[19]

It was there at a private dinner party that young Bernard Baruch claimed to have seen Gates place a $1 million bet in a baccarat game. Through the Empire Room and Peacock Alley, the billiard room and the Men's Cafe with its elegant four-sided mahogany bar, roamed the best-known men on the street, rehashing the day's events over a quiet drink or continuing a negotiation long after the financial district had shut down. During these hectic May days the Waldorf crowd found itself under pressure and on display as never before.

"This has been the most colossal week of speculative trading in the world's history," blared the *New York Herald* on Sunday, May 5. By noon Saturday more than 15.4 million shares had changed hands; the previous record, set only two weeks earlier, had been a mere 10 million shares. The leaders had been Union Pacific (2 million shares traded) and Atchison (1.5 million), and most pundits were still tracking a suspected corner in Milwaukee stock. The action in Northern Pacific had been strong but overshadowed by other stocks.[20]

The giddy, rarefied air of a bull market intoxicated the street. No one pretended to know what was happening, but speculators clambered aboard for what they hoped would be a prolonged ride. "When a man is in a wagon behind a runaway team," sighed a cautious broker, "the best thing to do is to clutch the back of the seat, hang on and make no predictions." One speculator, bathing his success in champagne at the Waldorf, was blasé enough to utter the wish that he might lose a million for a change. He was about to get his wish.[21]

At the House of Morgan, Bacon knew his task would not be easy. Finesse was out of the question; the market was already inflamed with speculative fever. To manage this difficult campaign he enlisted James R. Keene, one of the smoothest operators on the exchange. Keene had won and lost a dozen fortunes over his long career, and he had earned Morgan's confidence by his deft handling of the United States Steel offering. He never appeared on the floor during an operation, but his presence was felt through the army of brokers he employed.[22]

When the opening bell rang Monday morning, Keene's army rushed forward with fistfuls of buy orders. "In my entire career on the Stock Exchange," marveled Bernard Baruch, "I do not recall another opening similar to this one." The price of Northern Pacific catapulted nearly 18 points to 127½. "Screaming, leaping, scuffling, gesticulating and turning the group of Northern Pacific traders into one great football scrimmage," wrote one bemused reporter, "they scrambled madly for the stock." No one could account for the rise. Reporters badgered every Northern Pacific director they could find only to draw bewildered shrugs.[23]

Suddenly the phone in Harriman's bedroom began ringing off its hook. The reports on the tumult bothered him, as did the fact that he had received no final confirmation of his forty-thousand-share purchase. He rang up Heinsheimer to ask why and was greeted by an embarrassed silence. At last Heinsheimer blurted out the instructions Schiff had given him. Harriman gnashed his teeth in frustration. "I then became convinced," he said later, "that if I was ever going to get anywhere I would have to get men upon whom I could rely." These words would have mortified Schiff had he seen them. He never explained why he chose not to execute the buy order, though he admitted the fault was his alone. It was the one time he failed Harriman, and he could not have picked a worse time.[24]

For the moment Harriman was stumped. "I then knew," he declared, "... that the whole object of our work might be lost." Realizing the futility of trying to buy stock in a market gone mad, he dragged himself downtown to ask Schiff some hard questions "and to fight the question out with the material I had in hand." He had never been a good loser, and he did not even know whether he had lost. Whatever happened, his vast holdings in Northern Pacific gave him leverage.[25]

Wall Street was awash with wild rumors that only made traders even more frantic. On Tuesday Northern Pacific jumped another sixteen points while other stocks fell violently. "TITANS FIGHT FOR CONTROL OF BIG ROAD," screamed one headline as the truth dawned about who was fighting whom for what. By the day's end Morgan's men had the shares they needed, and Harriman realized the supply of actual stock had been cornered. The next morning Harriman informed the Union Pacific board of his latest stock purchases and got authority to buy or sell Northern Pacific. But there was nothing left to buy.[26]

The stage was set for disaster even though the major players had vanished into the wings. Speculators, who had been pouring sell orders into the market in hopes of profiting from the fall they believed was sure to come, realized to their horror that Northern Pacific had been cornered, and that the buying was for control. The stock would be kept off the market, which meant that none was available to fill their contracts at any price. As turmoil swept the floor, the price of Northern Pacific soared another 17 points to 160 while the rest of the list again dropped.[27]

That night throngs of haggard brokers surged through the halls of the Waldorf, talking, straining to overhear other conversations, moaning in despair over what the next day would bring, waiting anxiously for the London market to open and give them a sign. "One look inside the Waldorf that night was enough to bring home [the] truth of how little we differ from animals after all," observed

Baruch. "From a palace the Waldorf had been transformed into the den of frightened men at bay." Talk of losing a million had ceased to be blasé.[28]

All day Wednesday Harriman, Schiff, and Stillman held meetings with Gould, some Morgan men, Northern Pacific officers, and bankers seeking to arbitrate the fight. A reporter managed to intercept Schiff and asked if the Harriman syndicate had captured Northern Pacific. "We think that we have," came the terse reply. A mutual friend spotted Hill in Harriman's office chatting amicably.[29]

On Thursday morning a horde of ashen, bleary-eyed brokers stumbled through the drizzle to meet their fate. While wrecking crews were tearing down the old stock exchange building, the demolition on the Produce Exchange floor went on far more vigorously. After a ragged start, panic swept across the floor as trapped short sellers, unable to beg or borrow Northern Pacific, bid the stock up in rapid succession from 320 to 550 to 700 to an astonishing 1,000 in one 300-share transaction. Meanwhile, other stocks plunged 10 to 60 points, and the call loan rate shot up to 60 percent.[30]

Distraught brokers milled about the floor with stricken looks, unable to comprehend what was happening. Asked his opinion of the spectacle, Hill likened it to a ghost dance. "The Indians begin their dance," he intoned, "and they don't know why they are doing it; they whirl about until they are almost crazy. It is so when these Wall Street people get the speculative fever."[31]

An antidote for the fever was needed, and fast. As a by-product of their struggle for Northern Pacific, the rivals had triggered a major panic that threatened to bring the temple crashing down on all their heads. Harriman's fighting blood was still up, but even he recognized the need for a truce. The round of meetings that had begun on Wednesday resumed with fresh urgency, shifting from Harriman's office to Kuhn, Loeb to Morgan's. After some tough bargaining, Harriman and Bacon agreed to let the shorts settle at $150 a share without immediate delivery. When the announcement reached the exchange at three o'clock, the panic subsided at once. Northern Pacific closed at 325, up 165 for the day.[32]

As the story behind the fight leaked out, critics blasted both Harriman and Hill even though it was conceded that they had played no part in the panic itself except to stop it. Their only crime had been to start a fight that allowed eager speculators to slip their necks into a noose. But the panic quickly took on a broader significance as a graphic example of the dangers of letting titans wield unrestrained power. It became a prime exhibit for the gathering political storm against the abuses of big business.

Harriman noticed none of these danger signs or larger implications. Later he dismissed the panic as "the supposed contest between Morgan & Co. and ourselves" and insisted that "we were not in the supposed contest and had no hand in it." A weary operator was more candid. "The trouble has grown out of personal feeling between Mr. Harriman and Mr. Morgan," he declared. "It is an ugly thing all around."[33]

By coincidence, William K. Vanderbilt stepped off the boat from Europe on the very day of the panic. Rumor had pointed insistently to him as the titan behind the attempt to seize first the Union Pacific and then the Northern Pacific even though he had been abroad the whole time. Once on the scene, Vanderbilt neither looked nor sounded like a titan. A reporter watched him digest news of the panic, then asked his opinion. "I am not in the habit of talking for publication," Vanderbilt replied loftily, "but I am willing to say that I regard the condition of things in Wall Street as silly."[34]

The debris of battle lay scattered all over Wall Street and could not be easily swept up. Regardless of who had control of the Northern Pacific, some accommodation had to be made to prevent the war from breaking out again. Frustrated as he was, Harriman could not afford to let disappointment cloud his judgment. He knew that Schiff was beside himself with anxiety over the whole affair and fearful of what Morgan would think. When Schiff learned that Morgan was not returning at once from Europe, he hastened to write him a long explanation in tones that seemed to beg forgiveness.[35]

Three days after the panic Hill strolled into Kuhn, Loeb's office to see Schiff. Finding him out, he wandered over to the desk of Felix Warburg and asked, "How is Schiff?"

"Not very happy," answered Warburg.

Hill shrugged. "He takes these things too seriously."[36]

Harriman had no choice but to negotiate; to continue the fight was out of the question. The business community had joined in the public outcry against the panic, and a prolonged clash would inflame the rising political hackles against bigness and the abuse of power. Tactically a stalemate existed. The Harriman camp held a majority of all Northern Pacific stock, but Hill and Morgan owned a majority of the common. Later the rivals discovered that together they owned $79 million of the $80 million common stock.[37]

Who had control? If the company's annual meeting was held on schedule in October, Harriman could elect his own board. But if the present board postponed the meeting until after the first of the year, it could take up the preferred stock and prevent Harriman from putting in his own directors. One set of eminent lawyers assured Harriman that this could not be done; another set assured Hill that it could be done. With the stakes so high, no one cared to test the matter in court, where it might take months to resolve.[38]

A compromise was needed. Harriman was willing, but Hill did not want to be associated with him in any way. He did not like Harriman's style or his way of dominating anything that came within his reach. Earlier Harriman had ducked

Hill's overtures for a settlement in the Northwest; now Hill avoided Harriman while he scrounged for loose shares of Northern Pacific common. But there were none. Both men edged toward the bargaining table because they had nowhere else to go.[39]

Once there, they had to reconcile sharply contrasting visions of what should be. While Hill clung to the old notion of territorial division, Harriman had something far more ambitious in mind. Late in May he informed Bacon that he wanted not merely consolidation but integration on a grand scale. Compromise was possible if he and Hill could agree on "common methods of management and accounting" for all their roads. Hill regarded this notion more as threat than opportunity, but he was willing to trade vague gestures for something more concrete. Already a plan had formed in his mind for locking up the two northern systems in a giant holding company. Harriman would have to be part of this new company; the trick was to keep him in a minority position.[40]

On May 31 Harriman, Hill, Schiff, and Bacon slipped into New York's exclusive Metropolitan Club to thrash out terms. They came to agreement on two basic points. The first empowered Morgan to name the new Northern Pacific board. Harriman gave Hill and his friends control of the board to avoid a prolonged fight and to secure the second point. In return Hill agreed to join in devising a plan to establish uniform management and accounting methods for all the systems under their control. A complex formula for creating this plan was included in the agreement.[41]

The deal was announced with a fanfare of assurances that "complete and permanent harmony will result under the plan adopted." The smiles, however, went only skin deep. The Metropolitan Club agreement was vague enough to allow both men to think they had gained something, and each set out in quest of the object dearest to him. Early in June Harriman unveiled a plan to integrate control of all traffic on his and Hill's systems by placing it in the hands of two men, one selected by each party. Harriman chose John C. Stubbs, the gaunt, bespectacled Southern Pacific officer who had handled Collis Huntington's traffic affairs for thirty years. Hill picked Darius Miller, a genial executive with a knack for getting things done without antagonizing people.[42]

A dispute arose at once when Harriman insisted that the two men be given the same title of traffic director. "I fear Harriman loses sight of the danger of arousing unnecessary opposition from the public," complained Hill, who realized that both companies using the same title might suggest collusion and provoke an investigation by the ICC. While Stubbs settled into a Chicago office, Hill let Miller's status drift for a month before giving him the title of second vice president of the Great Northern.[43]

Harriman came grudgingly to see the need for disarming Hill's profound distrust of him. He accepted Morgan's slate of directors for the Northern Pacific without a murmur, and that summer he let his old antagonist do yeoman service bringing him together with Hill. In August Morgan invited both men aboard his yacht at Bar Harbor and elsewhere, nudging them toward agreement in his inimitable way. At one session Harriman listened to Morgan explain why it was necessary to retire the preferred stock, then surprised his host by giving cordial approval. Harriman then invited Hill to Arden and assured him that he meant to honor the agreement. A few days after Hill's departure, Harriman forwarded his proxies to Morgan for the October election.[44]

From Germany Schiff wrote Harriman rejoicing "that all shadows between Messrs Bacon, Hill & you have been pushed aside." Harriman bit his tongue. He loathed retiring the preferred on the terms offered and understood perfectly that Hill's holding company would reduce him to a stockholder, but Hill and Morgan had boxed him into a corner from which he could find no escape. The exchange of his Northern Pacific shares for stock in the new company, he admitted, "was a foregone conclusion unless we were prepared to commence litigation, which would be protracted and . . . detrimental to all railroad securities in view of the panic."[45]

He knew Schiff had no heart for a fight. As always, the banker took a more temperate view and appreciated better than Harriman the dangers through which they had just passed. By cable he prodded Harriman to resolve all differences with Hill. The fact that financiers throughout Europe spoke with great respect at what Harriman had accomplished was "a great 'stock in trade,' which you & we must be very careful not to imperil." Moreover, the recent market attack on the Union Pacific alerted Schiff that both it and the Southern Pacific were vulnerable to raids. Since they could not "permanently hold a sufficient amount of U P stock to absolutely control the Company," Schiff advised caution and vigilance "until we are absolutely certain that our rear is safe & that no attempts are likely to be made by others to get control of U. P."[46]

Harriman chafed at these realities, but he could not ignore them. With what little grace he could muster, he came to terms with Hill on the whole range of issues between them. He accepted the holding company plan and acquiesced in the kind of territorial agreement for the Northwest he had so long opposed. He gave Hill trackage rights to Portland in exchange for similar rights to Puget Sound. The old disputes in Idaho and Washington were resolved, with Stubbs and Miller handling the details. The press heard little of these matters and was too engrossed in the holding company to care anyway. The players, however, hailed the settlement as peace in their time and, in Schiff's view, "of the greatest importance and advantage to the Union Pacific."[47]

The Northern Securities Company, born November 12 in New Jersey, was a behemoth, its $400 million capital second only to that of United States Steel. For his Northern Pacific holdings Harriman received about $82.5 million worth of stock in the new company. Of its fifteen directors only three were loyal to Harriman; the rest were Hill and Morgan men. Hill was named president, and all of the officers were his men. From every angle Hill appeared to have won a decisive victory. He had locked up his properties safely and finally obtained from Harriman the territorial agreement he craved.[48]

But Harriman did get something he wanted. The fight had originated over the Burlington, which still posed a threat to the Union Pacific. In return for his concessions, Harriman wrung from Hill an agreement to create another holding company to lease the Burlington for 999 years. Half the stock in this new company would be owned by the Great Northern, the other half by the Union Pacific. The latter would not manage the Burlington but could block any expansion by it. The last obstacle to harmony would be removed.[49]

Harriman had used this device twice before—with the Alton and in December 1900, when he, Fish, and Kuhn, Loeb formed the Railroad Securities Company and exchanged its shares for their holdings in Illinois Central. But neither the Alton nor the Illinois Central was a parallel and competing line with the Union Pacific. The Burlington was, at least in part, and no one knew whether the courts would allow the Union Pacific to own its stock. Nor did anyone know whether Northern Securities itself could survive a legal challenge. Five days after its creation, Governor Samuel R. Van Sant of Minnesota denounced it as an "open violation of the plain intent and purpose of the law." With the zeal of a crusader who just happened to be up for reelection, Van Sant had Minnesota file suit against Northern Securities.[50]

The state suit bothered Harriman and Hill less than the threat of a federal attack. The Sherman Antitrust Act had yet to be applied to railroad mergers, and, as one analyst noted, "Union Pacific and Burlington . . . parallel each other throughout the State of Nebraska, in direct contravention to the constitution of that State." In December the ICC announced that it would hold an inquiry on the merger. No one feared the threat of an antitrust suit in an administration presided over by William McKinley, but something had happened to change the entire course of politics in Washington.[51]

On September 6, the same day Harriman had sealed the Metropolitan Club agreement by delivering his Northern Pacific proxies to Morgan, President McKinley was shaking hands with well-wishers at the Pan-American Exposition in Buffalo. One of those who approached him, an anarchist named Leon Czolgosz, pulled a gun and shot the president at close range. Eight days later McKinley died, elevating to the presidency a young, unpredictable dynamo named Theodore Roosevelt, who was to leave a fateful imprint on Northern Securities and on Harriman as well as the nation itself.

16 Seeking Hegemony

Harriman is not only a railroad man but a financier. Above all, he is a strategist. In the latter respect Morgan is said to be his inferior by capable judges. And he is ambitious; ambitious to surpass Morgan in the railroad world and perhaps if the real truth were known jealous of Morgan's great supremacy. . . . Harriman has never let slip an opportunity to benefit the great systems he controls in the West, and has always been on the alert to prevent any rival from breaking into his field.

—New York World, *May 12, 1901*

The spectacular fight over the Northern Pacific earned Harriman another honor: his first extended profile in a New York daily. His name had drifted through the press with mounting frequency since 1899, but this was the first time a reporter bestowed on him the kind of personal portrait reserved for big newsmakers. The illustration accompanying the profile was an example of the bad generic art used by newspapers before the use of photographs became common. Its well-stuffed body looked more like Morgan than Harriman, and the fleshy face with its neatly trimmed mustache bore a mild resemblance to William Howard Taft.[1]

If the artist missed the real Harriman, perhaps had never even seen him, the reporter captured his elusive subject well. His vivid account was echoed by later writers until it became the stuff of legend. The reporter admired Harriman for having the courage to challenge Morgan. Thousands of men might relish seeing Jupiter challenged, but not one in a thousand dared to lead the charge himself. Harriman was a battler with ability, supreme confidence, and a quick mind. And as the Northern Pacific fight demonstrated, he possessed the one quality reporters loved most: he made good copy.

Harriman's appearance left little impression except for an odd black derby that looked a size too large. He wore it two distinct ways: pulled forward, where the brim shielded his eyes, or jammed back on his head so that his ears stuck out. On the street he was as inconspicuous as the man with whom the reporter was the first to draw a comparison: Jay Gould. Both were small, slight, dark-skinned men with dark hair and eyes that glittered with hypnotic intensity. The reporter had heard men say that Harriman's eyes "could look through the steel side of a battleship."

During the next few years the black hair grew thin and gray, and the dark eyes glazed with fatigue, but the driving energy remained. "He goes about his work as if he were on springs," marveled the reporter. "He is chockful of nervous energy and bounds about from one place to another with never-ceasing restlessness. How he manages to buckle down to one thing long enough to complete it is a mystery to those who do not know him." That he got an enormous amount of work done was owing in part to his friendship with James Stillman. The reporter believed he understood the nexus of ambition that bound Harriman and Stillman together. Harriman longed to become the dominant railroad man in the nation, Stillman the supreme banker. The obstacle in both their paths was Morgan.

The portrait that emerged was that of a remarkable man who had amassed great power and craved still more yet was anything but a lone wolf. His position owed much to the resources behind him. Schiff, Stillman, the Rockefellers. The real mystery was the relationship among these titans. Were they associates or rivals? Who led and who followed? How tight was the bond among them? With so little information available, it was easy to regard Harriman as a puppet dangled by the big money behind him until the sheer force of his presence and the scale of his actions revealed the puppet to have a life very much its own.

Although Northern Securities became a landmark in the history of American business, it was a less original use of the holding company vehicle than Harriman had already conceived. The idea behind a holding company was to control several roads with a minimum of capital, but Harriman and his banker friends had something more in mind: to impose order on the chaotic rail industry. Large profits required a steady flow of capital from Europe, but the bankers could sell American securities to their overseas clients only if the emerging rail systems were efficient, well-managed, and free from the strife that had bled them to death earlier. Achieving this stability was the goal of community of interest, the voting trusts, the advisory board, and every other device of the era.

In puzzling through the maze of railroads west of the Mississippi River, Harriman came early to the holding company. Several of his Illinois Central cronies had formed one in February 1896 but left it dormant for two years. Harriman joined with Stillman and Fish to revive it as a vehicle for locking up $13.6 million worth of Illinois Central stock. It took Harriman until December 1900 to activate the Railroad Securities Company. By then he and his friends had created a holding company for the Alton as well, but the Northern Securities suit had a chilling effect on any further use of holding companies until the courts resolved their legality.[2]

Railroad Securities slipped quietly back into limbo while Harriman groped for other ways to expand and integrate his empire. The community of interest began to crack at the seams as it became clear that there were too many interests with too little sense of community among them. It was hard enough to keep track of events, let alone keep faith, during the frantic months of 1901 when everybody seemed to be buying a piece of somebody else. Until the courts resolved Northern Securities, Harriman had no choice but to improvise.

The Southwest theater was becoming as volatile as the Northwest. Since emerging from receivership in 1895, the Atchison had shown surprising strength under its capable new president, E. P. Ripley. Nevertheless, Schiff was convinced the "Atchison's independence cannot last very long," and he did not want it in unfriendly hands. In the spring of 1900 he and Harriman had started buying Atchison stock, but Schiff's efforts to enlist key foreign investors were blocked by Victor Morawetz, the financial maven of the Atchison.[3]

Schiff let the matter rest until a month after the Northern Pacific panic, then began picking up more Atchison stock. Hill urged him to make an offer directly to Morawetz, no doubt hoping to get Harriman looking southwest instead of northwest. After sounding his financial friends in Europe, however, Schiff concluded that Hill's approach could not be more wrong. "Morawetz is very jealous of his position," Schiff confided to Harriman, "& the least intimation to him that you & we want to get in will induce him to do everything he can to keep us out." The best course was to wait for Atchison stocks to slip from their present high prices. Then, Schiff urged, "we must have the courage to buy largely"—at least $40 or $50 million worth. The foreign investors would "go with us whenever we control enough stock to give us a chance in a contest, but we cannot count upon their help simply for love's sake, & it would be dangerous to even mention . . . what is in our mind."[4]

This advice offers a rare insight into Schiff's role in the partnership. To other eyes he was a quiet, dignified diplomat whose role consisted mainly of restraining the irrepressible Harriman. Yet part of the mortar binding them together was Schiff's ability to conceive bold plans and undertake great risks. They had already bought the Southern Pacific and were still carrying their huge load of Northern Pacific when Schiff wrote this meditation on yet another major investment. Stillman too possessed this improbable blend of caution, driving ambition, and daring. Harriman's partners were not just powerful and well connected; they also complemented him well.

Schiff differed from Harriman in knowing when to draw the line, and he drew it emphatically at the Rock Island. During the hectic spring of 1901, the men who dominated that road offered it to Harriman. He liked the property and the price, but when he took the proposal to Schiff, he received a polite lecture on the limits of human endurance. How could any one man, even a genius, Schiff asked tactfully, run the combined Union Pacific–Southern Pacific systems and take on additional burdens? Even if the Rock Island could be legally acquired, there was a limit to the economic advantages of scale. Make the combination too gigantic for one man, however able, to oversee properly and it would cease to be efficient.[5]

Harriman listened intently to this argument. "You are right," he conceded at last, "we had better leave it alone."

Nothing was more difficult for Harriman than leaving things alone. The Rock Island temptation took care of itself that summer when it passed into the hands of four promoters who soon became known on Wall Street as the "Rock Island crowd." But there were other properties lying around loose and plenty of raiders looking to piece together new systems or the facade of one to induce a buyout. A few brave souls were even building new lines. The toughest of them was Senator William A. Clark, who was pushing ahead on his proposed road from Los Angeles to Salt Lake. This was one challenge Harriman could not leave alone.

The Nevada desert seemed an unlikely battleground for the clash of titans. Visionaries had long dreamed of a direct line from Salt Lake City to southern California, where the burgeoning fruit business had begun to generate a large amount of traffic. But Los Angeles and San Diego were still small, sleepy towns, Las Vegas did not exist, and the mining industry in southern Nevada had faded with the decline of the legendary Comstock lode. The Union Pacific owned a line reaching as far south as Frisco, 277 miles from Ogden. In 1890 the Oregon Short Line had chartered a company to build from Milford, Utah, to Pioche, Nevada, but abandoned the project when money grew tight.[6]

The detritus of this project, consisting of some roadbed and tunnels, lay forgotten beneath the blazing desert sun and constant wash of shifting sands until 1898, when a new company called the Utah & Pacific built seventy-five miles of track from Milford to Uvada at the Nevada border. The Short Line gave this company its abandoned line in exchange for an option to buy the Utah & Pacific's stock within five years. It also created a new company to extend the line from Uvada through Nevada but did no work on the project.[7]

Harriman ventured into this remote arena earlier than most people realize. His first foray reveals how far ahead his thinking ran. In the winter of 1899, while organizing the Alaska expedition, he sent Samuel Felton to inspect the Los Angeles Terminal Railway and report on "its desirability as a terminus for a transcontinental line of railroad." At the time, Harriman had not yet reacquired the Navigation line and Huntington was very much alive; Harriman was looking at every possible avenue to the Pacific coast.[8]

The Terminal consisted of a twenty-eight-mile road from Los Angeles to the ocean at East San Pedro and three branches totaling another twenty-three miles of track. None of the lines did much business; it was a property waiting for a future that might never arrive. San Pedro, twenty-two miles south of Los Angeles, had a fine natural harbor. The federal government had plans to improve it and construct an inner harbor at Wilmington, where the Terminal company owned a large amount of salt marsh and tide land. No one considered this land of any value, and no one in the energy-starved Southwest dreamed that beneath it lay a vast reservoir of oil that would enrich the Union Pacific Railroad half a century later.[9]

Harriman was seeking an outlet to the sea for the flow of traffic along his Utah lines. The problem was that the route contained little local business to help support a new line. Moreover, Huntington had fought a masterful delaying action against the improvements at San Pedro to protect the port he was developing at Santa Monica. Any entrance into southern California would have to contend with Huntington's viselike grip on the region, and Harriman already had problems enough with Huntington at the Ogden gateway.[10]

The Terminal lines belonged to a promoter named R. C. Kerens, who had tried for nearly a decade to interest the Union Pacific in the project. In the spring of 1899 he found an unexpected supporter for the line. Kerens promptly sent an emissary to W. H. Bancroft, seeking this time not to enlist the Union Pacific as a partner but to buy or lease its line south of Salt Lake City. Bancroft got the message quickly. "I infer from his conversation," he telegraphed Harriman, "that W. A. Clark of Montana is behind him."[11]

This was a threat Harriman dared not ignore. The whole thrust of Clark's career had confirmed J. B. Bury's adage, "There is no force in nature more terrible than a young Scotsman on the make." Born in 1839 to Pennsylvania dirt farmers, Clark went early to Iowa and then Montana, where he endured incredible hardships to prosper as a merchant amid the brutal free-for-all of the gold camps. Gradually his interests spread to banking; then, in 1872, he made a daring leap into mining at a small, drowsy camp named Butte, where he erected the first smelter and acquired the lucrative Elm Orlu mine. In 1884 Clark happened on some ore samples from a remote mine in Arizona called the United Verde. Recognizing their value, he bought the mine and turned it into an enterprise that at its height fetched him profits of $10 million a year.[12]

By 1890 Clark had put together an empire of mines, mills, smelters, banks, stores, utilities, newspapers, and lumber holdings that made him one of the most powerful men in the West. A small, trim man standing five feet seven and weighing 140 pounds, Clark looked as forgettable as Harriman. Clear, cold blue eyes illuminated an otherwise drab face masked by a beard. His personality was a vacuum of austerity concealing a shrewd, calculating intelligence. "His heart is frozen and his instincts are those of the fox," said one of Clark's many detractors;

Formidable dandy: Mining millionaire turned social denizen W. A. Clark poses with his two daughters. (Montana Historical Society)

"there is craft in his stereotyped smile and icicles in his handshake. He is about as magnetic as last year's bird's nest."[13]

As Clark amassed wealth and success, however, the austere Scot turned into a dandy, a peacock addicted to things French, to attractive women, and above all to steady doses of public adulation. He took prolonged trips to Europe, began the obligatory art collection, and dabbled in cultural affairs. To hostile eyes he was vintage arriviste pure and simple, but nothing about him proved pure or simple. In 1900, when Clark was sixty-one, the whole bizarre range of his interests collided in a series of events that kept his name dancing through the headlines for weeks at a time.

Part of his new image involved a gargantuan mansion being constructed on Fifth Avenue and 77th Street, which sneering New Yorkers referred to as "Clark's Folly." Through the pages of the city's dailies, they followed avidly the progress of this latest addition to Millionaires' Row as well as the saga of the new wife Clark hoped to install there. Years earlier Clark had assisted the family of a miner killed in one of his mines. Two of the children were talented, attractive girls. Clark sent the eldest to France to study drawing. A widower since 1893, he soon fell in love with his protégé and proposed to her three years later. The idea infuriated his eldest daughter, Katherine, who was a year older than the step-mother she was about to inherit.[14]

Titillating as this soap opera was, it paled before the major scandal in Clark's life. His hunger for public adulation propelled him into politics. He went after a seat in the United States Senate in the only way he knew: he bribed the legislature to give it to him. His brazen tactics were too much even for the Senate, which refused to seat him. In desperation Clark resigned and had the lieutenant gover-nor reappoint him while the governor was absent, but that clumsy ruse fell flat. The Senate rejected him again, forcing Clark into a humiliating retreat from Washington.[15]

This episode earned Clark a different brand of public attention than he craved. "No election for a seat in the United States Senate has ever been so productive of scandal," sniffed the *New York Tribune*. Mark Twain paid Clark his own special brand of homage. "By his example he has so excused and so sweet-ened corruption that in Montana it no longer has an offensive smell," he wrote. "He is as rotten a human being as can be found anywhere under the flag; he is a shame to the American nation."[16]

None of this swayed or slowed Clark, who had the gall of a gambler and the certitude of a pope. While the critics raged, he moved serenely along with his mansion, his marriage, and his campaign for reelection to the Senate in the fall of 1900. Nor did he neglect his business affairs. Apart from Kerens's activities in Los Angeles, two developments called his attention to the Nevada desert that year. The discovery of a new bonanza mine, Tonopah, sent prospectors flocking into southwest Nevada and triggered a revival of the mining industry. Then Huntington died, removing the major obstacle to developing San Pedro as a port.

Clark saw that the proposed through line could tap the new mines in Nevada and open the mineral district of southwest Utah to development. Less than two weeks after Huntington's death, he announced that he would back the new line. The news caught Harriman while he was chasing the Southern Pacific and the Burlington as well as rebuilding the Union Pacific. While Harriman was preoc-cupied, Clark stole a march. In 1890 the Short Line had graded forty miles of line from Uvada to Caliente along with a branch from Caliente to Pioche. It had also surveyed a line through Meadow Valley Wash canyon and filed maps but done no work. The Union Pacific assumed that all rights to this route had passed to the Utah & Pacific, but Clark discovered that in 1894 it had been exposed for taxes and sold to the county. He also learned that a company called the Utah & California had surveyed the same route in 1897.[17]

It quickly became apparent that any feasible route from Ogden to Los Angeles had to pass through Meadow Valley Wash, which extended 110 miles southwest from Caliente. In March 1901 Clark incorporated the San Pedro, Los Angeles & Salt Lake Railroad, swept the Terminal properties into it, and announced that it would build the new road. He also acquired the defunct Utah & California and title to the original survey. His engineers commenced a new survey of Meadow Valley Wash, arguing that the Short Line route had been abandoned. When the federal land office upheld Clark's claim, he sent crews onto the entire Uvada-Caliente route.[18]

Caught by surprise, Harriman knew Clark well enough to waste no time on talk. He appealed the ruling, ordered the Short Line to exercise its option on the Utah & Pacific, and told Bancroft to rush construction on a new road from Ogden to Los Angeles. This was the kind of galvanizing order that railroad men loved. As Bancroft began pouring crews and material onto the disputed route, the outnumbered San Pedro crews tried to slow them by stringing barbed wire and filling cuts with rocks and timber. The mood grew tense but stopped short of violence.[19]

On April 24 the Department of Interior reversed the land office decision and awarded the old graded route to the Short Line. The struggle shifted to Meadow Valley Wash, where the prize would go to the first company that filed its map with the land office. Horace Burt rushed to the scene along with the engineer who had done the original survey in 1890. When the Short Line's engineers arrived in the narrow canyon, the dailies had the kind of spectacle they loved: two teams of surveyors racing to find separate lines in a cramped space with barely enough room for one decent line. In June the legal battle resumed at Carson City, where battalions of lawyers descended on the sleepy courthouse for a pitched battle of their own.[20]

In an age innocent of television, the clash of business titans was a favorite spectator sport for newspaper readers, and the bombast blowing in from the desert was a treat to relish. The court upheld the injunction against the San Pedro but allowed its work in the canyon to continue. The Short Line engineers whipped through their survey of Meadow Valley Wash in only twelve days and filed their maps first despite San Pedro protests that the maps were nothing more than copies of the original survey. Grimly the San Pedro crews threw up barricades across one end of the canyon while they graded frantically at the other. The Short Line men smashed through the barrier, but little fighting occurred. Clark got the court to enjoin the Short Line from doing any work in the canyon, which forced both sides to the bargaining table.[21]

Both Harriman and Clark were ready to compromise. The desert could barely support one line; moreover, Clark had no way to get into Utah or Harriman into Los Angeles without spending a lot more money. The question was what kind of deal to cut. It had to satisfy two tough bargainers and also stand up to the mounting attack on rail mergers. While dickering over terms, Harriman came to the realization that the answer lay in Clark's colossal vanity. The year had been kinder to Clark than to Harriman. He had reclaimed his seat in the Senate and married his young sweetheart. These pleasant distractions took some of the edge off Clark's business ambitions. He was willing to share the desert line with Harriman; all he wanted was the glory of building it. This, Harriman discovered, was the key to the solution.

In September the lawyers drew up a memorandum providing for a joint survey of Meadow Valley Wash and leaving all disputed points for Clark and Harriman to resolve personally. Publicly Clark encouraged every story that he was not only constructing the road but planning to link it with the Gould system. Privately, he assured Harriman of his intention to abide by the September memorandum until they could reach a broader agreement. Harriman understood the distinction between public posturing and private diplomacy. He did not mind the rumors, so long as they were not true; they might even deceive Gould.[22]

Harriman knew Clark was difficult to deal with and showed rare patience as the negotiations dragged out for months. On July 9 he was rewarded with a secret agreement in which Clark agreed to sell him a half interest in the San Pedro and the Empire Construction Company, which had been formed to build it. While this ensured Harriman ultimate control over the Los Angeles line, it also saddled him with Clark as a partner. The message was clear: Clark still wished to preserve the illusion that he was going it alone. As Harriman's chief adviser, W. D. Cornish, explained privately, "Mr. Clark is very sensitive on the point of his road being built as a San Pedro proposition. We are less tenacious about sentimental considerations but are looking to the final result."[23]

There was a good reason why Clark's vanity in demanding public recognition for building the road did not bother Harriman. The line was a crucial artery in his plan to dominate transcontinental traffic between Oregon and southern California and had to be kept out of rival hands. Having been burned by the furor over Northern Securities, Harriman saw an advantage in keeping the real ownership of the San Pedro disguised for as long as possible. The most remarkable thing about this deception was how well it succeeded. Rumors of a deal between Harriman and Clark abounded, but nobody knew who got what. When the Short Line transferred all its track south of Salt Lake City to the San Pedro,

Clark announced solemnly that it was "an absolute purchase, and Mr. Harriman retains absolutely no interest in the property." Even skeptics were convinced that Harriman had not gained control.[24]

On a bright Sunday morning in May 1903, Harriman and Clark sat down in San Francisco with their chief lieutenants to thrash out a procedure for building the road. The session lasted all day and produced the terms Harriman wanted. A few days earlier Clark had rejected them, but at the Sunday meeting Harriman dressed the same terms in different clothes and the senator swallowed them whole. Clark would get the glory and Harriman would get the road.[25]

But it did not come easy. Harriman and Clark agreed to create a committee of four to build and operate the road, with any dispute to be resolved by the two leaders personally. Harriman never liked doing things by committee, and he sensed from the outset that there would be trouble. His instincts proved correct; instead of the six months boldly predicted, the construction took nearly two years. But the secret remained intact. Not until October 1904, when Harriman mentioned the purchase in the Union Pacific annual report, did the news leak out that he owned a half interest in the road.[26]

Japanese doubts about the American way of business surfaced much earlier than most people realize. During the winter of 1901, when both community of interest and the merger mania were on the verge of a frenzied outburst, the director general of Japan's imperial railroads shook his head dubiously at the American example. "The amalgamation of roads does not strike me favorably," he admitted. "The community of ownership is fraught with danger and will work detrimentally to the interests of the people."[27]

A year later Harriman was coming to the same conclusion. As the Northern Securities fight graphically demonstrated, the community's members had failed utterly to devise ways of resolving their conflicts. Gradually the harsh truth dawned on them that cooperation among roads had limits that could not be overcome. Harriman learned this when he tried vainly to accommodate the traffic needs of both the Alton and the Illinois Central. Fish pressed him for more business at Omaha and protested vigorously when the Milwaukee demanded and got improved facilities there.[28]

Disputes flared over the exchange of traffic at Ogden and Denver as well. When a clash erupted in the Columbia River valley, Harriman had to assure a suspicious Hill that "I have done nothing to antagonize the situation and will not." Neither tact nor appeasement helped in most cases because concessions made in one direction annoyed some other interest, which promptly demanded new concessions in return. The community that appeared so united from without was a house divided within. The conflicts worsened steadily after 1901, eroding the enthusiasm and optimism that characterized the early faith in community of interest.

Harriman's relationship with George Gould had grown increasingly strained since the Southern Pacific purchase. They still sat together on several boards, but their interests were diverging in ways that hampered efforts to promote harmony. So far Gould had done nothing with his newly acquired Rio Grande roads, but east of the Mississippi River he launched a bold plan to forge a line to the Atlantic seaboard. No one had ever created a true coast-to-coast system, although Huntington had come close. Even Harriman had remained immune to this ambition.

Three major pieces of the line were already in place for Gould. The parent Missouri Pacific road reached Pueblo from St. Louis and Kansas City. From the latter cities the Wabash extended Gould's lines to Toledo and Detroit. In the fall of 1900 Gould had picked up the Wheeling & Lake Erie, which ran from Toledo to Wheeling, West Virginia. The key to Gould's grand scheme was reaching Pittsburgh, which generated an enormous traffic that was monopolized by the Pennsylvania Railroad. When one of Gould's officers discovered a good route from the Wheeling road to Pittsburgh, Gould decided to challenge the most powerful railroad in America.[29]

Stung by Gould's audacity, the Pennsylvania retaliated with every weapon in its arsenal—tying Gould up in court, in the state legislature, and on several other fronts. Unfazed, Gould sprang another coup in the spring of 1902 by acquiring the Western Maryland, which ran from Baltimore to Connellsville, Pennsylvania, only forty miles from Pittsburgh. To reach the seaboard, Gould had only to complete his new road to Pittsburgh and connect it to the Western Maryland.[30]

Gould's eastern forays had a subtle but profound effect on Harriman. While Harriman was delighted to see Gould's energies and resources squandered on a distant front, he could not ignore one danger signal. If Gould was endeavoring to forge a transcontinental line, he would need a line from Salt Lake City to the Pacific coast. Harriman had already shut him out of the Southern Pacific and the San Pedro (although Gould did not yet know about the latter). Would Gould dare to undertake construction of his own line?

One complex deal with Gould did little to reassure Harriman. During the fall of 1902 both men were drawn into the affairs of the Colorado Fuel & Iron Company (CFI), which was vital to them as a prime source of traffic for their roads and as the major independent steel company in the West. Railroads depended on steel companies for rails, bridge materials, and other needs. In 1900 only six firms produced steel rails, and they fixed prices on their own terms. This collusion frustrated Harriman's efforts to get better prices through large-scale buying. The formation of United States Steel in 1901 tightened this stranglehold by sweeping two of the largest firms together, and the traffic boon kept the mills humming with more orders than they could fill. In the bitter fight between the railroads and the rail makers, Harriman wanted to preserve CFI as an independent supplier.[31]

In the spring of 1901, however, the lynx eye of "Bet-a-Million" Gates fell on the property. Having just been elbowed out of the steel industry by Morgan, Gates viewed CFI as a promising reentry vehicle. But CFI president J. C. Osgood blocked Gates's efforts at every turn. The fight headed toward a showdown during the summer of 1902 amid a crossfire of threats and injunctions. By this time Harriman must have grown weary of Gates's portly shadow blighting his path. Whatever he thought of Gates personally, he regarded him as a rogue elephant lurching recklessly through companies in search of profits and indifferent to the debris left in his wake. Convinced that Gates only wanted CFI to unload on United States Steel at a blackmail price, he joined Gould and Edwin Hawley (whose Colorado & Southern also relied heavily on CFI traffic) in an already confused contest for control.[32]

Early in November Harriman invited Gould and Hawley to his office for a conference at which they agreed on a proposed board and composed a circular soliciting proxies. Their campaign succeeded in shoving Gates out of the picture. Then, inexplicably, Gould withdrew from the alliance and solicited proxies in his own name, claiming that Harriman and Hawley had used his name without his consent. "It is now taken for granted," wrote one pundit, "that Mr. Gould intends to play an independent part in the various schemes of rival interests."[33]

This was exactly what bothered Harriman. Did Gould's stand indicate that he was moving away from the community of interest to play a lone hand? The CFI fight was settled by a compromise giving each faction places on the board, but it was small change compared to what might follow if this breach was a prelude to larger ones. Then, in March 1903, a new line called the Western Pacific was chartered. Despite Gould's prompt denial, a Denver paper blared, "GOULD TO BUILD INDEPENDENT LINE TO PACIFIC COAST."[34]

While Harriman watched the Western Pacific for evidence of Gould's presence, he also had to deal with more immediate threats from the Atchison. In the summer of 1902 Atchison president E. P. Ripley decided to extend a small road called the Phoenix & Eastern from Phoenix to a connection with the Southern Pacific at Benson, Arizona. Ripley also wanted to push beyond San Francisco to the region between the ocean and the mountains, where a rich traffic in timber beckoned. But when he tried to buy a small road there that summer, Harriman snatched it up first. Undaunted, Ripley grabbed a tiny line that hauled redwood timber as a base in northwest California for what could turn into a construction war with the Southern Pacific.[35]

Faced with threats on so many fronts, Harriman told Atchison chairman Victor Morawetz bluntly that he considered both the Phoenix and northern

California lines an invasion of territory belonging to the Southern Pacific. That this stand was inconsistent with the one he had taken on territorial boundaries in the Northwest troubled him not at all. He saw in Arizona the possible evolution of a small local road into one paralleling the Southern Pacific; in California he feared the construction of a line all the way to Portland. This time Harriman's tough stand worked against him. The Atchison had neither the plans nor the money to undertake either project, but Harriman's obvious concern gave Morawetz unexpected bargaining power. When Harriman demanded that the Atchison sell him the Phoenix and abandon the region south of that town, Morawetz replied that any deal had to include a settlement for northern California as well. Later Morawetz admitted that he got the idea for a parallel line from these negotiations; Harriman had simply overplayed his hand.[36]

With negotiations at an impasse, Harriman and Schiff reconsidered their earlier plan to buy Atchison stock. But they could not buy everything. Breathless rumors of new construction or mergers sprouted faster than they could be denied, and Wall Street was addicted to rumor. Some were serious and some silly, but Harriman dared not ignore them lest he miss the ones that mattered.

By the end of 1902 the highly touted community of interest was crumbling as one interest after another marched in its own direction despite the pleas and threats of Harriman and others. Although his empire had grown, hegemony remained an impossible dream. He had found no way either to harmonize, or Harrimanize, his rivals. The diplomacy of big business had come to the same dreary impasse as that among nations: no one wished to fight, but no one could find terms on which to make peace.

Even worse, an uneasy public mood was fast turning the bigness of business into a political minefield. Few major business figures had yet grasped the importance of stepping gingerly through its explosive controversies. The attack on Northern Securities had already served warning; another came in December 1902, when the ICC decided to hold an inquiry into the community of interest. The hearings produced few revelations; both Harriman and Hill danced their way around questions with the usual blend of vagueness, temporary amnesia, and outright lies. But the commissioners delivered one pertinent message to Harriman. They zeroed in on the collusion implied in the roles of Stubbs and Miller as traffic chiefs and on the new holding company for the Burlington. These turned out to be the most vulnerable salients, just as Hill had said they would be. Although little was revealed about them, the commissioners left no doubt that the last word had not been heard on the subjects.[37]

What, then, could be done? The sun of prosperity still shone brightly on the railroads as it did on the nation, but the industry still had not put itself in position to wring maximum returns from it despite the record profits many roads were piling up. A dozen years earlier two giants of the industry, Jay Gould and

Collis Huntington, had tried to interest their peers in a bold plan. "When there is only one railroad company in the United States," Huntington had growled to a reporter, "it will be better for everybody concerned, and the sooner this takes place the better."[38]

The idea was far too visionary for other railroad men and was quickly dropped. Although the current craze for consolidation had alarmed the public into believing this was where the industry was heading, no one took such an idea seriously or talked in those terms—except possibly for one man who had a way of conceiving plans that others thought inconceivable. Not a word on the subject escaped his lips, but the full depth of Harriman's ambitions had yet to be plumbed. Was there ticking somewhere in the back of his indefatigable brain a variation on the theme of the One Big Railroad?[39]

17 Seeking the Perfect Machine

E. H. Harriman is not a railroad builder. He is not a pioneer. He took the labor off the hands of other men, Crocker, Stanford, Huntington, bought in a lump the life-labor of these men, greater perhaps than himself, and reared upon their hard-built foundations a structure of his own planning—the Harriman System. . . . He followed the path blazed out by the great pioneers—followed it and built it over anew upon a plan and scale of marvelous perfection. . . .

An executive officer must be judged by the results of his acts. His methods are a question of the day. His results are for all time.

—Wall Street Journal, *August 25, 1906*

One clue to Harriman's management style eluded all but a few observers sharp enough to look more at what than who his officers were. Nearly all the men who oversaw his roads had been trained as engineers: Horace Burt on the Union Pacific, Samuel Felton on the Alton, S. R. Knott of the Gulf line, and Julius Kruttschnitt of the Southern Pacific. Harriman wanted not merely top engineers to do the work but managers who understood what the engineers were telling them.

As the newest member of this team, Kruttschnitt had to undergo the usual Harriman rite of initiation. The man who would later be hailed as the "von Moltke of transportation" found himself walking a stretch of Southern Pacific roadbed with Harriman one day. Harriman's roving eye stopped on one of the bolts holding a rail in place.

"Why does so much of that bolt protrude beyond the nut?" he asked abruptly.

"It is the size which is generally used," said Kruttschnitt.

Harriman's eyes blazed. "Why should we use a bolt of such a length that a part of it is useless?"

"Well," admitted Kruttschnitt, "when you come right down to it, there is no reason."

They walked on in silence. Harriman stopped suddenly and asked, "How many track bolts are there in a mile of track?" Kruttschnitt did a quick calculation and produced a figure. "Well," retorted Harriman, "in the Union Pacific and Southern Pacific we have about eighteen thousand miles of track and there must be some fifty million track bolts in our system. If you can cut an ounce off from every bolt, you will save fifty million ounces of iron, and that is something worth while. Change your bolt standard."[1]

The Southern Pacific held the distinction of being the largest transportation system in the world. Its 9,441 miles of rail and 16,186 miles of water lines covered routes from New York to New Orleans and from San Francisco to the Far East. The railroad earned more per mile than any other transcontinental line but also cost more to operate. No western road had a more richly diversified traffic or was in a better position to make money on its local business. But it also had a whopping $350 million funded debt and had never paid a dividend, which made it unappealing to investors.[2]

The smart money on Wall Street thought Harriman had paid too high a price for a sprawling system that required heavy expenditures. The smart money, however, did not understand what Harriman was doing. He was not merely trying to assure control over the entire route to the coast; he intended to rebuild the Southern Pacific and turn it into a cash cow just as he had done with the Union Pacific. In that task Kruttschnitt assumed the role Berry had played in reconstructing the Union Pacific.

In November 1901 Harriman summoned Burt, Berry, Kruttschnitt, and William Hood, the Southern Pacific's able chief engineer, to New York. He was ready to implement several projects Huntington had started but left on the drawing board because of their cost. Kruttschnitt brought along a load of blueprints, maps, and statistics for Harriman to examine, but visitors kept interrupting their sessions. Finally, Harriman invited Kruttschnitt to his house for dinner. Afterward, poring over the plans and blueprints, he peppered the engineer with questions, scarcely pausing to hear the answer before asking another about the advantages of this method over that one, the economies to be gained, the increase in capacity to be derived. "The swiftness with which he covered the ground was astonishing," marveled Kruttschnitt.[3]

They finished in two hours, and Harriman told Kruttschnitt to be present at the executive committee meeting next morning. The plans called for spending $18 million. Harriman breezed into the meeting and explained the work, its costs and benefits, in concise terms almost before the other members had settled into their seats. Kruttschnitt was stunned to hear a unanimous vote of approval for everything. What kind of man, he wondered, could digest $18 million worth of work for a thousand miles of railroad in rugged country and spit it back so clearly that he got immediate approval? As he prepared to leave, Kruttschnitt asked Harriman cautiously how fast he should go in committing the funds.

"Spend it all in a week if you can," replied Harriman.[4]

Walking encyclopedia: Julius Kruttschnitt, the man of many facts, who became Harriman's chief operations officer. (Union Pacific Museum Collection)

Harriman proved to be as good as his word. Between 1893 and 1901 Huntington had spent about $12.4 million on improvements for the Southern Pacific. During the next eight years Harriman poured an astonishing $247 million into making it the equal of the Union Pacific. He followed the same master plan, shortening the Central Pacific fifty-one miles, cutting its maximum grades from 90 feet to 21.1 feet, reducing 16,625 degrees of curvature to 3,889 degrees, a savings of more than thirty-five complete circles. As a dinner speaker quipped, Harriman straightened out a line long accused of being crooked.[5]

The Montalvo-Burbank cutoff was well under way at the time of Huntington's death. Once Harriman completed it in 1904, he turned immediately to the Bay Shore cutoff, a radically improved entry into San Francisco. The original thirteen-mile line, a long, rugged detour to the west of the San Bruno Mountains blockading the southern approach to the city, had 796 degrees of curvature and a maximum grade of 158 feet. The growing city also bumped against the mountains, ruling out any possibility of improving the old line.[6]

This was precisely the challenge Harriman loved: a problem with no apparent solution except one so bold and costly as to defy the faint of heart. The answer was a direct route along the shore east of the mountains, shortening the line about 2.5 miles and drastically reducing grades and curvature. This required five tunnels, several bridges, and some heavy grading that brought the cost above $800,000 per mile. Completed in December 1907, the Bay Shore cutoff provided a double-track line into expanded terminal facilities at water level. A new bridge at Dumbarton Point enabled trains to cross the bay by rail instead of using ferries.[7]

By far the worst bottleneck on the system was the section that wound its tortuous way through the Promontory Mountains north of Salt Lake. Since the 1870s engineers had pondered the obvious solution of running track straight across the lake. This would lop forty-four miles off the route, eliminate vast amounts of curvature and grade, save hours of transit time, and slash operating costs. The problem was the lake itself. Although soundings had been taken since the 1860s, no one really knew where the bottom was; legend claimed that parts of the lake were bottomless. Since salt water was heavy, the waves whipped up by storms pounded with frightening force, and the salt might corrode building materials. No one knew for sure whether the lake was rising or retreating. In recent years it had receded several feet. Was this part of a natural cycle, or would it continue because irrigation projects were tapping its feeders?[8]

Huntington had finally decided to tackle the monster late in 1899 after receiving a report from Hood, but he died just as construction was about to begin. Harriman found himself in a ticklish position. Hood urged him to continue the project; Berry disagreed because he did not trust the lake's changing water level. Amid all the arguments, one point shone through with blinding clarity to Harriman: the challenge of doing what others said couldn't be done. This was no rash act of ego. Hood's thorough report made a compelling argument for the feasibility of the project, and the advantages of crossing the lake were obvious.[9]

The new line ran from Ogden across Bear River Bay to the tip of Promontory Point, crossed the large western arm of the lake to a point called Lakeside, and intersected the main line just beyond Lucin, fifty-eight miles from the lake. It required seventy-eight miles of new track along with eleven miles of permanent and sixteen miles of temporary trestle. Enormous loads of lumber flowed in

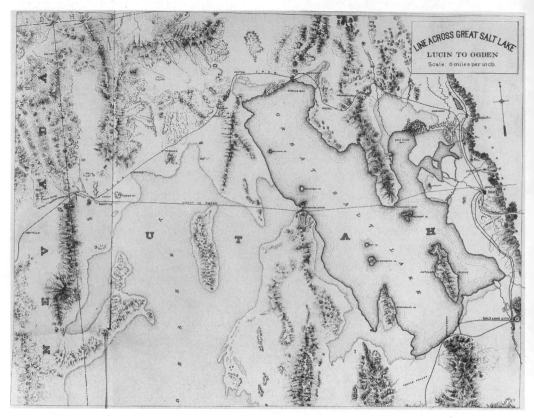

It looks simple on paper: A map of the Lucin cutoff line across the Great Salt Lake. The original Union Pacific–Central Pacific line can be seen skirting the northern edge of the lake. (Union Pacific Museum Collection)

from the forests of the Northwest for piles, bents, stringers, caps, and buildings. A steamboat had to be built on the lake and twenty-five giant pile drivers in San Francisco.[10]

To move a mountain of fill, Harriman purchased three hundred mammoth side-dump cars called "battleships," which carried eighty-ton loads. Eight giant steam shovels gouged rock and gravel from nearby quarries, and eighty locomotives hauled an endless procession of cars to the lake. The company scrounged every spare car it could for the work. Everything had to be brought to the site across a road already jammed with traffic. Water for the men, the steam shovels, and the locomotives—half a million gallons daily—was imported in tank cars from as far away as a hundred miles.[11]

An army of workmen three thousand strong worked ten-hour shifts around the clock seven days a week. They earned decent pay and kept it. There was no place for them to go; the ban on liquor was so strict that incoming parcels were

But in practice: One of the countless trains of gravel cars dumps its load into the seemingly bottomless Salt Lake. (Union Pacific Museum Collection)

searched. A station house was put up every mile across the lake and a boarding-house erected on a platform above the waves. The company supplied cooks and provisions and charged four dollars a week for board. To house men with families, it set up a camp of boxcars on sidings at Lakeside.[12]

Harriman demanded both safety and sobriety on the site. Despite the difficult and hazardous work, no lives were lost and only one man suffered a serious injury. On the subject of drinking on duty Harriman was a fanatic who resorted to any means to stop it or ferret it out. When a story reached him about an engineer whose work suffered because he was often drunk, he put Bancroft on the case personally and did not relent until the charge had been completely discredited.[13]

Despite Hood's careful preparations, the lake fought him at every turn. The first pile driven down for the temporary trestle at Bear River simply vanished. Another was placed atop it and also dropped out of sight at one blow. The engineers punched through fifty feet of soft mud before they hit a solid bottom. On the west side of the lake they found the opposite problem: a crust of nearly solid gypsum that yielded only an inch or two to the blow of a pile driver.

The straight and sinking road: A view of the Lucin cutoff line to the sink.
(Union Pacific Museum Collection)

Sometimes a pile went down easily for thirty feet only to spring back up when it struck the gypsum. In some places steam jets had to be used in place of the giant hammers.[14]

The engineers also learned to their dismay that ordinary fill simply floated away in the heavy salt water, forcing them to dump thousands of tons of rock into what seemed bottomless pits before they could use dirt and gravel. Hood had planned a twenty-foot-wide roadbed atop a permanent trestle fifteen feet above water no more than twenty-four feet deep. He assumed, therefore, that the largest embankment needed was about forty feet high. It turned out to be fifteen times that amount as ton after ton of fill simply vanished. Two places proved especially frustrating, one at Bear River and the other on the west arm of the lake at a station called Rambo.[15]

Hood completed the temporary track across the lake in March 1903, and the first locomotive puffed hopefully forward from Ogden. When it reached Bear River, the embankment suddenly sank out of sight, leaving the engine wallowing in two feet of water. Glumly the engineers realized that the real battle for the cutoff had begun. The problem was the lake's peculiar crust, which tended to crack and sink under the weight of the fill. No one could predict where, when, or how much this would happen; it had to be learned by trial and error at every weak point. The track was raised and filled anew; a week later it sank beneath a work train, scaring the wits out of the crew. Again and again it sank, always to a point just above the fill. The faint of heart looked anew at the legend that the lake was a bottomless pit.

For twenty-one months the battle raged. Nearly twenty-five hundred men toiled at the task day and night. An endless procession of "battleships" rumbled forward to drop loads of rock and gravel into a maw that swallowed them only to sink yet again. The engineers watched every dump anxiously, their hopes rising only to be deflated by the next collapse. "We know what it ought to do," cried one in frustration, "but what we don't know is why it doesn't do it."[16]

Harriman couldn't wait for them to find out. A week before Thanksgiving in 1903 he decided to tour the cutoff and surprised everyone by inviting a party of newsmen along with the usual cadre of rail officials. On Thanksgiving Day he led the large party onto the cutoff, where they poked around and posed for an endless array of photographs. In most of these pictures Harriman occupied an inconspicuous corner, as if he had wandered into the affair by accident. The occasion was a great success, but freight trains did not start running over the Lucin cutoff until March 1904.[17]

Gradually the sinking slowed, then stopped everywhere except at the two worst spots. Bear River finally held firm after one last disheartening drop of eight feet, but Rambo defied every attempt at taming. During the 287 days after April 1904, no less than 482 settling incidents occurred, 84 in August alone, 7 in one day, all in different places. Bizarre rumors persisted of locomotives being swallowed by the lake or of disastrous settlings. A sense of humor was needed to cope, but humor was not Kruttschnitt's long suit. He chased and crushed every rumor with grim determination, as did Hood, who grew weary of denying the "bottomless pit" theory so popular with reporters. When freight trains finally began running over the cutoff in March 1904, Hood balked at letting passenger trains test the new line until the sinking had stopped.[18]

The thought of losing a passenger train to Rambo filled everyone with horror, but the longer Hood delayed sending the trains over the cutoff, the more newspapers babbled ominously about lack of confidence in the work or floated new rumors about gigantic sinks. The operating department was eager to take responsibility for the trains, and even the cautious Kruttschnitt was ready to let passengers enjoy the glorious view over the lake. In September 1904 Hood finally agreed.[19]

Not until December, after receiving seventy thousand carloads of fill, did Rambo finally surrender. On January 1, 1905, the operating department formally took charge of the cutoff, but Hood placed a hundred cars loaded with rock on a

Celebration: E. H. Harriman and his guests at the Lucin cutoff opening ceremony. The front row includes J. C. Stubbs (left, holding overcoat with foot on rail), Julius Kruttschnitt (with hankerchief in pocket), William Hood, the Southern Pacific engineer who oversaw the project (behind Kruttschnitt's left shoulder), H. E. Huntington (straddling the rail next to Kruttschnitt), and Horace Burt (second from right, with beard). Harriman is the inconspicuous figure at far right clutching the post. He has removed his glasses for the picture. (Union Pacific Museum Collection)

nearby siding for emergency use and insisted on strict speed limits across the lake. By then the weary engineers knew what had become of all the loose fill they had poured into the lake: gradually it had coalesced into small islands or bars. One engineer, showing the work to a lady friend, heard her exclaim, "How fortunate it was that you found those little islands!"[20]

"Found them!" he groaned. "It took us two years to make them!"[21]

The Lucin cutoff soon established itself as one of the wonders of the West. One engineer hailed it as "perhaps the most noteworthy engineering achievement ever attempted in bridge and fill work." The ten passenger and fourteen freight trains that rumbled over it every day saved up to seven hours on their schedules along with the reduced costs of a straight, level route. The cutoff was more spectacular than some Harriman projects, but it fit one basic criterion: the savings paid for the cost many times over.[22]

Harriman shared the feelings of pride and exhilaration. "I am delighted with this piece of work," he beamed, "which I consider is almost unparalleled."[23]

Work on the Southern Pacific followed the Union Pacific model closely. On any project Harriman's first question was always whether the proposed plan was the best that could be devised. Once recovered from their shock at this largesse, Southern Pacific officers learned quickly to give Harriman what he wanted. Shoulders were widened, heavier rail laid, more ballast put down, and extra siding added. The busiest portions of the line were double-tracked; heavy iron bridges replaced wooden or light iron ones, new buildings went up, and 1,213 miles of block signals were installed in six years. A larger, heavier fleet of engines and cars replaced older equipment and raised the average tons hauled per train 51 percent between 1901 and 1909.[24]

But Harriman did not remain a slave to the Union Pacific model. He understood that certain peculiar features of the Southern Pacific required a different approach. It relied on oil to fuel locomotives, for example, because coal was scarce and expensive in the Southwest. To ensure supplies, Harriman expanded storage capacity, bought oil fields, and organized a subsidiary oil company. He also pushed to convert key roads to electric power, which offered a cleaner, more reliable source of energy in an age when the diesel engine had yet to be perfected for railroad use.[25]

Technical innovation always fascinated Harriman. In 1903, while touring France with his family by automobile, he wondered why some version of the vehicle could not be adapted to rails as a commuter car on lines lacking enough business to warrant full train service. On his return Harriman put his chief mechanical officer, William R. McKeen Jr., to work on the project. The enterprising McKeen came up with a self-propelled vehicle powered by a gasoline engine that could do forty to sixty miles an hour on sustained runs at lower cost than steam- or electric-powered cars. First tested in March 1905, the car evolved in little over a year to a model nearly twice as long with sealed porthole windows that kept out the weather and allowed stronger body construction.[26]

Harriman had this car sent east for a trial run over the Erie. At Arden he climbed aboard for the last leg and chatted freely with a reporter who called it a "submarine on wheels." Encouraged by the results, the Union Pacific installed the cars on regular routes throughout the system. For more than a decade the McKeen cars prospered, then fell on hard times after World War I. Nevertheless, Harriman's vision left behind an imposing legacy. Thirty years later the McKeen car became a design inspiration for the train that revolutionized rail travel: the streamliner. And the Union Pacific leader who developed this new train in the throes of the nation's worst depression was none other than Averell Harriman.[27]

Harriman resisted building branches on the Union Pacific, but he added considerable new track to the Southern Pacific. Following a principle he had embraced during his Illinois Central years, he often picked up existing roads and improved them. An earlier generation of rail leaders bought derelict roads just to get rid of the threat they posed, only to find themselves saddled with useless track. Harriman was far more selective, grabbing small roads that could improve his main line or feed it profitably and then bringing them up to his standard. If no lines existed in a region needing branches, he built as a last resort. Most of this work took place at the opposite ends of the system: northern California–Oregon and Texas-Louisiana.[28]

The most ambitious of these projects expanded the Southern Pacific's position in Mexico. Harriman had long been interested in Mexico and had sent a man there to gather information as early as 1899. The Southern Pacific had ventured into Mexico a year earlier, when Huntington leased the Sonora Railway, which ran from Nogales on the Arizona-Mexico border to Guayamas on the Gulf of California. He then bought up large parcels of undeveloped coal land in the state of Sonora and talked of building branch lines to mine coal for the energy-starved Southwest.[29]

Harriman lost little time reviving these plans. In February 1902 he took a special seven-car train on a trip to the Southwest and Pacific Coast that lasted four months. One of his first stops was Mexico City, where he met President Porfirio Díaz and leading members of his government. The timing of Harriman's visit was not accidental; Paul Morton of the Atchison was also in town paying calls at the palace. Nor had Harriman come merely to pay his respects. He looked at several roads with an eye to taking them over, then sat down with Díaz to negotiate for concessions to extend the Sonora road. His persistence brought two plums in the form of rights to lay new track up the Yaqui River valley to the mineral region Huntington had coveted and down the coast from Guayamas to Guadalajara.[30]

The Mexican venture turned out to be the largest new project undertaken by Harriman. After the work began in earnest in 1905, the Southern Pacific laid more than eight hundred miles of track in four years. To reduce costs, Harriman ransacked the globe for materials—importing ties from Japan, rails from Spain and Belgium, coal from Australia, machinery from Germany, and laborers from Russia, China, and Japan to toil alongside native Yaqui Indians. Harriman's strong sense of patriotism did not extend to paying high prices for materials he could get cheaper elsewhere.[31]

This was something new to railroading. No one had ever drawn from so wide a variety of sources for construction materials. Once it was completed to Guadalajara, the Southern Pacific owned the longest continuous line of railroad in the world, 3,750 miles of track stretching from Puget Sound to the Gulf of California. And there was talk of it growing still longer: in 1909 rumors swirled that Harriman might lay track all the way down to the Isthmus of Panama.[32]

The obsession of our own age with airplane crashes had its counterpart in the railway era, when headlines screamed lurid details of every major train wreck. During the early years of the century those headlines occurred with grim regularity as the number of accidents soared to record heights along with the amount of traffic. Between 1898 and 1908 an average of 363 passengers, 3,166 employees, and 5,661 other persons* lost their lives every year. But the averages were deceiving because the casualty count rose steadily to a peak in 1907, when more employees (4,534) and passengers (610) were killed than during any other year in American history.[33]

Railroad managers tended to duck the subject of safety because it was a public relations nightmare. Those who think that airlines hold a monopoly on grisly stories need only look at old accounts of people roasted alive in burning coaches or mashed in the impact of a rear-end collision or plunged to watery graves off a bridge. Pinning down responsibility became a familiar form of shell game. Rail officials blamed accidents on the negligence of employees; the unions charged them to faulty equipment, mismanagement, or overwork. Congress as usual talked much and did little on the subject. Railroad managers did not even care to talk, preferring a conspiracy of silence for two reasons: the negative effect on public opinion and their fear of liability suits. But they were hardly indifferent to the question. Good officers demanded safe operations and spent money willingly to get them.[34]

Of all the rail leaders who cared about safety, only one was fanatical in its pursuit. Harriman modernized a railroad's approach to safety much as he did its physical condition. Between 1898 and 1907 his roads invested nearly $12 million in improvements directly related to safety. No western system spent more money on maintenance, and no system anywhere installed more automatic signals, which were expensive to put in and keep up. But money alone was not enough. The best equipment and strictest rules did little good unless the men had the right attitude toward them.[35]

Early in 1907 a series of ICC reports on 448 railroad collisions revealed that 65 percent of them had been caused by the neglect of crewmen. The crush of business after 1900 dried up the labor pool, leaving every road short of skilled workers and forcing them to hire men whose "zeal and fidelity," as one trade

---

*The "other persons" category refers to accidents that do not involve trains or their movement but occur in shops or elsewhere on site. It is revealing that the public furor over railroad accidents ignored the fact that far more people were killed in nontrain accidents than in mishaps involving trains.

journal complained, "seem to be waning." Shippers and travelers did not help by sending mixed signals. On one hand, they clamored for safer conditions; on the other, they demanded faster schedules.[36]

Harriman tried to attack this problem through sheer force of will. Nothing infuriated him more than accidents caused by carelessness or negligence. He spurred officers not merely to wage safety campaigns but to hammer at prevention and slap harsh penalties on those who disobeyed rules as an example to the others. After one collision caused by the failure of a flagman to protect a stalled train during a blizzard, Harriman wired Burt angrily, "Something must be done to enforce the Company's regulations [and] someone who has force of character should be put on this particular matter, and see that the rules are carried out."[37]

Sometimes he delivered the message firsthand. On one inspection trip his train hit some rough track and nearly derailed because a work crew had failed to post a flagman. Harriman was livid when he learned the details and ordered Burt to fire the entire crew. "That's rather cruel," Burt protested. "Perhaps," retorted Harriman, "but it will probably save a lot of lives. I want every man connected with the operation to feel a sense of responsibility. Now, everybody knew that the man hadn't gone back with the flag. They could see it. And if he's responsible, that sort of thing won't happen again."[38]

Harriman demanded full accounts of every accident and its causes as well as monthly summaries. Any serious mishap sent telegrams flying at Burt. "I wish it were possible," sighed the hapless president after one collision, "to inspire operating force sufficiently to avoid accidents of this kind." Harriman decided to show that it was possible by challenging an industry taboo. For decades railroads had dealt with accidents by whitewashing them for public consumption, mainly to avoid suits. In the process officials often deceived themselves as well. "The evidence is often made to substantiate a preconceived conclusion," complained W. L. Park, "[and] the . . . testimony is shaped to meet the well-known views of a superior." The result soon became a way of life in the age of bureaucracy. The "science" of railroading, snorted Park, was "the art of shifting responsibility."[39]

Harriman wanted no more of it. In 1903 he set up boards of inquiry to investigate the cause of every accident. Four years later, with the accident rate soaring, he announced a bold new experiment: men of local prominence from outside the rail industry would be added to the boards and participate fully in the inquiry. The process would be opened up to public scrutiny to make the findings more credible. Kruttschnitt, who was himself a bear on the subject, admitted that civilians knew little about the composition of boiler plate or the intricacies of dispatching, but that was beside the point. "Whatever we do get in these reports," he stressed, "we will get no whitewashing. We will get the responsibility put squarely where it belongs."[40]

The legal department shuddered at the prospect, envisioning a steady parade of bogus damage and personal injury claims by every shyster in the West. But the reverse happened: an open inquiry left no mysteries or dark corners to explore. The public applauded the idea, and Kruttschnitt made sure the boards produced results by demanding that some cause be found for every accident. When the results fell short or were challenged, a second board was convened.[41]

These efforts made Harriman the undisputed leader in safety. While national figures continued to climb, the accident rate on Harriman's roads dropped sharply. No other rail leader left a greater mark on this sensitive area. After his death, Mary Harriman perpetuated the legacy by endowing a safety medal to be awarded by the American Museum of Safety. The Harriman Medal could not have had a more apt name.[42]

The men who worked for Harriman regarded him as fair if demanding. His rumpled, unassuming appearance and eagerness to talk to anyone with something to tell him impressed them, as did the fact that he knew his stuff and never put on airs. But no one got close to Harriman; he was too curt and imperious. The loyal Bancroft tried to portray him as beloved of the employees, but he was more admired than loved. One critic described him as "a singularly unemotional man, even among financiers." Another called him "cruel, hard, cold . . . full of strange contradictions, traits of real greatness mingling with traits of meanness and littleness."[43]

There was also a tender side to him that few people saw. Dr. E. L. Trudeau never forgot the night his son died, when Harriman dropped all other business to sit up with him and then arranged special cars to carry the body and mourners to the funeral at Paul Smith's. Or the time in 1902 when Trudeau's health broke down and Harriman sent him to California for two months, or the hunting and fishing club that Harriman and other friends sustained just so the doctor could use it. Utterly naive about business matters, Trudeau once asked Harriman if he would like to invest a few thousand dollars to add to the club's wild land. "It seems well worth the money to me," Trudeau said earnestly, "but you must decide, as I don't want you to get 'stuck.' "[44]

A huge, impish smile lit Harriman's face. He touched Trudeau's arm and said, "Ed, don't you ever worry about my getting stuck."

One Christmas Eve Harriman was confined to bed after a painful operation. Despite his agony, he summoned Southern Pacific auditor William Mahl and insisted on dictating a list of Christmas presents to be sent certain officials along with a letter thanking them for their loyalty and service. At the same time he decreed bonuses for the New York office staff equal to 10 percent of their salary. This was a revelation to Mahl, who had never seen Huntington do any such thing, and he marveled that it was Harriman, "a stranger to the Southern Pacific Company who in his humane character did for the employees of that Company that which was neglected by any of the four men in whose fortunes they had been instrumental in no small degree in building up."[45]

Harriman treated the men in the ranks well because it was the right thing to do and it was also good business. Sometimes he had to be shown the way. Once he asked W. L. Park to buy a safety shaving set for him. Park found one that was rather expensive, and when he said that it cost $15.75, Harriman examined it closely and remarked, "This is much better than the one I use. I had intended it for one of the boilermakers in the car ahead, who was complaining that he had had no opportunity to shave himself since leaving San Francisco. I guess I will keep this and give him mine."[46]

Harriman paused and looked quizzically at Park. "What would you do?" he asked abruptly.

"If I were going to give the fellow anything," suggested Park, "it would be something his grandchildren would talk about."

"I guess that's right," conceded Harriman. He snapped the case shut and ordered the steward to take it forward.

In an age when workers had virtually no benefits from either company or government, Harriman was among the first to introduce a pension plan on his roads. He helped put one into effect on the Illinois Central in 1901, when only four other railroads had plans, and the following year approved a plan for the Union Pacific and Southern Pacific systems. Modest as the pensions were, the men came quickly to prize them. One old veteran, clutching his first check, wrote in a wavering hand, "It is a noble thing for the Company to do."[47]

Other programs tried to serve the men still on the job. Like most railroads, the Union Pacific had long had a hospital plan, and some unions had organized their own relief plans to aid men and their families in times of death or injury. Harriman wanted something more—a program that would help bright, ambitious workers advance through the ranks. From this premise flowed the idea of creating a system to train men at all levels for any work they wished to learn.[48]

The plan took time to evolve; not until 1909 did the Union Pacific create its novel Bureau of Information and Education. Most major railroads provided special training for different classes of employees, but none extended it to all workers wishing instruction. The bureau offered training at company expense in any area and created a separate board to answer inquiries on any aspect of their work. Its programs aimed to improve efficiency, keep men abreast of new methods and technologies, and target promising candidates for promotion. Nothing better exemplified Harriman's desire to lead the industry into the new century. He created the first direct challenge to the tradition of older hands teaching younger ones to do things the way they had been taught.[49]

In his domineering manner Harriman was the same father figure to his rail workers as to the inhabitants at Arden: stern but just, demanding strict obedience and close attention to duty in return for good pay, decent working conditions, and other considerations. But Arden was a closed world without unions or a work force wildly divided by rank, skills, and ethnicity. Every railroad found it difficult to keep a stable work force, and the record flow of traffic wore down men as fast as it did equipment. Even the modernized Union Pacific–Southern Pacific systems struggled to handle 50 percent more business than their capacity.[50]

"The car shortage is worse than ever before," observed Kruttschnitt, "but the real trouble is to get labor." The influx of newcomers created a volatile mix of rookies and veterans just when peak efficiency was needed to handle the deluge of traffic. Rail managers complained that the shortage of labor made it impossible to impose discipline on the men, which meant more accidents as well as more labor strife. Sometimes workers resisted attempts to improve productivity. When this happened on the Union Pacific, Harriman found himself with a full-blown crisis.[51]

In June 1901 Harriman gave Horace Burt approval to convert the shops to piecework. The machinists, boilermakers, and blacksmiths promptly walked out. Burt managed to hire enough new men to keep the piecework system running. That winter he patched together an agreement with the strikers, but in June 1902 the boilermakers demanded a pay hike as well as rule changes. When Burt refused, they struck again and were followed by the machinists and blacksmiths.[52]

Neither the carmen, who made up half the work force in the shops, nor any other unions joined the strike, yet the strikers held out stubbornly month after month. An official warned that the fight meant "a great deal of money, to all of the Harriman lines; if we lose it, we practically lose control of the shops." Burt was so convinced of this that he staked his reputation on the outcome. Harriman gave him a free hand to deal with the crisis. Unmoved by the prolonged struggle or sporadic outbursts of violence, Burt took a hard line. In January 1903 the union men demanded the abolition of piecework. Burt replied curtly that they would never again work on the Union Pacific except under the piecework system.[53]

So far the road had kept up repairs well despite the strike, but the crush of traffic kept increasing the demands on equipment. The unions then threatened to hit the Southern Pacific, where Harriman already had problems. He loathed the idea of backing down on a vital issue, but his options were running out. In June 1903, two years after the strike began, he agreed to gradual withdrawal of the piecework system and a 7 percent pay hike for the shopmen. Under the agreement, the nonunion men, who by Burt's count made up 73 percent of the shop force, continued to do piecework, but when Harriman visited Omaha that Sep-

The first president: Horace G. Burt, first president of the reorganized Union Pacific, who resigned after repeated clashes with Harriman. (Union Pacific Museum Collection)

tember, the union leaders complained that the system was not being scrapped as promised. Reluctantly Harriman ordered it abolished.[54]

This was a rare retreat on Harriman's part, and it cost him dearly. A humiliated Burt turned in his resignation that same night. The nonunion shopmen, feeling betrayed, left the company or drifted into the unions. Harriman had hoped for greater efficiency; instead, he helped the unions entrench themselves more solidly than ever in the shops, setting the stage for later, more bitter battles.

Harriman understood that the future could not be based on the past. He agreed entirely with an editor who observed, "We cannot restore the conditions of 30 years ago, when so many managers were personally acquainted with their employees, therefore the only alternative is to increase the efficiency of the deputy managers." In his desire to create a new railroad, Harriman realized that he needed not only a new type of officer but also a new kind of organization.[55]

18 Seeking the Perfect Organization

E. H. Harriman and the Union Pacific represent the power of concentration in its highest phase. In the furthermost corners of the earth men are working for the benefit of Union Pacific and E. H. Harriman. The secret of it all is that the genius of Mr. Harriman has created a railroad system upon which more than its due portion of the traffic of the world must center. He has made the Union Pacific the main artery of commerce across the continent and he is reaping the reward of his foresight.
—Wall Street Journal, *December 11, 1905*

The mighty Pennsylvania Railroad took immense pride in calling itself the standard railroad of the world, but its officers were never so arrogant as to believe that they had nothing more to learn. They were always on the lookout for new ideas and techniques and kept a close watch on what other roads did. In 1908 the Pennsylvania sent a two-man team to inspect the Union Pacific. Their report, based on careful observation, carried a weight of authority far beyond public tributes in newspapers and magazines. It was the opinion of experts, it was private, and it was glowing in its praise of what Harriman had done.[1]

Such praise did not come easily to officers of eastern railroads, who tended to view western roads with an air of condescension if not disdain. But the Union Pacific possessed an organization the officers described as "departmental at the top and divisional at the bottom, there being a striking similarity between their organization and our own." Harriman made it the blueprint for a new and daring vision of how a railroad should be run and the instrument for his obsessive effort to create the perfect machine.

Much of what Harriman accomplished was the brilliant execution of existing ideas. In the case of organization, however, he carved out an original path that many railroad managers rejected as foolhardy. Nor was he ever content with his organization. To keep abreast of what was going on, he sent officers to tour other roads as the Pennsylvania did. As an industry steeped (some would say trapped) in tradition, railroads were not noted for their receptivity to innovation. Harriman sought to impress on his officers something even more basic than change: a higher learning curve.

The key to any organization lies in the quality of the men who run it. As Mohler and Frederick D. Underwood demonstrated, good men had a way of drifting into Harriman's orbit and staying there until he used them up. Harriman drove his officers mercilessly but gave them free rein to show what they could do. He combed the ranks of every road he acquired for its best talent. Within a few years after the Southern Pacific deal, several of its officers had moved to higher ranks within the parent Union Pacific.[2]

Aware that Hill had a reputation for cashiering older hands when they no longer measured up, Harriman told a reporter with relish, "When I take charge of a property I don't discharge the old men to make room for my pets. I don't have any pets. The way to reward faithfulness is not by discharging the old hands." But the reporter also knew Harriman's reputation for scourging a president or vice-president in tones that others would not use on an office boy. He concluded that the Union Pacific men "don't dislike Harriman like the Great Northern men dislike Hill. The trouble seems to be that everybody is afraid of Harriman."[3]

The perfect machine required three elements: the right organization to realize its full potential, the right men to make it run smoothly, and the right systems to maximize its efficiency. Harriman toiled incessantly to create a structure that delegated authority while still enabling him to keep his finger on everything that happened. The first step flowed out of the Metropolitan Club pact with Hill (see Chapter 15). Although nothing came of the provision to create uniform methods of management and accounting, Harriman at least got Hill's grudging consent to delegate all traffic matters. The authority vested in John Stubbs and Darius Miller made them traffic czars who bypassed the presidents of individual lines and reported directly to Harriman and Hill. Both men operated out of Chicago even though all the lines served by Stubbs lay west of the Mississippi River.

Two aspects of this arrangement disturbed traditional railroad men: centralizing so much authority in the hands of an officer outside the regular organization and locating that officer off the lines he supervised. Stuyvesant Fish shook his head at what he called a "novel experiment"; another, less tactful president sneered that no road could be run by two heads and, in an obvious jab at Harriman, grumbled that big systems should be "operated by men on the ground and not by financial people a thousand, or perhaps three thousand, miles from the seat of war."[4]

When Harriman acquired the Southern Pacific in 1901, the parent Union Pacific had a typically small organization. The board, vice-president, secretary, treasurer, and general counsel were in New York and the rest of the officers in

Traffic genius: J. C. Stubbs, the gaunt, schoolmaster-looking executive who came from the Southern Pacific to become traffic manager for the Harriman system. (Southern Pacific photo, Union Pacific Museum Collection)

Omaha. Once Harriman decided to unify the central commands of both systems, he revamped the management into six departments: executive, legal, traffic, accounting, treasury, and operating. The executive officers remained in New York and the railroad men in Omaha except for Stubbs.[5]

Harriman also extended the authority of Erastus Young, the Union Pacific's curmudgeonly auditor, over all the lines, brought William Mahl of the Southern Pacific to New York as comptroller for the combined systems, and turned the assistant secretary into a director of purchases. He summoned to New York as counsel Robert S. Lovett of the Southern Pacific, who became Harriman's closest confidant along with vice-president W. D. Cornish. Himself a lawyer, Cornish proved an invaluable cog in Harriman's machine. He was the perfect antidote to his truculent superior, a smooth diplomat who knew how to compromise and pacify when the occasion demanded.[6]

Once the departments were in place, Harriman took his boldest gamble. In 1904 he moved Kruttschnitt to Chicago as director of maintenance and operations for the combined systems. Railroad men gasped in bewilderment at this latest heresy. Harriman had placed the two most critical functions of a railroad, operations and traffic, in the hands of officers located hundreds of miles off the line and beyond the jurisdiction of the roads' presidents.

The men on the hot seat made the oddest of couples: the gaunt Stubbs, whose pinched, bespectacled expression gave him a professorial air, and the slow-moving Kruttschnitt, a walrus of a man who looked like a butcher. Stubbs had come to the Central Pacific shortly after it opened in 1869 and had been in charge of transcontinental traffic for a quarter-century; no one knew its complexities better. Kruttschnitt was a native of New Orleans who had earned a degree in civil engineering just in time to catch the depression of the 1870s. He did not land a railroad job until 1878, when he hooked on with a road that Huntington later leased. By 1900 he had risen to vice-president and general manager of all Southern Pacific lines. Already he had become a pioneer in the creation and use of statistics.[7]

Kruttschnitt and Stubbs were as dry and phlegmatic as Harriman was dynamic. "Harriman was rich in vision, in imagination," recalled the banker Frank Vanderlip. "There was in him something of the quality which a poet brings to his work. But Kruttschnitt had absolutely no imagination. His implements were facts; he was a living index of all railroad facts." All of Harriman's officers shared certain qualities invaluable to him: intelligence, loyalty, dedication to duty, and a voracious appetite for work. Harriman might complain that Stubbs, Mahl, or Kruttschnitt lacked vision, but he appreciated how their dutiful, plodding ways provided the raw materials that enabled his own imagination to soar. They were the ideal complement to Harriman's occasional tendency to let enthusiasm run away with his judgment.[8]

Harriman's new organization forced officials at every level to adjust their thinking radically. Railroad men were accustomed to hard work but not to fresh approaches. Mahl, who preferred Huntington as a boss, grumbled that Harriman did not develop men but rather shoved them about like pawns on a chessboard. Vanderlip conceded that "Harriman had the philosophy, the methods of an Oriental monarch." Those who had the stamina and ability to endure the grind flourished; those who balked or faltered in their traces were soon cut loose. Harriman played no favorites, but he did practice the survival of the fittest. The weeding out began early and claimed as one of the first casualties Charles M. Hays, president of the Southern Pacific.[9]

No road had a more unsavory reputation than the Southern Pacific. Company officials had long enriched themselves by investing in local land and oil companies that fed on inside information from the railroad. In March 1901, only a month after Harriman had finalized the acquisition, the novelist Frank Norris immortalized the road in *The Octopus* as a choking monopoly whose powerful tentacles swarmed deep into California politics and the pockets of shippers. Hays tried earnestly to undo this reputation, but his desire to manage the company his own way ran afoul of Harriman's plans to centralize functions like traffic and accounting outside the president's authority. After one clash Hays resigned in a huff, then regretted his impulsiveness and begged to be reinstated. But Harriman let him go even though he had no replacement in mind.[10]

Schiff, who had just sailed for Germany, was uneasy over rumors that Felton was to succeed Hays. He urged Harriman not to make the change "until the right man has been found in Felton's place. The responsibility for the Alton's success will long stick to us, whether we wish this or not, & we can therefore not afford to take any chances as to its physical management." Harriman agreed entirely and made a wholly unexpected choice for the Southern Pacific: himself. The arrangement was temporary, he explained, with Kruttschnitt handling the real work as his assistant.[11]

Schiff nearly gagged on the news. "The present state of affairs is unjust both to you and the Company," he sputtered. "I know of no other Company which so greatly needs a strong local management than the Southern Pacific." He stressed how unpopular the company was, how its officials were reputed to be lining their pockets at its expense, and how rival roads posed a constant menace. "From one end to the other of the system, a watchful eye is needed urgently & constantly," he pleaded. Where would Harriman find time to deal with these problems? "The existing situation fills me with anxiety and misgivings," Schiff concluded, "& I would not be loyal to you if I did not express this to you in entire frankness."[12]

But Harriman made the arrangement permanent. He realized that no traditional railroad president could feel comfortable in an organization where authority for so many key functions lay outside the traditional channels. The obvious solution was to make himself president and put operations in the hands of capable vice-presidents. This became clear when Horace Burt, that most dutiful of workhorses, finally wore down under the strain of Harriman's demands. Although he quit two years after Hays did, critics pointed at parallels between the two cases and circulated stories about how Harriman had forced Burt out by subjecting him to a series of humiliations.[13]

The climax occurred in the fall of 1903, when Harriman and W. L. Park met Burt in Cheyenne. The dispute with the shopmen still raged, and Harriman wanted to look into their complaints that his order abolishing piecework had been ignored. Burt still smarted from the order itself and was mortified at being suspected of disobeying it. When Harriman left for the shop, Burt grabbed Park and walked him up and down the platform. "When Mr. Harriman comes back to his car I am going to tender him my resignation," he confided. "I want you to know it now, so that later it cannot be said that I was dismissed." Park tried to dissuade him, but Burt only muttered, "I cannot be humiliated this way. These men around us know what is going on." Shortly afterward Harriman returned from the shop and gave Burt another tongue-lashing. That night he received the president's resignation.[14]

Several years later, when Harriman made what proved to be his last trip over the road, he fell into a reminiscent mood one night and told Park his side of the story. He denied firing Burt and gave him full due for the reconstruction work. But Burt, like many officers, never fully understood what Harriman was trying to do. He often had to force new ideas on Burt and sometimes new equipment even when the road was swamped with business. The struggle wore both of them down, Harriman always pushing and Burt resisting. Their parting had been friendly by Burt's own admission.[15]

After Burt's departure, Harriman assumed the presidency just as he had with the Southern Pacific. The following year he created Kruttschnitt's position as director of maintenance and operations for both systems. This arrangement eased the tidy minds of rail managers somewhat; on paper it preserved the chain of command by allowing Kruttschnitt to report to the president of both systems. But no organizational chart obscured the main point: the Harriman system was unique not merely in its structure but in having Harriman at its top.

Nor did any chart obscure the way Harriman shattered tradition in tackling the problem of organization. For years thoughtful railroad managers had debated whether to arrange their structures by departments or divisions. Most companies used the former, which organized the road by function and gave each department authority over the entire system. This highly centralized structure grew unwieldy as the system expanded and stunted the development of young officers, who tended to curry to superiors rather than rely on their own initiative.[16]

The divisional approach carved the system into separate spheres managed by officers who were held responsible for the performance of their domain. It was a horizontal rather than vertical structure which the Pennsylvania Railroad had pioneered as early as the 1870s with striking success. Except for the Burlington, surprisingly few other roads had adopted it even though their systems grew ever larger and more unwieldy to manage. The divisional method had its own shortcomings. Fierce rivalries tended to develop among the division heads, whose primary aim was often to make an impressive showing for their own realm without concern for the performance of the overall system.

These rivalries had ruined the Union Pacific's first experiment with the approach in the 1880s. Harriman devised a modified divisional system that tried to eliminate this flaw; the result was what the Pennsylvania's observers described as departmental at the top and divisional at the bottom. Stubbs and Kruttschnitt presided over the combined systems. While the vice-president and general manager of each major road had his own staff officers, two of these officials—the chief engineer and the superintendent of motive power—reported directly to Kruttschnitt.[17]

Beneath these officers six general managers presided over twenty-six division superintendents, each of whom ruled what amounted to a "separate but miniature railway." The division superintendents wielded the same authority in their domain as the vice-president did over the entire road, and they bore full responsibility for the results. Harriman also took care not to let his two chief officers become desk jockeys. He prodded Kruttschnitt not to turn his office into a "correspondence bureau" and urged him to get "out over the various lines and keep things smooth."[18]

Fifteen years earlier, in seeking a new organization for the Illinois Central, Harriman had insisted on making officers fit the plan and not the reverse. Now he could finally practice what he had preached by shuffling his officers to fit the new structure. The able Mohler was brought to Omaha to take charge of the Union Pacific, with the veteran E. E. Calvin replacing him on the Navigation line. C. H. Markham took Kruttschnitt's post as operating head of the Southern Pacific. W. H. Bancroft remained in charge of the Short Line but had his jurisdiction extended to all lines west of Green River, Wyoming. These were all men on whom Harriman could rely; in later years Mohler and Calvin rose to the presidency of the Union Pacific and Markham of the Illinois Central.[19]

The new organization enabled Harriman to accelerate his program of integrating every aspect of operations across the systems. All four major lines got the same operating rules. Uniform standards were devised for car and engine construction as well as other equipment, enabling Harriman to buy in bulk for all

TABLE 1. *Comparative Data on Selected Western Railroads, 1892 and 1902*

Category	Year	Union Pacific	Missouri Pacific	Atchison	Burlington	Rock Island
Revenue per mile	1892	$5,621	$5,146	$5,115	$6,043	$5,450
Revenue per mile	1902	$8,167	$6,680	$7,528	$6,634	$7,309
Operating Ratio	1892	66.7	72.6	69.2	68.1	69.9
Operating Ratio	1902	49.9	66.8	57.3	63.2	61.6

Source: All data are taken from company annual reports.

four lines at once. Centralized purchasing and common standards lowered unit costs, slashed inventories, made interchange of equipment easier, and cut downtime on equipment by making parts more available. Harriman hounded every officer to find new ways of "handling the largest possible business at the least possible cost."[20]

Kruttschnitt, the walking encyclopedia, needed little prodding. Once arrived in Chicago, he plunged joyfully into the creation of a clearinghouse to pool all cars on the Harriman lines as if the equipment was owned in common. This too was heresy to traditional railroad officers, who were loath to see their cars go even to other lines in the system. Harriman attacked this parochialism and demanded that officers use cars to full capacity. To wring the most use out of every locomotive, Kruttschnitt devised a formula for loading trains based on tonnage rating, tractive power, and speed. Heavier cars were put on longer runs to maximize their capacity, and shipments were combined to save equipment.

Every innovation became the stuff of statistics, which flowed into Kruttschnitt's office in unprecedented volume to monitor the system's efficiency. He calculated that the new system saved more than fifty-three million miles of empty car hauls in the first two years alone. Hauls grew longer, trainloads heavier, speeds slightly higher, and operating ratios lower. The Harriman roads spent more per mile on maintenance than any other western road between 1900 and 1909 yet managed to drive the operating ratio down, as Table 1 illustrates.[21]

Harriman pored over these statistics and attached special importance to average receipts and costs per ton-mile as well as trainload figures. The numbers revealed to him patterns of strength and weakness, beacons for his probing mind to follow. He not only did things by the numbers but used the numbers to show what he did. Once during an interview he hauled out a typewritten sheet of data on the Union Pacific and rattled off some figures. "As he read from it," wrote the surprised journalist, "I realized it was the apologia pro vita sua."[22]

"But the public assails and attacks you and impugns your motives and accuses you of all sorts of things," ventured the interviewer when Harriman had finished. "Doesn't the thanklessness of the job ever embitter you?"

In reply Harriman merely slapped the sheet of statistics and said defiantly, "That remains."

The numbers revealed something else about Harriman, something far more important to him than public adulation because it demonstrated in the clearest possible terms that his policies worked. Within a few years of acquiring his Pacific systems and pouring huge sums into modernization, he transformed them into two of the most lucrative cash cows in American business. The results of his management were not merely impressive; they were spectacular.

The swiftness with which this transformation occurred became apparent only in retrospect. Most observers saw vast amounts of money flowing into improvements but were slow to grasp how great a difference in performance it would make. In 1898 the Union Pacific's earnings amounted to $32.6 million gross and $13.1 million net. Over the next six years trainloads nearly doubled. Earnings rose steadily to $67.3 million gross and $30.3 million net in 1906, an increase of 106 and 131 percent. Once set in motion, the machine rolled relentlessly onward, its efficiency increasing every year as new betterments and equipment came on line. One analyst shook his head in wonder at how commonplace it had become "to see the gross and net earnings of the Harriman lines increase month by month at a phenomenal rate."[23]

To provide funds for this work, Harriman steadfastly resisted the clamor for dividends until he was convinced their time had come. After grudgingly paying the company's first dividend on common stock in 1900, he managed to hold the rate at 4 percent until July 1905, when it was advanced to 5 percent. A few months later Harriman let it go to 6 percent amid demands for still more. The stock also marched upward, crossing 50 in 1900 and climbing past 195 by 1906, when it became the bluest of blue chips. Awed observers saw the Union Pacific system transformed into a giant funnel across the heartland through which poured the swelling bounty of California, the Northwest, and the Orient. By 1906 Omaha had emerged as a grain and meatpacking center boasting seven new elevators in less than two years.[24]

The same pattern unfolded on the Southern Pacific. Between 1901 and 1906 the flood of traffic, coupled with increased efficiency, sent gross earnings up 37 percent and net earnings 33 percent. Harriman gave the system a careful inspection during the spring of 1902 and concluded that still more money had to be spent on betterments. His decision rankled stockholders hoping for dividends, especially one who had become the road's largest shareholder outside Union Pacific circles and its champion in the market.[25]

In the autumn of 1901 Harriman had received several visits from the crafty James R. Keene inviting him to join a pool to boost the price of Southern Pacific stock. Harriman could greatly aid the cause, Keene added, by relenting on his dividend policy. Harriman responded by giving Keene his standard lecture on why the Southern Pacific needed more outlays for improvements instead of dividends. The pool went ahead without him, buying stock at prices below 70, but its efforts were stymied by Harriman's stand on dividends. When Harriman reaffirmed that policy during his inspection tour in 1902, Keene countered by having his son-in-law, the broker Talbot J. Taylor, issue a glowing analysis of the Southern Pacific as "an almost inconceivably rich and powerful corporation," but the ploy was too transparent and made little impression.[26]

Harriman knew this game, had seen it many times on Wall Street. Men like Keene and Gates were called "strikers" because they were always looking to hit some company for quick speculative profits. He was not surprised when Keene tried another tack that fall by sending lawyer Edward T. Lauterbach to warn Otto Kahn that a suit was planned to remove the Union Pacific from the management of the Southern Pacific. The hostile suit could be avoided, Lauterbach suggested, if the Southern Pacific declared a 4 percent dividend or Harriman bought the pool's holdings. Kahn replied curtly that nobody was interested in buying the pool's stock and that dividends were a matter of policy, not negotiation.[27]

Once Harriman made it clear to Wall Street that he had no intention of paying a dividend, Southern Pacific stock tumbled to a low of 56 by December. For months he dodged Lauterbach's efforts to see him. Finally, the lawyer in desperation asked a mutual friend to tell Harriman that the proposed suit would be disastrous to his interests and that Keene was willing to drop it if Harriman would buy the pool's stock. Keene offered a sliding scale: a price around 70 for the 105,000 pool shares and 78 for his own 70,000 shares. Harriman spurned the offer, saying icily that he had nothing to fear from Keene, and he continued to duck Lauterbach's every attempt to see him. A frustrated Keene then tried to enjoin the Southern Pacific annual election on the grounds that the Union Pacific had no legal right to vote the shares it owned. He also asked that the managements of the Union Pacific and Southern Pacific be separated, adding piously that if the courts refused, "justice is dead in America."[28]

Unmoved by the threats, Harriman vowed to fight the suit and ruled out any change in dividend policy until the attack on the management ceased. The corporate charter of the Southern Pacific resided not in California but in the sleepy Louisville, Kentucky, suburb of Beechmont, whose 150 residents were treated to a brief media circus as lawyers invaded the town to do battle. After Harriman and Kahn detailed Keene's blackmail efforts, the court dissolved the injunction and ruled in Harriman's favor in the suit. Keene and his friends took heavy losses in selling off their shares.[29]

Harriman succeeded in routing Keene's raid, but the damage done was far greater than anyone realized. In their argument Keene's lawyers had denounced Union Pacific control of Southern Pacific as a direct violation of the Sherman

Act. This was the critical issue in the Northern Securities case, on which the Supreme Court had yet to rule. Keene's foray had poked another large nose under a very fragile tent and linked the Union Pacific–Southern Pacific combination to it. In time nearly every man on Wall Street would regret that the issue had ever been raised.[30]

Nor was that the only embarrassment. In the heat of battle Harriman had resorted to selling three hundred thousand shares of Southern Pacific stock controlled by the Union Pacific to William Rockefeller with a proviso that Rockefeller could sell them back to the company a year later. The object was to put enough stock beyond the reach of Keene's injunction to carry the election. It was, Harriman explained, "a protective measure, pure and simple," but it came back to haunt him. Investigators later jumped on the $187,500 commission paid Rockefeller for his services and charged that the real reason for the sale was to "show that the Union Pacific was not controlling a parallel and competing line."[31]

For the moment, however, Harriman had things his own way. Once Keene had been routed, the Southern Pacific continued its improvements program unopposed. Not until August 1906, more than five years after first gaining control of the Southern Pacific, did Harriman pay the first dividend on common stock. From then on, the dividend became as regular as the growth of earnings derived from an expanding business and remarkable operating efficiency.[32]

Neither threats nor criticism had deflected Harriman from his original goal. "The Harriman regime has been a drastic one," concluded one analyst. "The task . . . was the reconstruction of the Southern Pacific, without expanding fixed charges. To that task the management bent all its efforts, without regard to stockholders, petitions, threats and constant mutterings of discontent. This five years of Harriman autocracy . . . has been one of the most striking epochs in the history of American railroads."[33]

And one of the most ironic as well. An earlier generation of rail leaders had been roundly condemned for lining their pockets by paying dividends that had not been earned, taking it out of the road's hide by skimping on maintenance or fudging accounts. Harriman was attacked for pursuing exactly the opposite course: putting the road in superb condition at the expense of dividends even though the Union Pacific (and through it himself) would be the chief beneficiary of any dividends paid by the Southern Pacific.

Harriman had led the rail industry into a new era, shown open minds the path to the future. To those who opposed him he offered the same answer he had given the interviewer: a wave of an arm at the Southern Pacific and a defiant, "That remains."

19 Seeking the World

Far-seeing men realized that for the United States to maintain her position on the
Pacific it was necessary that diplomacy and commerce should go hand in hand and
that the political prestige, so necessary to the future of America in the East, could only
be secured by the creation of substantial vested interests. . . . It was Mr. Harriman
who saw the possibilities of this field and who laid the foundations for the
organisation which is now the chief instrument of American diplomacy in its
endeavor to secure for the United States recognition as a practical, not solely an
academic factor, in Far Eastern politics, and to assist China in her legitimate and
natural development.

—Willard D. Straight, untitled account, January 1911

Railroad tracks might stop at the water's edge, but transportation systems did not and neither did Harriman's imagination. He emerged as a railroad
man just as American interest in the Far Eastern trade was reviving in the wake
of the depression. The Open Door policy formulated in the last years of the century signaled a clear American intention to seek its share of the China market.

The flow of goods to and from the Orient passed over the transcontinental
railroads and was growing steadily. A long haul could be made even longer if this
traffic crossed the Pacific in American bottoms, but the United States had long
since lost the battle for supremacy on the high seas. Hill had been harping for
years on the value of the Far Eastern trade and the need for Americans to
dominate it. On this point Harriman agreed with his old adversary, but the
China market proved remarkably resistant to the American "can do" attitude
and had long twisted it into "how to" bewilderment.[1]

Until 1900, the American presence in China dwindled steadily while other
major powers carved the country into spheres of influence. Although direct
American investment jumped from $6 million in 1875 to $20 million in 1900, the
American business presence remained little more than a shadow. The United
States found itself on the premises without a clear sense of mission. It had
acquired Hawaii and, in the wake of the Spanish-American War, the Philippines
and Guam as well. By 1899 some seventy thousand American troops were em-

broiled in an ugly battle against Filipino insurrectionists. Secretary of State John Hay's celebrated Open Door policy had failed to halt the partitioning of China, and American troops were summoned there to help put down the Boxer Rebellion in the spring of 1900. The Russians were in Manchuria and edging toward war with Japan, leaving China a pawn between them.[2]

Several factors drew Harriman into these remote quarrels. The first may have been his role as a stockholder in the American China Development Company, which had been organized in 1895 to seek profitable investments in China. On paper the enterprise looked strictly blue chip, with Schiff, Stillman, a Morgan partner, and Levi P. Morton among the participants. In April 1898 the Chinese government granted the company the right to build a railroad from Hankow to Canton. Instead of laying track, the backers sold their interest to Leopold II of Belgium at twice the purchase price. The furor that erupted over the deal obliged Morgan's group to reacquire the concession, then sell it back to the outraged Chinese at a handsome profit. The result was a happy outcome for the investors but an embarrassment for the broader hopes of an American economic presence in China.[3]

Harriman had no hand in these events beyond the passive role of shareholder. Even before the American China Development Company folded, however, a second factor drew him into the strategic maze of the Far East. Acquisition of the Southern Pacific in 1901 brought with it control over the Pacific Mail Steamship Company, which along with a sister line was the only remaining American presence in the Far Eastern trade. The possession of a Pacific steamer line along with two rail systems touching the Pacific coast fixed Harriman's mind on the possibilities of the Far East. The fact that superior British and Japanese ships had all but swept American bottoms off the Pacific aroused two of his strongest instincts: patriotism and the love of a challenge.[4]

The outbreak of war between Russia and Japan in 1904 added another piece to the puzzle. Schiff involved his firm in the conflict by floating two Japanese war loans with help from Stillman's National City Bank. More than profit spurred Schiff to this effort; like many American Jews, he bitterly resented Russia's treatment of Jews. Harriman also favored Japan, believing that a Japanese victory would stimulate commerce across the Pacific.[5]

As the reconstruction of the Pacific roads progressed, Harriman grew restless for fresh challenges not to replace current projects but to supplement them. In this respect he was like a juggler, always adding one more ball to see how many he could keep aloft at once. Although the Far East posed as knotty a problem as could be found, Harriman viewed it as the shortest distance between a business problem and its solution without regard to diplomatic intricacies. Gradually a daring vision seized him. No one doubted that a huge increase in transpacific traffic was coming. "Granting the success of Japan in the present war," noted one analyst, "China, Manchuria, Korea and Japan will become immediately not only customers but shippers in tremendous volume to the United States ports. . . . Who is to handle the coming traffic?"[6]

Harriman leaped beyond the question of who to how it was to be handled. He conceived the notion of putting together a unified transportation system circling the globe. His plan assumed that Japan would win its war with Russia and acquire the South Manchuria Railway in the process. The first step was to secure control of this road and rebuild it, then buy the Chinese Eastern road from Russia and obtain trackage rights over the Trans-Siberian and other Russian lines from North Manchuria to the Baltic Sea. Since Harriman already controlled steamers crossing the Pacific and a system of transcontinental railways, he needed only a new steamship line plying the Atlantic between Russia and the United States to complete the circle.[7]

For years Harriman had toyed with the idea of visiting the Far East. One winter night in 1905 he invited to dinner Lloyd C. Griscom, a young diplomat whose wife was a friend of young Mary Harriman. Griscom had just been posted as minister to Japan and was eager to meet the man whose steamships were vying for the Pacific trade. The talk that evening was less about the Orient than railroads as Harriman dazzled Griscom with an account of how he had transformed the Pacific roads. As Griscom was leaving, he said casually to Harriman, "You ought to see what's at the other end of your line. Why not come out to Tokyo and visit us?"

"You may be getting more than you bargain for," Harriman shot back. "It sounds like a good idea to me."[8]

In June, shortly after hosting a luncheon for two Japanese visitors, Harriman announced that he would go to Japan in August. He would take along the entire family, as he had on the Alaska expedition, so they could share in another educational adventure. That summer he gathered information on Japan and related subjects, going so far as to collect data on Philippine railroads. The grand design had not yet come to him; he still did not know exactly what he wanted and so swept into his mind anything that contained a seed of possibility.[9]

Robert Goelet joined the Harrimans, along with R. P. Schwerin of Pacific Mail, Dr. W. G. Lyle, one of Harriman's physicians, two of Harriman's secretaries, and a tutor for the children. On August 16 they boarded one of Pacific Mail's new vessels, the *Siberia*, and steamed out of the Golden Gate in heavy seas. Five days later the travelers awoke to find Diamond Head shimmering on the horizon. The *Siberia* docked at Honolulu, having shattered the record for a run from San Francisco, and Harriman herded everyone into automobiles for a day of sight-seeing on the island.[10]

That same evening the *Siberia* hoisted anchor and headed for Midway Island, which it reached early on the fourth day. In 1905 Midway was a remote outpost manned only by employees of the Commercial Cable Company and a detachment of marines. Harriman went ashore long enough to pick up a wad of cables and scribble off answers. Six more days of cruising brought the *Siberia* to Yokohama, where Griscom gave them a warm welcome. He had arranged a special train to Tokyo and quarters for most of the party at the American legation.[11]

A steady stream of Japanese dignitaries and officials, as well as American businessmen, called to greet Harriman and shower him with invitations. Harriman told everyone he had come to learn and wished to talk with as many Japanese as possible, but there was a complication. Only a week before Harriman boarded ship for Japan, President Roosevelt had convened a conference at Portsmouth, New Hampshire, to mediate the Russo-Japanese War. On August 30, after two tense weeks, he produced an agreement that was to win him the Nobel Peace Prize. The terms gave Japan most of what it wanted from the war except for a huge indemnity it had hoped to wring from Russia. In Tokyo, however, the settlement was denounced as a national disgrace on the indemnity issue alone.[12]

The actual signing took place on September 5, the day before Harriman was to attend a dinner hosted by Baron Sone, the finance minister. On the afternoon of the sixth, opponents of the treaty staged a mass protest meeting in Hibiya Park. The police tried to block access to the park but were routed in the scuffle that followed. After passing resolutions against the treaty, the crowd surged toward the imperial palace only to be driven away. Angry and frustrated, they turned their wrath against the home minister, who had dispatched the police to break up their meeting.[13]

Earlier that day Griscom had been surprised to see troops from the Imperial Guard surround the American legation as a precaution. Harriman dismissed the idea that the fury of the crowd was directed against Americans. When his party set out for the residence of Baron Sone, however, they encountered large crowds in the streets, some of them carrying flags draped in black crepe. A few people noticed their carriage and chased after it, hooting insults but making no attempt to attack the riders.

Dr. Lyle and one of Harriman's secretaries had a more harrowing time getting to Baron Sone's home from the Imperial Hotel, which stood opposite Hibiya Park. As their rickshaws tried to weave a path through the crowd, people jeered and hurled stones at them. Lyle winced as a rock caught him in the neck, giving him a bruise as souvenir of his adventure, but they managed to reach Baron Sone's without further damage. All over the city the mob was growing in size and fury and venting its anger by smashing police kiosks and other small buildings. The baron, his drapes discreetly drawn to shut out the disturbance, greeted his guests as if nothing out of the ordinary was taking place.

As dinner proceeded, the Americans heard a dull roar every time the conversation paused. Suddenly the room went black. A servant rushed in to say that power was out all over the city and that bands of hoodlums were rampaging through the streets burning police booths and streetcars. The curtains were pulled open and everyone peered anxiously at tongues of flame licking the distant sky. A detachment of soldiers escorted the Americans back to the legation, where Harriman and his party ducked into the building while a line of soldiers with drawn bayonets held the screaming mob at bay. A police kiosk burned furiously a short distance away.

A dinner scheduled for Harriman the next evening was prudently canceled. As the rampage continued, Christian churches, trolleys, and some other buildings were torched before troops restored order and the emperor put the city under martial law. Harriman remained unperturbed even when the rioting took on an anti-American tone. He assured Baron Shibusawa, who called to express regrets, that Japan was not the only country where such things happened. Far from being frightened, the Harrimans seemed excited at being witnesses of history in the making. But Harriman had not traveled halfway around the world to be a spectator. He had people to meet and things to see, and the riots were costing him precious time.

Unwilling to burden Griscom with any more responsibility for the safety of his guests, Harriman took everyone to Nikko until things settled down. For three days the Harrimans enjoyed their favorite role of tourists, rummaging through the old resort town with its ancient temples and mausoleums; climbing a wild mountain gorge to glimpse beautiful Lake Chuzenji; riding along the avenue lined with giant cryptomeria trees; and buying armloads of booty at the curio shops.[14]

Averell was working against a deadline: the start of school at Groton. Harriman had asked permission for him to stay an extra two or three weeks, but the Reverend Endicott Peabody rejected the notion that more might be learned exploring the Far East than in a classroom at Groton. "Either he returns to the opening of school," Peabody decreed sternly, "or else he's not going to be admitted again." Glumly Averell crammed in a quick tour of Kyoto and two other cities before boarding ship.[15]

Harriman returned to Tokyo on the eleventh and plunged into a whirlwind of activities. Determined to meet everyone worth knowing, he endured receptions and dinners, gave interviews more freely than he ever had at home, and obtained an audience with the emperor. To the Japanese Harriman was unnaturally gracious but as blunt as ever. "The impression I have of the Japanese," he told one reporter, "is that they lack in the quality of working together. If Japan wishes to introduce foreign capital she must break off the habit of establishing small companies and try to carry on business on a larger scale."[16]

He pored over newspapers and maps, soaking up information without revealing his own thoughts. Then one evening Harriman stunned his host by saying, "Griscom, there's no doubt about it. If I can secure control of the South Manchuria Railroad from Japan, I'll buy the Chinese Eastern from Russia, acquire trackage over the Trans-Siberian to the Baltic, and establish a line of steamers to the United States. Then I can connect with the American transcontinental lines, and join up with the Pacific Mail and Japanese transpacific steamers. It'll be the most marvelous transportation system in the world. We'll circle the earth."[17]

The vision had arrived, and it was an extraordinary one. Harriman made his offer to the Japanese authorities at once, only to find them baffled by his direct style and slow to respond. Leaving negotiations in the hands of Griscom and a Japanese banker, he took to the road again. On September 14 he charged off to Kyoto, where he marched the family through the temples, museum, and ancient palace of the shoguns. He found Russian prisoners of war housed in one of the temples and went out of his way to talk to some of them before pushing on to Kobe.[18]

Harriman was rushing madly around the Far East as if intent on organizing it the way he had the Pacific railroads. He enlisted Griscom as a willing ally in expediting his travel plans as well as the negotiations. Harriman also wanted to see China and Korea, and he startled Griscom by asking to be the first civilian allowed into Port Arthur since the war. To Griscom's amazement, the Japanese government cheerfully granted Harriman's request.[19]

Harriman had a way of taking the removal of obstacles for granted. Even before the approval came through, he chartered a ship to take his group across the Sea of Japan. A member of the Japanese General Staff joined them for the trip to Dairen, where more Japanese officers came aboard. They went on to Port Arthur, threading their way gingerly into a harbor not yet cleared of mines. The Japanese proved gracious hosts and provided a full tour of the battlefields complete with a picnic lunch. Their civility contrasted oddly with the stench of death that still hung over the fields, where the arms and legs of partially buried bodies stuck aboveground like grotesque markers. Next day Harriman visited the war museum and was given a dinner at the Port Arthur Club.[20]

The experience gratified Harriman, but already his mind was racing ahead to the fulfillment of his plan. He wrote Secretary of War William Howard Taft on how to advance American interests and repeated the message to Griscom in terms that were vintage Harriman. "The way to find out what is best to be done," he stressed, "is to start doing something. . . . It is important that something be started that will save the commercial interests of the United States from being entirely wiped from the Pacific Ocean in the future."[21]

From Port Arthur Harriman hurried to Tientsin, where a special train took his group to Peking. There Harriman found an obstacle that would not yield.

The American minister, W. W. Rockhill, was the nation's foremost authority on the Chinese and had little use for businessmen or missionaries. Harriman asked to visit the imperial palace and was told the Manchu Court would never consent. When Harriman persisted, Rockhill reluctantly made the request and received the prompt rebuff he expected. Harriman vented his displeasure on Rockhill and threatened to let the State Department know just how poorly he had been served in Peking.[22]

The source of Harriman's pique was less a dislike for Rockhill than the frustration he always felt when balked. He could never escape the feeling that anyone who failed to accomplish what he wished had not really tried, had not moved heaven and earth the way he would in their position. Rockhill was convinced that Harriman intended making trouble for him in Washington, but Harriman had forgotten about the incident by the time he left China.

After three days of tramping through the dusty streets of Peking, Harriman's party steamed to Korea, where another special train took them to Seoul. They were but the latest in a stream of Western visitors descending on Korea that season, including President Roosevelt's daughter Alice. "Now Good Lord," groaned young Willard Straight, who was then stationed in Seoul, "we have the Princess Alice and her suite coming, the Harrimans the next week and I dont know who along the same line a little later, but I should judge from the geometrical progression that only the President, crowned heads from the Great Powers and Biblical characters can now compete."[23]

Straight put the Harrimans up at the American legation while parceling the others out to the Astor Hotel and a boardinghouse. The program of activities included luncheon with the emperor at the imperial palace and meetings with local Japanese. For the ambitious Straight these visitors were well worth the trouble. He got acquainted with Harriman, who was to help him advance both financially and socially, and made an even better impression on young Mary Harriman.

Harriman stayed three days in Seoul, then took a train to Pusan and a boat to Nagasaki, where he paused to inspect the dry docks and shipbuilding facilities before going to Kobe and Yokohama. After three weeks of constant movement and activity, Harriman allowed everyone a day's rest at Yokohama before hurrying back to Tokyo. Another dizzying round of luncheons, dinners, and receptions put him in touch with the remaining Japanese dignitaries he wished to meet.[24]

Griscom had been busy in his absence, having talked at length with the prime minister, the vice-minister of finance, and the distinguished elder statesman Count Kaoru Inouye. All responded favorably to Harriman's plan. The Western-minded Inouye was especially impressed, telling Griscom, "We would be very foolish to let such a great chance slip." But Griscom warned Harriman that more negotiation and patience were required. "The difficulty, as you know," he explained, "is to get them to decide anything or to work quickly. They do not understand our ordinary direct business methods."[25]

Worn down by the steady grind, Harriman pushed himself through the last round of amenities. On October 12 his persistence was rewarded with a preliminary agreement calling for a syndicate to buy and modernize the Manchurian Railroad under the joint ownership of Harriman and the Japanese government. The next day Harriman and his party boarded the *Siberia* in Yokohama and bade farewell to Japan. He had been abroad for two months and was eager to get home. "We believe there has been a beginning of an association which will end in a lasting commercial alliance between America and Japan," he said before departing. Events soon forced him to swallow that prediction. Eight days after putting out to sea, Harriman got word by cable that the Japanese government had been obliged to put the agreement in abeyance.[26]

Shortly after the *Siberia* sailed, Bertie Goelet offered a welcome distraction by wagering that the ship could not beat the record for the homeward run held by the *Korea*. Harriman leaped at the challenge and ordered the captain to push the ship full speed ahead despite rough, pounding seas. Alice Roosevelt was among the passengers and relished the whole episode. She knew, as Harriman did, that Goelet could not bear to part with his money and watched him grow so distraught over the ship's progress that his friends suspected him of trying to bribe a sailor to jump overboard.[27]

Harriman beat the record by a scant twenty-seven minutes and happily distributed his winnings among the crew before escorting his party to a special train that was to take them to New York. His sporting blood was still up; if the ship had made a record crossing, why not the train as well? As his special hurtled across the continent, eager reporters churned out stories of a mad, reckless dash at high speeds. Their accounts reached the desk of Alice's father, who fired off a wire to Harriman saying, "Please take care of the safety of my daughter on your train."

"You run the country," Harriman shot back. "I'll run the railroad."[28]

The record runs proved small consolation for Harriman. Only after reaching home did he learn why the agreement had collapsed. Three days after his departure, Baron Komura, the minister of foreign affairs, arrived in Japan with the final version of the treaty. Originally it had called for the Russians to surrender the South Manchurian Railroad to the Japanese; the final draft added a provision requiring Chinese consent to any such transfer and an agreement with Russia for connecting rail service. Komura had not known about the Harriman memorandum or his colleagues about the new provision, which prevented the Japanese from doing anything until these conditions were fulfilled.[29]

At every turn Harriman found his plans stymied. As complications piled atop one another, the realization dawned on him that no road through the Far East lay on a straight line or easy grade. The final blow came in January 1906, when he learned that the Japanese government had secured Chinese consent only by agreeing to place the South Manchurian road in the hands of a company composed exclusively of Japanese and Chinese stockholders. The Harriman agreement was dead.[30]

Despite this setback, Harriman had no intention of giving up on the Far East. "There will be large future developments, though not immediately," he predicted. If America was to get its share of the business, businessmen and diplomats would have to work in close alliance with the Japanese. Schiff was making the pilgrimage to Japan in the spring of 1906; perhaps he could smooth the way for future projects. Meanwhile, Harriman kept his Japanese contacts alive and continued to entertain visiting bankers and businessmen from that nation.[31]

The long sojourn to the Far East gave Harriman a unique experience among American businessmen. Although manufacturers and industrialists had long eyed overseas markets, few had yet probed the Far East and none dealt in land transportation. To his peers Harriman might as well have proposed laying track on the moon. He came close; at one point he toyed with the idea of building a road twelve hundred miles across the Gobi Desert along an ancient caravan route. The lack of any agriculture or other local business killed the scheme but not Harriman's fascination with the other side of the world.[32]

Schiff's efforts to revive the original project in the spring of 1906 failed. When Harriman got the bad news, he sent two experts to gather information on the trade, industry, and resources of northeastern China and enlisted Willard Straight to send him reports on railroad affairs in Manchuria and Siberia. Gradually Straight emerged as his most useful agent in the Far East. His accounts were to furnish Harriman information on which to fashion yet another bold plan. Harriman was far from done with the China market.

20 Seeking Relief

Any biography of Mr Harriman which omits his family life misses the point and loses the light of the whole story. . . . It was not unusual for him, in the midst of transactions of such importance as to make men dizzy from concentration, to stop in order to speak a word on the telephone, or send a message to Mrs Harriman about some engagement or matter of family interest. His attitude toward her was more than devotion. It was profound admiration, respect and unfailing attention and courtesy. Many times through the years business was interrupted or preceded by an order for flowers in commemoration of some anniversary. And as for the children, their education and welfare came before everything. Absolutely nothing was allowed to interfere with a visit to their schools, or the prosecution of any investigation or enterprise affecting their training or welfare.

—*Judge Robert S. Lovett, letter to George Kennan*

The more prominent Harriman became, the harder it was for him to live anything resembling a normal life. The upper class had always lived in a world apart, but American culture was undergoing a profound change by the 1880s. Industrialization had swollen the ranks of the wealthy and near wealthy just as immigration had increased the legion of the poor. There emerged a new material civilization in which business figures replaced politicians and soldiers as national heroes. The proliferation of cheap urban dailies fostered this process by splashing the exploits of tycoons across their pages and titillating readers with accounts of the lifestyles of the rich. By 1900 the yellow press had turned business titans and denizens of society alike into an early form of celebrity.

In this sense Harriman could measure his prominence by the growing amount of space he got in print. Some reporters made careers out of hounding the wealthy and depicting their antics in ways that were more vivid than accurate. The effect was to make the lives of the rich more accessible to the public while transforming their usual insularity into a siege mentality. For Harriman this posed a special problem. He had always belonged to the best social set, yet he also saw to it that his family shunned the worst excesses of the rich.

The Harrimans were a breed apart among a class apart. While denying their children none of life's pleasures, they were determined to imprint them with a sense of values and responsibility that could not be corrupted by their more feckless friends. This zeal made Harriman a domineering father and Mary a strict, demanding mother. It also placed a heavy burden on the children to measure up to the high standards expected of them. "Papa does want his children to be something & make something of themselves," Cornelia once lamented to her sister Mary. "He said that he started out wanting us to be different from other children & that's the reason we have been brought up so differently."[1]

The children staggered under the load, but none reared into rebellion. Young Mary, who was her father's favorite, came the closest. "I was ever so glad to get your letter," she repented to her father after one spat, "because it just set things straight and showed me how foolishly I had been acting. But besides being very 'babyish,' I think I have been selfish, and thinking only of my own pleasure and not doing my share a bit."[2]

Harriman prodded the children into reaching beyond what they thought themselves capable of doing. He expected of them the same perfectionist standards he demanded of himself and would not tolerate lack of effort or dishonesty. Averell learned this the hard way when he coaxed the chauffeur into letting him take his father's Mercedes out for a drive without first getting permission. Averell wrecked the clutch and had to confess his deed. "My father gave me quite unshaded hell," he recounted later. What bothered Henry most was that Averell had done it on the sly. "I'm straight with you," he admonished. "I expect you to be straight with me."[3]

Most of the Harrimans' friends commented glowingly on the closeness of their family life. What made it so remarkable was the way Harriman included his family in his business activities. His knack for mixing business and pleasure revealed the extent to which he found relief at home from the pressures of work. Yet family was also for him another form of business, one filled with joy and pleasure but no less demanding in the responsibilities it placed on him. Relief came hard for Harriman because he was always at work in whatever he did. The triumph of his life lay in learning not to escape this pressure but to thrive on it.

When the new century opened, Harriman was nearly fifty-two and the undisputed patriarch of his clan. His parents had long since died, and his eldest brother, John, followed them in 1898. Mary had lost her father in 1897, leaving her brother William more dependent than ever on Harriman for financial counsel. Another painful loss came in 1903 with the death of Harriman's youngest brother, William, who succumbed to Bright's disease. His loss touched Henry deeply; he had been closer to Willie than to any of his brothers and devoted to him during his long illness.[4]

Unlike his brothers, Willie never married. He became a club man and collector of art who loved sailing on his yacht, traveling, and hosting entertainments. As declining health forced him to surrender these pleasures, Henry tried to fill the vacuum. Whenever Willie fell ill, as he did late in 1892, Henry arranged for his care, providing a private car for him to travel south in the care of one of the family doctors. "I appreciate all the trouble you took then and all that you showed & did all thro my illness," wrote a grateful Willie as soon as he was able to grasp a pencil again.[5]

Willie's condition worsened in November 1902, and Henry sent him to Florida in Dr. Lyle's care. Late in February, hearing that Willie was failing, he rushed south despite being in the middle of negotiations with Hill. When Willie's condition seemed hopeless, Henry brought him back to New York to spend his last days among the family. A preferred way of handling illness or death among wealthy families in those days was to check the patient into a hotel rather than a hospital and arrange for treatment or care there. Willie was installed at the Plaza Hotel, where he died on April 4.[6]

Willie's passing cut Henry's last direct tie to his old firm, Harriman & Company. The house still had two of his cousins, Oliver Harriman Jr. and J. Borden Harriman, both sons of the uncle Oliver who had helped Henry buy his first seat on the New York Stock Exchange, and a nephew. By 1903, however, Henry had more than enough to occupy him elsewhere. He continued to favor his old firm, but his interest in it waned after Willie's death.

Harriman barely had time to mourn Willie's loss before heading west on an extended trip to inspect the railroad and deal with the shopmen's strike on the Union Pacific. Young Mary was the only family member who accompanied him. In mid-May Harriman finished his business in California and started east. He was on a tight schedule; the family was to sail for Europe at the month's end. As the train pulled out of Ogden, Harriman seemed in good spirits. He chatted with W. L. Park before going to bed around eleven o'clock. Half an hour later, Park was surprised to see Harriman's secretary, W. A. Ransom, rushing into his car. Mr. Harriman was ill, Ransom exclaimed, and needed a doctor at once.[7]

Park stopped the train and wired ahead for a doctor at the hospital in Evanston, Wyoming, less than an hour away. The doctor climbed aboard when the train arrived, but Park took no chances. He wired the company surgeon to meet the train in Cheyenne and also ordered the chief surgeon to hurry west on the next train. The doctors examined Harriman and agreed on their diagnosis: appendicitis. Everyone was in a state of near panic. The most important railroad man in the country lay ill in the middle of Wyoming with a condition that in 1903 was anything but routine. The surgery required was dangerous, and where was it to be performed?

An alarmed Park had to leave the train at Cheyenne. He stopped by Harri-

The squire at rest: E. H. Harriman in 1906, caught in a rare moment of relaxation.
(Union Pacific Museum Collection)

man's stateroom to say good-bye and found him sitting up in bed shaving himself. "These doctors of yours say I have appendicitis," Harriman growled. "They are mistaken. I am going to be all right soon." He had no intention of canceling the meetings he had scheduled with leaders of the shopmen's unions in Omaha. Park shook his head in amazement and reluctantly took his leave.[8]

Fortunately, Harriman had ordered Samuel Felton to meet the train at Cheyenne. Climbing aboard the Arden, he found a strikingly different Harriman: pale and drawn, his gaunt face wreathed with pain. "I am very sick," Harriman groaned in what was a startling confession from a man who never betrayed weakness. "I do not know what is the matter with me," he lied, "and the company doctor with me doesn't know, either."[9]

"Then of course you are going right through to New York," Felton ventured.

"Yes, I am going right through," Harriman replied. "But I have to meet a delegation of shopmen at Omaha. They wrote asking to see me, and I promised to see them." He brushed aside Felton's protest that the situation did not require the presence of a sick man. "Yes, I know all that," he snapped, "but I promised to see them, and I am going to see them."

Felton knew this obstinate streak of Harriman's all too well and did not waste any more words. Instead, he hurried off to consult the company's chief surgeon, who informed him of Harriman's ailment. The situation was both delicate and dangerous. No one knew how serious the inflammation was or how much time Harriman had before a crisis. Felton decided to take no chances. When the train reached Omaha, he hunted up the station master and countermanded the order to attach another car for the union delegates who were to accompany Harriman to Chicago. The delegates were told that Harriman was ill, and they offered no objections to postponing the meeting.

Another physician climbed aboard at Omaha and confirmed the diagnosis. When the train chugged out of that city, Felton heaved a sigh of relief and went reluctantly to tell Harriman what he had done. "Why did you interfere with my plans?" Harriman rasped peevishly.

"To save your life," Felton answered.

Harriman was not impressed. "What you have done," he said, "just means that I shall have to see them at Chicago. I said I would see them, and I am going to see them. Wire them to come on to Chicago."

Felton nodded wearily but ignored the order. Instead, he arranged for a top surgeon to meet the train in Chicago. When the doctor entered his stateroom, Harriman started up again about meeting the union delegates before doing anything else. The surgeon nodded impassively and proceeded to examine him. When he had finished, he said in a grave voice, "Mr. Harriman, you have appendicitis. You will go to my hospital at once and be operated on, or you will attach your car to the next train for New York and be operated on there."[10]

No longer able to deny his condition, Harriman allowed his car to be hitched onto a New York Central train for the trip home. By then the papers had got hold of the story and were spreading it rapidly despite Felton's attempt to downplay its seriousness. On Wall Street bears used the rumors to hammer the Harriman stocks. "With the exception of J. Pierpont Morgan," wrote one pundit, "there is no man . . . whose death would have a more depressing effect upon a large number of prominent stocks."[11]

When the train reached New York on the morning of May 16, Harriman had to be whisked to a suite in the Netherland Hotel because his house was under quarantine. During his absence Cornelia and Roland had come down with scarlet fever and were confined to the house with Averell, Carol, and their mother, leaving only young Mary to stay with her father. Doctors Lyle and Morris met him at the station, where Harriman made a brave show of denial to reporters while being eased into an automobile for the trip to the hotel.[12]

It was all bluff. Three days later a special platform was set up in the hotel suite, and Dr. William T. Bull performed the operation with half a dozen colleagues at his elbow. The surgery went smoothly, and once Harriman came out of the ether, he relished nothing more than telegraphing Hill that the doctor "took out the useless thing this morning. I am in fine shape." For years afterward he kept up a pretense of being angry with Felton for interfering with his plans, then finally wrote him a letter of appreciation.[13]

During his recovery he was surprised by a visit from John Muir, who happened to be in New York. "You must have suffered terribly," Muir sympathized, but Harriman ignored the remark and talked instead of his record dash across the continent. "Troubles seldom come singly," he added abruptly. "Now we are getting out of them all—strikes on the roads, scarlet fever in the family, etc.—and for the first time since these troubles commenced we are going to dine together this evening in my room. Join us and you will see all the family."[14]

Nothing made Harriman happier than to be reunited with his family and to share the moment with a friend. Muir could not accept, but he came away deeply impressed by what he called the finest "domestic weather" he had ever experienced. It was a warm, pervasive atmosphere that embraced all who fell under its spell and made them part of whatever the family happened to be doing at the time. For a time they became willing conscripts to whatever program Harriman had mapped out, and always it was he who called the tune they danced.

But the weather was not always fair. There were the inevitable tiffs and disagreements as well as the crises born of illness or injury. The pain Harriman endured from his own illness was nothing compared to his suffering when one of the children was afflicted. It was the one time he felt utterly helpless, unable to control his destiny. When Cornelia had to be operated on for appendicitis,

Harriman could only ask the minister at Arden to say a prayer for her recovery. The children got hurt often because they led such vigorous lives and their father had taught them to be plucky. Young Mary once found herself astride a wildly bucking horse but kept her composure and escaped with only a sore ankle. Later she would not be so lucky; her death in 1934 came from injuries suffered when her horse fell and rolled over her.[15]

To Harriman, the risks of vigorous activity were simply the price of doing life's business, and he drilled this attitude into the children. He gave them every means for improving themselves and expected them to take full advantage of their opportunities. All were sent to private schools; Roland went to one in Lakewood, New Jersey, with only six other students. Harriman often brought the family down in an automobile to visit him and once took all the students with them to Atlantic City for the night. They strolled the boardwalk, ate cotton candy, and posed for a family picture with Henry's head perched atop the cutout of a Teddy bear.[16]

The boys were congenial but awkward, eager to please and to learn because their father would have it no other way. Harriman saw that their schools had everything they needed. He believed so strongly in physical fitness that he had a bar attached to the bedroom roof of his railway car for chinning exercises. When Averell started at Groton in 1903, the school had no athletic director until Harriman helped defray the cost of one. Roland moved to Groton at eleven, a year younger than most of the boys, and struggled so badly that the headmaster suggested he repeat a year. Harriman had a better idea: he furnished the school with a tutor to help boys like Roland.[17]

Despite his frantic schedule, Harriman watched the boys' progress like a hawk. The school required them to write home on Sundays; the Harrimans demanded a postcard from each boy every night. Grades went home once a week and were scanned like financial reports. No one was punished outright for poor performance, but the somber mood in the house when they came home on holiday made clear how they stood in their parents' eyes. Yet not even frowns of disapproval could spoil the evening fun, when their competitive juices flowed out in games of dominoes, Parcheesi, or backgammon.[18]

When the boys showed an interest in rowing, Harriman took his yacht the *Sultana* up the Hudson to Poughkeepsie, where several college crews were training for a race. Although he knew nothing about rowing, he watched the crews work out, talked to the coaches, jotted down notes on their performance, and collected enough information to conclude that the best coach was Jim Ten Eyck of Syracuse. Ten Eyck was promptly invited to spend six weeks at Arden, where each day on Forest Lake he drilled the boys until they became good oarsmen.[19]

Although most children of the elite did some traveling, few could match the Harrimans. By the time Roland was twelve, he had visited every state except

Alabama and North Dakota along with Alaska, Siberia, Canada, Japan, China, Manchuria, much of Europe, and Mexico. In the United States they traveled by automobile before it became popular, enduring breakdowns, rugged terrain, and the taunts of bystanders shouting "Get a horse!" One summer Harriman piled the boys into a car and drove across the wilds of central Oregon, the first man to make the trip by car, so he could scout firsthand the prospects for a railroad line.[20]

Other trips were more tame but always with a purpose. One Sunday morning Harriman decided the time had come for the boys to see the rectory on Long Island where he had been born. The chauffeur drove them out to Hempstead, where they poked around the house in which the Reverend Orlando Harriman had lived. When they returned home, Mary asked if the boys liked the old homestead. "Well," shrugged Harriman with obvious disappointment, "the only one who was impressed was the chauffeur."[21]

Harriman expected no less of his daughters than of his sons. They too were educated in private schools and pushed to go as far as their abilities would take them. Mary blazed an impressive trail for the others to follow. She went to Barnard College, majored in biology and sociology, and developed an interest in eugenics that earned her the nickname "Eugenia" from classmates. She passed this interest along to her mother, who found herself in the unexpected role of sometimes having to restrain young Mary's enthusiasm for causes.[22]

In society no less than in education Mary veered from the usual path. A dark, pleasant girl with an infectious laugh, she liked to dance and enjoy the company of her friends. But when the time came for her debut in 1901, she balked at what she deemed a wasteful expense. Drawing together eighty other debutantes, she persuaded them to form a new organization that could be both fun and useful to the needy. Her zeal led to the founding of the Junior League.

Mary worshiped her father and was the child most like him. She was the most strong-willed and assertive, the most effervescent in personality, and the one most likely to challenge his authority. When they clashed over the issue of marriage, however, it was Mary who bowed in dutiful retreat. During the family's swing through the Far East, Mary fell under the spell of Willard Straight. Then stationed in Seoul, a vice-consul nursing grand ambitions in a backwater post, Straight was at twenty-five nearly two years older than Mary. Tall, charming, possessed of boyish good looks and brimming with talent, he had a bright, witty mind and a clever tongue. He wrote and drew well and had graduated from Cornell as an architect in 1901. He took a post with the Imperial Maritime Customs Service in China, then served as a Reuters correspondent in Korea during the Russo-Japanese War.[23]

The move to the legation at Seoul was the latest stop in Straight's search for his destiny. The Far East had fascinated him since a stay in Tokyo as a child, but it was not his only obsession. During these years Straight brooded endlessly over the contradictions in his life and ambitions. Both his parents had been school-teachers who died early, leaving Willard and his sister Hazel to be raised by two woman friends of their mother. Willard's increasing contact with the elite aroused in him a fierce desire to join them and a painful awareness of how unlike them he was. He was not only poor; he was an artist, with an artist's tempera-ment and sensitivity. His character was made of porcelain, theirs of marble—dense, polished, and solid. In October 1904 he poured out his doubts to his diary: "This playing with the Great is unsatisfactory. I am not of them. For the present by position and in virtue of money enough to dress well I am able to trot in their class. The celerity with which they would drop me should I make a mistake or appear in an old suit of clothes would be remarkable. Imagine going through life as an artist, a little brother to the Rich. Dawdling at Newport trying to catch orders. Painting portraits and being petted . . . a hanger on—a tail of a retinue. It is all wrong. One receives more than one can give."[24]

At the same time, Straight longed desperately to be "of them." He set his sights on capturing an heiress, and he had excellent if unorthodox tools with which to work. It was his blend of charm and artistic bent that captivated Mary. The company of her society chums amused but never fulfilled her. Men like Bertie Goelet were pleasant and charming but could not match Straight's cre-ative volatility, yearning ambition, and restless energy. There was a magnetism about him, a sense that he not only had a soul of more than ordinary depth but also wore it close to the surface.

During their brief time together, Mary fell in love with him. When Straight returned home in 1906 to attend the wedding of Alice Roosevelt and Nicholas Longworth, he saw Mary again. A romance between them bloomed before Straight went off to Cuba with the Longworths. That summer he returned to the United States and managed to secure an appointment as consul general to Mukden. Although his diary fell mysteriously silent during these months, there is no doubt he visited the Harrimans. Edwin Morgan, who had headed the legation in Seoul, thought it was Harriman's influence that got Straight his posting to Mukden.[25]

Harriman helped get Straight appointed because he had plans for the young diplomat. The vision of a global transportation system still danced in his brain. To keep it alive, he needed someone in the Far East who could keep him posted on the shifting scene there. Straight was eager to play this role; he viewed himself as a spearhead of American influence in Manchuria and China, opening a wedge for economic penetration by men of Harriman's caliber.[26]

Although Harriman did not know it, Straight also wanted something from him. Before his departure in October, he and Mary talked of marriage despite the enormous social and geographical gulf between them. They agreed to be engaged secretly, knowing that Harriman would be furious if he knew. Straight departed with a sense of relief, leaving Mary with the delicate task of how and when to tell her father. She was close to her father and the nearest thing to a free spirit in the family, yet the matter went unbroached for months.[27]

Meanwhile, Straight fed a steady stream of information to Harriman on the Manchurian and Siberian Railway, the political climate, investment opportunities, and other matters. While Harriman pondered these reports, Mary groped for an opening to present her own agenda. The only ones who knew her secret were Cornelia Harriman and Straight's sister Hazel. It did not help that her father had fallen into a bitter controversy with his old friend Teddy Roosevelt and come under attack by the ICC. Finally, in April 1907, she screwed up her courage and broke the news to him. "I don't quite know if he has recovered from the 'shock' of what I have told him," she sighed to a close friend afterward, "but now it is a question of waiting for Willard to be able to get leave."[28]

The shock waves were not long in coming. Harriman was livid not only over the engagement but also because it had been kept secret from him. Cornelia tried to intervene on her sister's behalf and received the same tongue lashing for being deceitful. "I don't think we're such despicable creatures as Papa made out us to be," she wailed. The trouble with Mary, Harriman told Cornelia pointedly, was that she insisted on making things so hard for herself. He also had serious reservations about Straight. If anything, Harriman noted harshly, he was too much like Mary—lacking in balance and stability. Harriman doubted he was as capable as Mary thought he was and doubted his sincerity even more. Was he after Mary or an heiress? Harriman conceded that he did not know Straight well, but that was the point: neither did Mary. She had been swept off her feet by a man she had seen only briefly and did not really know.[29]

Mary retreated in hurt and confusion. She talked of going to Mukden while her father remained implacable. Cornelia tried to help but confessed helplessly, "I feel so torn between you & Papa." The crisis remained private until one morning early in August when a reporter turned up at Arden asking to interview Mary, who happened to be the only one of the family there. Harriman had just taken the boys west on an inspection trip, and his wife had gone out with the other girls on the *Sultana*. Was it true, asked the reporter bluntly, that Mary was going to marry Willard Straight?[30]

Mary was aghast and could only blurt out a denial. "I don't know what to do about it," she cried frantically to a confidant. "I am terribly worried. How can they possibly have heard a rumour—& if any-thing comes out in the paper about it—Papa will be simply furious & it will make every-thing ten times worse. It is too dreadful." The story did appear, embellished with the juicy morsel that the couple had been secretly engaged for nearly a year. To the reporters chasing after him for his reaction, Harriman declared in steely tones that there had never been an engagement and would never be a marriage.[31]

The once and future engagement died aborning after this incident. Straight remained Harriman's contact in the Far East but had to seek his heiress elsewhere. He managed this with spectacular success, marrying Dorothy Whitney in 1911. Mary could not bear to be alienated from her father and hurried back into his good graces, but the rebel in her did not die. Social gossips soon paired her with Bertie Goelet, the son of Harriman's old Illinois Central friend and heir to one of the largest fortunes in America. Goelet was a pleasant specie of social butterfly—handsome, charming, utterly devoted to the ritual pleasures of those who fluttered between New York and Newport. In school he had written essays on such burning topics as "The Supposed Degeneracy of the Modern Racehorse."[32]

To society's eyes the match seemed a perfect one. Bertie ran in the same set as Mary, if far more vigorously, and his family had a place at Tuxedo conveniently near Arden. But Mary surprised society again by choosing Charles C. Rumsey, a sculptor from an old Buffalo family of modest means. Rumsey was the very creature Straight had dreaded becoming: the artist tied to society's tail. An excellent horseman and polo player, he met Mary at the Meadowbrook Club on Long Island, where they often rode together in hunts.[33]

"Pad" Rumsey did not fit Harriman's strict criteria for a son-in-law any better than Straight, but Mary had learned from experience. She did not marry Rumsey until eight months after her father's death. The only one of the girls to marry in Harriman's lifetime was Cornelia, who walked the straight and narrow by accepting Robert L. Gerry, the scion of a distinguished family that traced its lineage back to a signer of the Declaration of Independence. Their wedding at Grace Church in March 1908 was the lavish ceremony Mary never had, in which Harriman proudly gave his daughter away amid an overflow crowd of old friends and the social elite.[34]

On those rare occasions when Harriman found himself alone at Arden, he was quick to take refuge from his solitude in the company of friends or the disciplining of servants gone slack in their duties. His restlessness was as great as his need for his family, the "chicks" as he liked to call the children no matter how grown they were. He was incapable of sitting still or dwelling in the company of his thoughts except when working out business plans. The squire of Arden was always on duty even though he was seldom needed because Mary ran the household so efficiently.

Such was the case one sultry July day in 1906 when Mary and the children had gone off to Long Island, leaving Henry alone in New York awaiting a trip west. "I can see the cavalcade raising the dust for all Southampton," he teased Mary after wiring her a birthday present. He had spent a night at Arden during the week and had not liked what he found. The housekeeper was away; in her absence several boxes of berries had spoiled because no orders had been given about them. Harriman directed the gardener to start a ledger listing every item sent up to the house and ordered the cook to sign her name on receipt. Now he asked Mary to instruct the housekeeper "to stop the waste & carry out my new plan."[35]

At least the cook had shown good sense in not wasting a whole chicken on his solitary dinner, and the parts she served had been tasty. After dinner Ned Parrott stopped by to chat for a couple of hours. His father was dying, and Ned could only wait helplessly. "I feel very sorry for Ned," mourned Harriman. "The rest of them are cold." Another old friend, Rensselaer Weston, also ambled in to say hello. Their presence cheered Harriman only briefly. He felt adrift without someone from the family, and his only companion on the forthcoming trip was to be the lawyer Charles Peabody.[36]

Above all he missed Mary and her quiet, supportive dignity. Harriman understood that her formal manner masked a shyness that made her soft spoken even at the dinner table. She never competed with Harriman but made her wishes known when it counted. Society held little appeal for her; she dressed well but simply and had no desire to compete with the likes of Mamie Fish, whose social excesses were fast driving her husband to despair. Mary possessed a strong will and an even stronger loyalty to family, and she knew how to laugh.[37]

She was the ideal companion for a man who had always to command. Together with the children, she provided Harriman release from his duties as squire of Arden and Napoleon of the railways. Despite their occasional spats and tribulations, the family was never happier than when together. So important had Arden become as their haven from the outside world that in 1905 Harriman determined to build a new and far more ambitious house there. The squire wanted a castle set atop a mountain in splendid isolation, with breathtaking views across his domain in every direction.

But not a castle. Harriman wanted something palatial but with a unique twist: it was to be an American home, built entirely with native granite and other materials, designed by an American architect, constructed by his own workmen, and furnished with American art and artifacts. He selected a choice site atop one of the highest ridges in the Ramapo Hills even though everything used in the work had to be hoisted twenty-three hundred feet up on a private cable railway built for the project. This meant slow going and rugged handling, but that was fine with Harriman. Indeed, it was altogether fitting. Everything else in his life had been an uphill climb; why should his dream house be any different?

Part IV. Immolation

1904–1909

21 Fighting the Tide

E. H. Harriman . . . was a small, brown, taciturn man who never seemed to play. He gave the impression that what he did and made others do was never just "for fun," was always practical. . . . There was little of the pomp and none of the splurge of great wealth about him. What he wanted was power; quietly, deliberately, thoroughly, he worked to get it.

—*Alice Roosevelt Longworth,* Crowded Hours

Harriman sat atop the largest transportation empire in the world and presided over so many systems and companies that his associates had trouble remembering which one he served at any given time. Fish once asked him to read a letter and treat it "as written to you as Director of the Illinois Central R.R. Co., rather than any other capacity, as it would not do for me to go about telling tales concerning the alleged shortcomings of Officers of other Railroad Companies." This conceit of partitioning the self among corporate roles was typical of the era, but few titans had as many different personas as Harriman.[1]

A list published in 1905 revealed that Chauncey M. Depew, the longtime servant of the Vanderbilt roads, senator, and popular after-dinner speaker, served as director for seventy-four companies. Behind him came William K. Vanderbilt with fifty-six seats, Stillman with fifty-five, George Gould with fifty-two, and Harriman with forty-nine. Most of the boards on which Vanderbilt and Depew sat belonged to their own system; Stillman, Gould, and Harriman were far more diverse. Harriman's seats broke down into about thirty railroads, four or five traction companies, half a dozen steamship lines, some banks, trust companies, insurance, and telegraph companies along with the smaller concerns in which he had some personal interest.[2]

Critics brooded over the power wielded by fifty-seven men who together held a total of 1,460 seats on the boards of major corporations. The sheer size and scale of Harriman's empire, which to the public seemed to have mushroomed overnight, singled him out as a prime target for those alarmed by the growing influence of giant enterprises on society. A prudent man could see that controversy loomed on the horizon, but Harriman had never been prudent in the political sense. He could not easily change his style to suit a shift in the public mood. Like so many warriors risen swiftly to power, Harriman found himself thrown on the defensive by the enemies he had accumulated and the fears he had aroused. As always, the creation of an empire paled before the task of maintaining it against attacks from all sides.

Peace in the Northwest depended on implementing the Metropolitan Club agreement. In November 1901 Harriman again sat down with Hill and thrashed out a new memorandum elaborating on the issues covered in the May agreement. But Hill put off final approval of the draft, and Harriman bristled at the delays. Part of the problem lay in a clash of styles. Harriman was an engine of perpetual motion, eager to nail agreements down and get projects launched; Hill moved more deliberately, testing the legal ground gingerly before proceeding. Hill grew suspicious of Harriman for moving so fast, while Harriman grumbled over Hill's delaying tactics.[3]

The southeast corner of Washington State remained the most disputed ground. Both sides had agreed to construct jointly a series of lines radiating from the Snake River. Harriman wanted one key branch started at once but could not get Hill or Mellen of the Northern Pacific to budge. Finally his impatience exploded, and he started to let contracts for the work on his own despite Mellen's protests that the line's location had not yet been decided. Harriman assured a Hill associate that he wanted harmony but snapped that "the only way to get work started is to start it."[4]

The November memorandum wilted before this and other disputes that it was intended to resolve. Negotiations entered their second year under a cloud of distrust. The harder Harriman pushed, the more Hill dug in his heels, growling that if differences could not be "settled on a fair basis, the whole thing can go by the board." By the winter of 1903 an uneasy truce prevailed in the Northwest, and the efforts of Harriman and Hill to resolve their deadlock over the Metropolitan Club memorandum had been upstaged by the legal battle over Northern Securities.[5]

The state of Minnesota's suit against Northern Securities had been removed to a federal court and was regarded as little more than a nuisance (see Chapter 15). But late in February 1902, less than a month after the ICC concluded its inquiry into the community of interest, Theodore Roosevelt stunned business circles by bringing suit against Northern Securities for violating the Sherman Act. His motives in taking this action have puzzled historians as much as they did contemporaries. Roosevelt offered them little help; the editor of his voluminous correspondence turned up only one letter written in all of 1902 bearing directly on the Northern Securities case. In May of that year Roosevelt also told the writer Hamlin Garland in passing that he had "taken down the fences of a very great and very arrogant corporation."[6]

Both Roosevelt and Attorney General Philander C. Knox believed the time had come for the federal government to establish its right to harness the giant combinations that were emerging. But Roosevelt also had an eye cocked toward reelection to the office that fate had so unexpectedly delivered to him. Like all great politicians, he was a master at hitching self-interest in tandem with public policy. Northern Securities was the newest, most conspicuous target on the landscape and the one most likely to please the western interests Roosevelt needed to woo for the nomination in 1904. He understood that in politics timing and gesture count for more than deeds; from this one act he gained a reputation as "trust buster" that fooled even some historians.[7]

Harriman wasted little time on speculation over his friend Roosevelt's motives. Hearing the news just as he was about to go west on an inspection trip, he summoned Hill, Gould, Fish, Marvin Hughitt, and Samuel Spencer to an urgent meeting. Their discussion did little more than accentuate the friction between Harriman and Hill over the issues left dangling by the unresolved status of the Metropolitan Club memorandum. At a time when cooperation among rail leaders was urgently needed, the ranks were deeply divided.[8]

The memorandum itself had become a bone of contention. In testifying before the ICC that winter, Hill flatly denied that any such agreement existed on paper. Harriman let it be known privately that he had no qualms about furnishing the commission a copy if asked. Where Hill's political instincts told him that the memorandum would be misconstrued as a giant conspiracy, Harriman bristled indignantly at the idea of hiding anything he had done. So great was his contempt for the investigation that his first impulse was to duck out of testifying altogether. This naïveté gave Hill fits. "You should see Harriman at once," he wired Morgan partner Charles Steele, "making sure that no memorandum or paper of any kind is furnished to the Interstate Commerce Commission."[9]

Harriman finally yielded to Hill's pleas that he testify, but on the stand he was sullen and truculent, firing as many questions at the commissioners as they did at him. He was slow to grasp how dangerous the issues of collusion and conspiracy had become. For decades railroads had been the lightning rod for controversy over the abuse of power by giant corporations along with the favorite bogey of the era, Standard Oil. By the early 1900s, however, the merger movement had added an impressive array of financial and industrial firms to the roster of villains. Banks were an obvious target, especially Stillman's National City Bank with its close ties to the "Standard Oil crowd."[10]

It did not help that the public attitude, as in the 1980s, was soured by the stench of scandals emanating from Wall Street. The insurance industry found itself subjected to a major investigation that dragged Harriman's name through the mud as well. Charges of fraud and mismanagement were also leveled at the shipbuilders, the Beef Trust, the Gas Trust, and combinations such as Amalgamated Copper. Stories of financial irregularities paraded out of Wall Street with numbing regularity until even the *Wall Street Journal* blamed the trust controversy on "this passion for bigness, this misconception of the importance of size."[11]

A reform tide had been gathering since the turn of the century, drawing its strength from such disparate sources as the outrage over these scandals, the public fear of growing corporate power, the ability of Theodore Roosevelt to transform issues into a blend of conviction and political opportunism, and the desire of some special interests to use the issue for their own advancement. As the tide gained force, it swept with indiscriminate fury toward a debate over the extent of federal regulation, which emerged as both a major question of social policy and a potent political issue.

At the center of this controversy stood the Sherman Antitrust Act, which all sides agreed was defective and obsolete though barely a decade old. But when Congress showed no inclination to improve the law, the Northern Securities case emerged as a crucial test for how far the law could be applied. So far the Sherman Act had been applied to railroads only twice, and both times the Supreme Court had struck down rate agreements as collusive. The Northern Securities case marked the first challenge of a rail merger as being in restraint of trade.

The lawyers assured Harriman and Hill that "what Northern Securities has done is no more than has been done by every railway consolidation for nearly seventy years." But this was precisely what made the decision so crucial: it posed the threat of upsetting other rail mergers and might become a precedent for attacking combinations in other sectors as well. "Thoughtful men can see that the whole question of control of the transportation industry is up for decision," observed the *Wall Street Journal*, "not merely in the United States law courts, but in the great forum of public opinion."[12]

Slow as he was to fathom the danger, Harriman decided to lash back at the industry's critics. Breaking his usual silence, he paused at several stops on an inspection tour in May 1902 to tell reporters that "pools are obsolete in my opinion, and commissions are generally composed of men who know nothing about the operation of railroads." He denied vehemently that modern railroads were overcapitalized and accused politicians of attacking the carriers because it was the popular thing to do. "The people and the railroads should get closer together," he urged. "I believe the people are understanding this more every day."[13]

These remarks by a man who normally avoided reporters drew caustic responses from antirailroad circles, but less partisan observers praised his frankness. "The recent breach in Mr. Harriman's taciturnity was welcome in many ways," noted the *Wall Street Journal*. "We wish that he could be induced to do this kind of thing more often, for there is evidence that he knows what he is talking about—which is more than can be said for some who are much more often heard."[14]

Grudgingly Harriman found himself being pushed more into the national limelight on railroad policy issues. He was at a severe disadvantage there, possessing neither the tact nor the stump-speaking skills of Hill. Reporters found it easy to pounce on a phrase or sentence and twist it out of context. The fact that Harriman was quick and combative only whetted their sense of engagement. It also made diplomatic souls like Stillman and Schiff cringe every time Harriman opened his mouth to an eager band of reporters, especially in the wake of the Northern Securities decision.

For two years the case loomed like a ticking bomb above Harriman and Hill as the taking of testimony droned on until January 1903. Then, to expedite the decision, Congress took the unprecedented step of empowering a special panel of four federal circuit court judges to hear the case and certify their decision directly to the Supreme Court without the usual long delays in the appeal process. For three days in March the judges heard the arguments; on April 9, they ruled unanimously that Northern Securities had been created to eliminate competition, possessed the power to restrain trade, and was therefore illegal whether or not it actually used this power. The case was promptly appealed to the Supreme Court.[15]

The decision could not have come at a worse time for Harriman. He was distracted that winter by an injury, by the clash with Keene over Southern Pacific, and by the illness of his brother Willie, who died a few days before the decision was handed down. Then Harriman was stricken with appendicitis and laid up by the operation. It was the kind of situation he detested most: the stakes were huge and he could do nothing to affect the outcome.[16]

The question tormenting him was what would happen if the court ordered Northern Securities dissolved. Harriman had an enormous investment in the company, but Hill controlled its management. Schiff, too, was aware of the disaster that would unfold if the present arrangement came unraveled. He devised a fallback plan for the company and urged Hill to discuss it with Harriman. "Remember, the soup is never eaten as hot as it is cooked," he cooed in one of his interminable homilies, "and I am sure things will come out all right anyhow."[17]

In August another federal circuit judge, after hearing the suit brought by the state of Minnesota, contradicted his brethren by ruling that the formation of Northern Securities involved no restraint of trade. This case too was appealed, giving the Supreme Court a thorny package to ponder. All the judges construed the Sherman Act the same way and agreed on the facts of the case; they differed only in their views of whether the purchase of shares in a competing line by a single interest was criminal in intent or power.[18]

Nothing could be settled until the Supreme Court ruled. Once recovered from his operation, Harriman took his family to Europe. Before boarding ship he saw Hill, who had shown genuine concern during his illness. For a moment their relationship seemed to warm; the thaw vanished abruptly, however, once Harriman reached the other side. Determined to beard the lion in his own den, he breezed into London and called on two of Hill's closest associates, Gaspard Farrer and Lord Mount Stephen. It was his first meeting with both men. Farrer was a young, hard-nosed banker at Baring Brothers and nobody's fool. Harriman impressed him with his frankness, his breadth of vision, and his kind words about Hill despite their differences. Farrer came away quite taken with Harriman despite all he had heard about him.[19]

Mount Stephen was an older banker who had been close to Hill for a quarter-century, but he too fell under Harriman's spell. They met at a luncheon attended by the Harrimans and two of the girls and chatted for an hour. Afterward Mount Stephen invited them all to his estate for lunch. Harriman talked a little business with him and again lavished praise on Hill and his work. Mount Stephen found them "a very nice American family" and liked what he saw in Harriman. "He appeared to me to be an exceptionally able & clearheaded man and a man to be trusted," he wrote Hill.[20]

This was precisely the impression Harriman hoped to make. He would have relished its effect on Hill, who was quick to set Mount Stephen straight. "I am glad you met [Harriman] in London," he replied cautiously. "Privately speaking, he has a reputation of being able to turn a very sharp corner where he thinks it to his interest to do so. However, I have always treated him with open and fair consideration and I believe fully that this is the best course."[21]

Harriman came home refreshed and full of enthusiasm but still thin and lacking his old vigor. Although the signs were not yet obvious, the appendectomy marked the beginning of a physical decline. It was not that his health failed but rather that his body could no longer keep pace with his mind and will. Sheer determination came more and more to replace stamina as his driving force. Harriman never acknowledged his slipping vitality or the need to slow down. Every illness or setback merely summoned from him a greater capacity for denial and louder vows to press on.

After his return Harriman sparred fitfully with Hill without breaking the stalemate between them. In March 1904 the ax finally fell. The Supreme Court, by a five-to-four vote, ordered Northern Securities dissolved on the grounds that any combination with the power to restrain trade was illegal whether or not that power had actually been used. The swing vote belonged to Justice David J. Brewer, who argued in a separate opinion for a distinction between reasonable and unreasonable combinations. A few years later the Court would embrace Brewer's "rule of reason" dictum, but in this case he became the deciding vote for dissolution.[22]

Nothing better illustrated the confusion Americans felt over the corporate behemoths that had become so significant a part of their economic life. The issue revolved around the specter of "monopoly" threatening "competition" in an industry where the two worked in a unique way, and it invoked a flawed statute that was probably never intended to apply to railroads. Nevertheless, Americans clung to the axiom that competition was good, monopoly evil, and the concentration of power dangerous regardless of its purpose.[23]

The prolonged debate that erupted over the broader implications of the decision struck Harriman as academic compared to his immediate problem. Failure to reach an understanding on the Metropolitan Club agreement already had Harriman and Hill edging toward war in the Northwest. Now the court had dumped in their laps the problem of how to dismember the corpse of Northern Securities.[24]

There were two ways to dissolve the company. Each shareholder could receive the same amount of stock in Northern Pacific and Great Northern he had originally exchanged, or the holding company's assets could be distributed on a pro rata basis without regard to what stocks each holder had turned in when the company was formed. Under the first plan Harriman would retain control of Northern Pacific; the other option would give him large holdings in both companies but control over neither of them. One plan served Harriman's interests, the other Hill's, and no middle ground existed between them.[25]

Harriman demanded the first approach, but Hill dominated the Northern Securities board. On March 22 it approved the pro rata plan with Harriman the lone dissenter. Harriman then filed suit to enjoin the distribution. His suit tied everyone in knots. While the injunction stood, Northern Securities could not perform such corporate functions as paying dividends. Its earnings piled up in the treasury until the legal battle was resolved. This deadlock outraged Hill and his friends, who had grown accustomed to regular dividends. For three years they had waited anxiously for the court to decide the legality of Northern Securities; now they found themselves waiting yet again.[26]

As usual, Hill did most of the talking. For him the business rivalry had turned into a blood feud. He roared indignation at the suit, claiming that Harriman had agreed to the plan and then gone back on his word. "As a piece of conscienceless lying it is a rare effort," he said privately. "I would not, under any circumstances, be associated with them in any business. All they want to make them crooked is an opportunity to cheat some one." Harriman put off the reporters flocking to his office with the curt remark, "The court papers tell the whole story." Privately he told a friend that if he won the suit, he was willing to distribute the stock in a manner that left the management of the roads unchanged. This comment got back to Hill but did not budge his distrust of Harriman or his belief that Stillman and William Rockefeller were behind the suit.[27]

This suspicion that Harriman was an agent if not a puppet for Stillman and the shadowy William Rockefeller would not die. The Harriman persona had fragmented into conflicting images that confused business figures no less than the public. Hill believed firmly that the malign, treacherous version in his grasp was the real one, but his friends were not so sure. In July Harriman and Stillman went abroad to do some more lobbying in the enemy's camp. During their week in London, they allowed Gaspard Farrer and Lord Mount Stephen to take them in tow for extended visits. Again Harriman showed them a strikingly different figure from the one portrayed by Hill.

The face he presented was pleasant and temperate, the affable Dr. Jekyll off duty. He steadfastly refused to deal in personalities, and his anger flashed only once, when Mount Stephen suggested that William Rockefeller had prodded him into bringing the suit. The whole difficulty, as it had been from the start, lay in the threat posed to the Union Pacific by Hill's absolute control of the Burlington. He pressed on Farrer copies of the Metropolitan Club memorandum and the 1901 agreement in which Hill had agreed to share control of the Burlington with him. While Farrer realized that he had only one side of the case, the point had been rammed home. "It is not the Burlington per se but the Burlington in your hands, in your undivided control, that is the trouble," he informed Hill. "It is not the present but the future that Harriman fears; it is not Gould or the Moores but you."[28]

While insisting that he would welcome any settlement that protected his interests, Harriman coated his olive branch with a glaze of menace. If the suit failed, he reminded the banker, he would have $250 million in cash and securities for whatever measures might be required. Farrer did not have to guess what he meant and was quick to urge peace on Hill. "We do not believe that he is raising this trouble from vanity or greed," he emphasized, "but he is determined to safeguard what he has, and he will miss no opportunity to fight you on the present issue, and oppose you in all your future moves until that object is attained." Harriman echoed these same sentiments to Mount Stephen, speaking of Hill with great respect but insisting that only an equal voice in the Burlington management could safeguard Union Pacific interests. He uttered not even the hint of a threat, yet the same conclusion impressed itself on a fearful Mount Stephen as it had on Farrer: there would be no peace until Harriman and Hill came to terms. The prospect of renewed war was too terrible to behold.[29]

Harriman also revealed something else to Mount Stephen, something quite unintended. To the elderly banker's shrewd, appraising eyes, Harriman looked stronger than he had the year before but still far from well, "having a tired worn look for so young a man." After leaving London, Harriman went on to Aix-les-bains to take the cure for three weeks, but only after a stop in Paris. There too he made a good impression, convincing bankers of his reasonableness and his refusal to deal in personalities.[30]

Before going abroad, Harriman had boasted that he would return with Hill's friends in his pocket. This remark left Hill steaming when he heard it; now the reports that Harriman was turning his visit into a triumphal march drove Hill to stoop as low as an honorable man could go. To Farrer he poured out a fifteen-page torrent blasting Harriman's arguments and then Harriman himself in an ugly diatribe:

> It would take too much of your time and mine for me to go on and enumer-ate all these unreasonable things attempted by Mr. Harriman. . . . I am sorry to have to be compelled to say it, but it is no news to those who have known Mr. Harriman most intimately here,—his word is not accepted. Even Mr. George Clark, whom I think you know, and than whom no one stands higher as a business man, and from whose house Mr. Harriman married his wife, has told me repeatedly that while for family reasons he will always treat Mr. Harriman well, to look out for him, that he is not always to be trusted and that even in the matter of family estates he is not to be trusted.[31]

Late in August, before sailing home, Harriman paused briefly in London for another visit with the bankers. He came home satisfied with the impression he had made. Although he did not woo the bankers away from Hill, he had com-pelled them to revise their view of him. They saw gloomily that Hill's dislike of Harriman had grown blind, almost irrational, and that there could be no com-munity of interest in the Northwest. "The more I see of Mr. Harriman the more I like him," noted Farrer wistfully to Hill, "and the more I deplore that you and he cannot come together." Mount Stephen knew his old friend better. "It is quite clear," he sighed to Hill, "that the time has not yet come for you & Harriman to run in the same team & I doubt it ever will come."[32]

The suit dragged on until January 1905, when the circuit court ruled against Harriman and dissolved the injunction. Harriman then appealed to the Su-preme Court, where he lost again. By March 1905 Hill had finally won a com-plete victory, yet it did not slake his bitterness. When Schiff tendered him congratulations, Hill snarled, "I do not agree with you that the fight has been a fair one. I think it was the foulest and most unnecessary fight that I have ever known."[33]

This from the man who had remarked after the Northern Pacific panic that Schiff took such things too seriously.

Seven years of struggle and negotiation had brought all sides back to square one in the Northwest, the only difference being a heightened level of bitterness and distrust. While Farrer and Mount Stephen renewed their pleas for compromise, Schiff tried desperately to smooth a fresh path to the bargaining table. "There is no reason in the world," declared an editor, "why Mr. Hill and Mr. Harriman should not cement an honorable, business-like peace of a permanent character."[34]

But there was every reason, beginning with the enmity between the two men. After his return from Japan that fall, smarting from yet another setback, Harriman surveyed the landscape of struggle around him and remarked to a reporter, "We are going to run into an era of competitive railroad building just as we have passed through an era of competitive buying." His prediction made the rounds of the papers with lightning speed, tantalizing editors and alarming bankers and businessmen who were trying to divine what Harriman's next step was likely to be. They did not yet know the extent to which the initiative had passed from his hands.[35]

22 Fighting Formidable Foes

E. H. Harriman has come to blows since then with J. J. Hill, J. P. Morgan, the First National Bank, the Rock Island crowd, Edwin Hawley, George J. Gould, Stuyvesant Fish, and almost everyone else with whom he has been in contact. . . . If his ambition crossed theirs, he forgot about theirs. If his mood prompted he did not hesitate to insult them—in fact he did not know he was doing it.

—Wall Street Journal, *August 25, 1906*

Sitting with a well-known financial writer in the dregs of a gray afternoon, indulging himself in a rare moment of introspection, Harriman toyed with a familiar question: was it his withering candor that made him so unpopular? Did he pay a steep price for his lack of tact? "I suppose people think so because I don't truckle or toady to any of the big men," he answered earnestly. "I don't have to. Why should I?"[1]

The writer choked back a laugh at the idea of Harriman truckling to "big men" like Morgan or Hill, but knew he was dead serious. Once, in his excitement, Harriman had given H. H. Rogers so violent a scolding that the bewildered Rogers backed him off only by crying, "Do you know whom you are talking to?"

"I never fight unless somebody fights me," he continued. "As long as they pound I pound. But I'd rather be let alone. Let the other side go to work and succeed and prosper; so long as they leave me alone I'm satisfied. I drop all revenge. Often my associates have expressed their astonishment that I don't follow up a fight after it's stopped." He paused as if to share that astonishment, then added, "I am not vindictive."

These remarks drew cynical smiles in some quarters and outright guffaws in others. Like Jay Gould, Harriman had earned a reputation for prizing revenge as a beacon to guide his course. That this simplistic explanation made little or no sense did nothing to diminish its popularity. More to the point was his inability to leave alone anyone he thought posed the slightest threat to his own plans. Interference was to Harriman the most intolerable of crimes.

In the community of interest it was impossible for one man to move without jostling someone else. Every action posed a threat, immediate or potential, and therefore aroused suspicion. The most active of the players, Harriman was also the most suspicious of what others were doing. His hyper-kinetic engine bristled with ambition on offense and defiance on defense. The run at Northern Pacific had blended the two in brilliant fashion. On one hand, he acted to protect the Union Pacific from the threat posed by the Burlington in Hill's hands; on the other, he seized an opportunity to upstage Hill in his own territory.

But the campaign had ultimately failed. The Burlington remained in Hill's camp, and Harriman had yet to gain entry to Puget Sound. He also faced threats from Gould and the Atchison in the Southwest, as well as the erratic ambitions of the Rock Island crowd and the growing sense of isolation felt by the Northwestern and the Milwaukee. Peace was nowhere to be found west of Chicago.

The Northern Securities decision did not so much wreck the community of interest as drive the last decisive nail in its coffin. During the holding company's short life the strategic situation deteriorated in every theater. Harriman and Hill continued to squabble in the Northwest, their quarrel exacerbated by the schemes of the other Iowa roads seeking an outlet to the sea. George Gould toiled fitfully at his grand design of a coast-to-coast line, while Edwin Hawley quietly put together a string of roads under his command. The Rock Island plunged into a policy of belligerent expansion, and the Atchison flexed the growing strength of its modernized system with an aggressive campaign for new business.

The vaunted personal associations among these leaders did little to resolve conflicts spawned by the merger mania of 1901–4. No one found a way to satisfy one road without irritating others; closer ties between two lines usually provoked countermoves by rivals left outside the alliance. Harriman found it difficult to formulate a decisive policy because he could not get at his foes without hurting his friends. After William Rockefeller emerged as the leading figure in the Milwaukee, Harriman bought stock in the road and in October 1902 gave it equal status with the Northwestern over the Union Pacific to the coast.* This quashed rumors that the Milwaukee was about to build its own line to the Northwest, but it also raised Stuyvesant Fish's hackles that the Milwaukee got what he had long sought.[2]

The Atchison proved more difficult to subdue. As owner of the only unified line between Chicago and California, it made effective use of its shorter route and potential for faster schedules. Here was another vital reason for closer ties with the Iowa roads: the Union Pacific needed efficient connections with them to compete with the Atchison. Harriman also had to resolve the conflicts with

*This arrangement applied only to freight operations. The Northwestern remained the sole line whose passenger cars ran to the coast in Union Pacific trains.

the Atchison in Arizona and northern California (see Chapter 16). For months he insisted that the Atchison sell him the Phoenix & Eastern and stay out of the territory south of Phoenix. But Victor Morawetz adamantly refused to consider any settlement that did not also include the California dispute.[3]

Harriman had in mind relocating the Southern Pacific line between Lordsburg, New Mexico, and Yuma, Arizona, where the road crossed the Rocky Mountains. The best route lay along the Gila River, which was the only waterway on American soil that cut entirely through the mountains. Harriman wanted eventually to build his cutoff along this route but so far had done nothing. In December 1903 the crews building the Phoenix & Eastern reached the south bank of the Gila River west of Kelvin, then jumped the river and commenced surveying along the north bank toward a junction of the Gila and San Pedro Rivers. Without even filing location maps, the crews bridged the river and began construction work.[4]

The Atchison's move triggered a reprise of the fight for Meadow Valley Wash in Nevada. Harriman picked up the gauntlet by sending Epes Randolph, who had charge of Southern Pacific lines in Arizona and New Mexico, to lay track from Phoenix to Yuma and through Gila canyon to Lordsburg. Gila was a formidable box canyon eighteen miles long with walls that in some places towered a thousand feet above the river. Both companies slapped together location maps and rushed to file them, reaching the land office three hours apart on March 14, 1904. The two lines overlapped nearly everywhere, with Harriman's Arizona Eastern situated fifteen or twenty feet higher in the canyon. Grading forces from both sides arrived and blasted rock onto each other's line.

Journalists rushed to fill their columns with Bunyanesque accounts of a donnybrook that seemed a throwback to the golden age of railroading. Before much damage was done, however, the fight shifted to the drab battleground of the courtroom. Harriman's claim was upheld and appealed to the Supreme Court. While the lawyers traded volleys, Harriman revived the earlier scheme to buy Atchison stock. The object this time was not control but merely a voice on the board as leverage for a peaceful settlement. After he and his associates had acquired three hundred thousand shares of Atchison, Harriman demanded representation. Morawetz balked on the grounds that he thought it improper for directors of one road to sit on the board of another.[5]

Morawetz was playing a thin hand. The court fight had gone against him, and the Harriman group owned far too many shares to be ignored. Yet so anxious was Harriman to settle that he made the concession Morawetz wanted most. The result was a package compromise. Morawetz agreed to give Harriman two seats on the Atchison board provided the new directors were not Union Pacific officials. He also agreed to sell the Phoenix & Eastern to the Southern Pacific and to stay out of the disputed territory. In return, Harriman offered to put the competing northern California lines into a new company shared by the Atchison and Southern Pacific.

The deal enabled the two systems to live in harmony for many years despite occasional spats. It had taken Harriman's entire repertory of tactics. He had pushed hard, then shown restraint; overplayed his hand, then maneuvered carefully. He had responded to a threat with swift but measured strokes, then negotiated patiently for a settlement. Both sides could claim the outcome as a victory, yet in the long run it was Harriman who got his way. The Atchison was going to get into northern California anyway; Harriman got it there on terms acceptable to him and in a way that gave him a listening post on the board of the only rival he feared in the Southwest.[6]

In April 1904 Harriman accepted what was for him a rare assignment: an invitation to deliver a speech. The occasion was the World's Fair in St. Louis honoring the Louisiana Purchase. Harriman had passed through the city early in April on one of his swings through the West. During his brief stop the fair officials asked him to return at the end of his trip and give the opening-day crowd a few words on behalf of the "Domestic Exhibitors." Harriman agreed because it gave him a chance to expound on his favorite themes of progress and the large role played in it by the railroads. The timing could not have been better, coming only weeks after the Northern Securities decision.[7]

On April 30 Harriman stepped before a throng of curious onlookers eager for a sighting of so rare a specimen. After singing a hymn to the glories of material progress, he launched into a theme that must have astonished some of his business foes. "We have here collected the product of our artistic, scientific, and industrial life," he blared in his flat, colorless voice. What made it possible? The chief factor was "the co-operation of all our people. The first law of civilization is the co-operation of all individuals to improve the condition of life."

Modern railroads had made possible the remarkable strides in material civilization on display at the fair. "Within the present generation," Harriman reminded his listeners, "vast improvements have been made in railway transportation. It was impossible to supply the needs of our commerce by the railways originally constructed and operated. It became necessary to, not only reconstruct and re-equip these lines, but to bring them under uniform methods and management, all of which were possible only by the combination and unification of the original short lines of railway into systems each under one management of control, and this in turn was possible only by the combination of capital."

Nowhere did Harriman produce a more succinct summary of what he had tried to accomplish. His speech was a paean not only to progress but indirectly to himself, Hill, and others like them who had ushered in the new era of railroading. Their foresight had created the vital arteries on which the nation's swelling commerce moved, and for their pains they were being attacked from all sides. Harriman did not dwell on this latter theme; he conceded the need for regulation and urged government to cooperate rather than obstruct. "No one can escape this law of co-operation," he warned. "Self-interest demands that we must observe its just limitations."[8]

That Harriman would give a speech at all amazed many observers; that he would dwell at length on the theme of cooperation befuddled them. So little was actually known about Harriman's views and so much was assumed about them from his actions that few knew what to make of it. Was this a sop to the growing specter of government encroachment? Did it mean the elusive Harriman had decided to become more of a public figure? Could it be that Harriman, like Hill and other enlightened rail leaders, finally grasped the importance of his role as industry spokesman in an era of turbulent change?

No immediate answers were forthcoming. If nothing else, the St. Louis speech revealed a fatal contradiction in Harriman. The man who praised cooperation so fervently had never learned how to cooperate except on his own terms. He could leave associates alone to do the things they did best, but in his own domain he insisted on things being done his way. He always thought he knew the best way, and he was right often enough to give the term "Harrimanize" a pungent meaning.

But there were too many major players to Harrimanize, including George Gould. That most amiable of socialites still baffled observers with his erratic course. In the East he continued to fight the Pennsylvania Railroad like an impetuous general hurling his best battalions to be shattered against an impregnable position. In the West he persisted in denying any connection with the Western Pacific with an ingenuousness that left Harriman scratching his head. For two years after the road's incorporation in February 1903 analysts mused over the question of why Gould was playing ostrich on the subject.[9]

In March 1904 Gould responded to fresh rumors of his involvement by telling a reporter flatly, "I have not put a dollar into the undertaking, nor have I any intention to do so. I am not interested in the Western Pacific directly or indirectly, nor are any of the officials of the several roads with which I am connected." Six months later, amid rumors of growing tensions between Gould and Harriman, E. T. Jeffery and another man with ties to Gould joined the Western Pacific board. So did former Harriman ally Edwin Hawley. Still Gould played coy about his role, even after Jeffery was named vice-president of the Western Pacific in December 1904.[10]

Harriman watched this charade closely, not knowing whether to be angered or amused by Gould's antics. On March 8, 1905, he and Schiff lingered after a meeting of the Western Union board to ask Gould directly about his role in the Western Pacific. Gould again denied any interest in the road but added lamely that at some future time he might get involved. If so, he assured Harriman, he did not think it proper to remain on the boards of the Southern Pacific and Union Pacific.[11]

The next day Gould accepted reelection to the executive committee of the Union Pacific. If what he told Harriman and Schiff meant anything, this indicated that he was not involved in the Western Pacific despite overwhelming evidence to the contrary. Not until April 22, twenty-six months after the Western Pacific was chartered, did Gould admit publicly that he was behind the road. Then he waited three more days before notifying Harriman and resigning from the Union Pacific and Southern Pacific boards. Harriman promptly quit the Rio Grande and Rio Grande Western boards, leaving the community of interest in ashes.[12]

Once the news went public, Gould found ready underwriters for a $50 million bond issue and obtained a good route. Jeffery assumed the road's presidency and oversaw the project. One analyst predicted that Gould would get support from large interests who cared little for him but found the Western Pacific "a useful club to hit Harriman with." Beaming with confidence, Gould promised to build a first-class road in two years even though the first spade of earth had yet to be turned. "The Harriman monopoly west of the Great Divide," chortled an analyst, "is to be broken." There would be no stranglehold on all the lines reaching San Francisco, no Harriman "octopus" squeezing the West at will.[13]

In the euphoria surrounding the announcement, few observers paused long enough to see the absurdities in this thinking. Harriman knew the road Gould had undertaken was going to be fiendishly difficult and expensive. Once completed, how could it compete with the Harriman roads? At Salt Lake City the Western Pacific would connect with the Rio Grande, which had yet to be modernized. Beyond Denver it would use the Colorado division of the Missouri Pacific, which in 1905 still had light fifty-six-pound rail, dirt ballast, short passing tracks, and a host of other shortcomings.[14]

The same held true for much of the Gould system, which had become a dinosaur. In his scattershot way, Gould had neglected to bring his roads into the new century and had belatedly started to upgrade the parent road. He lacked an efficient organization, largely because he insisted on making all major decisions himself even though he was seldom well enough informed to do so. The capable managers he had gathered about him soon wore down from fighting caprice and indecision and broke with him. Jeffery alone remained, partly because Gould gave him a freer hand in the West and partly because, with so many defections, Gould depended on him more than ever for advice.[15]

By 1905 Gould's erratic behavior had also cost him most of his supporters on Wall Street, where he made the fatal error of antagonizing his friends in the syndicates that financed his eastern campaigns. The "Gould policy," concluded one analyst, "has become so inscrutable to Wall Street, that members of the financial community refer nowadays to the Gould situation only in terms of bewilderment." His response to these pressures in the summer of 1905 was typical: he sailed to Europe for a long vacation. One observer pinpointed the difference between Harriman and Gould: "The policies, ambitions, and apparent destinies of these two magnates are identical. Each is an autocrat. Each is impatient of advice, restraint and rivalry. Neither cares to share his power with his subordinate officers. Yet there is a very striking difference between the two. . . . Mr. Gould is swayed by incidental circumstances, while Mr. Harriman's vocation in life is to triumph over incidental circumstances."[16]

Harriman read Gould's character well enough to exploit its flaws. Aware that the building of the Western Pacific would be a monumental task, Harriman did what he could to make it even more monumental. Since supplies for the work had to pass over his roads, he extracted high rates and imposed delays. He was also accused of luring laborers away from Gould's line with promises of high wages only to set them adrift, but the charge was never proved. A fierce controversy over the issue of terminal space in Oakland did not get resolved until April 1907.[17]

By 1905 the elusive Edwin Hawley had joined Gould in the swelling ranks of Harriman's enemies. Like Harriman, Hawley had blossomed in midlife as a financier. Having entered railroading as a traffic man, he became one of Huntington's most trusted associates and helped negotiate the sale of the latter's stock to Harriman. Hawley remained with the Southern Pacific less than two years before drifting into Wall Street, where his railroad knowledge served finance instead of traffic. A shrewd and clever speculator, he emerged by 1904 as a rail operator to be reckoned with, having acquired the Minneapolis & St. Louis, the Iowa Central, and a large interest in the Colorado & Southern. A bachelor living in a midtown apartment, Hawley had a natural poker face with pale, cameo features and lips that barely moved when he spoke.[18]

Since leaving the Southern Pacific, Hawley had turned up on the opposite side of Harriman in several deals. Sometime around November 1903 he began buying Alton stock. Harriman made no secret of his willingness to sell the Alton; all his efforts to find a place for the road in his larger scheme of systems had failed. In the summer of 1904 Harriman returned from Europe to discover that Hawley and the Rock Island crowd owned 80 percent of the Alton's common and 30 percent of its preferred stock. Some way had to be found to share power in the road. Although Harriman loathed arrangements of this kind, he agreed grudgingly to a novel plan by which the two groups were to divide the seats on the board, create a voting trust, and take turns managing the Alton for a year at a time. The result was an uneasy alliance between strange bedfellows over a road that was soon racked with controversy.[19]

There was trouble too on the Kansas City Southern, which Harriman had dominated through a voting trust since the spring of 1900. The trust was due to expire in February 1905, and there had been loud grumbling over Harriman's management. Despite impassioned support from some local interests, Harriman had little desire for a fight over a property that had become marginal to his interests. He announced that he would not oppose a change in management and simply let the road go back to the Dutch holders, for whom Hawley acted as agent. If Harriman thought he was done with the Kansas City Southern, however, he was soon to discover that it was not done with him.[20]

After Harriman uttered his widely quoted remark that the country was about to enter a period of competitive building, reporters scurried eagerly to Hill for a response. "That view of the situation has not presented itself to me," he said with a broad smile. But months earlier Hill had begun organizing a project to build his own line to Portland along the north bank of the Columbia River. A few weeks after Harriman's remark, the Milwaukee announced that its long-awaited extension to Puget Sound would be built, whereupon Harriman declared that his projected line to Seattle would go forward. Farther south, Gould's Western Pacific lurched into action. The new age of competitive building had dawned.[21]

The Northern Securities decision had thrown the situation in the Northwest back to status quo ante bellum. In strategic terms Harriman controlled two key ports, San Francisco and Portland, while Hill had only Seattle. He wanted into Seattle and Hill into Portland, but the hard feelings between them made cooperation unlikely. Nor was the clash confined to the Northwest. Talk revived of Harriman buying into one or more of the other Iowa roads to counter Hill's hold on the Burlington. While similar rumors had been floating around for years, Harriman now had the huge war chest received in the breakup of Northern Securities. The securities from the dissolution armed Harriman with more than $100 million for whatever purposes his fertile brain conceived.[22]

Putting this huge sum in Harriman's treasury was like handing a brilliant general several crack divisions of troops. He and his friends had already bought into the Atchison and had strengthened their ties with the Northwestern. Early in 1906 Harriman bought ten thousand shares of Milwaukee stock; later that year he sent an agent to scout the Rock Island and two other roads. The prospect emerged of a giant coalition embracing the Harriman roads, the Milwaukee, the Northwestern, and the Atchison poised against the Hill interests. "Who is going to stop E. H. Harriman?" cried one rail manager. "Somebody has got to or he will have every trunk line in the country."[23]

With friends like the Clarks, Harriman hardly needed enemies. The construction of the San Pedro road dragged out into a far more serpentine fight than that

Harrimanizing the railroad interests: This cartoon depicts the growing public impression of Harriman as the czar of railroads. (Union Pacific Museum Collection)

against Gould's Western Pacific. The fault lay less with the senator, who like Harriman was far too preoccupied with other matters to oversee the work, than with his overweening brother, who shared the enormity of William's vanity if not his ability. Ross Clark viewed the work as an opportunity to make the usual profits in the usual way. The ordeal that followed graphically illustrated the gulf between the old style of railroad construction and Harriman's approach.

Building a road through desert country was a logistical puzzle requiring careful preparations. The route had to offer both economical operation and permanence in the fickle desert environment. Under the Clark-Harriman agreement, the project was to be overseen by a committee of four: Ross Clark, San Pedro chief engineer H. Hawgood, W. H. Bancroft, and Southern Pacific chief engineer William Hood. Every decision, every contract let, and every piece of work done was supposed to go through this committee.[24]

Ross Clark let it be known that he regarded the committee as a mere advisory body with the real power resting in his own hands, and he intended to let contracts for the entire road so that work could proceed everywhere at once. Bancroft was quick to confront Clark, who promised that no contracts would be let without the committee's consent. Harriman reinforced this stand by insisting that no financial commitment be made without prior approval from his representatives. Despite his vow, Clark went off chasing contracts like a hound sniffing rabbits. He planned to use the Empire Construction Company for building the road. Through this time-honored device the builders could siphon off profits from the construction work long before the road opened.[25]

The agreement gave Harriman a half interest in Empire, but unlike the

Clarks, he was more interested in completing the road as quickly and efficiently as possible than in making money from the process. The old tricks held no charm for him because they slowed progress and hiked costs. But Harriman was in Europe when the dispute arose, forcing everyone to mark time until he returned. When another squabble arose over how construction accounts should be audited, however, Harriman made his views unmistakably clear before returning home. "I insist that we have control Auditor, San Pedro Company and all companies," he cabled. "Permit nothing be done without."[26]

A flurry of telegrams flew between New York and Salt Lake City on these controversies, many of them in cipher code to conceal the contents from prying eyes. That Cornish, Hood, and Bancroft already had strong feelings about Ross Clark can be seen in the code name they assigned him: "Repulsive." They stood firm until Clark relented and gave Harriman what he wanted. The construction company was discarded, all contracts were made directly with the San Pedro, and a capable auditor was chosen to oversee accounts.[27]

Once the actual work began, Bancroft and Hood found fault with almost everything done by Clark and Hawgood. To get the best possible line, Hood sent his top engineer to examine all disputed points. His reports confirmed Hood's belief that his line was shorter and more economical than the San Pedro's, yet Hawgood clung to his own survey even though he did not visit the site or offer an argument in its favor. By fall Hood was discouraged enough to tell Bancroft, "I am convinced that the present organization of the [San Pedro] are not railroad builders." Two weeks later he muttered that Clark's crew, if left alone, would take ten years to complete the job. Cornish agreed that it would not suit Harriman "to have Mr. Clark dawdle along with the property as he has been doing."[28]

At the committee meetings Clark would agree pleasantly to everything and then go out and do something else. Hood thought one contractor did shoddy work, yet Clark promised him more work without telling Hood or Bancroft. As these squabbles increased, Hood began to suspect that something more was involved. In January 1904 he sent a young engineer named A. M. Bienenfeld to oversee the field work and report directly to Bancroft. Hood also let Hawgood know that Bienenfeld required more detailed reports than had yet been produced.[29]

Harriman learned of this struggle when he asked for a progress report in March 1904. He got an earful from Hood and Bancroft. Grading contracts had been let with little regard for costs, reliability of the bidders, or the requirements given by Bancroft and Hood. Months had been wasted bickering over these contracts and over the defects in Hawgood's route, which Hood considered a disaster. Hawgood had blocked Bienenfeld at every turn and even hired a stenographer to spy on him. Bancroft and Hood warned Harriman bluntly that nothing Clark or Hawgood said could be trusted without outside verification.

"It is exceedingly difficult," they concluded, "to do business where such complete lack of confidence exists as to the integrity of these parties."[30]

Bancroft sent the report to Cornish and suggested that it be shown to Harriman but not to Senator Clark. "It is very evident," he added, "that these people do not want anybody only their own 'gang' connected with the construction of this line." After pondering the report, Harriman decided to send an expurgated copy to Senator Clark, knowing that it would quickly find its way into Ross Clark's hands. A short time later Hood received an urgent call from Ross Clark to stop by the office. Clark complained that he felt mortified by the report, and he tried earnestly to convince Hood of his good faith. The impassive Hood remained polite but noncommittal.[31]

Harriman's warning shot led Clark and Hawgood to change their course but not their ways. Within weeks a showdown arose when one of the contractors, thwarted by Bienenfeld's rigorous screening of work, threatened suit. Clark and Hawgood supported his complaint; Bancroft and Hood rejected it as a scam concocted in league with Clark and Hawgood. Under the agreement, any such deadlock was referred to Harriman and Senator Clark, a prospect Hood relished. "I for my part am willing to say, and even desirous to say," he growled, "that Mr. Hawgood is both incompetent and dishonest."[32]

Before this happened, however, Hawgood threw down the gauntlet by firing Bienenfeld. Hood was furious, especially when he learned that Hawgood's intended replacement was a man who had been involved in an earlier rake-off scheme. He and Bancroft refused to accept the move or the other man. "What they know," muttered Hood, "is that the contract will be strictly carried out under Bienenfeld and no thieving allowed and they want a man who will be flexible." Ross Clark insisted that his decision was final; privately he told Hood that to back down would humiliate him. Hood snapped that his decision too was final, humiliation notwithstanding.[33]

Informed of this latest episode, Harriman shook his head in disgust. His first impulse was to fire off a telegram ordering Ross Clark to reinstate Bienenfeld, but Cornish persuaded him to let Bancroft and Hood handle it with the assurance of support from New York. Two days later, however, Harriman told Cornish to insist on Bienenfeld's retention and ignore Ross Clark's wounded feelings. Senator Clark was abroad and could be reached only by cable, but Harriman had lost all patience with the delays and chicanery.[34]

Early in May the construction committee thrashed out the dispute in four days of tense meetings. The testimony of several witnesses revealed that none of the contractors had any complaints about Bienenfeld other than that he held them strictly to terms and protected the company's interests like a hawk. The letters complaining about Bienenfeld had been written on the contractor's stationery by an employee using the firm's name without the contractor's knowledge. After hearing the contractors praise Bienenfeld, Bancroft and Hood demanded that he be reinstated, that the stenographer-spy be fired at once, and that copies of any order from Hawgood directing Bienenfeld to interpret contracts differently be sent to Bancroft and Hood.[35]

When Clark balked, Bancroft played the card Harriman had put in his hands for just such an occasion. Although Harriman owned half the San Pedro's stock, he had not yet asked for seats on its board. Unless these demands were met, Bancroft said stiffly, he would ask for positions on the board. Clark and Hawgood blanched at the threat. If Harriman's men went on the board, they would take an active role in the construction from the San Pedro side as well. Apart from replacing Hawgood as chief engineer, their peering over Clark's shoulder would shatter his image as the man in charge. Clark whined again about being humiliated. You have only yourself to blame, Bancroft growled before breezing out the door. At the next day's meeting Clark caved in to all the demands.

"When we came to leave Mr. Clark was very cordial," Bancroft snickered, ". . . and was overjoyed to think that I had come down to Los Angeles to see them." Clashes with the San Pedro men diminished sharply after this showdown. With only minor scrapes the road marched to completion in April 1905, giving Harriman a direct route to what later became the major traffic outlet on the West Coast. To observers the line across the desert wastes was a marvel of engineering and bold anticipation of traffic to come. To insiders it had been a grinding struggle between the old railroading and the new.

The fight showed Harriman at his best. He put the burden on his most capable officers, gave them marching orders and solid support, and let them fight the battle in their own way. By relying on men he trusted, he got the results he wanted despite all the delays and friction. Once the road was completed, Senator Clark proved an amenable partner until 1921, when he sold his half interest to the Union Pacific.

Although no one could have realized it at the time, the prize was well worth fighting for. In Harriman's lifetime the Los Angeles & Salt Lake barely had time to demonstrate its potential, but its traffic grew along with the West. During World War II the Los Angeles & Salt Lake emerged as the most heavily traveled of all transcontinental routes, and the oil beneath land owned by it provided the Union Pacific with a steady flow of income for decades.

23 Fighting Others' Fights

Mr. Harriman's "don't-give-a-damnitiveness" has been worse since the insurance

investigation began than ever before. He has delighted in offending public sentiment.

. . . His arrogance toward the public is beyond belief and rather emphasizes my

opinion that to be really effective in this world a man must have the elements of

stupidity in his make-up no matter how strong he may be.

—American Magazine, *April 1907*

"The history of Harriman," proclaimed one of an endless procession of Harriman watchers, "is a history of battle." Given his combative nature, this was hardly a revelation. What is surprising is the number of fights that came to him rather than emanating from him. "If there was any fighting going on within earshot, however little it might concern him," mused Otto Kahn, "he was tempted to take a hand in the fray, and the greater the odds against his side, the better." Three bitter, highly publicized struggles did much to blacken Harriman's name between 1905 and 1907. All were forced on him by circumstances or the actions of others.[1]

A peculiar flavor of irony hangs over these episodes. Although Harriman never backed down from a fight once drawn into it, he would have given much to avoid these clashes. They consumed enormous amounts of time and energy he could no longer spare. In different ways all were "no-win" situations that hurt the victor as much as the loser, with repercussions that extended far beyond the immediate issues. Finally, and most painful, all three fights pitted Harriman against men who had once been friends: James Hazen Hyde of Equitable Life, Stuyvesant Fish, and President Theodore Roosevelt.

The Equitable fight was an accident waiting to happen, and it was Harriman's misfortune to be in the right place at the wrong time. "Mr. Harriman had nothing whatever to do with the original trouble," sighed Kahn. "There was no earthly reason why he should have been drawn into the fierce and bitter contest which followed, but in he jumped with both feet and laid about with such vigor that in the end he became almost the principal and probably the most attacked figure of the conflict, both the warring factions pausing in their fight against each other to pour their fire of abuse and innuendo upon him."[2]

Insurance was another industry convulsed by growing pains at the turn of the century. Like railroads and banking, it had mushroomed from small companies into an industry dominated by giants. By 1903 Equitable had gross assets of nearly $380 million compared to $402 million for Mutual Life and $353 million for New York Life. This huge supply of capital served as the lifeblood for an age of industrial growth. The big three companies had more than 50 percent of their assets invested in securities, which prompted bankers like Morgan and Schiff to cultivate close ties with insurance companies. Morgan lured George W. Perkins of New York Life to his own firm, giving him a solid entry into that company, while Mutual had on its board George F. Baker and those denizens of Standard Oil, William Rockefeller and H. H. Rogers.[3]

Spectacular growth brought insurance companies the same dislocations that plagued large firms in other industries. The most common problem was a provincial form of management rooted in an earlier, simpler age. Every company owed its rise to the driving force of one individual who dominated its affairs during the early years. For Equitable this man was Henry B. Hyde, who founded the society on a shoestring in 1859 and built it into the largest firm in the world before his death in 1899. Despite this rapid growth, control of the Equitable still rested in its original $100,000 issue of stock. Most of this belonged to Hyde, giving him power over Equitable's $400 million in assets but income limited to a 7 percent dividend on the stock. Although Hyde paid himself and his officers handsome salaries, the real money had to be made through creative use of Equitable's huge capital pool.[4]

Hyde found one solution in financial subsidiaries. Equitable invested in several banks and trust companies and controlled two of them, Equitable Trust and Mercantile Trust. Hyde, his family members, and Equitable officers also bought shares in these institutions. Apart from drawing salaries for serving them, there were a dozen ways to reap rewards from this arrangement. The subsidiaries borrowed money from Equitable at low rates and loaned it out at higher rates. Hyde and his friends joined investment syndicates using funds borrowed at low rates from the company. They bought securities and sold them to Equitable at higher prices. Some of Equitable's investment funds were kept as cash balances in subsidiary banks for these purposes.[5]

Milking a large company in this manner was an abuse made possible by autocratic rule. Not that Hyde ever thought of it as milking; the company was his creature to do with as he pleased. He and his associate, James W. Alexander, wielded absolute power. The company's board of fifty-two prominent directors did nothing beyond read reports and approve them. Once when two new members were appointed to Equitable's fiscal committee, Alexander reminded them bluntly that it was "not their province to go into the management of the Company, or to express opinions about methods."[6]

An early court decision cast doubt on whether the federal government could regulate insurance companies, and state authorities had done little. But Hyde's death set in motion a chain of events that transformed Equitable and with it the entire insurance industry. His shares in Equitable passed to his son, James Hazen Hyde, with a provision that they be held in trust until he reached the age of thirty in 1906. Alexander assumed the presidency with Hyde moving up to vice president even though he had just graduated from college the year before. Since Alexander was nearly sixty, this arrangement was viewed as a sort of regency.[7]

Young Hyde carried the same burden in life as George Gould. He was the pleasant, underachieving son of a hard-driving, overachieving father, the doting parent who had started life with nothing and was determined to give his son every advantage even though the effect was to make him unfit for the hard knocks of business life. Henry Hyde lavished love and affection as well as material things on his only son. "You have brought me up rather extravagantly," James confessed in one of his many begging letters while at Harvard, where he lived an elegant lifestyle at his father's expense. "I am a hot house flower, edition de luxe," he sighed in another, "limited on fine paper, morocco binding, and I fear you never can make anything else out of me."[8]

The elder Hyde died before he learned the painful truth of this observation. His death thrust James into the same trap that held George Gould prisoner. As vice-president he drew a salary that reached $100,000 by 1903 and was supplemented by smaller amounts from subsidiary companies. At twenty-six he had become the key figure in one of America's top insurance companies, rubbing elbows with leading business and financial figures who treated him with a deference that led him to believe, as George Gould did, that his own talent and ability had earned him this exalted position.[9]

This was an illusion. As Henry Morgenthau observed sourly, fortune had given Hyde everything but character. Standing nearly six-four with handsome, aristocratic features, he dressed immaculately and spoke in a cultivated voice. The years at Harvard had given him a passion for things French. As a social denizen, Hyde made headlines not by his business coups but through lavish dinners and entertainments that drew the wrong kind of publicity to a man in charge of Equitable's vast resources. While Morgenthau dismissed him as a "perfumed dandy and spoiled child of quickly gotten riches," he was not a bad or dishonest man so much as a weak and shallow one.[10]

In society Hyde was a thoroughbred, sleek and fast; in business, however, he was a poodle among pit bulls. While Equitable's own business slipped and its organization fell into disarray, Hyde and Alexander milked the financial subsidiaries with renewed vigor. They joined several underwriting syndicates for themselves, Equitable, and other officers. These ventures brought Hyde into close contact with leading bankers like Schiff and Stillman.[11]

Although Harriman handled some securities transactions for Equitable during his days as a broker, he had nothing to do with the company beyond occupying offices in its building until the spring of 1901. During the Northern Pacific fight he borrowed $2.7 million from Equitable at the prevailing rate of interest with no special considerations. The loan was renewed several times until Harriman paid it off in January 1904 because he got cheaper rates elsewhere. None of the aspersions later cast on this loan produced a shred of evidence showing it to be anything other than a routine business transaction.[12]

On the same day Harriman got the loan, however, he joined Equitable's board. His duties were no more onerous than those of other directors, who merely rubber-stamped whatever was placed in front of them. In November 1902, when Harriman was putting together a syndicate to buy and hold $50 million worth of Union Pacific preferred as a defense against buyout threats, he offered Hyde a $2.5 million share. Hyde wanted the share put in Equitable's name; Harriman insisted that it be in Hyde's name because he did not want a corporation as a member of the syndicate. The result was a muddy transaction that later exposed both sides to undue criticism.[13]

Apart from the loan and the syndicate, Harriman had no dealings with Equitable other than attending board meetings. Given his habit of sticking his nose into everything around him, Equitable was probably the least he ever did in a corporation. This record might have continued unblemished had not a power struggle wracked the company. Since 1903 the insurance industry had been under attack for its high costs and arbitrary methods. The last thing prudent officers needed was publicity of the sort that would coalesce vague public discontent into hard demands for reform, yet that was exactly what Equitable produced in a fight for control that threw the company's inner workings into harsh relief and in behavior by Hyde that cast him in the role of feckless socialite living the high life at the expense of the policyholders.[14]

The closer time drew for Alexander to surrender the reins to Hyde, the more reluctant he became to do it. Aware that the industry was becoming a target for muckraking journalists, Alexander came to the sound (and self-serving) conclusion that it was no longer feasible for control of so great a company to rest in the hands of one man. At a board meeting on February 8, 1905, he made his move by presenting one petition to mutualize Equitable—which would allow policyholders to vote for directors—and another protesting Hyde's reelection as vice-president.[15]

An indignant Hyde saw these moves for what they were: a bald attempt to wrest the stock and the presidency from him. Nor was the timing an accident. Nine days earlier Hyde had thrown the most lavish of a long line of entertainments: a coming-out party for his niece at Sherry's in the form of an eighteenth-century costume ball meant to recall the glory of Versailles under Louis XVI and

Marie-Antoinette. Nothing like it had been seen since the infamous Bradley Martin ball in 1897. Harriman had been there along with William Rockefeller, George Gould, Stuyvesant Fish, and the cream of society.[16]

Although the papers treated the affair with restraint at first, the image of Hyde as a social butterfly played into Alexander's scheme to curb his power in Equitable. The board created a Committee of Twelve to consider the petitions and put Harriman on it along with Schiff and Henry Clay Frick. Hyde regarded Harriman as a friend who would support him in the fight, partly because Schiff was an ally and Harriman was close to Schiff. A few months earlier Hyde had asked Harriman to intervene in a suit brought against Mercantile Trust by Harriman's good friend Governor Benjamin B. Odell. Harriman obliged by bringing Odell and Hyde together in his office. After some negotiation, at which Harriman was not present, the two men agreed to a settlement.[17]

Later Hyde charged that Harriman had conspired with Odell to wring top dollar out of him by using threats of political influence against Mercantile Trust. At the time, however, he accepted Harriman's help gratefully. Mutualization required an amendment of Equitable's charter, which had to be approved by the legislature. Aware that anything was possible in Albany, Hyde dropped by Harriman's office after the fateful board meeting of February 8 and found him in conference with Odell. In discussing tactics, Odell assured them that a mutualization bill could be blocked but warned that it was always better to kill such bills early.[18]

When the Committee of Twelve met the next day, Harriman defended the existing system for electing directors and officers. Alexander countered with a lengthy report blasting Hyde and his influence in Equitable. He renewed the attack at a second meeting on February 14 and urged a quick settlement. Already the fight had gone public. When Schiff asked how the newspapers had got wind of the affair, Alexander admitted that he had sent two notices to agency managers in the Equitable system. In the uproar that followed, Harriman declared hotly that he would never vote for mutualization. Using this remark as an opening, Hyde then offered to place his stock in trust for five years and let the board vote it. Alexander dismissed the idea as merely postponing the issue for five years.[19]

Harriman was even more furious than Hyde. While patience was always his short suit, something in this brawl got his temper up in a way wholly out of proportion to his stake in it. He saw in Alexander's maneuvers a pattern of disloyalty that sickened him as it did Schiff. Angrily he asked whether Alexander had consulted counsel before acting, then snarled before Alexander could reply, "God damn you! I'll chuck you where you belong. I've got you where I want you, and I have the power to do it. And furthermore, you can repeat what I say in any private, personal or public way that you see fit." The startled Alexander replied that he had consulted no less than five lawyers, but Harriman was not appeased. The meeting broke up in hopeless disagreement over a report. As Harriman left the room he growled to Hyde, "Now, more than ever, Albany is yours."[20]

Hyde came away with the mistaken belief that the best and strongest men stood firmly behind his cause. He failed to grasp a subtle distinction: Harriman, Schiff, and others supported Hyde because they were outraged by Alexander and his tactics. They had no illusions about Hyde's shortcomings and had simply reserved judgment on what his role in Equitable was ultimately to be.

Two days later, the board met in an atmosphere charged with tension. Unable to get a consensus from the Committee of Twelve, it appointed two men to consider the conflicting claims. Schiff was to represent the Hyde interests, second vice-president Gage Tarbell the Alexander side. After an hour's discussion they brought in two recommendations: the society should mutualize, and the presidency should be left vacant for the present. Schiff tried to cut off debate only to be gaveled down by Alexander, who dismissed the report as an insult and vowed never to be legislated out of office.[21]

Only an eloquent plea from Chauncey Depew quelled the storm that threatened to rip the meeting apart. The sullen directors then rejected Hyde's offer, reelected all officers, approved mutualization, and created a committee to bring it about. The debate spilled over into the Metropolitan Club and Wall Street, where reporters hunted eagerly for juicy morsels. Schiff warned Hyde pointedly to regard the outcome as "not so much a victory for you personally, than a rebuke of the methods employed by Mr. Alexander."[22]

Harriman walked away from the meeting in disgust. The Equitable mess was deteriorating rapidly and eating up his time, but he saw no easy way out. A group of policyholders organized a committee to push for mutualization and hired as counsel Frank H. Platt, son of New York State Republican boss Thomas C. Platt. As an influential figure in the party, Harriman saw the potential for all sorts of conflicts brewing.

For nearly a month the war raged in the papers. On March 21 the board met again and approved a plan for policyholders to elect twenty-eight of the fifty-two directors and stockholders the other twenty-four. After creating one committee to consult the state insurance superintendent about amending the charter, the board appointed another, headed by Henry Clay Frick, to investigate the company's management. Harriman was among the five members of the Frick Committee, which became the storm center for the most explosive chapter in the Equitable fight.[23]

Afterward both sides cooed harmony to the press while privately feeding scurrilous accusations to reporters. Hyde remained confident that the Frick Committee would exonerate him, and he welcomed a second investigation by Francis Hendricks, the state superintendent of insurance. On March 19 Harriman got a taste of just how ugly the fight had grown when the *New York World* informed the city that he had taken complete charge of Hyde's campaign. By early April the Equitable was consuming most of his time and had drawn him into that open sewer known as New York state politics.[24]

Odell had gone to Europe in February, but his friends in Albany watched the legislature to prevent, in Harriman's words, "a condition which would, if once started, end nobody knows where as far as the Life Insurance Companies were concerned." But Harriman did not reckon with Hendricks. Both sides had approved the charter amendment and sent it to the commissioner for his blessing. Instead, he held it captive until Frank Platt and the policyholders' committee could file affidavits charging irregularities by the board and the management. Harriman spent two full days with Hendricks, who had first avoided him, trying to thrash out a solution.[25]

Gradually the game dawned on Harriman. He realized that Frank Platt and the policyholders' committee were Alexander's tools; that Alexander had secretly fed the committee the damaging material it released to the papers; and that he had captured Hendricks as well. "I must say," Harriman fumed to Odell, "that this is the first time I have been so far below the strata into indecency in my life, and I have a feeling that it will take a long time to get rid of the filth."

This long letter detailing his encounter with Hendricks reveals much about Harriman. As a private account to a close friend it may be assumed to contain no posturing or misleading statements. Harriman was furious over his rude treatment by Hendricks, but he also bellowed genuine shock and indignation at the political slime he found. "I can now understand," he told Odell, "why you at times became somewhat disgusted in the political situation when you are brought so much in contact with the outfit represented at the Superintendent's offices."

This response betrayed Harriman's curious naïveté about politics and his tendency to view complex matters in black-and-white terms shaped by the eternal verities that governed his life. Those verities imbued him with the strength and righteousness of the true believer who can do no wrong if his acts are in the service of the just. Like many businessmen, Harriman considered himself honest but did not hesitate to do the hard things his position required.

Lying was a classic example of this moral ambiguity. To men of delicate scruples, lying was wrong in any context. But even honest businessmen realized the practical necessity for lying in some situations. The real world was a clutter of clashing grays, not a stark skyline of black and white. While most men eventually came to terms with this contradiction, Harriman flew into a rage over any insinuation that he lied or hedged his principles. But he did lie. In April he told reporters flatly that he had never borrowed money from Equitable even though he had. Before the Armstrong Committee he denied ever having discussed the matter of a legislative investigation with Odell when in fact he had exchanged a flurry of cables with him during the spring of 1905.[26]

The fight had become grist for the newspapers and was being ground in large daily doses. Both sides kept feeding material to reporters, who added imaginative touches of their own. The dirt got so bad that the board finally begged both sides to stop talking to the press. Critics called for a new president untainted by past struggles. A second shrill cry rose from New York's two Democratic papers, the *World* and the *Sun*, and was picked up by others in the hinterland: Hyde was a pawn for Harriman, who was scheming to get hold of Equitable, merge it with the other insurance giants, and put Standard Oil astride "nearly all the available money in the country." The *Sun* warned that public opinion would never "tolerate a Harriman in the control of such a public institution as the Equitable Life." One cartoon showed Harriman and Morgan fighting over a huge pile of insurance money.[27]

Bad publicity seldom bothered Harriman personally. Not that he ignored it; he pored over the papers in search of every article and cartoon about himself with almost childlike curiosity. But the Frick investigation impaled him on a nasty dilemma: the evidence was as damaging to Hyde as it was to Alexander. Henry Morgenthau examined a satchel full of documents that convinced him the case against Hyde was solid. He showed them to Harriman, who sent him to Elihu Root, one of the most astute legal and political minds in New York. It was unheard-of, Root warned, to oust a man who owned a majority of a company's stock. How would public opinion respond, replied Morgenthau tersely, to having the life funds of widows and orphans at the mercy of a feckless young man?[28]

This last argument impressed Harriman deeply, as did the belief that Equitable had been badly mismanaged since Henry Hyde's death. During May the newspapers paraded one episode of financial abuse after another across their columns along with portraits of Hyde as a social dandy who used company funds for his personal entertainments. Reluctantly Harriman concluded with Schiff that Hyde had to surrender his stock. Despite the storm he knew it would create, Harriman helped draft a report that condemned Alexander and Hyde equally while calling for a reorganized management to curb the "loose and irregular methods" of the past.[29]

When the Frick Committee presented its thirty-eight-page report to the board on May 31, a furor erupted at once. Shocked and hurt by its findings, Hyde denounced the report as unfair and accused Harriman and Frick of betraying him. What Harriman really wanted, he charged bitterly, was to get control of Equitable for himself. Harriman, Frick, and Cornelius Bliss responded by storming out of the room. The most delicious irony in the situation was that Harriman had managed to bring Hyde and Alexander together—against himself. Threatened equally by the report, the two adversaries joined forces against the committee and filled reporters' ears with tales of a conspiracy to hand Equitable over to Standard Oil.[30]

Two days later the board met again and indulged in what M. E. Ingalls called "a cat and dog fight." Once adoption of the Frick report was moved, Alexander made a formal reply to its charges. Hyde then took up his defense, saying it was the crisis of his life, and consumed the rest of the morning rebutting the charges against him. At the afternoon session Tarbell took his whack at the Frick report. Schiff then tried to intervene as peacemaker by defending Tarbell and offering three resolutions for reform. While these were being debated, Hyde jumped up suddenly and accused Ingalls of giving the Frick report to the press. He also asked snidely whether Ingalls had received a $1,000 rebate on his own policy.[31]

"Young man," roared a livid Ingalls, "whom the gods would destroy they first make mad."

Before Ingalls could say more, Hyde turned his wrath on Harriman, Schiff, and Frick. They had posed as his friends and advisers, he snarled, and now were trying to snatch control from him. His attack grew so vituperative that Harriman jumped up several times to interrupt him but was so infuriated that he could only sputter, "Oh wow-wow-wow," in a manner that reminded some directors of a dog baying.[32]

Invectives flew back and forth until Frick bellowed, "I will no longer sit in the same board as that young man." Depew pleaded for harmony, but a flushed Harriman joined Frick in resigning on the spot and storming out. Cornelius Bliss soon followed; Hyde applauded their exit as purifying the board. "I have quarreled with Mr. Alexander and he with me," he said grimly, "and there is still bitter feeling between us, but he never tried to put me out of my property for the benefit of his own pocket, as these gentlemen have done."

In his wrath Hyde overlooked the fact that the whole fight had erupted because Alexander tried to do precisely that. The desperate embrace of Hyde and Alexander saved neither of them. The board rejected the Frick report but also asked Hyde to divest his stock. Conservative businessmen cringed at the headlines spawned by the fight, fearing that they might provoke a broader investigation of the industry. Ingalls and Schiff joined the parade of resigned directors, which reached a total of twelve.[33]

No one relished the fight more than Joseph Pulitzer. His *New York World* could not find columns enough to fill with the sensational revelations pouring out of the fight. Day after day his reporters hammered gleefully at inviting targets who happened also to be powers in the state Republican Party. A Harriman confidant was quoted as promising that his leader would revenge himself on Hyde. The Democratic *World* thought it knew how this would be done. So far Harriman's influence with Odell had protected Hyde from political interference; now Albany might take a keen interest in the young man.[34]

Damage control had become a giant problem. As one shrewd observer warned, the public might conclude from the Equitable mess "that there was a similar laxness in the management of other insurance companies and if such laxness existed in the insurance field, the public was likely to argue that it might also exist in the banking and railroad fields." Schiff worried that the affair might trigger a panic unless some settlement was reached fast. For Harriman, however, the issue remained intensely personal. He had been drawn into the fray because he felt obliged to help put Equitable's management right. His effort had been thwarted and heaped with abuse, but he never quit a fight under fire. Instead of getting out, he plunged deeper into the fray—thanks in part to a stunning, unexpected move by Hyde.[35]

The key to any resolution of the Equitable dilemma lay in prying Hyde's stock loose from him. Hyde's reluctance to sell had emotional as well as financial roots: the company was a monument to a father he adored, and he could not bear to let go of it. He offered to put the stock in trust or sell it to the society, but Equitable had no legal power to buy it. As the scandal lapped nearer his father's name, Hyde came to the sorrowful realization that he must sell. But to whom?[36]

Harriman wanted the stock but knew Hyde would never sell it to him under the circumstances. He was adamant that it be put in safe, impartial hands to ensure that the reforms within Equitable would proceed without interference. The board asked Hyde to divest within three months; he took less than a week. On Thursday, June 8, the *World*'s headline bawled, "$10,000,000 SCANDAL UNCOVERED BY STATE IN EQUITABLE SOCIETY." The next morning, as Harriman was hurrying from the Erie Ferry to his office, he heard that Hyde had sold the stock to Thomas Fortune Ryan.[37]

The news staggered Harriman. He brushed aside Hyde's slur that he would make a bonfire of his stock rather than let Harriman buy it, but he could not brush Ryan aside. Although not well known to the public, Ryan was a force on Wall Street. He had made his mark in railroads, tobacco, and banking and had a reputation as a brilliant organizer, tough bargainer, and stealthy operator. A towering six feet six inches tall with broad shoulders, cheerful eyes, and a slow Virginia drawl, Ryan was a commanding figure. "He was a mystery, always," declared Frank Vanderlip; "no one ever knew exactly what he was doing." The fact that Ryan was a Democrat did not stop Pulitzer from depicting him as a wolf grazing ravenously among the Equitable lambs.[38]

These qualities were precisely what worried Harriman about putting Equitable's stock in Ryan's hands. In that moment Harriman appointed himself guardian of Equitable's destiny even though he was no longer connected with the company. He did not pause to consider the ramifications for himself. The whole affair had already bled more time and energy than he could spare ("I want you and this committee, and everybody else, to understand," he later snapped at the

Armstrong Committee, "that I have something else to do besides devoting my time to life insurance"), yet he could not leave it so up in the air.[39]

Once at his office, Harriman called Ryan and asked if the rumor was true. It was, Ryan said in his slow way, adding that he wanted Harriman's cooperation. Harriman rushed over to Ryan's office and was told Ryan had done it to make a name for himself in a civic sense. He had made plenty of money but never done anything conspicuous; this was his bid to do something prominent. Harriman told Ryan bluntly that he could not help but doubt his motives, but if they were really unselfish, he could count on Harriman's assistance.[40]

Ryan asked him to help get Paul Morton elected chairman of Equitable's board, which was meeting that same afternoon. Harriman respected Morton, who had been a capable officer for the Atchison before serving as secretary of the navy. He talked to August Belmont, who opposed Morton's appointment, then telephoned Ryan to let him know Belmont had relented. Ryan thanked Harriman and promised to do nothing further without consulting him. He asked where Harriman would be that evening. Harriman was about to leave for Arden but agreed to wait at the Metropolitan Club for Ryan's call.[41]

He was still there at eleven that night, fidgeting impatiently when lawyer Paul Cravath rushed up to him full of apologies. He had been sent by Ryan to brief Harriman on what had been done that day. Ryan had asked three men headed by former president Grover Cleveland to serve as trustees for the stock until mutualization could be carried out. He had picked men "of such character as to command universal confidence and having no connection with Wall Street." Naturally, Ryan was sorry he had not been able to notify Harriman first.[42]

Enraged by the news, Harriman hissed at Cravath that he was not in the habit of being trifled with and would not tolerate this sign of bad faith on Ryan's part. Before Cravath could reply, Harriman spun on his heel and left. Next morning he got Ryan on the telephone, but nothing he heard satisfied him that Ryan was playing straight. On Monday he bounded into Ryan's office to settle matters. Cravath was there, as was Elihu Root. Without any amenities Harriman barked, "You want my co-operation?"[43]

"Yes," said the surprised Ryan.

"Well, I will tell you what I will do. I will take half your stock. I don't know what it cost and do not care—provided you agree to the appointment of two additional trustees who will be absolutely independent."

Ryan thought for a moment, then said, "I won't do it. That is not what you agreed to."

"What do you mean I agreed to?" snapped Harriman.

"You agreed that if you were satisfied that I was acting from an unselfish motive in the interest of the general situation and the society, that you would help me."

"Yes, I did," retorted Harriman, "and this is my way of satisfying myself."

Later Ryan testified that Harriman threatened to use "his whole influence" against him if the stock was not shared. Harriman could not remember whether he said any such thing, which was plausible given his temper, but insisted that his only interest was to see Equitable "protected and properly safeguarded." Ryan professed to want the same thing, but Harriman did not trust him, especially after Ryan had decoyed him. "It seemed to me," Harriman said, "that in denying the participation to myself or anybody else that . . . his motive was to center the control of the Equitable in himself." He was not alone in wondering why a man would pay $2.5 million for stock that could earn only $3,514 in dividends. Wall Street and the press alike tantalized over Ryan's real object, never believing for a moment that it might simply be what he said it was.[44]

Nor is civic duty alone a sufficient explanation for why Harriman got so wrought up over a fight in which he had so small an interest or why he was so blind to its repercussions. Paul Morton, who had just walked into the mess, offered a different slant. "We are likely to have a great row before we get through," he wrote his wife, "because Harriman is so mad—he got terribly left in the shuffle and is horribly broken up about it. He shook the tree for months and months and Ryan walked off with the plums and now Harriman is hostile."[45]

As Morton suggested, Harriman's cry of protest also came straight from his wounded ego. He never liked being thwarted, and nothing made him more furious than being used as a pawn in someone else's game. "I was brought forward . . . in the insurance matter by Hyde and Ryan, and by their request for my help," he later complained, "and in the case of Ryan I would probably have dropped the matter had it not been for my desire to save Belmont from taking a position for which he could have been criticized by the public press."[46]

In his wrath Harriman failed utterly to see how suspect his own motives looked to other eyes. As it did with Hyde, public attention clamped more onto the image of Harriman wielding threats like a club than onto the issues involved. Ryan was an outsider who had come into the fray as a neutral; Harriman had been slugging it out for months. The fight with Ryan only reinforced the suspicion that Harriman was serving as point man for the Standard Oil crowd's desire to get its hands on Equitable's assets. Rumors were already afloat that he and Schiff were secret partners with Ryan. Rival bankers like James Speyer insinuated with malicious glee that Harriman and Schiff, "having walked out the front door [of Equitable], are now walking in at the rear."[47]

These factors made it hard for anyone to view Harriman as fighting the good fight purely out of a sense of duty. The public could no more think that Harriman wanted nothing for himself than Harriman could believe it of Ryan. He looked like a man insatiable for power and ruthless in his drive to obtain it. Reporters had often portrayed Harriman as rude and ambitious but not as greedy or grasping. Now his image took on a new coloring that grew steadily more vivid as one improbable episode after another fed it.

Yet in the end Harriman got his way. Morton lost no time cleaning house, and Ryan kept his distance after handing the stock over to the trustees. Later, when public attention had moved past the insurance industry, Ryan quietly sold half of his Equitable stock to Harriman. Having reaped his dividend of glory, he was content to let Harriman share the load. The transaction was kept so secret that when Morgan later went to buy the Equitable stock from Ryan, he was unaware that Harriman owned half of it. Eventually Morgan acquired these shares not from Harriman but from his widow.[48]

In getting what he wanted, Harriman paid a steep price. The Equitable scandal set in motion a chain of events that put him on the defensive for two years. While Morton put the Equitable house in order, Superintendent Hendricks released his report condemning the company in terms that went beyond the Frick report. As the quagmire deepened, Frank Vanderlip moaned that it had "done more to lose to Wall Street and Wall Street men the respect of ordinary people than anything that has happened in my knowledge of affairs."[49]

The Democratic papers harped on the fact that Hendricks had not called Harriman to testify and asked whether it was because of the financier's influence in Albany. Harriman did not feel obliged to appear because he was no longer on Equitable's board. The *World* dissented in a lengthy feature entitled "HARRIMAN, THE HIDDEN FIGURE IN THE EQUITABLE SCANDAL," and even friendly papers agreed with the *Wall Street Journal* that "to stand upon technicalities in this affair at this time, is practically to confess wrong-doing." Governor Frank Higgins underscored this point by ordering what all sides feared most: a general investigation of the industry.[50]

The news caught Harriman as he was preparing to leave for Japan. He received a visit from the district attorney, who asked to see the Union Pacific syndicate agreement. Harriman showed him the document and said that all his other papers were in Judge Lovett's hands and available for inspection at any time. As Harriman left his office, he spied a reporter coming toward him. "Don't ask me anything about Equitable matters," he barked. The reporter inquired about his trip and received a curt answer. Then Harriman relented. "You fellows have a hard time, don't you?" he asked.[51]

"We have our troubles," the reporter admitted.

"There's altogether too blame many of you," Harriman observed. "Some of the papers have five or six men following me. That's too blamed many."

The next day Harriman released a statement categorically denying anything improper in his relations with Equitable, his loan, or the preferred stock syndicate. The real issue was mismanagement of the company rather than the transactions on which the papers had spilled so much ink. "There has been too much mystery surrounding the Equitable affairs," he concluded. "I have always been ready and willing to answer any questions asked by any one entitled to make inquiry and have never tried in any way to avoid it."[52]

With that explanation he departed for Japan, leaving in his wake a chorus of grumbling over who exactly qualified as "one entitled to make inquiry." During his absence the Armstrong Committee of the state legislature opened its investigation of the insurance industry. It proved a long-running show, lasting deep into December as it gathered testimony from all the major players. From it flowed a steady stream of revelations and controversies that splashed into business circles outside the insurance industry as well.[53]

Equitable emerged from this ordeal looking no worse than the other major insurance companies, but it provided the most fireworks. The gaudiest display came in mid-November, when Hyde, Harriman, and Odell took the stand on successive days and unleashed a torrent of sensations. Hyde led off with his sad tale of betrayal by men posing as his friends. He accused Harriman and Frick of treachery and charged Odell with using Harriman to gain a favorable settlement through what amounted to blackmail in his suit to recover losses in United States Shipbuilding bonds.[54]

The next day Hyde watched with a sardonic smile as Harriman flatly contradicted his version of events. He recited his answers in a dry voice without gestures, as if holding his emotions in rigid check. The hotter the questions, the colder grew his responses with their strange lack of inflection. His expressionless features contrasted oddly with the fire in eyes that stared intently at Charles Evans Hughes. Only once did his control slip, when Hughes turned to address a lawyer and Harriman snapped, "Mr. Hughes, I should like to have your attention."[55]

Odell then took the stand and issued the same sweeping rebuttal. The contradictions were so complete that no one knew what to believe. Since the committee did not allow cross-examination, the discrepancy could not be resolved. This left its members confused and the papers free to draw their own conclusions. Most of them roasted all three men. The *World* skewered Hyde in a devastating cartoon showing him as a peacock plucked of all his feathers, which were being bundled off by Harriman, Odell, and Ryan. Editors were no less charitable to Harriman and Odell, about whom there hovered an odor of ham-handed political influence.[56]

Ryan refused at first to discuss his meetings with Harriman, then let it be coaxed out of him that Harriman had threatened to use all his influence (which Ryan assumed meant political influence) against him if he did not sell half the stock. Recalled to the stand, Harriman gave events a different slant, but he could not deny the threats. They had burst out of him, as similar ones had so many times before. This remarkable performance gave the committee and reporters a tantalizing choice. Was Harriman's temper so explosive that he routinely fired off threats without even remembering them? Or, if he was lying about recalling the threats, why didn't he simply deny that any of it took place? The one constant in any interpretation was the image of a ruthless, overbearing bully who let nothing stand in the way of what he wanted.[57]

As the tide of criticism mounted, Otto Kahn tried to warn Harriman that it was becoming dangerous and required some response from him. But Harriman ignored him. "Let them kick," he shrugged. "They have the advantage because they will tell lies about me, and I won't about them. And as for the effect in the long run, why, the people always find out what's what in the end, and I can wait. Let those fellows continue to shout and to kick against air. I need my time and energy to do things."[58]

These were noble sentiments, but Harriman did not yet know just how loud his detractors would shout or how hard they would kick. Here as with so many other things, he had to find out the hard way.

24 Fighting a Former Friend

Lightning began to play around the head of Mr. Stuyvesant Fish, who had lectured
Mr. Harriman in the winter of 1905 on the subject of railroad ethics. Mr. Harriman
did not want a fight. Indeed, he much preferred to take the control of the Illinois
Central without one. . . . When this successful raid was accomplished, everybody felt
as though the house had been robbed in the night. All the highly respectable critics all
over the world view it with "extreme regret." . . . Mr. Fish has been unanimously
handed the crown of a martyr, whether he likes it or not.

—C. M. Keys, "Harriman: The Man in the Making"

If the Equitable fight had been an isolated incident, Harriman might have escaped with no more than the bruises of a distasteful experience. But it triggered an inextricable chain of events that together would create what Otto Kahn called the "Harriman Extermination League" and transform his reputation from builder to cold-hearted wrecker, a second-generation robber baron. The Harriman of legend, which had been slowly congealing since 1900, emerged as a bizarre Jekyll-Hyde creature mingling doses of good and evil in every deed.

This legend fit the schizoid character of American material civilization at the turn of the century. Victorian society was immensely pleased with itself and its accomplishments, yet beneath its smug, stolid exterior ran a deep vein of anxiety over the changes that were reshaping every facet of American life. Fear and hope, belief in both the idea of progress and the decline of civilization became a current that energized Progressive America with alternating jolts of optimism and alarm. Every aspect of American culture reflected this duality: art and architecture, business and industry, politics and reform.

The supreme creative skill of the age, which Harriman possessed in rare abundance, was the ability to organize on a grand scale. From the dedicated exercise of this skill arose the huge business enterprises that revamped not only the economy but everything else in American life. But this talent was itself a two-headed monster capable of performing great feats while trampling indifferently over anything in its path. The age preened and puffed over its monuments while ignoring the price paid for them in the form of social dislocation, grinding poverty, hideous slums, and a ravaged environment.

To catch a revealing glimpse of this Janus mask, one had only to look at the contrast between those two business titans of the era, Morgan and Harriman. The great banker, with his massive frame and ponderous movements, was a perfect emblem of the nineteenth century, as solid and indestructible as a piece of fine Victorian furniture. The House of Morgan stood for reliability, integrity, and conservatism. To the end of his life Morgan remained a colossus of tradition against the harsh, unfathomable winds of change that were blowing his world into oblivion.

The small, wiry Harriman was not only nimble but quick, a mercurial human computer ingesting data faster than most men could relay it and spewing back plans, ideas, correlations with incomprehensible speed. He moved with the driving thrust of a rocket, hell-bent on streamlining everything he touched into its most efficient and productive form regardless of the costs, financial or human; creating organization where none had existed; reducing every variable to a manageable component within some system and then integrating the systems into ever larger and more precise machines of performance while drumming out every anachronism with merciless pressure.

Morgan embodied the world going by, Harriman the world to come. Both possessed qualities Americans coveted and feared. The ideal world would contain the best features of both, which was what reformers of the 1900s longed desperately to attain without realizing it. But they could not have both; the two sets of qualities were utterly incompatible. When forced to choose between them, most Americans clung naturally to the most familiar. They came to resent Harriman as a catalyst of changes they dreaded, and they lashed out at him for tainting their pristine notion of progress.

To all appearances, the fight that erupted between Harriman and Stuyvesant Fish was purely a clash of business interests. Harriman wanted control of the Illinois Central; Fish stood in his way. The Illinois Central was a classic blue-chip road with a tradition of conservatism, Fish a businessman of the old school who took a dim view of modern practices and an even dimmer view of the consolidations that had reshaped the railroad world in recent years. Harriman needed the road for strategic purposes and was eager to reform its sound but archaic organization.

The Illinois Central's connection to the insurance scandal ran through Mutual Life, where the situation grew almost as ugly as that in Equitable during the fall of 1905. Fish had been put on a committee to investigate the company's management. Before the committee could dig very deep, however, a faction of directors led by H. H. Rogers and George F. Baker moved to reorganize the company "with the lid on," as one reporter termed it, hoping to prevent adverse publicity from leaking out. The longtime president Richard A. McCurdy was nudged out in favor of the lawyer Charles Peabody, who rebuffed efforts by the committee to get information. Fish antagonized Peabody by trying to pry data from the management. When his efforts failed, he resigned indignantly from the committee.

What had all this to do with Harriman? Knowing reporters thought they spotted a link. "Ever since the appointment of the Mutual Life's investigating committee last Fall," wrote one in February 1906, "the railroad fight and the controversy in the Mutual Life have been pretty much mixed up together."[1]

The key to this link was Peabody, who illustrated how incestuous the worlds of business and society had become. He sat on the boards of both the Illinois Central and the Union Pacific. His law partner was the brother of the powerful banker George F. Baker, a close Morgan ally. Peabody had also long been close to Fish, who had brought him into the Illinois Central as he had Harriman. He was counsel for the estate of Fish's father, and Fish had helped Peabody get the coveted position of counsel for the Astor estate. In recent years, however, the ambitious Peabody had drifted away from Fish toward men like Harriman, Stillman, and Rogers. To the public, Rogers's name was synonymous with Standard Oil, while Harriman was regarded by many people as "no more than the chief operating man for the Standard Oil railroad interests."[2]

Here were the ingredients for a delicious conspiracy theory. Harriman had nothing to do with Mutual Life, but to please his friends Rogers and Peabody he could punish Fish by snatching his railroad away from him. Two prominent Illinois Central directors, Cornelius Vanderbilt and John W. Auchincloss, also served on the Mutual Life board and disapproved of Fish's actions there. They might be enlisted in a campaign to oust Fish.

Early in February 1906, shortly before the Armstrong Committee released its report, rumors begin to surface that the Union Pacific was buying control of the Illinois Central. Harriman had remained a member of the Illinois Central board and chairman of its finance committee down through the years. Observers considered him its most influential director, but few realized how far back his association ran. What they saw instead were two more immediate explanations: the desire to add a strategic railroad to his collection and to exact revenge for Fish's behavior in the Mutual Life upheaval.[3]

But the whole story lay another layer or two deeper than reporters managed to dig. For years Fish's private life had been strained by the social excesses of his wife. Mamie Fish had become the coldest of warriors in the social arms race of New York and Newport. She had acquired a court jester in Harry "King" Lehr, who inspired her to such heights of malice as throwing one party for dogs and another for friends to meet a prince who turned out to be a monkey. One social gossip hinted that she had "for some time been steadily succumbing to the lure of alcohol." Fish wanted no part of this scene and distanced himself from it as much as possible. But he was still expected to pay for his wife's indulgences, and the tab taxed even his considerable resources.[4]

This pinch led Fish into some dubious investments and even more dubious practices of the sort that he regularly condemned in others. During the spring of 1903 he deposited $500,000 of Illinois Central money in a small bank of which he was a trustee, then trooped off to Europe without telling his directors about the move or asking their advice. Shortly afterward the bank overextended itself to help finance an enterprise called United States Shipbuilding, which was to blacken the names of half the prominent men on Wall Street. Fish had invested in the company and persuaded a reluctant Harriman to put $50,000 into the venture.[5]

That spring Harriman was in the West, mourning his brother's death and dealing with the shopmen's strike before being stricken with appendicitis. During his convalescence some Illinois Central directors informed him of what Fish had done and voiced doubts about the bank's soundness. An irate Harriman tried to retrieve the money only to find that the bank could not stand losing the whole sum at once. He agreed to draw it out a little at a time and eventually got the entire amount back.[6]

A weary Harriman then took his family off to Europe. When he returned in the fall, the same directors greeted him with fresh tales of alarm. With the bank on the brink of a financial crisis, Fish had again deposited Illinois Central funds on his own, withdrawn them, and put them in a third time. He had also personally borrowed $1.5 million from the Illinois Central without approval from the board, giving collateral that was later found to be inadequate. The directors wanted to bring these matters before the board and demand Fish's resignation.[7]

Harriman urged them to reconsider. Distasteful as the whole affair was to him, he had known Fish long enough to realize that the trouble lay in his devotion to a wife who was, in Melville Stone's words, "a vain, silly extravagant woman." Harriman felt obliged to help because Fish had been his friend for a long time, and there was also a practical consideration: if the matter went before the board, it would go public and tarnish the company as well as Fish.[8]

There was another way. Harriman lent Fish $1.2 million to clean up his financial obligations without the incident becoming public knowledge. Unfortunately, the relief proved temporary. In January 1904, still beset by exorbitant bills from his wife's demanding social calendar, Fish again deposited Illinois Central funds in a bank of which he was a trustee. The few directors who knew what Fish was doing complained bitterly to Harriman about it. One of them grumbled that Fish "looked upon the Illinois Central as his personal property, to be used as he personally saw fit."[9]

This attitude had been common for years, but it was fast going out of style. The emergence of larger, more impersonal organizations demanded a new code of ethics with a clear definition of conflict of interest. The first man to denounce impropriety in others, Fish did not believe that he was doing anything improper. Nor did he sense the growing revulsion against these practices even though the directors who objected to his behavior were men who had known him socially and in business for many years, not fiery reformers. Desperation had made Fish blind to the most obvious signals.

The situation presented Harriman with a classic dilemma. Fish was his friend and in some respects his mentor. They had run together in society before Mamie Fish's ambitions outdistanced her judgment, and they still turned up at the same dinners or soirees where the best men of business and politics gathered to discuss affairs in the congenial privacy of their own kind. But what Fish had done was clearly wrong and could not be allowed to continue. For all the boorish behavior Harriman sometimes displayed, he believed ardently in the gospel of propriety. So did Fish, yet he had violated it while staunchly denying that he had.

Moral scruples can never be absolute so long as human nature remains the flawed thing it is. Harriman was no saint; he never hesitated to play the game close to the rules while seldom admitting that he broke them. Once he nearly shattered the spirit of his closest adviser, Judge Robert S. Lovett. The high-minded judge found himself in a terrible bind: honor demanded that he tell Harriman something in the strictest confidence and that the confidence not be violated in any way that harmed the source. To Lovett's horror, Harriman promptly went out and used the information. "I don't see how you could have done such a thing to me," moaned the despairing judge, who seriously considering resigning.

"I understand these things so much better than you do," snapped Harriman in a tone he used to scold one of his boys. "Of course, I can't respect a confidence that ties my hands in a matter of momentous consequence to the operations in which I am engaged. I must be the judge of what is right and wrong in these things."[10]

The contrast among these three men, all of whom considered themselves ethical, upright persons, was striking. To Lovett's stern, old-fashioned sense of honor, right was always right and wrong always wrong regardless of the situation or the stakes. Fish was no less rigid in his integrity, yet he had a peculiar habit common to certain businessmen of assuming that because he was a man of strict honor, anything he did must be honorable; because he would not knowingly commit an unethical act, any act he committed must be ethical. Harriman belonged to a different breed who believed in honor and integrity but even more in the superiority of their own judgment to discern what behavior those qualities entailed in a given situation.

In this case Harriman's discomfort over the Fish dilemma moved him to rare patience and tact. Again he fended off the directors anxious to bring the matter before the whole board and managed to keep a lid on the affair for two years. Unfortunately, during that time the insurance imbroglio and other scandals had brought the perils of Fish's practices into stark relief. By the autumn of 1905 the problem for Harriman was no longer how to keep the Illinois Central matter quiet but also how to detach it from the insurance battle that had caught up so many of the same people.

To Harriman's chagrin, Fish himself blew the lid off with his demand for an investigation of Mutual Life's affairs before it could be handled in-house. An irate Charles Peabody countered by asking Fish to explain his personal handling of Illinois Central funds. Fish dissembled with a statement giving details on a variety of matters other than the transactions involving himself. While these maneuvers took place behind the scenes, public attention riveted on the alleged effort by Harriman to gain control of the Illinois Central. There, too, Fish had a personal stake in the form of his holdings in the Railroad Securities Company.[11]

Originally Harriman and Fish each held a half interest in the holding company, which owned ninety-five hundred shares of Illinois Central stock, but shortly after it was formed, Harriman persuaded Fish to let Kuhn, Loeb take a one-third interest in the company. During the summer of 1905, when Schiff and other Harriman allies began accumulating Illinois Central stock, Harriman assured Fish that the purchases were merely for investment. As the takeover rumors grew louder, however, Fish began drumming up support against it on the grounds that the Illinois Central owed its proud record to being managed in favor of no other interest than its own. In staking this high ground, Fish shrewdly advanced himself as the champion of stockholders who had for years entrusted their proxies to him on this basis of local management.[12]

While Fish sincerely believed in this role, he also knew it was an effective tactic. The Illinois Central had an unusually large number of small stockholders. Editors regularly showered him with praise, and European investors held him in high esteem as a railroad man. He was in a perfect position to portray himself as the defender of widows and orphans who depended on Illinois Central dividends against the machinations of big-money interests like Harriman and Standard Oil. Honor would not prevent Fish from using this defense to keep his place; to his mind, honor demanded its use.

The newspapers aided his cause by portraying Fish as another victim of the Standard Oil behemoth using Harriman and Peabody as its tools. Peabody denied vehemently but in vain that he had any connection to Standard Oil or Harriman to Mutual Life. For Harriman the fight had taken the worst possible turn: it had gone public and on Fish's terms, as a struggle by noble David against wicked Goliath rather than on the real issue of Fish's financial irregularities. Once again Harriman found himself set up as the villain of a piece in which he had little personal interest. He did want control of the Illinois Central, or at least he wanted it out of Fish's hands, but he did not wish to embarrass Fish. By March 1906, however, events were fast assuming a life of their own as Fish made a loud exit from the Mutual Life board and entered into a war of words with the exasperated Peabody.[13]

Jacob Schiff tried to intervene by reminding Fish that "in the end you will both be much happier if you settle your differences among yourselves in a conciliatory spirit," but his advice fell on deaf ears. The absence of any loose Illinois Central shares in the market convinced observers that a fight loomed in October, when elections for three directors were to be held. The Illinois Central, like many railroads, held staggered elections in which only part of the board stood for election in any given year. Everything depended on the outcome, for Harriman had the support of six of the road's thirteen directors. One more vote would enable him to do what he pleased with the presidency.[14]

To complicate matters, another director had died and had to be replaced. Desperate to have his own man in this seat, Fish sent out a circular to stockholders seeking proxies to be voted by himself or one of his representatives. In past years Harriman had been among those representatives; this time his name was conspicuously absent. At the next board meeting Peabody moved to create a joint committee for receiving proxies. Fish denounced the resolution as part of a plot to turn the Illinois Central over to the Union Pacific, and he stalked out of the meeting to prevent a quorum. A furious Peabody promptly tendered his resignation as an Illinois Central director.[15]

The fact that Harriman, Peabody, and Bertie Goelet were all Union Pacific directors lent credence to Fish's charge, and he held another interesting hole card. One of the proxies in his pocket belonged to Joseph Pulitzer, who had contacted Fish through a mutual friend and was itching to join the fray. Having originally bought his *New York World* from Jay Gould and then turned it against him, Pulitzer was well versed in the art of manufacturing unsavory legends.[16]

So explosively had Harriman burst into prominence that he had sneaked up on Pulitzer and the other New York publishers. During the past year, however, the *World* had been paying more attention to Harriman. In February 1905, when word leaked out that Harriman had bought a large block of Atchison stock and would go on its board along with Frick and Rogers, the *World* dubbed him the man "who runs Standard Oil Railroads." Next day the paper printed a cartoon of Harriman and John D. Rockefeller clutching hands around a globe with the caption "The Earth is Ours!" From then on, the image of Harriman as a ruthless power monger joined the stable of *World* stereotypes.[17]

Even with Pulitzer in his corner, Fish hesitated to start an open fight with Harriman. He sought advice from Melville Stone, who knew both Fish and Harriman well. Stone passed him along to H. H. Rogers, who obliged by arranging a conference at his office with Harriman, Peabody, and Fish on the morning of July 27. Both sides were eager to compromise and came quickly to terms. The three outgoing directors would be reelected, Peabody would withdraw his resignation, and the vacant seat on the board would be filled by a majority vote of the directors. On this basis Harriman agreed to give his proxies to Fish for reelection.[18]

The press hailed the agreement as a victory for Fish even though neither Harriman nor Fish had ever admitted there was a fight. Four days later, a Union Pacific committee chaired by Frick recommended that the company purchase a total of 195,000 shares of Illinois Central stock owned by Kuhn, Loeb, Rogers, Harriman, and Stillman at a price of $175 per share. Once the deal was completed, the Union Pacific would not only have men on the Illinois Central board but would also be its largest stockholder. On October 9, eight days before the Illinois Central annual meeting, seven directors, including Harriman, informed Fish that they had chosen Henry W. DeForest to fill the vacant seat. DeForest was a lawyer with impeccable credentials except for one that made him anathema to Fish: he was a director in the Southern Pacific.[19]

Harriman surely suspected that Fish would balk at the choice; whatever else DeForest was, he was in Fish's eyes a Harriman tool. At a board meeting the next day Fish announced that he could not accept DeForest because it would make him a party to handing the Illinois Central over to Union Pacific control. Harriman flatly denied that he had assured Fish that no director connected to another road would be appointed. "It passes the bounds of credulity," he declared, "to suppose that we would give Mr. Fish the right to nullify the very agreement we were signing, and to veto the selection to be made by a majority of the directors."[20]

On October 11 Fish asked Harriman to buy his Railroad Securities shares. Harriman agreed to give Fish 8,769 shares of Illinois Central stock and slightly over $1.5 million for them. Since Fish could not control the Illinois Central shares owned by Railroad Securities anyway, the effect was to give him a block of stock he could control while leaving Railroad Securities in the hands of Harriman and his Kuhn, Loeb allies. The deal took place five days before the annual meeting. Harriman later claimed he had no inkling of Fish's ulterior motives. "Had I known of his intention to break faith," he wrote in another of those position papers disguised as a letter, "I would not have made this transaction."[21]

But he at least suspected that Fish might pull a fast one, for on the evening of October 16 he called Melville Stone to remind him that he had been responsible for the July agreement and should prod Fish to honor its terms. Stone rang up Rogers, and together they drafted a telegram to Fish confirming that they, like Harriman, distinctly heard Fish say at the meeting that he would be satisfied with anyone the other directors chose. "In light of this fact," the telegram concluded, "do you not feel bound by this pledge?"[22]

The answer came at the stockholders' meeting the next day. When the election of the replacement director came up, Fish paused to read some prepared remarks giving his version of recent events. The issue, he declared solemnly, was "whether the Illinois Central Railroad Company shall or shall not continue to be an independent corporation." Attendance at board meetings averaged seven directors, which was also the number for a legal quorum. The Union Pacific already had three directors on the board; DeForest as an ally would make four, enough for a majority in most meetings. For twenty years, the stockholders had relied on Fish to keep the company independent. "For the first time I am called upon in behalf of these stockholders to withstand a forcible and organized effort to change the policy of the company, and . . . turn it over to those who control another railroad system."[23]

Having claimed piously that he acted for others rather than himself, Fish proceeded to nominate his own candidate for the seat. The Harriman representative protested at once, touching off an acid exchange of arguments. When the parliamentary smoke cleared, Fish's man had been elected by an overwhelming majority. The newspapers flocked to Fish's support; wiser heads, however, understood that Fish had won a battle but could not possibly win the war. A majority of directors still stood against him, including one whose defection to Harriman surprised some observers: J. T. Harahan, the man who had replaced Harriman as vice-president and served as Fish's chief operating officer for well over a decade.[24]

The showdown would take place on November 7 at a special board meeting to elect officers for the coming year. Harriman needed every vote at his command, but Bertie Goelet was in Paris with his mother on the first leg of an extended world tour. Harriman fired off a cable reporting what Fish had done and urging Goelet to hurry back in time for the meeting. "Make every effort [to] come here," he stressed, "returning plenty time for India trip."[25]

Bertie read the cable in dismay. "Impossible to persuade Mama," he replied. "How can I disobey her? She has her mind made up." To emphasize the point, Henrietta Goelet sent her own message to Harriman: "Have seen your cable. Positively forbid my son to leave me. If he does, he disobeys me." Devoted as he was to family loyalty, Harriman gnashed his teeth at the spectacle of a twenty-six-year-old man being held on a leash by his mother. Goelet writhed in misery over his dilemma. "Mama has just returned from country visit," he cabled the next day. "There has been hell to pay. She absolutely forbids me to return. What shall I do?"[26]

"Remind your mother of our talk four years ago about filling your father's place in Illinois Central," Harriman fired back. "This is serious crisis and will turn on one vote. Ask her for me to spare you if only for two weeks to fulfill your trust."[27]

At this plea Henrietta relented, and a chastened Bertie sailed for the United States to do his duty. Fish put up a brave front, but even partisan papers saw that he had no chance. The meeting went like clockwork as the seven Harriman directors elected Harahan the new president. "FISH PUNISHED FOR HIS HONESTY IN MUTUAL LIFE," cried the *World*'s headline. Other papers mourned his downfall in more restrained voices. "This isn't my fight," Harriman demurred to a reporter. "Personally, I had not a word to say at to-day's meeting." But one close student of his career saw the whole event as a stunning example of his "incalculable power in American railroad affairs."[28]

The deposing of Fish sent the Harriman legend into orbit. For some observers in search of a suitable parable, the victory smacked too much of Goliath trampling a game but outmanned David. Others saw a Judas element in the form of Harahan, the vice-president who had turned on his master to claim his place as a reward. No one noted the fact that Harahan and Harriman had known each other for nearly twenty years. Harriman emerged as the "Colossus of Roads" and the "Man of Mystery." Editors tumbled over one another in their eagerness to blast this naked display of power and overweening ambition. A Richmond paper denounced him for hoisting the "black flag of piratical high finance."[29]

Thoughtful critics conceded that Harriman had made a brilliant addition to his system, one comparable to Hill's scoop of the Burlington. The Illinois Central gave Harriman his long-coveted route to the Gulf and was the strongest of the systems reaching that outlet. Its lines met the Union Pacific at Omaha and the Southern Pacific at New Orleans. The real question, however, was not how far Harriman's empire stretched but how far his ambition reached. "Does he look forward to a time when his personality should completely dominate the railroads of the United States?" asked one editor. If so, he was courting a public outcry against monopoly that could lead to government ownership. "It may be well to remind Mr. Harriman," noted the editor tersely, "that the Colossus of Rhodes was destroyed by an earthquake."[30]

The Colossus of Roads was not as cold-hearted as he seemed. He still regarded Fish as an old friend, and he knew that Fish clung to the presidency partly because he needed the salary. Harriman offered to keep Fish in a nominal position as chairman of the board and sent Stone to discuss the proposition with Fish, who for all his pride was willing to listen. But Mamie Fish would have none of it. With a fine disregard for reality, she spurned the idea as beneath her husband's dignity and station.[31]

Helpless to oppose his wife, Fish found himself stripped of his office and its income. He still retained his seat on the board, but the next year he and Harriman both had to stand for reelection. In weighing his prospects, Fish noted the rising tide of sentiment against Harriman's power and saw how it might be used against him. If he had any doubts about making the attempt, Harriman dispelled them when, testifying before the ICC that winter, he insisted on making public the details of Fish's dubious handling of Illinois Central funds. After first playing coy, Fish seized his favorite outpost on the high ground by accusing the management of running the road in the Union Pacific's interest and padding accounts to boost its showing. The fight turned ugly in August 1907, when Fish and Harahan nearly came to blows at a board meeting, after which both sides took refuge in pious mud-slinging. Fish hammered relentlessly at the sources of Harriman's soaring unpopularity, while Harriman had Harahan counter with details of Fish's financial improprieties.[32]

This was the kind of fight Harriman hated because it took place through intermediaries and brought out the worst of both sides. He made a perfunctory effort to resolve it, then settled back gloomily for a long struggle only to have Fish nettle him with the same ploy Harriman had used back in 1887 to snatch the Dubuque & Sioux City road from Morgan. Fish enjoined the Illinois Central election on a technicality and the court postponed the election, keeping the controversy in the headlines for several more months.[33]

In February 1908 the court tossed out the injunction and allowed Harriman to vote all his stock. Fish lost his seat on the board and gradually sold off his holdings in the Illinois Central. For all his bitterness, Fish came later to see a brighter side to these dark days. In 1921, a dozen years after Harriman's death and two years before his own, he told a friend that Harriman had done him "a great service" by taking over the management and boosting the price of Illinois Central stock to a level where Fish could sell at a handsome profit.[34]

Harriman found no solace in the struggle beyond the victory he expected all along. He had lost an old friend and been slathered with mud in the bargain, yet he showed less resentment than Schiff, whose blood boiled at the tactics Fish had used. News of the victory reached Schiff in Cairo, where he was about to embark on a tour of Palestine. After showering Harriman with congratulations, Schiff drew the proper moral. "With all of this," he lectured gently, "the lesson you have no doubt learnt is that it will not do to try to control too much, without regard to public opinion."[35]

But the lesson came hard to Harriman, especially during these months. The strain of his ordeal went beyond the mental and emotional; his vitality had begun to decline noticeably. In a rare admission of weakness, he later confided to Otto Kahn that there had not been a day in 1906 during which he had not been tormented by severe pain. The ravages of this suffering were etched in Harriman's drawn and haggard features. There was no one cause but a series of ailments, the worst of which was a continuing bout with hemorrhoids.[36]

Early in January 1907 Harriman underwent minor surgery for an undisclosed ailment that was probably hemorrhoids. The wound healed slowly and kept

Harriman at home for a month. While the family denied rumors that there was any cause for concern, a friend visiting Harriman late that month was shocked to find him "looking wretchedly and suffering intensely." By early February he seemed his old feisty self, but in September he reluctantly submitted to the knife again for the same complaint. Although he bounced back more quickly this time, pain remained a constant companion.[37]

It was hard to know what pained Harriman most during the grim days of 1906 and 1907: the physical suffering, the daily bombardments of vituperation from the press and his foes, or the desertion of longtime friends through quarrels or differences over policy. Harriman bore it all in his stoic, tight-lipped manner, never seeking sympathy or vilifying those who attacked him. To solicitous friends he murmured, "It will all come out right in the end."[38]

But the end seemed very far away as his troubles mounted. Before him loomed the ugliest and most vicious fight of all, pitting him against a man who was not only an old friend but the most powerful and formidable figure in America.

25 Fighting a Formidable Friend

[Harriman] was a dominant factor in the inner circles of the greatest banking institutions. The vast resources of the New York life insurance companies were at his disposition. Ramifications of his political power, Federal and State, extended to every quarter of the land. State and even national conventions took his orders. Members of Congress did his bidding. Laws were enacted at his will. Only two men ever dared to block his path. The late J. P. Morgan stood between him and the possession of the Northern Pacific Railroad in 1901; and Theodore Roosevelt thwarted his purpose to become an absolute dictator of the transportation affairs of the United States.
—William Z. Ripley, "Federal Financial Railway Regulation"

On a wall in Harriman's office hung a picture taken during an inspection trip through Mexico. The party had paused to examine a small railroad servicing a copper mine, and the photographer captured a dozen men, including Stillman, William Rockefeller, and Epes Randolph. By far the most inconspicuous figure in the group was Harriman, who was ignoring the camera in favor of a Mexican policeman with whom he was shaking hands. The policeman towering above the slight man in the baggy clothes and battered felt hat looked far more important and impressive.[1]

Anonymity had served Harriman well for many years, but now it was gone just when he needed it most. He had become a public target at a time when he needed to husband his fading strength for the work at hand but instead had to spend it fending off attacks. The economy had turned sluggish and many financiers thought hard times lay ahead. Harriman's properties required close attention to remain at the high standard of performance he had established. He was approaching the age when many leaders think of retirement or begin grooming a successor. Harriman did neither. Time had not slaked his ambition nor attacks dented his determination. He knew only one way to fight, and that was to stand his ground until the right prevailed. "I would give up the whole business," he told Alex Millar, "if I could be sure my plans would be carried out."[2]

But Harriman knew there was no one able to carry out his plans. Far from looking to get out, he was looking to get deeper in. The problem was that his way of doing things consumed enormous amounts of energy. He relied on an asser-tive personality that took command in everything; on a bulldog tenacity that argued for a policy until he wore others down; on knowing more than anyone else by doing his homework; and on sound judgment that required clear, fresh thinking. The Harriman style taxed both mental and physical stamina, and it permitted no shortcuts. To maintain this high level of dedication while engaged in prolonged controversies and blocking out constant pain asked much of his ebbing vitality.

The drain on his strength forced him to economize in every way, made him more imperious and impatient, more curt even to his friends and more peevish when thwarted. A man already renowned for his lack of charm grew even more brutal as he pared every action down to its essence. Eventually, of course, death would block his plans, but death was a subject he scrupulously avoided. It was not to be thought of or discussed. In fact, Harriman had lived with the fear of death all his life, only he knew it by another name: failure.

During 1906 two incidents occurred amid the Equitable and Illinois Central fights that twisted what should have been personal triumphs into examples of how the prevailing climate of public opinion warped everything Harriman touched. Both arose as protests to Harriman's dividend policy, which one critic labeled "conservatism run mad." The first involved the Wells Fargo company. Few people knew that Harriman had anything to do with this fabled banking and express firm until headlines blared the news in the summer of 1906. He had gained control of it shortly after buying into the Southern Pacific. The big four express companies—Adams, American, United States, and Wells Fargo— depended on railroad contracts for their business. Harriman wanted Wells Fargo to handle the express business on all his western roads. The fact that it owned a bank especially appealed to him.[3]

After taking charge of Wells Fargo, Harriman separated the bank from the express business and in April 1905 merged it with a Nevada bank run by an associate. The bank stopped issuing annual reports and gave out no information on its assets, earnings, and activities. It was an open secret that Harriman tapped Wells Fargo's surplus for loans to finance his rail operations. Rumors about these low-interest loans exposed him to the same charges that arose in the Equitable scandal then unfolding. No one accused him of damaging Wells Fargo; on the contrary, trouble arose when some stockholders complained that he was paying only an 8 percent dividend while the company netted more than 30 percent on its stock.[4]

In May 1906 some minority holders launched a drive for higher dividends and access to financial information. Harriman grudgingly hiked the dividend to 10 percent and released some figures, but neither move appeased the dissidents.

A proxy battle with a novel twist erupted. The minority holders had no desire to change the management; they wished only to compel it to pay larger dividends. As the fight heated up, however, it developed what one observer delicately called "glimpses of feeling entirely outside of the matter at issue." A minority circular bluntly defined the struggle as one "between Mr. Harriman on the one hand and the entire body of 1,900 stockholders on the other."[5]

Here was a fight Harriman neither wanted nor needed, yet he could not avoid it or keep it from overlapping the other controversies splashing his name across headlines. One group of Wells Fargo holders filed suit against him and engaged the flamboyant Samuel Untermyer, who had defended Hyde in the Equitable fight. Harriman countered with William Nelson Cromwell, a high-powered attorney capable of dueling Untermyer in any battle of mouths. When the stockholders convened early in August, Harriman won a decisive but costly victory. During the meeting, Cromwell delivered an impassioned defense of the management in which he said of Harriman, "It is not on the business acumen of the officers but on his wonderful executive genius on which the stockholders must rely if the prosperity of the company is to continue. He cannot be replaced, for he moves in a higher world into which we may not enter."[6]

Critics across America pounced gleefully on Cromwell's "higher world" phrase as the perfect emblem of Harriman's aloofness, arrogance, and high-handed methods. Wells Fargo flourished while the other express companies struggled, but public attention ignored performance in favor of an image that fit the current perception of Harriman. A second incident at almost exactly the same time reinforced the impression, this one involving a dividend on the Union Pacific. For years analysts had heaped praise on Harriman's handling of the Union Pacific. While most of this attention went to its operation and reconstruction, thoughtful observers recognized that its financial record was no less brilliant.[7]

Early in 1906, as the road rolled up new records in traffic hauled and the surplus mushroomed, Harriman let the dividend go from 5 percent to 6 percent and fended off the clamor for more with his usual lecture on the need for conservatism. During the spring and summer, however, record earnings continued to pile up on both Pacific systems. The Union Pacific produced a surplus exceeding $25 million; it also owned $90 million worth of Southern Pacific stock on which Harriman had finally decided to pay a 5 percent dividend. This would put another $4.5 million into the Union Pacific treasury, and the securities acquired in the breakup of Northern Securities also poured dividends into the Union Pacific's coffers.[8]

At a board meeting on August 15 the directors absorbed these figures and agreed with Harriman to raise the dividend to 10 percent. Although the Union

Pacific had never paid so large a dividend, the size provoked less of an uproar than the circumstances.[9]

Normally the board released news of a dividend at once, but several key directors missed the meeting and Harriman wished to inform them before it went public. The board left the timing of the release to the executive committee, which was to meet the next morning. That session was postponed until three in the afternoon so that Harriman could attend the funeral of an old friend. By then the absent directors had been contacted, but the New York Stock Exchange had closed. If the news went out at once, the London market would get the benefit of it before New York. "We decided that it was best to have the announcement made in New York before it was in London," Harriman explained, "that is, while the New York market was open." The "We" consisted of Harriman, Stillman, and Judge Lovett, the only members present that day.[10]

Normally news of a dividend was hardly the stuff of headlines, but in this case rumors of a major increase in the payment had excited Wall Street for weeks. When the announcement was delayed, two dozen reporters flocked to the Union Pacific office in the Equitable Building on the morning of the sixteenth only to learn that Harriman was absent and the meeting would be held later. When at last the news went out the next morning, an already boiling market sent Union Pacific and Southern Pacific soaring. Those who had lost heart over the delays and sold out or sold short howled in protest.[11]

Angry voices crying fraud soon drowned out the message of the remarkable dividends. "HARRIMAN DIVIDENDS AMAZE WALL STREET," blared a *Times* headline, while beneath it in smaller caps ran the accusation that "THE INSIDERS MADE MILLIONS." Harriman was charged with delaying the announcement so that he and his friends could buy Union Pacific stock heavily and profit from the rise they knew the dividend would bring. The *Times* estimated that Harriman alone pocketed $10 million from this maneuver, which even a moderate journal deplored as a "wrongful use of corporate power." Criticism rained down on Harriman from every quarter even though no one had produced a shred of evidence that any director had bought stock.[12]

The fact that the dividends for both roads represented a sharp reversal of Harriman's past policy lent a veneer of plausibility to the charges. This was exactly the sort of insensitivity to public opinion that made Harriman's friends shudder. Schiff, Kahn, and Stillman tried repeatedly to warn Harriman that he lived in a world where the presence of smoke always heralded fire. "A man at the head of a great corporation," stressed Otto Kahn, "must not only do right, but he must be very careful to avoid even appearances tending to arouse the suspicion of his not doing right." But none of them could curb Harriman's tendency to ride "roughshod over conventionalities and amenities."[13]

Together these episodes imprinted on the public an image of Harriman as a sinister force worthy of the legendary Jay Gould. This negative image completely reversed his actual role and could not have been more distorted, yet it gained credence. Instead of rewarding him for his vision, the march of events elevated him into an unwitting symbol for a host of ills, real and imagined, in the body politic.

This transmutation of Harriman in the public mind did not go unnoticed by the first citizen of the land, who had his own quarrel with the little man. If there was one American who exceeded Harriman in physical and mental vigor, it was Theodore Roosevelt. Whatever one thought of him—and the range of opinions could not have been wider—Roosevelt was one of the most remarkable men who ever lived. His mind was less deep than cavernous, a vast closet of information through which he rattled at lightning speed to fetch what he needed. There was scarcely a topic on which he did not hold strong views and scarcely a prominent figure on whom he had not pressed them.[14]

He looked as much larger than life as he seemed. His body resembled an Easter Island icon with its square, solid head atop a squat but powerful trunk hardened by the outdoor life on which he thrived and which he relished as the supplicant embraced the cleansing blows of flagellation. His hair was short and thick, like his neck, and his complexion ruddy. The one flaw in his appearance, a pair of pitifully weak eyes, darted restlessly behind wire glasses or a pince-nez and were overshadowed by the famous, formidable teeth—shining rows of white tile that came together so perfectly they reminded one of a row of dominoes.[15]

They were strikingly alike in many ways, Roosevelt and Harriman. One had been born the child of privilege, the other of privilege denied. Both had come into the world frail and weak-eyed and challenged their physical limitations with a defiance bordering on recklessness. Both had voracious appetites for work and play. Their minds moved at speeds incomprehensible to most men, stoked by sources of energy that were apparently unlimited. They bristled with great plans which they were impatient to realize and hurtled toward them without regard for obstacles or setbacks, inspiring their followers to match the impossible pace they set, contemptuous of the weak, the slow, and the incompetent who fell by the wayside. They were unabashed in their hunger for power and delight in using it; full of themselves and their work, which they linked always to the greater good of patriotic duty.

One major difference separated them and proved decisive in their conflict: Roosevelt was a politician and Harriman was not. He knew how to manipulate and placate people as Harriman did not. And he could never conceal the colossus that was his ego. While Harriman subsumed his vanity beneath the work at hand, content to operate in the wings, Roosevelt craved the limelight. It was once said of him that he had to be the bride at every wedding and the corpse at every funeral. Ultimately his hunger for center stage cost him as dearly as Harriman's arrogance and remoteness did him.

But it served Roosevelt well in politics. He had that gift of solipsism, so necessary to politicians, for standing firmly on principles that could later be bent or broken when necessary under the guise of some belligerent denial or earnest rationalization. It was this quality that led his detractors to regard him as a fraud and charlatan if not a demagogue. Ironically, Harriman and Roosevelt were alike in realizing how radically industrialization had altered American life and institutions and how necessary it was to devise new instruments for harnessing these forces. But Roosevelt came later than Harriman to this revelation and never got past a tendency to put political expediency above his larger visions.

During the 1880s the two men had lived only a few blocks apart in New York, Roosevelt at 6 West 57th Street and Harriman at 14 East 55th Street. But they were distant neighbors with little in common beyond their membership in the Republican Party. State politics was what drew them together, which meant that most of their relationship was played out on Roosevelt's turf. Harriman was a neophyte in politics. No businessman with large concerns could avoid politics, but Harriman never grew comfortable with it. The netherworld of dealing and compromise was too slippery in its footing and spongy in its results. He could not help viewing politicians as the Luddites of their age, ever willing to smash the machinery of progress if it threatened them.

Harriman owed his connection with New York state politics to Benjamin B. Odell Jr., who had grown up in the Orange County city of Newburgh. Six years younger than Harriman, the bright, ambitious Odell had taken early to politics and climbed onto the Republican state committee at the age of thirty. He served two forgettable terms in Congress, during which his eye never strayed far from the state arena. In 1898 he came home purged of national ambitions and happily installed as chairman of the state executive committee, which put him near the throne of state Republican rule occupied by the wily Senator Thomas C. Platt.[16]

The relationship between Harriman and Odell began with their mutual interest in Orange County affairs and ripened into a close personal friendship. By coincidence, the year 1898 marked a crucial juncture in the careers of both men. Harriman made his decisive move into the Union Pacific; Odell decided to back Theodore Roosevelt, who had just come home from Cuba a national hero, as the candidate for governor of a troubled Republican Party. He persuaded a reluctant Platt that Roosevelt was the only man who could save the party that fall, and his instincts proved sound. An arduous campaign enabled the Rough Rider to squeak out a narrow victory.[17]

Harriman had little to do with the campaign, but shortly after the election he hosted a dinner in honor of Odell at the Metropolitan Club. The guest list ranged from political heavyweights like Platt, Mark Hanna, Chauncey Depew, and Elihu Root to businessmen like Stillman, Schiff, and D. O. Mills. Harriman sat at the center on one side of the banquet table flanked by Odell and Roosevelt. It was an impressive position for a man who played no major role in politics and had only that month joined the board of the reorganized Union Pacific. His presence at the dinner suggests that Harriman occupied a prominent place in New York financial and political circles before the public even knew his name.[18]

The celebration turned out to have a deeper significance, for both Harriman and Roosevelt launched the national phase of their careers during that November of 1898. Roosevelt's term as governor led to his being put on the Republican ticket in 1900. Some said the nomination as vice-president was intended more to bury than to praise him, but fate transformed it into an early residence in the White House. His successor as governor was none other than Odell, who served two terms and became a vital conduit for the political support Roosevelt counted on at home. Odell in turn relied heavily on men like Harriman to keep the Republican organization well financed.[19]

As governor, Odell stressed reform, economy, and pro-business policies. He struck impressive blows against waste and corruption and pushed through controversial changes in the tax system. On appointments he boldly separated himself from the aging Platt and strengthened his own power base by resuming his post as party chairman. While this dual role enabled Odell to maintain his independence from Platt, it drew harsh criticism and made the support of men like Harriman all the more vital.[20]

Harriman needed no invitation to gravitate toward any center of power, even one he did not personally wish to occupy. So interlaced were the worlds of finance and politics in New York that he could not have escaped the pull. Most of his friends were rock-ribbed Republicans, and few rivaled Harriman in their patriotic ardor. He was a regular contributor to the party coffers and did not hesitate to ask for favors or to express his views on legislation. Occasionally the Democratic papers linked his name to some local scandal or power play, as the *New York Herald* did in April 1901 when it charged Harriman with using Odell's help to grab control of a strategic bridge.[21]

Party leaders formed the habit of consulting Harriman on financial and economic questions. Roosevelt did not hesitate to sound his views along with other Wall Street men like Morgan. Harriman received frequent invitations to the White House for a meal and conversation. Always eager to pick the best brains he could find, Roosevelt considered Harriman a key figure in New York and the top man in his field. For his part Harriman asked an occasional favor and sought appointments for men he favored or had been asked by friends to support.[22]

All this was the normal stuff of politics, yet things had a way of never being quite normal with Roosevelt. While his left hand stroked the big business interests, the right hand attacked Northern Securities or Standard Oil as well as the character of the men who ran them. "The big New York capitalists seem to me to have gone partially insane in their opposition to me," Roosevelt complained late in 1903, "but I have long been convinced that the men of very great wealth in too many instances totally failed to understand the temper of the country and its needs, as well as their own needs."[23]

No mention was made here of Roosevelt's own needs, especially his burning desire to capture the presidency on his own in 1904. It was this ambition that led to the disastrous break between Roosevelt and Harriman. Like most political divorces, it was neither clean nor clear-cut. The muck dredged up by their quarrel clung more to Harriman than to Roosevelt only because the latter was the most artful dodger.

By 1904 New York state politics were in the throes of transition. Odell was at the height of his power, having dethroned Platt and taken charge of the party slate for the fall elections. Over Platt's bitter objections, he chose Frank Higgins, his dutiful lieutenant governor, to head the ticket and drummed up support for Roosevelt's reelection campaign. That spring Odell coaxed Harriman into serving as a delegate to the Republican national convention. Harriman had been asked, claimed one Roosevelt man, because he was "a little cool toward the Roosevelt cause." The reason for Harriman's coolness was no mystery: the Supreme Court had just handed down its decision on Northern Securities. Roosevelt welcomed Harriman's support, invited him down to Washington before the convention met, and took care to solicit his views on some appointments in which Harriman had an interest.[24]

Roosevelt had compelling reasons for courting Harriman. Teddy the Trust Buster needed money to finance his campaign, and he looked privately to the very business leaders he had savaged in public for the funds to keep the nation safely in Republican hands. A Senate inquiry later found that corporate donors provided nearly three-fourths of the party war chest in 1904. Harriman was a key figure in a key state whose influence extended through a wide circle of businessmen. But he sailed off to Europe on June 29 and did not return for two months. "As soon as you come home I shall want to see you," Roosevelt wrote him. "The fight will doubtless be hot then. It has been a real pleasure to see you this year."[25]

After his return, Harriman cleared his desk and on September 20 offered to run down to Washington even though it seemed to him "that the situation could not be in better shape." Evidently Roosevelt agreed, for he told Harriman not to trouble himself. By early October, however, things had changed radically. Roosevelt learned that the campaign in New York State had run out of money and was floundering. Raising funds proved more tricky than usual. Earlier Odell had agreed with Republican national chairman George B. Cortelyou and national treasurer Cornelius N. Bliss that the national committee would do all fund-raising and disburse the proceeds to individual states as needed. New York needed $200,000, but the national committee had no money to give it.[26]

Roosevelt was aghast at the news. "I would rather lose the election in the country than be defeated in my own State," he growled at Senator Nathan Scott on the phone. After being told that his own campaign was safe but that Higgins was in danger of losing, Roosevelt dashed off a note asking Harriman to come talk to him about "the trouble over the State ticket in New York." Harriman was already aware of the problem and had delayed a trip west to do some work for the party. "I am giving a very large part of my time to correcting the trouble here," he told Roosevelt, and offered to come to Washington in a few days if conditions did not improve.[27]

Two days later Harriman received from Roosevelt one of those cryptic letters that sound as if they had been written more for the record than for the recipient:

> A suggestion has come to me in a roundabout way that you do not think it wise to come on to see me in these closing weeks of the campaign, but that you are reluctant to refuse, inasmuch as I have asked you. Now, my dear sir, you and I are practical men, and you are on the ground and know the conditions better than I do. If you think there is any danger of your visit to me causing trouble, or if you think there is nothing special I should be informed about, or no matter in which I could give aid, why of course give up the visit for the time being and then a few weeks hence, before I write my message, I shall get you to come down to discuss certain government matters not connected with the campaign.[28]

The "government matters" referred to the railroad question and what Roosevelt planned to say about it in his annual message. Harriman had been led to believe that he would be consulted on the draft of this statement. Two items, then, were on the agenda of any meeting between them: the campaign in New York and Roosevelt's views on railroad regulation.

Well might Harriman have puzzled over this adroit piece of circumlocution. He had suggested no such uneasiness and probably had no inkling of what the president was driving at. The object was to create evidence that any visit to Washington was being made on Harriman's initiative for business of his own. Roosevelt was responding to a series of attacks launched by the *New York World* on October 1, when Joseph Pulitzer noted in a signed editorial that the Bureau of Corporations had been in existence for 583 days and accomplished nothing. Was it a coincidence that the bureau's chief, George B. Cortelyou, happened also to be head of the Republican national committee? Were the corporations pouring money into the Republican war chest buying protection? Could a man soliciting money from corporations also regulate them?[29]

Day after day Pulitzer hammered at this theme. The *New York Times* and the

Brooklyn Eagle joined the attack, which grew steadily more shrill. Never a man to leave his flank unguarded, Roosevelt created the letter to Harriman as a form of protection. Harriman could not go to Washington at once anyway; he had to be in Rochester for a funeral. After his return, he telephoned Roosevelt for another appointment to see him. By then Pulitzer's crusade had begun to sputter.[30]

But the problems in New York remained. When Harriman came back from Washington, he told Judge Lovett, "They are in a hole, and the President wants me to help them out. I've got to do it, and I'm going to raise the money." He told the same thing to Odell, Charles Peabody, and other friends, all of whom recalled this fact later when Roosevelt denied that he had ever asked Harriman to raise money for the campaign. True to his word, Harriman came up with $250,000 for the national committee, including $50,000 from his own pocket. Of this sum, $200,000 went back to the New York state committee and helped Higgins eke out a victory.[31]

All should have been well that ended well, but one item of unfinished business still clouded New York's political agenda. Chauncey Depew hoped to retain his Senate seat and had the support of Platt and Roosevelt; Odell preferred former governor Frank S. Black. To devise a graceful exit for Depew, Odell got Harriman to extract a quid pro quo from Roosevelt during their conference in late October: Harriman would raise money for the party in New York if Roosevelt promised to make Depew ambassador to France after the election.[32]

Largely on the basis of this pledge, Odell announced that Black was his choice for the Senate seat. The wily Platt, fortified by a talk with Roosevelt, rose gleefully from his political grave to drum up support for Depew. Harriman had taken his family to Virginia on a short vacation trip. On the return trip he stopped in Washington to see Roosevelt, who blithely told him that he favored Depew's reelection to the Senate. This position was remarkable in two respects: it violated a pledge Roosevelt had given (though he later denied giving it), and it put him behind a man who, whatever his other credentials, was exactly the type of corporate Hessian Roosevelt was fond of railing against in public.[33]

Harriman found himself in an impossible position. Depew could not be pushed out of the Senate without having another place to go. He was a friend, a colleague on several boards, and an officer in the New York Central system. But Odell had already come out for Black; if Depew kept his seat, Odell would be left out on a limb that Platt was waiting eagerly to saw. As a reward for the service he had rendered, Harriman had to disappoint one of his closest friends. The grand irony was that none of it had to do with anything Harriman wanted for himself. Seething with resentment, he saw no choice but to persuade Odell to eat crow by switching to Depew. Only a close friend could have asked such a favor or agreed to it. Odell swallowed his pride and withdrew his support of Black, allowing Platt to hail the change as proof of his resurrection. Some papers unwittingly rubbed salt in the wound by charging that Harriman had inspired Odell's change of front as part of a secret deal: Depew kept his Senate seat while Harriman got one on the board of the New York Central.[34]

Harriman walked away with his reputation soiled and Odell with his prestige and power in New York badly damaged. Although Harriman said little about it, this act of duplicity soured him on Roosevelt and politics. Nor was it an isolated incident. The president had said repeatedly that he wanted Harriman's input on that part of his annual message dealing with railroad affairs, but he never got around to consulting him. "When you were down here," Roosevelt explained in another of those letters that sound as if they were written to be read by someone else, "both you and I were so interested in certain of the New York political developments that I hardly, if at all, touched on governmental matters."[35]

"It was natural," retorted Harriman, "for me to suppose that railroad matters would be included in any discussion you and I might have before writing your message." At issue was a paragraph urging Congress to strengthen the ICC's power over rates. Harriman wanted it left out, arguing that it would cause more harm than good. "While, as I say, I should have been delighted to go over it with you," declared Roosevelt in his inimitable way, "I must also frankly say that my mind was definitely made up."[36]

Harriman remained on friendly terms with Roosevelt and that winter arranged to have his portrait done for the state capitol in Albany. He also advised the president on some appointments but found his views ignored. Then in 1905 the Equitable bombshell exploded, dragging Harriman, Odell, and Depew through the heat of publicity that scorched the entire New York political machine with allegations of influence peddling. It did not help that Francis Hendricks, the state superintendent of insurance who so infuriated Harriman, owed his place to Roosevelt and remained a staunch loyalist.[37]

The Armstrong investigation set in motion a series of fateful changes in New York. As public indignation swelled in the wake of revelations from the hearings, Roosevelt smelled political blood. He saw an opportunity to deal the old machine a death blow by allying with Higgins against Odell and Platt. The investigation delivered him a perfect reform candidate for governor in the person of Charles Evans Hughes, who had gained wide respect for his handling of the hearings. At the Republican convention in September 1906 the Roosevelt-Higgins forces won a sweeping victory over Odell and what one Buffalo paper called the "corporation pirates."[38]

Harriman watched these events with mounting anger. His own distrust of Roosevelt had grown during 1905, and now the president had gone after his good friend Odell. After a visit by Harriman to Oyster Bay in July, contact between the two men dwindled; after the wedding of Alice Roosevelt in February 1906, which the Harrimans attended, it ceased almost entirely. Still another issue soured relations between them: railroad regulation.[39]

After ignoring Harriman's advice to drop the subject from his 1904 message, Roosevelt launched a concerted effort to get a railroad act. By the winter of 1906 the president was trying to herd through Congress the Hepburn bill, which would increase the ICC's power over rail rates. Harriman opposed the bill and lashed out at what he called an "anti-railroad conspiracy" bent on destroying the credit of the railroads in order to promote Roosevelt's pet project, the Panama Canal. "I am not opposed to the canal," he insisted, "but the attack on railroads, apparently, is to create a sentiment in favor of some other method of transportation."[40]

These remarks did not endear Harriman to Roosevelt or slow the bill's progress. During 1906 the president's keen political nose sniffed the shift of public sentiment against Harriman as the Armstrong investigation unfolded its sordid revelations, the fight with Fish splashed through the daily headlines, and a furor erupted over the timing of the Union Pacific 10 percent dividend. The fact that Harriman and Odell were close friends made it easy for Roosevelt to lump them together in his own thinking. Apart from the real issues that separated the two men, Harriman had become to Roosevelt that most dreaded of creatures: a political liability.

As the state campaign of 1906 approached, the Republican convention nominated Hughes as a reform candidate for governor and dumped Odell as party chairman. In this strange campaign Hughes was pitted against William Randolph Hearst, whose papers had long blasted the corrupt Republican machine. Republicans running for state office made a display of shunning corporate contributions in favor of direct appeals to the voters, but the congressional candidates had no intention of jettisoning the big donors. James S. Sherman, head of the Republican Congressional Committee, remembered Harriman's key role in the 1904 campaign and decided to ask his help again.[41]

Sherman's timing could not have been worse. For months Harriman had been brooding over Roosevelt's breaches of faith and the problems they had spawned. Late in 1905 he had received a letter from Sidney Webster, his old friend from the Illinois Central board, warning him against being drawn into politics because he was not fit for it. The advice struck a chord in Harriman and prompted a lengthy reply that revealed his curious mix of naïveté and guile:

> The trouble originated in my allowing myself to be drawn into other people's affairs, and partly from a desire to help them and at their request. I seemed to be like the fellow who got in between the man and his wife in their quarrel. As to my political instincts . . . I am quite sure I have none, and my being made at all prominent in the political situation is entirely due to President Roosevelt

and because of my taking an active part in the autumn of 1904 at his request, and his taking advantage of conditions then created to further his own interests. If it had been a premeditated plot it could not have been better started or carried out.

With this preface Harriman launched into a detailed account of his role in the 1904 campaign and Roosevelt's reneging on his pledge to appoint Depew. "So you see," he concluded, "I was brought forward by Roosevelt in an attempt to help him, at his request, the same as I was in the insurance matter by Hyde and Ryan by their request for my help."[42]

Clearly Harriman was venting months of frustration and anger toward Roosevelt's behavior as well as the insurance fiasco, which was then marching toward the Armstrong hearings. Both episodes represented to him something sordid and unclean, and he wanted desperately to wash his hands of them. Yet he was also taking care to protect himself the same way Roosevelt had, by putting down his version of events as a matter of record. Behind his well-known impulsiveness lay a layer of guile he took pains to conceal as best he could. He sent the letter to Webster but kept a copy for himself.

James Sherman knew nothing about this letter, but he did know that Harriman still harbored resentments from the 1904 campaign. Before approaching him for a contribution, he asked Maxwell Evarts, who was counsel for the Southern Pacific, to see Harriman about it. Evarts broached the matter several times only to be rebuffed. Harriman declared irritably that he had better uses for his money; privately he was also bitter over Odell's ouster from the inner circles of the party. Roosevelt had managed this by getting Higgins, who had ridden Odell's coattail to the statehouse, to defect and join the president. In a letter to Harriman, Odell denounced Higgins as "the worst ingrate I know of . . . a weak-kneed & spineless man." Neither Odell nor Harriman cared for Hughes as a candidate, and both were tired of being made scapegoats by men they considered nothing more than rank opportunists.[43]

This was Harriman's mood when he finally agreed to see Sherman. Fortunately for Harriman, Evarts came along as well. The meeting took place in September, less than a month after Harriman had received Odell's letter blasting Higgins and at a time when criticism of the 10 percent dividend still rang in his ears. In this combative mood, eager to give someone a piece of his mind, Harriman wasted no time on amenities when the unsuspecting Sherman walked in. He reached into his desk, pulled out a copy of the letter to Sidney Webster, read it to Sherman in his flat voice, and said again that he would not give one dollar to the Republican campaign.[44]

Evarts's jaw dropped almost as far as Sherman's at this performance; he could not fathom what bearing the letter had on the issue at hand. Why Harriman chose this peculiar way to refuse Sherman can be explained only by the circumstances. He was a tired man wracked with pain and forced to endure in silence one frustrating controversy after another. Here was a chance to unleash some of his deep resentment over the shabby treatment accorded him and his friend Odell. He had poured those frustrations into the letter and now the letter exploded out of him to Sherman, who was merely a surrogate target. In fact, Harriman had once before hauled out the Webster letter and read it to an old friend after swearing him to silence.[45]

Unfortunately, there was no vow of secrecy this time. A short time later, Sherman told Roosevelt about the interview with Harriman. The president took so keen an interest in the account that he sat down that same afternoon and wrote Sherman a letter restating what Sherman had told him. Here was yet another of those letters written for the record, and this one recorded hearsay with a vengeance. It summarized what Roosevelt said Sherman had said about what Harriman had said.

In Roosevelt's version, Sherman described Harriman as being so dissatisfied with the president that he said in effect that "as long as I [Roosevelt] was at the head of the Republican party or as it was dominated by policies which I advocate and represent, he would not support it, and was quite indifferent whether Hearst beat Hughes or not, whether Democrats carried Congress or not." Roosevelt adamantly denied that he had made any promise to appoint Depew or asked Harriman to help raise money. Choosing his words carefully, he said, "I never requested Mr. Harriman to raise a dollar for the presidential campaign of 1904." This was true; the money had been solicited for the New York state campaign.[46]

The account Roosevelt set down was hardly casual. It filled more than six pages and included copies of his correspondence with Harriman except for one crucial omission betraying his assertion that he had asked Harriman for help in raising money. Then, in an astonishing paragraph, Roosevelt quoted Sherman as having told him that Harriman did not care who won the election because "those people were crooks and he could buy them; that whenever he wanted legislation from a State legislature he could buy it; that he 'could buy Congress' and that if necessary he 'could buy the judiciary.'" This remarkable allegation allowed Roosevelt to rise to the full height of his well-practiced indignation: "It shows a cynicism and deepseated corruption which make the man uttering such sentiments, and boasting, no matter how falsely, of his power to perform such sentiments, at least as undesirable a citizen as Debs, or Moyer, or Haywood. It is because we have capitalists capable of uttering such sentiments and capable of acting on them that there is strength behind sinister agitators of the Hearst type. . . . I was horrified, as was Root, when you told us today what Harriman had said to you." After this pious and patently calculated outburst, Roosevelt authorized Sherman to show the letter to Harriman but not to make it public without the president's permission.

In the bizarre annals of American politics there are few controversies stranger than this one. Harriman had written a private letter to a friend and read it to someone else who repeated its contents and accompanying remarks by memory to the president some days later. Roosevelt then penned a private letter summarizing what Sherman had told him and adding his own rebuttal of Harriman's alleged charges along with a vigorous denunciation of Harriman. How much Roosevelt embellished on Sherman's remarks, or how accurate Sherman's report was in the first place, cannot be established. Sherman left no account of the episode; his version comes entirely from Roosevelt's hands. Some years later, however, Evarts released a statement denying that Harriman had said much of what Roosevelt claimed Sherman said he had said.[47]

Since neither letter had been made public, no one knew about the controversy except those directly involved. That fall the bad blood between Harriman and Roosevelt grew worse. Hughes eked out a victory over Hearst, but most of the other Republicans on the ticket were defeated. Three days after the election, rumors circulated that the ICC was considering an investigation of the Harriman roads. Early in December the ICC announced it would examine "relations between the Union Pacific and Southern Pacific Railway systems growing out of their common management and control."[48]

The news caught Harriman at a bad time. He spent much of November on a trip west, going more public than usual, giving interviews to reporters and talks to business and civic groups. Early one morning he arrived in Chicago and had his car switched to a side track to conduct business until his connection arrived. Four stenographers and secretaries took down the letters and telegrams he rattled off while welcoming a procession of rail officials and bankers. Breakfast sat cooling in the galley, unable to penetrate the flow of business. A reporter slid through a seam in the line of visitors and was rewarded with a brief interview on the platform. Harriman stood before him draped in an oversized steamer coat "of loud pattern, such as can be bought for $15 or $16," the inevitable derby jammed down over his forehead.[49]

Despite the crush of business and lack of breakfast, Harriman showed unusual patience and courtesy. No, he was not a financial king and had no desire to be. He didn't run a single railroad by himself. Yes, he had bought into the Chicago subway because it would help reduce the cost of transportation, but he had no plans to move to Chicago. "Do you understand that?" Harriman asked often. "Do I make that clear?" He tolerated the interruptions because he was anxious to get across a message he repeated everywhere he went: the railroads were crucial to national prosperity and should not be hamstrung by suspicion and regulation.[50]

The trip wore Harriman down just as he faced a major investigation. Young Roland added to his worries by breaking his collarbone at school when his pony stumbled and rolled over him. Harriman himself was fighting intense pain from the hemorrhoids, which had grown worse. He tried to get the ICC to postpone the hearings and was told the commission had too crowded an agenda to change its schedule. He went so far as to appeal to Roosevelt, who spoke to the chairman but told Harriman he could do nothing.[51]

Disappointed, Harriman decided to try a more personal approach. He had no way of knowing what role Roosevelt had played in urging the investigation, but the timing seemed more than coincidence. For once Harriman was in no mood to fight. Leaving aside his personal feelings, a prolonged feud with a popular, newly elected president meant disaster for his interests, the interests of his friends, the Republican Party, and perhaps the country as well. The time had come for overtures of peace.

26 Fighting Nature

As recently as the year 1900, the Imperial Valley had not a single civilized inhabitant, and not one of its hot, arid acres had ever been cultivated. It now has a population of more than forty thousand, with churches, banks, ice factories, electric-light plants and fine school buildings, in half a dozen prosperous towns, and its 400,000 acres of cultivated land have produced, in the last six or eight years, crops to the value of at least $50,000,000. The history of this fertile oasis in the Colorado Desert will forever be connected with the name of E. H. Harriman. He did not create the Imperial Valley, nor did he develop it; but he saved it from ruinous devastation at a time when the agency that had created it threatened capriciously to destroy it, and when there was no other power in the world that could give it protection.

—George Kennan, The Salton Sea *(1917)*

Amid his trials of 1906, Harriman found to his dismay that the list of foes arrayed against him included nature itself, which unleashed its wrath in the form of two major catastrophes. Although the last thing Harriman needed was more fights, these offered a refreshing difference. They were clean and elemental, pitting force against force with the stakes clear and the outcome uncluttered by human conniving. Or so Harriman thought when he took up the challenges.

Information was vital to the running of a far-flung empire. To get it reliably and privately, Harriman had in 1901 leased a private wire from Western Union between New York and Chicago, then built an extension from Chicago to Omaha. By using the Union Pacific's wires west of Omaha, Harriman had a communication link that enabled him to talk to people in the West by telegraph as a later generation would by telephone. He would fire messages at his secretary, who tapped them out on the key and then read him the response when it came.[1]

Sometimes nature thwarted this system. In November 1903, just as Harriman was preparing to leave for the ceremonies opening the Lucin cutoff, a monster storm knocked out telephone, telegraph, and rail service, isolating Harriman at Arden for more than a week. A secretary named W. V. Hill managed to get a brief message to him by a circuitous route and was told in reply to get to Arden the best way he could. Dutifully Hill started out, trudging through the rain on foot along the railroad track. As he neared Arden, a small figure in rubber boots came striding down the track toward him. It was Harriman, who had come to meet his man and make sure he was all right after so soggy a journey. This was Hill's first glimpse at the human side of Harriman. In the office, Harriman had a way of keeping his staff constantly on edge awaiting his call that rang out like a rifle shot.[2]

When they were finally free to leave Arden, Harriman asked Hill if he had ever been out west. The young man shook his head. "I'm going in a few days," Harriman said, "and I want you to come along." In this abrupt way Hill, who was not yet a stenographer, found himself in charge of Harriman's deluge of correspondence, interviews, and appointments on a trip lasting several weeks. This trial by fire prepared Hill for many such trips, including one that arose unexpectedly on the morning of April 18, 1906, when a series of violent tremors shook the Pacific coast and engulfed San Francisco in a wall of fire.

Hill got word of the disaster that same morning and rushed to Harriman's residence in New York with the news. Harriman went at once to his office and ordered no expense spared in restoring communications with San Francisco. A line was patched through to Oakland Pier, which had escaped damage. For much of the day Harriman digested reports from his men on the scene and sent out a steady stream of orders. Southern Pacific trains were to carry survivors out of and relief supplies into the city at no charge and cooperate in every way with civic and military officials.[3]

No one could match Harriman in his ability to direct a complex operation far from the scene, but that was not good enough for him. He told Hill to get ready to leave the next morning for San Francisco. Civic leaders had rebounded well from the shock, and the army was there in force. Hundreds of people were already toiling furiously to contain the damage and organize the relief effort, yet Harriman felt obliged to join them. The Southern Pacific controlled most of the city's transportation arteries and was vital to the relief work. Harriman wanted to make sure the work got done the right way—his way—and he wanted to meet the challenge directly.

For three days his special train rumbled across the continent, scooping up hundreds of telegrams at every stop. Harriman exhorted his officials to keep supply trains moving at all costs and to make all company facilities available to local authorities. Early on the morning of April 22 his train rolled into Oakland and parked on the outer edge of the yard, where his car became command headquarters. The devastation had spared Oakland and most of the waterfront area. Harriman's order to general manager E. E. Calvin had been a laconic "Do all you can," and he was gratified to learn how much had already been done. Calvin had sent agents to buy carloads of food in nearby towns and run them into San Francisco for army troops to distribute. Company ferries carried hundreds of refugees to Oakland at no charge and returned with tons of supplies. Company riverboats also brought in supplies.[4]

Since the Ferry Building had escaped damage, Calvin threw open its gates for use as a relief center. The railroad opened information bureaus throughout the city and evacuated thousands of people at no charge. With connecting roads also providing free tickets to whatever destination the riders chose, more than two thousand cars filled with refugees left San Francisco in the two days after the quake. The staff of the company hospital worked to exhaustion tending victims of the quake and twice had to flee when flames overtook first the hospital and then the car barns used as a temporary site. They finally settled their patients on an athletic field near the yards in San Mateo.[5]

Shortly after his arrival, Harriman met with a committee of state, local, and business leaders formed to deal with the crisis. He listened to their plans for rehabilitation, then fired off a stream of suggestions to get the work started. After all of them were adopted, the Southern Pacific men secured an office building for themselves and set to work rebuilding it. For nearly two weeks Harriman stayed at the pier, orchestrating the flow of supplies, firing telegrams in all directions, issuing studiously upbeat statements to the press, stamping the crisis with his unique blend of energy, efficiency, and optimism.[6]

No other business figure rushed to the scene; for once, Harriman had center stage to himself. Every report from him stressed two themes: the marvelous spirit of everyone on the scene and the determination to rebuild. "The rich and the poor have to be cared for alike," he noted in one telegram home, "and it is wonderful how courageous and hopeful they all are. It is the kind of spirit upon which can be depended the successful return of upbuilding and prosperity." The earthquake was history; all eyes must turn to restoring the glory that was San Francisco. His positive attitude boosted everyone's spirits, and it was not confined to words. The barrage of telegrams from his car included appeals, public and private, for funds to help this work as well as the victims. Harriman put $200,000 from his own roads into this kitty.[7]

Even to his critics Harriman emerged in this crisis as a symbol of conquering adversity through sheer will. In one stroke he had done more to clean the tarnished image of the Southern Pacific in California than had been managed in three decades. His response, declared one editor, put Harriman "before the people of the Pacific coast in an entirely new and entirely favorable light." Another hailed the "Harriman monopoly" for proving itself "in the hour of need the strongest and most faithful friend that the city of San Francisco could have had."[8]

Harriman was surely aware of the public relations coup he had scored, but it was strictly a fringe benefit. He had not planned the trip west or calculated its effect; he had simply reacted to a crisis and gone instinctively to the scene. The workload had been staggering—thousands of telegrams to handle as well as meetings, inspection tours, reports, interviews, and decisions large and small. One day he was standing with Calvin on the deck of a ferryboat when a stranger approached Calvin with a hard-luck story about his wife having died from the shock. The man had no money, knew no one in the city, and desperately needed transportation back east for himself and his wife's remains. Without hesitation Calvin wrote out an order for free travel.

"How do you know the man's story was true?" Harriman demanded after the man had left. Calvin admitted that he didn't, but he thought it was better to take a chance than run the risk of denying help to someone in need. Harriman nodded. "It is well that you reached that conclusion," he said, "because if you had not done so, I would have taken the case out of your hands and given him the money myself."[9]

When the pace finally slowed, Harriman turned wearily to Hill and quipped, "We have been a little busy." The secretary replied hesitantly that there were still hundreds of telegrams that Harriman had not yet seen. Harriman lugged the bundles to his bed, where he fell asleep reading them. On the trip home he asked first for a slow run so he could rest, then changed his mind and ordered full speed ahead. When his special train paused at Green River, Wyoming, he sent for the engineer and fireman. They trudged back to his private car slathered in coal dust, expecting to be reprimanded for something. Instead Harriman shook their hands, thanked them for running through the rugged canyons without disturbing his sleep, and gave them a week off with full pay.[10]

Harriman was in an expansive mood, tired but pleased with himself. The trip home turned into another record run, landing him back in New York in just under three days. The papers loved it, and a larger than usual gaggle of reporters was waiting for him at Grand Central Station. After greeting his family, Harriman joked with the reporters, then planted himself against a wall to field their questions. He wanted to talk about San Francisco, not the record run, and he deluged them with facts, figures, and opinions on the city. Later he even put together a short article on the subject.[11]

Ironically, Harriman's response to the disaster was about the only thing that earned him public praise during 1906, and its benefits were quickly subsumed by the parade of negative publicity that summer and fall. Even his response to the quake had unfortunate repercussions. In his tributes to those on the scene, Harriman had lavished praise on Mayor Eugene E. Schmitz, who was widely considered corrupt and unscrupulous. A few months later Schmitz and an ally were indicted on charges of bribery and extortion, which tainted Harriman's own falling star. The usually voluble Theodore Roosevelt said not a word of praise for Harriman's work in the earthquake crisis, but he was quick to note his role in another catastrophe.[12]

In his year of discontent, when so much else was going wrong, Harriman could not have predicted that an earthquake would compound his miseries. Neither could he have guessed that a runaway river in the West would complicate his difficulties with Roosevelt. Like most of the controversies that plagued Harriman, this one began somewhere else with someone else and somehow managed to find him.

Today the Imperial Valley of southern California is a garden of breathtaking beauty and fertility from which flows a large portion of the nation's fruits and vegetables. In 1900, however, it was a barren alluvial plain without a single inhabitant—most of it lying below sea level, its parched surface swept by howling sandstorms and scorched by blazing sunlight that sent temperatures well past a hundred degrees. To the northwest lay a huge basin known as the Salton Sink, once the home of an ancient sea the size of Great Salt Lake.[13]

A hundred miles long, thirty-five miles wide, and a thousand feet deep at its lowest point, the sink had been dry for centuries. A salt company working its bed provided the region's only industry. The Southern Pacific's tracks passed alongside the sink, taking full advantage of the land's low profile. Both the sink and the valley owed their origins to the volatile Colorado River, which carved a jittery route between California and Arizona. Long ago the river had flowed into a Gulf of California that extended a hundred miles farther north, but its fast-moving current deposited so much silt that a dam formed, cutting the gulf in half and creating the Salton Sea. Over the centuries the river emptied into the lower gulf until the sediment built up high enough to divert it back to the Salton; then, after following this route for years, it reversed course again and returned to the gulf.

The plain created by this process was a natural hothouse with ideal soil and sunlight for growing almost anything if a source of water could be found. As early as 1853 a geologist named William P. Blake, who was the first to examine the sink closely, declared boldly that the plain if irrigated would "yield crops of almost any kind." The obvious source was the Colorado River, which was dangerous to tamper with because of its fast currents and unpredictability at flooding times. Nevertheless, in 1900 the California Development Company (CDC) started work on an irrigation channel and created a Mexican subsidiary to extend the work below the border.[14]

In May 1901 the company completed its first cut into the river just opposite Yuma. To skirt a series of sand hills between the river and the valley, a canal was dug in Mexico toward one of the dried riverbeds that once carried water to the sink. On this riverbed water flowed northward into the valley. The promoters

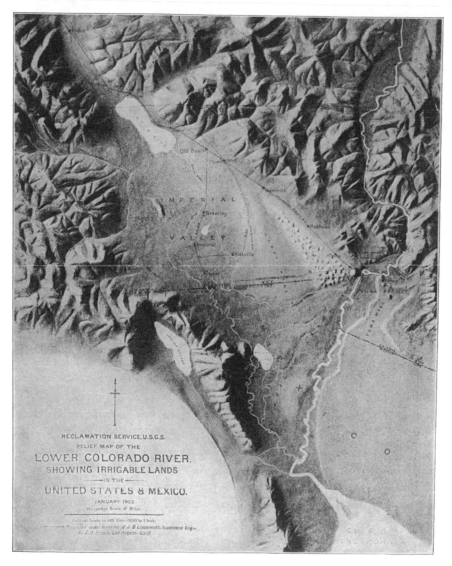

Nature's battleground: This map shows the Imperial Valley, the Colorado River, and the Salton Sink that was soon to become a sea. The island in the river can be seen right center, just above the Yuma Project. (Smithsonian Institution Report, 1907)

sold water rights and organized a land company to lure settlers. They succeeded beyond their wildest dreams; settlers arrived so rapidly that by 1905 the Imperial Valley boasted ten thousand inhabitants. A network of irrigation ditches spread across the plain, 120,000 acres of land went under cultivation, towns sprang up, and the Southern Pacific laid a branch line into the valley.

Prosperity meant a growing demand for water. Giddy with the ease of their success, the promoters were happy to oblige. Their engineering costs had been remarkably low, and they saw no reason to increase them. In their euphoria they ignored the fragility of the resource on which all life in the Imperial Valley depended. By one estimate, a single day's water supply for the valley carried enough silt to form a levee twenty feet high, twenty feet wide, and a mile long. While the demand for water soared, the supply declined as silt clogged the canal and ditches. Yet the company did nothing to dredge or sluice or create settling basins for the canal.

By 1904 the main canal had become so clogged that it could no longer meet the valley's needs. When some crops failed for lack of water, disgruntled farmers filed damage claims. Once the summer flood level dropped, the promoters faced a crisis. The dredging tools at their disposal could not possibly clear the clogged four-mile section of the main canal in time to provide an adequate water supply for the coming season. Their only hope was to open a new heading from the river to a point on the canal beyond the silted section.

Opening a new cut involved the risk of winter flooding, but records kept at Yuma showed that the river had flooded only three times in the past twenty-seven winters. Late in September a cut was made about four miles south of the original heading at a point where the river divided around an island. From this spot the engineers could reach the main canal by dredging only a quarter-mile through easy material. The new opening looked to be the perfect shortcut; it turned out to be the gateway to disaster.

The company did not install a head gate. It did not yet have formal permission from the Mexican government (the cut was on Mexican soil), and it wanted to keep the cut open until summer to maximize scouring action. But the river had other ideas. By an unhappy coincidence it chose that season to launch one of its periodic reversals of pattern. Two February floodings served notice of this intent but caused no damage. An engineer estimated that the heading could have been closed then for $5,000. In March the company protected the cut with a dam of piles, brush, and sandbags only to have a third flood sweep it away. "This was sufficient notice to us," wrote the company engineer with masterful understatement, "that we were up against a very unusual season."[15]

Hurriedly the company threw up another dam; still another flood carried it away. Normally the Colorado began its rise in the spring, peaked in July, and subsided in August. This year the waters began rising in the winter and kept rising. The series of floods sent water surging over the banks of the canal toward its ancient repository, the Salton Sink. If this flow continued, the old, long-dry riverbeds would spring to life, the sink would fill, and the Colorado might shift from its present to its ancient bed.

By the spring of 1905, the promoters saw bankruptcy or worse staring them in the face. Lacking the funds and equipment to contain the river, they approached the largest corporation in the valley, the Southern Pacific. A skeptical Julius Kruttschnitt heard their plea for a loan and sent them packing. Desperate for money, they went directly to Harriman, who had no personal interest in the valley and learned of its situation for the first time in this interview. Nor was he yet aware how serious a danger the river posed. The promoters assured him that the heading could be closed for $20,000 at most; the rest of the $200,000 they sought would go to pay off old debts and expand the irrigation system.[16]

Harriman could not help but be impressed at the bold idea of transforming a desert into a garden. He was familiar with irrigation projects elsewhere along his lines and quick to grasp the potential business Imperial Valley might generate for the Southern Pacific. But he also liked to control anything he went into, and he disliked going into ventures with men he did not know. In his usual fashion, he sent a trusted official to investigate the matter.

Something in the official's report struck a responsive chord in Harriman. He decided to grant the loan even though Kruttschnitt and others advised strongly against it, but on terms that gave him working control. The Southern Pacific held 51 percent of CDC's stock as collateral and got the right to name the president and three directors. Shortly after signing the papers on June 20, 1905, Harriman asked Epes Randolph to take the presidency of CDC. A gifted civil engineer, Randolph had already served Harriman well as the head of Southern Pacific's Arizona and Mexican lines.

Events soon made Harriman wish that he had not been so adamant about controlling the company. At the time, however, the project was for him a small-change operation. No one yet grasped how vulnerable the valley was to the whims of the river. It was, observed an engineer later, "a Holland—500,000 acres of an American Holland." Late in June an engineer from the federal Reclamation Service examined the cut and described the situation as "not serious, but sufficiently alarming to require some attention." A few weeks later Randolph went down to inspect the heading for the first time and was appalled by what he found.[17]

Already the river had widened the new cut from forty to one hundred feet and deepened it from eight to twenty feet, and its current was scouring furiously. The flow of water through the cut had reached an estimated eight thousand cubic feet per second and was increasing by quantum leaps. Randolph realized that the river was overwhelming the gap and shifting its course. If that process continued, the Imperial Valley would be wiped out. The fall of the Colorado River from the break to the gulf was only a hundred feet compared to four hundred feet from the break to the bottom of the valley. Since the distance was about the same either way, the river, if it broke through, would follow the steeper decline with a velocity that would make it almost impossible to contain.[18]

And it was gathering force fast. Although the river was falling, the amount of water pouring through the cut was rising. Already the overflow accumulating in the Salton Sink had flooded out the saltworks there; before long it would threaten the Southern Pacific tracks. Randolph hurried to tell Harriman that the situation was far worse than he had been told. Not only the Southern Pacific tracks but the valley itself was in jeopardy. The entire $200,000 would not touch the job; no one could predict how much was needed, but the tab might run as high as $750,000. The work, Randolph added gravely, would be "a very difficult undertaking."[19]

Harriman chewed on this information, then asked, "Are you certain you can put that river back into the old channel?"

"It can be done," Randolph assured him.

"Go ahead and do it."

Randolph and his engineers tried first to divert the river around the eastern side of the island by erecting a barrier on the side nearest the cut. When the opening continued to widen, he got Harriman's consent to try a more elaborate barrier dam across the west fork. Randolph started work in September and had not quite completed the dam by November. There seemed no reason to hurry; the river was at low ebb and flood season was months away. Yet he barely had time to admire the new barrier before disaster struck.[20]

The only thing more unpredictable than the Colorado River was the Gila River, which drained into the Colorado at Yuma and was notorious for sudden, violent floods. On the last two days of November the Gila sent a raging wall of water clogged with driftwood roaring down on Yuma. Rising at the rate of a foot an hour, this torrent overflowed the island and carried much of it away, ripped the new barrier dam to shreds, and poured into the heading with a fury that widened the breach to six hundred feet. Through it the river flowed with mounting force, spreading over the plain in search of old riverbeds on its way to Salton Sink.

Randolph's worst fears had come true. The canal and ancient bed had become the river, carrying its waters to the sink, which was fast becoming a sea again. If the heading could not be closed before next spring's flood season, the Colorado might keep its new course. The Imperial Valley would then become a freshwater lake, and the Southern Pacific would find sixty miles of its track under water. Two threats faced the residents of the valley: the surging waters might submerge their land, or they might destroy the system of irrigation ditches on which all life in the valley depended. They might drown or die of thirst.

The river could not be shut out entirely; it had to be contained and controlled. After a testy debate among the engineers over what to do, Randolph decided to pursue two plans at once. A concrete head gate set in rock would be installed at a point where the river could be turned into a newly dredged channel as a permanent source of water for the valley. In addition, a wooden head gate would be put just above the breach to divert the river while a permanent dam was constructed. Through the winter Randolph pushed both projects only to find himself in a losing race. The concrete gate was not finished until late June 1906; the wooden gate was not ready until mid-April despite round-the-clock efforts.

Throughout 1906 the Colorado remained at near record levels, discharging that year more than twice its usual annual flow. The concrete gate could not be made ready in time, and the wooden one was overwhelmed by the river. When Harriman rushed to San Francisco in April to help fight the earthquake, Randolph went to meet him with more bad news. All efforts to force the Colorado back into its bed had failed, and the river was pouring unchecked into the valley. A giant dredge under construction in San Francisco and urgently needed in the valley had been delayed by the earthquake. The funds loaned to CDC had been used up. Randolph shrugged helplessly and asked what Harriman wanted him to do.

Standing amid the debris of one disaster, pondering the momentum gathering around another one, Harriman did not hesitate. The earthquake had already disrupted business on the Southern Pacific and tied up its lines. There was no way of knowing what effect the runaway river would have or how much it would ultimately cost. Nor was there a compelling reason why he should get deeper into it other than his love of a challenge and his instinct for doing what should be done when adversity struck. He had shown that instinct by hurrying to San Francisco, and he revealed it again by giving Randolph another $250,000 to spend on harnessing the river.

While Harriman battled the earthquake, the feisty Randolph returned to the valley with renewed determination. When the summer flood crested late in June, the river poured through a cut now half a mile wide at a rate of seventy-five thousand cubic feet per second. Its restless waters spread across a ten-mile area on their way to the Salton Sea, which had grown to an area of four hundred square miles and was rising seven inches every day. Five times that summer the Southern Pacific moved its track to higher ground. The saltworks lay beneath sixty feet of water, two towns had been damaged, and thousands of acres of crops were flooded or badly eroded. Another thirty thousand acres lay parched because their irrigation ditches had been swept away.

In the water's relentless path the soft, powdery delta soil crumbled into new beds and rapids, which soon turned into cascades and then falls, some of them eighty feet wide and a thousand feet high. One engineer estimated that in nine months the surging river dumped into the Salton Sea an amount of silt four times the entire yardage of the Panama Canal. "The water simply tore things in

Runaway river: One of the channels cut by the Colorado River as its runaway waters headed toward the Salton Sink. Note the lone figure standing above the cut on the right. (Smithsonian Institution Report, 1907)

the valley to pieces," he exclaimed. "It was perhaps the most extensive and remarkable geological action of recent geological times."[21]

Randolph found himself staring at a crisis that had no precedents. Other rivers had overflowed their banks and then receded; no one had ever tried to force a runaway river back into its bed. Forty or fifty top engineers visited the site and could agree only on what would not work. Randolph decided to go with his gut feeling, which was to erect a rock dam. An ordinary barrier dam could not withstand the enormous pressure of the water pouring through the gap, so Randolph tried a deceptively simple notion: keep piling rocks into the breach until more remained than were washed away and the flow gradually diminished. Once the gap was closed, a permanent system of dams and levees could be built.

Nearly all the engineers dismissed Randolph's plan as impractical, yet Harriman supported it at once. This was an extraordinary commitment given the high stakes and the doubts of so many distinguished engineers, but Randolph was his man and he had confidence in him. "I do not believe," Randolph marveled later, "that any man whom I have ever known, except Mr. Harriman, would have undertaken it."[22]

Feeling the full weight of the responsibility thrust on him, Randolph spared no effort in mounting his campaign. The Southern Pacific ran a spur line to the site and furnished all the work trains needed. Randolph borrowed three hundred of the giant side-dump cars or "battleships" used on the Lucin project. The

Lost towns: A view from temporary dikes of the submerged towns of Calexico and Mexicali in the Imperial Valley. (Smithsonian Institution Report, 1907)

CDC deployed its fleet of three light steamers and several barges. To get the vast amount of rock needed, Randolph tapped every quarry within four hundred miles and opened a new one. Clay came from a deposit just north of the Mexican border and gravel from the Southern Pacific's huge pit forty miles west of the opening. Massive quantities of timber and steel cable poured in from Los Angeles, along with pile drivers, steam shovels, and other heavy equipment. Randolph recruited laborers wherever he could find them—Indians from six different tribes in the region, Mexicans, and drifters.

On August 6 they went to work in earnest. The plan was to dam the breach enough to shunt the water to the bypass where the wooden gate had been installed and then close the heading permanently. It took two shifts of men working around the clock twenty days to fashion a brush mattress as a base for the dam. Once this was put in place, the crews threw a railway trestle across the gap. On September 14 the first battleships rumbled across the trestle to dump loads of rock on the mattress. Gradually the flow shifted to the bypass, but with it came masses of driftwood banging against the gate. On October 11 the gate broke off and floated away. Behind it came the river, turning the bypass into the main channel and leaving the new dam standing dry.

Harriman responded to the bad news with a shrug and sent Randolph back to work. The dam had acquitted itself well, convincing Randolph that he was on the right track. The trestle was extended across the bypass, and three thousand loads of rock were dumped into the bypass until both openings were dammed and connected by huge levees to form a barrier half a mile long. Gobs of clay and gravel were pumped into the openings to seal the dams. On November 4 the river slid grudgingly back into its old bed.

Everyone breathed a sigh of relief and turned to the task of dismantling the works they had built. Then, on December 7, the fickle Gila River sent another of its killer floods boiling into the Colorado. The new dams held firm, but one of the earthen levees south of them developed a leak. Originally built by CDC, the levees had been reinforced but not rebuilt. In short order the river gnawed a hole in the levee; three days later it was pouring through a thousand-foot-wide gap on its way to the Salton Sea. A disheartened Randolph, watching all his work come undone, realized that it was not enough to dam the river. Full protection required a twenty-mile system of levees along the bank as well.

The bad news brought by Randolph this time put Harriman in a dilemma. He had already spent $1.5 million trying to contain the river, and Randolph estimated it would take at least that much more. The twenty miles of levees would be expensive because they required excavations as deep as ten feet to anchor them on material that could not be eroded away again. The total traffic from the valley did not come close to the cost, let alone the profits. Harriman could move the road's tracks again for only $60,000, but another, more sensitive issue nagged at him.[23]

The responsibility for this mess clearly belonged to the CDC, which had opened the original heading, but this fact might easily get lost in a controversy over who was to blame. The Southern Pacific had put itself in the position of being morally and legally responsible for what the CDC had done, bearing out yet again the truism that no good deed goes unpunished. The full implications of this dawned on Harriman when Randolph suggested that he had done all any private citizen could be expected to do in fighting the river. The time had come to enlist government aid in the fight rather than drain the railroad's treasury. In that dreary December of 1906 the last thing Harriman wanted to do was ask Theodore Roosevelt for help. But Randolph was right: the more Southern Pacific assumed the burden on its own, the more liable it became for whatever went wrong.[24]

Reluctantly Harriman on December 13 sent Roosevelt a lengthy telegram outlining the situation. "In view of the above," he concluded, "it does not seem fair that we should be called to do more than join in to help the settlers." Two days later he got exactly the reply he expected from Roosevelt. "I assume you are planning to continue work immediately on closing break in Colorado River," the president said blandly. "I should be fully informed as to how far you intend to proceed in the matter."[25]

Harriman glowered at the reply, his eyes red with fatigue and his body clenched in pain from hemorrhoids that required surgery again. To the growing list of grievances between himself and Roosevelt had been added a runaway river, a catastrophe that could easily be blamed on him by one so practiced at the art as the president. Harriman had no choice now but to play the controversy through, and to his dejected spirit it was difficult to know which posed the gravest threat: the river or the president.

27 Fighting for Survival

In the short time of Harriman's rise he has succeeded in making himself the most cordially disliked man, personally, in the whole financial community. Men who are associated with him in great enterprises make no bones of commenting on it, probably because no one has ever heard that Harriman cared whether people liked him or not. His brusqueness of manner, inversely proportional to his physical size, has gone along with an absolute intolerance of dissenting opinion and a sheer inability to see that any one else cannot grasp a point as quickly as he does, to make a board meeting with Harriman at the table something to be looked upon in the same light as a visit to the dentist. Having jumped to his conclusion by performing in a minute the mental processes that might require a day in average men, he considers it time wasted to sit around while other slower mortals are pondering the things out, and the marvellous clearness of perception and accuracy of his thinking have made his conclusions right so often that the possibility of being mistaken does not enter his mind.

—New York Times, *May 13, 1906*

All the disparate forces bearing down on Harriman in this worst year of his life came together in December 1906 like strands of a tapestry woven by a malevolent fate. Against this inescapable weave Harriman fought with dwindling strength but undiminished resolution. To his friends he made no complaint regardless of how much pain and frustration he endured, but those near him saw the agony in his eyes and the drawn, pinched features. The fight was taking its toll; for the first time Harriman began to look like an old man.

The month opened on a gloomily prophetic note with the funeral of Samuel Spencer, the brilliant president of Morgan's Southern Railway, who had died in a shocking accident when one of his passenger trains smashed into the rear of another. Harriman had known Spencer for years and thought highly of him. On a crisp December afternoon he slipped unobtrusively into St. John's Episcopal Church, one of the last to arrive, and brooded through the service, his mind flashing from the image of an old friend departed to the grisly accident that killed him. It was the kind of carelessness Harriman had fought against for years, and it was a harbinger of the year to come, the bloodiest in railroad history.[1]

The railroads got a bad name that winter as overtaxed crews and equipment tried to move a record traffic under trying conditions. Shortly after Spencer's death, another collision killed more than forty people in Maryland; an investigation showed the engineer who caused the crash had been on duty for thirty-three hours and had slept for only eight out of the past fifty-seven hours. Even the proud Union Pacific was not immune to this rash of tragedies. Two of its crack passenger trains collided in Nebraska and killed three passengers, one of them a well-known actor. A few days later the Los Angeles Limited caught fire in a bizarre accident that claimed one life.[2]

Harriman raged against these tragedies but could not stop them. Public resentment against the carriers was rising and transferred easily to the men who ran them, whose arrogance of power and control of vast resources seemingly made them indifferent to the needs and safety of those who patronized the railroads. This assumption led easily to the belief that only the federal government could curb their excesses and abuses. Politicians were not alone in hopping on this bandwagon. On December 7 a federal grand jury in Utah indicted some subsidiary companies owned by the Harriman and Gould systems for alleged fraud in their control of coal lands. Although the charges did not involve Harriman directly, they splashed his name across the headlines and fed the growing image of him as a corporate predator.[3]

The cloud of suspicion gathering about Harriman tainted even his triumphs. Everyone conceded his genius as a railroad man, but few realized how much the Union Pacific's success owed to his masterful handling of finances. To the public he remained a pawn of the powerful money interests behind him: Schiff, Stillman, William Rockefeller, Rogers, and the dark empire of Standard Oil. In fact, Harriman had formulated the policies that enriched the Union Pacific with help from his friends but not as their pawn. Two policies in particular had proved spectacularly successful: the convertible bonds of 1901 and the investment in Northern Securities.

The $100 million in bonds Harriman had issued in 1901 to buy Southern Pacific and Northern Pacific stock paid 4 percent and could be converted into stock any time before May 1906. No one expected many shares to be converted because the stock paid only a 4 percent dividend, but the spectacular growth of earnings over the next two years made higher dividends inevitable. The result was a stampede by bondholders to convert before the dividend rose; by the summer of 1906 nearly all the bonds had been converted to stock. In effect, Harriman had reduced the fixed debt by $100 million and released the collateral on the bonds for other use. This saved $4 million a year in interest and put $83 million of the company's unpledged bonds into its treasury for other use.[4]

Through these and other steps, Harriman revamped the asset base of the Union Pacific into a tower of strength. Yet this major achievement was overshadowed by another spectacular move. By 1906 the prices of the Great Northern and Northern Pacific shares received in the dismantling of Northern Securities had soared to record levels. Harriman decided the time had come to sell them off and put the money to other use. Altogether the Union Pacific had invested $89 million in Northern Securities; the sales eventually brought back $144 million, a profit of 62 percent from what had been universally hailed as a ringing defeat for Harriman. Any financial wizard could make success pay handsomely, but none matched Harriman's profits from a losing battle. While this coup did much to enhance the Harriman legend, it attracted less attention than what Harriman did with the proceeds.

The sale of these stocks in 1906 alone put nearly $100 million into the company treasury. Harriman invested this money in the stock of other railroads friendly to the Union Pacific. This brought the Union Pacific income from dividends, created a closer harmony of interest among the roads, and gave Harriman leverage in their management. By the end of 1906 he had acquired large blocks of Atchison, Baltimore & Ohio, Illinois Central, Milwaukee, New York Central, Northwestern, and Railroad Securities Company stock.[5]

From a purely financial point of view the moves were bold and brilliant strokes. The investments paid the Union Pacific an income of nearly $16 million by 1909. In 1906 the road earned more from this outside income than its entire gross receipts had been for the year before Harriman took control. No carrier in America, not even the Pennsylvania, boasted so diversified a portfolio. Good financial policy, however, proved to be political dynamite; the purchases drew immediate cries of alarm. One analyst depicted the Union Pacific as a railroad, a bank, and a holding company. Why a bank? By the end of 1906 the company had outstanding nearly $35 million in demand loans, a figure exceeded only by six or seven of the largest banks in New York. It also had large cash reserves even after making the stock purchases.[6]

To public eyes this hydra-headed monster took on a sinister aura as the Standard Oil of railroads, its tentacles of power and influence coiling far and deep into the economy under Harriman's direction. This image emerged on the eve of the ICC investigation into the Harriman roads. It built on the shocking (and distorted) revelations that erupted out of the insurance investigation, the Fish imbroglio, and the other controversies that implanted Harriman in the headlines.

The ICC investigation culminated this invention of a new public enemy. As Harriman well knew, observers were smacking their lips in anticipation over the disclosures the inquiry would elicit. Like the Armstrong sessions, which had vaulted Charles Evans Hughes into the governor's office in New York, it was going to be a messy affair with reporters gleefully sensationalizing every nugget of information dropped in their path. Harriman also had the problem of a runaway river that had yet to hit the New York dailies but would quickly be linked to his name when it did. Then there was the pain, the constant drain on his energy that grew steadily worse, like the gap in the levee through which the Colorado had again poured its waters in recent days.

While the papers fashioned their portrait of him as an invincible titan, the gaunt Harriman felt more like a fugitive being pushed into a corner by his gathering enemies. Whatever his feelings about Roosevelt's behavior, he could not afford a prolonged vendetta with so powerful a foe. He and Roosevelt were among the dignitaries invited to the annual Gridiron dinner on December 8. Harriman summoned Maxwell Evarts and asked if he remembered the earlier talk with James Sherman. Evarts said that he recalled it perfectly. Harriman then asked if he would be willing to see Roosevelt. Evarts said yes. "Well, we are going to Washington to the Gridiron dinner," Harriman told him.[7]

The dinner was a glittering affair at the New Willard Hotel, where, in a banquet room filled with cigar smoke and bonhomie, enemies put aside their feuds for an evening of fun. Roosevelt roared his approval at a skit bashing his handling of Panama and Cuba, and Harriman laughed at a "bulletin" announcing that William Howard Taft had resigned as secretary of war to act as peacemaker between Harriman and Stuyvesant Fish, who was also present. Next day Harriman arranged for Evarts to visit the White House. Evarts arrived at five in the afternoon and found Roosevelt polishing up a letter that was his rejoinder in another controversy. "I suppose you know what Harriman wanted you to come to see me about?" he said.[8]

"Yes," replied Evarts. He related his version of the interview between Harriman and Sherman. Roosevelt interrupted to ask what Harriman had said about him. Nothing, Evarts assured him, that could not have been repeated to him or anybody else. What about the remarks Harriman made as to getting anything he wanted by buying it? Roosevelt demanded. "Nothing of that kind was ever talked about," Evarts insisted. "Mr. Sherman must have misunderstood the conversation."

"Why, my conversation with Mr. Sherman would show Harriman to be the most wicked, cynical man in the world," cried Roosevelt. "It was so bad that I had Mr. Sherman repeat it to Root, and then I had Sherman write out the whole conversation in a letter to me. Now, why did Sherman tell me all this?"

Evarts shrugged. A misunderstanding, surely.

"I want party harmony in New York," Roosevelt emphasized, "and . . . I want you to see Sherman and get him to write me that his conversation was all a misunderstanding."

After Evarts agreed to do this, Roosevelt asked his views on the forthcoming investigation. Evarts protested that it had gone public too fast, that there should have been a quiet private inquiry to determine whether a public investigation was warranted. That might be true, Roosevelt conceded, but the matter was in the hands of the ICC, over which he had no power. Roosevelt did not mention that two weeks after penning his letter to Sherman, he had written an ICC commissioner applauding the idea of an inquiry into the Union Pacific–Southern Pacific systems. The idea had been prompted by the commissioner's recent report on coal land abuses and a string of shipper complaints over high rates. "It seems to me," Roosevelt added pointedly, "that these complaints are sufficiently widespread to justify a thoro investigation."[9]

Evarts left the White House convinced that Roosevelt had lied about having a letter from Sherman and had merely written down what Sherman had told him—or what he claimed Sherman had told him. Yet Evarts also thought there was no hurry about asking Sherman to put his version of events on paper. On that point events proved him tragically wrong.[10]

Fate took Harriman and Roosevelt in opposite directions that month. The president was in an expansive mood, having learned the day after seeing Evarts that he had been awarded the Nobel Peace Prize. By contrast, everything went wrong for Harriman. He felt so poorly that he asked Roosevelt to use his influence to delay the investigation for a few weeks. Roosevelt made a gesture in that direction without success. On December 13, the day after receiving Roosevelt's reply to his request, Harriman sent the telegram notifying Roosevelt of the runaway river and asking for federal assistance.[11]

Sending this second plea for help was the last thing Harriman wanted to do, but he had little choice. The president's tough reply did not surprise him. Six days later he tried another lengthy telegram outlining the work to be done and offering to put all his men and facilities at the disposal of the government's Reclamation Service. Roosevelt shot back an even longer reply the next day rejecting the offer. The Reclamation Service could not act without authority from Congress and permission from Mexico, neither of which could be obtained fast enough. "It is incumbent upon you to close break again," admonished Roosevelt. The CDC had caused the crisis and should be responsible for solving it. There was not "the slightest excuse for the California Development Company waiting an hour for the action of the Government. It is its duty to meet the present danger immediately." Later the government would do what it could about compensation.[12]

Harriman read this telegram with clenched teeth. The president had done it to him again. He had taken a public position throwing the blame squarely on the CDC, which deserved it, but also holding Harriman responsible for the CDC as a Southern Pacific subsidiary. It was another magnificently contrived piece of grandstanding. The papers treated it exactly as Harriman feared they would,

praising Roosevelt for his forceful handling of the crisis and for pinning responsibility on the reckless business interests who had caused it; linking Harriman to
the issue as somehow to blame for it with no recognition of what his actual role
had been or what he had already done to keep the river at bay.[13]

The only thing Harriman could do was make the best of a bad situation
because the river would not wait. That same day he sent Roosevelt a long reply
adamantly denying that the Southern Pacific was in any way responsible for the
CDC or the crisis. "However, in view of your message," he added, "I am giving
authority to the Southern Pacific officers in the West to proceed at once with
efforts to repair the break, trusting that the Government . . . will assist us with
the burden." Roosevelt pronounced this decision "very satisfactory."[14]

Most newspapers portrayed Harriman as marching to a tune whistled by the
president, yet it is hard to dispute Epes Randolph's belief that Harriman would
have tackled the challenge even if Roosevelt had explicitly refused any aid. By
then the break in the levee exceeded eleven hundred feet and was forty feet deep
at points. The engineers threw a pair of trestles over the breach despite losing
three sets of pilings to the raging water, and late in January the first dump cars
rolled across to deposit their load of rock.[15]

To push the work, Harriman all but shut down two entire divisions of the
Southern Pacific for three weeks to deliver equipment and supplies to the crews
toiling around the clock. "We handled rock faster than it was ever handled
before," boasted one engineer. Gradually the rising wall of rock turned the river
back until it resumed its old course on February 10. After filling the rock dam
with finer material, the crews began erecting a double row of dikes twelve miles
long behind it. If another break occurred, these would trap the flow long enough
for workers to put up a defense.[16]

But there was no other break. The Imperial Valley had been saved to blossom
into the garden of the West. As a bonus it kept the newly filled Salton Sea, which
did not evaporate as some experts predicted. Roosevelt kept his promise by
seeking compensation for the work from Congress. Harriman asked only for
$1.6 million, the amount spent in the last phase of the work. Congress held
hearings, received a clear picture of events, delayed action for years, then refused
to pay a dime because the work had benefited the railroad. Nor did it bother
thanking Harriman with a resolution.

Settlers in the valley took a more generous view. "We believe," one farmer told
a congressional committee, "that Mr. Harriman felt a very human interest in our
troubles." Besides singing his praise, they offered the Southern Pacific a package
of land and irrigation bonds to help defray the cost. Most of the engineers who
took part in the work agreed that it would never have been done without
Harriman behind it. "Those of us who actually handled the work," murmured
Randolph, "were merely instruments in the hands of the Master Builder."[17]

The Master Builder himself felt a keen sense of pride even if his labor went unrecognized at the time. "The best single thing we did and which gave me most satisfaction was this," he told Otto Kahn. "I used every ounce of driving power I possessed to hustle the job as I have never hustled any job before." Near the end of his life Harriman paid a visit to the Imperial Valley and took a last, lingering look at the levee. On his way back a reporter from the *Los Angeles Examiner* asked, "Mr. Harriman, the Government hasn't paid you that money and your work here does not seem to be duly appreciated. Do you not, under the circumstance, regret having made this large expenditure?"[18]

Harriman turned to the reporter, his tired eyes gleaming with certainty. "No," he said softly. "This Valley was worth saving, wasn't it?"

"Yes," said the reporter.

"Then we have the satisfaction of knowing we have saved it, haven't we?"

As Christmas of 1906 drew near, two distasteful prospects still faced Harriman: a grilling at the hands of the ICC and another operation to relieve him of the pain that wracked him daily. Of necessity the surgery came first, though not before one last sorrow intervened. For Harriman the month closed as it had begun, with the funeral of a friend. This time it was A. J. Cassatt, president of the Pennsylvania Railroad, who had died suddenly of heart disease. Some said he had died of a broken heart from recent revelations of graft in the proud Pennsylvania system.[19]

On the day of Cassatt's funeral in Philadelphia, Harriman was in New York submitting to the knife. It did not go as well this time. The impatient patient was slow to recover, and he chafed against Dr. Lyle's dictum of strict rest. A friend visiting him nearly a month after the operation was alarmed to find him "looking wretchedly and suffering intensely." Harriman did not leave the house until the month's end. When he finally ventured downtown on February 7, reporters flocked to him at once. His manner was relaxed, his mind as sharp as ever, and his humor in fine form. Asked when he was coming downtown again, he teased, "What is the use? I have been away for a month or more. Everything has been going along smoothly and they appear to be able to get along just as well without me as with me. Why should I not stay home altogether?"[20]

The reporters knew Harriman was incapable of staying home unless held prisoner there. Besides, he had a date with the ICC that could not be ducked. Rumor hinted that the commission's target was much broader than coal lands, that it wanted an entry into the whole of Harriman's empire. The order called for an inquiry into "the consolidation and combination of carriers; relation between such carriers and community of interest therein, their rates, facilities and practices." This title gave the commissioners ample room for fishing expeditions.[21]

Everyone understood the order was aimed at Harriman's roads. The basic target was assumed to be the relationship between the Union Pacific and Southern Pacific as well as the investments made by the Union Pacific in other railroads. But the commissioners displayed a keen interest in a wholly unrelated topic: the Alton deal. To neutral eyes this seemed an odd choice. The Alton episode was old business; the road had never been a major player and had no significance in the present relationship of roads. But Harriman knew why the subject was being exhumed: it was the most vulnerable chink in his armor, the one deviation from his usual business practices and therefore the most inviting target.

The hearings opened on January 4, 1907, and produced good copy for two months, vying for headline space with the lurid murder trial of Harry K. Thaw, the slayer of architect Stanford White. The mood on Wall Street was apprehensive. Apart from the Harriman inquiry, there was raging debate over railroad rates at both the state and federal levels, snarling talk of strikes, the government suit against Standard Oil, and other incidents that led even moderate businessmen to suspect the government of harassing corporations. Some lashed out angrily at Roosevelt, who tried vainly to convince business leaders that he was doing them a favor.[22]

The trusts had become a political issue of astonishing virulence, bringing together in improbable alliance the unwashed masses and the overwashed gentility, who viewed the new economic order as a menace not only in its concentration of power but also as a distasteful form of new barbarism. In this war of social and political images Harriman found himself thrust into the role of icon for all the fears and hatreds of those opposed to the new corporate world.

Since Harriman was still recuperating from his operation, the ICC summoned his colleagues and officials to testify before going after the star witness. For seven weeks a parade of prominent rail men and financiers marched before the commissioners to tell their tales in the veiled language elicited by such inquiries. Long before Harriman's appearance it was a foregone conclusion that the government would bring suit to separate the Union Pacific and Southern Pacific roads after the hearings concluded. Even the sympathetic *Railroad Gazette* conceded that the evidence showed that "Mr. Harriman's power in the conduct of railroads of which he is the head is to all intents absolute." The papers wrung every dollop of sensationalism they could from the testimony, thereby whetting appetites for whatever pearls Harriman himself might drop.[23]

On February 25, his fifty-ninth birthday, Harriman strode into the oppressive gloom of the Federal Building and took the stand for the first time. Those who expected fireworks were not disappointed. Despite his recent illness, Harriman was his old feisty, combative self, frank and stubborn by equal turns, trading repartee with the lawyers, giving information freely but dictating the terms on which he gave it, pulling back only when his own counsel insisted that the question poked unduly into his private affairs. At the prompting of his lawyer, Harriman read a long statement explaining his role in the Alton and justifying the syndicate's actions.

After he stepped down, a reporter asked him which birthday he was celebrating. "The fifty-ninth," Harriman shot back. "When I'm sixty, I'll retire." It was a flippant remark, but he came to regret it.[24]

The next day sparks flew in earnest. Harriman was kept on the stand all day, and the strain wore on him. One line of inquiry pursued Harriman's purchase of stocks in other roads during 1906 and arrived at the doorstep of the Illinois Central fight. Before the questioning got far, Harriman insisted on relating the entire story behind the fight to remove Fish from the presidency. Both the ICC and his own counsel tried to restrain him, but he would not be stopped. As with the reading of the Webster letter to Sherman, it spilled out of him like a torrent of rage and frustration dammed up too long and demanding an outlet.[25]

"In view of serious charges you have made in regard to Mr. Fish—," began one commissioner after he had finished.

"I have not made any charges," retorted Harriman. "I have only stated facts. I do not want to be put in the position of making charges." Moments later he noted pointedly, "The funds of the Union Pacific have never been used by any Director for their own personal benefit."

While the commissioners fumbled with papers on their desk and the lawyers fumbled for a new line of questioning, reporters scribbled furiously. Most accounts portrayed it as a bitter personal assault on Fish, who refused to comment on the matter. Frank Vanderlip thought Harriman had acquitted himself well "with the glaring exception of the attack on Mr. Fish which was something he insisted upon." At least it showed Harriman in fighting trim, no longer on the defensive but meeting questions with his old slashing style, yearning to say more than his lawyers wished him to say and restrained only by their insistent pleas, trying at every turn to orchestrate not only his answers but the questions as well.

"Now, wait a minute," he told chief examiner Frank B. Kellogg repeatedly, "let me have my way about this."

"You always have it your way," sighed Kellogg wearily.[26]

Harriman wrapped up his appearance the next morning. As he mounted the stand, he quipped to reporters that he would rather be a newspaperman than a witness and was promptly offered a job. He was detained only briefly, then stepped down and took a seat among the reporters to watch Otto Kahn testify. Afterward he chatted for nearly an hour with the newsmen and seemed so affable that some suspected him of "cultivating pleasant relations." He obliged one photographer by whipping off his silk hat for a picture.[27]

From the crossfire emerged one clear issue that lay near the heart of the trust issue: how much power should any one man be allowed? Ironically, the issue had come to public attention less through the behavior of individuals than through the power amassed by their creations, the giant corporations. Few men had become so closely or conspicuously identified with the performance of his companies as Harriman, who forced people to confront this oldest of questions in its newest guise of the industrial setting, where wealth and power had accumulated on a scale never before witnessed.

It was easy to condemn scoundrels who had accumulated power, but Harriman was the most benevolent of despots. Even his harshest critics conceded that he had wrought miracles of productivity with the railroads under his command. The worst of his ideas had more value than the best of ordinary men, and the ideas kept flowing in endless, surging procession. His response to the earthquake (little was yet known of his work in the Imperial Valley) was only the most recent display of what a good citizen he could be. He was the most ardent of patriots, the most dedicated of servants, who asked only that he be allowed to do things his way without interference.

There was the rub. He asked for the one thing that could not be granted. Fearing nothing more than the concentration of power in individual hands, the public had just begun to grasp the distinction between corporations and the men who dominated them. The age of titans had entered its twilight when Harriman appeared, and to most observers he was literally too much of a good thing. "No one man should have so great power to speculate with the resources of a great and rich system of railroads," declared the *Railroad Gazette*. "It is wrong economically and morally, if not legally." Harriman was, added the genteel *Nation*, the "feudal lord of our ancien regime, crushing the individual by an irresistible weight."[28]

While the hearings droned on and pundits pondered this paradox, Harriman took his family off to Virginia for a few days' vacation. On the way home he paused in Washington to show Roland the sights, including the White House. Roosevelt received them politely if briefly and took Roland by the hand for a whirlwind tour through his store of bearskin rugs, heads, and other trophies. That night Harriman hosted a dinner for some of his comrades from the Alaska expedition.[29]

To reporters Harriman dismissed the visit as purely social. The papers rang with rumors that Roosevelt planned to chastise the Harriman system as a "horrible example" of the evils of overcapitalization by bringing suit against it and that the icc might extend its inquiry to the Northern Pacific panic. Pressed for a response, Harriman muttered ruefully, "I've been a pack-horse all my life, and if I am to be required to pack this new burden, I will be able to do it."[30]

But he was plainly tired of packing both burdens. Some accommodation had to be reached with Roosevelt and the icc. He had not ambled into Washington just to see the sights but had summoned Maxwell Evarts to meet him there. On

Monday, March 4, Harriman and Evarts paid a surprise call on the ICC. The commissioners were assembled in chairman Martin A. Knapp's office when Harriman and Evarts walked in. One of them broke an awkward silence by asking Harriman what was the most important engineering feat he had undertaken. Harriman launched enthusiastically into a description of the Colorado River fight, which had just reached its climax. Everyone settled into a pleasant conversation in which Harriman made a strong impression on the commissioners.[31]

Encouraged by this visit, Harriman asked Evarts to see Roosevelt again and arrange a meeting between them. Evarts telephoned for an appointment and went over to the White House on Wednesday. "Here comes Harriman's ambassador," Roosevelt bawled out as he liked to do when he spotted Evarts. They went into Roosevelt's office, where Evarts asked him to sit down with Harriman and discuss the railroad situation.[32]

"How can I do it?" Roosevelt cried, throwing up his arms. "What will the newspapers say?"

What could the newspapers do about it, countered Evarts. The burning issue of the day was railroad regulation. Roosevelt had crucial decisions to make on the carriers, and who could better advise him than Harriman? "No man has the knowledge of this subject that he has," Evarts reminded him, "and no man knows better what ought to be done."

"Well, you don't know what Morgan and some of these other people say about Harriman," Roosevelt demurred.

"Mr. President," replied Evarts, "I know one thing: you never heard Harriman say one word about Morgan or any of the rest of them." Besides, Morgan was a banker, not a railroad man. If the president wanted information on the railroads, why was he reluctant to see the man who knew more about the subject than anyone else?

Roosevelt nodded assent and promised to discuss the matter with his cabinet. Evarts left with the belief that the wound was on its way to healing. Next day Roosevelt wrote Evarts that he would be glad to see Harriman, but as usual there was a hook. "The visit is evidently expected by the outside world," Roosevelt added, "as numerous newspaper correspondents have been inquiring about it." He asked that when the meeting took place, nothing said in it be released without his prior approval.[33]

The overtures to Roosevelt and the ICC marked a dramatic change of front by Harriman. He finally accepted that a new climate of opinion had emerged and that his imperious ways had become a serious liability. If he could not alter his personality, he could at least temper its roughest edges by invoking in word and deed the theme he had sounded so emphatically at the exposition in 1904: the necessity for cooperation. To that end he announced a stunning reversal of past

Harriman's ambassador: Maxwell Evarts, who tried in vain to mediate the quarrel between Harriman and Theodore Roosevelt. (Union Pacific Museum Collection)

policy: hereafter he would make himself more accessible to reporters and speak out on the issues.

"Harriman ends policy of silence," blared the *New York Times* after receiving the announcement on March 6, the same day Evarts saw Roosevelt. "It has never been my idea to concern myself much about the relations of the public to the railroads," Harriman admitted in his clumsy way, "but I propose hereafter to give the public information; to take it into my confidence as to matters it is entitled to know about." He went so far as to invite reporters into his home for an interview, gathering them in the library to scribble furiously while he paced the thick carpet firing observations at them, pausing only to pound his fist on the desk for emphasis. This was a Harriman the boys had never seen and quickly came to relish. Having come in from the cold, Harriman too discovered that he liked this new role.[34]

He offered opinions on a wide range of topics from the tariff to the needs of the railroads in a time of crisis. Yes, the government should regulate, but it must not destroy the roads' ability to do their job in the most efficient way. "Unless we can educate people up to this proposition," he lectured, "we might just as well stop trying to do our share in the development of the country. I said in Washington, and I say now, that there has got to be co-operation on the part of the railroads on the one hand and the public and the Government on the other." Later, Harriman took the interview, revised it, and let it appear under his name as an article called "The Railroads and the People."[35]

This new role captivated many listeners because it seemed as alien to Harriman as it did natural to Hill. Asked why he had changed, Harriman said with disarming candor, "The creating of public sentiment by our enemies, has reached such a stage that we will have to take the matter in charge for ourselves. It can no longer be left to subordinates and others." A few railroad presidents chimed agreement with Harriman's remarks. For a moment the door to reconciliation seemed open; then something peculiar happened.[36]

On March 11 J. P. Morgan hurried to Washington for a meeting with Roosevelt. Later it was said he had gone at the urging of several railroad presidents who knew that Morgan was about to depart on his annual pilgrimage to Europe and were nervous about what the administration might do in his absence. Afterward, Morgan told reporters that Roosevelt had agreed to meet with four prominent rail presidents "to allay the public anxiety as to the relations between the railroads and the Government." Uncertain as to where this left his own meeting with Roosevelt, Harriman asked Evarts's advice. "We will wait until after these fellows get through," Evarts suggested, "and when the matter quiets down we will go down on our trip." Privately Evarts believed that the real reason for Morgan's sudden visit was his fear that Harriman was scoring too many points in the right circles.[37]

Events then took a series of bizarre, unexpected turns that left everyone confused. Morgan departed for Europe and Harriman went to work preparing maps and tables for his meeting with Roosevelt. The highly touted session between the rail presidents and Roosevelt never took place; no explanation was offered. On March 13, the day Morgan sailed, the market suffered a contraction so severe that many observers thought it signaled a panic. The convulsion lasted two days, long enough for wild rumors to spread and strong men to waver in their judgment.[38]

When Harriman told Frank Vanderlip that he thought the worst had passed, he should have called the president instead. Roosevelt interpreted the decline as "a demonstration arranged by Mr. Harriman to impress the administration," and he smelled a concerted effort by Wall Street to put pressure on him. A procession of financial men had visited him to urge that he do nothing to disturb the market in general and railroad securities in particular. The collapse seemed too timely to be coincidental, and it snapped something in Roosevelt. His attitude toward businessmen hardened that week. On March 15 he asked the ICC for recommendations on how best to strengthen the agency's regulation of railroads.[39]

Word spread that Roosevelt blamed Harriman for the market break and was out to get him. The temperate Jacob Schiff tried to ease tensions with two long letters to Roosevelt pleading for conferences to iron out differences before the situation exploded. "It is difficult for me to understand," came the exasperated reply, ". . . why there should be this belief in Wall Street that I am a wild-eyed revolutionist." On March 21 Senator Shelby Cullom of Illinois called on Roosevelt to discuss Harriman's activities in his state and told reporters afterward, "If I could have my way and there was a law to do it, I would put Harriman in the penitentiary for his work in the Alton deal."[40]

Harriman was at Sherry's that evening, hosting a dinner for his Boys' Club. A reporter found him there and repeated Cullom's remark. "If Senator Cullom said that," snapped Harriman, "he could not have been sober."[41]

Harriman had emerged as the point man in the worsening feud between Roosevelt and the financial community. As the skirmishing grew heavier, both sides sought ways to avoid a pitched battle. The long-deferred meeting between Harriman and Roosevelt offered one hope of clearing the air. With the mood in both New York and Washington darkening, something had to be done fast. Unfortunately, the something turned out to be an explosion no one could have anticipated.[42]

The detonator was a disgruntled stenographer named Frank W. Hill, who had been discharged by Harriman. Hill took away with him notes of some letters he had taken down, including the one to Sidney Webster. In March he made the rounds of the New York papers trying to peddle the Webster letter. Evidently one editor alerted Harriman, who asked all the papers not to print it. The *Times* obliged with a notice saying only that some of Harriman's papers had been stolen. William Randolph Hearst's *New York American* bought the letter but did not print it. Hill then sold it again, this time to the *World*. Pulitzer was not only willing to print it but sent a reporter to get Harriman's reaction before publication.[43]

The reporter found Harriman in conference with John G. Milburn, one of his lawyers and the man in whose house President McKinley had died in Buffalo. After Milburn left, Harriman came out to see the reporter. He shook hands, sat down, crossed his legs, and said abruptly, "That letter must not be printed."

"Didn't you write it to Mr. Webster?"

"Yes; I wrote it, but I went further than the copy you have there. You only have part of it. You have it about as imperfectly as an inferior stenographer could get it from old notes. Now, I know you got that from a discharged employee of mine. You're not the only ones that have it. He has been to others with it and I warn you not to print it."

Harriman emphasized again and again that the letter would do "irreparable harm," but to no avail. Sidney Webster, hunted down in Newport by the paper for his response, was so shaken by the news that he left for New York despite his poor health. The *World* printed the letter on April 2 along with a full account of Harriman's reaction to it.

Roosevelt responded in predictable fashion by hauling out the "letter" he had written after his talk with Sherman and releasing it to the papers along with a barrage of rhetoric about a "rich man's conspiracy" against him by Harriman, Hearst, and William Rockefeller. The object, he hissed, was to shatter the Republican Party and put the reactionary Hearst in the White House in 1908. Harriman himself had longed to be elected senator in 1904, Roosevelt added, to help defeat adverse legislation.[44]

In one stroke the road to reconciliation gave way to a shooting war of the sort at which the president excelled. Publication of the letters embarrassed everyone involved. The president spouted charges and denials with the regularity of Old Faithful but never succeeded in removing doubts about his role. The controversy came back to haunt him again in 1912, when he made another run at the presidency. Harriman was also badly tarred, especially by Roosevelt's lumping of him with three labor leaders under the label of "undesirable citizen." Worst of all, the image of Harriman as a cynical corruptionist willing to buy judges or legislators reinforced the caricature of him that had recently emerged in the public mind.

This was a war neither side could win. At first, Harriman tried to duck the fire. Asked his response to Roosevelt's charges, he said blandly, "This has been an unusual Winter, both as to politics and as to weather." But Roosevelt would not relent. Harriman, he wrote a senator, "lies about private conversations just as he swindles in railway transactions. . . . The real trouble with Harriman and his associates is that they have found themselves absolutely powerless to control any action by the national government. There is no form of mendacity or bribery or corruption that they will not resort to in the effort to take vengeance."[45]

In Roosevelt's personal iconography Harriman became the leading symbol for the evils in American business, the wicked example he invoked in his frequent tirades against the forces impeding progress in American life. Harriman could do little to counter this attack, for he lacked the forum and the immense personal popularity at Roosevelt's command. At home the land rang with denunciations of Harriman; in Europe, where investors owned vaults full of American securities, abuse was heaped on the man who had been wildly praised only months earlier. None of this was an accident in Otto Kahn's view: "A few of [Harriman's] bitterest enemies had set out the year before on a carefully planned, astutely prepared, campaign of destruction against him. . . . The Harriman Extermination League—if I may so call it—played the trump-card by poisoning President Roosevelt's mind against Mr. Harriman . . . which caused him to see in Mr. Harriman the embodiment of everything which his own moral sense most abhorred and the archetype of a class whose exposure and destruction he looked upon as a solemn patriotic duty."[46]

Kahn's charge of an Extermination League can neither be proven nor easily dismissed. Certainly Roosevelt's mind was receptive to being poisoned against others, especially when it served his own needs. Harriman was aware of the forces arrayed against him, whether separately or in a league of conspirators. Tired, haggard, coping yet again with pain that surgery had failed to alleviate, he plodded doggedly onward, asking no one's sympathy and issuing no complaints except about government policy. The strain made him even more irascible than usual, more impatient in his dealings with everyone. Critics denounced his manner as well as his crimes, derided his utter lack of grace and tact, his handling of men like cattle, and his insistence on having his own way.[47]

The critics did not understand that Harriman had no time to waste on pleasantries, that time was now more than ever his true enemy. Nor did they understand how the pain lashed and drove him like a spur. Life had stripped away the amenities for Harriman, yet his appetite for challenge was as unquenchable as ever. Near the end of his testimony before the ICC there occurred a remarkable exchange when the ICC interrogator asked what would happen if Harriman got hold of the Santa Fe.

"You would not let me get it," retorted Harriman.

"How could we help it?"

"How could you help it? I think you would bring out your power to enforce the conditions of the Sherman Anti-Trust Act pretty quick." Harriman paused, then added, "If you will let us, I will go and take the Santa Fe tomorrow."

"You would take it tomorrow?"

"Why, certainly I would; I would not have any hesitation; it is a pretty good property."

"Then it is only the restriction of the law that keeps you from taking it?"

"I would go on as long as I lived."

"Then, after you had gotten through with the Santa Fe and had taken it, you would also take the Northern Pacific and Great Northern, if you could get them?"

"If you would let me."[48]

To some extent, Harriman was toying with his inquisitor, but the commission and the press took these remarks at face value and paraded them as an example of his unquenchable lust for power. In one sense Harriman was deadly serious: he would go on as long as he lived. For the moment, however, the president and the ICC and the Extermination League held him at bay. In the public mind he had become a monster pounding savagely against the door of conquest held shut by Roosevelt and the antibusiness reformers. Privately Harriman was no longer fighting for empire; he was fighting for survival.

28 Fighting Back

At the present moment Mr. Harriman enjoys more genuine ill-will than any other

man in the country. . . . In the minds of the ever-fickle public he has even threatened

to dispossess the veteran John Rockefeller. . . . For three months I have sat in this office

and firmly dealt with a procession of writers who asked, nay begged, for the privilege

of writing about Harriman. It seemed at one time as if the Literature of the Twentieth

Century would consist entirely of one subject. A hundred years hence anthologists

would speak of 1907 as the opening of the early Harriman period.

—American Magazine, April 1907

James Stillman never forgot the evening he had settled comfortably into his box at the opera to enjoy a pleasant evening of music. As the performance swelled, Harriman appeared suddenly at the entry and said, "Stillman, I want to see you a minute." Reluctantly, Stillman left his seat and went into the hallway. "Come this way," Harriman motioned, leading him downstairs past the cloak-room to the street, where, to Stillman's surprise, a brougham stood waiting. They got inside, and the driver pointed the horses toward East 55th Street. "Well, Harriman," asked the perplexed Stillman, "what is it you want of me?"[1]

"Well, wait a few minutes," replied Harriman. "We will soon be there."

The coach stopped in front of Harriman's house. They went inside and up the stairs to the library. By this time Stillman's curiosity was pushing hard against his formidable reserve. "Harriman," he said finally, "what is it?"

Harriman fetched a box of cigars and offered it to Stillman, then went over and stirred the fire to life.

"Well, Harriman, I am still waiting," Stillman said yet again. "What is it you want?"

"Oh! You must have been tired of that opera," Harriman said without smiling. "I know I was, and I thought we might pass the time better at home."

This to Stillman was vintage Harriman. He decided what he wished to do and did it. He didn't bother asking Stillman what he wanted to do but whisked him away for a quiet evening of cigars and conversation. As they sat talking amid thick, bluish curls of smoke, Stillman asked, "Harriman, what is it in life that most interests you and gives you most pleasure?"

The little man cupped his face in his hands and pondered the question. "Well," he said finally, looking up, "I would rather think of some big helpful thing to be done, get all the people I could opposed to it and to say that it couldn't be done, and then set both feet and go ahead and do it."

That, too, thought Stillman with a wry smile, was the quintessential Harriman.

In the bleak year of 1907 the little man had lined up all the opposition he could handle. The ICC wound up its inquiry and threatened legal action forcing Harriman to answer the nearly one hundred questions he had ducked while on the stand. Harriman vowed that he would resist any such suit to the utmost. The commission's report, released on July 13, showed its priorities by devoting nearly a third of the text to the Alton deal alone. It excoriated the spread of Harriman's control and influence, deplored its effect on competition, warned of threats it posed to the national interest, but recommended no action against Harriman.[2]

A disappointed Roosevelt thought the commission had rushed to judgment and then made too little judgment. Its "milk-and-water" report, as he called it, gave him little or no help in deciding what to do about Harriman. Roosevelt urged his attorney general, Charles J. Bonaparte, to take his time reaching a conclusion. "It is important to be sure that we can stand on whatever we do," he admonished. So important was the Harriman report to Roosevelt that he went over the draft personally.[3]

Harriman faced several threats. The government could file suit forcing the Union Pacific to divest its control of the Southern Pacific as well as its holdings in the Atchison and the San Pedro. It could also bring criminal charges against Harriman for his handling of the Alton transactions. The government had just won a huge victory against Standard Oil of Indiana, which had been hit with an unprecedented $20 million fine by a federal court. Exhilarated by this triumph, Bonaparte informed reporters that "a better moral effect would be produced by sending a few prominent men to jail than by a great deal of litigation . . . against the corporations they controlled."[4]

Harriman dismissed the ICC report as "a political document and part of a personal pursuit of me." In August, after huddling with Roosevelt, Bonaparte filed suit to compel Harriman to answer the ICC's questions on the Alton. Harriman could easily have pleaded ill health and taken refuge in Europe until the clouds parted, but that was not his way. He would admit neither weakness nor wrongdoing, and any form of retreat amounted to the appearance of both. "I doubt," wrote an admiring Otto Kahn, "whether any more superb courage in bearing and daring has ever been demonstrated than was shown by Mr. Harriman in those long months of incessant onslaught."[5]

His close friends never deserted him, partly because they were swimming in the same rough seas. No one understood this better than Stillman, whose subtle mind sorted out the nuances of the attack on Harriman better than most. In August 1906, amid the furor over the Union Pacific 10 percent dividend, Stillman had observed to Harriman that the animosity of the *New York Sun* toward both of them, the City Bank, and their Standard Oil friends derived from the paper's vindictiveness toward Harriman personally.[6]

Harriman took this insight to heart and two days later sent Stillman his resignation as director of National City Bank, saying that it "should not be exposed to any criticism because of relations of one of its directors which might antagonize other interests which might be of advantage to it." Stillman replied at once that he had been misunderstood:

> I do not believe that the criticisms leveled against all of us by the press are provoked by any means by you alone. It is because we are prominent & because this or that newspaper . . . is hostile to the large interests with which we are identified that gives occasion for the onslaught against us. It is quite immaterial which one of us is singled out at any particular time, the rest of us get the same treatment at other times. If newspaper attacks on prominent men governed their qualifications as directors, corporations would be weakly organized. You are too valuable a director & too much esteemed by your co-directors to permit of the course proposed by your letter. Accordingly, I return your resignation & beg that you tear it up & not think any more about the matter.

Harriman deeply appreciated this response. It revealed not only Stillman's loyalty to him but also his refusal to be cowed by public clamor. As a banker with a velvety style, he detested loud controversy of the sort Harriman attracted as a lightning rod, yet he realized that it could not be avoided and must not be intimidating.[7]

A year later Stillman's support remained unwavering, as did that of Schiff, Rockefeller, and others. Melville Stone, who drafted Harriman's reply to Roosevelt's release of the Sherman letter, later characterized the president's behavior as disingenuous and dishonorable, "the sort of thing for which a man ought to be expelled from a club." For the present, however, Roosevelt was in charge of the club and had things his way. He and Harriman never met face to face again.[8]

Harriman did what he could to bolster his position, giving interviews freely through the summer and remaining bullish about the economy when the market stumbled badly in August. He had always been an incorrigible optimist, and not even the combined horrors of recent years could shake his unquenchable faith in the future. Reporters were surprised at how mild his manner was with them. He waved off questions about Roosevelt and the Bonaparte suit, saying, "Really, I am not interested in them." Instead, he hammered at a theme that was fast becoming a leitmotif with him: "The time will come when the things that I have done will be understood and not misunderstood. . . . The time may come when I am dead."⁹

Even his pleasures sometimes brought him bad press. Late in June he took Averell and a group his friends on the *Sultana* to New London for the Harvard-Yale regatta and carefully anchored near the finish line. But the race was postponed until evening and the course was reversed, leaving Harriman in position to see only the start. Although the *Sultana* was too big to move upstream, Harriman had no intention of missing the race. He packed the boys into the launch and took off after the racing crews despite government restrictions against ships following them.¹⁰

Several unpleasant incidents in the past had prompted officials to curb the practice vigorously. As Harriman followed the crews upstream, a revenue cutter repeatedly hailed him to turn about. Harriman ignored the order until the cutter pulled in front of him. The officer in charge warned him that he would be arrested if he did not change course, adding some language Harriman found offensive. "You don't dare to, you coward!" Harriman shouted back. The officer stiffened, then bellowed, "You are under arrest, sir!"

The boys accompanied Harriman aboard the cutter, and everyone missed the race. Afterward, Harriman was contrite, offering an apology for his actions. It was Harriman at his most imperious. He did not want to miss the race and so let nothing stand in his way. He followed his objective in a straight line until he met an obstacle that could not be overcome. Only then did he pause to consider what he had done and how it looked to others.

Part of it was the ever-present pain that corroded his temperament like acid. By late September he could stand it no longer and submitted again to surgery. He returned to the office a few days later and had scarcely settled back into his routine when disaster struck Wall Street. The collapse of a brash attempt to corner the stock of United Copper ruined F. August Heinze, closed two brokerage houses, sent a bank to the brink, and triggered a run on the Knickerbocker Trust Company amid reports that its president was knee-deep in Heinze's collapsed scheme. By closing time on Saturday, October 19, the Knickerbocker had barely weathered the run.¹¹

For months, men like Morgan, Stillman, and Schiff had fretted over softening business conditions. During the summer of 1907 money grew tight; railroad earnings drooped, as did steel orders; a large shipping combine collapsed; an iron manufacturer failed; the city of New York could not find a market for two of its bond issues; the New York street railway combination slipped into receivership along with giant Westinghouse Electric. Speculators like Heinze swam doggedly upstream against these negative signals until the tide of contraction hurled them back with a vengeance. Now the awful stench of panic hung over Wall Street.

For months, too, conservatives had been warning Roosevelt that his attacks on the business community were aggravating an already serious situation. The president, feeling pressure from all sides, mistook these alarms as threats like the brief panic on the stock exchange the past winter, demonstrations arranged by Harriman and others to force him around to their point of view. When the crisis broke, the president was off chasing bears through the canebrake of Louisiana. No one on Wall Street doubted that he would blame them for whatever disaster occurred.

Morgan learned of the crisis while attending an Episcopal convention in Richmond. He hurried back to New York and set up shop in his magnificent library, where his collection of paintings, rare books, and manuscripts provided a strange backdrop for the command headquarters of a financial panic. There for more than two weeks Morgan took charge of a banking community that was divided, confused, and in utter disarray. George F. Baker and Stillman served as his lieutenants; they were not only the most powerful bankers but the most stalwart as well, capable of sound judgment under fire and of rallying men with less ability and still less backbone.[12]

It was a leadership role at which Harriman too excelled, but this crisis belonged to the bankers and no one doubted who should take charge. He joined the stream of prominent men filing into Morgan's library to pledge their moral and financial support. However much Harriman hated not being at the center of the action, he recognized the importance of giving Morgan his unwavering support regardless of their past differences. Later that day he heard rumors were afloat that he had just had a row with Morgan. "It has gotten," growled Harriman in disgust, "so that I cannot go over to Mr. Morgan's office to have a talk with him without people criticizing and looking for trouble."[13]

After deciding that the Knickerbocker Trust was too far gone to save, Morgan and his lieutenants browbeat the other bank and trust company presidents into joining forces to stop the runs on other institutions. A fund was raised to provide loans that saved all but three smaller banks. When the call loan rate on the New York Stock Exchange shot up to 125 percent, Morgan raised $23.5 million to ease the money crunch. Stillman led the way by putting $8 million of National City Bank funds into the loan kitty. The city of New York then found it impossible to borrow funds to meet its payroll, forcing Morgan, Stillman, and Baker to arrange another loan to save the city's credit.

No sooner had this crisis passed than word came that the prominent brokerage firm of Moore & Schley had $25 million in call loans coming due and no cash to pay them. The collateral for the loans included a large block of Tennessee Coal & Iron Company stock, which might get dumped on the market at low prices. Hurriedly Morgan and his associates worked out a scheme to save Moore & Schley by having United States Steel buy the stock in Tennessee Coal & Iron with its own bonds, which could be used to secure the loans falling due. This solution, however, allowed the nation's largest corporation to swallow a major competitor. Everyone agreed this could not be done without prior approval from Roosevelt.[14]

Roosevelt had returned from harassing wildlife in the South and was busy writing up the adventure for a new edition of his *Outdoor Pastimes*. On November 4 he interrupted his breakfast to meet with the leaders of United States Steel. After hearing their plea, Roosevelt replied that he "felt it no public duty of mine to interpose any objection." Judge Elbert H. Gary, head of the steel giant, took this to be "tacit acquiescence" and hurried back to New York with the news. Moore & Schley lived to speculate another day, and within a few days the panic eased.[15]

Harriman's role in these events was minor, yet the panic was to haunt him in unexpected ways. His enemies tried to use the crisis as evidence that he was in trouble. One day during the panic a prominent financier warned broker Clarence Housman to get clear of Harriman because the latter was certain to fail. Housman was then only thirty-seven and had just taken charge of the firm founded by his brother A. A. Housman, who had died suddenly in August. He was carrying more than $6 million in securities for Harriman, more than enough to bring the firm down if Harriman failed.[16]

For Housman it was an agonizing decision. Possible ruin faced him, yet he could not bring himself to abandon the man who had been his best client. Harriman had stood beside him after his brother's death and had never failed to meet a margin call with more than was required. In his personal bearing Harriman evinced not the slightest trace of concern or anxiety. Housman decided to stick with him; he never had cause to regret it.[17]

Later critics charged that the Moore & Schley crisis was merely a scheme to deliver a major competitor into United States Steel's arms. Whether Roosevelt believed this or not, it is clear that the panic fed the brooding suspicions he already had about Wall Street's way of bending him to its will. During the weeks after the panic his private railing against unprincipled businessmen grew ever more shrill. "That the Harriman and Rockefeller interests and those closely allied with them," he wrote William Allen White, "have been willing to see a panic and desirous of precipitating it, with the purpose of discrediting my administration, I am quite prepared to believe."[18]

Roosevelt stopped short of charging that his foes had brought on the panic, but his complaints took on the tone of a persecution complex. While his wrath extended to a wide circle of financiers, Harriman was the most immediate target. The ICC already had Harriman in court seeking to pry answers from him. In January 1908 Attorney General Bonaparte announced that he would sue the Union Pacific to divest its holdings in the Southern Pacific, San Pedro, Santa Fe, and Oregon Short Line roads. If successful, the action would dissolve the entire Harriman system.[19]

Harriman countered with sweeping denials of all charges. Although the hearing would not take place for months, the suit loomed like an avenging angel above not only Harriman but the entire financial and railroad community. Everyone, including Roosevelt, agreed the Sherman Antitrust Act needed revising, yet it was again being used to attack railroads. If the government won its case, no major system in America would be safe from prosecution. The outcome would not be known for months (in fact years), adding one more element of uncertainty to an already difficult situation for railroads and the owners of their securities.[20]

The ICC won the first round of its suit, but Harriman got it reversed by the Supreme Court. On December 1 the antitrust suit against the Harriman system commenced. Harriman served notice that he would oppose the government to the limits of his resources. He was fighting to preserve his life's work—not only a vast rail system but a way of doing things, an intelligent, efficient form of management that was threatened by the suffocating ooze of politics. To lose the suit was in his mind to lose the rational basis for a national transportation system.[21]

On the evening before the suit opened, Harriman attended a dinner given by the Economic Club of New York. To his surprise, a clamor arose for him to speak. He demurred, then strode to the "pulpit," as he called it, and protested that he did not know what to talk about—or rather that he could not talk about what they wished to hear. "I am sort of an economic subject myself," he said whimsically. "I am a subject of contention—a bone of contention if you like—an economic morsel, and this morsel, or this bone . . . has been pursued by a pack and the scent is getting slim, and I do not intend to do anything to renew that scent."[22]

But he teased them with a little story that carried his pet moral: "A good deal of what you have been hearing is not right, and some day you will find it out." Three years earlier, Harriman added, he had warned the president that amending the Interstate Commerce Act without also amending the Sherman Act would create nothing but trouble. Having seen this unhappy situation come to pass, Harriman predicted that Roosevelt would soon seek to amend the Sherman Act. A week later, in his farewell message, Roosevelt did exactly that.[23]

Harriman's back had begun to bother him a great deal, forcing him to endure long stretches in bed where he was reduced to commanding by telephone. When he did get downtown, the pain made him look even more frail, his gaunt frame bent like a wilted plant and his features twisted in grim determination. But he did not need to be downtown so often anymore, and he could do more by telephone in a day than most men making their rounds could in a week. From his bed he managed a deal that did more than any other single act to cleanse his tarnished image in the public mind.

The October panic left several enterprises on shaky ground, including the Erie Railroad, which had been using short-term notes to fund its rehabilitation. One issue worth $5.5 million was due to mature on April 8, 1908. The Erie had planned to take the notes up with the proceeds from a new issue until the panic scuttled its already fragile credit. The holders of the old notes let it be known that they would not accept the new notes in payment.[24]

The Erie had been considered a Morgan road since its reorganization in 1895, but Harriman had his own stake in it. He commuted on the Erie from Arden, and it bothered him that the road was not as well run as his own system. After 1900 he itched to be on the Erie board, but the Northern Pacific fight killed any inclination Morgan had to accommodate him. When a seat fell vacant in September 1903, however, President Frederick D. Underwood and some of his directors urged Morgan to appoint Harriman. Morgan left the decision to the board, which promptly offered Harriman the seat. Analysts interpreted the move as a healing of the breach between Harriman and Morgan. This view gained strength in June 1905, when Harriman moved to the executive committee.[25]

Underwood could not have been happier. He was struggling valiantly to modernize the Erie, not only its physical plant but also the thinking of its directors, who had always been slow to appropriate money for work. Their old-fashioned style was reflected in a provision that did not allow the president to spend more than $500 without approval from the executive committee. Work had already begun on a new low-grade line, but lack of bond sales in a dead market forced Underwood to curtail construction in 1905.[26]

Convinced that the new line would greatly improve the Erie's capacity for handling its large traffic efficiently, Harriman took hold of the project and revitalized it. He also drummed his familiar themes into the other members of the board. "You have fixed your railroad, but it is worth nothing unless properly equipped," he reminded them. Pay no dividends, load the road with equipment trusts, anticipate a growth in business, and be ready for it even if this meant having surplus equipment for a time. "No matter how much business there is," he lectured, "you cannot get it if you have not got the equipment."[27]

Harriman left his imprint on the Erie executive committee with what amounted to a cameo appearance. At one of the first meetings he attended, the other members entered into the usual solemn discussion over a request to spend $12,000 on new mules for the coal mines. A director asked for more details on mule consumption. Harriman fidgeted through this performance, then snapped, "My time is worth a mule a minute." If the manager in question could not be trusted to make this decision on his own, he growled, then he should be replaced. Harriman voted for the request and stalked out of the meeting.[28]

But he stayed with the Erie, supporting Underwood's work at every turn. When two strikes tied up the road, Harriman helped Underwood fight them vigorously even though it cost the road $1.8 million along with lost business. The strikes were over piecework, a battle Harriman had already fought and lost on the Union Pacific. There circumstances had forced him to back down and cut the ground out from under Horace Burt's strong stand. Perhaps he still smarted from that experience, for he took an unyielding position this time.[29]

Now the Erie was in trouble again. Through the winter the road's directors had issued comforting statements about taking care of its obligations without offering any definite plan. As the deadline for the maturing notes drew near, the board postponed its meeting. Wall Street was nervous. The House of Morgan was supposed to be behind the Erie, but Morgan himself was abroad and no reassuring statement had come from his partners. A meeting was called for the evening of April 7 in the absent Morgan's library to discuss the problem. Harriman took Judge Lovett with him and on the way over predicted that the Morgan partners would let the Erie go into receivership. If that happened, he added gloomily, the panic might return with a vengeance. No one had any idea of how to avert this disastrous chain reaction.[30]

They filed quietly into the library and took chairs by the fireplace. Most of the Erie's directors were there along with some of the Morgan partners. Francis Lynde Stetson, the counsel for both Morgan's firm and the Erie, passed around papers asking for a receivership. A New York statute, he said in a dry voice, forbade operating a business after it had defaulted on maturing obligations. If the Erie notes were not paid by three o'clock the next afternoon, the board had no choice but to seek receivership.

In solemn, hesitant voices they discussed ways to raise the money. Every suggestion met the same obstacle: the Morgan partners adamantly refused to provide the funds even though they had been the Erie's bankers for a decade. Harriman's hunch had been correct; he wondered what Morgan would have done if he had been present. Then he spoke up abruptly with an offer to lend the Erie half the money if the Morgan men and the other directors would put up the other half. They looked at him in surprise, then withdrew to the far end of the library to discuss it among themselves.

Harriman sat silently by the fire, smoking and staring at the flames with that absent, reflective expression so familiar to Lovett. The judge had never discussed the Erie's affairs with Harriman, but he felt obliged to speak up now and launched into a vigorous objection to Harriman's offer. Compared to the others, Harriman had a small interest in and smaller responsibility for the Erie. The money would come out of his own rather than a corporate pocket. The key to being a successful financier was never having to dig into one's own pockets except in the direst of emergencies. Why do it for the Erie?

It was the general situation that concerned him, Harriman replied. The recession had almost run its course; the Erie failure might revive it. But, retorted Lovett, your own roads are sound and will not be affected. Harriman made no response but sat gazing at the fire, the reflection of its flickering flame dancing on his spectacles. The library hummed with the silence of its opulent furnishings into which stray sounds disappeared almost apologetically.

Why couldn't the others see it, Harriman wondered. The Erie must not be allowed to fail; its importance went far beyond any intrinsic value. European investors held large amounts of Erie and might regard its receivership as a signal to pull back their overseas investments. The Erie's board contained some of the most prominent men in American finance, starting with Morgan; if they let it go to the wall, what confidence would investors at home or abroad have in any of them? Did they not realize what a blow this would be to their reputations? How could Morgan possibly turn his back on the Erie?

The others marched like pallbearers back to Harriman and with strained expressions declared their unwillingness to put up any part of the money. Harriman shook his head in disgust. "Rather than see such a disaster come about," he said, "I am disposed to lend the Erie the entire amount myself if you will lend me the money. I could borrow it from others downtown if there was time for me to take the matter up and make the necessary arrangements." The bankers and directors again retreated to a remote corner of the library to confer. After they had huddled a long time in earnest discussion, their muffled tones drifting like clouds toward the fireplace, they returned to Harriman. If he could borrow downtown, they preferred that he do it there.

By then it was two in the morning, too late to do anything. Harriman said that he had not definitely made up his mind but would decide the next morning. He asked that all receivership proceedings be delayed until the notes actually came due at three in the afternoon. This much, at least, the others granted. On the way home Lovett renewed his case against the whole idea. Harriman seemed to relent, and Lovett left him thinking that the issue had been settled.

Sleep was short and tortuous that night. When Harriman awoke next morning, he could not get out of bed. The day was cold and gloomy; sheets of rain pounded the windows or sputtered into snow. The strain of the late meeting coupled with the damp chill left Harriman writhing in pain from the rheumatism that plagued him. At seven o'clock he reached for the phone and asked Lovett to come over as soon as possible. The judge got there by eight and blanched at the sight of Harriman. He was even more shocked to hear Harriman say that he had decided to go ahead with the Erie loan on condition that Underwood remain president until it was repaid.

The soul of rectitude: Judge Robert S. Lovett, the earnest, upright Texan who became one of Harriman's closest advisers and ultimately his successor as head of the Union Pacific System. (Union Pacific Museum Collection)

Since Harriman couldn't get out of bed, he sent Lovett downtown to arrange the loan with Frank Vanderlip at the National City Bank and fetch the necessary collateral from the safe deposit vault. Harriman called Vanderlip in advance and also telephoned George F. Baker, who had been present for part of the meeting the previous night. Vanderlip was willing to make the loan, but there was a problem: under existing law the bank did not have sufficient capitalization and surplus to make so large a loan. Vanderlip promised to see what he could do while Lovett hurried off to see Baker.

Asked whether he would lend Harriman $1 million if needed for the Erie loan, Baker replied without hesitation, "I will lend Harriman one million or two millions or three millions if he wants them." This was a noble gesture from the man who was Morgan's closest banking ally. As it turned out, Vanderlip managed to swing the entire amount and the Baker loan was not needed, but Harriman never forgot the offer. Baker was his kind of man, willing to provide help when it was most needed.

Harriman had already put the House of Morgan on notice by telephone. After Lovett informed them that the loan had been arranged, the Erie directors assembled on cue and passed the necessary resolutions. No one objected to Harriman's condition that Underwood be retained. When all the papers had been signed, Stetson noted sententiously that Harriman had done a brave thing without realizing the irony of his remark. The press agreed entirely once the word got out. "HARRIMAN CASH SAVES THE ERIE," announced the *New York Times*, adding in a subhead, "MORGAN PLAN A FAILURE."[31]

Secluded at home, Harriman told reporters only, "The situation speaks for itself." Two questions tantalized Wall Street: why had Harriman put up the money, and why had Morgan's men refused to do so? Inevitably speculation arose that Harriman would take charge of the Erie, but he was quick to deny any such intention. Gradually observers came to appreciate the larger significance of what Harriman had done. Since no recession occurred, it was impossible to prove that his bold action had prevented one. There was, however, widespread agreement that he had done much to restore confidence on Wall Street at a time of great anxiety.[32]

News of Harriman's action, recalled Lovett, "created one of the greatest sensations in the financial district that has occurred during my acquaintance with it. He at once became a hero and by all factions was acclaimed leader where before he had for years been bitterly and almost daily criticised." Although this overstates the case, the Erie loan did mark a turning point in the rehabilitation of Harriman's reputation. The Extermination League slowly waned and withered, as did the image of the cold, ruthless operator preying on friend and foe alike.[33]

The loan also marked a turning point in Harriman's tortured relationship with Morgan. The banker had gone abroad in February that year but returned briefly in June to receive an honorary degree from Yale and again in July. During this last trip he conferred with Harriman and saw him again shortly after coming home in September. Observers hailed these meetings as signs of a reconciliation; in fact, the thaw had begun much earlier. Whatever Morgan's personal feelings about Harriman, he had to admit that the little man had been right about the Erie for a long time. He had opposed Morgan's reorganization plan in 1894, and events had forced Morgan to revise it in the direction Harriman had urged. Then there was the Cincinnati Hamilton & Dayton deal.[34]

In 1905, while Harriman was in the Far East, Morgan had, at Underwood's urging, bought that financially wobbly road and sold it to the Erie. Harriman was so disturbed by the deal that he prodded Underwood into asking Morgan to rescind the transaction. The surprised Morgan agreed to take the road back at cost, relieving the Erie of a white elephant. Despite his outrage at the original transaction, Harriman considered this a fine gesture and thanked Morgan for it. He also argued incessantly for applying earnings to improvements instead of dividends and for spending large sums to transform the Erie into an efficient modern road. He had been right on those matters, and he was right in saving the Erie from what would have been a needless and disastrous receivership. In time Morgan came to appreciate what Harriman had done.[35]

Still the question lingered: why had Harriman done it? Was it a grand gesture, like Ryan's purchase of the Equitable stock, to demonstrate his civic responsibility to the public? He surely knew it would bring him good ink and do wonders for his reputation, yet the real answer may have been far simpler—just as Harriman himself was simpler than critics realized. In the closed, intensely patriotic world of eternal verities by which he lived, Harriman had acted to save the country from what might have been a financial calamity. He had done his duty, done the right thing, and was proud of it.

Only a month before saving the Erie, Harriman had stood up proudly in Grace Church and given his daughter Cornelia to Robert L. Gerry. In recent months he had quashed Mary's engagement to Willard Straight, but he harbored no ill will toward the young diplomat. On the contrary, while he did not want Straight as a son-in-law, he was happy to have him as an agent, for his Far East ambitions were stirring to life again.

In June 1906 Straight had been named consul general at Mukden. Before his departure in August he spent a weekend at Arden, during which Harriman asked to be kept informed of any railroad developments in Manchuria. Eager to oblige, Straight toured the Manchurian and Siberian rail lines and sent back detailed reports to Harriman. The ethics of what Straight was doing while on the government's payroll were hazy at best, but the question never troubled him or Harriman. Both of them believed ardently that it was their patriotic duty to plant an American presence in the Far East.[36]

Straight learned that the Russians were interested in discussing sale of the Chinese Eastern road to Americans. While this negotiation limped along for two years without result, the Chinese sounded Straight on ways of encouraging American investment in Manchuria. Straight evolved a plan he thought ideal for

American interests and Harriman. The key involved a loan of $20 million and creation of a Manchurian bank that would act as government agent for a wide range of development schemes. Harriman would secure the right to build a Manchurian line that would connect with an extension being undertaken by a British consortium. By August 1907 Straight had the necessary agreements lined up and sent the scheme along to Harriman with a strong plea to take hold of it.[37]

His timing could not have been worse. Harriman was ill and distracted by the fights swirling around him. Then the October panic threw financial markets into chaos. "Unsettled money conditions make it impracticable," Harriman cabled. A disappointed Straight urged Harriman to reconsider. Some progressive younger men had vaulted to positions of influence in China and were eager for American capital to underwrite their development plans. Two men in particular had emerged as key players: Yuan Shih-k'ai, who had moved to an important post in Peking, and American-educated T'ang Shao-i, who had been made governor of Manchuria's southernmost and most populous province. "The opportunity is a rare one," Straight stressed, "for it offers a chance to direct rather than to make a simple investment."[38]

Harriman fell ill with the grippe and did not reply until January, when he dictated a letter from his bed. "It would be utterly impossible under the conditions here," he told Straight, "to successfully negotiate anything in the matters you present. It could only be done in times of confidence, prosperity and easy money." He also wished Straight to understand why the proposal did not appeal to him. "What interests me," he emphasized, "are the transportation and development problems and the doing of them, and not the money which can be made by banking or other such enterprises."[39]

Problems and the doing of them. There it was again, the same theme Harriman had confided to Stillman. Despite being ill and under constant attack, the fiery flame of creativity still burned in Harriman. Young Straight, struggling to make it in life and hungry for the emoluments of wealth and power, could not understand that Harriman had gone past these things as the polestar for what remained of his life. What Harriman wanted most to do was build railroads under trying circumstances, make them run well, and then link them together in a gigantic system circling the globe.

His vision was as elemental as his instincts, but the Far East was no place for elemental instincts. In his politically naive way Harriman viewed railroads as tools of transportation rather than as instruments of national policy or battlegrounds of international rivalries. He was not so naive as to think he could merely buy control of "Manchuria, Inc.," as Michael Hunt has suggested. His experience with the Japanese had taught him this slow and intricate manner of doing business. He understood that to do anything in the treacherous corridors of power in the Far East took time, but time was the one commodity he had in shorter supply than patience.[40]

The Chinese were hungry for American capital, and Straight believed Harriman was the best man for the task. He wrote Harriman again, arguing that the bank was merely the doorway to the railroads. Through the winter and spring he plied Harriman with information and sent along a book on Chinese railways, hoping to tickle his interest. Preoccupied with other matters, Harriman did not respond until June 1908. Again he dismissed the bank and financing features of the scheme. "I would be interested only in doing the thing itself," he repeated, "that is, in the construction and operation of the railroad lines. . . . The simply making money out of such an enterprise does not appeal to me."[41]

But Harriman was interested. A week later he had Alex Millar send Straight a letter outlining Harriman's views. "Anything done with the Chinese must be of immediate result," Millar stressed, "because with them the future means a century or more. The only thing that would induce Mr. Harriman to consider any proposition would be an immediate, clear, offer on the part of the Chinese Government, which would be comprehensive and leave nothing for future consideration." In September Harriman arranged with Secretary of State Elihu Root to summon Straight home for consultation. "He desires to talk with you regarding Japanese and Manchurian matters," Millar told Straight delicately. "Something may come up in relation to the Steamship matters with Japan, and the old matter of management of the Manchurian railroads."[42]

Something indeed. Harriman had eliminated his objection to the Manchurian bank by interesting Schiff in the financial side of the transaction. Before leaving Manchuria, Straight secured from T'ang a signed memorandum as the basis for a $20 million loan. The money would be used to organize a bank, which would disperse it for building railroads, purchasing the Chinese Eastern road, and other developmental purposes. Schiff let both the Chinese and the Japanese know that his firm would consider taking this loan.[43]

From these maneuvers emerged a grand plan. American and Chinese interests would join forces with the British company that owned the right to build the road joining the proposed line at Tsitsihar, and perhaps together they would construct a trunk line from the Gulf of Chihli to the Amur River. T'ang came to the United States in November to conduct negotiations personally. Schiff arranged a dinner for him with Harriman, Lord Revelstoke of Baring Brothers, Robert Fleming, the Scottish financier who had made a career out of American railroads, and other prominent New York financial figures.[44]

Then everything went wrong. T'ang arrived in the United States only to learn that at home both the emperor and the empress dowager had died unexpectedly. Their deaths set in motion a power struggle that threatened T'ang and his mentor, Yuan Shih-k'ai. The strictures of mourning forced T'ang to miss Schiff's dinner. Harriman fell ill and could do little to help Schiff. The Manchurian scheme dropped into limbo despite dogged efforts to keep it alive. From his sickbed Harriman tried to stay abreast of developments, but even he had to concede that "nothing can be done definitely until Mr. Tang's status with the new outfit is determined."[45]

The answer came in January 1909. Yuan was shoved into retirement, and T'ang was ordered to Europe. Harriman asked to see T'ang before his departure, hoping to reach some personal understanding so that someone in China would know his views regardless of what happened there. They held a brief get-acquainted meeting before a dejected T'ang left the United States on January 19 and Harriman retreated to South Carolina for some rest. Despite his faltering health and the uncertainty in China, Harriman kept the vision of development there dancing in his own mind.[46]

Something else had changed as well. That winter King Theodore surrendered the White House to William Howard Taft and went off on an extended world tour to annoy big game in Africa and then to flatter the crowned heads of Europe. His prolonged absence lifted the weight of his personal and official animosity from Harriman's shoulders. Taft was a man Harriman found entirely congenial even though he would not relent on the government's suit to unmerge the Union Pacific and Southern Pacific.

The change of administrations left Straight up in the air. He could not go back to Mukden and did not want to stay in Washington as a special hand rather than a regular. Harriman put in a word with Philander C. Knox, Taft's secretary of state, to use Straight where his experience would be more useful. Within a short time Harriman and his friends had a new plan to revive the Far Eastern plan, and in their scheme Straight was to play a crucial role.[47]

The circle of Harriman's enemies was breaking up, chastened in part by the financial panic of October 1907 that had frightened them as much as it had outraged Roosevelt. None felt the pinch more than George Gould, whose pasteboard empire was collapsing under the combined weight of debt and mismanagement. For years the erratic Gould had pursued the opposite policy of Harriman's: he had paid dividends by cutting improvements and service to the bone, practiced the fine art of "skinning the road," as Commodore Vanderbilt called it. To build the Western Pacific and his eastern roads, he had mortgaged subsidiary lines to the hilt. Even before 1907 he was paddling in troubled waters; the panic served notice that the day of reckoning was near.

While Harriman's lines basked in record earnings, Gould struggled to keep his overworked and undernourished roads afloat. The Western Pacific continued to swallow money as it inched painfully toward completion. E. T. Jeffery had boasted in 1906 that the new road would "be self-supporting from the day it is fully opened to business," but opening day did not come until 1910 and the road never fulfilled that brash hope. Gould's eastern system crumbled into financial embarrassment when the overtaxed Wabash could no longer sustain the demands made on its limited resources. The Pittsburgh Terminal and Wheeling & Lake Erie roads slid into receivership.[48]

After all his stocks tumbled sharply during 1907, Gould swallowed his pride and sought peace with Harriman. They met several times, sparking rumors that Harriman would return to the boards of the Gould properties. "Nothing would give me greater pleasure," George told one inquiring reporter, "than to have Mr. Harriman with us." Harriman provided Gould some financial help but stayed clear of the management of his roads. It was the bankers who were closing in on the Gould empire; within a few years they would depose the emperor.[49]

By the fall of 1908, the dark, savage storm of controversy raging over Harriman had vented its fury and moved on, leaving in its wake the soft, sweet serenity of sunlight and silence. The once formidable Harriman Extermination League scattered like wisps of departing clouds, its fierce roars of thunder reduced to distant peals. The little man had stood like a monument against his foes, absorbed everything they could hurl at him, and emerged with his reputation intact. For all his defiance, the experience had chastened and mellowed him, left him more attuned to the importance of public opinion and the need to cultivate it.

As the turning leaves splashed wild, glittering patterns of color across the face of Arden that fall, Harriman had every reason to feel satisfied. He had routed his enemies, or rather stood firm long enough for time and changing circumstances to rout them. But there was one enemy he had not vanquished and who would not submit. It was the one foe he could not defeat or banish by force of will, and in the golden sunshine of that triumphant autumn his dark presence moved steadily closer.

29 Fighting the Inevitable

The kindest and perhaps the fairest thing that can be said about him is that he has been Napoleonic both in his aspirations and in his superiority to scruple. But that won't do. Napoleons are too dangerous. It is not so much that they break too many eggs, as that the omelet when they get it done is apt to be their omelet. Mr. Harriman has made an omelet, but it is too much his. We wish he could be employed to make one for us. He ought to do penance for his misdeeds, and the particular penance we would choose for him would be to build the Panama Canal. If he could be put in charge of that, we would be willing to lend him the key of the United States treasury, and ask him no more than to leave us the change when the job was done.

—Wall Street Journal, *March 16, 1907*

During the turbulent winter of 1907, as Harriman prepared to testify before the ICC on his fifty-ninth birthday, he had remarked that another year might well find him ready to quit the game. When that milestone approached in February 1908, however, he told a reporter that things were too unsettled for him to call it a career. "It isn't a case of changing my mind," he explained, "but of not having had time to think about retirement."[1]

Talk of retirement was very much in the air that winter among Harriman's friends. Stillman and Schiff both felt an urgent need to cut back their workloads. The October panic had left Stillman drained and his nerves frazzled. For some time he had been working on a plan to make Frank Vanderlip president of the bank and himself chairman of the board. The bank's opulent new building was scheduled to open the first of the year; perhaps, mused Stillman, that was the time for the change. Schiff too was reducing his commitments and looking to turn more work over to younger men. After talking for years of going to Egypt, he finally embarked in the winter of 1908 and boarded a houseboat provided by his old friend Sir Ernest Cassel for a leisurely cruise down the Nile.[2]

Floating along those historic waters put Schiff in a philosophical mood. "Here I am on board of a Nile steamer, thinking of you," he wrote Harriman, "while the imposing ruins on shore remind me how hollow everything earthly is; how we strive so often for naught; how short a time we live, & how long we are then dead. Take my advice, my good friend, do not work so constantly, be not so fond of power, & do not go back on what you have told me on the eve of my departure—that you would give up the different Presidencies & content yourself with the chairmanship of the boards & executive committees, placing moreover men of experience on the boards & executive committees to share responsibilities with you. I wonder whether you have done anything in this direction?"[3]

Harriman knew that both Stillman and Schiff wanted him to surrender the day-to-day grind to other men and move with them to what Stillman called an "advisory" capacity. Stillman had urged this course on Harriman several years earlier only to be met with suspicion and resentment. Harriman took Stillman to mean that the Union Pacific would be better off without him and responded by clutching his position tighter than ever. Now he knew better: far from wanting to get rid of Harriman, Schiff and Stillman knew Harriman's obsessive nature and feared for his health if he kept up the old pace.[4]

The time seemed ripe for their campaign in 1908. Despite the panic and other negative forces, the Harriman roads astounded the railroad world by rolling up one new earnings record after another. During fiscal 1908 the road netted $11 million above the 10 percent dividend despite large outlays for improvements. The Harriman policy, like Harriman himself, seemed fully vindicated. One analyst called the 1908 Union Pacific report "a story of growth, progress and wealth so remarkable that it cannot be easily understood or realized." The railroad's performance was augmented by Harriman's investments in other roads, which showed a huge gain despite the blow dealt prices by the panic.[5]

Stillman and Schiff saw in these holdings a way for all of them to cash in their chips. They urged Harriman to spin off the outside holdings into a new holding company and distribute its stock to Union Pacific stockholders as a special dividend. This would provide them all with a fat dividend, eliminate the objection that the Union Pacific owned shares in other railroads, and enable all of them to slide gracefully into reduced workloads. The bankers also wanted the Union Pacific executive committee enlarged. It was time, they suggested gently, for Harriman to start grooming his successors by delegating some power to younger men or other strong figures. Such a move would blunt public apprehension over the autocratic power he wielded.[6]

Harriman endorsed the idea in principle but offered little encouragement to those working on the holding company plan. The ICC investigation prodded their efforts along, as did the shock of recognition by Wall Street, which for the first time in the winter of 1907 grasped how much income the outside investments were pouring into the treasury. "The Union Pacific," noted one analyst, "has come necessarily to be regarded as much as an investing company as a railroad." But a holding company could also serve as a vehicle for controlling railroads through stock ownership along the lines of Northern Securities. The

Family man: This close-up from a group photograph shows an obviously worn and tired Harriman (top left) with his sons at the Omaha Field Club in 1908. Roland sits at his father's feet; Averell is at right. The man next to Harriman is Euclid Martin, president of the Omaha Chamber of Commerce. (Union Pacific Museum Collection)

ICC investigation planted this fear firmly in the public mind, as did observers like one who predicted the new company would be "a Mightier Weapon to E. H. Harriman Than Ever Union Pacific was."[7]

Nevertheless, the bankers persisted. By October 1907 the value of the assets exceeded $301 million, and a board meeting was called to discuss the idea. "We have at last persuaded Harriman to recommend a distribution in the way of dividends of the shares of a holding or investment company," reported Stillman hopefully, but the panic wreaked havoc with the plan. Harriman withdrew his support at once, growling to a reporter, "You may rest assured that the whole matter will be settled on a proper basis, when the time comes; but this is not the time to discuss it."[8]

The time never came. A committee appointed to formulate a plan grew discouraged over the legal obstacles and gave up. The government suit to dissolve the Harriman empire dealt another blow to the idea, which drifted into limbo. Harriman was content to let it stay there. He had never really cared for the notion and said so in the summer of 1908, when it flickered briefly to life again. What bothered him was not the government suit or the legal barriers or the ghost of Northern Securities; it was the surrender of power. The distribution would enable him to walk away with piles of money into the semiretirement that his good friends envisioned for all of them. But he didn't want to give up even part of his empire; if anything, he wanted to expand it.[9]

Schiff's plea from the Nile moved Harriman but did not budge him. "I told him in confidence what I had in mind eventually to do, but made no promise," he scribbled on the bottom of Schiff's letter as if trying to convince himself. "His advice is good if matters are looked upon only from a selfish view-point." In May 1908 Schiff used the occasion of the tenth anniversary of Harriman's coming to power in the Union Pacific to salt his tribute with another reminder that life and glory alike were fleeting.[10]

Again Harriman was deeply touched, but his reply sounded as much prelude as valedictory. "Your reminder of our long past together . . . gratified me very much," he told Schiff. "You put it so well, & to me it is the greatest satisfaction that we 'still stand together' & are looking forward as well as back. Of course it has been nerve wearing & taken some of our vitality, & sometimes I have questioned whether it has been worth while. Maybe it would not have been had only the UP & ourselves been the gainer."[11]

But of course they had not been the only gainer. In a remarkable passage Harriman summed up the achievement of his lifetime, much as he had with the writer at whom he had flung the sheet listing his accomplishments. "Where would have been those whom it serves," he declared, "had we not straightened, improved, & improved again, enlarged, made better, & so increased its capacity that it permitted the enlargement of every enterprise, & establishment of new ones in all the territory adjacent to it & the systems under its influence." Nor was that all. "Besides," he said proudly, "its method introduced like methods by other important systems. Where would we all now be without them? It has all made for advancement in civilization & will someday be understood."

Harriman made it clear that he did not intend to retire on these laurels. "There is much in the future to be worked for improvement," he added, "& I hope we will still be found standing together when the opportunities & responsibilities present themselves." This was not what Schiff wanted to hear. He realized that the sheer weight of his duties was wearing Harriman down, causing him to let things slip because he had so much on his mind. Stillman felt the same way. From Paris he urged Harriman to retire to an advisory position and put "two big able independent presidents on the spot to manage those two great properties."[12]

Even if Harriman agreed with this idea, where would he find the men? He had an impressive stable of good officers, but none qualified as a replacement for himself. He had always considered himself indispensable, and those who knew him doubted he could long confine himself to an advisory position. One of them laughed at reports that Harriman was about to create a consulting board to ease his workload. "It would be unconstitutional for him to do it," he smiled, "his constitution being so constructed that he consults nobody except himself."[13]

Harriman was willing to take vacations. During the summer of 1908 he spent a happy August at his lodge on Klamath Lake in southern Oregon, where a steady of stream of visitors—politicians, railroad men, friends of the children— arrived to keep him company. The boys trudged off to camp in the wilds at the head of the Rogue River atop the Cascades. Little Roland got the thrill of his young life by killing his first bear, while Averell had to content himself with a small buck. Harriman beamed with pride at their trophies.[14]

Once back at Arden, he basked in a surprising number of "lazy days here in which I do nothing but loaf. Don't even think or try not to." Arden itself occupied his attention as he followed work on the new house with the same zeal he devoted to the reconstruction of railroads. The work had made good progress while Harriman was in Oregon even though there was no contractor. Harriman used plans drawn by an architect friend and a force of local workmen under their own foreman. Men, supplies, materials, even visiting automobiles rode the cable railway up the mountain to the summit, which could also be reached by a gentle, zigzag road.[15]

The forest had been cleared, a site for the house, lawn, and garden blasted out of the granite ridge, and drilling begun on an artesian well. Most of the granite for the house came directly from the mountain. The views from the terraces thirteen hundred feet above sea level were breathtaking. To the west lay the valley of the Ramapo River with its cluster of houses and behind it the blue shadows of the Shawangunk range. In the opposite direction stood wild ravines of thick forest broken only by two or three small lakes.

The house would not be ready to occupy for at least another year, and by autumn Harriman was growing restless over what for him was a leisurely pace. The children had dispersed to school or visits to friends. The election came and went, elevating Taft to the White House as expected, and the business world seemed unusually quiet. The signs for a return of prosperity looked good. Harriman's usual robust optimism grew mellow as the attacks against him slowed, then ceased, and hostility in the West toward railroads diminished. He had noticed this at every stop on his trip to and from Oregon. "The communities could not do enough for us," he reported impishly, "and all are willing that we should have charge of all the Railroads in sight, whether competing or not so long as we had them and for improvements, etc."[16]

For months Harriman had been flinging bullish statements into the teeth of the doubts spawned by the panic of 1907; now events seemed at last to be shifting in his direction. During the past year he had pursued with a vengeance his new policy of going public, and it had paid dividends. He got on well with reporters and held the old Harriman waspishness in check. During a trip to San Francisco that summer, he did not hesitate to express his disappointment at the slow progress the city had made since the earthquake. But he stayed resolutely clear of politics or any of the old controversies that once got him into so much trouble.[17]

Late in July 1908 he welcomed Stillman, who had come back from Paris and traveled up to Arden for the weekend. Stillman was gratified to find Harriman improved not only in both health and spirit. "His position here is better in every respect," he wrote a European friend, "and in fact the entire situation as to relations and co-operation between the large interests could hardly be more satisfactory than they are at present, so different from what has prevailed at times in the past." The change pleased Stillman because it boded well for his plans to cut back on his duties. "When I see the high-tension of everyone here I am convinced of the wisdom of getting into an advisory position," he confessed, "and I am more determined than ever to do so."[18]

True to his word, Stillman handed the presidency of the bank to Vanderlip in January 1909 and moved up to the newly created chairman's position. His sojourns in Paris grew longer and his visits to America less frequent; he did not even bother to attend the meeting that approved the change but orchestrated it from Paris. Stillman had crossed the bar, joined those who wanted to "take things easier and get something more out of life than work." The question in his mind was whether he could persuade Harriman to follow suit.[19]

The answer came that same January, when Harriman bought half the shares in Guaranty Trust Company owned by Mutual Life, then got himself elected to the board of the New York Central Railroad. His entry into the Central's board, long expected and long delayed, touched off an orgy of speculation over what role he would play in the Vanderbilt family firm. It was no secret that the road had been poorly managed and lagged well behind its chief rival, the Pennsylvania, in modernizing its operation. There had long been grumbling among some stockholders that the ruling Vanderbilts knew more about throwing a party than running a railroad. One critic, comparing the Vanderbilt, Harriman, and Hill systems, made the damning observation, "The third stands for one-man construction; the second stands for one-man reconstruction; the first stands only for inheritance."[20]

To analysts the Central was a disturbing conundrum. Its board included the three most powerful bankers in America—Morgan, Stillman, and Baker—as well as William Rockefeller, yet its financing was criticized for lacking cohesion or any semblance of a broad plan. Two Vanderbilts also held seats along with H. M. Twombley, who was married to a Vanderbilt, and the venerable Chauncey Depew. Two other directors were antiques dating back to when Commodore Vanderbilt had formed the Central out of smaller roads in 1869; one of them had been in the company's service since 1854.[21]

The board urgently needed a transfusion of fresh blood and fresh thinking. One faction of stockholders wanted Harriman to work the same miracle for their road that he had for his own lines; another group feared he would dominate the board as he did anything he touched. Although Harriman had long known the Vanderbilts socially and in business, their close ties to Morgan formed a barrier to his entry into the management. In January 1908, after the Union Pacific bought a large block of Central stock, Harriman hinted that he would like a seat on the board only to be told by William K. Vanderbilt that there were no places available.[22]

As always, Harriman took the setback not as a snub but as a challenge. During 1908, while the Central continued to draw criticism for its managerial anemia, Harriman enhanced his reputation by saving the Erie from default. In December the Central's president resigned, paving the way for an overhaul of the management. The two antiques on the board surrendered their seats to Harriman and J. Ogden Armour, the first westerner to be made a director, spurring rumors that Harriman would be made chairman and given charge of the road. The stories were quickly denied, but others insisted that he was also after the Delaware & Hudson and the Boston & Maine.[23]

Was Harriman looking to reorganize the East's feeble rail system? Whatever his plan, he had exasperated his friends by spreading himself even thinner when he barely had the strength to handle the load he was already carrying. Stillman voiced this concern from Paris as delicately as possible and received a curt reply that bruised his feelings. He let Harriman know about the hurt as well and touched a surprising chord of sensitivity. "There was no sting in my message," Harriman cabled, adding plaintively, "wire that you understand."[24]

When Harriman returned to New York from Pelican Lodge in the summer of 1908, friends and reporters alike marveled at how tanned and well he looked. Yet a picture taken at Omaha, where he paused on the way back, tells a different tale. Sitting among a covey of civic leaders with his sons at his feet, Harriman looked dapper and rested. But his features bore a worn, aged expression, and he looked frail and wizened, like an old mountain eroded into a shrunken hump of its former majesty. The ordeal of 1906–7 had etched its horrors into his features as well as his nervous system.

Rumors about his health, always a sure ticket for bears on Wall Street, dogged his steps. One had him undergoing treatment for a back ailment. In December the red flag flew in earnest when Harriman was felled by what appeared to be ptomaine poisoning. The problem seemed trifling at first, then developed into something more serious. "I really had a nasty breakdown just before Christmas," he admitted to Stillman, "apparently poisoned by something eaten at one of the big functions. It got completely into my system."[25]

The holidays passed and still Harriman was not strong enough to venture downtown. When Frank Vanderlip stopped by his house on the evening of January 8 for a chat, Harriman insisted that he would make it downtown for the bank's annual meeting. But a week later Harriman headed south on a trip combining rest with some business. Since his daughters were tied up with social engagements, he took Bertie Goelet along for company. They went first to Aiken, South Carolina, where Harriman took things slowly. "I have been idling here with the idlers for a week and in normal condition again," he reported. The "idlers" included the venerable John D. Rockefeller, with whom Harriman chatted twice before pushing on to Savannah, Atlanta, Macon, and Augusta.[26]

The march through Georgia had more to do with business than pleasure. Late in 1907 Harriman had acquired control of the strategic Central of Georgia rail system for the Illinois Central, but complications forced him to put the road into a voting trust for nearly two years. Aware that strong antirailroad sentiment in Georgia discouraged investment in new lines or modernization, Harriman did a little politicking. He visited the mayor of Savannah and attended a banquet given by the Chamber of Commerce in Augusta, where Harriman also owned the local street railways. Asked to make some remarks, he proclaimed, "If the State will cease to be antagonistic to the railroads' interests I will spend ten million dollars on the Georgia Central Railroad."[27]

After returning to New York, Harriman was too weak to do anything except crawl back to bed. Even there, Vanderlip marveled, he was "quite as active as ever and he does about as much business over the telephone as a half dozen ordinary men would do in their offices." Yet the sight of him struck Vanderlip as "little short of tragic." Telephone in hand, Harriman dispatched business and ideas in every direction, his brain more active than ever, as if released from any need to tend the body. Something else was wrong that could not be explained by ptomaine. It was his back, he explained. The muscles were misbehaving; except for that, he was fine.[28]

The ritual of denial had begun even though Harriman did not yet know what he was denying. There was no quit in him, no ability to submit to weakness or defeat of any kind. The more his body failed, the harder he drove it. He dismissed every setback as temporary and not worthy of concern. One day he surprised Vanderlip with a call demanding a lower interest rate on a loan he was about to renew. Despite his faltering voice, which stirred pangs of pity in Vanderlip, Harriman argued the case as if his life depended on the half-percent difference. In the end Vanderlip yielded.[29]

Nothing drove Harriman to despair more than having to miss important meetings because he could not get out of bed. He kept promising to be on hand only to renege at the last minute. In February the Union Pacific executive committee had only Vanderlip and Marvin Hughitt on hand, one shy of a quorum because Harriman telephoned belatedly to say that he could not attend. It had taken the combined efforts of three doctors and his wife to keep him at home, he grumbled. Vanderlip delivered this explanation to the venerable Hughitt with a wry smile and was startled to get an explosion in return.[30]

Hughitt needed no examples of Harriman's obstinacy. One had only to look at the sad state of affairs on his system: the whole management was drifting badly; the New York office lacked vitality; large matters hung in abeyance because Harriman was too ill or distracted to handle them and would not delegate the work; the experiment of putting Kruttschnitt and Stubbs in Chicago had been a disaster. Hughitt was fed up and worried because his beloved Northwestern depended so heavily on the Union Pacific as a feeder. Vanderlip passed this outburst along to Stillman, who had heard it before and assured him that things were not as bad as Hughitt thought. The government suit had everyone on edge; nothing would settle down until it was resolved. But Hughitt had a point: the little man clutched the reins of power too tightly in his own hands. With the system so dependent on having Harriman at its head, Hughitt was hardly alone in wondering what would happen to it when Harriman was gone.[31]

Harriman had planned an inspection trip to the Southwest. The doctors encouraged him to go, thinking it would help him avoid the harsh New York winter. If he must be in bed, the bed could be aboard a moving train. In mid-February he headed west at the head of a large entourage and set up camp in tents near San Antonio. After having a private telegraph wire strung, he called special meetings of the executive committees of both Pacific roads and pro-

Ailing but indomitable: This photograph of Harriman was taken in Denver during his last trip to the West in 1909. (Collection of Fred and Jo. Mazzula)

ceeded to hand them details of a major new bond issue without having given either Vanderlip or Hughitt prior notice about it.[32]

"He is a sick man," sighed Vanderlip, "but his illness has not laid the slightest hold on his ambition." In distant Paris Stillman shook his head at the news. Harriman was a wonder, he consoled Vanderlip. "Still he cannot go on forever expending his energies as he has been doing and I hope to do some missionary work with him on my return. I am very fond of him and admire him immeasurably in spite of everything." Two questions haunted Stillman, though he kept them to himself: what was the illness, and what was the ambition?[33]

From San Antonio Harriman swung down into Mexico, basking in the warm sun and dry air. He was gratified to find the Mexican project in splendid shape. From modest beginnings it was marching toward 1,780 miles of track amid insistent rumors that Harriman would extend it to Panama. Prosperity still shone over his systems; every month brought fresh reports of record earnings on both Pacific roads. Critics who had once denounced the 10 percent dividend as obscene now wondered what Harriman would do with all the cash the Union

Pacific earned above that figure. He had shown them all that his approach was the best one for modern conditions.[34]

On the way back he paused in Los Angeles to discuss the trip with reporters, then went on to Santa Barbara for a week and from there to try the baths at Paso Robles. Along the way he grappled again with the old rumors in language that could not be mistaken. "There is absolutely no foundation," he snapped, "for any assertion that I intend to retire from active business." In fact, his aching, restless eyes looked far beyond Mexico and gazed longingly at the distant, shimmering mirage of the Far East.[35]

Harriman blew back into the East like a warm front, full of optimism and high spirits about the signs of prosperity and improved public sentiment in the West. He arrived on April Fool's Day, looking tanned and rested, though his voice seemed to lack strength. The newsmen and photographers found him full of mischief; when they commenced taking pictures, he and his daughters whipped out cameras and snapped shots of them photographing him. After having his little joke, he stood patiently for a lengthy interview with plenty of pictures. He did not go downtown regularly but turned up at enough meetings to deflect attention from his health for a time. To casual observers he seemed to have regained his vigor and was slipping gradually back into harness. Then, one afternoon late in April, he summoned Vanderlip to his house and confided that he planned to go abroad as soon as Mary was ready.[36]

He was not going on his own account, Harriman explained at length, but for his wife, who was suffering from nervous prostration and needed rest. He had no itinerary; they would wander the Continent and perhaps spend some time with a German doctor who could attend Mary. As for himself, he was feeling first-rate but might take the cure somewhere, not because he needed it but because it would help him get into a regular routine of simple meals and proper hours that he could follow after he came home. Since everything the American doctors knew came from some German, he laughed, he might as well look up the original source.[37]

Vanderlip had a dozen questions but could not ask them because Harriman orchestrated the conversation in his usual manner and turned at once to business matters. Anyone who saw Harriman knew something was wrong. Although he complained mostly about his back, the problem appeared to be more with his digestive tract. He was losing weight and looked even more emaciated than usual. He had little energy and less appetite—symptoms that he usually managed to conceal. What Harriman actually thought about his condition remained hidden behind his mask of good cheer and optimism. Then something caused the mask to slip briefly. On May 20, amid his preparations for the trip, Harriman learned that his good friend H. H. Rogers had died of a stroke early that morning.[38]

The news touched Harriman deeply. Rogers had always been a workhorse like himself until he suffered a stroke in July 1907. Although his pace had slowed since then, he had been at his desk the previous afternoon and had a full slate of appointments the day of his death. At the Union Pacific board meeting the next day Harriman surprised everyone by delivering a heartfelt tribute to Rogers. Perhaps in the passing of his friend Harriman saw for the first time the shadow stalking him in a way he could no longer ignore.[39]

A week later, on the eve of his departure, Harriman held a Southern Pacific board meeting at his home. As it broke up, he asked Vanderlip to stay on a while. Harriman was in a gentle, almost affectionate mood. He talked in stirring language about his plans and the need for cooperation in developing the country. Vanderlip used the opening to chide him for ignoring the executive committee in his recent decisions. Harriman smiled an apology and reiterated what had become an obsessive theme with him: the importance of cooperation among all interests and the public as well.[40]

Vanderlip was but one of a stream of visitors to the house as Harriman wrapped up his affairs in a way that had a curious finality to it. He told the broker Clarence Housman abruptly, "I have closed my account with you, and if I ever do anything in Wall Street again I shall remember you, as I have enjoyed our pleasant relations." Harriman paused, then added with a twinkle in his eye, "Now, I suppose you want my opinion on the market." This surprised Housman as much as the closing of the account; Harriman had never offered his views before. "It all depends upon the crops," Harriman said. "Big crops will mean a big market; small crops, stocks will go down."[41]

Before sailing, Harriman had one other piece of personal business to wrap up. More than ever in these last difficult years he had come to appreciate the unspoiled beauty of Arden. The thousands of acres he had added to its domain secured it as a refuge, but threats remained nearby. Quarriers still blasted stone from the magnificent face of the riverfront Palisades, lumbermen coveted the towering stands of timber in Orange and Rockland Counties, and recently the state of New York had acquired a patch of wild land near Bear Mountain to use for a new prison.

A prison in the midst of Arden's wilderness! The very thought drove Harriman into a rage. Some years earlier the state had moved to protect the cliffs by acquiring strips of land along the river for what became the Palisades Interstate Park. Harriman personally had beaten back the timbermen by buying parcels of land as fast as he could get them, but how to save his paradise from being defiled by a prison? Late in 1908 he concluded that the best solution was to fold as much of the land as possible into a giant state park that would make the presence of a prison untenable.[42]

Early in 1909 he broached the idea to Governor Hughes in the form of an offer to give the state a large part of his own estate and an endowment to sustain it if the state would make it part of an enlarged park. For months he tried to see Hughes in person, but the governor was too busy to come to New York and Harriman could not make it to Albany. Finally, Hughes offered to see Harriman in New York on June 1, which happened to be the day Harriman sailed for Europe. When neither man would budge from his schedule, Harriman wound up dictating his proposal to Hughes while standing on the dock waiting to board the *Kaiser Wilhelm II*.[43]

His plan was to donate about twelve thousand acres of his estate along with $1 million to help acquire land between his own and the Interstate Park. Other property owners would surely help secure the entire wilderness between the Hudson and Ramapo Rivers from West Point down below Stony Point. If this was done, "the State's Prison should be moved again to the other side of the river so as not to destroy the natural beauty which can never be replaced."[44]

Leaving that idea for Hughes to chew on, Harriman boarded ship. For once he did not have a flock of reporters trailing after him. He managed that miracle by inviting forty of them to his house the day before and granting an interview with the kind of give-and-take they had come to expect from him. Nor did he have a large entourage; only his wife, Mary, and Union Pacific secretary Alex Millar accompanied him on the voyage. He did not seclude himself from other passengers but joined in conversations on deck and in the smoker, listening keenly to the views of other businessmen and offering his own to their eager ears. He took a little exercise, stuck his face willingly into a bracing wind, and left the impression that there was still plenty of life in him.[45]

Those who thought Harriman weak in the legs, noted one bemused reporter on the other side, "should have seen him sprinting for the first section of the train at Cherbourg." There were no private cars or trains for him; he endured the first-class sleeper and marched along the rocking, jolting train to the diner like any other passenger without complaint. He went at once to visit Stillman in Paris and grew weaker during the few days they spent together. He begged Stillman to stay longer, but the banker had already postponed his departure to see Harriman and was anxious to get back.[46]

Disappointed, Harriman moved on to Vienna and consulted a nerve specialist named Adolf Struempel, who agreed to take charge of his case. While in Vienna, Harriman's problem with his digestive tract worsened. Uneasy over the alarming reports that were already flying back to New York, he insisted that his trouble was no more than nerves and that rest was the only cure he needed.

Struempel advised him to find it at the mountain resort of Semmering in the eastern Alps.[47]

Harriman went willingly, hoping to bask in fresh air and glorious scenery. Instead, he found cold, heavy rain and fog. "It's awful dull and stupid," he complained to Stillman, but some of the children were coming to join him at his next stop, Bad Gastein, and he hoped they would cheer him up. At least he was satisfied with Struempel, who was as charmless and blunt as Harriman himself, with the same lack of airs or frills. To the press Struempel recited the party line that Harriman's problem was not dangerous or organic but merely a nervous condition that needed curing. Privately he was moving toward a very different diagnosis.[48]

While Struempel pondered his case, Harriman went on to Bad Gastein. There he endured the prescribed baths, which he loathed, ate the required diet, and found solace in long walks through the gardens. Carol and Roland came to keep him company for a while, and Willard Straight arrived for a brief visit. Whatever sparks had flown from his fling with young Mary were long gone. They greeted each other like old friends, though Straight confided to his diary that Harriman "seemed down on his luck." Harriman invited Straight to join them for dinner and spent the entire next day in discussions with him. They talked late into the night, Harriman sitting by his bed wrapped in a delicate Chinese dressing gown. When they parted at eleven, Straight gently helped him to bed and tucked in the comforter at its foot.[49]

Their animated exchange brightened Harriman's mood somewhat. The Far East adventure had sprung to life again. Although T'ang's future remained clouded, Schiff, at Harriman's urging, had pursued the loan question. What had been the interest of one man and one banking house in Manchurian railways took a broader turn in May 1909, when the Chinese government signed a contract with bankers of three European nations to construct some railroads. The State Department reminded the Chinese of their promise to let American capital participate in this work and suggested forming a consortium of leading American bankers to play this role. That same month the houses of Morgan and Kuhn, Loeb joined with Baker's First National and Stillman's National City banks to create what became known as the American Group, which promptly hired Willard Straight as its agent in the Far East.[50]

This was the business that had brought Straight to Europe for a round of meetings. Harriman had been apprised of every development and wanted Straight to take charge of the tortuous negotiation to pry the Chinese Eastern Railway from the Russians. While in Paris, Harriman had met with a Russian financier and given him a proposal to take to the Russian minister of finance. Clearly he had lost none of his zest for a challenge. "I like to work with brains, you know," he told Stillman. "The doing the thing is what interests me."[51]

He had summoned Straight to Gastein on the heels of Otto Kahn, who had visited a few days earlier. After going over several matters with Kahn, Harriman penned a lengthy report to Schiff. "I fear you will all be disappointed in outcome of Chinese matter," he warned. "It is going to need patience, and not too much expected too soon." The clash aroused the old pangs of patriotism in Harriman. "I fear the European groups will resort to methods in China which will not be credible in method of construction & dealing gently with China," he wrote. "I hope for a purely American influence in some one thing, so we can show them how to do it right, & thus get a real & lasting American influence." For Harriman the Chinese Eastern could be that one thing.[52]

This remarkable letter reaffirmed the best of Harriman's creative instincts. Even now his tired eyes were fixed on the future with as much tenacity as ever. The old values were still there: do things the right way, do them on a grand scale, and take the long view of things. His brain was still fired with fresh challenges and projects, each more ambitious than the next. He could not retire because he did not know what that was. "You were right, Stillman, all the time," he admitted to his friend during their brief visit in Paris. "I ought to have quit and laid back. But it is too late now. I am in deeper than ever, and must go on, on, on."[53]

No one heard him complain about his health. If anything, he improved the art of denial. "This is a queer little place & has been & is doing us much good," he wrote Schiff from Gastein. "The only trouble with me is that I have no trouble except my back, which will always be stiff, but not dangerous in the least. All my organs are like a childs—only necessity is to give my nerves a chance to become normal again & this I'm doing & intend to continue in the work."[54]

Variations on this explanation became the official line on Harriman's condition, but it could not conceal the fact that he had grown worse during his stay at Gastein. The cure did him no good; he lost ten pounds from a body that could not spare it and still had no appetite. His personal physician, Dr. Lyle, made a hurried crossing to join Harriman. Struempel came from Vienna to examine him and shook his head gloomily. Everything confirmed the diagnosis he had feared: the trouble was not nerves but cancer, a carcinoma of the stomach, and it had been discovered too late to be operable.[55]

The bluntness Harriman wanted from Struempel hit him hard. He took the news without flinching but decided to consult Professor Gustav Hoesslin, a prominent specialist in Munich. He had planned to remain in Europe until September 4 but no longer had that much time to spare. At once he revamped his plans and headed by automobile for Munich with a brief stop in Salzburg. "Gastein took too much of my reserve weight," he explained to Straight, "and I am going home to get it back, with the good food and air of America. The German hotels and food are not the kind on which I would thrive."[56]

How much he told Mary and the children remains a mystery. Never did the family admit that Harriman suffered from cancer, yet Mary at least must have known the truth. He had never withheld anything from her, and now he needed her support more than ever. Most likely he swore her to secrecy on the subject. A more intriguing question is how much he admitted to himself. No amount of will or denial could conceal the fact that he was going home to die, to see his beloved Arden for the last time, and that he dare not linger long in getting there. Yet even with that knowledge he did not submit to the inevitable. For business and personal reasons he had to maintain a pretense of recovery, and his own fighting spirit compelled him to believe in it as well.

What seemed business as usual to others became for Harriman a race against time that he could not acknowledge. Letters and telegrams poured in on business matters and were duly answered. At Munich he interviewed one of Straight's friends as a possible agent. To the Russian financier helping him with the Chinese Eastern deal he explained, "I have not time to work out combinations and groups and alliances, and mix diplomacy with business. Let us have, if anything, a plain straight-forward transaction."[57]

While keeping up his business face, Harriman submitted himself to Professor Hoesslin, who took sixteen X-rays and confirmed what Struempel had told him. Discouraged, Harriman left Munich on August 14 by automobile only to find that he was too weak to endure the trip to Paris. With as little commotion as possible, the family switched to the train and, once arrived in Paris, hurried to Stillman's vacant house. There he remained for three days, giving Mary and the children time for a little sight-seeing and shopping while he arranged a special train to Cherbourg so that he might travel with as much privacy as possible.[58]

During these few days Mary did a strange thing that suggests she knew the diagnosis. The family and Thomas Price, who had relieved Millar as secretary, vigilantly shielded Harriman from visitors, yet Mary persuaded him to sit for sculptor Auguste Rodin. It was her way of getting a last—and lasting—likeness of the man she loved, one with more life and character than Napoleon's death mask.

Harriman agreed reluctantly to the sitting, then found himself fascinated at watching the sculptor work. They sat eyeing each other in silence, the celebrated sculptor and the famous entrepreneur, two artists of rare genius who worked in different mediums. "Rodin . . . manipulated a bunch of clay into form which was supposed to be my foundation," Harriman observed wryly to Straight. "He will try to do the rest from memory. Whether he makes me a German or a Frenchman, or a mixture, I suppose I will have to take my chances. Anyway, it was a mighty good experience, and he was a close observer, and I am now wondering whether he will see what good there is, or will leave all the defects standing out so as to overshadow it."[59]

The sittings became a welcome relief from the mounting speculation over his health. Despite all precautions, the reporters had struck his trail thanks to his abrupt changes of itinerary and the pall of secrecy cast over his movements. A *World* correspondent tracked him to Stillman's house only to receive the standard line from Price: Harriman had no organic trouble but needed to recover from the ordeal of the cure at Gastein. He believed the best place to do that was at home, and he planned to sail soon.[60]

This explanation satisfied no one. In New York rumors sent the Harriman stocks into wild fluctuations. They were not abated by the presence of Dr. Lyle and Mary Harriman, who had hurried over to join her father for the return trip. Somehow Harriman managed to procure a special train, and passage was booked on the *Kaiser Wilhelm II* for August 18. Delays caused the train to reach Cherbourg three hours late, but the giant Lloyd steamship waited for him. At the station waiting attendants hurried forward with a wheelchair, but Harriman, swallowed by an overcoat shielding him from the wind, waved them off and walked resolutely to the car.[61]

He found the correspondents waiting for him at the dock and endured their questions briefly before climbing aboard. Their descriptions of his feeble appearance sent fresh tremors through the New York Stock Exchange, which Harriman did little to counter on the crossing. He rejoiced at finding Odell among the passengers but was too weak to socialize as he had done on the trip over. Rough weather early in the voyage gave him an excuse to remain secluded. Only on the final day did he venture out on deck to talk a little; the rest of the time he kept to his stateroom behind a palace guard of family and servants, admitting only close friends like Odell.[62]

He was mustering strength for the ordeal he knew awaited him once the ship touched shore in New York. He had cabled ahead his willingness to meet with reporters, but he wanted no fanfare on his arrival. Once past quarantine, a Southern Pacific tug would meet the *Wilhelm* in New York Harbor and take Harriman to the Erie station at Jersey City, where a special train waited for the trip to Arden. The transfer would be his coming out, the first glimpse newsmen would get of him in person. When the ship docked at the Hoboken pier, he waited until the other passengers had disembarked. "I guess I might as well show them that I am still on earth," he muttered with a smile, then started forward in halting steps.[63]

Judge Lovett rushed forward to help him reach the port gangway. Harriman stood at the rail, looking down at a throng of fifty reporters and sixteen photographers along with the usual coterie of the curious. For a moment it was deathly still; then someone began clapping and a ripple of applause floated up from the dock. Harriman doffed his hat and bowed. "Hello, boys," he called in a weak voice. "Hello, Mr. Harriman," came the response. "Glad to see you back."[64]

Suddenly it became the longest and most important journey he had ever made, as if every fight he had ever fought was distilled into this moment. With

The long walk: Photographer George Bain captured the gaunt, terminally ill Harriman leaving the ship after his return from Europe in 1909. (Union Pacific Museum Collection)

clenched teeth he let go of Judge Lovett and started down the gangplank, clutching the rail with both hands. The reporters and photographers watched silently as stronger arms helped Harriman walk toward the stairway to the lower pier where the tug waited. But he could not make it. After about two hundred feet he staggered toward collapse and allowed himself to be wheeled the rest of the way. His head sagged wearily onto his chest.

The newsmen gasped at the sight of his pinched, pallid face and frail, shrunken body that seemed to swim in its clothes. What shocked them most was his yellow, parchment-like skin and his lusterless eye. But the fight was still there. When half a dozen photographers dashed forward to snap his sagging head, Harriman motioned feebly to a *World* reporter. "I don't like these photographers snap-shooting me when I have this sick spell," he protested. "Just ask the newspaper boys to stand around me, please, and keep those photographers away." He offered the reporter a hand that was clammy and cold despite the August heat.

He stood up weakly and explained that the ship's motion while in quarantine had upset his stomach. "But I will be all right in a few minutes," he wheezed, "and ready to get up and kill one of those photographers." Playing with them was all he could do. He was public property now; he understood this at last and no longer fought it as he once had. Even at this bleak time, he was public property.

With help he made it to the tug, where he submitted to one last pose at the rail with his family while the photographers snapped away furiously. When young

Mary could stand it no longer and stepped away, Harriman motioned her back to the rail. At Jersey City he was helped aboard his private car and settled onto a couch where, his head propped up with pillows, he said, "Bring on the reporters." They jammed together in the coach, their faces dripping sweat from the stifling heat. Mary hovered near the couch along with Judge Lovett, so solicitous and anxious to be rid of the reporters that Harriman finally said, "Won't you ask her to go away, it makes me nervous."[65]

He felt bound to give the interview he had promised. Not that he had anything new to tell them. "I have come home to get well," he said, contradicting the expressions that wreathed the faces around him. He brushed aside questions about his business interests, joked with the boys in a feeble way, and insisted on continuing despite the lack of air in the crowded car and Judge Lovett's dogged attempts to terminate the proceedings. To Mary's chagrin he poured out details of the cure at Gastein, the special diet he had submitted to, the X-rays taken of him. "They gave me a worse racket than the photographers," he laughed. Then, pointing to his head, he added, "They got everything but what's inside here."

Finally, Judge Lovett announced in firm tones that the engine was starting. Harriman invited the reporters to come along on the trip to Arden, but a glare from the judge told them to decline. As the perspiring newsmen filed out of the car, one of them threw a last question at Harriman. "In selecting brainy executives," he asked, "do you let the matter of dress count for anything?"

Harriman paused, then laughed with more energy than he had yet shown. "It is all in the shape of their heads, my boy," he answered.

The boys thanked him and went back to their offices to write one of the fullest and most sympathetic accounts of Harriman they had ever produced. He had never before seemed so human to them. It had been a gutsy, magnificent performance. It was also the last time Harriman gave an interview or was seen in public.[66]

During the days of late August and early September Harriman had time as never before to watch the sun trace its gleaming arc across the sky, filling his beloved Ramapo valley with shafts of golden light through the mist. Sitting on the sun porch, his withered body swaddled in a deck blanket, the squire of Arden gazed longingly across the canopy of trees to the distant river, inhaling the pungent odor of pine, then turned back toward his unfinished house where the ring of hammers and grunts of workmen punctuated the silence. The noise of the workmen bothered Harriman no more than the irony of them racing to complete a house he would not live to enjoy. He relished their activity and occasionally summoned one of them to talk with him. The carpenters, masons, and painters were for him a sign of progress, the frenzy of creation that had always been his own life force.

Now more than ever he had become the squire of Arden, isolated in his unfinished castle on Tower Hill atop the village he ruled, which depended on him for its survival. Work on the house alone generated a payroll of $30,000 a month, and the villagers, like the stock market, trembled with alarm at every fresh tale of Harriman's failing health. A battalion of reporters swelled the population, loitering about the village in hopes of garnering a scrap of news or spying someone worth interviewing; bored from waiting for a story with too open an end; seeking in vain some access to the castle that would get them past the palace guards.[67]

The world below the castle snatched at every rumor, wrung meaning from every random detail. Why had young Averell, who had been working that summer on a railroad survey crew, been called home early? Was Harriman desperately ill with cancer and about to undergo an operation? A specialist on abdominal surgery had been summoned from Cleveland. Tanks of oxygen were seen being hoisted up the railway along with a portable bed that could serve as an operating table. Dr. Lyle and others dismissed these tales and insisted Harriman was feeling better and gaining back some of the weight he had lost. Somehow the reporters missed the special mission of C. C. Tegethoff, who rose early one morning and personally delivered to Arden a container of radium for Harriman's treatment.[68]

The only regular visitor to Arden was the faithful Judge Lovett, who came every afternoon to give Harriman the day's news and receive orders. Family members gave out uniformly encouraging reports to reporters and to all appearances went about their business as if nothing was wrong, but all of them remained at or near Arden. No one knew what to believe, least of all the Wall Street vultures agonizing over which way to play the Harriman stocks.

On the last Saturday in August Jacob Schiff came to visit Harriman and was pleasantly surprised at what he saw. Despite being weak, Harriman was in good spirits. So confidently did he speak of his plans for the future that Schiff came away believing he would recover. He had no trouble assuring the reporters that Harriman looked much better and was a well man. Behind him came Stillman, who marveled at Harriman's good humor. Harriman seemed to him as well as he had been in Paris that spring, perhaps a touch weaker. He too went home feeling that his friend was on the road to recovery.[69]

On the heels of their visits Harriman sent the papers a prepared statement assuring them that he was doing well in his program of rest. The specialists who had examined him as a precaution had found nothing wrong. "I appreciate the interest shown in my welfare by the press and my friends in all sections, and perhaps by some others," he said wryly, the last reference a shot at the Wall Street bears hungry for bad news about his health. He asked the reporters to leave Arden village and promised to let them know of any change in his condition. All the New York editors withdrew their men at once, and the Harriman stocks took a welcome flight upward.[70]

In their haste to shake the village dust from their feet, the departing reporters missed the arrival of a visitor who would have provided them a scoop. A surprised J. P. Morgan had received a message from Harriman urgent enough for him to drop everything and board a special train for Arden. A painter working on the library window casings happened to look down at the loggia below and saw Harriman sitting with a heavy-set visitor who wielded an enormous black cigar. The painter knew who he was, having done work for Morgan. It mattered little to the painter that he was the only outside witness to the final meeting between the two most powerful men in America, a privilege for which men on Wall Street would have killed. He turned back to his casings.[71]

The sight of Harriman's withered body melted Morgan's gruff reserve. Harriman sat in a steamer chair with a blanket over his legs and an overcoat draped about his frail shoulders as if on the deck of a ship. He had asked Morgan to come because some matters between them needed clearing up. After taking care of business, they talked for an hour about the differences that had divided them for so long. If there had been any ill feelings, Harriman assured his guest, they were long forgotten. Morgan replied that he understood everything now and held not the slightest grudge or animosity; he wished only for Harriman to regain his health. They shook hands warmly, and Morgan took his leave.[72]

Of the meeting Morgan said only that he was happy for the chance to clear the air of old antagonisms, but thereafter he referred to Harriman as if he were an old and intimate friend. Harriman was no less pleased to make his peace at last with a man who would in better circumstances have been the best of allies to him. Morgan had been present at the opening of Harriman's rise in business circles, and he was there to help close it down.

The din of construction, the scrape and pounding of masons cutting stone, was the only music of creation Harriman heard during these last days. He had put his affairs in order and told Schiff on the phone of his business plans in a strong, determined voice. Then, late on the evening of Sunday, September 5, Harriman was wracked by a violent attack of diarrhea. Dr. Lyle hurriedly summoned two nurses to Arden. Behind them came the army of reporters, alerted once again to the possibility of a crisis. To allay their suspicions, Mary Harriman allowed a *World* reporter to visit the house and see for himself that no one was alarmed.[73]

No one was convinced. The Harriman stocks nosed downward again as more doctors and equipment were rushed to the house on Tower Hill. Harriman was put on oxygen and packed in ice to keep his fever down. The fight against the diarrhea was exhausting him, yet he held on. With the last of his strength he clung fiercely to the things that mattered most to him. At 10:30 on the morning of September 9, Tegethoff was astonished to hear his special phone ring and to find Harriman on the line. In the throes of his agony Harriman remembered that the next day was his thirtieth wedding anniversary. "Don't forget that tomorrow will be Pearl Day," he instructed Tegethoff, "and buy a nice pearl for Mrs. Harriman."[74]

A few hours later, Tegethoff received another call, this one telling him that Harriman was dead.

Epilogue: The Good That Men Do

It is conceded that Harriman's desire was not wealth, but power; that he made far more money for others than for himself; that he never failed to increase the efficiency and earning power of the roads that he acquired; that whatever may be said of his methods of warfare, he was ever a railroad builder, never a railroad-wrecker. In fact, the post-obit portraits of Harriman lack the horns and tail that featured in sketches of the same model a few years ago.

—Literary Digest, *September 18, 1909*

The workmen who had been Harriman's most constant companions during his last days turned their efforts to a less cheerful task after his death: blasting and carving a place in the ledge of solid rock for his crypt. Years earlier, when the Harrimans had first come to Arden, they had chosen a family plot in the far corner of the churchyard at Arden parish. It was the only spot in the enclosure where a ridge of bluestone rose to the surface. Little Harry had been buried there, and now his father was to join him. It was only fitting that Harriman's grave had to be wrenched from solid rock; in death, as in life, he let no obstacle deter him.[1]

A pouring rain drenched their efforts and those of the men toiling on the new road winding up to the house. Mary, struggling to maintain her composure with help from the children, planned a simple funeral limited to family and close friends. The latter included villagers as well as titans of business and finance. "At times he seemed a workmen like ourselves," said one of the men. "Just an older workman whom we cared a good deal about."[2]

The skies had cleared by Sunday, September 12, when the funeral took place. At nine that morning Mary opened the house for employees of the estate. A procession of five hundred workmen trudged up the new road to pay their last respects to the squire of Arden. The family chaplain, J. H. McGuinness, held a private communion for the family at ten before the regular church service an hour later. There, in fervent tones, McGuinness delivered the only eulogy Harriman was to have on this bleak day.[3]

At three o'clock a special Erie train arrived bearing dignitaries from New York and two cars overflowing with flowers. They were driven to the church in vehicles sent over from Tuxedo. A squad of Tuxedo police guarded the church, and teams of workmen were deployed along the road to turn away the uninvited. Inside the little chapel prominent millionaires squeezed into pews alongside locals in a curious mix that would have pleased Harriman enormously. Mary saw to it that longtime servants and old villager friends got some of the choicest seats.

At three o'clock, too, the church bell commenced pealing its dirge at half-minute intervals. The cortege started slowly down the dusty road from the house, past clumps of villagers standing in tribute. Beneath the towering canopy of oak, hemlock, birch, and maple, lush stands of woodbine and ferns draped the bases of the old stone walls along with goldenrod, lavender, and wild caraway. On this last trip through his domain the squire of Arden was escorted by eight superintendents from the estate acting as pallbearers.

The service was brief, lasting barely twenty minutes, and simpler than that rendered many a departed villager. After the recessional, hundreds of villagers stood on an overlooking slope while the funeral procession moved to the burial plot for the interment. The most spectacular tribute to Harriman came not at the grave site but across the continent. At precisely 3:30 every train and every workman on the Harriman lines, as well as the Erie, paused for one minute of silence to honor him. Trains rumbled to a stop, telegraph operators silenced their keys, laborers dropped their shovels, and clerks stood at their desks with bowed heads.

At Arden the steel, hermetically sealed coffin was lowered into place and covered with lilies on which the archdeacon of New York sprinkled a handful of dirt. When the service had ended, the two men who had been so close to Harriman for so long walked away with similar feelings ringing in their hearts. "Yesterday we laid the little hero at rest," wrote Stillman to a close friend. A sorrowful Schiff put his loss in stronger language. "When we laid the little man into the grave near the quiet village church," he mourned, "a power was buried which it will hardly be possible to replace."[4]

It would have amused Harriman, and pleased him immensely, that a later generation came to regard his eldest son as the most celebrated Harriman with a father who made a lot of money in railroads or something. All the children did well in life but none more than Averell, who shone first in business and then in a distinguished career as a diplomat and political statesman. There was in Averell something of his father's fierce competitive drive and hunger for power, the need always to seek greater challenges in larger arenas. Roland did not have this urge and contented himself with a quiet but highly successful career in banking. A dignified, unassuming man, he started at the top and stayed there.

There would be no Harriman dynasty. Neither Averell nor Roland produced a son to carry on the family name; the Harrimans that endured came from other branches of the family. Nor would there be a major foundation bearing Henry's name even though Mary and the children practiced good works as zealously as religion. Mary carried out her husband's plan for donating ten thousand acres of Arden's land to the state as part of a park and succeeded in diverting the prison elsewhere. The new house at Arden ultimately wound up in the hands of Columbia University as a conference center. Most of the Harriman children got deeply involved in charitable work; Roland was for years a leading figure in the Red Cross.

Apart from the accomplishments of his family, the true legacy of E. H. Harriman lay in his continuing influence on the industry he dominated. The Harriman Safety Medal endowed by his wife symbolized the way he had not only turned safety into a crusade on his own systems but also revamped the way other roads thought about it. He had brought a dark subject out of the closet at a critical time and given the industry a credibility with the public it had long lacked.

By sheer force of example, Harriman dragged the railroad industry into the new era of high-volume traffic carried at low rates. He was not the first to recognize these forces or to devise the correct strategy against them. What he did was implement the strategy on a grand scale from which other rail managers shrank because they lacked the vision or the backbone. "I have more imagination than they," he once said of other businessmen. "I see what they saw, but I see it larger, because I see its possibilities." Harriman not only saw, he had the courage to act—sinking huge sums into modernizing railroads on what the conventional wisdom regarded as little more than a theory.[5]

Harriman's vision extended to the entire railroad map. In 1901 he had joined together two giant systems that some thought should have been one from the beginning: the Union Pacific and the Southern Pacific. His management turned them into an efficient, modernized, well-integrated system that was one of the financial wonders of the era. Shortly afterward, his ill-fated clash with Hill led him reluctantly but vigorously into yet another giant merging of systems in the Northern Securities Company. The Supreme Court undid both of these creations in decisions that history has shown to be unwise, and much later both systems came back together again. The Burlington Northern, after much jousting with the courts, finally saw life in 1970; the Union Pacific and Southern Pacific were rejoined in September 1996 with results far less smooth and happy than in their original merger. It is tantalizing to wonder what the modern history of railroads might have been had the original combinations been allowed to endure throughout the twentieth century.

Of all the monuments to Harriman's foresight, none is more enduring than the Union Pacific Railroad, which ninety years after his death remains one the largest and strongest carriers in a nation where railroads went out of fashion half a century ago. The holding company Harriman resisted in 1907 finally came in 1969, turning the company into a diversified industrial empire. The outside investments have since moved from other railroads to such fields as energy, real estate, minerals, industrial development, waste management, and trucking. While the railroad has become one division of the giant parent company, it continues to turn a profit.

Harriman did more than create the new Union Pacific Railroad after 1898. He also gave it the leadership and the principles to ensure continuity through rapidly changing times. He was succeeded by Judge Lovett, who ruled the company with a firm and wise hand. The judge had long been close to Averell, who spent much time after his father's death with the older man, while Roland became close friends with the judge's only son, Robert A. Lovett. All three boys went into banking and in 1931 merged their interests in the new firm of Brown Brothers Harriman, which remains one of the last private banking houses.

The judge smiled on their success but did not let them wander too far from the railroad that had made their fortunes. When he died in 1932, Averell replaced him as chairman of the board with Roland and young Bob Lovett as directors. Averell stayed on the job until the siren's call of New Deal politics lured him to Washington. The approach of war led to his being sent first to England and then to Russia on diplomatic missions. Bob Lovett soon followed him into government service, leaving Roland to mind the railroad.[6]

Their absence was supposed to be temporary, but in 1946 Averell became secretary of commerce and never returned to the Union Pacific. Bob Lovett did rejoin the company only to be summoned back to Washington to serve in several positions, including secretary of defense. Not until 1953 did he come back to the Union Pacific, where he became chairman of the executive committee. With Roland as chairman of the board, the two lifelong friends ushered the venerable railroad into the modern era much as E. H. Harriman had done half a century earlier. Together they held power until Lovett stepped down at the end of 1966. Two years later Roland also retired as chairman, although both men remained on the board until 1978.

Here was a legacy that might have surprised the elder Harriman himself, though it would have greatly pleased him. Two close families had ruled the Union Pacific for more than seventy years. The first generation had made it strong; the second had kept it that way through a changing economy, a transportation revolution, two world wars, and the Great Depression. In good times and bad the Union Pacific never missed paying a dividend. It had fulfilled every promise E. H. Harriman saw in it that bleak winter of 1897–98 when he first climbed aboard.

On a spring day in 1967, nearing his own retirement, Roland Harriman posed before a new memorial to his father in Salt Lake City. The picture was a fitting capstone to an era of leadership that could never be duplicated, but the monument was hardly needed. Not only a rail empire but the West itself was E. H. Harriman's true monument, especially those shining markers of his personal commitment: the Imperial Valley and the Lucin cutoff. Another, less obvious memorial could be found in the volumes of information and museum exhibits generated by the Alaska expedition.

These were the tributes Harriman would have most appreciated because they were active and enduring. As he had said many times, it was the doing of things he liked best.

Notes

ABBREVIATIONS USED IN THE NOTES

AF   Materials found at Arden Farms, Harriman, New York

AJA   Jacob H. Schiff Papers, American Jewish Archives, Cincinnati, Ohio

BA   Burlington Archives, Newberry Library, Chicago, Illinois

Batson Minutes   Excerpts of Executive Committee minutes by G. W. Batson, AF

Chronicle   *Commercial and Financial Chronicle*

DAB   *Dictionary of American Biography*

FAV   Frank A. Vanderlip Papers, Butler Library, Columbia University, New York City, New York

GK   George Kennan Papers, Library of Congress, Washington, D.C.

HBH   Henry B. Hyde Collection, Baker Library, Harvard Business School, Boston, Massachusetts

IC   Illinois Central Archives, Newberry Library, Chicago, Illinois

ICI   Records in possession of IC Industries, Chicago, Illinois

JA   Records of the Los Angeles & Salt Lake Railroad in possession of Jim Ady, Salt Lake City, Utah

JJH   James J. Hill papers, James J. Hill Reference Library, St. Paul, Minnesota

JS   James Stillman papers, Butler Library, Columbia University, New York City, New York

NCAB   *National Cyclopedia of American Biography*

OK   Otto Kahn Papers, Firestone Library, Princeton University, Princeton, New Jersey

RGD   R. G. Dun & Co. Collection, Baker Library, Harvard Business School, Boston, Massachusetts

SF   Stuyvesant Fish Papers, Butler Library, Columbia University, New York City, New York

SMF   Samuel M. Felton papers, Baker Library, Harvard Business School, Boston, Massachusetts

TR   Theodore Roosevelt papers, Library of Congress, Washington, D.C.

UPL   Union Pacific Railroad Company collection, Nebraska State Museum and Archives, Lincoln, Nebraska

UPN   Union Pacific Railroad Company records, Union Pacific Corporation, New York City, New York (these records have since been moved to Omaha).

UPO   Union Pacific Railroad Company records, Union Pacific System, Omaha, Nebraska

WDS   Willard D. Straight Papers, Cornell University Library, Ithaca, New York

WSJ   *Wall Street Journal*

PROLOGUE

1. This George Kennan should not be confused with George F. Kennan, who emerged as an authority on Soviet affairs during the 1940s. They are distantly related and often mistaken for each other. See George F. Kennan, *Memoirs, 1925–1950* (New York, 1969), 6–7, and Walter Isaacson and Evan Thomas, *The Wise Men* (New York, 1986), 75–76, 228.

2. David Fairchild, "George Kennan," *Journal of Heredity* 15 (Oct. 1924): 403.

3. Unless otherwise indicated, this sketch is drawn from Kennan's manuscript autobiography and chronology in GK.

4. Diary of Willard D. Straight, July 6, 1904, WDS.

5. *DAB*, 10:331.

6. Isaacson and Thomas, *Wise Men*, 76.

7. Straight diary, Sept. 4, 1904.

8. Ibid., July 6, 1904.

9. Fairchild, "George Kennan," 404–5.

10. Diary of George Kennan, May 3, 1912, May 12, 1913, GK.

11. Kennan diary, Mar. 12, 1912.

12. *New York Times*, Nov. 8, 1932; E. Roland Harriman, *I Reminisce* (Garden City, N.Y., 1975), 60.

13. Otto Kahn to Mary Harriman, Jan. 5, 1909 [1910], materials at AF.

14. Persia Campbell, *Mary Williamson Harriman* (New York, 1960), 2–3; Reverend J. D. Morrison, "Recollections and Impressions of the Late E. H. Harriman," 1, AF.

15. Campbell, *Mary Harriman*, 10–17.

16. Ibid.; *New York Times*, Aug. 23, 1911, Apr. 20, 1913; *Railroad Age Gazette*, 55:160.

17. Otto H. Kahn, "Edward Henry Harriman," in Stuart Bruchey, ed., *Three Railroad Pioneers* (New York, 1981), 37–43.

18. Ibid., 43; Kennan to his wife, Nov. 28, 1912, GK; Campbell, *Mary Harriman*, 5.

19. *New York Times*, May 15, 1912; *New York Tribune*, May 15, 1912. For the article, see *Metropolitan Magazine* 32 (May 1910): 141–55.

20. R. Fulton Cutting to Mary Harriman, Aug. 12, 1910, GK; Bayard Cutting to Mary Harriman, Sept. 13, 1910, GK; L. F. Loree to Mary Harriman, Nov. 10, [1910], AF; Batson to Mary Harriman, Oct. 22, Nov. 29, 1910, Mar. 14, 1911, AF; W. F. Herrin to Mary Harriman, Oct. 28, 1910, GK; Alex Millar to Mary Harriman, Nov. 4, 1910, GK; George C. Clark to Mary Harriman, Nov. 7, 1910, GK.

21. Batson to Mary Harriman, May 11, Sept. 13, 21, Oct. 27, Dec. 22, and undated, 1911, AF. A partial list of those interviewed by Batson, along with clippings from several New York papers on the forthcoming appearance of the book, are in AF.

22. Batson to Mary Harriman, Dec. 22, 1911, AF; Lovett to Frank A. Vanderlip, Jan. 16, 1912; FAV; *New York Times*, Jan. 10, 1912; *New York Tribune*, Jan. 10, 1912; Union Pacific Exec. Com. minutes, Jan. 9, 1912, UPN; Lovett to William Sproule, Jan. 10, 1912, UPN.

23. Interview with W. Averell Harriman, June 23, 1981; Harriman, *I Reminisce*, 62; Kennan notes, 1-0-12, AF; *New York Tribune*, Jan. 10, 1912. In June 1915 Lovett told C. W. Barron that all his own letters from Harriman, as well as those in the Union Pacific offices and legal department, were destroyed in the fire.

24. *New York Times*, May 15, 1912; *New York Tribune*, May 15, 1912.

25. Kennan diary, Mar. 12, 1912.

26. Ibid., Jan. 10, Feb. 12–14, 1914.

27. Kennan to E. D. Kenna, Jan. 30, 1916, AF. The letter to Kenna, like many of those at AF, is in draft form.

28. Kennan diary, Mar. 1, 12, 17, 26, 28, 1914, Feb. 20, 1915.

29. Ibid., Apr. 15, 20, 21, 27, 1914; Kennan to his wife, Apr. 16, 1914, GK.

30. Kennan to his wife, Oct. 26, 1914, GK; Kennan diary, Oct. 24, 1914.

31. Kennan diary, Oct. 25, 1914.

32. Ibid., Nov. 4, 5, 11, 17, Dec. 16, 1914, Mar. 3, 5, 1915; Kennan to Lawrence Abbott, Nov. 26, 1914, GK.

33. Kennan diary, Nov. 8, 1914, Aug. 7, 1920; *NCAB*, 33:380–81.

34. Kennan diary, Dec. 8, 1914, June 14, Aug. 26, 28, 30, Oct. 3, 6, 22, 26, 28, 29, Nov. 8, 1915; Kennan to Mary Harriman, Aug. 1, 1915, AF; Mary Harriman to Kahn, Oct. 15, 1915, OK; Kahn to Kennan, Oct. 27, 29, Nov. 15, 29, 1915, AF; Kennan to Felton, Nov. 2, 1915, AF.

35. Kennan to C. Hart Merriam, Jan. 11, 1916, GK; *NCAB*, 32:65; William Z. Ripley, *Railroads: Finance and Organization* (New York, 1915), 77, 112, 262–67.

36. Kennan to Mary Harriman, Aug. 1, 1915, AF; Kennan to Tegethoff, Aug. 29, 1915, AF.

37. Kennan to Mary Harriman, Oct. 25, Nov. 6, 1915, AF; Abbott to Kennan, Nov. 8, 1915, AF; Kennan diary, Oct. 6, 7, 29, Nov. 6, 1915.

38. Mary Harriman to Kennan, Nov. 7, 1915, AF; Kennan to Merriam, Jan. 11, 1916, GK; Kennan diary, Nov. 9, 10, 1915. The books were George Kennan, *The Chicago and Alton Case: A Misunderstood Transaction* (Garden City, N.Y., 1916) and *Misrepresentation in Railroad Affairs* (Garden City, N.Y., 1916).

39. Mary Harriman to Kennan, Dec. 31, 1915, AF; Kennan to Mary Harriman, Jan. 2, 17, 1916, AF; Lane to Kennan, Jan. 22, 1916, AF.

40. Ripley to Kennan, Jan. 19, 1916, AF.

41. Kennan to Ripley, Jan. 22, 1916, AF; Ripley to Felton, Feb. 14, 1916, AF; Kennan to Felton, Feb. 14, 1916, AF; Walker to Kennan, Feb. 15, 18, and 28, 1916, AF; Kennan to Walker, Feb. 16, 19, 29, 1916, AF; Walker to Ripley, Feb. 18, 1916, AF.

42. Kennan to Walker, Feb. 29, 1916, AF. See, for example, the review in *WSJ*, Feb. 10, 1916.

43. Kennan diary, Jan. 29, Feb. 15, 1916; Mary Harriman to Kennan, Mar. 19, 1916, AF.

44. Seligman to Mary Harriman, Apr. 8, 1916, AF; Ripley to Seligman, Mar. 18, 1916, AF; Kennan to Kahn, Mar. 21, 1916, AF; Kahn to Kennan, Mar. 22, 1916, AF; Mary Harriman to Kennan, Apr. 4, 1916, AF. Ripley also told Judge Lovett, "I am urging Mrs. Harriman to have the matter [biography] treated in a more dignified and literary fashion" (Ripley to Lovett, Apr. 14, 1916, AF).

45. Ripley to Kennan, Mar. 10, 1916, AF; William Z. Ripley, "Federal Financial Railway Regulation: The Alton as a Test Case," *North American Review* 203 (Apr. 1916): 538–52. The source Ripley denounced was a piece by Frank Spearman, a noted popular railroad writer.

46. Mary Harriman to Kennan, Apr. 1, 1916, AF; Ripley, "Federal Financial Railway Regulation," 538; Kennan, *Misrepresentation in Railroad Affairs*. Like his original piece, a shortened version of Kennan's reply appeared first in *North American Review*, May and June 1916, and was published in full as the separate volume given here.

47. Ripley, "Federal Financial Railway Regulation," 548–51. Kennan's rebuttal is included in his *Misrepresentation* volume.

48. Ripley to editor of *North American Review*, May 18, 1916, AF; Kennan to Mr. Brennan, May 28, 1916, AF; Ripley to Lovett, Apr. 14, 1916, AF; Lovett to Ripley, Apr. 20, 1916, AF; Lovett to Kennan, Apr. 26, 1916, AF; Kennan diary, May 3, 1916.

49. Arthur Pound and Samuel Taylor Moore, *They Told Barron: Conversations and Revelations of an American Pepys in Wall Street* (New York, 1930), 58–59.

50. Kennan to Mary Harriman, Jan. 17, 1916, AF.

51. Kennan to Slason Thompson, Nov. 21, 1915, AF. A copy of the Alton statement is at AF.
52. Mary Harriman to Kennan, Mar. 1, 1916, AF; Kennan diary, Mar. 1, 6, 1916. Mary's note includes a list of the memoirs, copies of which are at AF.
53. Kennan diary, Mar. 6, 9, 1916. Even after this find, however, Kennan still maintained that "most of the Harriman papers and documents were destroyed in the burning of the Equitable Building" (Kennan to Miss Dawes, Nov. 2, 1916, GK).
54. Kennan diary, Apr. 26, 29, May 2, 3, 1916; Kennan to Mary Harriman, Apr. 30, 1916, AF; Mary Harriman to Kennan, Nov. 12, 1916, AF.
55. Kennan diary, May 5, 31, 1916, Jan. 5, Feb. 14, 22, 1917; Kennan to his wife [Jan. 5, 1917], GK.
56. Kennan diary, Aug. 18, Sept. 8, Oct. 1, 3, 5, 11, Nov. 16, 24, 25, 28, 1916, Jan. 11, 12, 18, Mar. 6, 1917; Mary Harriman to Kennan, Jan. 27, 1917, AF; Kennan to Mary Harriman, Feb. 12, 1917, May 8, 1919, AF.
57. Averell Harriman to Kennan, Feb. 15, 28, May 3, 1917, AF; Kennan to Averell Harriman, Feb. 16, 28, 1917, AF; Kennan to Schiff, Mar. 12, Oct. 17, 1917, AJA; Schiff to Kennan, Mar. 13, June 18, Oct. 22, 1917, AJA, Mar. 14, 1917, AF; Kennan to Mary Harriman, Mar. 15, 1917, AF.
58. Kennan to Mary Harriman, July 17, 1921, AF; Kennan diary, Jan. 4, 1919, July 17, 1921.
59. Kennan to Mary Harriman, July 17, 1921, AF; Kennan diary, Jan. 4, 1919, July 17, 1921.
60. Kennan diary, Mar. 15, 1917; Isaacson and Thomas, *Wise Men*, 158.
61. Kennan to Tegethoff, May 5, 1917, AF; Kennan to Schiff, May 18, 1917, AJA; Kennan diary, Apr. 27, 1917, Jan. 3, 31, May 16, 1919; Kennan to Mary Harriman, Feb. 7, 1918, May 8, 1919, AF.
62. Kennan to Schiff, May 7, 1920, GK; Kennan to Mary Harriman, Nov. 20, 1918, GK.
63. Kennan to Mary Harriman, Jan. 18, 1920, GK.
64. Ibid., Oct. 1, Dec. 3, 1920, Feb. 5, 1921, AF. Kennan's diary provides a running chronology of when he worked on each episode.
65. Kennan to Mary Harriman, Oct. 1, 1920, Apr. 19, 1921, AF; Kennan diary, Mar. 17, June 21, 26, July 2, 1921.
66. Kennan diary, Apr. 16, 29, June 27, July 2, 6, 1921; Kennan to Mary Harriman, Feb. 5, Apr. 19, 1921, AF; Lovett to Mary Harriman, May 12, 1921, AF; Lovett to Kennan, Apr. 25, 1921, AF; Kennan to Lovett, Apr. 28, July 2, 1921, AF.
67. Ferris Greenslet to Kennan, Oct. 8, 10, 1921, AF; Kennan to Mary Harriman, Oct. 10, 1921, Feb. 13, 1922, AF; Kennan diary, Sept. 29, Oct. 6, 10, 15, 21, 24, Nov. 6, Dec. 12, 20, 1921, Jan. 11, Feb. 28, 1922. See also the series of letters from Mary Harriman to Kennan in early 1922, GK.
68. Kennan to Mary Harriman, Feb. 28, June 12, 22, 1922, AF; Mary Harriman to Kennan, Mar. 6, 1922, GK; Kennan diary, Apr. 17, 18, June 12, 1923.
69. Kennan to Mary Harriman, June 12, 14, 22, July 27, 1922; Kennan diary, Oct. 3, 31, 1922, Apr. 9, 1923.
70. Kennan to Mary Harriman, Sept. 6, 1923, AF.
71. Ibid., Nov. 23, 1923, Feb. 13, 1924, AF; Mary Harriman to Lena Harriman, Nov. 30, 1924, AF; *New York Times*, Nov. 8, 1932, May 28, 1940.
72. Kennan to Mary Harriman, June 14, 1922, AF; Mary Harriman to Kennan, Nov. 5, 1922, GK.

CHAPTER 1

1. Rosamond Harriman Owen, family reminiscence, 2, AF. Rosamond was Orlando's youngest child.

2. I am grateful to William J. Rich III for providing me with a genealogical chart of the Harriman family. A briefer version drawn up by Tegethoff is in AF.

3. The date of William's move is uncertain. George Kennan, *E. H. Harriman*, 2 vols. (New York, 1922), 1:3, gives it as 1800, but Rosamond Owen, reminiscence, 3, said she did not know the date. William first appeared in a city directory in 1803–4. See Thomas Longworth, *New-York Register and City Directory* (New York, 1804), 164. See also Longworth, *Directory*, 1811, 126.

4. Owen, reminiscence, 4.

5. Ibid., 2.

6. Ibid., 6.

7. Ibid., 4–5; Margaret Armstrong, *Five Generations: Life and Letters of an American Family, 1750–1900* (New York, 1930), 266.

8. The essay, dated April 6, 1832, and evidently written for a young men's debating association, is at AF.

9. Owen, reminiscence, 6–7; Armstrong, *Five Generations*, chart just before index.

10. Armstrong, *Five Generations*, 264, 267; Kennan, *Harriman*, 1:5.

11. Kennan, notes of talk with Cornelia Simons, Aug. 19, 1917, AF; C. M. Keys, "Harriman," *World's Work* 13 (Jan. 1907): 8459–60; Kennan, *Harriman*, 1:6.

12. Kennan, *Harriman*, 1:6–7. Parts of Orlando's story can also be found in fragments of Batson's manuscript, AF.

13. RGD, New York City, 268:509; John Daggett Jr., *The New-York City Directory* (New York, years cited), 1842–43, 148, 1844–45, 157, 1846–47, 176, 1848–49, 187, 1849–50, 192; Charles R. Rode, *The New-York City Directory* (New York, 1853–54), 286.

14. RGD, New York City, 225:133, 268:509; Rode, *Directory*, 1856, 363, 1856–57, 356.

15. Keys, "Harriman," 8460; Batson fragment, AF; Kennan, *Harriman*, 1:8–9.

16. Carl Snyder, "Harriman: 'Colossus of Roads,'" *Review of Reviews* 35 (Jan. 1907): 39.

17. Kennan, *Harriman*, 1:9–11; Snyder, "Harriman," 39.

18. Kennan to Cornelia Simons, Feb. 4, 1918, AF. See, for example, Keys, "Harriman," 8459; Edwin Lefevre, "Harriman," *American Magazine* 64 (June 1907): 115.

19. Keys, "Harriman," 8460; Kennan, *Harriman*, 1:11–12.

20. Committee on Admission minutes, July 28, 1870, New York Stock Exchange; Francis L. Eames, *The New York Stock Exchange* (New York, 1968), 73, 123; Kennan, *Harriman*, 1:12–13.

21. Maury Klein, *The Life and Legend of Jay Gould* (Baltimore, 1986), 68–71.

22. James K. Medbery, *Men and Mysteries of Wall Street* (New York, 1870), 11.

23. Eames, *New York Stock Exchange*, 121.

24. John Moody and George Kibbe Turner, "Masters of Capital in America," *McClure's Magazine*, Jan. 1911, 335.

25. RGD, New York City, 225:133, 268:509; John F. Trow, *The New-York City Directory*, 1863–64, 364, 1864–65, 376, 1865–66, 412, 1867, 431, 1868, 440, 1869, 462; E. C. Stedman, *The New York Stock Exchange* (New York, 1905), 146.

26. Committee on Admissions minutes, July 28, 1870, New York Stock Exchange; Stedman, *New York Stock Exchange*, 147; Eames, *New York Stock Exchange*, 51, 85, 127; Moody and Turner, "Masters of Capital," 336. In 1864 the initiation fee had been raised to $3,44, but in October 1868 memberships were made salable from a retiring member to newcomers on approval by the committee on admissions. Tegethoff thought Harriman had paid $5,51 for his seat. See Kennan to Rensselaer Weston, Jan. 22, 1917, AF.

27. Moody and Turner, "Masters of Capital," 335.

CHAPTER 2

1. John Moody and George Kibbe Turner, "Masters of Capital in America," *McClure's Magazine*, Jan. 1911, 335–36.
2. Francis L. Eames, *The New York Stock Exchange* (New York, 1968), 96.
3. Moody and Turner, "Masters of Capital," 336; George Kennan, *E. H. Harriman*, 2 vols. (New York, 1922), 1:16.
4. Weston to Kennan, Jan. 5, 1917, AF; Kennan interview with Cornelia Simons, Aug. 19, 1917, AF; Kennan, *Harriman*, 1:18–19. For background on the Livingston family, see Clare Brandt, *An American Aristocracy: The Livingstons* (Garden City, N.Y., 1986).
5. James K. Medbery, *Men and Mysteries of Wall Street* (New York, 1870), 111.
6. Kennan, *Harriman*, 1:17–18; C. M. Keys, "Harriman," *World's Work* 13 (Jan. 1907): 8461.
7. *Literary Digest*, Sept. 18, 1909, 420; Keys, "Harriman," 8461; Edwin Lefevre, "Harriman," *American Magazine* 64 (June 1907): 118; J. B. Berry, "Notes on J. B. Berry's Association with Mr. E. H. Harriman," 8, AF.
8. RGD, New York, 397:300L; John F. Trow, *The New-York City Directory*, 1868, 440, 1869, 462.
9. RGD, New York, 397:300A1, 300A44; Trow, *Directory*, 1874–75, 544.
10. Committee on Admissions minutes, June 15, 1877, New York Stock Exchange; RGD, New York, 397:300A1, 300A44; Trow, *Directory*, 1877–78, 571–72; *New York Times*, Dec. 30, 1911.
11. RGD, New York, 397:300A44.
12. *Galveston News*, Sept. 10, 1909.
13. Moody, "Masters of Capital," 335; Kennan, *Harriman*, 1:19–20.
14. Edward Livingston Trudeau, *An Autobiography* (Garden City, N.Y., 1916), 78–81.
15. Ibid., 82–83.
16. Ibid., 15–16.
17. Ibid., 71–96.
18. Ibid., 90–91.
19. Kennan, *Harriman*, 1:22–23.
20. Ibid., 1:23–24.
21. Kennan dairy, Mar. 6, 1917, GK; George C. Clark to Kennan, Mar. 12, 1917, AF; Kennan to Clark, Mar. 13, 1917, AF.
22. Clark to Kennan, Mar. 15, 1917, AF; Kennan interview with H. S. Brooks, undated, AF. Brooks was an officer in the Boys' Club. See also Kennan to Moody, Feb. 4, 1918, AF.
23. Kennan interview with Brooks, AF.
24. Kennan, *Harriman*, 1:28.
25. Ibid., 1:29; Kennan interview with Brooks, AF.
26. Clark to Kennan, Mar. 12, 1917, AF.
27. Kennan to Moody, Feb. 6, 1918, AF.
28. Harriman to the President and Board of Directors of the Illinois Central Railroad, Feb. 20, 1889, IC.
29. Kennan, *Harriman*, 1:30–58.
30. Francis H. Tabor, "Mr. E. H. Harriman and the Boys' Club," AF.
31. Ibid.
32. RGD, New York, 552:251, 553:424.
33. Ibid., 268:509, 553:433, 442, 565, 568, 711; Persia Campbell, *Mary Williamson Harriman* (New York, 1960), 3.

34. RGD, New York, 397:300A44. There are pictures of young Henry and Mary in Campbell, *Mary Williamson Harriman*, 4.

35. Kennan notes on recollections of R. Fulton Cutting, Sept. 6, 1910, AF.

36. J. D. Morrison, "Recollections and Impressions of the Late E. H. Harriman," 1–2, AF; Kennan, *Harriman*, 1:61; Henry V. Poor, *Manual of the Railroads of the United States* (New York, 1879), 205, *Manual*, 1880, 196. There is a curious contradiction about the wedding. Kennan says it took place at the Averell home, while Morrison, who presided at the wedding, says it occurred at St. John's Church before an "immense congregation." Mary did not correct Kennan's version even though Kennan later quoted Morrison's version of events. See Kennan, *Harriman*, 1:61, 2:389.

37. Trow, *Directory*, 1880–81, 648, 1883–84, 704, 1885, 724, 1886, 811. Roosevelt lived at 6 West 57th Street.

38. Lewis R. Morris, "A Successful Life, Edward Henry Harriman," 4, AF.

39. Kennan to Mary Harriman, May 15, 1921, AF, quoting Lovett's letter.

40. Eames, *New York Stock Exchange*, 80–81; RGD, New York City, 397:300A44.

41. *Chronicle*, 33:11.

42. RGD, New York, 397:300A44, 300A116.

43. Ibid.; Eames, *New York Stock Exchange*, 133.

CHAPTER 3

1. Computed from *Chronicle*, 42:41. The nonrail issues included five telegraph, four express company, eleven coal and mining, and six other issues.

2. *DAB*, 6:397–403; S. Fish, *1600–1914* (Privately printed, 1942), 162–73, 191. This family volume by Fish's son contains some extracts from Fish's letters of the period. George Kennan, *E. H. Harriman*, 2 vols. (New York, 1922), 1:18, suggests that Harriman met Fish during his early years on Wall Street but has no hard evidence on the subject in his notes.

3. *DAB*, 6:402–3; *New York Times*, Apr. 11, 1923; Margaret Armstrong, *Five Generations: Life and Letters of an American Family, 1750–1900* (New York, 1930), 375–76.

4. William K. Ackerman, *Historical Sketch of the Illinois-Central Railroad* (Chicago, 1890), 142–43; John F. Stover, *History of the Illinois Central Railroad* (New York, 1975), 144–71, 208, 210.

5. Edward Chase Kirkland, *Men, Cities and Transportation*, 2 vols. (Cambridge, Mass., 1948), 1:158–72, 174–80; Henry V. Poor, *Manual of the Railroads of the United States for 1871–1872* (New York, 1872), 293–94, 419, 1872–73, 79, 1873–74, 316, 1875–76, 185, 446, 1876–77, 678, 1877–78, 159; *Chronicle*, 28:526.

6. Poor, *Manual*, 1877–78, 157, 1878, 197, 1879, 204–5.

7. Ibid., 1881, 157, 1882, 162; *Chronicle*, 30:118, 144, 323, 358, 494, 622, 31:358, 429, 484, 560, 34:686, 36:212, 622, 42:753.

8. Poor, *Manual*, 1870–71, 330, 1872–73, 226, 1873–74, 341; RGD, New York, 618:283, 407, 418.

9. RGD, New York, 366:207, 300, 300Q, 364:100A2.

10. Ibid., 34:100A2, 618:407, 454, 462, 473; Poor, *Manual*, 1870–71, 330, 1872–73, 226, 1873–74, 341, 1874–75, 149, 1875–76, 200, 1876–77, 220, 243, 1877–78, 158, 1878, 199.

11. RGD, New York, 618:473, 582; Poor, *Manual*, 1879, 206, 1880, 164, 1881, 124, 1882, 125–26; *Chronicle*, 30:434, 466, 33:412.

12. J. B. Berry, "Notes on J. B. Berry's Association with Mr. E. H. Harriman," June 21, 1911, 1, AF.

13. Ibid., 2.

14. RGD, New York, 619:32; Kennan, *Harriman*, 1:61–66; *Annual Report of the State Engineer and Surveyor of the Railroads of the State of New York* (Albany, 1881), 304, 1883, 579, 1884, 617; Poor, *Manual*, 1883, 197; *Chronicle*, 35:132, 313. Kennan's version of this episode contains numerous factual errors.

15. H. B. LeFebore to W. W. Webb, Jan. 31, 1911, AF; Batson notes from interview with W. W. Webb, undated, AF; *Annual Report of the State Engineer and Surveyor*, 1884, 617; Poor, *Manual*, 1884, 189–90; Berry, "Notes," 1–2. LeFebore and Webb are the only sources for the assertion that Harriman bought the others out and took charge of the road, and their accounts conflict at points.

16. Poor, *Manual*, 1885, 189–90.

17. Data on the Sodus Bay during these years can be found in *Annual Report of the State Engineer and Surveyor*, 1880, 684–88, 1881, 810–16, 1882, 304–7, 1883, 578–79, and its successor, *Annual Report of the Board of Railroad Commissioners of the State of New York* (Albany, 1884), 2:617–22, 1885, 2:745–55. See also Poor, *Manual*, 1873–74, 341, 1874–75, 149, 1879, 206, 1880, 164, 1882, 125–26, 1884, 189–90. Unfortunately, the data are scant for 1881 and 1882.

18. LeFebore to Webb, Jan. 31, 1911, AF. All figures are calculated from data in sources listed in above two notes.

19. Poor, *Manual*, 1884, 189–90.

20. Batson notes from interview with W. W. Webb, undated, AF; Kennan, *Harriman*, 1:64–65. Kennan emphasizes repeatedly that Harriman had "rebuilt and reequipped" the road.

21. Batson notes from interview with W. W. Webb, undated, AF; *Chronicle*, 39:48, 784; Poor, *Manual*, 1885, 189–90; Kennan, *Harriman*, 1:65; Fish to J. T. Harahan, Sept. 18, 1894, IC; Charles C. Tegethoff to Fish, Jan. 21, 1901, SF; W. W. Webb to Fish, May 13, 1910, SF. Kennan says Harriman "happened to be absent from his office" that morning, but it is hard to believe that his absence was not calculated.

22. Ackerman, *Historical Sketch*, 95, 112–20; Stover, *History of the Illinois Central*, 15, 127–71; *Chronicle*, 34:144.

23. *Chronicle*, 30:218, 33:357–58, 34:144, 36:298–99, 310, 38:243–45; Clarke to Ackerman, May 10, 1877, IC. Figures computed from data in company annual reports.

24. Ackerman, *Historical Sketch*, 134–37; Stover, *History of the Illinois Central*, 177–78.

25. IC Directors minutes, June 18, 1879, Mar. 17, Oct. 20, 1880, Mar. 25, 1881, Feb. 7, 1882, records in possession of ICI; Clarke to W. H. Osborn, Dec. 26, 1881, IC; *Chronicle*, 34:144.

26. IC Directors minutes, June 23, July 11, 1881, ICI.

27. Ibid., Sept. 21, 1881, ICI; John Moody and George Kibbe Turner, "Masters of Capital in America," *McClure's Magazine*, Jan. 1911, 337–38; Kennan, *Harriman*, 1:70. Kennan takes his version almost entirely from Moody.

28. Poor, *Manual*, 1880, 769–70.

29. *Chronicle*, 30:91, 34:177, 489, 35:637, 36:310; Clarke to Fish, Jan. 16, Oct. 5, 1882, IC; Clarke to Ackerman, Nov. 1, 1882, IC; Clarke to W. H. Osborn, Apr. 3, Nov. 29, 1882, IC; IC Directors minutes, Mar. 16, 1882, ICI; Clarke notice, Jan. 1, 1883, IC.

30. IC Directors minutes, Nov. 15, 1882, Jan. 17, Apr. 21, 1883, ICI; Clarke to Ackerman, Nov. 20, Dec. 9, 1882, IC; Ackerman to W. Bayard Cutting, Mar. 9, 1883, IC; Clarke to Fish, Mar. 27, 1883, IC; Clarke to Osborn, Feb. 2, Apr. 2, 1883, IC.

31. *Chronicle*, 36: 298; IC Directors minutes, Nov. 3, 1881, ICI; Poor, *Manual*, 1882, 691, 1883, 725.

32. IC Directors minutes, May 31, 1882, May 30, 1883, ICI; Moody and Turner, "Masters of Capital," 338.

33. Clarke to Fish, May 24, 1883, IC; Ackerman to John Elliott, Aug. 11, 1883, IC; IC Directors minutes, July 18, Aug. 15, 1883, ICI. Ackerman was formally made first vice-president during his leave, then resigned at the end of it.

34. IC Directors minutes, Dec. 5, 19, 1883, ICI.

35. Ibid., Dec. 19, 1883, ICI.

36. Ibid., Feb. 26, 1884, ICI; Clarke to Fish, Feb. 29, 1884, IC.

37. IC Directors minutes, Mar. 12, Apr. 16, 1884, ICI; *Chronicle*, 38:332, 40:337; Poor, *Manual*, 1884, 701.

38. *Chronicle*, 38:87, 243–45; Moody and Turner, "Masters of Capital," 338.

39. IC Directors minutes, May 21, July 16, 1884, Mar. 21, 1885, ICI.

40. *New York Times*, Apr. 11, 1923; Elizabeth Drexel Lehr, *"King Lehr" and the Gilded Age* (Philadelphia, 1935), 168–69.

41. Lehr, *"King Lehr" and the Gilded Age*, 169–70.

CHAPTER 4

1. RGD, New York City, 397:A116, A140; Harriman to Stuyvesant Fish, Oct. 22, 1887, IC; DAB, 6:398. See George Kennan, *E. H. Harriman*, 2 vols. (New York, 1922), 1:74, for the standard version of Harriman's departure from Wall Street.

2. RGD, New York City, 397:A140; Dissolution notice, Jan. 3, 1888, IC.

3. Carl Snyder, "Harriman: Colossus of Roads," *Review of Reviews* 35 (Jan. 1907): 40.

4. Clarke to Fish, Mar. 2, 1886, IC; *Chronicle*, 42:338.

5. Clarke to James Fentress, Mar. 23, 1887, IC; *Chronicle*, 44:653; IC Directors minutes, Mar. 16, May 18, Sept. 28, Dec. 21, 1887, Apr. 18, 1888, ICI; William K. Ackerman, *Historical Sketch of the Illinois-Central Railroad* (Chicago, 1890), 134, 137.

6. John Moody and George Kibbe Turner, "Masters of Capital in America," *McClure's Magazine*, Jan. 1911, 338; Kennan, *Harriman*, 1:74; Harriman to Fish, July 17, 1884, Apr. 7, 1886, IC; *Chronicle*, 41:585, 612, 42:306, 43:245, 44:310; Harriman to Vermilye & Co., July 9, 1886, IC; IC Directors minutes, Feb. 17, 1886, ICI; IC Exec. Com. minutes, June 30, Sept. 6, 1886, ICI.

7. Harriman to Fish, May 25, 1888, IC.

8. Harriman to Fish, Oct. 15, Nov. 15, 1886, Jan. 6, 12, 22, 24, July 8, 11, 12, Aug. 1, 4, 5, 9, 20, Sept. 19, 1887, IC; *Chronicle*, 43:607, 671, 44:118, 310, 526, 808, 46:383; *Railroad Gazette*, 19:427. These citations are but a sample of the large amount of correspondence by Harriman and his firm on borrowing and lending money for the Illinois Central.

9. Clarke to Fish, Jan. 6, 1885, IC; Harriman to Fish, Dec. 18, 1885, Mar. 3, Apr. 7, Oct. 15, Nov. 5, 29, 1886, Jan. 3, Feb. 1, 1887, IC; B. F. Ayer to Fish, Jan. 6, Oct. 7, Nov. 3, 1886, IC; Fish to Harriman, Nov. 4, 1886, IC.

10. Clarke to Fish, Aug. 27, 1885, Sept. 25, Oct. 8, Dec. 13, 1886, Jan. 27, Feb. 3, 1887, IC; Clarke to Osborn, Mar. 2, Apr. 10, 1883, IC; *Chronicle*, 37:479, 40:716, 43:190; John F. Stover, *History of the Illinois Central Railroad* (New York, 1975), 201. The 112-mile Chicago, Madison & Northern ran from Chicago to Freeport, with a 59-mile branch to Madison, Wisconsin, and a shorter one to Dodgeville.

11. Stover, *History of the Illinois Central*, 532.

12. *Chronicle*, 42:306, 46:382; *Bill of complaint, Edward C. Woodruff vs. The Dubuque & Sioux City Railroad Company, Anthony J. Drexel, John Pierpont Morgan et al.*, Jan. 29, 1887, 4–5, AF.

13. Clarke to Fish, Mar. 31, 1887, IC.

14. Jeffery to Fish, Apr. 11, 1886, IC; *Chronicle*, 43:766, 44:21; *Bill of complaint*, 4–15, AF. The committee consisted of Jesup, Morgan, Roosevelt, and Lorenzo Blackstone.

15. Fish to Harriman, undated, IC; *Answer of Anthony J. Drexel and others, Woodruff vs. The Dubuque & Sioux City Railroad Company, Anthony J. Drexel et al.*, Feb. 7, 1887, 2–3, AF.

16. Harriman to Fish, Feb. 11, 12, 1887, IC.

17. *Bill of complaint*, 21–22, AF; Minutes of the annual meeting of the Dubuque & Sioux City Railroad, Feb. 14, 1887, IC; *Chronicle*, 44:235. The minutes are actually a detailed transcript.

18. *Chronicle*, 44:235, 362, 433–34, 494, 46:382; Ackerman to Clarke, Mar. 17, 1887, IC; IC Directors minutes, Apr. 6, 1887, ICI; Drexel, Morgan & Co. to Fish, Apr. 7, 1887, IC; Jesup et al. to Fish, Apr. 7, 1887, IC.

19. Herbert L. Satterlee, *J. Pierpont Morgan: An Intimate Portrait* (New York, 1939), 243–44.

20. Webster to Fish, Nov. 23, 24, 1887, IC.

21. James M. Fry letter, Jan. 20, 1988, IC. For the legal issues involved, see the brief by Clarence A. Seward, Nov. 29, 1887, IC, and *Chronicle*, 46:38, and the plaintiff's amended petition of Feb. 1888, AF.

22. Harriman to Fish, Feb. 28, May 16, 1888, Nov. 2, 1891, IC; Fish to Harriman, Sept. 17, 1888, Feb. 12, 1889, July 26, Aug. 10, 1893, Nov. 3, 15, 1894, Feb. 6, Apr. 1, May 1, June 11, July 30, 1895, IC; C. A. Clark to Harriman, Oct. 10, 1888, IC; Harriman to Clark, Dec. 6, 1888, IC; *Chronicle*, 44:291, 539–40; 59:919, 60:82, 794, 61:1154, 62:588, 63:29.

23. *Chronicle*, 44:526–27; IC Directors minutes, Jan. 20, Dec. 15, 1886, ICI; Stover, *History of the Illinois Central*, 204–5.

24. The difference in the names used to address Harriman and the places he frequented during the summer are both revealed in the correspondence cited throughout this book.

25. Referees Deed: William Vanamee to Edward H. Harriman, Nov. 3, 1886, AF; RGD, New York, 497:214, 521:130; Marian Gouverneur, *As I Remember* (New York, 1911), 119–23.

26. RGD, New York, 497:214, 226, 521:130.

27. Ibid., 497:37, 42, 214, 226, 443, 462, 521:130, 522:253.

28. Ibid., 498:462; *DAB*, 14:261; Kennan, *Harriman*, 1:74–75, 2:30–32. Kennan says the Parrotts were boyhood friends of Harriman; Roland Harriman says his father met the Parrotts during the 1870s, before he was married (*I Reminisce* [Garden City, N.Y., 1975], 254). The account of this affair in Kennan contains several errors, including the incorrect date of 1885 for the sale.

29. Referees Deed: William Vanamee to Edward H. Harriman, Nov. 3, 1886, AF; Harriman, *I Reminisce*, 255–56; Kennan, *Harriman*, 2:30–31. I am indebted to George Paffenbarger of Arden Farms for providing me a copy of this deed.

30. Edwin Wildman, "The Jekyll-Hyde Harriman," *Overland Monthly* 51 (Mar. 1908): 3, 210.

31. *DAB*, 11:411–12.

32. Cleveland Amory, *The Last Resorts* (New York, 1948), 77–122.

33. A picture of the house can be found in Harriman, *I Reminisce*, 64–65.

34. Fish to Harriman, May 24, 1887, IC.

CHAPTER 5

1. E. Roland Harriman, *I Reminisce* (Garden City, N.Y., 1975), 6.

2. IC Directors minutes, Feb. 20, 1889, ICI.

3. Rush Loving Jr., "W. Averell Harriman Remembers Life with Father," *Fortune*, May 8, 1978, 202.

4. Evidently this episode was a sensitive one in the family because Kennan omits all reference to Harry or his death or its effect on Harriman's later career.

5. IC Directors minutes, Mar. 21, 1888, ICI; Fish to Harriman, Mar. 6, Mar. 14, 15, 16, 1888, IC.

6. E. T. Jeffery to Fish, June 6, 7, 1888, IC. For an overview of the development of railroads as business enterprises, see Alfred D. Chandler Jr., *The Visible Hand: The Managerial Revolution in American Business* (Cambridge, Mass., 1977), 77–121.

7. IC Exec. Com. minutes, Apr. 5, 1888, ICI; IC Directors minutes, May 15, 1889, ICI; Harriman to Fish, June 27, 1888, IC; John F. Stover, *History of the Illinois Central Railroad* (New York, 1975), 204.

8. Harriman to Fish, Apr. 12 (two letters), 1888, IC; Fish to Harriman, Apr. 13, 14, 1888, IC.

9. Fish to Harriman, May 12, 22, 23, 26, 28, 1888, IC; Harriman to Fish, May 17, 24, 25, 1888, IC; Fish to Jeffery, May 22, 1888, IC.

10. Harriman to Fish, June 11, 27, 1888, IC.

11. Jeffery to Fish, July 3, 1888, IC; Ayer to Fish, July 12, 1888, IC.

12. Luttgen to Fish, Sept. 27, 1888, Jan. 23, May 13, 1889, IC; Webster to Fish, Jan. 22, 1889, IC; IC Directors minutes, May 15, 1889, ICI.

13. IC Directors minutes, Apr. 4, 17, 1889, ICI; Finance Com. minutes, May 8, 1889, ICI.

14. For more detail, see Maury Klein, *The Life and Legend of Jay Gould* (Baltimore, 1986), 177–79.

15. IC Directors minutes, July 25, 1888, ICI; *Chronicle*, 48:112–13, 128; Fish to Jeffery, July 30, 1888, IC; *Railroad Gazette*, 21:62, 68, 198. The dividend was handled on a semiannual basis so that each meeting declared a rate for half the year. The July 1888 rate of 3.5 percent was cut to 2.5 percent in January 1889.

16. *Railroad Gazette*, 19:582, 595, 596, 644, 821, 847, 854; Jeffery to Fish, July 22, 1888, Jan. 10, 1889, IC; Fish to Jeffery, Sept. 10, 1888, Jan. 8, 1889, IC; IC Directors minutes, Feb. 20, 1889, IC; Fish to Jeffery, Jan. 11, 12, 1889, IC; Fish to Ayer and Fentress, Jan. 12, 1889, IC; Jeffery to Fish, Jan. 26, 1889, IC; Ayer to Fish, Feb. 18, 1889, IC; Fish to Charles F. Adams et al., Feb. 20, 1889, IC.

17. IC Directors minutes, Apr. 17, 1889, ICI.

18. Fish to Harriman, Jan. 23, Feb. 4, 16, Aug. 3, 1888, May 6, 1889, IC; Harriman to Fish, Dec. 29, 1887, Jan. 9, Feb. 29, Apr. 2, May 19, 23, 29, July 11, 20, 1888, IC; Levi P. Morton to Fish, May 9, 1888, IC; *Railroad Gazette*, 20:97, 196, 263; Speyer & Co. to Fish, Mar. 29, 1888, IC.

19. Harriman to Fish, Feb. 1, 12, 1889, IC; Harriman to E. K. Wright, Feb. 6, 1889, IC; Harriman to John A. Stewart, Feb. 11, 1889, IC; Fish to Harriman, Feb. 12, 1889, IC; Harriman to Frederic Cromwell, Feb. 13, 1889, IC; Harriman to James Fentress, Feb. 26, 1889, IC.

20. Fish to James Fentress, Sept. 21, 1888, IC; Harriman to Fish, Oct. 5, 1888, IC; *New York Sun*, Feb. 17, 1889. For more on Ives, see Klein, *Gould*, 384, 467. The accounting error that probably inspired the *Sun*'s attack is discussed in *Railroad Gazette*, 21:198.

21. Boissevain Brothers to Fish, Mar. 2, 1889, IC; *New York Sun*, Mar. 5, 1889; Harriman to Fish, Mar. 2, 14, 1889 (several items), IC; Fish to Harriman, Mar. 14, 1889 (several items), IC.

22. Fish to Boissevain Brothers, Mar. 15, 1889, IC; *Chronicle*, 48:368; Harriman to Fish, May 15, 1889, IC.

23. Jeffery to Judge Thomas M. Cooley, Apr. 1, Apr. 2, 1889, IC; Jeffery to Fish, Apr. 12, 1889, IC; Jeffery to C. H. Chappell, Apr. 29, 1889, IC.

24. Fish to Jeffery, May 31, June 11, 1889, IC; Fish to George Bliss, May 31, 1889, IC; Fish to Board of Directors, June 11, 1889, IC; Jeffery to Fish, June 17, 1889, IC; Jeffery to Harriman, Sept. 2, 1889, IC. This version of events is mostly Jeffery's.

25. Jeffery to Fish, July 1, 6, 8, 1889, IC; IC Directors minutes, June 19, 1889, ICI; Jeffery to James Fentress, July 21, 1889, IC; Jeffery to Harriman, Sept. 2, 1889, IC.

26. Fish to Jeffery, July 5, 6, 1889, IC; Fish to Morton, Rose Co., June 28, 1889, IC; Fish to Harriman, July 9, 1889, IC.

27. Harriman to James Fentress, July 11, 1889, IC.

28. IC Directors minutes, May 15, 1889, ICI; Harriman to H. B. Plant, July 10, 1889, IC; Harriman to J. C. Welling, July 10, 1889, IC.

29. Jeffery to Harriman, July 15, 20, 1889, ICI; Harriman to S. V. R. Cruger, July 22, Aug. 14, 1889, IC; Harriman to Jeffery, July 16, 30, Aug. 5, 1889, IC; Jeffery to T. J. Hudson, July 15, July 20, Aug. 7, 1889, IC; G. M. King to Harriman, Aug. 12, 1889, IC; Hudson to Jeffery, Aug. 12, 1889, IC; Jeffery to Fentress, July 21, 1889, IC; Jeffery to John Deary, July 24, 1889, IC; *Railroad Gazette*, 21:500–501. Several of Jeffery's letters to friends about his resignation are in IC.

30. Harriman to Fish, Aug. 16, 1889, IC; Fish to Harriman, Sept. 1, 1889, IC.

31. Harriman to Jeffery, Aug. 13, 1889, IC; Jeffery to Harriman, Aug. 15, Sept. 2, 1889, IC; Jeffery memorandum, Sept. 2, 1889, ICI; Harriman memorandum, Sept. 2, 1889, ICI. The two accounts of the meeting agree on essential facts but differ slightly on sequence and give different coloring to their depiction.

32. Harriman memorandum, Sept. 2, 1889, ICI; Harriman to Jeffery, Sept. 2, 1889, IC; Jeffery circular, Sept. 2, 1889, IC; *Chronicle*, 49:316–17; *Railroad Gazette*, 21:588; Harriman to Fish, Sept. 2, 9, 24, 1889, IC.

33. Harriman to Board of Directors, Sept. 9, 1889, ICI; Harriman to Fish, Sept. 2, 9, 1889, ICI.

34. Fish to Harriman, Sept. 15, 1889, IC. For the conventional version of this incident, see George Kennan, *E. H. Harriman*, 2 vols. (New York, 1922), 1:82–87.

35. *Chronicle*, 49:316–17; Harriman to Hudson, Sept. 20, 21, 1889, IC.

36. Harriman to Beck, Sept. 2, 1889, IC; Harriman circular, Sept. 2, 1889, IC; Fentress to Harriman, Sept. 9, 1889, IC; Harriman to Fish, Sept. 2, 1889, IC.

37. John G. Mann to Harriman, Sept. 5, 1889, IC.

38. Ibid., Sept. 12, 1889, IC; Harriman to Mann, Sept. 9, 1889, IC; Chandler, *Visible Hand*, 175–82.

39. T. J. Hudson to J. C. Welling, Oct. 5, 1889, IC; Mann to Welling, Oct. 13, 1889, IC; Organization Board minutes, Oct. 25, 1889, IC. A copy of the new code is in ICI.

40. Harriman to Fish, Oct. 7, 1889, IC.

41. W. E. Ruttan to Harriman, Oct. 24, 1889, IC; Fish to Harriman, Oct. 26, 1889, IC.

42. Harriman to Fish, Nov. 11, 1889, IC; Fish to Board of Directors, Nov. 18, 1889, IC; Fish to Welling, Nov. 27, 1889, IC.

43. IC Finance Com. minutes, Dec. 5, 1889, ICI; IC Directors minutes, Nov. 20, Dec. 16, 1889, IC; *Railroad Gazette*, 22:33; Fish to Fentress, Dec. 16, 1889, IC.

44. IC Finance Com. minutes, Nov. 18, 1889, ICI; IC Directors minutes, Dec. 18, 1889, ICI; Harriman to Fish, Jan. 9, 1890, IC; Harriman to Fentress, Feb. 11, 1890, IC.

45. Fish to Jeffery, Jan. 28, 1889, IC; Jeffery to Fish, Apr. 7, 1889, IC; C. A. Beck to Harriman, Sept. 11, 1889, IC.

46. Fish to Jeffery, Jan. 28, 1889, IC; Jeffrey to Fish, Apr. 7, 1889, IC; C. A. Beck to Harriman, Sept. 11, 1889, IC; Fish to RRE com., Jan. 17, 23, 1890, IC.

47. RRE com. minutes, Jan. 20, 1890, IC; "Report of Committee on Rates, Revenues and Expenditures," Jan. 24, 1890, ICI.
48. Harriman to A. G. Hackstaff, Jan. 24, 1890, IC; IC Directors minutes, Jan. 4, 1890, ICI. The italics are in the original.
49. Kennan, *Harriman*, 1:88–92. Later writers picked up and embellished this same theme.
50. Harriman to Fentress, Feb. 11, 1890, IC; IC Directors minutes, Feb. 19, 1890, ICI; Fish to Harriman, Feb. 28, 1890, IC; Fish to Sidney Lawrence, Feb. 8, 1890, IC.
51. Fish to Harriman, Feb. 28, Mar. 1, 1890, IC; Harriman to Fish, Mar. 2, 1890, IC.
52. Harriman to Fish, Mar. 2, 1890, IC; IC Directors minutes, Mar. 19, 1890, ICI.
53. IC Directors minutes, Mar. 19, 1890, ICI.
54. Fish to William Boissevain, Mar. 25, 1890, SF.
55. Ibid.
56. IC Directors minutes, June 18, Oct. 20, 1890, ICI; IC Exec. Com. minutes, Oct. 15, 1890, ICI; IC Finance Com. minutes, Nov. 17, 1890, ICI; Fish to Messrs. Boissevain Bros. and Teixeira de Mattos Bros., Oct. 23, 1890, IC; *Railroad Gazette*, 22:744; *Chronicle*, 51:569. All improvements figures computed from data in Illinois Central annual reports for the period 1890–97.

CHAPTER 6

1. IC Directors minutes, June 18, Oct. 20, 1890, ICI; *Railroad Gazette*, 22:708; *New York Tribune*, Oct. 9, 1890; Fish to editor of *New York Tribune*, Oct. 18, 1890, ICI; *Chronicle*, 51:417.
2. Fish to Boissevain Bros. and Teixeira de Mattos Bros., Oct. 23, 1890, IC; *Chronicle*, 51:400, 418.
3. IC Finance com. minutes, May 19, 1890, July 13, Aug. 19, 1891, ICI; Fish to Walther Luttgen, Jan. 23, 1890, IC; Harriman to Speyer & Co. and August Belmont & Co., Jan. 31, 1890, IC; Harriman to Fish, Aug. 21, 1890, IC; Fish to J. W. Auchincloss, July 16, 1890, IC; Fish to Boissevain Brothers, Oct. 27, 1890, IC; Harriman & Co. to Fish, Feb. 5, Aug. 11, Sept. 21, Oct. 26, Dec. 14, 1891, IC; *Chronicle*, 51:114, 400, 418, 457, 493, 53:71, 455–57, 55:255–56, 528–29, 639; IC Directors minutes, May 21, July 23, 1890, Jan. 21, 1891, ICI.
4. *Chronicle*, 55:546; Harriman to Fish, Oct. 5, 1892, SF.
5. Otto H. Kahn, "Edward Henry Harriman," in Stuart Bruchey, ed., *Memoirs of Three Railroad Pioneers* (New York, 1981), 1; George Kennan, *E. H. Harriman*, 2 vols. (New York, 1922), 1:93.
6. Harriman to Fish, Nov. 29, Dec. 8, 1892, SF; Fish to Harriman, Aug. 3, 1893, Sept. 18, 1894, IC; *Chronicle*, 56:103, 127, 57:533–34, 60:391, 61:558, 966, 62:988, 63:76; *Railroad Gazette*, 25:736, 26:670, 27:144, 663, 814; Fish to Speyer & Co., Jan. 28, 1896, IC; Fish memorandum, Feb. 10, 1896, IC; Harriman to National Bank of Scotland, July 17, 1896, IC; Harriman to Bell, Cowan & Co., Jan. 26, 1897, IC; Harriman to Fish, July 22, 1896, IC.
7. Harriman to Fish, Apr. 2, 1897, IC.
8. Ibid.
9. Harriman to Fish, Mar. 10, 1892, IC.
10. Ibid., Dec. 18, 1888, Feb. 9, Mar. 20, June 1, Dec. 30, 1889, Feb. 25, 1890, IC; Fish to Harriman, Feb. 12, Mar. 30, Apr. 9, 1889, Oct. 28, 1892, IC; Harriman to Fentress, Dec. 19, 1888, Mar. 18, 20, Apr. 11, 18, Nov. 25, 1889, IC; *Chronicle*, 48:462, 54:939, 964, 55:59, 679, 57:550.
11. *Chronicle*, 57:763, 1083, 58:716, 59:1006; IC Directors minutes, July 31, Nov. 15, 1893, ICI; Fish to Harriman, Nov. 17, Dec. 5, 1893, Jan. 2, Feb. 16, Mar. 10, 13, 20, 26, Apr. 16, 24, May 7, 31, June 8, 28, 30, Sept. 27, Dec. 31, 1894, Feb. 1, 19, 25, July 30, 1895, IC; Fish to

August Belmont, Dec. 5, 1893, Feb. 16, May 7, 15, 31, June 8, 1894, IC; Belmont to Fish, Feb. 27, 1894, IC.

12. Harriman to Fentress, June 29, July 22, Aug. 7, 1896, IC; Harriman to Fish, July 6, 1896, IC; Fish to Harriman, May 5, Nov. 28, Dec. 3, 31, 1896, Feb. 3, Apr. 12, 17, 22, 24, July 21, 26, 27, 29, Dec. 10, 1897, IC; Agreement between E. H. Harriman and Western Contract Co., Aug. 4, 1890, IC; Harriman to George W. Norton, Nov. 2, 1896, IC; Harriman to Post & Pomeroy, Dec. 8, 1896, IC; *Chronicle*, 64:42, 755, 65:111, 235, 415, 516; *Railroad Gazette*, 29:756.

13. Figures taken from company annual reports.

14. Kennan, *Harriman*, 1:93.

15. Vincent P. Carosso, with Rose C. Carosso, *The Morgans: Private International Bankers, 1854–1913* (Cambridge, Mass., 1987), 373–75; *Chronicle*, 58:43, 178, 223, 263–64.

16. *Chronicle*, 58:383, 408, 430, 474, 595, 636, 716, 941, 1073; Edwin Lefevre, "Harriman," *American Magazine* 64 (June 1907): 121.

17. *Chronicle*, 58:1109, 59:291, 781, 880, 920, 945, 965, 1031, 1058, 60:83, 302, 349, 392, 432, 657, 795, 874, 968, 1105, 61:240, 325, 366–73, 449, 472, 559, 750, 831, 871, 925, 1013; Carosso with Carosso, *Morgans*, 375–78.

18. Kennan, *Harriman*, 1:102–3; Herbert L. Satterlee, *J. Pierpont Morgan: An Intimate Portrait* (New York, 1939), 272.

19. Fish to Harriman, July 9, 17, 1895, July 2, 1897, Nov. 3, 1898, Dec. 4, 14, 1900, Aug. 21, 1901, IC; "Analysis of Sample Beets . . . ," Nov. 28, 1896, IC; M. R. Spelman to E. P. Skene, Nov. 30, 1896, IC; Skene to J. C. Welling, Jan. 29, 1897, IC; Welling to Fish, Feb. 1, 1897, IC; Spelman to Fish, Feb. 16, 1897, IC; Harriman to Fish, Dec. 28, 30, 1896, July 12, 1897, Mar. 1, 1898, IC; John E. Searles to Fish, Feb. 3, 1897, IC; A. L. Walburn to Fish, Sept. 21, 1898, IC.

20. S. M. Connico to Fish and Harriman, June ?, 1886, IC; J. T. Harahan to Fish, Jan. 28, 1897, IC; L. C. Fallon to Harahan, Jan. 26, 1897, IC; Fish to Harriman, Aug. 21, 1901, IC; Fish to Clarence F. Parker, Apr. 8, 1896, AF.

21. J. B. Berry, "Notes on J. B. Berry's Association with Mr. E. H. Harriman," June 21, 1911, 11, AF; Harriman to ?, Oct. 15, 1901, AF.

22. RGD, New York, 168:65; E. T. Jeffery to Harriman, Apr. 2, 1889, IC; G. Wallace Chessman, *Governor Theodore Roosevelt* (Cambridge, Mass., 1965), 15–17; W. W. Webb, "Some Recollections of Edward H. Harriman," 3–6, AF.

23. Tegethoff to Fish, Feb. 27, 1903, SF.

24. E. Roland Harriman, *I Reminisce* (Garden City, N.Y., 1975), 2.

25. Russell Headley, ed., *The History of Orange County, New York* (Middletown, N.Y., 1908), 761–64.

26. Telephone interview with George Paffenbarger, Arden Farms, Jan. 25, 1989; RGD, New York, 502:6; Harriman, *I Reminisce*, 257. Letters from Harriman with the Arden Farms letterhead can be found in IC.

27. Headley, *History of Orange County*, 759–60; Harriman, *I Reminisce*, 232.

28. Headley, *History of Orange County*, 751–59; Kennan, *Harriman*, 1:103–4; Harriman, *I Reminisce*, 231–32.

29. RGD, New York, 502:6; Harriman, *I Reminisce*, 256–57; W. E. Ruttan to Harriman, Aug. 9, 1895, IC; *WSJ*, Aug. 8, 1897.

30. RGD, New York, 501:319.

31. Carl Snyder, "Harriman: 'Colossus of Roads,' " *Review of Reviews* 35 (Jan. 1907): 45; Lefevre, "Harriman," 127; Harriman, *I Reminisce*, 258.

32. Snyder, "Harriman," 45–46; Harriman, *I Reminisce*, 259; C. M. Keys, "Harriman," *World's Work* 13 (Jan. 1907): 8464.

33. J. H. McGuinness to Kennan, Dec. 27, 1918, AF.

34. Harriman to men residents of Arden, Oct. 13, 26, 1895, AF. These letters are contained in a document titled "For Church Organization at Arden, New York, during Winter Months," AF.

35. Harriman to men residents of Arden, Oct. 26, 1895, AF.

36. Harriman to McGuinness, undated, AF; J. H. McGuinness, "The Personal Side of E. H. Harriman," 7, AF. A shorter, less useful version of McGuinness's article was printed in *Sunset*, Aug. 1911, 196–98.

37. McGuinness, "Harriman," 5, 7–8.

38. Ibid., 6.

39. Ibid., 6–7.

40. Ibid., 6.

41. Ibid.

42. Harriman to Fish, Sept. 13, 1888, IC.

43. McGuinness, "Harriman," 2–3.

44. Ibid., 4–5.

45. Ibid., 4; McGuinness to Kennan, Dec. 27, 1918, AF; Snyder, "Harriman," 46; J. H. McGuinness, "The Other Side of E. H. Harriman," *Sunset*, Aug. 1911, 197.

46. Harriman, *I Reminisce*, 260–61.

47. McGuinness, "Harriman," 7; C. Hart Merriam, "Recollections and Impressions of E. H. Harriman," 20, AF.

48. Notes of Kennan interview with Melville E. Stone, 6, AF.

49. Lefevre, "Harriman," 127.

CHAPTER 7

1. W. E. Ruttan to Harriman, Aug. 9, 1895, IC; Fish to J. T. Harahan, Apr. 14, 1896, IC; *WSJ*, Sept. 8, 1899; Harriman to Fish, Jan. 26, 1899, SF; Tegethoff to Fish, Mar. 14, 1902, SF; undated memorandum, SF.

2. Jeffery to W. H. Holcomb, Nov. 24, 1888, IC.

3. Ibid., Nov. 21, 24, 1888, IC; Holcomb to Jeffery, Nov. 23, Dec. 21, 1888, IC; Jeffery to Fish, Dec. 22, 1888, IC; John W. Doane to Fish, June 22, 1892, Jan. 26, 1894, IC. For the Union Pacific's problems, see Maury Klein, *Union Pacific: The Birth of a Railroad, 1862–1893* (New York, 1987), 584–658.

4. For background, see Klein, *Union Pacific: Birth*, 285–305, 367–84, 465–68, 531–49.

5. Maury Klein, *Union Pacific: The Rebirth, 1894–1969* (New York, 1990), 17–18; *Chronicle*, 65:800–801; *WSJ*, Mar. 9, 1895.

6. For more detail on these points see Klein, *Union Pacific: Rebirth*, 19–20.

7. This portrait of Schiff is drawn largely from Frieda Schiff Warburg, *Reminiscences of a Long Life* (New York, 1956), 51–57.

8. Ibid., 43; Cyrus Adler, *Jacob Schiff: His Life and Letters*, 2 vols. (Garden City, N.Y., 1928), 2:340.

9. Adler, *Schiff*, 1:1–10.

10. Ibid., 2:344.

11. Ibid., 2:341–46.

12. Ibid., 1:50.

13. Batson interview with Schiff, Mar. 20, 1911, 1–2, AF; George Kennan, *E. H. Harriman*, 2 vols. (New York: 1922), 1:119–21; G. W. Batson to Mary Harriman, Mar. 20, 1911, AF; Schiff to Mary Harriman, Aug. 11, 1910, AF; Jacob H. Schiff, "E. H. Harriman: An Appreciation," AF; Vincent P. Carosso, with Rose C. Carosso, *The Morgans: Private International Bankers, 1854–1913* (Cambridge, Mass., 1987), 387–88. Kennan drew his version almost entirely from Batson's interview after sending it to Schiff for correction. Schiff found some minor errors in the text but later approved Kennan's final version as correct in every sense. Since he also gave Mary Harriman essentially the same story, it must be assumed that this is the version Schiff preferred. There is also a manuscript copy of Batson's version of the reorganization with corrections by Schiff and notes by Kennan, AF. See Kennan to Schiff, Mar. 12, 1917, AF; Schiff to Kennan, Mar. 13, Oct. 22, 1917, AJA, and Mar. 14, 1917, AF.

14. *WSJ*, Oct. 11, 14, 1895; *New York Times*, Oct. 12, 15, 1895. Klein, *Union Pacific: Rebirth*, 22–23, has more details on the plan, a copy of which is in *Chronicle*, 61:705–7.

15. Klein, *Union Pacific: Rebirth*, 24; Schiff interview, 2–3, AF.

16. Finance Com. minutes, Dec. 19, 1894, ICI; Fish to Harriman, Jan. 2, 1897, IC; Harriman to Fish, Jan. 14, 1897, IC; Adler, *Schiff*, 1:93, 121.

17. Fish to George Gould, Dec. 28, 1896, IC; Fish to Harriman, Jan. 7, Mar. 31, Apr. 17, 1897, IC. The quotation is from the Jan. 7 letter.

18. For more detail on this myth see Chapter 8. The views of the *Wall Street Journal* are best obtained by scanning the paper for the period 1896–98. See, for example, *WSJ*, Jan. 27, 29, Feb. 20, Apr. 8, 9, 21, 30, Sept. 2, Oct. 21, 1896.

19. Fish to O. O. Telerton, Dec. 28, 1896, IC.

20. Fish to Harriman, Jan. 2, 1897, IC; Joel D. Hubbard to Fish, Jan. 5, 1897, IC; Fish to Hubbard, Jan. 7, 1897, IC; Harriman to Fish, Jan. 14, 1897, IC; Fish to J. T. Harahan, Jan. 20, 1897, IC.

21. Schiff interview, 3–4, AF; Batson manuscript on reorganization as corrected by Schiff, AF.

22. Harriman to Fish, Jan. 14, 1897, IC.

23. *WSJ*, Jan. 11–15, 19, 21–27, 1897; *New York Times*, Jan. 12, 15, 16, 21–26, 1897; *Chronicle*, 64:136, 235; Hubbard to Fish, Feb. 3, 1897, IC; J. C. Welling to Fish, Feb. 5, 1897, IC; Harahan to Fish, Feb. 5, 1897, IC; Russell Sage to Fish, Feb. 9, 1897, IC; Fish to George P. Harrison, Feb. 9, 1897, IC; *Chicago Inter Ocean*, Feb. 9, 1897; *Philadelphia American*, Feb. 13, 1897; John C. Bell to Fish, Feb. 27, 1897, IC; John F. Shafroth to Fish, Mar. 1, 1897, IC; George D. Perkins to Fish, Mar. 2, 1897, IC; John C. Coombs to Fish and Harriman, Mar. 5, 1897, IC; *Railroad Gazette*, 29:88; Klein, *Union Pacific: Rebirth*, 26.

24. John Moody and George Kibbe Turner, "Masters of Capital in America," *McClure's Magazine*, Jan. 1911, 341; *Railroad Gazette*, 29:738.

25. *New York Times*, Feb. 4, 1897; *WSJ*, Feb. 4, 8, 1897.

26. *WSJ*, May 24, 1897; Schiff interview, 4–5, AF.

27. Schiff interview, 4–5, AF; Kennan, *Harriman*, 1:126. The date of this meeting is unknown, but it probably took place in the spring of 1897. Curiously, one contemporary writer got hold of this story. See Moody and Turner, "Masters of Capital," 340–41.

28. Fish to Harriman, July 2, 1897, IC. Details on Harriman's share in the syndicate are in Harold van B. Cleveland and Thomas F. Huertas, *Citibank, 1812–1970* (Cambridge, Mass., 1985), 36.

29. *Chronicle*, 66:17; *WSJ*, Feb. 13, May 5, 17, July 27, Aug. 12–14, 1897.

30. Klein, *Union Pacific: Rebirth*, 27–28; Notes of Kennan interview with Schiff, Apr. 21, 1917, AF.

31. Pierce to Stillman, Dec. 7, 1897, UPN; Schiff to Pierce, Nov. 4, Dec. 6, 1897, Jan. 2, 1898, UPN; *WSJ*, Nov. 8, Dec. 27, 1897, Jan. 6, 1898; *Railroad Gazette*, 29:877, 936, 30:88; *Chronicle*, 66:290; *New York Times*, Nov. 9, Dec. 28, 1897; Pierce to Oliver W. Mink, Dec. 20, 1897, UPN; Burt to Schiff, Dec. 31, 1897, UPN.

32. *Chronicle*, 66:39.

33. Otto H. Kahn, "Edward Henry Harriman," in Stuart Bruchey, ed., *Memoirs of Three Railroad Pioneers* (New York, 1981), 10–11; Batson interview with Stillman, Feb. 10, 1911, 1–2, AF.

34. Schiff to Pierce, Jan. 2, 1898, UPN; Harriman to Pierce, Jan. 17, 1898, UPN.

35. Schiff to Pierce, Apr. 11, 1898, UPN; Batson minutes, 1–2, AF; *Railroad Gazette*, 30:382. The Union Pacific minute books for the Harriman years were lost in the Equitable Building fire of 1912. Batson examined the books before the fire and made some notes from them.

36. Fish to Harriman, June 28, Sept. 30, 1898, IC; *Railroad Gazette*, 30:905; Fish to John Jacob Astor, Oct. 6, 1899, IC; John F. Stover, *History of the Illinois Central Railroad* (New York, 1975), 142–43.

37. Batson manuscript on struggle for possession of Burlington, 14, AF.

38. Alexander Millar, *Edward H. Harriman and the Union Pacific Railroad* (New York, 1910), 5.

CHAPTER 8

1. George Kennan, *E. H. Harriman*, 2 vols. (New York, 1922), 1:143; Jacob H. Schiff, "E. H. Harriman: An Appreciation," 2, AF; *Fortune*, May 8, 1978, 202. Virtually every source on Harriman cited in these notes follows this same theme.

2. *WSJ*, Jan. 27, 1896, Oct. 15, 1897. See also *WSJ*, Dec. 12, 1893, Nov. 2, 1895, Jan. 29, Apr. 8, 21, Sept. 2, Nov. 16, 1896, Jan. 20, Aug. 12, Oct. 12, Nov. 18, 1897, Mar. 15, 1898. For a description of the road's original condition, see the testimony of W. L. Park in *United States of America v. Union Pacific Railroad Company et al.*, U.S. Circuit Court for the district of Utah, docket no. 993, 9:4280–81; hereafter cited as *USA v. UP*.

3. Alexander Millar, *Edward H. Harriman and the Union Pacific Railroad* (New York, 1910), 4; W. H. Bancroft, "Impressions of Mr. E. H. Harriman," 1, AF; *WSJ*, May 12, 1898.

4. Edward Livingston Trudeau, *An Autobiography* (Garden City, N.Y., 1916), 95. Details on the trip are taken from J. B. Berry, "Notes on J. B. Berry's Association with Mr. E. H. Harriman," June 21, 1911, 5–11, AF; Mary Harriman and Cornelia Harriman, *Diary of a Trip* (Privately printed, 1898), UPO. The diary kept by the girls enables one to reconstruct the trip's itinerary and provides details not found elsewhere.

5. Berry, "Notes," 6, AF.

6. Michael P. Malone, *The Battle for Butte: Mining and Politics on the Northern Frontier, 1864–1906* (Seattle, 1981), 103; Berry, "Notes," 8, AF.

7. Berry, "Notes," 6, AF; Harriman and Harriman, *Diary*, 12.

8. Berry, "Notes," 11, AF. Berry is probably wrong on the price he quotes; the highest price at which Union Pacific preferred sold during July 1898 was 62⅛. See *Chronicle*, 68:25. For evidence of the buying, see *WSJ*, July 19, 1898.

9. Otto H. Kahn, "Edward Henry Harriman," in Stuart Bruchey, ed., *Memoirs of Three Railroad Pioneers* (New York, 1981), 12–14.

10. Ibid.; Batson minutes, 2–3.

11. Kahn, "Harriman," 14–15.

12. Edwin Lefevre, "Harriman," *American Magazine* 64 (June 1907): 126.

13. Kennan to Mary Harriman, May 15, 1921, AF. Lovett's statement is contained in this letter.

14. Stillman interview, 5, AF.

15. *Galveston News*, Sept. 10, 1909.

16. W. L. Park, "Personal Recollections of Mr. Harriman in connection with the Union Pacific," 6, AF; George Kennan, "Notes of Talk with Mr C. B. Seger," Jan. 7, 1917, AF.

17. Julius Kruttschnitt, "Three Business Giants for Whom I Worked," *American Magazine* 92 (Nov. 1921): 37.

18. *New York Times*, June 30, 1898; *Chronicle*, 67:30; *Railroad Gazette*, 30:502.

19. Berry, "Notes," 4, 10, 12; Berry to Kennan, Apr. 10, 1917, AF; Samuel M. Felton, "The Genius of Edward H. Harriman," *American Magazine* 99 (Apr. 1925): 9–10, 184; Bancroft, "Impressions," 2–4; W. F. Herrin, "Personal Impressions of E. H. Harriman," 4, AF.

20. Herrin, "Impressions," 4; Berry, "Notes," 8, 10; Felton, "Genius of Harriman," 9, 12; Kennan interview with F. D. Underwood, Feb. 11, 1916, 2, AF.

21. Felton, "Genius of Harriman," 10–11; William Mahl, "Memoirs, 1860–1910," 44, William Mahl Papers, University of Texas Library. I am indebted to Kenneth Lipartito for calling the Mahl Papers to my attention.

22. Felton, "Genius of Harriman," 184.

23. Millar, "Harriman," 13; W. V. Hill, "Mr. Edward Henry Harriman," 4, AF. Hill was one of Harriman's secretaries.

24. Harriman to Burt, Feb. 6, 1899, UPL.

25. Felton, "Genius of Harriman," 9.

26. Kahn, "Harriman," 2.

CHAPTER 9

1. J. B. Berry, "Notes on J. B. Berry's Association with Mr. E. H. Harriman," June 21, 1911, 2–5, AF; *WSJ*, Sept. 16, Nov. 21, 1898, Jan. 24, Mar. 3, 1899.

2. Batson minutes, 5–6.

3. Ibid., 4; Alex Millar to Winslow Pierce, Nov. 1, 1898, UPN; *New York Times*, Oct. 13, 1898; *WSJ*, Dec. 2, 1898; *Railroad Gazette*, 30:884.

4. Harriman to Burt, Sept. 2, 5, 1898, UPO.

5. Kennan memorandum of talk with C. B. Seger, Jan. 7, 1917, AF; W. L. Park, "Personal Recollections of Mr. Harriman in connection with the Union Pacific," 2, AF. See also Harriman to Burt, July 22, 1898, UPO.

6. Batson minutes, 2; Park, "Recollections," 2–3. Between 1901 and 1909 the Union Pacific acquired 522 new locomotives, 258 passenger cars, 12,499 freight cars, and 707 work cars. These figures are taken from annual reports.

7. *WSJ*, Aug. 18, 1899.

8. Park, "Recollections," 4; Burt to Harriman, Apr. 3, 1899, UPL; Millar to Burt, July 2, 1898, UPO; *Annual Report of the Union Pacific Railroad Company*, 1899, 9; hereafter cited as *UP Report*.

9. Kennan interview with Seger, Jan. 7, 1917, AF. The following incident occurred after Harriman had acquired other roads to create a system exceeding nine thousand miles in all.

10. Samuel M. Felton, "The Genius of Edward H. Harriman," *American Magazine* 99 (Apr. 1925): 11.

11. The 1899 figures are calculated from data in *UP Report*, Nov. 1899, 11. There are two annual reports for 1899, one dated June 30, the other November 1.
12. Rail figures are calculated from data in *UP Report*, 1902, 15, and 1909, 19.
13. Batson minutes, 6; *Kansas City World*, Sept. 17, 1903; Berry, "Notes," 7; *Railroad Gazette*, 31:180; *WSJ*, Apr. 4, 18, 1899.
14. See, for example, *WSJ*, Jan. 11, 1902.
15. *Scientific American*, 86:240; *Railroad Gazette*, 33:186.
16. *Railroad Gazette*, 33:186–87, 36:226–27. These articles are good summaries of the reconstruction work. One is by Berry himself, the other by a subordinate engineer.
17. *Railroad Gazette*, 36:226–27; Park, "Recollections," 12–13. The old line would do as a second track because the worst grades could be used for descending instead of ascending.
18. Park, "Recollections," 7.
19. *Railroad Gazette*, 33:187.
20. Park, "Recollections," 7.
21. Maury Klein, *Union Pacific: The Rebirth, 1894–1969* (New York, 1990), 59.
22. For more detail on the Aspen tunnel, see ibid., 60–61.
23. Batson minutes, 6–10; Harriman to Burt, Sept. 9, 1902, UPL; Klein, *Union Pacific: Rebirth*, 56–57. For the story of the original oxbow see Maury Klein, *Union Pacific: The Birth of a Railroad, 1862–1893* (New York, 1987), 57–61.
24. For details on the construction of the Lane cutoff, see *Railroad Gazette*, 41:549–52.
25. Klein, *Union Pacific: Rebirth*, 61; Park, "Recollections," 30.
26. Park, "Recollections," 21.
27. *WSJ*, Aug. 18, 1899; Klein, *Union Pacific: Rebirth*, 61.
28. *United States of America v. Union Pacific Railroad Company et al.*, U.S. Circuit Court for the District of Utah, docket no. 993, 9:4281–82, hereafter *USA v. UP*.
29. Ibid., 4195, 4281, 4283.
30. Robert S. Lanier, "Harriman the Absolute," *Review of Reviews* 40 (Oct. 1909): 469.
31. Klein, *Union Pacific: Rebirth*, 62.
32. Ibid., 62–63; *USA v. UP*, 9:4192, 4196, 4280, 4284–85.
33. Klein, *Union Pacific: Rebirth*, 64.
34. *USA v. UP*, 9:4299; Park, "Recollections," 18–20.
35. Park, "Recollections," 18.
36. Klein, *Union Pacific: Rebirth*, 65.
37. Ibid., 66.
38. *WSJ*, Jan. 18, 1905.
39. Berry, "Notes," 13–14.
40. *USA v. UP*, 9:4123–25, 4286. The figures in this and the next paragraph are calculated from the table on p. 4125.
41. Klein, *Union Pacific: Rebirth*, 67; *WSJ*, Sept. 13, Oct. 3, 1898.
42. Batson minutes, 10; *WSJ*, Sept. 19, 23, 1898; *New York Times*, Sept. 23, 1898; *Chronicle*, 67:635.
43. *Chronicle*, 68:25; *WSJ*, Oct. 3, 14, 20, Nov. 10, 11, 1898.

CHAPTER 10

1. Carl Snyder, "Harriman: 'Colossus of Roads,'" *Review of Reviews* 35 (Jan. 1907): 45; E. Roland Harriman, *I Reminisce* (Garden City, N.Y., 1975), 9.
2. Harriman, *I Reminisce*, 10; *Fortune*, May 8, 1978, 197.

3. John Muir, *Edward Henry Harriman* (N.p., n.d.), 21–24. This brief tribute was privately printed. I am grateful to the late W. Averell Harriman for giving me a copy.

4. Harriman, *I Reminisce*, 17.

5. Muir, *Harriman*, 24–26.

6. Maury Klein, *Union Pacific: The Rebirth, 1894–1969* (New York, 1990), 70–71. Late in 1898 the Gulf road was reorganized into the Colorado & Southern Railway.

7. For more detail on these developments, see Maury Klein, *Union Pacific: The Birth of a Railroad, 1862–1893* (New York, 1987), 559–65.

8. Klein, *Union Pacific: Birth*, 560.

9. For more detail on these intrigues, see ibid., 566–83.

10. The definitive biography of Hill is Albro Martin, *James J. Hill and the Opening of the Northwest* (New York, 1976). For a brief portrait, see the fine sketch by Martin in *Encyclopedia of American Business History and Business: Railroads in the Nineteenth Century* (New York, 1988), 169–76.

11. This account follows closely the version in Martin, *Hill*, 434–59.

12. Ibid., 455, 458–59. For one unsavory episode of Mellen's earlier career, see Klein, *Union Pacific: Birth*, 612–21.

13. W. H. Bancroft, "Impressions of Mr. E. H. Harriman," 5–6, AF; Harriman to Burt, Sept. 16, 1898, UPN. For more detail, see Klein, *Union Pacific: Rebirth*, 72–74.

14. Klein, *Union Pacific: Rebirth*, 73.

15. Ibid., 75.

16. Ibid., 76.

17. Hill to Morgan, Aug. 2, 1898, JJH; Hill to E. D. Adams, Mar. 28, Apr. 4, 1898, JJH; Hill to W. L. Bull, Apr. 4, 1898, JJH; Mohler to Hill, Jan. 16, Feb. 2, 1898, JJH; Hill to Mohler, Jan. 25, May 14, 1898, JJH; *WSJ*, Jan. 17, 1898; *Railroad Gazette*, 30:82, 107. For Mohler, see *NCAB*, 33:197.

18. Hill to D. S. Lamont, July 17, 1898, JJH; Hill to Bull, July 2, 1898, JJH.

19. Hill to Lamont, July 17, 1898, JJH; Harriman to Burt, July 22, Aug. 4, Sept. 2, 1898, UPO.

20. The following scene is taken from "In the matter of the Oregon Railroad & Navigation Company: Minutes of Conference," Oct. 3, 1898, JJH.

21. *DAB*, 10:563–64; *Who Was Who in America, Historical Volumes, 1897–1942* (Chicago, 1942), 1:164, 700, 1229.

22. Hill to Bull, Oct. 31, 1898, JJH; *WSJ*, Nov. 16, Dec. 14, 1898; *Railroad Gazette*, 30:852, 886, 904; Mohler to Hill, Dec. 30, 1898, JJH.

23. *WSJ*, Jan. 10, 13, Feb. 10, 25, Mar. 15, Apr. 14, 24, June 13, July 15–18, 1899; *Railroad Gazette*, 31:33, 73, 108, 132, 236, 305, 393, 483, 515, 532; Hill to J. P. Morgan & Co., Mar. 25, 1899, JJH; Hill to Coster, Apr. 15, 1899, JJH; *Chronicle*, 69:181.

24. Hill to Mohler, July 19, Aug. 1, 1899, JJH; *WSJ*, July 22, 31, 1899.

25. *Omaha Bee*, Aug. 9, 1899; *WSJ*, Aug. 15, 28, 31, 1899; Harriman to Mohler, Aug. 7, 31, 1899, UPO; *Railroad Gazette*, 31:620. The truce was renewed in January 1900 and then again in 1901 for an indefinite period. For details, see Harriman to Mohler, Jan. 16, Oct. 2, 1900, UPO; memorandum of understanding between Harriman and Mellen, Jan. 12, 1900, UPO; B. Campbell to Mohler, Apr. 1, 1901, UPO.

26. UP Exec. Com. minutes, Aug. 31, Sept. 13, 1899, UPL; Oregon Short Line Exec. Com. minutes, Sept. 12, 1899, UPL; *Chronicle*, 69:492, 542, 592, 695; *WSJ*, Oct. 10, 1899; *Railroad Gazette*, 31:620, 634, 649, 668, 702, 720; Harriman to Mohler, Aug. 31, 1899, UPO.

27. Harriman to Mohler, Aug. 7, 1899, UPO.

28. Hill to Bull, Aug. 18, 1899, JJH; Hill to Coster, Aug. 19, 1899, JJH; Hill to Harriman, Sept. 12, 1899, JJH.

29. J. B. Berry, "Notes on J. B. Berry's Association with Mr. E. H. Harriman," June 21, 1911, 14, AF; Klein, *Union Pacific: Rebirth*, 81–82.

30. Frank H. Spearman, "Building Up a Great Railway System," *Outlook* 91 (Feb. 1909): 443; Kruttschnitt to Batson, Apr. 11, 1911, AF.

31. Kruttschnitt to Batson, Apr. 11, 1911, AF; Harriman to Burt, Sept. 15, 1899, UPL.

32. Spearman, "Building Up a Great Railway System," 443–44; Burt to Harriman, Sept. 16, Oct. 2, 1901, UPL; UP Exec. Com. minutes, Dec. 1, 1906, UPL.

33. Berry, "Notes," 8; George Kennan, "Notes of Talk with F. D. Underwood," Feb. 11, 1918, 3, AF.

34. W. L. Park, "Personal Recollections of Mr. Harriman in Connection with the Union Pacific," 15–17, AF.

CHAPTER 11

1. Anna Robeson Burr, *The Portrait of a Banker: James Stillman* (New York, 1927), 196; Frank A. Vanderlip, *From Farm Boy to Financier* (New York, 1935), 113–14.

2. Vanderlip, *From Farm Boy to Financier*, 112; Henry Morgenthau, *All in a Life-Time* (Garden City, N.Y., 1922), 65; Burr, *Portrait of a Banker*, 72.

3. Burr, *Portrait of a Banker*, 7–83; *DAB*, 18:25–26; Harold van B. Cleveland and Thomas F. Huertas, *Citibank, 1812–1970* (Cambridge, Mass., 1985), 32–35; *New York World*, Apr. 24, 1901.

4. Edwin Lefevre, "James Stillman," *Cosmopolitan* 35 (July 1903): 334; Cleveland and Huertas, *Citibank*, 33.

5. *DAB*, 18:25–26; Burr, *Portrait of a Banker*, 182–94; Morgenthau, *All in a Life-Time*, 77.

6. Cleveland and Huertas, *Citibank*, 33, 37.

7. Ibid., 37, 40. Stillman took a $5.8 million share for himself and a $1.8 million share for City Bank in the selling syndicate. Kuhn, Loeb underwrote the entire reorganization and took a $6.5 million share in the selling syndicate. The latter totaled $105 million.

8. Stuart Daggett, *Railroad Reorganization* (Boston, 1908), 1–29; Cyrus Adler, *Jacob Schiff: His Life and Letters*, 2 vols. (Garden City, N.Y., 1928), 1:143–45; Henry V. Poor, *Manual of the Railroads of the United States* (New York, 1899), 70; Hill to W. H. Newman, Sept. 21, 1898, JJH; Hill to E. T. Nichols, Nov. 26, 1898, JJH; Harriman to Fish, Oct. 25, Nov. 14, 1898, SF; *Chronicle*, 69:128.

9. Albro Martin, *James J. Hill and the Opening of the Northwest* (New York, 1976), 433; Hill to John K. Cowen, Oct. 30, 1898, JJH; Hill to Underwood, Feb. 18, 1899, JJH; *WSJ*, Jan. 16, 1899; Hill to Schiff, Sept. 7, 1899, JJH. For Underwood, see *DAB*, supplement 3:783–84.

10. George Kennan, "Notes of Talk with F. D. Underwood," Feb. 11, 1918, AF; *WSJ*, Jan. 4, Mar. 22, 1899.

11. Daggett, *Railroad Reorganization*, 31–32; Hill to W. R. Lawson, Jan. 19, 1900, JJH; Hill to Schiff, Jan. 27, June 20, 1900, JJH; Hill to A. J. Cassatt, Apr. 16, 1901, JJH; Adler, *Schiff*, 1:145–46.

12. Carl Snyder, "Harriman: 'Colossus of Roads,' " *Review of Reviews* 35 (Jan. 1907): 48.

13. For Stilwell and his career, see Keith L. Bryant Jr., *Arthur E. Stilwell: Promoter with a Hunch* (Nashville, 1971). The Pittsburg in the road's name was a small town in the coal region of Kansas.

14. Ibid., 20–38, 59–139, 148–50, 162; George Kennan, *E. H. Harriman*, 2 vols. (New York, 1922), 1:216–17; *WSJ*, Apr. 13, 1899; L. F. Loree to Kennan, Jan. 29, 1920, AF. Bryant

disputes Kennan's assertion that Stilwell weakened his line by trying to include as many town sites as possible. Loree's letter was the basis for Kennan's statement.

15. Arthur E. Stilwell, *Cannibals of Finance* (Chicago, 1912), 50, 78–81; Bryant, *Stilwell*, 138–39, 154–57; *WSJ*, Aug. 30, Oct. 24, 27, 1898, Jan. 3, 14, 20, 21, 1899; Loree to Kennan, Jan. 29, 1920, AF.

16. *WSJ*, Jan. 3, 14, 20, 21, Feb. 4, 16, Mar. 4, 17, 1899; *Chronicle*, 68:187, 524, 618; Otto H. Kahn, "Edward Henry Harriman," in Stuart Bruchey, ed., *Memoirs of Three Railroad Pioneers* (New York, 1981), 3; Kennan, *Harriman*, 1:218; Loree to Kennan, Jan. 29, 1920, AF. Loree later became president of the road.

17. *Chronicle*, 68:672, 723–24, 772, 824; *WSJ*, Mar. 27, 30, Apr. 5–7, 12, 13, 18–20, 29, May 2, July 8, 13, Aug. 8, 1899; Bryant, *Stilwell*, 154–57.

18. *WSJ*, Apr. 29, July 25, Aug. 3, Sept. 25, 1899; *Chronicle*, 68:1024. There was, said the *Wall Street Journal*, "so much of a 'get-rich quick' atmosphere surrounding the whole enterprise, and so much 'milking' of the railroad by other organizations and companies, that it was foredoomed to failure from the outset."

19. Samuel M. Felton, "Report on the Kansas City Pittsburgh [*sic*] & Gulf Railroad," July 1899, SMF; *Chronicle*, 68:871, 1024–25, 1225–26, 69:27, 283, 384–85, 440. Bryant, *Stilwell*, 152, argues that Felton "desired engineering and operational perfection and the changes asked for were too drastic." He fails to grasp that Felton was viewing the road from the Harriman perspective that creating a modern line capable of hauling a large tonnage at low cost was its only chance for a profitable future. To say, as Bryant does, that the Gulf road "was a pioneer railroad through a wilderness most of its length, not a major trunk line from Chicago to New York," is to miss the point. By 1900 the age of "pioneer" roads had passed, and no road forming part of a through line could compete with other major systems unless it had been modernized.

20. *Chronicle*, 69:333, 491–92, 591, 645; *WSJ*, Aug. 11, 18, 21–23, 25, Sept. 1, 13, 1899; Bryant, *Stilwell*, 158–59; Stilwell, *Cannibals*, 79; Kahn, "Harriman," 3; Kennan, *Harriman*, 1:219–20. Kennan, relying on Kahn's version, asserts that Stilwell and his friends sold all their holdings to Gates without telling Harriman. Bryant is vague on how much Stilwell sold but leaves the impression that he still had some holdings even though he lost control of the Philadelphia committee.

21. *WSJ*, Aug. 22, 1899; Kahn, "Harriman," 3. Kahn's version is the only "inside" account of what happened, but it must be used carefully.

22. Kahn, "Harriman," 4–5; Kahn to Kennan, Jan. 20, 1919, AF.

23. *DAB*, 7:188–90; *New York Times*, Aug. 9, 1911; *WSJ*, Jan. 9, 1899; Lloyd Wendt and Herman Kogan, *Bet a Million! The Story of John W. Gates* (Indianapolis, 1948). The Wendt and Kogan book is colorful but not reliable.

24. Bernard M. Baruch, *My Own Story* (New York, 1957), 145.

25. *WSJ*, Sept. 22, Sept. 25, Oct. 27, 28, 30, 1899; Stilwell, *Cannibals*, 85. After this remark Stilwell added, "(the details of which I will not reveal in this book as it involves names and trickery which under no circumstances would I reveal now.)" His reticence seems odd since he did not hesitate to reveal what he deemed trickery elsewhere. His version of events is, to say the least, selective.

26. Kahn, "Harriman," 5; Bryant, *Stilwell*, 160–61; *Chronicle*, 69:955, 1012, 1062, 1247, 1301, 1346, 70:280, 584, 633, 945, 1149, 1249, 71:84; *WSJ*, Oct. 30, Nov. 1, 6, 17, Dec. 15, 1899, Jan. 4, 10, 13, 17, 20, 27, Feb. 2, Mar. 20, 29, Apr. 3, Aug. 30, 1900; Harriman to John J. Mitchell, May 15, 1900, AF; Harriman to W. F. Harrity, May 16, June 13, 1900, AF; Harriman to S. R. Knott, July 6, 1900, AF. Kahn's account combines and telescopes events.

27. *WSJ*, Feb. 15, 1898, Jan. 21, Aug. 12, 17, 21–26, 1899; *Chronicle*, 69:743, 906; Bryant, *Stilwell*, 149, 159–61.

28. *Chronicle*, 71:863; *WSJ*, May 9, 11–14, 1900. The voting trust had seven members, four of whom were controlled by Gates.

29. Harriman to Gates, Oct. 12, 1900, AF; Harriman to Mercantile Trust Co., Oct. 18, 1900, AF; Kahn, "Harriman," 5; Gates et al. to John J. Mitchell, Oct. 26, 1900, AF; *Chronicle*, 71:863, 913; *New York Times*, Oct. 31, 1900; *WSJ*, Oct. 27, 29, 31, 1900.

30. *WSJ*, Nov. 6, 1900; *New York Times*, Oct. 31, 1900; *Chronicle*, 71:913, 963–64.

31. *WSJ*, Nov. 28, 1900, Feb. 1, 28, Mar. 15, 16, Apr. 30, May 18, 1901; Bryant, *Stilwell*, 165.

32. *NCAB*, 20:203–4; Poor, *Manual*, 1881, 616, *Manual*, 1888, 357, *Manual*, 1896, 444.

33. All figures taken from Poor, *Manual*, 1881, 617, *Manual*, 1889, 345, *Manual*, 1897, 347, *Manual*, 1899, 246. The statement by Ripley that for many years before 1898 the Alton had enjoyed a "constantly expanding business" is so inaccurate that one wonders if he ever looked at the relevant data. See William Z. Ripley, *Railroads: Finance and Organization* (New York, 1915), 263.

34. Quoted in Kennan, *Harriman*, 2:231.

35. *WSJ*, Mar. 3, 4, Oct. 1, Nov. 14, 16, 1898.

36. Ibid., Nov. 16, 17, Dec. 2, 3, 10, 16, 1898; *Chronicle*, 67:1054, 1262; "Statement by Mr. E. H. Harriman in Answer to Report of Interstate Commerce Commission," July 17, 1907, 3, AF. According to Kennan's cover notes, this statement was prepared from Harriman's dictation by noted corporation lawyer Samuel C. T. Dodd. There are two versions of this statement, which was never released publicly (see prologue). The draft version was given Kennan by Mary Harriman, the finished one by M. E. Stone. Copies of both versions are at AF. The second one is a revision of this earlier draft; unless otherwise stated, my citations come from this original version. Kennan's defense of the Alton transaction is derived largely from this statement.

37. Harriman, "Statement," 3–4; *NCAB*, 20:203; *WSJ*, Nov. 16, 1898, Oct. 28, 1903.

38. Samuel M. Felton, "The Genius of Edward H. Harriman," *American Magazine* 99 (Apr. 1925): 9.

39. Ibid., 10; *WSJ*, Dec. 16, 1898, Jan. 4, 10, 1899.

40. Felton, "Genius of Harriman," 10; Samuel M. Felton, "Report on the Chicago and Alton Railroad," Jan. 7, 1899, SMF.

41. Felton, "Report on the Chicago and Alton," 38, 43; Harriman, "Statement," 4–5.

42. Harriman to Fish, Apr. 19, 1899, SF.

43. Harriman, "Statement," 6–7; *WSJ*, Dec. 21, 22, 1898, Jan. 14, 25, 26, 30, Feb. 1–4, 7–10, 14, 20, 23, 25, 27, Mar. 2, 3, Apr. 3, 1899; *Chronicle*, 68:249–50, 281, 427, 617. Blackstone lived only until May 1900.

44. Harriman, "Statement," 7; *WSJ*, Mar. 14, 16, 22, Apr. 12, 19, May 20, 23, 1899; *Chronicle*, 68:670; Fish to Harriman, Apr. 11, 13, 1899, IC. For differing interpretations of these transactions, see Kennan, *Harriman*, 2:228–310; Ripley, *Railroads*, 262–66; William Z. Ripley, "Federal Financial Railway Regulation: The Alton as a Test Case," *North American Review* 203 (Apr. 1916): 538–52; George Kennan, *The Chicago and Alton Case: A Misunderstood Transaction* (Garden City, N.Y., 1916), and Kennan, *Misrepresentation in Railroad Affairs* (Garden City, N.Y., 1916); James C. Bonbright, *Railroad Capitalization* (New York, 1920), 169–85.

45. *WSJ*, Aug. 14, 1899; *Chronicle*, 69:178, 228, 70:739; Kennan, *Harriman*, 2:236, 247–50; "In the matter of Consolidations and Combinations of Carriers, Relations between such

Carriers, and Community of Interests Therein, Their Rates, Facilities, and Practices," 12 *ICC Reports* 943 (1907), 296–97.

46. *Chronicle*, 70:279, 291, 429; *WSJ*, June 8, 1900; Kennan interview with Stone, Apr. 29, 1915, AF.

47. Felton to Harriman, May 26, 27, 29, 1899, UPL; *Chronicle*, 69:26, 129, 384, 541, 645; *WSJ*, June 23, Aug. 14, 17, 30, Dec. 23, 1899, Jan. 31, 1900, May 21, 27, 1901; Schiff to Harriman, Aug. 8, 1899, UPL; *Railroad Gazette*, 31:649.

48. *WSJ*, May 25, July 19, Aug. 8, 1899, Mar. 26, Apr. 5, May 15, 16, 18, 29, 31, June 5, July 11, Aug. 10, 1900; Fish to J. T. Harahan, Nov. 10, 1899, IC; Fish to Harriman, Nov. 24, 1899, IC; Fish to Felton, Nov. 24, 1899, IC; 12 *ICC Reports* 943 (1907), 298–99; *Chronicle*, 69:1147, 70:686, 736, 894; Bonbright, *Railroad Capitalization*, 171–72. Both the ICC report and Bonbright cover these events in the wrong sequence. The total of $39 million of Railway stock was exchanged for the syndicate's $18.3 million of Railroad stock, while the bonds were sold to pay for the syndicate's $3.5 million of Railroad preferred and the Peoria line.

49. *WSJ*, May 12, 18, 29, 31, 1900; *Chronicle*, 70:944, 995; Kennan, *Harriman*, 2:235–37; Bonbright, *Railroad Capitalization*, 171.

50. Harriman, "Statement," 9–10; Felton, "Chicago and Alton," 43. Here, as elsewhere, all figures are rounded off for convenience.

51. *WSJ*, May 1, 12, 15, 16, 18, 29, 31, Aug. 30, 1900. The commission's final report is in 12 *ICC Reports* 943 (1907), 295–306.

52. To give a specific example, the ICC, Ripley, and Bonbright all compare the Alton in 1898 with its position in 1906, just before Harriman surrendered control. None of them try to look at the situation as it existed in 1900, when the syndicate reshaped its financial structure.

53. Adler, *Schiff*, 1:131.

54. Kennan notes of talk with Stone, Apr. 29, Nov. 23, 1915, AF.

55. See, for example, Robert N. Burnett, "Edward Henry Harriman," *Cosmopolitan*, Mar. 1903, 593–96.

56. Figures based on data taken from Poor, *Manual*, 1902, 307, 1908, 33; Harriman, "Statement," 10–11.

57. Felton, "Chicago and Alton," 40–43.

58. Ibid.; Felton, "Kansas City, Pittsburgh & Gulf," 46–47, 51–53.

59. Poor, *Manual*, 1900, 656, 1908, 363; Harriman, "Statement," 11. For the political fight, see Albro Martin, *Enterprise Denied: Origins of the Decline of American Railroads, 1897–1917* (New York, 1971).

60. See, for example, Bonbright, *Railroad Capitalization*, 182–83, which ignores entirely the effect of inflation on the Alton's decline.

61. There was in fact a controversy over whether the proper way to pay for betterments was to use earnings or capital funds. See, for example, *WSJ*, Aug. 31, 1900; Ripley, *Railroads*, 267–80; Edward S. Mead, *Corporation Finance* (New York, 1930), 270–79.

62. In addition to earlier citations, see, for example, *WSJ*, Oct. 24, Nov. 1, 17, 27, 1900, July 30, 1901, Aug. 20, Nov. 11, 1902; printed circulars, Oct. 24, 1900, AF. Bonbright, *Railroad Capitalization*, 183–84, argued that "the public notices of the transactions, though they may have conformed to the customary requirements, were wholly insufficient to protect investors against the deceptive appearances of the transactions." This statement borders on the ludicrous. Leaving aside the obvious fact that investors are not obliged to invest in anything and that the burden of understanding the risks involved in

whatever investments they choose is theirs, the fact remains that every Alton transaction was both fully reported and analyzed in detail by such organs as the *Wall Street Journal* and the *Commercial and Financial Chronicle*. Some of the transactions were complex but no more so than dozens of other issues. Bonbright's argument is a classic case of imposing different standards born of hindsight and of imposing a generic demand on a situation in which he lacks sufficient knowledge of its specific context.

63. Barron to Kennan, May 24, 1915, AF; *WSJ*, Sept. 13, 1909.
64. Barron to Kennan, May 24, 1915, AF; *WSJ*, Sept. 13, 1909; Arthur Pound and Samuel Taylor Moore, eds., *They Told Barron: Conversations and Revelations of an American Pepys in Wall Street* (New York, 1930), 58–59.

CHAPTER 12

1. George Kennan, *E. H. Harriman*, 2 vols. (New York, 1922), 1:185.
2. For Harriman's version, see his preface in C. Hart Merriam, ed., *Harriman Alaska Series* (New York, 1901–14), 1:xxi–xxiii. This is the first of thirteen volumes on the expedition published at Harriman's expense. Hereafter cited as *HAE*.
3. C. Hart Merriam, "Recollections and Impressions of E. H. Harriman," 20, AF.
4. William H. Goetzmann and Kay Sloan, *Looking Far North: The Harriman Expedition to Alaska, 1899* (Princeton, 1982), 6–7, 14. This study is a good account of the expedition, but it contains some serious flaws. The authors know little about Harriman and even less about business history in general and railroads in particular. The result is chronological errors and sloppy generalizations compounded by a tone belonging to the old "Robber Baron" school of history: a peculiar mix of "gee whiz" and disdain. Although the authors note that Harriman's career "stood at a turning point" in 1899 (p. 5), they proceed to describe him in the rest of the book as a tycoon of vast power who collected railroads as the scientists gathered specimens. They also wrongly tie Harriman's motives to the round-the-world project, which was conceived several years later. As a final example, the authors repeatedly describe Harriman as a famous railroad leader, which he was not in 1899.
5. Alex Millar to T. M. Orr, Aug. 16, 1899, UPN.
6. Merriam, "Recollections," 1.
7. Ibid., 2–3.
8. Ibid., 3; Goetzmann and Sloan, *Looking Far North*, 8–9; Harriman preface, *HAE*, 1:xxii.
9. The most convenient roster is in Goetzmann and Sloan, *Looking Far North*, 207–12, which is taken from *HAE*, 1:xxxiii–xxxvii. There are also lists in AF and UPN. The idea of having assistants for the scientists was apparently dropped.
10. Goetzmann and Sloan, *Looking Far North*, 9–14; *HAE*, 1:1; John Muir, "Tribute to the Memory of E. H. Harriman," 4–5, AF. This is a draft version of Muir's printed booklet and contains some detail omitted in the final version.
11. Memo for Burt, May 13, 1899, UPO; C. Hart Merriam journal, May 23, 1899, C. Hart Merriam Papers, Library of Congress. Those who imagine that trains got put together and moved with ease need only look at the sheath of telegrams in UPL relating to the creation and movement of this one special train to appreciate the work involved. Goetzmann and Kay, *Looking Far North*, 17, refer to "a luxurious train of 'palace cars'" as if it had special equipment instead of regular Pullman Palace cars. Nor do they understand what a "special" train is—i.e., one run apart from the regular schedule.
12. Harriman to Burt, May 30, 1899, UPN; Goetzmann and Sloan, *Looking Far North*, 17. The latter authors assert that Harriman named the car, but it was Pullman's own name.

See "Itinerary and Consist of Special Train Carrying the Harriman Alaskan Expedition," June 2, 1899, UPN.

13. Harriman to Mrs. E. H. Harriman, May 18, 1899, AF; Goetzmann and Sloan, *Looking Far North*, 17. The same form letter went out to every member of the expedition.

14. Thomas H. Kearney, "Reminiscences of the Harriman Expedition," 1, Waldo L. Schmitt Papers, Smithsonian Institution Archives. Kearney's recollections were gathered in 1948. See Kearney to Schmitt, Sept. 14, 1948, ibid.

15. Merriam journal, May 24, 1899; Merriam, "Recollections," 3–4; Lewis R. Morris, "A Successful Life, Edward Henry Harriman," 2, AF. For the membership of committees, see Goetzmann and Sloan, *Looking Far North*, 210–12.

16. Bancroft to Harriman, May 24, 25, 1899, UPL; Harriman to Bancroft, May 25, 1899, UPL; *HAE*, 1:4–12; Merriam, "Recollections," 5; Merriam, journal, May 27, 28, 1899; Goetzmann and Sloan, *Looking Far North*, 20, 22–24.

17. Merriam journal, May 29, 1899; Merriam, "Recollections," 5; William H. Dall diary, May 29, 1899, Smithsonian Institution Archives; *Railroad Gazette*, 31:236, 393; *HAE*, 1:14–16; Goetzmann and Sloan, *Looking Far North*, 24–26. The latter authors, unaware of the courtesies rail officers routinely extended to one another, have some silly stuff about the Northern Pacific special.

18. Muir, "Tribute," 5.

19. *HAE*, 1:17–18; Merriam journal, May 31, 1899; Goetzmann and Sloan, *Looking Far North*, 3–4.

20. *Omaha Bee*, June 11, 1899; E. L. L. memorandum, June 2, 1899, UPN. The "E. L. L." is probably E. L. Lomax.

21. Merriam, "Recollections," 7; Goetzmann and Sloan, *Looking Far North*, 112.

22. Merriam, "Recollections," 7–8; Muir, "Tribute," 6; E. Roland Harriman, *I Reminisce* (Garden City, N.Y., 1975), 4.

23. John Burroughs, *My Boyhood* (Garden City, N.Y., 1922), 220.

24. *HAE*, 1:17–26; Merriam journal, June 1–4, 1899; Dall diary, June 1–4, 1899; Linnie Marsh Wolfe, ed., *John of the Mountains: The Unpublished Journals of John Muir* (Boston, 1938), 380–82; Goetzmann and Sloan, *Looking Far North*, 38–42; Merriam, "Recollections," 6.

25. *HAE*, 1:26–30; Merriam journal, June 6, 1899; Wolfe, ed., *John of the Mountains*, 382–83; Goetzmann and Sloan, *Looking Far North*, 48–53.

26. Goetzmann and Sloan, *Looking Far North*, 53.

27. Ibid., 55–61; *HAE*, 1:30–34.

28. Merriam journal, June 7, 1899; Dall dairy, June 7, 1899; Goetzmann and Sloan, *Looking Far North*, 61–64.

29. *HAE*, 1:32–33.

30. Ibid., 35–38; Goetzmann and Sloan, *Looking Far North*, 68–74.

31. *HAE*, 1:38–40; Wolfe, ed., *John of the Mountains*, 384–85; Goetzmann and Sloan, *Looking Far North*, 75–76; Merriam journal, June 9, 1899; Merriam, "Recollections," 8–9.

32. Wolfe, ed., *John of the Mountains*, 384–85; Merriam journal, June 9, 1899.

33. Wolfe, ed., *John of the Mountains*, 385–86; Merriam journal, June 10, 11, 1899; Goetzmann and Sloan, *Looking Far North*, 76–85.

34. Merriam journal, June 13, 1899; Wolfe, ed., *John of the Mountains*, 386–87; Merriam, "Recollections," 9.

35. *HAE*, 1:48–52; Goetzmann and Sloan, *Looking Far North*, 86–92.

36. Merriam journal, June 14–17, 1899; Dall diary, June 14–17, 1899; Wolfe, ed., *John of the Mountains*, 387–88; Merriam, "Recollections," 6–7.

37. Goetzmann and Sloan, *Looking Far North*, 92–94.

38. Ibid., 95–96; Merriam journal, June 18, 1899.

39. Goetzmann and Sloan, *Looking Far North*, 97–104; *HAE*, 1:52–63; Wolfe, ed., *John of the Mountains*, 390–91; Merriam journal, June 18, 1899; Dall diary, June 18, 1899.

40. *HAE*, 2:261; Merriam journal, June 23, 1899; Wolfe, ed., *John of the Mountains*, 390–91.

41. Goetzmann and Sloan, *Looking Far North*, 102; Merriam, "Recollections," 11; Kearney, "Reminiscences," 2.

42. *HAE*, 1:63–64.

43. Ibid., 63–71, 74; Merriam journal, June 24, 1899; Wolfe, ed., *John of the Mountains*, 393–94. For details on the canning industry, see *HAE*, 2:337–55.

44. *HAE*, 1:63–71; Wolfe, ed., *John of the Mountains*, 394–95; Merriam journal, June 25, 1899; Dall diary, June 25, 1899; Goetzmann and Sloan, *Looking Far North*, 108–15.

45. *HAE*, 1:70–74.

46. Merriam journal, June 26, 1899; Merriam, "Recollections," 14; Wolfe, ed., *John of the Mountains*, 396; Muir, "Tribute," 7.

47. Muir, "Tribute," 6.

48. Ibid., 7–8; Merriam, "Recollections," 15; Goetzmann and Sloan, *Looking Far North*, 110–12.

49. Merriam, "Recollections," 15; Goetzmann and Sloan, *Looking Far North*, 112; *HAE*, 1:73; Merriam journal, June 26, 1899.

50. *HAE*, 1:76; Merriam journal, June 27–30, 1899; Dall diary, June 27–30, 1899; Goetzmann and Sloan, *Looking Far North*, 114–17.

51. *HAE*, 1:70–86; Merriam journal, July 1, 2, 1899.

52. *HAE*, 1:xxvii, 85; Merriam journal, July 3, 1899; Goetzmann and Sloan, *Looking Far North*, 119–21.

53. Merriam journal, July 4, 1899; Dall diary, July 4, 1899; Wolfe, ed., *John of the Mountains*, 401–2; Goetzmann and Sloan, *Looking Far North*, 122–26.

54. Goetzmann and Sloan, *Looking Far North*, 126–36; *HAE*, 1:87–94, 98; Merriam journal, July 7, 8, 1899.

55. *HAE*, 1:94–98; Merriam journal, July 9, 1899; Wolfe, ed., *John of the Mountains*, 406–7.

56. Merriam, "Recollections," 16; *HAE*, 1:98–99; Merriam journal, July 9, 1899; Dall diary, July 9, 1899.

57. *HAE*, 1:99–102; Goetzmann and Sloan, *Looking Far North*, 137–41.

58. Wolfe, ed., *John of the Mountains*, 407–8; Merriam journal, July 11, 1899.

59. Wolfe, ed., *John of the Mountains*, 408–9; Merriam, "Recollections," 12–13; Merriam journal, July 12, 1899; Dall diary, July 12, 1899.

60. *HAE*, 1:107–14; Merriam journal, July 13, 1899; Wolfe, ed., *John of the Mountains*, 409–10; Goetzmann and Sloan, *Looking Far North*, 146–51.

61. Goetzmann and Sloan, *Looking Far North*, 136.

62. Wolfe, ed., *John of the Mountains*, 413. For a survey of the scientific results, see ibid., 193–206.

63. Goetzmann and Sloan, *Looking Far North*, 152.

64. Merriam journal, July 17–22, 1899; Dall diary, July 20–22, 1899.

65. Kearney, "Reminiscences," 3.

66. Goetzmann and Sloan, *Looking Far North*, 161–70; *HAE*, 1:115–17; Merriam journal, July 26, 1899.

67. Merriam journal, July 26, 27, 1899. The temperature was in the mid-eighties.

68. Dall dairy, July 27, 1899; Merriam journal, July 27, 1899; Wolfe, ed., *John of the Mountains*, 420.

69. Interview with W. Averell Harriman, June 23, 1981; Burroughs to Albert Kendrick Fisher, Sept. 24, 1899, Albert Kendrick Fisher Papers, Library of Congress.

70. Merriam journal, July 30–Aug. 2, 1899. The movements of Harriman and the train can be tracked in the sheath of telegrams between July 31 and August 9, 1899, UPL.

71. *New York Times*, Aug. 16, 1899. For other examples of publicity, see *New York Tribune*, Aug. 14, 1899; *Kansas City Journal*, July 31, 1899; *Denver Republican*, July 31, 1899; *Deseret Evening News*, July 31, 1899; *Seattle Post-Intelligencer*, July 31, 1899; *Omaha Bee*, Aug. 8, 1899; *Omaha World-Herald*, Aug. 8, 1899.

CHAPTER 13

1. Henry Morgenthau, *All in a Life-Time* (Garden City, N.Y., 1922), 73.

2. Ibid., 70.

3. Maury Klein and Harvey A. Kantor, *Prisoners of Progress: American Industrial Cities, 1850–1920* (New York, 1976), xii.

4. These paragraphs are drawn from ibid., 44–51. For a more detailed account, see Alfred D. Chandler, Jr., *The Visible Hand: The Managerial Revolution in American Business* (Cambridge, Mass., 1977), 1–344.

5. Klein and Kantor, *Prisoners of Progress*, 51–52; Ralph L. Nelson, *Merger Movements in American Industry, 1895–1956* (Princeton, 1959), 34, 37.

6. Maury Klein, *Union Pacific: The Rebirth, 1894–1969* (New York, 1990), 85.

7. *New York Tribune*, Jan. 6, 7, Mar. 24, Apr. 13, 1900; *WSJ*, Jan. 9, Mar. 23, 1901.

8. Klein, *Union Pacific: Rebirth*, 90–91.

9. *WSJ*, Jan. 10, 1901.

10. Ibid., Apr. 5, 1901.

11. For details see Chapter 10.

12. *United States of America v. Union Pacific Railroad Company et al.*, U.S. Circuit Court for the District of Utah, docket no. 993, 4:1666–68; Harriman to A. F. Walker, June 5, 1900, AF; *WSJ*, Nov. 14–16, Dec. 5, 1899; *New York Times*, Mar. 2, Apr. 6, 1900; *San Francisco Chronicle*, Apr. 9, 1899, June 29, 1900.

13. Klein, *Union Pacific: Rebirth*, 93.

14. Ibid., 93–94.

15. *WSJ*, Jan. 9, 1900; Fish to Harriman, June 28, 1898, IC.

16. *WSJ*, Apr. 25, June 9, Aug. 8, Nov. 2, 18, 1899.

17. Quoted by Kennan from Batson manuscript, AF.

18. Lamont to Hill, July 31, 1900, JJH.

19. Harriman's movements can be tracked in the file of telegrams for this period in UPL. The telegrams inviting officers to the luncheon are also in UPL.

20. The file of telegrams inviting officers to the second luncheon is in UPL.

21. Harriman to Burt, Aug. 21, 1899, UPL; Perkins to Harris, Aug. 15, 1899, BA.

22. *WSJ*, Nov. 14, 15, 20, 21, Dec. 5, 1899; Hill to Coster, Sept. 30, 1899, JJH.

CHAPTER 14

1. *WSJ*, May 3, 1905.

2. *New York Times*, July 28, 1908; Carl Snyder, "Harriman: 'Colossus of Roads,'" *Review of Reviews* 35 (Jan. 1907): 45.

3. W. L. Park, "Personal Recollections of Mr. Harriman in Connection with the Union Pacific," 25, AF; Kennan notes, AF; Arthur Pound and Samuel Taylor Moore, *They Told*

Barron: *Conversations and Revelations of an American Pepys in Wall Street* (New York, 1930), 136.

4. C. M. Keys, "Harriman," *World's Work* 13 (Jan. 1907): 8659; Frank A. Vanderlip, *From Farm Boy to Financier* (New York, 1935), 144; Edward J. Wheeler, ed., *Index of Current Literature* 42 (Jan.–June 1907): 154; Edwin Lefevre, "Harriman," *American Magazine* 64 (June 1907): 125.

5. Wheeler, *Index of Current Literature* 42 (Jan.–June 1907): 154; Snyder, "Harriman," 44; *Fortune*, May 8, 1978, 197; Edwin Wildman, "The Jekyll-Hyde Harriman," *Overland Monthly* 51 (Mar. 1908): 3, 212; Samuel M. Felton, "The Genius of Edward H. Harriman," *American Magazine* 99 (Apr. 1925): 9; E. Roland Harriman, *I Reminisce* (Garden City, N.Y., 1975), 9.

6. Richard C. Overton, *Burlington Route: A History of the Burlington Lines* (Lincoln, Neb., 1965), 248–50.

7. C. C. Tegethoff to Kennan, Jan. 30, 1919, AF; Schiff to Kennan, Apr. 18, 1919, AF; *WSJ*, May 17, 19, 1900; Kennan notes, AF. Kennan's notes, taken from original documents, provide details on the pool.

8. *United States of America v. Union Pacific Railroad Company et al.*, U.S. Circuit Court for the district of Utah, docket no. 993, 10:4727–28, 4947–48, 11:5058, 5062, hereafter cited as *USA v. UP*; *WSJ*, Aug. 15, 1900.

9. Overton, *Burlington Route*, 250.

10. *USA v. UP*, 11:4954; Robert G. Athearn, *The Denver and Rio Grande Western Railroad* (Lincoln, Neb., 1977), 191.

11. *WSJ*, Aug. 29, 1900.

12. Ibid., Feb. 1–3, 1901; *USA v. UP*, 3:1216–22, 11:4948–52; *New York Times*, Feb. 2, 1901; *Journal of Commerce and Commercial Bulletin*, Feb. 2, 1901; UP Exec. Com. minutes, Feb. 5, 1901, UPL.

13. Maury Klein, *Union Pacific: The Rebirth, 1894–1969* (New York, 1990), 89–90.

14. *USA v. UP*, 10:4713, 4737–38, 11:4953–57; George Kennan, *E. H. Harriman*, 2 vols. (New York, 1922), 1:241.

15. Schiff to Hill, Feb. 4, 1901, JJH; Kennedy to Hill, Feb. 6, 1901, JJH.

16. Burton J. Hendrick, "The Passing of a Great Railroad Dynasty," *McClure's Magazine* 38 (Mar. 1912): 488.

17. Ibid., 484.

18. *USA v. UP*, 11:4954.

19. Ibid.; *WSJ*, Feb. 8, 14, 1901; *New York Times*, Feb. 14, 1901; *Railroad Gazette*, 33:120, 292.

20. J. P. Morgan et al. to President and Board of Directors of the Chicago, Burlington & Quincy System, Jan. 19, 1901, BA; extract from Proceedings of Conference of Executive Officers of Western, Northwestern and Southwestern railroad companies, Dec. 5–7, 1900, BA.

21. Perkins to W. J. Palmer, Dec. 24, 1900, BA; Perkins to George B. Harris, Jan. 5, 1901, BA; *WSJ*, Mar. 23, 1901. For more detail, see Klein, *Union Pacific: Rebirth*, 92–93.

22. *WSJ*, Mar. 30, 1901; *Journal of Commerce and Commercial Bulletin*, Jan. 8, 1901.

23. *Railroad Gazette*, 33:96. For the steel merger, see Vincent P. Carosso, with Rose C. Carosso, *The Morgans: Private International Bankers, 1854–1913* (Cambridge, Mass., 1987), 466–74.

24. Harriman to Hill, Jan. 24, Feb. 6, 7, 1901, JJH; Cyrus Adler, *Jacob Schiff: His Life and Letters*, 2 vols. (Garden City, N.Y., 1928), 1:90–91; Hill to Harriman, Jan. 29, Feb. 6, 1901, JJH; Hill to Robert Bacon, Feb. 7, 9, Mar. 2, 1901, JJH.

25. Albro Martin, *James J. Hill and the Opening of the Northwest* (New York, 1976), 487–88; Klein, *Union Pacific: Rebirth*, 97.

26. *WSJ*, Nov. 1, 1900, Jan. 3, Jan. 9, 15, 1901; *Journal of Commerce and Commercial Bulletin*, Dec. 15, 19, 1900; Klein, *Union Pacific: Rebirth*, 98.

27. Hill to Perkins, Feb. 18, 1901, JJH; Perkins to Hill, Feb. 19, 1901, JJH; Hill to Morgan, Feb. 20, 1901, JJH; Overton, *Burlington Route*, 256–57.

28. Robert Bacon to Hill, Mar. 2, 1901, JJH; Adler, *Schiff*, 1:103. Hill was also denying any interest in the Burlington to the press. See *WSJ*, Mar. 20, 1901.

29. Hill to Schiff, Apr. 9, 1900 [1901], JJH; Hill to J. S. Kennedy, May 16, 1901, JJH; Martin, *Hill*, 496–98; Kennan, *Harriman*, 1:296–97.

30. *WSJ*, Mar. 30, Apr. 3, 1901; Overton, *Burlington Route*, 258; Batson fragment, 10, AF. Baker had also accompanied Hill to some of the meetings with Perkins.

31. Adler, *Schiff*, 1:103–4; Batson fragment, 10, AF; *New York Times*, May 13, 1901.

32. Adler, *Schiff*, 1:104–5.

33. *St. Paul Globe*, Dec. 22, 1901; Hill to Lord Mount Stephen, June 4, 1901, JJH; Herbert L. Satterlee, *J. Pierpont Morgan: An Intimate Portrait* (New York, 1939), 354.

34. Schiff to Hill, Apr. 8, 1901, JJH; Hill to Schiff, Apr. 9, 1900 [1901], JJH; *WSJ*, Apr. 13, 26, 1901; Perkins to Hill, Apr. 30, 1901, JJH.

CHAPTER 15

1. B. H. Meyer, *A History of the Northern Securities Case* (Madison, Wisc., 1906), 232.

2. *WSJ*, Apr. 16–27, 1901; *Journal of Commerce and Commercial Bulletin*, Apr. 25, 1901; Batson fragment, AF. The Batson fragment quotes correspondence on the Northern Pacific transactions.

3. Albro Martin, *James J. Hill and the Opening of the Northwest* (New York, 1976), 498–500; Herbert L. Satterlee, *J. Pierpont Morgan: An Intimate Portrait* (New York, 1939), 350; Hill to Lord Mount Stephen, Apr. 26, 1901, JJH. Hill's movements are confirmed in the Mary T. Hill diary, Apr. 15–27, 1901, JJH. I am grateful to W. Thomas White for providing me copies of the relevant entries.

4. Martin, *Hill*, 498–500; Hill to Lord Mount Stephen, Apr. 26, 1901, JJH; *WSJ*, Apr. 27, 1901; G. B. Schley to Hill, Apr. 27, 1901, JJH. Martin has Hill arriving in New York on April 29 but then going to meet Schiff the same day. Schiff wrote Morgan less than two weeks after the meeting, stating explicitly that he saw Hill on the morning of May 3. See Cyrus Adler, *Jacob Schiff: His Life and Letters*, 2 vols. (Garden City, N.Y., 1928), 1:106.

5. *New York Times*, Apr. 30, May 1, 1901; *WSJ*, Apr. 30, 1901; *New York Herald*, Apr. 30, 1901; *New York World*, May 5, 1901; Mary T. Hill to Clara and Rachel Hill, Apr. 29, 1901, JJH; C. W. Woolford to Hill, Apr. 30, 1901, JJH; Hill to Gaspard Farrer, Apr. 30, 1901, JJH; Mary T. Hill diary, May 2, 1901, JJH.

6. *WSJ*, Apr. 30, 1901; *New York Tribune*, Apr. 30, 1901; *New York Sun*, Apr. 30, 1901; *New York World*, Apr. 30, 1901; *New York Herald*, Apr. 30, 1901; Perkins to Hill, Apr. 30, 1901, JJH.

7. *WSJ*, Apr. 24–May 4, 1901; *Chronicle*, 72:874, 937; *New York Tribune*, Apr. 26, 1901; *New York Sun*, Apr. 30, May 1, 1901; *New York Herald*, Apr. 30, May 1, 1901; *New York Times*, May 1, 1901; *New York World*, May 1, 1901.

8. *New York Herald*, May 2, 1901; *New York Times*, May 2, 1901; *New York World*, May 1, 2, 1901; *New York Sun*, May 2, 1901; *WSJ*, May 2, 1901; *Journal of Commerce and Commercial Bulletin*, May 2, 1901.

9. UP Exec. Com. minutes, May 2, 1901, UPL; *New York Herald*, May 3, 1901; *New York Times*, May 3, 1901; *New York World*, May 3, 1901; *New York Sun*, May 3, 1901; *WSJ*, May 3, 1901; *New York Tribune*, May 3, 1901.

10. *New York Herald*, May 4, 1901; *New York Times*, May 4, 1901; *New York Sun*, May 4, 1901; *WSJ*, May 4, 1901; *New York Tribune*, May 4, 1901; *Chronicle*, 72:874.

11. Adler, *Schiff*, 1:106. Two weeks later, both Schiff and Hill wrote private letters of explanation that are utterly irreconcilable. The two versions are Schiff's letter to Morgan dated May 16, 1901, in Adler, *Schiff*, 1:102–7, and Hill to John S. Kennedy, May 16, 1901, JJH. Hill elaborated twice on his version in letters to Lord Mount Stephen, June 4, 1901, July 22, 1904, both JJH.

12. Satterlee, *Morgan*, 354; Martin, *Hill*, 502. Hill's version is pieced together from Hill to John S. Kennedy, May 16, 1901, JJH; Hill to Lord Mount Stephen, June 4, 1901, July 22, 1904, JJH.

13. Hill to Lord Mount Stephen, June 4, 1901, JJH.

14. Batson fragment, AF. This story is taken from a direct quotation. Batson claims Harriman gave him this account but does not say when. George Kennan reprinted it in *E. H. Harriman*, 2 vols. (New York, 1922), 1:305–6.

15. Charles E. Perkins maintained that Harriman's "truculence" over the episode "reflected his great mortification at having overlooked the point." See Martin, *Hill*, 648. While this response fits Harriman's personality, it ignores one basic fact: if Harriman was not aware of the problem, why did he attempt to buy more common stock?

16. Adler, *Schiff*, 1:106; Frieda Schiff Warburg, *Reminiscences of a Long Life* (New York, 1956), 62; Batson fragment, AF.

17. Satterlee, *Morgan*, 355–56.

18. See, for example, Crawford Livingston to Hill, May 6, 1901, JJH.

19. Bernard M. Baruch, *My Own Story* (New York, 1957), 126–27.

20. *New York Herald*, May 5, 1901; *New York Tribune*, May 5, 1901.

21. *New York Herald*, May 5, 1901.

22. For a sketch of Keene see Baruch, *My Own Story*, 135–43.

23. *New York Times*, May 7, 1901; *WSJ*, May 7, 1901; *New York Herald*, May 7, 1901; *New York Sun*, May 7, 1901; Baruch, *My Own Story*, 128.

24. Batson fragment, AF; Kennan to Mary Harriman, Jan. 15, 1920, AF.

25. Batson fragment, AF.

26. Ibid.; *New York Times*, May 7, 8, 1901; *WSJ*, May 8, 1901; *Journal of Commerce and Commercial Bulletin*, May 8, 1901; *New York Tribune*, May 8, 1901; *New York World*, May 8, 1901; *New York Herald*, May 8, 1901; UP Directors minutes, May 8, 1901, UPL.

27. *WSJ*, May 9, 1901, *New York Times*, May 9, 1901; *Journal of Commerce and Commercial Bulletin*, May 9, 1901; *New York Tribune*, May 9, 1901; *New York Herald*, May 9, 1901; *New York World*, May 9, 1901; *New York Sun*, May 9, 1901.

28. Baruch, *My Own Story*, 136–37.

29. *New York Sun*, May 9, 1901; *New York Herald*, May 9, 1901; Kennan notes, AF.

30. *New York Times*, May 10, 1901; *WSJ*, May 10, 1901; *New York Herald*, May 10, 1901; *New York World*, May 10, 1901; *New York Tribune*, May 10, 1901; *New York Sun*, May 10, 1901.

31. *New York Herald*, May 10, 1901.

32. *WSJ*, May 10–13, 1901; *New York Tribune*, May 10–12, 1901; *New York Times*, May 10–13, 1901; *New York Herald*, May 10–12, 1901; *New York World*, May 10–12, 1901; *New York Sun*, May 10–13, 1901.

33. Batson fragment, AF; *WSJ*, May 9, 1901.

34. *New York Sun*, May 10, 1901.

35. Adler, *Schiff*, 1:102–7.

36. Ibid., 107–8.

37. Maury Klein, *Union Pacific: The Rebirth, 1894–1969* (New York, 1990), 107; Martin, *Hill*, 506. See also the figures in Vincent P. Carosso, with Rose C. Carosso, *The Morgans: Private International Bankers, 1854–1913* (Cambridge, Mass., 1987), 477.

38. Meyer, *History of the Northern Securities Case*, 234; Batson fragment, AF; W. D. Travers(?) to Hill, May 30, 1901, JJH.

39. UP Exec. Com. minutes, May 10, 1901, UPL; Hill to Harriman, May 19, 1901, JJH; E. T. Nichols to Hill, May 23, 1901, JJH; Hill to Bacon, May 23, 1901, JJH; Hill to Hughitt, May 22, 1901, JJH; *WSJ*, May 14–17, 1901; *Journal of Commerce and Commercial Bulletin*, May 15, 1901; *New York Tribune*, May 15, 1901.

40. Hill to Hughitt, May 22, 1901, JJH; Bacon to Hill, May 23, 1901, JJH. Hill's plan is outlined in Hill to Lord Mount Stephen, May 25, 1901, JJH.

41. Memorandum of understanding, May 31, 1901, JJH. Details on the integration plan are in the memo and summarized in Klein, *Union Pacific: Rebirth*, 107–8.

42. Harriman to Burt, June 10, 1901, UPL; Hill to Bacon, June 12, 1901, JJH; Klein, *Union Pacific: Rebirth*, 108.

43. Hill to Bacon, June 12, July 19, 1901, JJH; Hill to Schiff, July 19, 1901, JJH; Hill to Harriman, July 19, 1901, JJH; Schiff to Hill, July 22, 1901, JJH; *Railroad Gazette*, 33:535.

44. Hill to Mount Stephen, May 25, July 22, 1901, JJH; Hill to Edward Tuck, June 13, Aug. 14, 1901, JJH; Hill to Lord Strathcona, Aug. 13, 1901, JJH; Hill to Bacon, Sept. 2, 1901, JJH; UP Directors minutes, Sept. 4, 24, 1901, UPL; J. S. Kennedy to Hill, July 22, Sept. 6, 1901, JJH; Hill to Lefevre, Sept. 6, 1901, JJH; *WSJ*, Aug. 21, 1901; Hill to Gaspard Farrer, Aug. 31, 1901, JJH. The directors included Hill, Harriman, William Rockefeller, banker Harrison M. Twombley (a Vanderbilt man), and Samuel Rea of the Pennsylvania Railroad.

45. Schiff to Harriman, Sept. 11, 1901, AF; Kennedy to Hill, Sept. 6, 1901, JJH; Martin, *Hill*, 506; Harriman to Schiff, Oct. 16, 1901, AF; *WSJ*, Oct. 30, 1901; Klein, *Union Pacific: Rebirth*, 109.

46. Schiff to Harriman, Sept. 11, 1901, AF. It is not clear what "financial measures" Schiff refers to.

47. *WSJ*, Nov. 4, 15, 1901; Adler, *Schiff*, 1:110; Klein, *Union Pacific: Rebirth*, 109.

48. *WSJ*, Nov. 15, 1901; *Chronicle*, 73:1062; *Railroad Gazette*, 33:815–16. Details on the new company are in Meyer, *History of the Northern Securities Case*, 225–41.

49. *WSJ*, Nov. 8–11, 14, 15, 22, 23, Dec. 2, 1901; *Chronicle*, 73:1062; *New York Times*, Nov. 16, 1901; *Chicago Chronicle*, Dec. 17, 1901; W. P. Clough to Hill, Dec. 26, 1901, JJH.

50. *New York Times*, Nov. 18–23, 29, 1901; *WSJ*, Nov. 21, 26, Dec. 2, Dec. 4, 9, 1901; *Chronicle*, 73:1112, 1264, 1314; Meyer, *History of the Northern Securities Case*, 242–44.

51. *WSJ*, Dec. 4, 5, 7, 9, 19, 1901; Clough to Hill, Jan. 8, 1902, JJH; *Chronicle*, 73:1264; Martin A. Knapp to Horace G. Burt, Dec. 28, 1901, UPL; Burt to Harriman, Dec. 31, 1901, UPL; Harriman to Burt, Dec. 31, 1901, UPL; *New York Times*, Dec. 31, 1901.

CHAPTER 16

1. *New York World*, May 12, 1901.

2. Draft charter, Oct. 23, 1901, SF; Harriman to Stillman, Mar. 31, Apr. 1, 1898, JS; Harriman to Fish, Sept. 24, [1900], SF; Railroad Securities Co. circular, Oct. 6, 1901, SF; *Journal of Commerce and Commercial Bulletin*, Feb. 16, 1901; *WSJ*, Feb. 16, 20, 1901.

3. *WSJ*, Feb. 2, 11, 12, 26, Apr. 2, 20, July 26, 1901; Schiff to Harriman, Sept. 11, 1901, AF.

4. Schiff to Harriman, Sept. 11, 1901, AF.

5. *United States of America v. Union Pacific Railroad Company et al.*, U.S. Circuit Court for the district of Utah, docket no. 993, 10:4720, 4758; hereafter cited as *USA v. UP*.

6. Ibid., 2:113; "History of Corporations whose Property is Now Owned or Operated by San Pedro, Los Angeles & Salt Lake Railroad Company," JA, 2.

7. Maury Klein, *Union Pacific: The Rebirth, 1894–1969* (New York, 1990), 113.

8. "Report on the Los Angeles Terminal Railway," Apr. 29, 1899, 1, SMF.

9. Ibid., 1–3; Klein, *Union Pacific: Rebirth*, 114.

10. French Strother, "Swinging the March of Empire Southward," *World's Work* 11 (Jan. 1906): 7073–74.

11. Ibid.; Bancroft to Harriman, May 25, 1899, UPL.

12. This portrait of Clark is drawn largely from Michael P. Malone, *The Battle for Butte: Mining and Politics on the Northern Frontier, 1864–1906* (Seattle, 1981), 12–15, and *DAB*, 4:144–46.

13. Malone, *Battle for Butte*, 82–83.

14. *New York World*, Apr. 26, 27, May 13, 1900; *DAB*, 4:145.

15. *New York World*, Feb. 25, 1900; *New York Tribune*, Mar. 16, Apr. 11, 18, 24, May 16–19, 1900; Malone, *Battle for Butte*, 80–130.

16. Malone, *Battle for Butte*, 199; *New York Tribune*, Mar. 16, 1900.

17. *WSJ*, Aug. 29, Oct. 6, 29, 1900; *New York Times*, Oct. 1, Nov. 23, 1900; Klein, *Union Pacific: Rebirth*, 115.

18. *USA v. UP*, 10:4790–4800; *WSJ*, Jan. 4, 1901; *Chronicle*, 72:184, 581; *Railroad Gazette*, 33:152, 229–30.

19. *Salt Lake Tribune*, Apr. 5, 1901; *Denver Post*, Apr. 8, 1901; Bancroft circular, Apr. 9, 1901, UPL; *Chronicle*, 72:723.

20. Klein, *Union Pacific: Rebirth*, 116; *Salt Lake Tribune*, Apr. 25–27, June 30, July 4, 5, 1901; *Railroad Gazette*, 33:286; *WSJ*, Apr. 30, June 12, 27, July 8, 1901; *Deseret Evening News*, June 21, 1901; *Salt Lake Herald*, June 28, 30, July 26, 1901.

21. *Deseret Evening News*, July 23, 30, 1901; *Salt Lake Tribune*, July 27, 30, 31, Aug. 10, 1901; *Salt Lake Herald*, July 31, Aug. 3, 1901; *Chronicle*, 73:237; *New York Commercial*, July 12, 1901; *Railroad Gazette*, 33:637, 640–41, 679–80.

22. *WSJ*, Aug. 8, 15, 28, Oct. 17, 1901, Jan. 18, Mar. 3, Apr. 8, 29, May 27, 1902; Burt to Harriman, Sept. 15, 1901, UPL; Cornish to P. L. Williams, Oct. 5, Nov. 1, 1901, JA; Ashton to Bancroft, Jan. 3, 20, 1902, JA; *Railroad Gazette*, 33:900, 34:68; Bancroft to Cornish, Dec. 10, 1901, Jan. 20, 1902, JA.

23. Cornish to Williams, Feb. 5, 1902, JA; Williams to Ashton, Apr. 16, 1902, JA; T. E. Gibbon to Bancroft, May 6, 1902, JA; Bancroft to Harriman, May 21, 1902, JA; Harriman to Bancroft, May 21, 1902, JA; Bancroft to Cornish, May 30, June 3, 1902, JA; Ashton to Bancroft, July 28, 1902, JA; Cornish to Bancroft, Aug. 13, 1902, JA. The text of the entire agreement is in *USA v. UP*, 1:87–108.

24. *Chronicle*, 75:907, 76:920, 1193; *WSJ*, Dec. 13, 1902, Apr. 30, 1903; Perkins to Hill, Jan. 2, 1903, JJH; Hill to Perkins, Jan. 8, 1903, JJH; memorandum, Jan. 18, 1903, JA; *New York Times*, Apr. 20, 1903; *Railroad Gazette*, 34:316.

25. Bancroft to Cornish, May 11, 1903, JA; W. R. Kelly to P. L. Williams, July 24, 1903, JA.

26. Cornish to Bancroft, June 8, 1903, JA; *WSJ*, Oct. 24, 1904.

27. *WSJ*, Jan. 22, 1901.

28. Klein, *Union Pacific: Rebirth*, 112.

29. John L. Cowan, "Freeing a City from a Railroad's Control," *World's Work* 9 (1905): 5713–16; *New York Times*, Feb. 26, May 2, 25, 1901; Joseph Frazier Wall, *Andrew Carnegie* (New York, 1970), 779–80.

30. W. L. Burton, "History of the Missouri Pacific," 769–70, unpublished manuscript, copy in author's possession; *New York Times*, Apr. 6, May 5, 7, 1902; *WSJ*, Apr. 9, 29, 30, May 12, 13, 16, 23, 24, July 2, 1902; *Chronicle*, 74:938, 989, 1091, 75:31, 79.

31. *Journal of Commerce and Commercial Bulletin*, Oct. 18, 19, 1900; Fish to Horace Burt, Oct. 19, 1900, UPL; *WSJ*, Oct. 25, 1900.

32. *WSJ*, Dec. 12, 20, 1900, Apr. 12, 19, 23, 25, 26, June 22, July 16, Aug. 22, Dec. 24, 1901; Jan. 13, Feb. 5, Mar. 8, 22, April 10, 19, May 19, 22, June 11, 19, 25, 28, July 3, 9, 17, 21, 25, Aug. 2, 19–22, Sept. 3, 6, 12, 23, Oct. 6, Nov. 25, 1902; Lloyd Wendt and Herman Kogan, *Bet A Million! The Story of John W. Gates* (Indianapolis, 1948), 247–49.

33. *WSJ*, Nov. 14, 20, 25, 1902; *St. Louis Globe-Democrat*, Aug. 28, 1902; *Denver Republican*, Nov. 13, 1902; *New York Commercial*, Aug. 13, 1902.

34. *Denver Post*, Feb. 6, 1903; *WSJ*, Nov. 25, Dec. 3–5, 8, 11, 1902, Mar. 7, 1903; *Chronicle*, 76:655; G. H. Kneiss, "History of the Western Pacific Railroad," *Western Pacific Mileposts*, Spring–Fall 1978, H3–8.

35. *USA v. UP*, 2:525, 3:1133–34; statement by Hugh Neill, Nov. 28, 1911, 3, AF.

36. *USA v. UP*, 3:1134–36.

37. Interstate Commerce Commission, "In the Matter of Consolidations and Combinations of Carriers Subject to the Act to Regulate Commerce, Including the Method of Association Known as the 'Community of Interest Plan,' " (Washington, D.C., 1902). This hearing was prompted by the Northern Pacific panic and the formation of Northern Securities. Only six witnesses were called: Harriman, Hill, Mellen, Stubbs, Miller, and George Harris of the Burlington.

38. Maury Klein, *The Life and Legend of Jay Gould* (Baltimore, 1986), 437.

39. Klein, *Union Pacific: Rebirth*, 112–13.

CHAPTER 17

1. George Kennan, *E. H. Harriman*, 2 vols. (New York, 1922), 1:278.

2. Maury Klein, *Union Pacific: The Rebirth, 1894–1969* (New York, 1990), 122. For the condition of the Southern Pacific, see *WSJ*, Feb. 12, Aug. 29, 1901.

3. Harriman to Burt, Nov. 15, 1901, UPL; Burt to Harriman, Nov. 15, 1901, UPL; Burt to Kruttschnitt, Nov. 15, 16, 1901, UPL; Kruttschnitt to Burt, Nov. 15, 1901, UPL; Hood to Kennan, June 21, 1922, with accompanying memorandum, GK; Kennan, *Harriman*, 1:244–45.

4. Kennan, *Harriman*, 1:244.

5. Klein, *Union Pacific: Rebirth*, 2:124; Kruttschnitt to Batson, Apr. 11, 1911, AF.

6. Kennan, *Harriman*, 1:250; Hood memorandum, June 21, 1922, GK.

7. *Railroad Gazette*, 37:566, 42:328–31, 43:729, 44:176–77.

8. For a good summary of the project, see Oscar King Davis, "The Lucin Cut-Off," *Century* 71 (Jan. 1906): 459–68. See also Herbert I. Bennett, "Building across Great Salt Lake," *Scientific American Supplement* 57, no. 1481 (May 21, 1904): 23726–27.

9. Hood memorandum, June 21, 1922, GK; Klein, *Union Pacific: Rebirth*, 125; *WSJ*, Nov. 17, 1899, Apr. 16, Sept. 28, 1901; *Salt Lake Herald*, June 28, 1900; *Railroad Gazette*, 32:488, 502, 532, 33:358, 712; Kruttschnitt to Burt, Feb. 1, 2, 3, 1902, UPL; Millar to Burt, Feb. 3, 1902, UPL; Burt to Kruttschnitt, Feb. 3, 1902, UPL; Harriman to Burt, Feb. 3, 1902, UPL; Burt to Harriman, Feb. 3, 1902, UPL; Hood to W. H. Bancroft, Feb. 27, 1905, JA; Hood to

Kruttschnitt, Jan. 13, 1902, UPL; Kruttschnitt to Harriman, Jan. 27, 1902, UPL; *New York Times*, Jan. 28, 1902.

10. Klein, *Union Pacific: Rebirth*, 127; Davis, "Lucin Cut-Off," 463.

11. Hood memorandum, June 22, 1901, GK; Davis, "Lucin Cut-Off," 463–65; Bennett, "Railroading across Great Salt Lake," 23727; Hood to Kruttschnitt, Jan. 13, 1902, UPL.

12. Davis, "Lucin Cut-Off," 465; *Kansas City Journal*, Aug. 17, 1903.

13. Davis, "Lucin Cut-Off," 465–66; W. D. Cornish to Bancroft, Mar. 19, 29, 1904, JA; Bancroft to Cornish, Mar. 21, 1904, JA.

14. Davis, "Lucin Cut-Off," 465–66; Klein, *Union Pacific: Rebirth*, 127.

15. Davis, "Lucin Cut-Off," 467.

16. Ibid.

17. Millar to Bancroft, Nov. 17, 20, 1903, JA; Bancroft to Kruttschnitt, Nov. 20, 21, 23, 25, 1903, JA; Kruttschnitt to Bancroft, Nov. 20, 21, 1903, JA; Burt to Bancroft, Nov. 25, 1903, JA; Bancroft to Burt, Nov. 25, 1903, JA; *Railroad Gazette*, 35:878.

18. Klein, *Union Pacific: Rebirth*, 128; W. R. Scott to Bancroft, Apr. 18/19, 20, 21, 1904, JA; Kruttschnitt to Bancroft, Dec. 30, 1903, Aug. 9, 1904, JA; Bancroft to Kruttschnitt, Dec. 31, 1903, Aug. 9, 1904, JA; D. S. Spencer to Bancroft, Dec. 31, 1903, JA; *Railroad Gazette*, 36:54; Hood to Bancroft, Apr. 4, Aug. 8, 9, 11, 1904, JA; Bancroft to Hood, Aug. 8, 1904, JA.

19. Hood to Bancroft, Aug. 22, Sept. 2, 6, 1904, JA; E. Buckingham to Bancroft, Aug. 29, Sept. 2, 1904, JA; Kruttschnitt to Bancroft, Sept. 6, 1904, JA; Bancroft to Buckingham, Sept. 3, 6, 1904, JA; Bancroft to Kruttschnitt, Sept. 6, 1904; W. E. Marsh to Hood, Sept. 11, 1904, JA.

20. Hood to Bancroft, Sept. 15, 1904, JA; Hood to W. E. Marsh, Sept. 15, Dec. 29, 1904, JA; Bancroft to Hood, Sept. 18, Oct. 11, Dec. 29, 1904, JA; Hood to Kruttschnitt, Oct. 4, 1904, JA; Bancroft to E. Buckingham, Jan. 2, 1905, JA; Buckingham to Bancroft, Jan. 13, 1905, JA; Bancroft to E. E. Calvin, Sept. 26, 1905, JA.

21. Davis, "Lucin Cut-Off," 468.

22. Bennett, "Railroading across Great Salt Lake," 23726; *Railroad Gazette*, 42:691.

23. *Omaha Bee*, Nov. 28, 1903.

24. Kruttschnitt to Batson, Apr. 11, 1911, AF; Klein, *Union Pacific: Rebirth*, 124; *Railroad Gazette*, 34:14, 766, 35:585, 37:318, 40:223–25, 298, 41:48, 51, 194–95, 42:516, 43:40, 75, 573, 669, 783, 44:234, 45:661–62; *WSJ*, Apr. 19, 1902, Dec. 19, 1903, Nov. 21, 1904, Oct. 17, 1905; *Chronicle*, 74:1197–98.

25. *Chronicle*, 74:1197–98; *Railroad Gazette*, 41:502–4, 43:249, 340; *Scientific American*, 97:254.

26. *New York Times*, May 27, 1906; *WSJ*, Apr. 6, May 6, 1905; Klein, *Union Pacific: Rebirth*, 296–97.

27. *Railroad Gazette*, 40:609, 652–53, 41:437–38, 42:761–62, 43:199–200, 242; *WSJ*, Nov. 27, 1906.

28. Kruttschnitt to Batson, Apr. 11, 1911, AF; *Railroad Gazette*, 33:408, 422, 764, 38:151, 216, 39:63, 72, 135, 159–60, 40:161–62, 41:58, 42:322, 760, 43:228, 765, 45:47, 555, 982, 1610; *WSJ*, Mar. 28, 1902, May 4, Nov. 22, 1907; SP Exec. Com. minutes, June 5, 1902, Oct. 29, 1903, Feb. 11, June 16, Nov. 23, 1904, Aug. 31, 1905, Oct. 25, 1906, UPL; Don L. Hofsommer, *The Southern Pacific, 1901–1985* (College Station, Tex., 1986), 42–46.

29. Keith L. Bryant Jr., *A History of the Atchison, Topeka and Santa Fe Railway* (New York, 1974), 80–82, 170; Hofsommer, *Southern Pacific*, 45; *Railroad Gazette*, 46:9, Fish to J. T.

Harahan, Apr. 11, 1899, IC; Harriman to Fish, Nov. 1, 1899, IC; Fish to Harriman, Nov. 1, 1899, IC; *WSJ*, Dec. 6, 1899.

30. Kennan notes from Harriman material, AF; Fish to Harahan, Feb. 10, 12, 1902, IC; Joseph Stanley-Brown to Fish, Feb. 20, 1902, IC; *WSJ*, Feb. 12, Mar. 18, 27, 1902; Harriman to Limantour (?), Oct. 29, 1902, AF; Alexander Millar, *Edward H. Harriman and the Union Pacific Railroad* (New York, 1910), 11. A description of the new lines is in *Railroad Gazette*, 46:8–11.

31. *Railroad Gazette*, 38:175, 39:144, 40:29, 41:6, 31–32, 69–70, 130, 42:195–96, 458, 43:215–16; *WSJ*, Oct. 22, 1907.

32. *WSJ*, Nov. 20, 1907, Jan. 23, May 5, 1908, Feb. 18, Mar. 24, June 7, 1909; *Railroad Gazette*, 44:169, 430, 591, 45:694, 1664; *New York Times*, June 12, 13, 1909.

33. All figures computed from data in U.S. Bureau of the Census, *Historical Statistics of the United States from Colonial Times to 1970* (Washington, D.C., 1975), 2:740. See also Klein, *Union Pacific: Rebirth*, 130.

34. *Railroad Gazette*, 43:2–3.

35. Ibid., 42:720; Kruttschnitt to Batson, Apr. 11, 1911, AF; *United States of America v. Union Pacific Railroad Company et al.*, U.S. Circuit Court for the district of Utah, docket no. 993, 9:4108–13, 4134.

36. *WSJ*, Mar. 21, 1907.

37. Klein, *Union Pacific: Rebirth*, 130–31; Edward Dickinson to Burt, June 7, 1900, UPL.

38. Interview with W. A. Harriman, June 23, 1981; *Fortune*, May 8, 1978, 197.

39. Burt to Harriman, Nov. 23, Dec. 18, 19, 1901, Jan. 8, Feb. 6, Mar. 20, July 2, 1902, Jan. 24, Mar. 16, 1903, UPL; Harriman to Burt, Dec. 18, 19, 1901, Jan. 8, Feb. 6, 1902, Jan. 24, 1903, UPL; W. L. Park to E. Buckingham, Feb. 2, 1902, UPL; *Railroad Gazette*, 46:984.

40. *Railroad Gazette*, 45:2–3; Klein, *Union Pacific: Rebirth*, 131–32.

41. Klein, *Union Pacific: Rebirth*, 131–32; Frank H. Spearman, "Building Up a Great Railway System," *Outlook* 91 (Feb. 1909): 447.

42. *Railroad Gazette*, 54:400, 55:708.

43. Bancroft to Mary Harriman, Nov. 17, 1911, AF; *WSJ*, Nov. 27, 1906; C. M. Keys, "Harriman," *World's Work* 13 (Jan. 1907): 8552.

44. Edward Livingston Trudeau, *An Autobiography* (Garden City, N.Y., 1916), 94, 276–77.

45. William Mahl, "Memoirs, 1860–1910," 26–28, William Mahl Papers, University of Texas Library.

46. W. L. Park, "Personal Recollections of Mr. Harriman in Connection with the Union Pacific," 23–24, AF.

47. Klein, *Union Pacific: Rebirth*, 140. The earlier pension plans belonged to the Grand Trunk (1874), Baltimore & Ohio (1884), Pennsylvania (1900), and Chicago & Northwestern (1901).

48. Ibid., 139–40; *Railroad Gazette*, 48:1419.

49. For details on how the bureau operated, see *Railroad Gazette*, 48:1419–22.

50. J. B. Berry, "Notes on J. B. Berry's Association with Mr. E. H. Harriman," June 21, 1911, 8–9, 16, AF; *WSJ*, Aug. 18, 1903, Jan. 8, Sept. 10, Nov. 9, 12, 1906.

51. Klein, *Union Pacific: Rebirth*, 140; *WSJ*, Mar. 21, Apr. 17, Oct. 2, 1907.

52. Klein, *Union Pacific: Rebirth*, 140–41.

53. Ibid.; *New York Times*, Jan. 7, 31, 1903.

54. Klein, *Union Pacific: Rebirth*, 141.

55. *Railroad Gazette*, 47:306.

CHAPTER 18

1. H. M. Carson and R. N. Durborow to W. W. Atterbury, Dec. 2, 1908, Pennsylvania Railroad collection, Hagley Library, Wilmington, Delaware.

2. Alexander Millar, *Edward H. Harriman and the Union Pacific Railroad* (New York, 1910), 12.

3. Edwin Lefevre, "Harriman," *American Magazine* 64 (June 1907): 127.

4. Fish to Thomas Lloyd, June 28, 1901, IC; Maury Klein, *Union Pacific: The Rebirth, 1894–1969* (New York, 1990), 132–33.

5. These changes are best followed by looking at the list of officers in the company annual reports for 1901–9. Originally there was a seventh department, construction and maintenance, but it was merged with operating.

6. Harriman to Burt, Oct. 25, 1901, UPL; *WSJ*, Nov. 2, 1901; William Mahl, "Memoirs, 1860–1910," 38, William Mahl Papers, University of Texas Library.

7. Klein, *Union Pacific: Rebirth*, 133–34.

8. Frank A. Vanderlip, *From Farm Boy to Financier* (New York, 1935), 202–3; Mahl, "Memoirs," 40.

9. Vanderlip, *From Farm Boy to Financier*, 203; Mahl, "Memoirs," 4, 44, 49.

10. *New York Times*, May 25, July 19, 1901; Schiff to Harriman, July 28, 1901, AF; *San Francisco Chronicle*, Aug. 17, 1901; *Los Angeles Times*, Aug. 18, 1901; *Omaha Bee*, Aug. 21, 1901; *WSJ*, Aug. 19, 20, 24, 1901.

11. Schiff to Harriman, Sept. 11, 1901, AF; *WSJ*, Sept. 30, 1901.

12. Schiff to Harriman, Nov. 10, 1901, AF.

13. Klein, *Union Pacific: Rebirth*, 135.

14. W. L. Park, "Personal Recollections of Mr. Harriman in connection with the Union Pacific," 25–27, 33, AF.

15. Ibid.; Klein, *Union Pacific: Rebirth*, 136.

16. For more detail on the department versus division issue, see Ray Morris, *Railroad Administration* (New York, 1920), 46–89, and Alfred D. Chandler Jr., *The Visible Hand: The Managerial Revolution in American Business* (Cambridge, Mass., 1977), 176–85. Morris includes details on the Harriman system.

17. Carson and Durborow to Atterbury, Dec. 2, 1908, 1–5 and attached organizational chart. The chief engineer handled construction, maintenance, and certain facilities; the superintendent of motive power took care of shops and all matters relating to equipment, tools, and power plants.

18. Ibid., 2; Frank H. Spearman, "Building Up a Great Railway System," *Outlook* 91 (Feb. 1909): 441; Klein, *Union Pacific: Rebirth*, 138–39; Don L. Hofsommer, *Southern Pacific, 1901–1985* (College Station, Tex., 1986), 27–30.

19. Klein, *Union Pacific: Rebirth*, 139.

20. Ibid., 137.

21. *United States of America v. Union Pacific Railroad Company et al.*, U.S. Circuit Court for the district of Utah, docket no. 993, 11:5043–47, hereafter *USA v. UP*; Carson and Durborow to Atterbury, Dec. 2, 1908, 12–17. The average expenditures per mile of road for western systems during 1900–1909 were as follows: Union Pacific, $2,329; Southern Pacific, $2,807; Northern Pacific, $2,203; Atchison, Topeka & Santa Fe, $2,305; Great Northern, $1,804; Denver & Rio Grande, $1,799; Canadian Pacific, $1,518.

22. William Mahl to Burt, Jan. 16, 1903, UPL; Lefevre, "Harriman," 129–30.

23. Klein, *Union Pacific: Rebirth*, 153; *Chronicle*, 79:1674–76. All figures are compiled from company annual reports and *Railroad Gazette*, 35:869–70. To make the figures compa-

rable, the 1898 earnings include the Navigation and Short Line roads even though the system had not yet been reunited.

24. *WSJ*, May 7, 1902, Dec. 9, 1903, July 21, 27, 1905, Jan. 8, 1906.

25. Ibid., May 30, 1902; Southern Pacific income account statement, July 16, 1912, FAV; Thomas Warner Mitchell, "The Growth of the Union Pacific and Its Financial Operations," *Quarterly Journal of Economics* 21 (Aug. 1907): 587.

26. Excerpt from Harriman affidavit, Mar. 27, 1903, AF; Talbot J. Taylor & Co., "Southern Pacific Company," AF; *WSJ*, Aug. 24, 1902. The excerpt appeared in *New York Times* and *WSJ*, Apr. 2, 1903.

27. *WSJ*, Apr. 2, 1903.

28. *WSJ*, Aug. 29, 1902, Mar. 7, Mar. 10–14, 16, 19, 20, 1903; *Chronicle*, 76:28, 78:27; *New York Times*, Mar. 10–14, 18, 19, 1903.

29. *New York Times*, Mar. 15, 23, 24, Apr. 2–4, 7, 10, 1903; *WSJ*, Mar. 24, 26, Apr. 1–4, 8, 9, 13, 1903; *Railroad Gazette*, 40:76; *New York News Bureau*, Apr. 1, 1903.

30. *WSJ*, Apr. 6, 1903.

31. Ibid., Apr. 7, 1903; Oregon Short Line Directors minutes, Nov. 12, 1903, UPL; *USA v. UP*, 2:750–55. Rockefeller sold the shares back to the Oregon Short Line (through which the Union Pacific controlled them) in November after the legal battle had been won.

32. *Railroad Gazette*, 36:129–30, 41:46; *WSJ*, July 31, 1904, July 26, 1905, Aug. 4, 1906.

33. *Railroad Gazette*, 41:568; *WSJ*, Aug. 15, 1906.

CHAPTER 19

1. Albro Martin, *James J. Hill and the Opening of the Northwest* (New York, 1976), 474.

2. Michael H. Hunt, *The Making of a Special Relationship: The United States and China to 1914* (New York, 1983), 143–83; Michael H. Hunt, *Frontier Defense and the Open Door: Manchuria in Chinese-American Relations, 1895–1911* (New Haven, Conn., 1973), 1–38.

3. Howard K. Beale, *Theodore Roosevelt and the Rise of America to World Power* (Baltimore, 1956), 200–211; Hunt, *Making of a Special Relationship*, 150–51, 277–78; Hunt, *Frontier Defense*, 26–27, 41–42.

4. Fish to Harriman, Dec. 19, 1901, IC; Felton to Harriman, Dec. 26, 1901, IC. The sister company was the Occidental & Oriental Steamship Company, which was originally owned jointly by the Union Pacific and Southern Pacific. For background on both steamship companies, see Maury Klein, *Union Pacific: The Birth of a Railroad, 1862–1893* (New York, 1987), passim.

5. *WSJ*, May 5, Nov. 14, 1904, Feb. 2, 1905.

6. Ibid., June 27, 1905.

7. Thomas J. McCormick, *China Market* (Chicago, 1967), 78–84; George Kennan, *E. H. Harriman's Far Eastern Plans* (Garden City, N.Y., 1917), 6–7. Two American promoters came up with a similar plan during the 1890s, but it died from lack of capital and political miscalculations.

8. Lloyd C. Griscom, *Diplomatically Speaking* (Boston, 1940), 223.

9. Harriman invitation to Fish, June 15, 1905, SF; *WSJ*, June 28, 1905; Kennan notes, AF.

10. "A Brief Record of a Trip to the Orient by Mr. E. H. Harriman and Party," 1, AF.

11. Ibid., 1–2, 6.

12. Beale, *Theodore Roosevelt*, 277–312; Griscom, *Diplomatically Speaking*, 261.

13. These events are reconstructed from "Brief Record," 3–5; Griscom, *Diplomatically Speaking*, 261–63; *New York Times*, Sept. 8, 9, 1905. Griscom's account, written later, somewhat confuses the events of September 5–7.

14. "Brief Record," 13; Kennan, *Harriman's Far Eastern Plans*, 16.

15. "Brief Record," 13; *Fortune*, May 8, 1978, 208.

16. "Brief Record," 13–15.

17. Griscom, *Diplomatically Speaking*, 263.

18. Ibid., 263–64; "Brief Record," 15.

19. Griscom, *Diplomatically Speaking*, 263–64; Griscom to Harriman, Sept. 25, 1905, AF.

20. "Brief Record," 15–17; E. Roland Harriman, *I Reminisce* (Garden City, N.Y., 1975), 15.

21. Harriman to Griscom, Sept. 16, 1905, AF.

22. Paul A. Varg, *Open Door Diplomat: The Life of W. W. Rockhill* (Urbana, Ill., 1952), 71–72.

23. "Brief Record," 17–18; *New York Times*, Oct. 1, 6, 1905; Straight to Henry Schoellkopf, Sept. 17, 1905, WDS.

24. "Brief Record," 18.

25. Griscom to Harriman, Sept. 25, Oct. 7, 1905, AF; "Memorandum of Mr. Griscom's Remarks to Count Katsura (Prime Minister), Count Inouye, and Mr. Sakatani (Vice-Minister of Finance) in Separate Interviews," n.d., AF.

26. Press statement, Oct. 13, 1905, AF; K. Uyeno to Harriman, Oct. 21, 1905, AF. A copy of the memorandum is in AF. It is reprinted in Kennan, *Harriman's Far Eastern Plans*, 23–25.

27. Alice Roosevelt Longworth, *Crowded Hours* (New York, 1933), 107.

28. Ibid.; Harriman, *I Reminisce*, 23–24.

29. J. Soyeda to Harriman, Oct. 30, 1905, AF; Kennan, *Harriman's Far Eastern Plans*, 26–27.

30. Undated cable, AF; Soyeda to Harriman, Nov. 13, Dec. 18, 1905, Jan. 15, 1906, AF; Griscom to Harriman, Feb. 15, 1906, with enclosure, AF. Some of this correspondence is reprinted in Kennan, *Harriman's Far Eastern Plans*, 27–37.

31. *WSJ*, Oct. 25, 1905; Harriman invitation to Fish, Jan. 4, 1906, SF; *New York Times*, Jan. 10, 1906; K. Matsumoto to Harriman, Apr. 29, 1906, AF.

32. Kennan, *Harriman's Far Eastern Plans*, 39–40.

CHAPTER 20

1. Cornelia Harriman to Mary Harriman, undated, AF.

2. Mary Harriman to her father, undated, AF.

3. *Fortune*, May 8, 1978, 198.

4. Louis Husbrouck to Fish, Feb. 26, 1897, IC; *New York Times*, Apr. 5, 1903.

5. *New York Times*, Apr. 5, 1903; Willie Harriman to E. H. Harriman, Dec. 3, 1892, AF.

6. Kennan notes on Harriman letter, Nov. 19, 1902, AF; Harriman to Hill, Feb. 26, Apr. 9, 1903, JJH; Fish to Harriman, Mar. 7, 1903, IC; *New York Times*, Apr. 5, 1903.

7. *New York Times*, May 21, 1903; W. L. Park, "Personal Recollections of Mr. Harriman in connection with the Union Pacific," 24, AF.

8. Park, "Recollections," 24–25.

9. Samuel M. Felton, "The Genius of Edward H. Harriman," *American Magazine* 99 (Apr. 1925): 185–86.

10. Ibid.; *New York Commercial*, May 16, 1903; *New York Times*, May 16, 1903; *Chicago Chronicle*, May 16, 1903.

11. *New York Times*, May 16, 1903; *Chicago Chronicle*, May 16, 1903.

12. *New York Times*, May 17, 1903; *New York Commercial*, May 17, 1903.

13. *New York Commercial*, May 21, 1903; *New York Times*, May 21, 1903; Bancroft to Cornish, May 22, 1903, JA; Mary Harriman to Hill, May 27, 1903, JJH; Harriman to Hill, May 28, 1903, JJH; Felton, "Genius of Harriman," 186.

14. John Muir, "Tribute to the Memory of E. H. Harriman," 10, AF.
15. Harriman to J. M. McGuinness, undated, AF; *Chicago Tribune*, Mar. 26, 1902; *New York Times*, Dec. 19, 1934.
16. E. Roland Harriman, *I Reminisce* (Garden City, N.Y., 1975), 13.
17. Ibid., 7, 27–28.
18. Ibid., 13, 28.
19. Ibid., 36–37; *Fortune*, May 8, 1978, 198; *New York Times*, June 30, 1908.
20. Harriman, *I Reminisce*, 16–19.
21. Ibid., 12.
22. *New York Times*, Dec. 19, 1934; Persia Campbell, *Mary Williamson Harriman* (New York, 1960), 22, 42.
23. *DAB*, 18:121; Herbert Croly, *Willard Straight* (New York, 1924), 1–158.
24. Diary of Willard Straight, Oct. 27, 1904, WDS.
25. Croly, *Straight*, 197–200.
26. Michael H. Hunt, *Frontier Defense and the Open Door: Manchuria in Chinese-American Relations, 1895–1911* (New Haven, Conn., 1973), 154.
27. Croly, *Straight*, 202.
28. Straight to Harriman, Oct. 31, Nov. 15, Dec. 7, 27, 1906, Mar. 19, 1907, WDS; Mary Harriman to Mrs. C. C. Davis, Apr. 15, [1907], AF; Hazel Straight to Willard Straight, June 3, 1907, WDS.
29. Cornelia Harriman to Mary Harriman, undated, AF.
30. Ibid.; Mary Harriman to Charles Davis, undated but Aug. 1907, AF.
31. Mary Harriman to Charles Davis, undated; Davis to Mary Harriman, Aug. 8, 1907, AF; *New York Times*, Aug. 6, 1907.
32. *New York Times*, Dec. 19, 1934. Two of Goelet's school essays are in my possession.
33. *New York Times*, Dec. 19, 1934.
34. Ibid., Mar. 4, 1908.
35. Harriman to his wife, July 20, 1906, AF.
36. Ibid.
37. Campbell, *Mary Williamson Harriman*, 67–68.

CHAPTER 21
1. Fish to Harriman, Nov. 18, 1901, IC.
2. *WSJ*, May 4, 1905.
3. Maury Klein, *Union Pacific: The Rebirth, 1894–1969* (New York, 1990), 145–46. A copy of the new memorandum is in D. Miller to Hill, July 30, 1902, JJH.
4. Louis W. Hill to Hill, June 16, 1902, JJH; Mellen to W. P. Clough, June 16, 1902, JJH; Clough to Hill, June 18, 1902, JJH; Hill to Harriman, Mar. 31, Apr. 9, 1902, JJH; Hill to Schiff, Mar. 31, 1902, JJH; Harriman to Hill, Feb. 22, Apr. 1, 2, 12, 1902, JJH; Schiff to Hill, Apr. 2, 1902, JJH.
5. George Harris to Hill, Sept. 14, 19, 1902, JJH; Hill to D. Miller, Sept. 16, 30, 1902, JJH; Hill to Mellen, Sept. 30, 1902, JJH; Clough to Hill, Sept. 30, Oct. 3, 1902, JJH; Hill to Clough, Oct. 4, 1902, JJH.
6. *WSJ*, Feb. 12, 21, 22, 25, 1902; *New York Times*, Feb. 20–22, 1902; B. H. Meyer, *A History of the Northern Securities Case* (Madison, Wisc., 1906), 242–43, 257–58; Elting E. Morison and John M. Blum, eds., *The Letters of Theodore Roosevelt*, 8 vols. (Cambridge, Mass., 1951–54), 3:236, 257, 590–91; Albro Martin, *James J. Hill and the Opening of the Northwest* (New York, 1976), 515.

7. Martin, *Hill*, 513.

8. J. Stanley-Brown to Hill, Feb. 26, 1902, JJH.

9. Harriman to Hill, Feb. 17, 1902, JJH; Hill to Steele, Feb. 19, 1902, JJH; Hill to Harriman, Jan. 15, Feb. 19, 1902, JJH.

10. *New York World*, Dec. 24, 1899.

11. *WSJ*, June 14, July 17, 1905.

12. Ibid., Mar. 21, Sept. 17, 1902; *New York Times*, Jan. 17, 1903; Kennedy to Hill, Feb. 21, 1903, JJH; Hill to Kennedy, Feb. 25, 1903, JJH; "Memo for Mr. Hill," Feb. 24, 1903, JJH.

13. *New York Times*, May 27, June 3, 1902; *Omaha World-Herald*, May 28, 1902; *Omaha Bee*, May 28, 1902; *WSJ*, June 3, 4, 1902.

14. *WSJ*, June 4, 1902.

15. *New York Times*, Mar. 19–22, Apr. 10, 1903; *Chronicle*, 76:654; *WSJ*, Apr. 1, 9, 10, 1903; Meyer, *History of the Northern Securities Case*, 258–59, 272–74.

16. *WSJ*, Apr. 13, 1903; M. D. Grover to Hill, Apr. 18, 1903, JJH; Hill to C. E. Perkins, Apr. 21, 1903, JJH.

17. Schiff to Hill, Apr. 9, 19, 1903, JJH.

18. Meyer, *History of the Northern Securities Case*, 274–78; *New York Times*, Aug. 1, 1903; *Railroad Gazette*, 35:570.

19. Farrer to Hill, Aug. 20, 1903, JJH.

20. Mount Stephen to Hill, Aug. 21, 1903, JJH.

21. Hill to Mount Stephen, Sept. 10, 1903, JJH.

22. Meyer, *History of the Northern Securities Case*, 279–89, contains a full analysis. See also *Chronicle*, 78:1138; *Railroad Gazette*, 36:212; *New York Times*, Mar. 15, 1904.

23. Frank Parsons, "The Merger Tangle," *Arena* 31 (June 1904): 588; Klein, *Union Pacific: Rebirth*, 148.

24. *WSJ*, Mar. 18, 1904.

25. Klein, *Union Pacific: Rebirth*, 148.

26. Ibid., 148–49; *Railroad Gazette*, 36:274; *WSJ*, Mar. 25, 29, Apr. 2, 1904; Hill to William B. Dean, Apr. 1, 1904, JJH; *Denver Republican*, Apr. 9, 1904; *Chronicle*, 78:1392–93, 1447.

27. *WSJ*, Apr. 5, 1904; *New York Commercial*, Apr. 5, 1904; D. Willis James to Hill, Apr. 25, 1904, JJH; Schiff to Mount Stephen, May 8, 1904, JJH; W. P. Clough to Hill, May 14, 1904, JJH; Hill to Mount Stephen, June 15, 1904, JJH.

28. Farrer to Hill, July 11, 1904, JJH.

29. Mount Stephen to Hill, July 15, 1904, JJH.

30. Ibid.; Baker to Hill, July 26, 1904, JJH; E. T. Nichols to Hill, Aug. 5, 1904, JJH.

31. Hill to Farrer, July 22, 1904, JJH.

32. *WSJ*, July 30, 1904; Mount Stephen to Hill, July 1, Aug. 10, 1904, JJH; Farrer to Hill, Aug. 25, 1904, JJH.

33. *WSJ*, Jan. 4–6, 25, Mar. 7, 1905; *New York Times*, Jan. 4, 31, Mar. 7, Apr. 4, 1905; *Railroad Gazette*, 38:4, 93, 197; Hill to Schiff, Mar. 10, 1905, JJH.

34. Schiff to Hill, May 14, 1905, JJH; *WSJ*, May 19, 1905.

35. *WSJ*, Oct. 25, 1905; Klein, *Union Pacific: Rebirth*, 149.

CHAPTER 22

1. Edwin Lefevre, "Harriman," *American Magazine* 64 (June 1907): 126–27.

2. *Denver Post*, Mar. 20, 1902; *Kansas City Journal*, May 10, 1902; *Denver Republican*, Oct. 21, 1903; Harriman to Millar, Mar. 6, 1903, IC; W. C. Taylor to L. W. Hill, July 8, 1902, JJH; Fish to Horace Burt, Aug. 9, 1902, IC; *WSJ*, July 8, 9, 26, 29, Sept. 9, 11, 25,

Oct. 11, 20, 24, Dec. 15, 1902; *Omaha Bee*, Oct. 13, 15, 1902; Fish to Harriman, Oct. 22, 1902, IC.

3. Stubbs to William Sproule and J. A. Munroe, July 8, 1902, UPL; *United States of America v. Union Pacific Railroad Company et al.*, U.S. Circuit Court for the district of Utah, docket no. 993, 3:1132–64, 11:4918–21; hereafter cited as *USA v. UP*.

4. Stubbs to Sproule and Munroe, July 8, 1902, UPL; *USA v. UP*, 3:1132–64, 11:4918–21; Hugh Neill to Batson, Nov. 28, 1911, AF. Unless otherwise indicated, this episode is drawn from these sources.

5. *USA v. UP*, 3:1104–8, 1134–38, 1164, 10:4722, 4759–62.

6. Ibid.; *WSJ*, June 29, 1904; *New York Times*, Jan. 13, 1907; *Railroad Gazette*, 42:96, 600.

7. "Address Delivered by E. H. Harriman at the Opening of the Louisiana Purchase Exposition at St. Louis, Missouri, April 30, 1904," 1–4, AF.

8. Ibid., 5–6.

9. *Chronicle*, 76:655; *Denver Post*, July 2, 1903; *New York Times*, Feb. 6, 1904; *WSJ*, Feb. 8, 1904, Jan. 13, 1905.

10. *WSJ*, Aug. 29, Sept. 21, Oct. 13, 1904; *New York Times*, Sept. 10, 1904; *Chronicle*, 78:1168, 79:1024, 1267, 2749.

11. Harriman to Gould, Apr. 26, 1905, reprinted in *USA v. UP*, 1:208–9.

12. Ibid.; *WSJ*, Apr. 25, 1905; *New York Times*, Apr. 23, 28, 1905.

13. *New York Times*, Mar. 20, June 8, 1905; *Chronicle*, 80:1364, 1480, 1730; *WSJ*, Apr. 24, 25, 29, May 2, 4, 1905.

14. *New York Times*, Apr. 23, 1905; *WSJ*, May 11, 12, June 5, 1905; W. L. Burton, "History of the Missouri Pacific," 802–3, unpublished manuscript, copy in author's possession.

15. Burton, "History of the Missouri Pacific," 790–803.

16. *WSJ*, July 23, 1904, Apr. 25, May 6, 17, July 15, Sept. 28, Oct. 4, 1905, Apr. 14, 1906; *New York Times*, Oct. 1, 1905.

17. Maury Klein, *Union Pacific: The Rebirth, 1894–1969* (New York, 1990), 151–52.

18. *USA v. UP*, 2:834–36; Bernard Baruch, *My Own Story* (New York, 1957), 151, 164.

19. *WSJ*, Oct. 14, 22, 28, Nov. 3, 12, 27, Dec. 30, 1903, Jan. 8, 13, 14, Feb. 12, 19, 26, July 9, Sept. 5, 9, 10, 21, Oct. 5, 1904; Harriman to Felton, Apr. 14, 1903, AF; *New York Times*, Sept. 19, 1904; Union Pacific Exec. Com. minutes, Sept. 29, 1904, UPL; *Chronicle*, 80:417; Cyrus Adler, *Jacob Schiff: His Life and Letters*, 2 vols. (Garden City, N.Y., 1928), 1:139–40.

20. C. M. Keys, "Harriman," *World's Work* 13 (Jan. 1907): 8550–51; *WSJ*, Apr. 15, June 9, Aug. 4, Oct. 12, Nov. 8, 18, 1904, Jan. 25, Feb. 8, 24, Mar. 3, 4, Apr. 6, May 2, 3, 9, 1905; *Railroad Gazette*, 38:80.

21. *New York Times*, Oct. 28, 1905; Hill to Louis Hill, July 20, 1905, JJH; *WSJ*, Oct. 28, Nov. 21, Dec. 2, 1905, Jan. 27, Feb. 14, 1906; *Railroad Gazette*, 43:406.

22. *WSJ*, Sept. 22, 1905.

23. *New York Times*, Oct. 25, Nov. 5, 1905, Mar. 23, 1906; *Railroad Gazette*, 43:406; Unsigned cable to Hill, Oct. 6, 1904, JJH; Hill to Mount Stephen, Dec. 12, 1904, JJH; *WSJ*, Jan. 27, 31, Feb. 9, Mar. 7, Oct. 25, 28, Nov. 17, 1905, July 28, Dec. 25, 1906; Stillman to Harriman, Mar. 2, 1906, AF; Harriman to Stillman, May 27, 1906, AF; Harriman to Charles D. Hine, Dec. 26, 1906, AF.

24. William Ashton to Bancroft, June 19, 1903, JA; *Deseret Evening News*, June 18, 1903.

25. Hood to Bancroft, June 19, 1903, JA; Bancroft to Hood, June 25, 1903, JA; P. L. Williams to W. R. Kelly, July 21, 1903, JA; Cornish to Bancroft, July 30, 1903, JA.

26. Bancroft to Cornish, July 31, Aug. 3, 4, 8, 9, 1903, JA; Cornish to Bancroft, Aug. 4, 5, 8, 18, 27, 1903, JA; Hood and Bancroft to Cornish, Aug. 5, 1903, JA; Bancroft to W. R. Kelly,

Aug. 12, 1903, JA; P. L. Williams to Bancroft, Aug. 17, 1903, JA. The agreement gave Harriman a half interest in Empire and in the California Improvement Company, which owned the stock of the San Pedro and the Los Angeles Terminal Land Company. Harriman bought this interest on behalf of the Short Line. See Oregon Short Line Exec. Com. minutes, July 16, 1903, UPL.

27. Cornish to Kelly, Aug. 28, 1903, JA; Cornish to Bancroft, Aug. 28, 1903, JA; Kelly to Cornish, Aug. 28, 29, 1903, JA; Kelly to T. E. Gibbon, Aug. 29, 1903, JA; Hood to Bancroft, Aug. 31, 1903, JA; Bancroft to Hood, Sept. 4, 1903, JA.

28. William Ashton to Hood, June 19, 1903, JA; Hood to Ashton, June 23, 1903, JA; Hood to Hawgood, June 24, Sept. 23, 1903, JA; Hood to Bancroft, June 30, Sept. 23, Oct. 5, 13, 1903, JA; Hawgood to Hood, Oct. 2, 1903, JA; Bancroft to Cornish, Oct. 6, 8, 1903, JA; Cornish to Bancroft, Oct. 29, 1903, JA.

29. Bancroft to Cornish, Dec. 29, 1903, JA; Hood to Hawgood, Jan. 15, Feb. 5, 6, 10, 1904, JA; Hawgood to Hood, Feb. 3, 1904, JA; Bancroft to Hood, Feb. 13, 25, 1904, JA; Hood to Bancroft, Feb. 27, 1904, JA.

30. Bancroft to Hood, Mar. 4, 1904, JA; Bancroft and Hood to Harriman, Mar. 12, 1904, JA.

31. Bancroft to Cornish, Mar. 13, 24, 1904, JA; Hood to Hawgood, Mar. 17, 30, 1904, JA; Hood to Bancroft, Mar. 17, 30, Apr. 1, 1904, JA.

32. Hood to Bancroft, Apr. 7, 11, 12, 20, 1904, JA; Bancroft to Hood, Apr. 4, 10, 22, 1904, JA; Hood to Hawgood, Apr. 6, 1904, JA; Clark and Hawgood to Bancroft and Hood, Apr. 2, 1904, JA; Bancroft and Hood to Clark and Hawgood, Apr. 8, 1904, JA; John H. Norton to Hawgood, Apr. 16, 1904, JA; Erickson & Petterson to Hawgood, Apr. 22, 1904, JA; Hawgood to Bienenfeld, Apr. 27, 1904, JA.

33. Hood to Bancroft, Apr. 29, May 2, 3, 1904, JA; Bancroft to Hood, May 1, 3, 1904, JA; Bancroft to Cornish, May 1, 1904, JA; Hood to H. I. Bettis, May 2, 1904, JA; Hood to Ross Clark, May 3, 1904, JA.

34. Bancroft to Hood, May 3, 4, 1904, JA; Hood to Bancroft, May 4, 1904, JA; Bancroft to Cornish, May 4, 1904, JA; Cornish to Bancroft, May 4, 6, 1904, JA; Ross Clark to Bancroft, May 4, 1904, JA.

35. "Minutes of Construction Committee Meeting," May 7, 9, 10, 11, 1904, JA; Bancroft and Hood to Cornish, May 12, 1904, JA; Bancroft to Cornish, May 13, 1904, JA. The account of the meeting is taken from these sources.

CHAPTER 23

1. Charles P. Norcross, "Owners of America," *Cosmopolitan*, July 1909, 170; Otto H. Kahn, "Edward Henry Harriman," in Stuart Bruchey, ed., *Three Railroad Pioneers* (New York, 1981), 18.

2. Kahn, "Harriman," 18–19.

3. R. Carlyle Buley, *The Equitable Life Assurance Society of the United States, 1859–1964*, 2 vols. (New York, 1967), 1:572–77.

4. Ibid., 3–485; *Report of the Joint Committee of the State of New York Appointed to Investigate the Affairs of Life Insurance Companies* (Albany, 1906), 68–69, 76–77; hereafter cited as *Armstrong Report*.

5. *Armstrong Report*, 78–98.

6. Ibid., 75; James W. Alexander to James H. Hyde, Nov. 14, 1904, HBH.

7. Buley, *Equitable*, 1:535, 540; *NCAB*, 15:249.

8. Quoted in Buley, *Equitable*, 1:516, 523.

9. *Armstrong Report*, 76.

10. Henry Morgenthau, *All in a Life-Time* (Garden City, N.Y., 1922), 66, 80; Buley, *Equitable*, 1:589–93.

11. Buley, *Equitable*, 1:577–86, and *Armstrong Report*, 91–103, detail some of these ventures.

12. *Armstrong Report*, 87; Harriman testimony, *Testimony Taken before the Joint Committee of the Senate and Assembly of the State of New York to Investigate and Examine into the Business Affairs of Life Insurance Companies Doing Business in the State of New York* (Albany, 1905), 3081; hereafter cited as *Armstrong Hearings*.

13. *Armstrong Report*, 101–3; Harriman testimony, *Armstrong Hearings*, 3081–87; Buley, *Equitable*, 1:632. Harriman's acceptance of the seat on Equitable's board, dated May 3, 1901, is in AF.

14. Harriman testimony, *Armstrong Hearings*, 3104–6.

15. Buley, *Equitable*, 1:603–12. The petition asked that all policyholders with policies of $5,000 or more be allowed to vote for directors.

16. Ibid., 598–603; *New York Times*, Feb. 1, 1905; *New York World*, Feb. 5, 1905.

17. Harriman testimony, *Armstrong Hearings*, 3090–96; *New York Times*, Nov. 15, 1905.

18. Buley, *Equitable*, 1:612. The source for this meeting is a memorandum made by Hyde at the time.

19. Ibid., 612–18; *New York World*, Feb. 13, 15, 1905.

20. Buley, *Equitable*, 1:618–19. Buley's chief source for most of these events is detailed notes left by Hyde, which must be regarded as partisan. The intriguing question is why Hyde, never the most precise of men in business, took such care from the outset of the fight to compile detailed notes and memorandums of every meeting and event.

21. Ibid., 619–20; *WSJ*, Feb. 20, 1905.

22. Buley, *Equitable*, 1:620–21; *New York World*, Feb. 16–19, 1905; Schiff to Hyde, [Feb. 17, 1905], HBH; Frank Vanderlip to Stillman, Mar. 1, 1905, FAV.

23. Buley, *Equitable*, 1:622–24. The Frick Committee originally had seven members, but two declined to serve.

24. *WSJ*, Apr. 4, 1905; *New York World*, Mar. 15, 19, 22, 28–31, 1905; Harriman to Odell, Apr. 4, 1905, AF.

25. Harriman to Odell, Apr. 4, 1905, AF.

26. *WSJ*, Apr. 4, 1905; Harriman testimony, *Armstrong Hearings*, 5152; note on telegrams between Harriman and Odell, Apr.–May 1905, AF.

27. Buley, *Equitable*, 1:627–35; *WSJ*, Apr. 20, May 4, 9, 11, 25, 1905; *New York World*, Apr. 1–27, May 4, 1905; *New York Sun*, Apr. 8, 1905.

28. Clarence J. Housman, "Recollections of E. H. Harriman," 1, AF; Morgenthau, *All in a Life-Time*, 81–82.

29. *New York World*, May 8, 9, 11, 13, 20, 27, 1905.

30. Buley, *Equitable*, 1:640–42; *New York Times*, June 2, 1905; *New York World*, May 31, June 1, 3, 1905.

31. *New York Times*, June 3, 1905, contains a full account of the meeting.

32. *New York World*, June 2, 3, 1905.

33. *WSJ*, June 5–10, 1905; *New York Times*, June 5, 1905; *New York World*, June 4–8, 1905; Frank Vanderlip to Stillman, June 6, 7, 1905, FAV.

34. *New York World*, June 4–6, 1905.

35. Vanderlip to Stillman, June 7, 1905, FAV.

36. *Armstrong Report*, 71.

37. *New York World*, June 8, 1905; Harriman testimony, *Armstrong Hearings*, 5135; Buley, *Equitable*, 1:644–46.

38. *New York World*, June 9–11, 1905; Harriman testimony, *Armstrong Hearings*, 5136; Frank A. Vanderlip, *From Farm Boy to Financier* (New York, 1935), 150; Bernard M. Baruch, *My Own Story* (New York, 1957), 104, 111; Buley, *Equitable*, 1:648–49.

39. Harriman testimony, *Armstrong Hearings*, 5142.

40. Ibid., 5135–37; Ryan testimony, *Armstrong Hearings*, 4800–4801. Ryan's version differs somewhat from Harriman's. He claimed that Harriman told him he had spent a lot of time on the Equitable and should have been consulted before the purchase and that Ryan could not carry out his plans without Harriman's aid.

41. Harriman testimony, *Armstrong Hearings*, 5140–41.

42. Ibid.; Buley, *Equitable*, 1:644–46.

43. Harriman testimony, *Armstrong Hearings*, 5142–51.

44. Ryan testimony, *Armstrong Hearings*, 4803–5; Harriman testimony, ibid., 5142–51, 5149.

45. Buley, *Equitable*, 1:658.

46. Ibid., 654–57; *WSJ*, June 13, 1905; *New York World*, June 20, 1905; Harriman to Sidney Webster, Jan. 2, 1906, AF. For the significance and context of this letter, see Chapter 27.

47. Vanderlip to Stillman, June 14, 1905, FAV.

48. Kennan notes, 9-10-09, AF; *WSJ*, Apr. 30, 1910. Herbert L. Satterlee, *J. Pierpont Morgan: An Intimate Portrait* (New York, 1939), 516–17, says that Morgan bought all the stock from Ryan. Buley, *Equitable*, 2:757, could find no evidence that Ryan had sold the shares to Harriman, but in fact they were listed in the official tally of Harriman's estate. See *New York Times*, Mar. 18, 1913. It is not known when Harriman bought them from Ryan.

49. *WSJ*, June 23, 30, 1905; *New York World*, June 16, 20–22, July 11–13, 1905; Vanderlip to Stillman, June 23, 30, July 12, 1905, FAV.

50. Vanderlip to Stillman, July 12, 1905, FAV; *WSJ*, July 13, 14, 17, 22, 1905; *New York World*, July 11–13, 15, 16, 21, 1905.

51. *New York Times*, July 22, 1905.

52. Ibid., July 26, 1905; *New York World*, July 25, 26, 1905. A copy of the full statement is also at AF and in George Kennan, *E. H. Harriman*, 2 vols. (New York, 1922), 1:417–18. Kennan errs in saying that Harriman never published the statement.

53. *WSJ*, July 27, 29, Sept. 30, 1905; *New York World*, Aug. 2, Sept. 1, 7, 16, 24, 30, Oct. 11, 1905; Buley, *Equitable*, 1:674–84.

54. *WSJ*, Nov. 15, 1905; *New York Times*, Nov. 15, 1905; *New York World*, Nov. 15, 1905.

55. *WSJ*, Nov. 16, 1905; *New York Times*, Nov. 16, 17, 1905; *New York World*, Nov. 16, 17, 1905. See also the relevant testimony in *Armstrong Hearings*.

56. *WSJ*, Nov. 16, 1905; *New York Times*, Nov. 16, 1905; *New York World*, Nov. 16, 17, 1905.

57. Ryan testimony, *Armstrong Hearings*, 4800–4809; Harriman testimony, ibid., 5135–65.

58. Kahn, "Harriman," 19–20.

CHAPTER 24

1. *New York Times*, Feb. 22, 1906.

2. Ibid., Feb. 22, July 8, 1906.

3. *WSJ*, Feb. 7, 1906; *New York Times*, Feb. 22, 1906.

4. Mary Cable, *Top Drawer* (New York, 1984), 138, 188–89.

5. George Kennan, *E. H. Harriman*, 2 vols. (New York, 1922), 2:44–47; *New York Herald*, Sept. 25, 1907. The dreary saga of U.S. Shipbuilding is best followed in the *Wall Street Journal* for these years. A list of the syndicate members is in SF. The Odell suit in the Equitable fight (see Chapter 23) involved this same company.

6. Harriman to Fish, Nov. 2, 1905, SF.

7. *New York Times*, Feb. 27, 1907; Kennan, *Harriman*, 2:44–45. Kennan based his version on papers furnished him by Mary Harriman. Copies of some of this material are in AF.
8. Harriman to Fish, Nov. 2, 1905, SF; Kennan interview with Stone, Apr. 29, 1915, AF.
9. C. C. Tegethoff to Fish, Nov. 5, 1903, Jan. 28, 29, June 29, Oct. 18, Dec. 30, 1904, Feb. 24, Apr. 12, June 29, Sept. 29, 1905, SF; *New York Times*, Feb. 27, 1907; Fish to Harriman, Oct. 2, 1905, AF; Harriman to Fish, Nov. 2, 1905, SF; Fish to Harriman, Nov. 29, 1905, AF; Kennan, *Harriman*, 2:46–48. Kennan's copies of these letters make it clear that the versions appearing in his biography are excerpts from longer letters rather than full text.
10. Frank A. Vanderlip, *From Farm Boy to Financier* (New York, 1935), 203–4.
11. Fish to Peabody, Feb. 17, 19, 1906, SF; Peabody to Fish, Feb. 20, 1906, SF.
12. Fish to Edward J. Parker, Feb. 9, 1906, IC; Mayes & Longstreet to Fish, Feb. 10, 1906, IC; Fish to Mayes & Longstreet, Feb. 15, 1906, IC. For the early history of Railroad Securities, see Chapter 16.
13. *New York Times*, Feb. 22, Apr. 8, July 8, 1906; *WSJ*, Feb. 27, 28, Mar. 6, 1906; Frank Vanderlip to Stillman, Feb. 27, 1906, FAV; Fish to F. T. Bacon, Feb. 28, 1906, IC; Fish to Peabody, Feb. 28, Mar. 5, 1906, SF; Peabody to Fish, Mar. 2, 1906, SF.
14. Cyrus Adler, *Jacob Schiff: His Life and Letters*, 2 vols. (Garden City, N.Y., 1928), 1:123; *WSJ*, Apr. 3, 7, 9, 11, 18, 1906. The directors who stood with Harriman were John W. Auchincloss, Cornelius Vanderbilt, Bertie Goelet, Walther Luttgen, and Peabody.
15. Kennan, *Harriman*, 2:51–52, 56–57; Stuyvesant Fish speech to Illinois Central stock-holders, Oct. 17, 1906, AF; Harriman to Stone, Oct. 25, 1906, AF. Kennan's version of Fish's actions is drawn from the speech cited above.
16. Fish to Pulitzer, July 28, 1906, Joseph Pulitzer Papers, Butler Library, Columbia University.
17. *New York World*, Feb. 9, 10, 1905.
18. Kennan, *Harriman*, 2:52–53, 56–57; Harriman to Stone, Oct. 25, 1906, AF. A copy of the agreement is in AF.
19. UP Directors minutes, July 19, 31, 1906, UPL; Fish speech, Oct. 25, 1906, AF; *New York Times*, July 28, 1906; *WSJ*, July 31, 1906; *Railroad Gazette*, 41:89–91; John W. Auchincloss et al. to Fish, Oct. 9, 1906, AF. As was typical in such cases, Harriman, Stillman, and Rogers were present at the meetings but did not vote on the issue because they had a personal interest in it.
20. Fish speech, Oct. 17, 1906, AF; Kennan, *Harriman*, 2:54–55; Fish to Kuhn, Loeb & Co., Oct. 15, 1906, AF; Kuhn, Loeb & Co. to Fish, Oct. 15, 1906, AF; *WSJ*, Oct. 22, 1906. A copy of the original statement is in AF.
21. Harriman to Stone, Oct. 25, 1906, AF. Harriman paid Fish with Illinois Central shares bought earlier by the Union Pacific and then transferred the Railroad Securities Company shares to the Union Pacific at cost. See UP Exec. Com. minutes, Oct. 25, 1906, UPL.
22. Kennan, *Harriman*, 2:57; Stone to Fish, Oct. 17, 1906, AF.
23. Fish speech, Oct. 17, 1906, AF.
24. *Proceedings of the Annual Meeting of the Stockholders of the Illinois Central Railroad*, Oct. 17, 1906, AF; *New York Times*, Oct. 17–19, 1906; *WSJ*, Oct. 18, 19, 1906.
25. Harahan to Harriman, Oct. 20, 1906, AF; Harriman to R. W. Goelet, Oct. 21, 22, 1906, AF.
26. Goelet to Harriman, Oct. 24, 25, 1906, AF; Henrietta Goelet to Harriman, Oct. 24, 1906, AF.
27. Harriman to Goelet, Oct. 25, 1906, AF.

28. Ibid., Oct. 25, Nov. 1, 1906, AF; Goelet to Harriman, Oct. 25, 1906, AF; Fish to W. W. Astor, Nov. 1, 2, 1906, IC; Charles H. Wenman to Fish, Nov. 3, 1906, IC; F. S. Winston to Harriman, Nov. 4, 1906, AF; Harahan to Harriman, Oct. 25, 1906, AF; Harriman to Harahan, Oct. 25, 1906, AF; *New York World*, Nov. 8, 1906; *New York Times*, Nov. 6–9, 1906; *WSJ*, Oct. 20, Nov. 6–9, 1906.

29. *WSJ*, Nov. 8, 9, 1906; *New York Times*, Sept. 23, Nov. 10, 1906; *Railroad Gazette*, 41:397.

30. *WSJ*, Nov. 8, 10, 1906; *New York Times*, Nov. 12, 1906.

31. Kennan interview with Stone, Apr. 29, 1915, AF.

32. *WSJ*, July 19, Aug. 2, 30, Sept. 6, 12, 26, 28, 1907; *New York Times*, Aug. 3, 12, 29–31, Sept. 12–14, 24–28, Oct. 4, 1907.

33. *New York Times*, Sept. 8, Oct. 5–8, 14–17, 20–22, Nov. 16, 21, 24–26, Dec. 1, 6, 7, 14, 18–20, 1907; *WSJ*, Oct. 7, 9, 16, 22, 23, Dec. 18, 1907; *Railroad Gazette*, 43:413, 474, 510, 606, 638, 670, 734, 766.

34. *New York Times*, Feb. 21, 1908; *WSJ*, Feb. 21, June 25, 1908; S. Fish, *1600–1914* (Privately printed, 1942), 238.

35. Adler, *Schiff*, 1:123; Schiff to Harriman, Mar. 7, 1908, AF.

36. Otto H. Kahn, "Edward Henry Harriman," in Stuart Bruchey, ed., *Three Railroad Pioneers* (New York, 1981), 38; Alexander Millar, *Edward H. Harriman and the Union Pacific Railroad* (New York, 1910), 3; Kennan interview with Stone, Apr. 29, 1915, AF.

37. *New York Times*, Jan. 3, 6, 8, Mar. 1, Sept. 27, 1907; Vanderlip to Stillman, Jan. 25, 1907, FAV; *WSJ*, Jan. 23, 30, Feb. 9, 1907.

38. Millar, *Harriman,* 3.

CHAPTER 25

1. *New York Times*, Sept. 23, 1906.

2. Alexander Millar, *Edward H. Harriman and the Union Pacific Railroad* (New York, 1910), 3.

3. *WSJ*, July 21, 1905; Noel M. Loomis, *Wells Fargo* (New York, 1968), 278–84.

4. *WSJ*, Feb. 14, July 13, 1902; Harriman to Fish, Mar. 24, 1902, IC; Loomis, *Wells Fargo*, 284–89, 309. The express company became the major stockholder in the newly merged bank but did not operate it.

5. *New York Times*, June 27, July 7, 17, 20, 1906; *WSJ*, May 12, July 7, 13, 16, 20, 1906.

6. *New York Times*, July 28, 31, Aug. 10, 1906; *WSJ*, July 27, Aug. 1, 9, 10, 1906.

7. *WSJ*, Dec. 11, 1905; *Chronicle*, 81:266; *Railroad Gazette*, 39:554–55.

8. Maury Klein, *Union Pacific: The Rebirth, 1894–1969* (New York, 1990), 153.

9. *United States of America v. Union Pacific Railroad Company et al.*, U.S. Circuit Court for the district of Utah, docket no. 993, 1:223–25, 251–52, 2:789–90.

10. Ibid.; Klein, *Union Pacific: Rebirth*, 153–54.

11. *WSJ*, Aug. 4, 17, 18, 1906.

12. *New York Times*, Aug. 18, 1906; *Railroad Gazette*, 41:151–52; Klein, *Union Pacific: Rebirth*, 154–55.

13. *New York Times*, Aug. 18, 1906; *Forum*, 38:194; Otto H. Kahn, "Edward Henry Harriman," in Stuart Bruchey, ed., *Three Railroad Pioneers* (New York, 1981), 17.

14. The best portrait of Roosevelt is found in the splendid biography by Edmund Morris, *Theodore Roosevelt* (New York, 1979).

15. Ibid., 489.

16. *DAB*, 13:622–23.

17. Morris, *Roosevelt*, 665–87.

18. The menu, list of thirty-six guests, and seating arrangements for the banquet are in AF.

19. Morris, *Roosevelt*, 711–30, details Roosevelt's leap from the state to the national ticket.

20. *DAB*, 13:623; *WSJ*, Apr. 1, 1903. For details on New York's political infighting, see Harold F. Gosnell, *Boss Platt and His New York Machine* (Chicago, 1924).

21. *New York Herald*, Apr. 28, 1901; *WSJ*, Apr. 21, 1903. The Kennan notes in AF contain several Harriman letters dealing with legislation.

22. Roosevelt to Harriman, Nov. 12, 1901, Aug. 16, Sept. 15, 1902, Oct. 2, 9, Dec. 30, 1903, TR; Roosevelt to Odell, July 8, 1902, TR; Harriman to Roosevelt, Sept. 19, 1902, Oct. 8, 1903, Jan. 8, 1904, TR.

23. Elting E. Morison and John M. Blum, eds., *The Letters of Theodore Roosevelt*, 8 vols. (Cambridge, Mass., 1951–54), 3:679.

24. Gosnell, *Boss Platt*, 299–300; Louis J. Lang, ed., *The Autobiography of Thomas Collier Platt* (New York, 1910), 420–46; *WSJ*, Jan. 14, Apr. 11, 13, 1904; *New York Times*, Apr. 10, 1904; Roosevelt to Harriman, May 12, 17, 28, June 3, 25, 1904, TR; Harriman to Roosevelt, May 15, 27, June 2, 24, 1904, TR.

25. Henry F. Pringle, *Theodore Roosevelt* (New York, 1931), 251–52; Harriman to Roosevelt, June 28, 1904, TR; Roosevelt to Harriman, June 29, 1904, TR.

26. Harriman to Roosevelt, Sept. 20, 1904, TR; Roosevelt to Harriman, Sept. 23, 1904, TR; George Kennan, *E. H. Harriman*, 2 vols. (New York, 1922), 2:180–81.

27. Quoted in Kennan, *Harriman*, 2:181–82; Roosevelt to Harriman, Oct. 10, 1904, TR; Harriman to Roosevelt, Oct. 12, 1904, TR.

28. Roosevelt to Harriman, Oct. 14, 1904, TR.

29. Kennan, *Harriman*, 2:183–89; *New York World*, Oct. 1, 1904; Pringle, *Roosevelt*, 249–50. Later, when a controversy arose between them, Roosevelt used the letter in exactly this way and also testified to that effect.

30. *WSJ*, Oct. 15, 1904; Kennan, *Harriman*, 2:186–87.

31. Kennan, *Harriman*, 2:188–94. A receipt for the $50,000, signed by C. N. Bliss, is in AF. Harriman's version of events is given in his letter to Sidney Webster, written in late December 1905 but not made public until the *New York World* published it April 2, 1907. Kennan's version is drawn largely from this letter.

32. Ibid., 194–96; Lang, ed., *Platt*, 460.

33. *New York World*, Apr. 2, 1907.

34. Ibid.; *WSJ*, Jan. 11, 1905; Lang, ed., *Platt*, 460–61; Gosnell, *Boss Platt*, 300–301.

35. Harriman to Roosevelt, Nov. 30, 1904, TR; Roosevelt to Harriman, Nov. 30, 1904, TR.

36. Harriman to Roosevelt, Dec. 2, 1904, TR; Roosevelt to Harriman, Nov. 30, 1904, TR.

37. Harriman to Roosevelt, Jan. 24, 30, Feb. 1, Mar. 1, 1905, TR; Roosevelt to Harriman, Jan. 25, 29, 31, Mar. 2, 1905, TR; Gosnell, *Boss Platt*, 208–11.

38. Gosnell, *Boss Platt*, 301–4.

39. Roosevelt to Harriman, July 1, Nov. 25, 1905, Feb. 18, 1906, TR; Harriman to Roosevelt, July 5, 1905, TR.

40. *WSJ*, May 9, 1906; Pringle, *Roosevelt*, 293–98; Vanderlip to Stillman, May 18, June 20, 1906, FAV.

41. Gosnell, *Boss Platt*, 303–6; George Kennan, *E. H. Harriman*, 2 vols. (New York, 1922), 2:198.

42. Harriman to Webster, Jan. 2, 1906, AF. This celebrated letter is reprinted in *New York World*, Apr. 2, 1907. Kennan, *Harriman*, 2:197, contains only excerpts. A full version in galley form is in UPN.

43. Statement by Maxwell Evarts, 1, AF; Odell to Harriman, Aug. 17, 1906, AF. The excerpts of Evarts's statement given in Kennan, *Harriman*, 2:203–6, 218–19, 223–26, are edited and do not include some revealing asides.

44. Evarts statement, 1.

45. Ibid., 2–3; W. W. Webb to Mary Harriman, June 6, 1922, AF.

46. Roosevelt to James S. Sherman, Oct. 8, 1906, TR.

47. For this controversy and excerpts from Evarts's statement, see Kennan, *Harriman*, 2:203–27.

48. Gosnell, *Boss Platt*, 305; *New York Times*, Nov. 10, Dec. 7, 1906; *WSJ*, Nov. 14, 21, Dec. 6, 1906.

49. *New York Times*, Nov. 19, 1906.

50. Ibid., Nov. 19–21, 1906; *WSJ*, Nov. 23, 24, 1906.

51. *New York Times*, Nov. 23, 1906; Roosevelt to Harriman, Dec. 11, 12, 1906, TR.

CHAPTER 26

1. W. V. Hill, "Mr. Edward Henry Harriman," 1, AF. Hill was one of Harriman's secretaries from December 1901 to September 1907 and often traveled with him.

2. Ibid., 1–2.

3. Ibid., 2.

4. E. E. Calvin to Kennan, Apr. 10, 1921, AF; Calvin report to Harriman, June 18, 1906, AF; *WSJ*, Apr. 25, 1906.

5. Calvin report, 1–14, AF.

6. Calvin to Kennan, Apr. 10, 1921, AF; Maury Klein, *Union Pacific: The Rebirth, 1894–1969* (New York, 1990), 155–57.

7. *WSJ*, Apr. 23–28, May 4, 1906; Vanderlip to Stillman, May 1, 4, 1906, FAV.

8. *WSJ*, Apr. 23, 25, May 2, 1906. See also Klein, *Union Pacific: Rebirth*, 157.

9. Calvin to Kennan, Apr. 10, 1921, AF.

10. Hill, "Harriman," 3.

11. *New York Times*, May 9, 1906; *New York Tribune*, May 9, 1906; *WSJ*, May 9, 10, 1906; *Railroad Gazette*, 40:499; *Sunset*, June 1906, 37–41.

12. *WSJ*, May 9, 1906; *New York Times*, Nov. 15, 16, 1906; Elting E. Morison and John M. Blum, eds., *The Letters of Theodore Roosevelt*, 8 vols. (Cambridge, Mass., 1951–54), 5:219.

13. Except where noted, this account is drawn from George Kennan, *E. H. Harriman*, 2 vols. (New York, 1922), 2:88–173; *Railroad Gazette*, 41:144, 420, 42:489–92; F. H. Newell, "The Salton Sea," *Annual Report of the Board of Regents of the Smithsonian Institution*, 1907 (Washington, D.C., 1908); "Southern Pacific Imperial Valley Claim: Evidence, Statement, and Argument before the Committee on Claims," House bill 13997, 60th Cong., 1st sess. (1908). Copies of the latter documents are at AF.

14. Kennan, *Harriman*, 2:97, 101–6.

15. Quoted ibid., 2:118.

16. Epes Randolph to Kennan, Nov. 16, 1916, AF; "Southern Pacific Imperial Valley Claim," 7.

17. "Southern Pacific Imperial Valley Claim," 9.

18. Kennan, *Harriman*, 2:123; *Railroad Gazette*, 42:492.

19. Randolph to Kennan, Nov. 16, 1916, AF.

20. Randolph to F. H. Newell, Mar. 9, 1917, AF. Although these early plans were executed by the CDC chief engineer, Randolph accepted "entire responsibility for the plans adopted . . . in fact they were of my own design."

21. "Southern Pacific Imperial Valley Claim," 8.

22. Randolph to Kennan, May 19, 1916, AF.

23. Ibid., Nov. 16, 1916, AF.

24. Klein, *Union Pacific: Rebirth*, 162–63.

25. Kennan, *Harriman*, 2:148–49; Roosevelt to Harriman, Dec. 15, 1906, TR.

CHAPTER 27

1. *New York Times*, Dec. 3, 1906.

2. Ibid., Jan 4, 6, 7, 21, 1907.

3. Ibid., Dec. 7, 8, 1906.

4. For more detail on these financial matters, see Maury Klein, *Union Pacific: The Rebirth, 1894–1969* (New York, 1990), 165–68.

5. For a list of the purchases see ibid., 2:167.

6. *WSJ*, Nov. 15, 17, 29, Dec. 1, 1906, Jan. 11, 1907; *New York Times*, Dec. 3, 1906.

7. This scene is drawn from Statement by Maxwell Evarts, 1–6, AF.

8. For the dinner, see *New York Times*, Dec. 9, 1906.

9. Roosevelt to Judson C. Clements, Oct. 21, 1906, TR; Elting E. Morison and John M. Blum, eds., *The Letters of Theodore Roosevelt*, 8 vols. (Cambridge, Mass., 1951–54), 5:461–62.

10. "I had planned to take care of the matter immediately after the adjournment of Congress," Evarts recalled. "In the meanwhile, Roosevelt went to Panama, and before he came back all the correspondence was made public and the whole thing was off" (Evarts statement, 4–5). But the trip to Panama took place in November. Roosevelt returned on the twenty-sixth, before their meeting, so his trip could not have influenced later events. See *New York Times*, Nov. 9, 27, 1906.

11. Morison and Blum, eds., *Roosevelt Letters*, 5:524; *New York Times*, Nov. 11, 1906; Roosevelt to Harriman, Dec. 11, 12, 1906, TR.

12. Harriman to Roosevelt, Dec. 19, 1906, AF; Roosevelt to Harriman, Dec. 20, 1906, TR; George Kennan, *E. H. Harriman*, 2 vols. (New York, 1922), 2:149–50.

13. *New York Times*, Dec. 21, 1906.

14. Harriman to Roosevelt, Dec. 20, 1906, TR.

15. Morison and Blum, eds., *Roosevelt Letters*, 5:531; Roosevelt to Harriman, Dec. 20, 1906, TR; *New York Times*, Dec. 22, 1906; Randolph to Kennan, Nov. 16, 1916, AF.

16. "Southern Pacific Imperial Valley Claim: Evidence, Statement, and Argument before the Committee on Claims," House bill 13997, 60th Cong., 1st sess. (1908), 11–12; Kennan, *Harriman*, 2:154–59.

17. Kennan, *Harriman*, 2:165; Randolph to Kennan, May 19, Dec. 2, 1916, AF.

18. Otto H. Kahn, "Edward Henry Harriman," in Stuart Bruchey, ed., *Three Railroad Pioneers* (New York, 1981), 34–35; Randolph to Kennan, Nov. 16, 1916, AF.

19. *New York Times*, Dec. 29, 1906.

20. Ibid., Jan. 1, 3, 6–8, Feb. 9, 1907; Vanderlip to Stillman, Jan. 25, 1907, FAV; *WSJ*, Jan. 30, Feb. 9, 1907. The *Times* reports Harriman as being present at the services in Philadelphia, but it is unlikely he went to Philadelphia and had surgery that same day.

21. 12 *ICC Reports* 277; *New York Times*, Dec. 21, 1906.

22. *New York Times*, Dec. 30, 1906.

23. Ibid., Jan. 6–Feb. 23, 1907; *WSJ*, Jan. 6–Feb. 22, 1907; *Railroad Gazette*, 42:33. The other major New York dailies contain equally full coverage of the hearings.

24. *New York Times*, Feb. 26, 1907; *WSJ*, Feb. 26, 1907. The actual testimony is in *United States of America v. Union Pacific Railroad Company et al.*, U.S. Circuit Court for the district of Utah, docket no. 933, 2:740–805; hereafter cited as *USA v. UP*.

25. *New York Times*, Feb. 27, 1906; *WSJ*, Feb. 27, 1906; Vanderlip to Stillman, Feb. 28, 1907, FAV.

26. *New York Times*, Mar. 3, 1907.

27. *WSJ*, Feb. 28, 1907; *New York Times*, Mar. 3, 1907.

28. *Railroad Gazette*, 42:34; *Nation*, Jan. 17, 1907, 51.

29. *New York Times*, Mar. 1, 3, 1907.

30. Ibid.

31. Evarts statement, 7; *WSJ*, Mar. 6, 1907; *New York Times*, Mar. 7, 1907.

32. This scene is drawn from Evarts statement, 7–9.

33. Ibid., 9; Morison and Blum, eds., *Roosevelt Letters*, 5:607.

34. *New York Times*, Mar. 7, 9, 10, 1907.

35. Ibid., Mar. 10, 1907; *Independent*, 62:699–704.

36. *New York Times*, Mar. 11, 1907.

37. Ibid., Mar. 12, 1907; Herbert L. Satterlee, *J. Pierpont Morgan: An Intimate Portrait* (New York, 1939), 439; Morison and Blum, eds., *Roosevelt Letters*, 5:617; Evarts statement, 9–10.

38. Satterlee, *Morgan*, 439; Evarts statement, 10; *WSJ*, Mar. 14, 1907. "It is extraordinary but true," wrote Satterlee, "that the railroad presidents named by Mr. Morgan did not go down to Washington as he had arranged, and no one ever explained this." Roosevelt claimed that the presidents themselves refused to adopt Morgan's suggestion. See Morison and Blum, eds., *Roosevelt Letters*, 5:631.

39. *New York Times*, Mar. 16, 1907; Vanderlip to Stillman, Mar. 15, 1907, FAV; Morison and Blum, eds., *Roosevelt Letters*, 5:621–23.

40. E. M. to Willard Straight, [week of Mar. 19, 1907], WDS; Vanderlip to Stillman, Mar. 22, 1907, FAV; Cyrus Adler, *Jacob Schiff: His Life and Letters*, 2 vols. (Garden City, N.Y., 1928), 1:44–50; Morison and Blum, eds., *Roosevelt Letters*, 5:631; *New York Times*, Mar. 22, 1907.

41. *New York Times*, Mar. 22, 1907.

42. Ibid., Mar. 23, 1907.

43. Ibid., Apr. 5, 1907; "Reprint of Newspaper Articles in Reference to Publication of Letter to Sidney Webster," UPN. The following scene is taken from this reprint, which is from the *New York World*, Apr. 3, 1907.

44. *New York World*, Apr. 2, 1907; *New York Times*, Apr. 3, 4, 1907; *WSJ*, Apr. 3, 1907.

45. *New York Times*, Apr. 4, 1907; Morison and Blum, eds., *Roosevelt Letters*, 5:642–43.

46. Kahn, "Harriman," 26–27, 37–38.

47. Ibid. This point is confirmed in an example given by Clarence J. Housman, "Recollections of E. H. Harriman," 4–5, AF.

48. *USA v. UP*, 2:803.

CHAPTER 28

1. This scene is taken from Batson interview with Stillman, Feb. 10, 1911, AF.

2. *New York Times*, Apr. 5, 6, June 5–8, 12, July 14, 1907; *WSJ*, Apr. 6, 10–12, May 16, July 15, 1907; 12 *ICC Reports* 277–306.

3. *WSJ*, July 15, 1907; Elting E. Morison and John M. Blum, eds., *The Letters of Theodore Roosevelt*, 8 vols. (Cambridge, Mass., 1951–54), 5:715–16.

4. Maury Klein, *Union Pacific: The Rebirth, 1894–1969* (New York, 1990), 175.

5. *New York Times*, Aug. 8–10, 13, 1907; *WSJ*, Aug. 14, 15, 1907; Otto H. Kahn, "Edward Henry Harriman," in Stuart Bruchey, ed., *Three Railroad Pioneers* (New York, 1981), 41–42.

6. Harriman to Stillman, Aug. 21, 1906, JS.

7. Ibid.; Stillman to Harriman, Aug. 21, 1906, AF.

8. Kennan interview with Stone, Nov. 23, 1915, AF; Morison and Blum, eds., *Roosevelt Letters*, 5:797, 845, 855, 859.

9. *WSJ*, Aug. 10, 20, 23, 24, Sept. 10, 11, 1907; Clippings from San Francisco newspapers, Aug. 1907, AF.

10. *New York Times*, June 28, 29, 1907.

11. Ibid., Sept. 27, 1907; Harriman to Willard Straight, Oct. 7, 1907, WDS; Herbert L. Satterlee, *J. Pierpont Morgan: An Intimate Portrait* (New York, 1939), 454–58; Vincent P. Carosso, with Rose C. Carosso, *The Morgans: Private International Bankers, 1854–1913* (Cambridge, Mass., 1987), 534–36.

12. The panic of 1907 is treated in Satterlee, *Morgan*, 454–91; Carosso with Carosso, *Morgans*, 534–49; Anne Robeson Burr, *The Portrait of a Banker: James Stillman* (New York, 1927), 216–38.

13. *New York Times*, Oct. 23–25, 1907; Clarence J. Housman, "Recollections of E. H. Harriman," 3–4, AF.

14. Carosso with Carosso, *Morgans*, 544–45.

15. Ibid., 545; Satterlee, *Morgan*, 484–88; Morison and Blum, eds., *Roosevelt Letters*, 5:821–23, 830–31.

16. Housman, "Recollections," 4–5.

17. *WSJ*, Apr. 14, 1908.

18. Morison and Blum, eds., *Roosevelt Letters*, 5:845–46, 855–56, 859.

19. *New York Times*, Nov. 13, 14, 1907, Jan. 2, 17, 26, 1908; *WSJ*, Nov. 14, 15, 1907, Jan. 27, 1908.

20. *New York Times*, Jan. 27, Feb. 2, 1908; *Nation*, 86:96–97; *WSJ*, Feb. 5, 1908; *Railroad Gazette*, 44:141, 170, 520; *Chronicle*, 86:255–56, 287, 443–44. For more detail see Klein, *Union Pacific: Rebirth*, 175–76.

21. *New York Times*, Feb. 15, Dec. 1, 1908; *WSJ*, Dec. 2, 15, 1908; *Chronicle*, 87:1567; *Railroad Gazette*, 45:1494, 1581–82; 22 *ICC Reports* 17–20.

22. *New York Times*, Dec. 1, 1908.

23. Ibid.; *Boston Post*, Dec. 10, 1908.

24. George Kennan, *E. H. Harriman*, 2 vols. (New York, 1922), 2:312–13.

25. F. D. Underwood to Kennan, Jan. 31, 1921, AF; *WSJ*, Oct. 13, 1903, Jan. 7, 9, 23, 1905; *New York Times*, June 29, 1905.

26. For more detail on Underwood and the Erie, see William D. Burt, "Erie's River Line: Leap for the Brass Ring," *Diamond* 5, no. 2 (1990): 4–17.

27. Underwood statement to Batson, 1–3, AF; Underwood to Kennan, Feb. 8, 1921, with accompanying memorandum, AF.

28. Underwood statement to Batson, 5–6, AF; Underwood memorandum, Feb. 8, 1921, 2.

29. The major strike can be followed in the *Hornell* (N.Y.) *Daily Times*, Nov. 1906–Dec. 1907. I am grateful to William D. Burt for providing me information and materials on this and other aspects of the Erie's history.

30. *WSJ*, Mar. 25, Apr. 4, 1908. This episode is drawn largely from R. S. Lovett to Kennan, Jan. 17, 1922, GK.

31. *New York Times*, Apr. 9, 1908.

32. Ibid., Apr. 9, 10, 13, 1908; *WSJ*, Apr. 9, 1908.

33. Lovett to Kennan, Jan. 17, 1922, GK.

34. Satterlee, *Morgan*, 498–500; *WSJ*, June 19, 1908; *New York Times*, July 30, Aug. 12, Sept. 17, 1908; *New York World*, Dec. 2, 1905. For details on the Cincinnati Hamilton & Dayton matter see "Interstate Commerce Commission Report No. 6833," Mar. 13, 1917, 44 *ICC Reports* 1–263.

35. 44 *ICC Reports* 174; *WSJ*, Apr. 14, 1908.

36. Straight to Harriman, Oct. 31, Nov. 15, Dec. 7, 27, 1906, WDS; Michael H. Hunt, *Frontier Defense and the Open Door: Manchuria in Chinese-American Relations, 1895–1911* (New Haven, Conn., 1973), 154.

37. Straight to Blando [J. O. P. Bland], July 16, 1912, WDS; Straight, "Notes on the late Mr. E. H. Harriman's Interest in the East," 3–4, AF; Straight, untitled manuscript on Harriman in the Far East, 2, AF; Michael H. Hunt, *The Making of a Special Relationship: The United States and China to 1914* (New York, 1983), 204–5; Straight to Harriman, Mar. 19, 1907, WDS; Straight diary, Aug. 7, Sept. 3, Oct. 6, 1907; Alex Millar to Straight, Oct. 5, 1907, WDS.

38. Millar to Straight, Oct. 5, 1907; Straight to Harriman, Oct. 7, 1907, WDS; Hunt, *Frontier Defense*, 119–32.

39. Straight to William Phillips, Oct. 10, Dec. 18, 1907, WDS; Harriman to Straight, Jan. 8, 1908, WDS; Straight to Harriman, Jan. 30, 1908, WDS.

40. Hunt, *Frontier Defense*, 157.

41. Straight to Harriman, Feb. 16, Apr. 30, 1908, WDS; Harriman to Straight, June 5, 1908, WDS.

42. Millar to Straight, June 12, Sept. 15, 22, 1908, WDS; Phillips to Straight, Oct. 9, 1908, WDS; Straight, untitled manuscript, 3; Straight to Blando, July 16, 1912, WDS.

43. Cyrus Adler, *Jacob Schiff: His Life and Letters*, 2 vols. (Garden City, N.Y., 1928), 1:247–48; Schiff to Straight, Nov. 18, 1908, WDS; Straight, untitled manuscript, 3.

44. Straight, untitled manuscript, 3; Schiff to Straight, Dec. 1, 1908, WDS.

45. Hunt, *Special Relationship*, 207–8; Straight to Blando, July 16, 1912, WDS; Schiff to Straight, Dec. 3, 7, 10, 14, 28, 31, 1908, WDS; Straight to Schiff, Dec. 15, 18, 1908, WDS; Harriman to Straight, Dec. 25, 1908, Jan. 5, 1909, WDS; Straight to Harriman, Dec. 31, 1908, WDS.

46. Straight to Harriman, Jan. 6, 20, 1909, WDS; Straight to Schiff, Jan. 6, 1909, WDS; Harriman to Straight, Jan. 7, 1909, WDS; Schiff to Straight, Jan. 7, 1909, WDS; T'ang to Straight, Jan. 7, 1909, WDS; Straight to T'ang, Jan. 20, 1909, WDS; Straight to Robert Collins, Jan. 22, 1909, WDS.

47. Harriman to Knox, Feb. 5, 11, 1909, WDS; Knox to Harriman, Feb. 8, 1909, WDS; Straight to Knox, Feb. 18, 1909, WDS.

48. Jeffery to Messrs. Blair & Co. et al., Apr. 16, 1906, Western Pacific Papers, Baker Library, Harvard Business School; *WSJ*, Jan. 28, Apr. 8, 11, May 7, 30, June 3, 4, 10, 1908.

49. *New York Times*, May 20, Aug. 6, 7, 1908; *WSJ*, May 22, June 10, 13, 16, July 28, 29, Aug. 3–6, 1908.

CHAPTER 29

1. *New York Times*, Feb. 23, 1908.

2. Stillman to Mary Cassatt, Dec. 12, 1907, JS; Stillman to Samuel Sloan Jr., Dec. 14, 1907, JS; Stillman to Vanderlip, Mar. 17, 1908, FAV; Cyrus Adler, *Jacob Schiff: His Life and*

Letters, 2 vols. (Garden City, N.Y., 1928), 2:336–38; Anne Robeson Burr, *The Portrait of a Banker: James Stillman* (New York, 1927), 250.

3. Schiff to Harriman, Feb. 2, 1908, AF.
4. Stillman interview with Batson, 3, AF.
5. *WSJ*, Oct. 11, Nov. 15, 27, Dec. 21, 24, 1907, July 4, 14, 30, Sept. 11, 1908; *Railroad Gazette*, 44:12–14.
6. *New York Times*, Apr. 11, 12, 17, May 3, 1907.
7. Ibid., Dec. 3, 1906; *WSJ*, Nov. 15, 17, 21, 29, Dec. 1, 1906, Jan. 10, 11, Feb. 26, Apr. 30, 1907; *Chronicle*, 84:1053.
8. Stillman to Prince Andre Poniatowski, Oct. 30, 1907, JS; *WSJ*, Oct. 14, 25, 26, 30, 1907; *Chronicle*, 85:1083.
9. *WSJ*, Oct. 31, Nov. 5, Dec. 3, 1907, Oct. 15, 1908; *New York Times*, Oct. 31, 1907, Oct. 21, 1908; *Railroad Gazette*, 43:542; *Chronicle*, 85:1144.
10. Schiff to Harriman, Feb. 2, 1908, AF.
11. Harriman to Schiff, May 23, 1908, AF.
12. Stillman to Harriman, Jan. 10, 1908, JS; *New York Times*, Jan. 26, 1908; *New York Herald*, Jan. 26, 1908; Vanderlip to Stillman, Jan. 29, 1908, FAV; Stillman to Vanderlip, Feb. 11, Mar. 14, 1908, FAV.
13. *WSJ*, Mar. 29, 1909; Alexander Millar, *Edward H. Harriman and the Union Pacific Railroad* (New York, 1910), 3.
14. Burr, *Portrait of a Banker*, 240–42; E. Roland Harriman, *I Reminisce* (Garden City, N.Y., 1975), 17–20.
15. Burr, *Portrait of a Banker*, 241; George Kennan, *E. H. Harriman*, 2 vols. (New York, 1922), 2:337–39.
16. Burr, *Portrait of a Banker*, 242; *WSJ*, Aug. 2, 10, 23, Sept. 10, 11, 1907, Mar. 19, Oct. 6, 1908; *New York Times*, Dec. 5, 1907, May 17, Aug. 8, Sept. 9, 1908.
17. *New York Times*, Aug. 24, Sept. 8, 1908.
18. Stillman to Prince Andre Poniatowski, July 27, 1908, JS.
19. Burr, *Portrait of a Banker*, 249, 255–57; Harold van B. Cleveland and Thomas F. Huertas, *Citibank, 1812–1970* (Cambridge, Mass., 1985), 55; Vanderlip to Lord Revelstoke, Jan. 19, 1909, FAV.
20. *WSJ*, May 26, 1908, Jan. 28, Feb. 27, 1909.
21. Ibid., Dec. 30, 1908.
22. Ibid., Jan. 5, May 15, 26, Aug. 24, 1908; W. K. Vanderbilt to Harriman, Jan. 28, 1908, AF.
23. *WSJ*, Dec. 23, 1908, Jan. 15, 21, 28, 1909; *New York Times*, Jan. 28, 1909; *Chronicle*, 88:256.
24. Burr, *Portrait of a Banker*, 260.
25. Ibid., 260–61; *WSJ*, Sept. 30, Oct. 6, 1908; Vanderlip to Stillman, Dec. 21, 1908, FAV; *New York Times*, Dec. 22, 1908.
26. Vanderlip to Stillman, Jan. 12, 1908, FAV; *New York Times*, Jan. 29, 30, 1909.
27. *New York Times*, Nov. 2, 1907, Mar. 9, 10, 1908, Jan. 24, 27, 29, 30, 1909.
28. Vanderlip to Lord Revelstoke, Feb. 4, 1909, FAV; Vanderlip to Stillman, Feb. 4, 1909, FAV.
29. Vanderlip to Stillman, Feb. 12, 1909, FAV.
30. Ibid.
31. Stillman to Vanderlip, Mar. 12, 1909, FAV.
32. Vanderlip to Stillman, Feb. 18, 22, 1909, FAV.
33. Ibid.; Stillman to Vanderlip, Feb. 19, 1909, FAV.
34. *WSJ*, Mar. 4, Apr. 20, May 1, 1909.

35. Ibid., Feb. 18, Mar. 24, June 7, 1909; *New York Times*, Mar. 19, June 12, 13, 25, 1909; *San Francisco Chronicle*, Sept. 10, 1909.

36. *New York Times*, Apr. 2, 1909; Vanderlip to Stillman, Apr. 22, 1909, FAV; *WSJ*, Apr. 3, 1909.

37. Vanderlip to Stillman, May 4, 1909, FAV.

38. *WSJ*, May 20, 1909.

39. Vanderlip to Stillman, May 21, 1909, FAV.

40. Ibid., May 28, 1909, FAV.

41. Clarence J. Housman, "Recollections of E. H. Harriman," 8–9, AF.

42. Kennan, *Harriman*, 2:344.

43. Robert H. Fuller to E. H. Harriman, Feb. 6, 1909, AF; Thomas Price to Fuller, Feb. 9, Apr. 8, 14, 20, May 24, 1909, AF; Fuller to Price, Apr. 10, 15, 21, May 25, 1909, AF; Price memorandum to Harriman, May 18, 1909, AF. Fuller was Hughes's secretary; Price was Harriman's secretary.

44. Price to Fuller, June 1, 1909, AF.

45. *WSJ*, June 8, July 14, 1909.

46. Ibid., July 14, 1909; Stillman to Vanderlip, June 8, 1909, FAV; Millar, *Harriman*, 15.

47. *San Francisco Chronicle*, Sept. 10, 1909; *New York Times*, July 25, 1909.

48. Burr, *Portrait of a Banker*, 268; *San Francisco Chronicle*, Sept. 10, 1909.

49. *San Francisco Chronicle*, Sept. 10, 1909; *New York Times*, July 25, 1909; Straight diary, July 19, 20, 1909, WDS; Straight, untitled account, 7, AF.

50. Herbert Croly, *Willard Straight* (New York, 1924), 281–92; Straight, "Notes," 8; Straight to Messrs. J. P. Morgan et al., June 16, Aug. 1, 1909, WDS.

51. Straight to Harriman, July 12, 23, 1909, WDS; Harriman to Straight, July 16, 1909, WDS; Straight, "Notes," 8; Straight to Blando, July 16, 1912, WDS; Croly, *Straight*, 295–96; Burr, *Portrait of a Banker*, 268–69.

52. Harriman to Schiff, July 21, 1909, AF.

53. Batson interview with Stillman, 4, AF.

54. Harriman to Schiff, July 21, 1909, AF.

55. Harriman to Ed. Noetzlin, Aug. 18, 1909, WDS; C. C. Tegethoff to Kennan, May 12, 1921, AF; *New York American*, Aug. 25, 1909; *Oakland Tribune*, Sept. 10, 1909; *Salt Lake City Herald-Republican*, Sept. 12, 1909. Tegethoff says that Harriman went back to Vienna to consult Struempel, but his correspondence shows that he went to Salzburg and then Munich, from which he started for Paris.

56. Harriman to Straight, Aug. 18, 1909, WDS; Harriman to Noetzlin, Aug. 18, 1909, WDS.

57. Straight to Harriman, Aug. 2, 3, 6, 8, 13, 1909, WDS; Harriman to Straight, Aug. 3, 4, 1909, WDS; J. O. Bland to Straight, Aug. 17, 1909, WDS; Harriman to Ed. Noetzlin, Aug. 18, 1909, WDS.

58. Harriman to Straight, Aug. 18, 1909, WDS; *New York American*, Aug. 25, 1909; *Denver Republican*, Sept. 10, 1909.

59. Harriman to Straight, Aug. 18, 1909, WDS.

60. *New York World*, Aug. 18, 1909.

61. Ibid., Aug. 18, 19, 1909.

62. Ibid., Aug. 19, 20, 23–25, 1909; *WSJ*, Aug. 19, 21, 1909.

63. *New York World*, Aug. 22–25, 1909.

64. Ibid., Aug. 25, 1909.

65. Ibid.; *New York American*, Aug. 25, 1909.

66. A full account of the day, varying in details, can be found in every major New York daily for August 25, 1909.
67. *New York Times*, Aug. 26, 1909; *New York World*, Sept. 7, 9, 1909.
68. *New York World*, Aug. 26–28, 1909; *New York Times*, Aug. 26, 1909; Tegethoff to Kennan, May 12, 1921, AF.
69. Adler, *Schiff*, 1:117; *New York World*, Aug. 29, 1909; Stillman to Princess Poniatowski, Sept. 13, 1909, JS.
70. *New York World*, Aug. 31, 1909; *WSJ*, Aug. 31, 1909.
71. Herbert L. Satterlee, *J. Pierpont Morgan: An Intimate Portrait* (New York, 1939), 513; *New York World*, Sept. 12, 1909.
72. Satterlee, *Morgan*, 513–14.
73. Stillman to Prince Poniatowski, Sept. 10, 1909, JS; *New York World*, Sept. 7, 8, 1909.
74. Tegethoff to Kennan, May 18, 1921, AF.

EPILOGUE
1. *New York Times*, Sept. 10, 1909; *New York World*, Sept. 11, 1909.
2. *Salt Lake City Herald-Republican*, Sept. 12, 1909.
3. *New York Times*, Sept. 13, 1909; *New York World*, Sept. 13, 1909.
4. Stillman to Princess Poniatowski, Sept. 13, 1909, JS; Cyrus Adler, *Jacob Schiff: His Life and Letters*, 2 vols. (Garden City, N.Y., 1928), 1:117.
5. *Portland Oregonian*, Sept. 10, 1909.
6. For more detail on their later careers, see Klein, *Union Pacific: Rebirth*, passim.

Index

Bacon, Robert: and Burlington Railroad, 223, 224; and Northern Pacific Railroad, 225, 231–32, 233, 235, 237, 238; and J. P. Morgan, 226

Baker, George F.: Stillman compared to, 163; and Burlington Railroad, 222–23; and Mutual Life, 330, 345, 346; and J. P. Morgan, 407; and Erie Railroad, 413, 414; and New York Central Railroad, 426; and American Group, 433

Baltimore & Ohio Railroad, 162–63, 166–67, 181, 208, 226, 388

Bancroft, W. H.: and Union Pacific Railroad, 119; and Oregon Short Line, 152, 247, 278; and standardization, 160; and Alaskan expedition, 186; and Kerens, 244; and safety, 259; and Harriman's management style, 267; and San Pedro, Los Angeles & Salt Lake Railroad, 325–28

Bankers and banking: and G. Kennan, 2; and S. Fish, 49; banker syndicates, 91, 113; and Union Pacific Railroad, 107, 388; and Harriman, 163, 212; and competition, 205, 209; and railroad industry, 208, 209, 316; and community of interest, 209; and western advisory committee, 220; and Northern Pacific Railroad, 235; and mergers, 309; and Northern Securities Company, 312, 314–15; and insurance industry, 330; and Wells Fargo company, 357; and panic of 1907, 407; and Manchuria, 416, 417

Barron, Clarence W., 17, 179

Barry Glacier, 193

Baruch, Bernard, 169, 233, 235

Batson, George W., 9, 10, 11, 13, 19, 22, 23, 32

Bay Shore cutoff, 257

Beard, Charles A., 15

Beck, C. A., 82

Beef Trust, 309

Belmont, August, 36, 39, 58, 92, 93, 339, 340

Berry, J. B.: and Harriman's inspection trip, 119–23; and Harriman's management style, 126, 255; and operating costs, 130–31, 135, 137, 139; and railroad growth, 145; and improvements spending, 146, 158; and Oregon Railway & Navigation Com-

pany, 157; and Union Pacific Railroad, 255; and Southern Pacific Railroad, 257

Bienenfeld, A. M., 326, 327–28

Black, Frank S., 365

Blackstone, Timothy B., 171–72, 176

Blagden, Samuel, 41

Blake, William P., 376

Bliss, Cornelius N., 336, 337, 363

Boissevain, William, 87

Boissevain Brothers, 57

Bonaparte, Charles J., 404, 405, 408

Boston & Maine Railroad, 426

Boston fire, 37

Boxer Rebellion, 284

Brewer, David J., 312–13

Brown Brothers Harriman, 446

Bryan, William Jennings, 110

Bull, W. L., 154

Bull, William T., 297

Bureau of Information and Education, 268

Burlington Northern Railroad, 445

Burlington Railroad: and western theater of operations, 206; and Union Pacific Railroad, 210, 212–13, 216–17, 221–23, 230, 239, 314, 318; and J. J. Hill, 221–23, 225, 228, 318, 324, 353; and holding company, 252; management of, 278; statistics on, 279

Burroughs, John, 184, 186, 187, 189, 192, 193, 195, 200

Burt, Horace G.: as president of Union Pacific Railroad, 115, 128, 131; and Harriman's inspections, 119–23; and Harriman's management style, 135, 254, 255, 269–70, 277, 411; and double-tracking, 142; and Oregon Railway & Navigation Company, 154, 157; and standardization, 160; and Harriman's train journey to Seattle, 186; and midwest theater, 212; and Oregon Short Line Railroad, 247; and safety, 266

Bury, J. B., 244

California Development Company (CDC), 376–79, 381, 383, 384, 390–91

Calvin, E. E., 278, 373–74, 375

Cannon, George Q., 115

Carnegie, Andrew, xiii, 183

Cassatt, A. J., 208, 392
Cassel, Ernest, 420
Cassidy, Butch, 160
Cedar Falls & Minnesota Railroad, 66
Central America, xiv
Central of Georgia rail system, 427
Central Pacific Railroad, 120, 122, 210, 216, 219, 256, 275
Central Vermont Railroad, 50
Chesapeake, Ohio & Southwestern Railroad, 92
Chicago, Madison & Northern Railroad, 64
Chicago, Milwaukee & St. Paul Railroad, 163
Chicago, St. Louis & New Orleans Railroad, 49
Chicago & Alton Railway, 13–17, 163, 174, 175–76. *See also* Alton Railroad
Chicago & Northwestern Railroad, 37, 109, 115
Chicago fire, 37
Chicago World's Fair, 90
China: Harriman's railroad lines in, xiv, 418; and G. Kennan, 4; and Open Door policy, 207, 283–84; and trade, 285; Harriman's visit to, 288–89, 291; and W. D. Straight, 300, 416, 417; and American capital, 433, 434
Chinese Eastern Railroad, 285, 288, 415, 417, 433, 434, 435
Cincinnati Hamilton & Dayton Railroad, 415
Civil War, 34, 68
Clark, Dodge & Co., 41
Clark, George C., 41, 44, 315
Clark, Katherine, 246
Clark, Ross, 325, 326, 327, 328
Clark, William A., 217, 243, 244–49, 325, 327, 328
Clarke, James C., 54, 55, 56–57, 58, 62, 64, 79
Clark family, 37, 324–26
Cleveland, Grover, 110, 113, 339
Colorado & Southern Railroad, 251, 323
Colorado Fuel & Iron Company (CFI), 250–51
Commercial Cable Company, 286
Community of interest: and Harriman, 173, 208, 211, 217, 220, 222–24, 242, 249–50,

252, 318, 322; and Alton Railroad, 173, 208, 217; and competition, 205, 209; and Oregon Railways & Navigation Company, 208; logistics of, 209–10, 317–18; and G. Gould, 217, 220, 251, 322; and Burlington Railroad, 222, 223, 228; and Northern Pacific Railroad, 229; and Northern Securities Company, 241, 249, 318; and Railroad Securities Company, 242; and J. J. Hill, 249–50, 315; and Interstate Commerce Commission, 252, 308, 392
Cooke, Jay, 37, 40
Cooley, F. B., 78
Coolidge, T. Jefferson, 115
Cornish, William D., 126, 248, 275, 326–27
Cortelyou, George B., 363, 364
Coster, Charles H., 65, 153, 154–56
Cravath, Paul, 13, 339
Cromwell, William Nelson, 358
Cruger, S. Van Rensselaer, 58
Cullom, Shelby, 399
Custer, George Armstrong, 189
Cutting, R. Fulton, 52
Cutting, W. Bayard, 56, 58
Cutting family, 37
Czolgosz, Leon, 239

Dall, William Healey (Will), 6, 10, 184, 192, 197, 199
Daly, Marcus, 121
Dead Horse Trail, 189
DeForest, Henry W., 351, 352
Delaware & Hudson Railroad, 426
Dellenbaugh, Frederick, 185, 199
Depew, Chauncey M., 307, 334, 337, 361, 365–66, 368, 369, 426
Depression of 1870s, 36, 54–55, 75
Depression of 1873, 37, 38, 50, 68, 107
Depression of 1893–97: and railroad industry, xiii, xvi, 48, 114, 206; and Illinois Central Railroad, 87, 89, 90–91; and Harriman, 88–89, 93; and Erie Railroad, 93; and Union Pacific Railroad, 106, 119; and J. J. Hill, 151; and Baltimore & Ohio Railroad, 166; and Kansas City, Pittsburg & Gulf Railroad, 167; and Alton Railroad, 171–72, 176; and G. Gould, 217

Goelet, Henrietta, 352–53
Goelet, Robert, 58, 70
Goelet, Robert (Bertie), 285, 290, 300, 302, 350, 352–53, 427
Gould, George: and Union Pacific Railroad, 109, 113, 115, 116, 131, 173–74, 322; and Kansas City Southern Railroad, 171; and Alton Railroad, 175, 177; and Missouri Pacific Railroad, 208; and Harriman, 211, 224, 250, 318, 321–23, 325, 419; and Wabash Railroad, 211; and Burlington Railroad, 216; and Southern Pacific Railroad, 217, 219, 220, 250, 322; and Rio Grande Railroad, 217, 220, 221, 250; character of, 219–20; and western advisory committee, 220; and Northern Pacific Railroad, 235; and W. A. Clark, 248; and Colorado Fuel & Iron Company, 251; boards served on, 307; and Northern Securities Company, 309, 314; and Pennsylvania Railroad, 321; and Western Pacific Railroad, 321–22, 324, 325; and J. H. Hyde, 331, 333; and coal lands, 387; and panic of 1907, 418–19
Gould, Jay: Harriman compared to, xiv–xvi, 240, 317, 360; and Wall Street, 34; and Harriman's brokerage firm, 36, 37; "Jay Gould method," 65; and J. P. Morgan, 65–66; and Burroughs, 184; and G. Gould, 217; management style of, 219; railroad industry consolidation, 252–53; and Pulitzer, 350
Government, U.S.: and Union Pacific Railroad, 106–7, 110, 111–12, 114; and railroad ownership, 110, 205, 353; and industrial development, 204; and railroad crashes, 265; and federal regulation, 310, 321, 364, 367, 370, 387, 396, 398, 400, 401, 409; and insurance industry regulation, 331; and Imperial Valley, 391; and corporate harassment, 393
Grammercy Sugar, 94
Granger Railroad, 206, 207, 210
Grant, Ulysses S., 49
Great Northern Railroad: and J. J. Hill, 151, 222, 226, 237, 273; and Oregon Railway & Navigation Company, 152, 154, 155; and western theater of operations, 206; and

competition, 207; and Burlington Railroad, 224, 225, 239; and Harriman, 230, 402; and Northern Securities Company, 313, 388
Greenwood Iron Works, 68
Griscom, Lloyd C., 285, 286, 287, 288, 289–90
Guam, 283
Guaranty Trust Company, 425

Hadley, Arthur T., 15
Hanna, Mark, 361
Harahan, J. T., 352, 353, 354
Harriman, Alfonso, 27
Harriman, Anna (b. 1846), 29
Harriman, Anna Ingland, 28
Harriman, Carol, 12, 95, 119–22, 297, 433
Harriman, Charles, 28, 34
Harriman, Cornelia (b. 1850), 30
Harriman, Cornelia (b. 1884), 45, 67, 98, 192, 199, 293, 297–98, 301, 302, 415
Harriman, Cornelia Neilson, 29, 30, 31, 45, 80
Harriman, E. H.
—business interests: titans compared to, xiii, 345; enemies, xiv, xv, 8, 320, 344, 355, 401, 402, 418, 419, 425; controversies, xiv, 8, 11, 20, 358, 369, 370, 388, 419, 425; as broker, xv, 33–35, 37, 38, 61, 62, 93; papers of, 9–10, 17–18; and G. Kennan's biography, 13, 20; E. H. Harriman & Company firm, 36–38, 44, 46–47, 48, 55–56, 57, 58, 61, 63; railroads, 47, 49–50; boards served on, 49, 57, 70, 166, 181, 307, 332, 333, 405, 425; Sodus Bay grain elevator, 52; Harriman & Co., 62, 78, 89, 90, 93, 294; depression of 1893 interests of, 94; streetcar line, 94–95; mining, 95, 96–97, 105; and West, 105, 111, 115, 117, 122, 123, 146; and frontiers, 117; oil companies, 263; American China Development Company, 284; Equitable Life, 332, 333–43, 344, 366, 368, 388; United States Shipbuilding, 347; Wells Fargo company, 357–58; and panic of 1907, 407, 408
—myths concerning: and G. Kennan's biography, xiv, 13; G. Gould compared to, xiv–xvi; context of, xvi; childhood, 32;

and Ontario Southern Railroad, 51; and
Sodus Bay & Southern Railroad, 52–53;
and improvements spending, 52–53, 85,
87; and Garfield's death, 56; and Wall
Street business, 61; and Erie Railroad,
93–94; and Union Pacific Railroad, 118–
19, 126, 134; and S. Fish, 353; and Northern Securities Company, 388
—personal life: intensity of, xiii, xv, 214–15,
241, 345, 357; ruthlessness, xiv; family
devotion of, xv, 31, 45–46, 67–68, 73–74,
148, 187, 196, 292–93, 297–303, 441; ath-
leticism, xv, 32, 38–39, 41, 96, 100, 187,
298; combativeness, xv, 33, 66, 115, 317,
329; will, 6, 211, 266; disagreeableness of,
13; G. Kennan's biography, 19–20; family
background, 27–33, 42–43, 44, 89; education, 32, 33; Jekyll-Hyde personality, 38,
67; and nature, 39–41, 68, 69, 100, 109,
117, 144, 149, 182, 198; charity of, 41–44,
45, 71, 96, 374; marriage, 45, 46, 67, 302–
3, 441; names used to address, 67; illnesses, 84, 111, 128, 230, 267, 294, 296–97,
311, 312, 314–15, 347, 354–55, 371, 384, 386,
390, 392, 393, 401, 406, 409–10, 412, 416,
418, 421, 427–39; weaknesses, 88; mental
processes, 125; and order, 148–49, 215,
241; and public recognition, 183, 200; and
power, 211; honesty, 335–36, 348
—railroad career: and modernization, xiii,
xvi, 163, 168, 211–12, 445; management
style, xiii, 82–83, 91–92, 124–29, 132–35,
137, 146–47, 159–61, 165, 173–74, 176, 207–
8, 211–12, 254–55, 259, 267–73, 275–81,
282, 320, 324, 409; and global transportation system, xiv, 18–19, 182, 285, 300, 416;
and J. H. Schiff, 13, 78, 105, 109, 110, 112,
113, 118, 147, 163, 166, 173, 181, 228, 241,
242, 311, 359, 362, 387, 405, 420–21, 423–
24, 434, 439, 440, 444; controversies, 13–
17, 78, 173, 174, 180, 388; Alton Railroad,
13–17, 91, 171–80, 181, 208, 211, 212, 239,
472–73 (n. 62); Ogdensburg & Lake
Champlain Railroad, 45, 49–50, 57; and
S. Fish, 49–52, 54, 55–56, 61, 67, 74, 77–
79, 81–94, 99, 106, 111, 112, 128, 211, 249,
347–51, 354; Sodus Bay & Southern Railroad, 51, 52–53, 57; Ontario Southern

Railroad, 51–52; Chicago move, 71, 73;
Erie Railroad, 93–94, 410–13, 426; Oregon Short Line, 152, 155, 247–49; and
Mellen, 153–54; Baltimore & Ohio Railroad, 162–63, 166–67, 181; Kansas City,
Pittsburg & Gulf Railroad, 162–63, 167–
70, 181; and community of interest, 173,
208, 211, 217, 220, 222–24, 242, 249–50,
252, 318, 322; and holding company, 175,
241, 252; Burlington Railroad, 210, 212–
13, 216–17, 221–24, 246; Northern Pacific
Railroad, 225–26, 230–31, 234, 235, 236–
38, 240; Railroad Securities Company,
239, 351; railroad industry consolidation,
253; and safety, 265–67; and international
trade, 284–85, 288–91; Northern Securities Company, 310, 311–13, 320, 324, 387,
445; San Pedro, Los Angeles & Salt Lake
Railroad, 326–28; and dividends, 357;
and convertible bonds, 387, 411, 421, 423–
24, 426, 428–29; legacy, 445–47. *See also*
Arden; Illinois Central Railroad; Southern Pacific Railroad; Union Pacific
Railroad
Harriman, Edward (b. ca. 1817; E. H.'s
uncle), 28, 30, 31, 34–35
Harriman, Edward (b. 1787; son of William
Harriman), 27
Harriman, Frederick (b. 1828), 28
Harriman, Henry Neilson (b. 1883), 45, 67,
71, 73, 74, 77, 95, 443
Harriman, J. Borden, 294
Harriman, James (b. 1818), 28, 35
Harriman, John Neilson, 29, 35, 37, 38, 45,
293
Harriman, Mary (b. 1881): birth of, 45; Harriman's relationship with, 67, 293; and
inspection tours, 119–22, 294; and Alaskan expedition, 195; and Griscom, 285;
and W. D. Straight, 289, 299–302, 415,
433; and Harriman's illnesses, 297, 436,
438; and horses, 298; education of, 299
Harriman, Mary W.: and philanthropy, 6,
8; and business, 6, 73; and Alaskan expedition, 8, 10, 188, 189, 199; and Roosevelt,
9; and Harriman's biography, 9–23; family background, 44–45; marriage, 45, 46,
67, 302–3, 441; and charity, 98, 445; and

Los Angeles Limited, 387
Los Angeles Terminal Railway, 243–44, 247, 248
Louisville, New Orleans & Texas Railroad, 92
Louisville & Nashville Railroad, 92, 109, 206
Lovett, Robert A., 446
Lovett, Robert S.: and Mary Harriman, 6; and Harriman's biography, 9, 10, 13, 19, 21; and Ripley, 16–17; and Harriman's marriage, 46; and Harriman's mental processes, 125; and Alton Railroad, 179–80; as Harriman's confidant, 275, 348; and Harriman's papers, 341; and Union Pacific Railroad, 359, 446; and Roosevelt, 365; and Erie Railroad, 411–14; and Harriman's illness, 436–39
Lucin cutoff, 257–63
Luttgen, Walther, 58
Lyle, W. G., 285, 286, 294, 297, 392, 434, 436, 439, 440

McClure, S. S., 3, 4
McClure, William, 46, 47, 61
McCurdy, Richard A., 345–46
McGuinness, J. H., 97, 99, 443
McKeen, William R., Jr., 263
McKenna, Joseph, 113
McKinley, William, 110, 111, 140, 146, 215, 239, 400
Macy, Josiah, 50
Macy, Sylvanus J., 50–52
Macy, William, 50–51
Macy & Sons, 51
Mahl, William, 267–68, 275, 276
Manchuria, xiv, 284, 285, 291, 300, 415–18
Manchurian and Siberian Railway, 301, 415
Mann, John G., 82–83
Markham, C. H., 278
Martin, Albro, 226
Medbery, James K., 37
Mellen, Charles S., 151, 153–54, 156, 157, 158, 186, 210, 212, 308
Mercantile Trust, 330, 333
Merriam, C. Hart: and Mary Harriman, 8, 10; and Alaskan expedition, 183–84, 185, 187, 190, 192, 195, 196, 197, 198, 199
Mexico: Harriman's railroad lines in, xiv,

264–65, 356, 429; and California Development Company, 376, 378
Midway Island, 285–86
Milburn, John G., 400
Millar, Alexander, 117, 118–19, 214, 356, 417, 432, 435
Miller, Darius, 237, 238, 252, 273
Miller, Roswell, 115
Mills, D. O., 362
Milwaukee Railroad: and Miller, 115; management of, 210–11; expansion of, 213; and Southern Pacific Railroad, 217; and J. P. Morgan, 221; and stock market, 225, 227, 233; and Harriman, 249, 318, 324, 388; and railroad competition, 324
Minneapolis & St. Louis Railroad, 323
Mississippi & Tennessee Railroad, 70, 92
Missouri Pacific Railroad, 109, 174, 206, 208, 250, 279, 322
Mitchell, John J., 172–74
Mobile & Ohio Railroad, 62
Modernization: and Harriman's mission, xiii, xvi, 211–12, 445; of Russia, 4; and Illinois Central Railroad, 84; of Union Pacific Railroad, 123, 130, 132–43, 145, 153, 159, 280; of Oregon Railway & Navigation Company, 158, 210; and Harriman's reorganization efforts, 163, 168; and Alton Railroad, 172, 177; and safety, 265; and Atchison, Topeka & Santa Fe Railroad, 318; and Rio Grand Railroad, 322; and New York Central Railroad, 426
Mohler, A. L.: and Oregon Railway & Navigation Company, 153, 156, 157, 158, 210; and standardization, 160; and Harriman, 186, 200, 212; and management, 273; and Union Pacific Railroad, 278
Monopoly, 205, 353
Montalvo-Burbank cutoff, 257
Moore & Schley, 407–8
Morawetz, Victor, 242, 251–52, 319
Morgan, Edwin, 300
Morgan, J. P.: Harriman compared to, xiii, 345; and Northern Pacific Railroad, 16, 151, 225–26, 229, 231, 234, 235, 236, 237–38; and Illinois Central Railroad, 64–66; and J. Gould, 65–66; and Harriman, 65–66, 93–94, 96, 112, 154, 212, 224, 229, 236,

Oregon railroads, 116, 135, 150

Oregon Railway & Navigation Company: and Union Pacific Railroad, 121, 150–51, 154–56, 158, 159, 181; and voting trust, 152–53; and Northern Pacific Railroad, 153, 154–55, 157–58, 186; and Harriman, 153–55, 182, 224, 228, 243; modernization of, 158, 210; and community of interest, 208; and Calvin, 278

Oregon Short Line: and Union Pacific Railroad, 121, 150, 152, 155, 156, 159, 409; and Oregon Railway & Navigation Company, 152, 153, 155, 156; and Harriman, 152, 155, 156, 159, 181; and Utah & Pacific Railroad, 243, 246–47; and San Pedro, Los Angeles & Salt Lake Railroad, 248; and Bancroft, 278

Osborn, Charles J., 36

Osborn, W. H., 58

Osgood, J. C., 251

Pacific Mail Steamship Company, 284, 285, 288

Palisades Interstate Park, 8, 431

Panama Canal, 367

Panic of 1857, 33, 68

Panic of May 1884, 46

Panic of 1907, 43, 407, 416, 418, 420, 421, 423, 425

Panic of September 1873, 37

Park, W. L., 136, 137, 144, 266, 268, 277, 294, 295

Parrott, Ned, 303

Parrott, Peter, 68, 69

Parrott, Robert, 68

Parrott Iron Company, 68, 97

Peabody, Charles, 303, 346, 349, 350–51, 365

Peabody, Endicott, 287

Pennsylvania Railroad: and New York Central Railroad, 52, 53, 426; management of, 82, 278; and Union Pacific Railroad, 140, 272; traffic on, 145; and Baltimore & Ohio Railroad, 166–67, 208; as trunk line, 206; and Cassatt, 208, 392; and G. Gould, 250, 321; portfolio of, 388

Perkins, Charles E., 210, 212–13, 216, 220, 221–22, 224

Perkins, George W., 226, 330

Philippines, 3, 4, 207, 283–84, 285

Phoenix & Eastern Railroad, 251, 319

Pierce, Winslow S., 109, 112, 113, 115, 116, 131

Pittsburgh Terminal Railroad, 419

Platt, Frank H., 334, 335

Platt, Thomas C., 361, 362, 363, 365

Political issues: and railroad industry, 110, 205, 235, 236, 252, 307–8, 313, 409; and J. J. Hill, 166; and Harriman, 175, 335, 342, 360, 362–63, 365–70, 400, 404, 409, 425, 427; and large corporations, 205, 215, 252, 309, 310, 407, 408; and W. A. Clark, 246; and insurance industry, 337–38; and Roosevelt, 360–61, 367, 407; and trusts, 393, 394–95

Populism, 110

Press: Harriman's relations with, xv, 8, 240–41, 279–80, 290, 317, 336, 340–41, 343, 350, 353, 355, 357, 359–60, 367, 375, 396–98, 405–6, 425, 430; and Illinois Central Railroad, 78, 80, 81, 351, 352, 353; and Harriman's wealth, 78, 292; and Harriman at Illinois Central, 89–90; and Arden, 101; and Union Pacific Railroad, 110, 111, 118, 132, 226–27, 359, 423; and Harriman's management style, 159, 273; and Stillman, 163; and Alton Railroad, 175; and Alaskan expedition, 183, 187, 200; and Burlington Railroad, 222; and Northern Pacific Railroad, 228, 234, 235, 238; and stock market, 233; and W. K. Vanderbilt, 236; and W. A. Clark, 246, 248; and Oregon Short Line Railroad, 247; and G. Gould, 251; and Lucin cutoff, 261; and Southern Pacific Railroad, 261; and self-propelled vehicle, 263; and railroad crashes, 265; and business tycoons, 292; and Harriman's health, 297, 392, 432, 433, 435–40; and Mary Harriman, 301–2; and Harriman's view of railroad industry, 310–11, 316, 370, 398; and Northern Securities Company, 313; and Atchison, Topeka & Santa Fe Railroad, 319; and J. J. Hill, 324; and insurance industry, 332; and Equitable Life, 333, 334–38, 340–43; and Mutual Life, 345–46; and S. Fish, 349; and Roosevelt, 364–65; and Harriman's San Francisco earthquake aid,

374–75; and Harriman as corporate predator, 387, 395; and Harriman's Imperial Valley crisis, 389, 390–92; and Harriman's Interstate Commerce Commission investigation, 392–96, 399–400; and Bonaparte, 404; and Standard Oil, 405; and Erie Railroad, 414
Price, Thomas, 435, 436
Prince William Sound, 192–93
Progressive era, 8, 344
Pulitzer, Joseph, 337, 338, 350, 364–65, 399

Railroad industry: and depression of 1893–97, xiii, xvi, 48, 114; Harriman's modernization of, xiii, xvi, 211–12, 445; and J. Gould, xv; and Chicago & Alton deal, 13–17; and gold rush, 33; and Wall Street, 48; and industrial revolution, 48, 204; and S. Fish, 49–50; and competition, 54, 75, 85, 153, 204–7, 209, 316, 324; expansion of, 54–55, 63, 76; and railroad rates, 63, 64, 75–76, 85, 90, 170, 171–73, 177, 178, 209, 212, 366, 367, 393; and pools, 76; and banker syndicates, 91; and West, 119; lack of vision in, 124; and increase in traffic, 145; and voting trusts, 151, 152, 170, 241, 323, 324, 427; and community of interest, 173, 205, 208–11, 217, 220, 222–24, 228, 229, 241, 242, 249–50, 251, 252, 308, 315, 317, 318, 322, 392; Harriman's desire to impose order on, 177, 215–16, 398; Harriman's need to reflect on, 182; and stock market, 204, 225, 226–28, 399; and mergers, 205, 209, 213, 219, 220–21, 248, 249, 309, 318; and collusion and combination, 205, 221, 309, 345; theaters of operation, 205–6; and reorganization, 208; stability in, 241; and consolidation, 252–53; and railroad crashes, 265–67; and safety, 265–67, 387, 445; and Roosevelt, 364, 366; and panic of 1907, 410; and Harriman's legacy, 445
Railroad Securities Company, 239, 241–42, 349, 351, 388
Randolph, Epes, 319, 356, 379–84, 391
Randolph, L. V. F., 58
Ransom, W. A., 294
Ream, Norman B., 166

Reclamation Service, 379, 390
Reform movements, 310, 345, 348, 402
Republican Party, 362, 363–64, 367, 389, 400
Revelstoke, Lord, 417
Rio Grande Railroad, 206, 207, 217, 220, 221, 250, 322
Rio Grande Western Railroad, 206, 217, 322
Ripley, E. P., 242, 251
Ripley, William Z., 13–17, 176, 179
Rockefeller, John D., xiii, 174, 183, 350, 427
Rockefeller, William: and Stillman, 163, 165; and Milwaukee Railroad, 211, 318; and J. H. Schiff, 226; and J. P. Morgan, 229; and Southern Pacific Railroad, 282; and Harriman, 314, 387, 405; and Mutual Life, 330; and Hyde, 333; and Mexico, 356; and Roosevelt, 400, 408; and New York Central Railroad, 426
Rockefeller family, 241
Rockhill, W. W., 289
Rock Island Railroad, 206, 210, 242–43, 279, 318, 323, 324
Rodin, Auguste, 19, 435
Rogers, H. H., 214, 317, 330, 345, 346, 350, 351, 387, 431
Roosevelt, Theodore: Harriman's split with, xiv, 8–9, 14, 16, 20, 21, 301, 329, 363, 400–402; and G. Kennan, 4, 14, 22; and Mary Harriman, 10, 12; presidential bids of, 10, 16, 363, 400; and Alton Railroad, 14, 175; and Harriman, 45, 239, 309, 360–61, 362, 363–70, 371, 375–76, 384–85, 389–90, 395, 396–401, 404, 405, 408; and wilderness, 69; and West, 105; and Burroughs, 184; and Northern Securities Company, 239, 308–9, 363; and Russo-Japanese War, 286; and trusts, 309, 310; personality of, 360–61; and Odell, 361; and J. P. Morgan, 362, 398; and Imperial Valley, 384, 391; and panic of 1907, 408; and Sherman Antitrust Act, 409; and Taft, 418
Root, Elihu, 336, 339, 362, 369, 389, 417
Rumsey, Charles Cary, 12, 302
Russia: and G. Kennan, 1–2, 3, 17, 20; modernization of, 4; and Japan, 284; and Chinese Eastern Railway, 433, 435
Russo-Japanese War, 4, 284–85, 286, 299

Spencer, Samuel, 154, 156, 309, 386, 387

Speyer, James, 216, 217, 220, 340

Spindletop oil field, 171

Stalin, Josef, 200

Standard Oil: and Macy family, 51; and Rockefeller, 229, 330; as large corporation, 309; and Hyde, 336; and Equitable Life, 337, 340; and Harriman, 346, 350, 387, 388; and Illinois Central Railroad, 349; and Roosevelt, 363; government suit against, 393, 404; and press, 405

Stanley-Brown, Joseph, 13, 199

Steele, Charles, 309

Stetson, Francis Lynde, 154, 411, 414

Stillman, James: and Harriman, 13, 44, 115, 125, 163, 173, 212, 241, 311, 359, 362, 387, 403–5, 416, 424, 426–27, 429, 432, 433, 434, 435, 436, 439; and J. H. Schiff, 113, 165; and Union Pacific Railroad, 115, 116, 131, 146–47, 165, 359; and banking, 163, 165, 203; and Kansas City, Pittsburg & Gulf Railroad, 167; and Kansas City Southern Railroad, 171; and Alton Railroad, 174, 175; and railroad industry, 208; and J. P. Morgan, 212, 229–30, 241, 407; and Burlington Railroad, 216; and railroad cooperation, 220; and Northern Pacific Railroad, 225, 229, 235; and holding company, 241, 421, 423; and American China Development Company, 284; and Russo-Japanese War, 284; boards served on, 307; and mergers, 309; and Northern Securities Company, 314; and Equitable Life, 331; and C. Peabody, 346; and Illinois Central Railroad, 351; and Mexico, 356; and business conditions, 406; and retirement, 420, 421, 425; and New York Central Railroad, 426; and Hughitt, 428; and American Group, 433

Stilwell, Arthur E., 167–70

Stock market: and railroad industry, 204, 225, 226–28, 235; growth of, 204–5; and mergers, 221; and press, 233; contraction of, 398–99, 407; and panic of 1907, 407; and Harriman's health, 436, 439–40

Stone, Melville E., 17, 175, 177, 347, 350, 351, 353, 405

Straight, Hazel, 300, 301

Straight, Willard D., 2–3, 289, 291, 299–302, 415–18, 433–34, 435

Streamliner, 263

Struempel, Adolf, 432–33, 434, 435

Stubbs, John C., 237, 238, 252, 273, 275, 278, 428

Sturges, Frederick, 57, 58

Sultana, 298, 301, 406

Sundance Kid, 160

Sunset Route, 207

Supreme Court, U.S.: and Cedar Falls & Minnesota Railroad, 66; and Louisville & Nashville Railroad, 92; and Northern Securities case, 282, 311–13, 315, 324, 363, 445; and Southern Pacific Railroad, 319; and Interstate Commerce Commission, 409

Tabor, Francis H., 43

Taft, William Howard, 240, 288, 389, 418, 425

T'ang Shao-i, 416, 417–18, 433

Tarbell, Gage, 334, 337

Taylor, Talbot J., 281

Tegethoff, C. C.: and Mary Harriman, 6; and Harriman's biography, 10, 14, 18, 19; and G. Kennan, 12; and Harriman, 13, 439, 441

Telegraph industry, xv, 1, 33, 37, 143, 149, 160, 204

Telephone industry, 143, 204

Ten Eyck, Jim, 298

Tennessee Coal & Iron Company, 407–8

Thaw, Harry K., 393

Thomas, E. B., 154

Thomson, Frank, 53

Tlinkit Indians, 191

Tolstoy, Lev, 3

Tompkins Square Boys' Club, 8, 42–43, 96

Trans-Siberian Railroad, 285

Trudeau, E. L., 8, 40, 119, 184, 195, 214, 267

Tuxedo Park, 69–70, 96, 302, 444

Twain, Mark, 246

Twombley, H. M., 426

Underwood, Frederick D., 166, 273, 410–12, 414, 415

Union Pacific, Denver & Gulf Railroad, 149–50
Union Pacific–Central Pacific Railroad, 206
Union Pacific Railroad: Harriman's rebuilding of, xiii, xv, 85, 246, 255; J. Gould's rebuilding of, xv; and Harriman's charity, 43; reorganization of, 88, 106–7, 109–14, 165, 362; Harriman's interest in, 105, 106, 361; and Illinois Central Railroad, 106, 110, 111, 112, 114, 116–17, 123, 211, 346, 350, 351, 353, 354; and depression of 1893–97, 106, 119; and J. H. Schiff, 107, 109–16, 118, 124, 131, 223; and Harriman's reorganization plans, 110–16; and Northwestern Railroad, 112, 115, 210, 213, 217; management of, 114, 115–16, 159, 272, 278, 294, 428; Harriman's stocks in, 114, 123, 124; Harriman as board member of, 115–16, 123–24, 131, 146, 173, 181; improvements spending of, 118, 123–24, 130–45, 177, 280; and Harriman myths, 118–19, 126, 134; Harriman's inspections of, 119–23, 133–34, 135, 144, 146, 152; and Oregon Short Line, 121, 150, 152, 155, 156, 159, 409; and Oregon Railway & Navigation Company, 121, 150–51, 154–56, 158, 159, 181; modernization of, 123, 130, 132–43, 145, 153, 159, 280; and Harriman's management style, 124–29, 132–35, 137, 146–47, 159–61, 165, 173–74, 207–8, 268, 269, 272–73, 275–76, 411, 421, 423–24; and Pennsylvania Railroad, 140, 272; and meeting points, 145–46; and dividends, 146, 358–59, 367, 368, 388, 405, 421, 423, 429, 446; earnings of, 146–47, 358, 421, 429–30; branch lines of, 149–59; and Northern Pacific Railroad, 151, 228, 234, 238; and standardization, 159–60, 278–79; and train robberies, 160–61; and Harriman's legacy, 162, 446; and Alton Railroad, 174, 177; and western theater of operations, 206; and competition, 207–8; and Burlington Railroad, 210, 212–13, 216–17, 221–23, 230, 239, 314, 318; and Southern Pacific Railroad, 213, 217, 218, 243, 256, 273, 281–82, 370, 393, 404, 408–9, 418, 445; and Milwaukee Railroad, 225; and stock market, 226–28, 233, 238; and

W. K. Vanderbilt, 236; and Nevada, 243; and Los Angeles Terminal Railway, 244; and oil, 244, 328; and San Pedro, Los Angeles & Salt Lake Railroad, 249; and McKeen car, 263; statistics on, 279, 280; and G. Gould, 322; and W. A. Clark, 328; and Hyde, 332; and Equitable Life, 341; and Peabody, 346; and convertible bonds, 387; and safety, 387; and Northern Securities Company, 387–88; assets of, 388; and New York Central Railroad, 426; and Harriman's illness, 428; and Rogers, 431; and holding company, 446
Union Pacific–Southern Pacific system, xiii, 269, 390
United Copper, 406
United States express company, 357
United States Shipbuilding, 342, 347
United States Steel, 170, 221, 233, 238, 250, 251, 407, 408
Untermyer, Samuel, 358
Utah & California Railroad, 247
Utah & Pacific Railroad, 243, 246–47

Van Buren family, 37
Vanderbilt, Cornelius, 34, 36, 346, 418, 426
Vanderbilt, William K., 228, 236, 307, 426
Vanderbilt family, 208, 210, 219–20, 225, 226, 227, 307, 426
Vanderlip, Frank: and Harriman, 215, 275, 276, 399, 429; and Ryan, 338; and Equitable Life, 341; and Interstate Commerce Commission, 394; and Erie Railroad, 413–14; and Stillman, 420, 425; and Harriman's health, 427–28, 430, 431
Van Sant, Samuel R., 239
Villard, Henry, 150–51, 152
Voting trusts, 151, 152, 170, 241, 323, 324, 427

Wabash Railroad, 174, 211, 419
Walker, Roberts, 14–15
Wall Street: J. Gould's career on, xv; Harriman's career on, xv, 33; changes in, 33–34; and E. H. Harriman firm, 36–38, 44, 46–47, 48, 61, 62; depressions and, 38; and railroad industry, 48, 228, 252, 310–11, 393; and S. Fish, 49; and anti-Semitism, 78; and Union Pacific Railroad, 111, 116,